The Moral Organization

Naomi Ellemers • Dick de Gilder

The Moral Organization

Key Issues, Analyses, and Solutions

Springer

Naomi Ellemers
Faculty of Social and Behavioral Sciences
Universiteit Utrecht
Utrecht, Utrecht, The Netherlands

Dick de Gilder
Faculty of Social Sciences
Vrije Universiteit Amsterdam
Amsterdam, Noord-Holland
The Netherlands

ISBN 978-3-030-84174-4 ISBN 978-3-030-84175-1 (eBook)
https://doi.org/10.1007/978-3-030-84175-1

This Springer imprint is published by the registered company Springer Nature Switzerland AG
The registered company address is: Gewerbestrasse 11, 6330 Cham, Switzerland

Acknowledgments

December 2020

Preparation of this book was made possible through the months we were able to take our leave from regular activities, granted by our employers, the University of Utrecht and the VU Amsterdam, the Netherlands. We greatly benefited from the hospitality we enjoyed as guests (in 2018) and honorary professors (in 2019) at the Centre for Research in Social Psychology, University of Queensland, Australia, as well as the fellowship enabling our stay at the Institute for Advanced Studies, University of Bologna (in 2019).

We are particularly grateful to our hosts who allowed us to participate in the activities of the Social Identity and Groups Network (headed by Professor Jolanda Jetten and Professor Catherine Haslam) at the University of Queensland, and the Socialab research laboratory in psychology at the University of Bologna (headed by Professor Monica Rubini). At both these locations, we found a home away from home. We felt privileged to be so warmly welcomed by our colleagues and their students, and were much inspired by the intellectual interactions as well as the personal support and encouragement we received from our friends. To our delight, we also found highly engaged and professional dance teachers and a welcoming community of fellow dancers allowing us to continue our practice and improve our ballroom and Latin technique at both locations.

While finalizing the manuscript, we prevailed on a number of friends and colleagues, whose feedback and comments helped improve the book for accessibility and completeness.

We thank Tamar Almor, Bianca Beersma, Tatiana Chopova, Alex Haslam, Wiebren Jansen, Maryam Kouchaki, Félice van Nunspeet, Floor Rink, Daan Scheepers, Nik Steffens, Elianne van Steenbergen, and Jojanneke van der Toorn for their encouragement and helpful suggestions. We are grateful to Nadia Buiter, Jamie Breukel, and Miriam Wickham who assisted with literature searches, preparation of case descriptions, and compilation of reference lists.

Professor Stefano Pagliaro, from the University of Chieti-Pescara in Italy, generously offered feedback and comments for all chapters, cheering us all the way. Our lifetime friend and faithful supporter Irene Idema tactfully indicated sections that are less accessible for the broader audience of readers we hope to attract. Hanneke Sanou prevented us from writing too much Dunglish, and Isabella Klaassens checked all the sources and references. We completed preparation of the manuscript during the COVID-19 pandemic and multiple lockdowns in 2020. During these months, our dance teacher René Versteege helped us preserve our sanity and retain our focus. We are grateful to them all.

Amstelveen, The Netherlands Naomi Ellemers
Dick de Gilder

Contents

List of Figures

Chapter 1
Moral Behavior in Organizations

Abstract People generally want to do what is morally right This is also true in the workplace, as research consistently shows. Yet every day we encounter situations in which people in organizations act in ways that appear immoral. How can this be? This chapter explains the *paradox of morality* as a **key issue**: it is exactly *because* people are so motivated to think of themselves as morally good that they are reluctant to acknowledge or consider the moral flaws of their actions. Our **analysis** reveals why it is not always easy to do what is morally right, despite good intentions. Even where people agree about key moral principles, they may differ on what these would prescribe in specific situations. In a moral dilemma, people often disagree which is the lesser of two evils. When facing such dilemmas in the workplace, people turn to others to help determine what decisions and actions are appropriate. Standard **solutions** aiming to improve moral behavior of people in organizations can be optimized by taking into account these hidden forces relating to social identities and self-views. Explicit efforts to influence moral behavior in organizations are unlikely to be effective if they are not aligned with more implicit forces defining the ethical climate in the workplace.

N. Ellemers, D. de Gilder, *The Moral Organization: Key Issues, Analyses, and Solutions*, https://doi.org/10.1007/978-3-030-84175-1_1

1.1 Key Issues: We All Want to Be Moral

Across the world, people tend to subscribe to very similar moral values and principles, raising their children to be honest and fair, loyal and sincere (Haidt, 2012; Schwartz, 1992). Also in pursuing their own goals and interests, most people take care not to harm others, and to help them if they can. Research consistently shows that – if forced to choose – most people find it more important to be honest, reliable, and sincere than to be competent and smart, or even likeable (Ellemers et al., 2008; Pagliaro et al., 2011; Pagliaro et al., 2016). For instance, people invest more effort in showing a good task performance when they think they are being evaluated for their moral values than when they think they are demonstrating their ability to learn new skills (Ståhl & Ellemers, 2016; Van Nunspeet et al., 2015). This desire to do what is morally right and to be seen as moral by others is very strong and has been consistently documented with various research methods across a broad variety of populations in different countries (for overviews see; Ellemers, 2017; Ellemers, Pagliaro, & Barreto, 2013).

The desire to be moral extends to the workplace. Research shows that people prefer employment in teams and organizations that are seen as moral, and that this benefits their well-being as well as their task performance (see Fig. 1.1). For instance, in seeking employment people are more attracted to work teams and organizations that have a reputation for being honest and treating customers fairly rather than focusing on profit or offering attractive career prospects – if they can't have both (Van Prooijen & Ellemers, 2015; Van Prooijen et al., 2018). Employees are more satisfied with their job and more committed to their organization when it engages in socially responsible activities that make the organization seem moral (e.g., Ellemers et al., 2011). When getting to know their co-workers or forming impressions of organizations and institutions, people seek information about the moral stature of these individuals or groups before anything else, and this

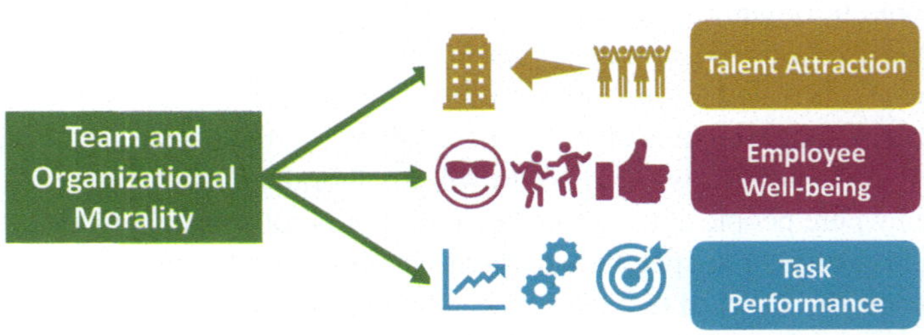

Fig. 1.1 The moral organization. Summarizes findings from many scientific studies. Together, these demonstrate that individuals who perceive a work team or organization as moral are: (a) more attracted to apply for a job in that organization or to work in that team, (b) report greater satisfaction and wellbeing, and (c) show higher performance when working in such an environment. (Ellemers et al., 2008; Ellemers et al., 2011; Pagliaro et al., 2011; Pagliaro et al., 2013; Ståhl & Ellemers, 2016; Van Prooijen & Ellemers, 2014; Van Prooijen et al., 2018; Van der Lee et al., 2017; Van Nunspeet et al., 2014)

information weighs heavily in the overall impression they form (Brambilla et al., 2013; Goodwin, 2015; Pagliaro et al., 2013).

No wonder that people ask organizations and their leaders to account for their moral guidelines, as well as the moral consequences of the choices they make or the actions they take. As citizens, and employees, as consumers and clients, as investors or as regulators, they question organizations regarding their social responsibilities and moral behavior – increasingly pressuring them when they are not satisfied with the answers they get. And organizations respond: they have to explain their moral position, even if they are not totally convinced this benefits their key mission or outcomes. Some organizations enthusiastically engage in activities that attest to their corporate social responsibility (CSR), but even those that are less passionate about such goals will nowadays at least pay lip service to these concerns and communicate to their stakeholders that they find this important.

1.1.1 Immoral Behavior Galore

Seemingly in sharp contrast to such statements and efforts, examples abound of cheating employees, lying managers, fraudulent organizations, and corrupt institutions. Given the importance people attach to morality, it is not surprising this often leads to public outrage – damaging the organization and its members in ways that are costly and not easy to fix.

A classic example is the 1970s Ford Pinto case, in which the American automobile manufacturer decided not to adapt defective fuel systems that might explode. Allegedly they reasoned that the total expense of making the Pinto safer – said to cost 11 US dollars per car at that time – would be larger than the cost of deaths, injuries and car damages resulting from accidental explosions (Gioia, 1992). Stepping up external production regulations does not necessarily resolve such issues. This was evident from the more recent “Dieselgate” fraud, where German car manufacturer Volkswagen manipulated emission tests, in order to make the car meet regulatory requirements in the USA.

Such morally questionable decisions are not only made in manufacturing industries, but also in other sectors, as we will see throughout this book. Since the global financial crisis we are well aware of all the things that can go wrong in the financial services industry, and the measures that have been taken to reduce such risks. Nevertheless, ING, a Dutch bank with an international network, neglected to conduct the required background checks on many of its customers. Their computer systems restricted the number of suspicious transactions that were filtered out for closer inspection, to make them fit the limited resources the bank had made available to follow up on such cases. This facilitated the laundering of large sums of criminal money over many years – a liability of which the bank was fully aware. When this came to light, this resulted in an unprecedented out-of-court settlement of close to 800 million Euros. It also forced the bank to heavily invest in upgrading their controls. The public outrage over this scandal and the loss of reputation for the bank was huge. In social media it was graphically symbolized in the bank's logo with the orange lion. The adapted version depicted one of its claws showing the middle finger, symbolizing the supposed disdain towards the bank's clients and the general public. Notwithstanding the financial settlement made by the organization, CEO Ralf Hamers still faced criminal charges. The court ruled to open a case against Hamers because he had failed to take public responsibility for his actions.

Irresponsible or immoral decisions are made not only at the expense of reputations or profits but also at the cost of human lives. This was the case at Boeing. The US aviation company was aware of problems with its newly developed flight control system MCAS. Yet it continued to install the system in its 737 Max jet airplanes. In 2018 and 2019 this resulted in two airplane crashes in which 346 people died. Safety regulation did not prevent this: the new airplanes and their control systems had passed certification procedures at the (US) Federal Aviation Administration (FAA). Email correspondence displayed in a public investigation by the American Congress revealed that Boeing had simply lied to the regulator.

Blatant breaches of relevant guidelines, disregard for the costs and well-being of customers and clients, and neglect of the public interest not only occur in organizations whose primary motive is making profit. All these problems also emerge in public institutions, even at national level. Perhaps this does not come as a surprise in countries that are seen as high on the list of public sector corruption by experts and business people. For instance, systematic doctoring of athletes' doping tests occurred in Russia, ranked number 137 of 180 countries in the 2019 corruption perception index (Transparency International, 2020). However, similar problems emerge in countries where the rule of law is held in high esteem, such as the Netherlands, which ranked number 8 of 180 in the same index. Even in institutions that aim to maintain public order and compliance with regulations, corruption and unethical behavior is tangible. For instance, the Dutch justice ministry of Justice was found to have deliberately misrepresented research results that did not support its policies, ongoing nepotism was revealed at the Dutch public prosecution office ("Public Prosecutor Placed under Stricter Supervision," 2020), and discrimination, misbehavior and bullying emerged as persistent problems in the Dutch national police (Pieters, 2019). In fact, forms of behavior that unambiguously violate key moral principles are also perpetrated, condoned, and sometimes actively covered up in not-for-profit organizations whose core mission it is to care for the wellbeing of others. Well-documented examples include the harassment and sexual abuse of Haiti hurricane victims by humanitarian aids working for Oxfam (O'Neill, 2018), as well as the long-term abuse and rape of children by priests and cardinals of the Catholic Church (Böhm et al., 2014; see also Box 2.2).

And on it goes. In different media, we can see a never-ending stream of examples documenting fraud, corruption, negligence, breaches of trust and misbehavior of individual workers, entrepreneurs, organizations or whole sectors of industry (see also Soltani, 2014). This would seem to suggest that people are inherently selfish and that it is common practice for individuals as well as businesses to avoid, bend or break rules and regulations. Apparently, this is all for their own gain and benefit, showing a general lack of care for others and their interests. It is no wonder that many have developed a cynical view on human morality and the moral standards of entrepreneurs and business people in particular (e.g., Cohn et al., 2014).

1.1.2 The Paradox of Morality

The more such examples come to light, the more they beg the question of what is driving the flawed choices made by these organizations and the people working in them. Citing selfish motives only makes this question more pressing, in view of all the damages those involved are likely to suffer. Even problems that seem to remain unnoticed for many years, eventually backfire at great cost to the organization, the individuals responsible for its actions, as well as the private and public investors who finance these organizations. The reputational and financial costs associated with legal procedures and fines, liability and compensation payments, expenses for product recall and improvement, and loss of business can be quite substantial. Some organizations never fully recover, or are even forced out of business. If the outcome of getting caught is so severe – effectively killing brand reputations, ending successful careers, causing organizations to go bankrupt or even resulting in the slow death of whole industries – why would they even take this risk?

This question is even more puzzling given all the research evidence cited at the start of this chapter, showing that people generally do care about morality and try to be fair, caring, and loyal to others. In fact – and fortunately – most entrepreneurs, employees, teams, and organizations would not consciously decide to go against known rules, nor would they deliberately harm clients, the environment, the government, other institutions, or the general public. Yet there is no direct relation between moral intentions and moral outcomes. Of course, we are not the first to have noted that even good people can do bad things. This can happen, for instance, because they do not pause to consider the impact of their actions on others, underestimate the force of their emotions and habits, or neglect the wider implications of their business decisions (Mazar et al., 2008; Moore, 2008; Moore et al., 2012; Shalvi et al., 2015). In this book, we build on these prior insights but also extend them. A key aspect of our analysis is what we call 'the paradox of morality': How intentions to do what is morally right, can prevent people from seeing their own actions as morally wrong – and make them persist in their moral failures. We argue that people prefer to explain and justify how past behaviors align with their good intentions, rather than working towards moral improvement. Defensive responses also reinforce and maintain existing work habits, task efforts, and strategic decisions of individuals and groups in the workplace – even if these are morally flawed.

Throughout this book, we will present evidence to reveal that it is precisely the desire to do what is moral, and (anticipating) the social pain of being seen as immoral by others, that prevents people from fully considering the harm of their actions to others. We build on experiments showing the extent to which people get upset and feel threatened if they are criticized for the moral choices they make (e.g., failing to correct a cashier who gives back too much change), or when they are asked to reflect on their own moral failures (e.g., lying to a friend). Even when people choose not to share their emotions, this can be captured from involuntary physical indicators. It is visible for instance in changes of their brain activity, heart rate, and blood pressure (e.g., Kouzakova et al., 2014; Van Nunspeet et al., 2014). Such responses occur autonomously, revealing when people are stressed, alert, engaged, or emotionally affected, even if they are unable to consciously recognize this or unwilling to acknowledge this is the case (Blascovich & Tomaka, 1996; Greenwald et al., 1998; Seery, 2013). The discrepancy between self-stated intentions and involuntary physical and emotional responses reveals the intensity of the stress people experience when they fail to live up to their moral intentions.

In general, people are quite reluctant to admit – sometimes even to themselves – that they feel guilty or ashamed about their own moral behavior. People can call on different strategies to deal with such emotions (blaming the situation or other distractions), to convey that this is not how they 'really' are. On the one hand, this can help them alleviate the sense of threat raised by the thought that their acts may be morally flawed. On the other hand, use of such self-protective strategies also causes people to defend and justify misguided choices, or to ignore the broader implications of their actions (Bandura, 1999; Giner-Sorolla, 2012; Shalvi et al., 2015). The more people invest in highlighting their good intentions and defending what they did, the less likely they are to seriously consider the moral flaws of their actions. Yet admitting that problems exist is a necessary first step to improve individual and organizational moral behavior. Hence the term paradox of morality.

Considering the nature of this social pain and the conditions that foster it, explains why so many people tend to look away from the moral implications of their actions. They prefer to seek approval for their moral decisions rather than exposing themselves to moral critique. This is not to deny that pathological liars, professional fraudsters, and accomplished con-artists also exist. However, our current goal is to understand the day-to-day psychological mechanisms that can explain more common occurrences of morally questionable behavior demonstrated by 'normal' people – who try to do what is moral but fail. Acknowledging these mechanisms – and adapting the organizational circumstances that invite them – is needed to effectively promote moral behavior in organizations. Our aim is to offer a comprehensive understanding of the aspects of organizational life that may unwittingly invite and perpetuate immoral behavior in and of organizations. This can inform and strengthen efforts that invite people to behave in line with their own moral ideals – also at work.

1.1.3 The Search for a Quick Fix

When blatant breaches of moral guidelines (and the harm this causes) are publicly exposed, this raises the urge to 'do something'. Such calls from the general public, government institutions or own staff often press management to 'take decisive action'. The priority is to convey commitment to change, even when the primary goal only is to prevent further reputational damage for themselves as well as the

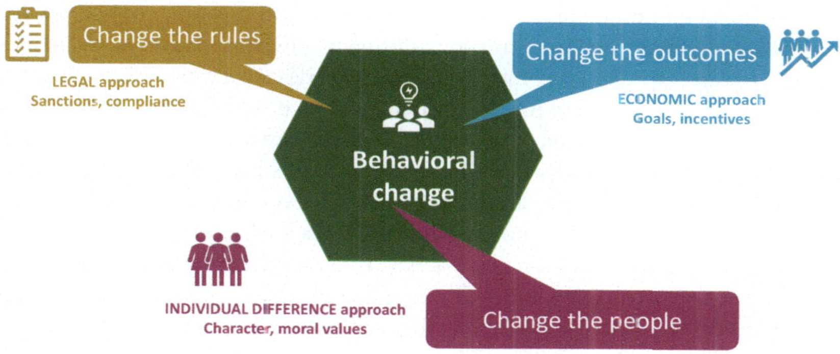

Fig. 1.2 Three quick fixes to curb unethical behavior. Depicts three common strategies that are used as 'quick fixes' to achieve behavioral change in organizations. Throughout this book we note limitations of attempts to curb unethical behavior simply by changing the rules, changing the outcomes or changing the people

organization. Not surprisingly, this approach tends to promote the search for a quick fix instead of a thorough analysis of underlying causes and psychological mechanisms that have led to these problems. So what would a quick fix be in the case of Boeing? Would everything change if the CEO resigned? Might compensation payments or legal fines prompt Boeing to conduct more extensive tests before new technology is installed in its airplanes? Would setting up more elaborate rules and stricter controls by the FAA rule out future safety issues at Boeing?

Each of these fixes points to at least one of three common ways to explain and influence behavior in organizations: by searching for individuals with other character traits and moral outcomes ('changing the people'), by adapting key goals and incentives ('changing the outcomes'), or by introducing sanctions and stricter compliance monitoring ('changing the rules'; see Fig. 1.2). The first represents the tendency to attribute the causes of strategic choices and the prioritization of particular outcomes (e.g., profit) over others (e.g., safety) to the stable personality characteristics of specific individuals. This would suggest that hiring and firing the right people is key to organizational success. We will refer to this as *the individual difference approach*. Second, most businesses and other organizations rely heavily on motivation models and cost/benefit calculations informed by economic reasoning. We will refer to the wide-spread use of material incentives (rewards and sanctions) to understand and influence the behavior of the members of the organization as the *economic approach*. Third, there is a strong tendency by regulators both from within the company and external bodies to harness control mechanisms in order to enforce compliance. Here we refer to the regulatory practice of imposing increasingly comprehensive rules and developing ever more detailed procedure manuals as the *legal approach*.

It is for good reason these three approaches exist. Human behavior is influenced by personality characteristics, instrumental concerns, and control mechanisms to some extent at least, and we will consider these approaches more thoroughly further on in this chapter. However, despite the wide-spread use of measures tapping into these three most common approaches, these do not seem to stop people from lying and cheating, or from making irresponsible decisions time and again. Incidents recur not only in commercial companies but also persist in a range of other sectors, including sports (match fixing in soccer, doping in speed cycling and athletics), science (plagiarism, misrepresentation, and fabrication of research findings), as well as politics and public offices (nepotism, lobbying and bribery). This not only seems to attest to the inherent fallibility of human morality – even despite good intentions – but also reveals the limits of common solutions to fix such problems.

We go beyond these common approaches, by systematically analyzing the *psychological mechanisms* that contribute to a range of organizational problems relating to morality. We delve deeper into the intricate social processes at play in organizations, to provide an additional layer of understanding. Explicit strategies to realize moral intentions tend to highlight selection and development of individuals, try to steer their behavior with sanctions and incentives, and hope to control this through regulation and monitoring – acting in line with the three quick fixes we identified. However, in addition to these visible ways to influence moral behavior, standard organizational procedures and practices also define the *implicit moral climate* – which influences moral behavior in less visible ways (see Fig. 1.3). We argue that common organizational practices and procedures relying on the three quick fixes can unwittingly undermine rather than promote the circumstances under which organizations and their members are likely to behave in ways that can be seen as moral. If organizations don't take these implicit and less visible mechanisms into account, their explicit attempts at moral improvement are unlikely to be successful.

The *first* key feature of to our approach is the observation that individuals and the (work-related) decisions they make are also guided by *group memberships*, organizational roles, and implicit demands of specific situations. *Second*, we demonstrate that these group memberships, roles, and situations raise emotions, social concerns, and *post-hoc justifications*. These can overrule cost/benefit calculations or

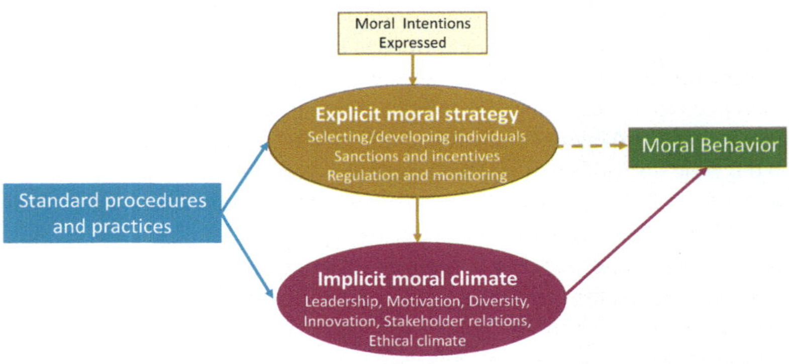

Fig. 1.3 What stands in the way of moral behavior? Illustrates that there is no direct link between moral intentions and moral behavior. Standard procedures not only capture the explicit moral strategy, but also define the implicit moral climate. The implicit climate often is a less visible but more powerful determinant of moral behavior than the explicit strategy

economic incentives that guide behavioral choices, especially in the moral domain. *Third*, we note that top-down imposition of rules invites tick-the-box compliance and prevents *norm internalization* that would allow people to more fully engage with the moral responsibilities associated with their organizational roles. Without an analysis of such 'soft' factors, moral behavior in organizations cannot be fully understood, nor can it be promoted to such an extent that it has a long term impact.

1.2 Analysis: It Is Not as Easy as It Seems to Do What Is Morally Right

A word of warning is appropriate: morality is extremely difficult to define. It is a much more elusive concept than most people think (see Box 1.1), and the roads leading to moral behavior are thorny and have surprisingly winding side paths.

Box 1.1 Defining morality
This book is about moral behavior in organizations. But what do we mean by this? In line with the Stanford Encyclopedia of Philosophy (Gert & Gert, 2020), we define morality as indicating *standards for acceptable vs unacceptable behavior* that allow people to work and live together in communities and societies (for a more extensive discussion see Ellemers, 2017).

The *behavior* that people display thus is an important cue to determine their moral standing. Such evaluations are not only made for individuals, but also for whole professions, teams, or even organizations (Ashforth et al., 2020). However, there often is no one-to-one relation between specific behaviors and key moral principles. Attempts to define and evaluate which behaviors are acceptable (and which are not) often refer to abstract principles and human virtues, such as fairness, care, and loyalty. As we note in Chapter 1, in many concrete situations such general guidelines are not very helpful. What would be fair, who deserves our care, and how much should we sacrifice to display our loyalty?

One of the key points in this book is that it is not possible in every case to specify ahead of time what is morally acceptable and what is not. In practice, people and groups therefore often *disagree* about the precise behaviors they consider morally acceptable. In fact, they may refer to different interpretations of the same moral standards. This doesn't mean that anything goes. However, people tend to shift the boundaries of what they consider acceptable behavior also as a strategy to justify their own choices and mitigate identity threats (Ellemers, 2017; Ellemers & Van der Toorn, 2015).

How then do people evaluate the moral standing of individuals, groups, and organizations? They do this mostly by trying to *infer the (true) goals and intentions* of actors whose behaviors they can see. In line with standard models of social evaluation, such inferences about underlying and sometimes 'hidden' intentions can be distinguished from friendly vs unfriendly displays in social interactions (Abele et al., 2020).

In considering behavior in and of organizations, people try to assess whether the actions and statements they observe seem *honest, reliable, and sincere* (Ellemers & Van den Bos, 2012: Leach et al., 2015). In this context, honest mistakes may be accepted or even forgiven. However, deliberately misleading regulators or subordinates, intentionally cheating customers or investors, or systematically lying to employees or supervisors would all qualify as examples of immoral organizational behavior, and indicate unethical business practices.

Even if this definition does not offer a clear list of do's and don'ts, in daily practice it can be relatively easy to test the morality of specific actions and choices. Based on our definition that morality indicates the social acceptability of one's behavior, three simple questions can help (see also Kouchaki & Smith, 2020). These explicitly consider the social implications of specific actions by testing: (1) is this something you would be proud to share with your loved ones? (2) is this something you would like to be remembered for? (3) is this how you would like to be treated yourself? A regular and open discussion of such questions in the workplace can guard against actions that are not socially acceptable, and benefits the transformation towards a moral organization.

In philosophy different schools of thought defend different moral principles, but all tend to refer to implicitly shared ideals to capture 'universal' rules of conduct to define what is moral (Churchland, 2011; Morris, 1997). For instance, consequentialist approaches emphasize the beneficial vs harmful *outcomes* of people's actions to decide what is morally right. Helping others is morally right, harming them is not. Deontological ethics, however, refers to 'sacred duties', arguing that some *rules* (always be fair, always protect human lives) should never be violated, regardless of how this helps or harms people in other ways. Even though there is something to be said for both these principles, in any given situation, they do not necessarily point to the same course of action. This already clarifies that it is not so easy to do what is morally right. It is also in line with Nietzsche's thesis that good and evil do not exclude each other, as what is a moral act for one person can be an immoral act for others (Nietzsche, 1894).

Attempts to align different principles, for instance in the 'Golden Rule' (don't do to others what you would not have others do to you; Churchland, 2011; Morris, 1997), or striving for 'the greatest good for the greatest number' (Mill, 1861/1962) do not necessarily resolve this. These are the moral dilemmas faced for instance by those having to decide about military peace keeping operations: Is it all right to sacrifice the lives of some innocent citizens if this helps prevent a larger conflict that is likely to cause many deaths? Or should killing people never be seen as a moral cause of action, regardless of the circumstances? Even if there is political and legal approval for such actions, the trauma experienced by the military personnel involved attests to the emotional costs and long-term implications of breaching such basic principles of human morality.

In psychological research, these and similar dilemmas are commonly used to examine the moral development of individuals, or to specify the intuitive and rational aspects of deciding about acceptable vs unacceptable courses of action (for an overview see: Ellemers et al., 2019; see Box 1.2). However, if there is one thing both contrived and more realistic dilemmas reveal, it is that it is not always easy to decide what is moral. Are all lives equally precious? Are all rules equally sacred? What about cases of civil or organizational disobedience? Sometimes people deliberately decide to violate organizational rules and receive praise for their moral courage – even when breaking the law. This happens for instance when people offer employment to illegal migrants so that they can earn a living, when doctors treat patients without medical insurance, or when schools educate students who can't pay tuition. The COVID-19 pandemic clearly highlights how each decision raises new moral issues. Who is to say what is moral and what is not?

Box 1.2 How psychologists examine morality

In the development of psychological thinking about morality and moral behavior, three prominent traditions can be distinguished, which we summarize below (Ellemers et al., 2019; Giner-Sorolla, 2012; Greene, 2013; Haidt, 2012). In this book we adopt a fourth, more recent approach, that examines moral behavior in relation to people's self-views and identities.

1. *Morality as a stage in human character development:*

This developmental approach assumes that children gradually advance in their moral judgment through lessons learned from adults, such as their parents or teachers. Over time they are increasingly able to recognize standards of morally acceptable behavior (Eisenberg et al., 2002). In this view, children ideally progress through different stages of moral development, in which they come to internalize important social norms (e.g., do no harm), and learn how to exercise self-control to curb selfish impulses (Heilbrun & Georges, 1990; Kohlberg, 1971, 1978; Rest, 1986). The assumption then is that moral failures are tied to lack of developmental maturity in specific individuals.

2. *Morality as an individual difference variable:*

The personality approach assumes that the tendency to behave morally represents a fixed character feature, that predicts people's behavior across many different situations. Expanding the well-known 'Big Five' model of personality traits (Goldberg, 1990; McCrae & Costa Jr., 1987, 1996), the

HEXACO model proposes Honesty/Humility as a separate personality aspect (Ashton & Lee, 2007, 2008a, 2009; but see De Raad et al., 2010), which indicates people's ideas about social relations (Chirumbolo & Leone, 2010). People with lower ratings on the Honesty/Humility trait are more inclined to display remorseless and unethical behavior, for instance in business contexts (Ashton & Lee, 2008b; Paulhus & Williams, 2002). This view assumes that moral failures can be avoided by selecting people with the 'right' personality.

3. *Morality as a way to decide in difficult situations:*
   This cognitive approach is most closely connected to philosophical debates on how to define right vs. wrong. A prominent way to examine this is by asking people to make decisions where they are forced to choose the least of two evils (Bauman et al., 2014). Experimental paradigms examine which areas of the brain are involved in such decisions, and reveal when these are made intuitively, and when they require more deliberate reasoning (Haidt, 2001; Haidt & Graham, 2007; Graham, 2014). This approach addresses moral behaviors that result from deliberate individual decisions.

4. *Morality as a class of behaviors that elicits self-reflection:*
   A social approach to morality explicitly considers people's self-views and their relations to others (Rai & Fiske, 2011). In this view, moral principles offer 'supremely important' guidelines for social control, where transgressions may lead to social exclusion (Beauchamp, 2001; Ellemers & Van den Bos, 2012; Giner-Sorolla, 2012). The shared definition of which behaviors are seen as morally acceptable or unacceptable define the social value people assign to themselves in relation to others. Others who share similar standards for morally acceptable behavior help people define who they are, where they belong, how they should behave, and whose judgments they should ignore (Ellemers, 2017; Skitka & Mullen, 2002). This is the approach to morality that captures team and organizational level mechanisms relevant to moral behavior, and guides the analyses in this book.

If these examples show one thing, it is this: We tend to think it should be obvious what is moral (helping others) and what is not (harming them). But in reality things are not so black and white. In fact, observing how people behave does not necessarily reveal their underlying intentions (see also Fiske & Rai, 2014). Some would resists 'helping' another person because they know the immediate benefits requested mask long term disadvantages that will cost the person much more (López-Pérez et al., 2017). Decisions that are 'cruel to be kind' occur for instance when a bank turns down irresponsible loan requests, or when a doctor refuses to approve a popular treatment that will only make the patient suffer more. In a more general sense, it would be too simple to take people's visible actions as valid indicators of their underlying intentions. People don't always stop to consider the wider implications of their decisions, and even if they do, it may not be that obvious how their actions impact on the outcomes of others. When shopping for jeans and finding a bargain, would everyone realize that production at this price is only possible through sweatshop labor that violates human rights? And if so, would people think they can make a difference by refusing to buy the jeans already in the store? This is why the morality of human behavior lies as much in the *reasoning* about relevant concerns and *interpretation* of likely outcomes as in the behavior itself (see also Ellemers, 2018).

1.2.1 Two-Faced Individuals and Organizations

The ambiguity about what is morally right or wrong is also visible in the behavior of individuals and organizations. Let's consider some examples.

In 2017, Whole Foods Market Inc. was named a 'legend' for being on Fortune Magazine's list of the "100 best companies to work for", 20 years in a row (Cloud, 2017). The company motto: 'whole foods, whole people, whole planet', expressed the outspoken position of founder and CEO John Mackey on environmental issues through sustainable agriculture and a commitment to responsible business practices and community citizenship. Yet the same John Mackey used a false name to post on-line messages discrediting Wild Oats, a competitor in the market for wholesome food products. Allegedly he did this to lower the Wild Oats stock price before making a takeover bid (Manz et al., 2008). So how would you view John Mackey and his company? As an attractive employer and a model for responsible food production, or as yet another example of a ruthless and greedy commercial business?

Paul Polman, CEO of Unilever in 2009–2019 became well known for his 'sustainable living plan'. This specified that he aimed to double the company's financial turnover while reducing its environmental footprint with 50 per cent, and improving the health and working conditions of millions of people around the world. He defended his plans against those who thought his ideas were misguided and naïve, and inspired other business people to adopt similar goals. In 2017, however, the same Paul Polman was heavily criticized by employees, investors, and the media when he accepted a 51% pay increase which was clearly disproportionate compared with the salary raises enjoyed by the rest of the company. Further, in an attempt to fend off an attempt at hostile take-over by Heinz-Kraft, Unilever decided to abandon some of its social and environmental goals so as to increase short term profits (Smit, 2019). In retrospect then, would you think Paul Polman and the business strategy he advocated were really driven by the moral concerns cited in his sustainable living plan? Or was this just a smart way of playing on public sentiments to promote the company and advance his own reputation and legacy as a visionary business leader? Perhaps it was a bit of both.

And what to think about the philanthropy of the Sackler family? Highly admired and well respected patrons of the arts and sciences the Sacklers made large donations to museums and universities across the world for many years. The family capital they shared so generously was built on the profits of their pharmaceutical company Purdue Pharma. However, everything changed in 2019, when the company faced legal charges because of the addictive nature of their opioid pain killer OxyContin, which resulted in thousands of deaths from drug overdose in the United States alone. The family and its donations were no longer welcomed (Harris, 2019). Again, what to think about these people and their family company? Should we separate their commitment and generosity to the cultural and scientific community from their business practices? Can the good they tried to do somehow compensate for the bad that was caused by their family firm? Might they – at some point – have cultivated their status as community benefactors deliberately, to distract the media and the general public from asking questions about how this money was generated?

The same companies can be seen as moral or as immoral, and moral and immoral behaviors apparently co-exist, even within the same individuals. Billionaire software entrepreneur Bill Gates has been accused of breaking tax laws, but also seeks to give away a considerable proportion of his estate to charitable purposes. The same is true for many other wealthy entrepreneurs and investors. The frontman of rock band U2 'Bono' is well-known for his outspoken opinions about the moral responsibilities of governments and business leaders towards poor people in third world countries. Nevertheless, the 'paradise papers' revealed that Bono does not show more social responsibility than many companies and citizens in seeking out opportunities for tax avoidance, even while donating money to charity (Goff, 2017).

The cynical view – one often voiced by the media and members of the general public – is that all this is strategy. Individuals and organizations alike publicly pledge their commitment to socially responsible goals, hoping to improve their own or their company's reputation for their own personal benefit – or so it is thought (Ormiston & Wong, 2013). In reality things are rarely that simple. Every organization has to contend with multiple stakeholders, whose interests do not necessarily align (see also Chap. 7).

Companies are often forced by their shareholders to enhance their profits so as to avoid losing the financial security that allows them to select their own strategic priorities – for instance to become more socially responsible. In the light of the hostile take-over bid by Kraft-Heinz, Unilever decided to placate shareholders by starting a share buy-back program, increasing dividends, and reducing costs by 2 billion US dollars, even if this went against its sustainable living plan. CEO Polman stated "We had to make some practical compromises… which I frankly would not have done"… "We just deliver and let the numbers talk, but unfortunately that's not possible for the majority of how the financial markets still operate" (Edgecliffe-Johnson, 2018; see also Smit, 2019).

Or take Boeing. Core values of this company emphasize high standards and accountability for engineering excellence. The pledge to prioritize safety, quality, and integrity in its production methods and services explicitly states: 'that's why we will always take the time to get the engineering right' (Boeing, n.d.). Yet the accidents with the 737 Max were attributed to pressure placed on the construction department to deliver this new airplane ahead of competitors in the market. As the single surviving airplane manufacturer in the USA, the profitability of the company not only determines CEO bonuses, but also has national significance. It is needed to secure continued investment in new aviation technologies, and retain specialized expertise and production capacity for the USA. Boeing is also the main employer in the city of Seattle, providing jobs for over 150.000 employees worldwide (Statista Research Department, 2020). This makes it very likely that a range of different concerns prompted the company to speed up production to bring their new aircraft to market. It would be too easy to conclude that the people running this company simply are greedy individuals, or that the decision to cut corners in safety testing was prompted only by profit motives.

The clashes between multiple interests and the weighing of incompatible concerns not only burden organizational leaders who have to make strategic decisions. In their more mundane activities many employees face similar dilemmas on a daily basis. Some face so much 'red tape' that compliance with all the rules and regulations would prevent them from finishing their assignments on time. Others may feel compelled to perform tasks that are not allowed in their protocol. For instance, some teachers go against school policy by giving away food or school supplies to children living in poverty. Some healthcare workers ignore requests from management to work more efficiently when they take time to sit down with elderly clients to prevent them from feeling lonely. In fact, these unauthorized initiatives may contribute more to the educational or health outcomes that define the mission of their organization than protocolled tasks. All of these examples attest to one thing: people who try to do what is morally good often have to balance different principles, interests and outcomes against each other. The moral choices they make tell us about how they prioritize these different concerns in a specific situation, but this does not imply they are immoral. After all, the good Dr. Jekyll and the evil Mr. Hyde simply are different character reflections of one and the same person (Padnick, 2012).

1.2.2 *Do We Even Agree on What Is Moral?*

In part, the dilemmas people face in situations such as these stem from the problem that there is no direct relation between the abstract moral principles so many people endorse (being loyal or fair, caring for others) and the concrete behaviors these moral principles prescribe in a particular situation. This can give rise to cross-national differences in what are considered acceptable business practices, due to specific cultural interpretations of key organizational responsibilities and desired outcomes (Ahmed et al., 2003). For instance, Maori values in New Zealand have been found to translate into a focus on organizational stewardship and well-being as relevant business concerns, which are less prominent elsewhere in the world (Spiller et al., 2011).

We will see examples of similar issues, for instance in Chap. 5 on diversity and inclusion, where we show that even if all employees in the organization value fairness in career opportunities, they may still disagree on whether the adoption of a particular diversity policy makes the process more fair or unfair. For instance, talent programs for women may seem fair to those who think that the organization currently fails to notice the leadership potential of female employees. However, these same programs may seem grossly unfair from the perspective of men who feel excluded from the guidance and mentoring offered to women only. At the same time, the tendency of both groups of people to anchor their view on this specific issue (the talent program) in broader moral principles (importance of fairness) makes it very difficult to acknowledge that opposing views (for or against the talent program for women) may be driven by very similar moral concerns (the desire to secure fair procedures for career advancement).

These types of disagreements are not easy to resolve and can invite intense conflict. Conflicts sometimes are fueled by leaders of political factions or religious groups, who all claim their specific way of showing fairness, loyalty or care is the only acceptable way (Harinck & Ellemers, 2014). Disagreements about moral issues may come about not because some people adhere to moral principles while others do not, but because different people prioritize different moral principles (Haidt, 2012). In fact, this lies at the root of many political conflicts, where people disagree on whether to prioritize individual freedom over authority (should people have the right to abortion), loyalty over fairness (should we help the weak), or contrast purity with harm (should people be allowed to refuse vaccination; see Box 1.3).

Box 1.3 Moral principles and moral identities

Different theoretical approaches highlight the importance of socially shared moral principles for people's sense of self and identity. These often take a *normative* perspective, in that they define moral behavior as people's tendency to adhere to specific issues and principles. The final approach listed below is the one we favor in this book, because it addresses the *process* through which different views and behaviors can come to be seen as moral or immoral. This process is guided by situational factors that play a role in the workplace.

Moral Foundations Theory distinguishes between different types of *moral reasoning*. The assumption is that different principles that can be used to make moral decisions (so-called 'moral foundations' such as individual fairness and care or group loyalty and authority) are relevant for different people. The realization that others prioritize similar moral principles may tie people together, and is used to characterize and separate groups with distinct political or religious views (Graham & Haidt, 2010; Graham et al., 2009; Graham et al., 2011; Haidt, 2008, 2012). However, this does not explain how these broader principles translate into specific guidelines for acceptable behavior, for instance in the workplace.

Moral Mandates indicate *specific worldviews* characterized by behaviors that seem fundamentally right or wrong (such as female circumcision or gay marriage). Considering these convictions as universally valid and objectively true, makes people hostile towards others who contest their views, and can induce aggression between groups. The seemingly mandatory nature of such convictions causes them to resist new information or majority opinions countering their views. It can even make people reluctant to comply with legal authorities (Mullen & Skitka, 2006; Skitka et al., 2005; Skitka & Mullen, 2002; Skitka, 2010; Skitka et al., 2008). The cultural values and life choices central to this approach are not obviously useful to explain moral transgressions in organizations.

Moral Identity refers to the extent to which people use specific traits (such as honesty or care), as defining their *ideal self-views*. These internalized moral identities are seen to guide the behavioral choices people make, and impact on how far they extend their 'circle of moral regard'. This approach emphasizes individual differences in moral behavior. Yet evidence reveals that group-level and situational factors – such as performance-based financial incentives – can make internalized moral ideals seem less relevant as behavioral guidelines (Aquino et al., 2009; Aquino & Reed II, 2002; Reed II & Aquino, 2003; Shao et al., 2008; Smith et al., 2014).

The Behavioral Regulation Model highlights concerns for inclusion and social esteem as key *social mechanisms* that groups and their leaders use to regulate individual moral behaviors. By defining which behaviors emulate 'moral goodness' groups actively contribute to inviting, rewarding, and perpetuating specific behaviors in their members. Group-specific interpretations (e.g., don't cheat customers) of more abstract moral guidelines (care for others), are used to separate those who are respected and included from those who are devalued and shunned (Ellemers, 2017, 2018; Ellemers et al., 2013; Ellemers & Van den Bos, 2012; Ellemers & Van Nunspeet, 2020). This approach is central to the analyses in this book because it focuses on ways in which individual moral choices in workplace behavior can be influenced by situational forces represented by professional groups, work teams and organizations.

In a nutshell then, the problem is this: what is moral for some, is not moral for others – yet both parties are convinced of their own morality, sometimes even referring to the same considerations. Moreover, it is hard to compromise on morality and values, or to accept different viewpoints on – often – inherently emotionally involving topics. This is where we begin to see why it is so difficult to resolve choices that are morally charged. In the next chapter we will further explain why it is impossible to understand such moral conflicts without taking into account people's social roles and group memberships. The different roles and responsibilities people have at work and in life, and the groups to which they belong, color their perspective on the situation that drives their moral convictions. The reverse is also true, as supporting and enacting specific guidelines for moral behavior also communicates loyalty to specific groups, and secures acceptance and inclusion by others. Considering these social influences and group-level mechanisms is crucial to understanding how people deal with moral dilemmas in organizations, as we will elaborate in Chap. 2, when explaining the social identity approach to moral behavior in organizations.

So how can people in organizations do what is morally right? By definition, organizations are made up of many different individuals who have to work together as employees and managers. Yet they may disagree about the importance of different moral principles as well as the specific courses of action these prescribe for their behavior in the workplace. Moreover, those on the 'inside' of the organization may weigh the likelihood and severity of specific outcomes differently than those on the outside, simply because they view these from a different perspective. For instance, a study found that professionals in the packaging industry were less inclined to consider the ethical implications of depicting attractive graphics on hazardous products than their customers, even if all endorsed the same moral values (Bone & Corey, 2000). Such moral disagreements that refer to the prioritization of different concerns or outcomes usually cannot be resolved simply by seeking additional information or weighing the costs and benefits of different options. In fact, as we have seen, the paradox of morality implies that especially when people are motivated to do what is morally right, they find it painful to consider that others might disapprove of their moral choices. The net result is that people tend to feel extremely uncomfortable engaging with the question of how and why their moral preferences deviate from those of others. In people's personal lives they can resolve this by seeking out others (for friendship, or political action) who endorse the same moral principles and approve of their moral choices, instead of challenging them. In the workplace, people usually do not have the luxury of choosing with whom to interact.

1.2.3 Moral Disengagement as a Way Out

At work, people are compelled to spend time and join forces with others who might have very different views on important moral choices. What happens then? More often than not, this will lead to frustration and conflict. Scientific research shows that people tend to experience discomfort when others make them consider the moral implications of their behavior. This was the response observed in a study where individuals went along with the request to argue for something they disagreed with, before confronting them with 'moral rebels' – who refused the same request on the grounds of it being unethical. Participants in this research disliked and even discredited the moral rebel. Instead of reconsidering the moral rectitude of their own actions, they resented the person who exposed the moral hazards of their own unthinking compliance (Monin et al., 2008). Likewise, it was revealed that employees who report unethical behavior in the organization (employee theft or fraud) are seen as highly ethical but are also disliked by their co-workers (Treviño & Victor, 1992).

A popular way out of this moral minefield is to simply avoid considering morality in the workplace – by ignoring the moral implications of choices that are made. Following Milton Friedman and his influential 'Chicago School' approach to economics, separating moral judgments from business decisions (considering these to be 'amoral' – not relevant to moral concerns) is what many business schools teach future generations of business leaders (e.g., Bayer & Rouse, 2016; Derks et al., 2018; Painter-Morland & Slegers, 2018; Parker, 2018; Rosati et al., 2018). Just focusing on the financial costs and benefits to determine the business outcomes of different actions, or monitoring whether decisions are acceptable from a legal point of view makes the discussion about appropriate vs inappropriate forms of behavior in the workplace more realistic and manageable. This seems a viable, commonly used strategy which encourages organizations to consider different stakeholders merely as self-interested agents instead of incorporating moral and other-regarding concerns into their decision making (Jones et al., 2007). However, neglecting moral concerns can also lead organizations to develop 'ethical blind spots' that put them at risk of inviting or condoning practices that clearly violate common moral principles (Martin et al., 2014; Moore et al., 2006; Sezer et al., 2015). Focusing one's attention away from moral concerns can alter important priorities, and prevent people from considering how the achievement of business goals may jeopardize social responsibilities of the organization and its members (Stachowicz-Stanusch et al., 2017). This is a relevant risk, especially in organizations that focus on short term goals and outcomes (Bazerman & Tenbrunsel, 2011; Burrows, 1993; Moore & Gino, 2013).

The decision to only consider cost/benefit calculations or legal implications, implicitly conveys messages about human nature and the moral values that are (not) important in the organization (Rehn, 2008; Treviño & McCabe, 1994). This happens for instance in the common practice of labeling human workers as organizational 'resources' or social 'capital' (Ayios et al., 2014; Greenwood, 2011). Even without meaning to, using these business terms can facilitate the tendency of considering people only as a potential asset or liability in relation to business interests (Mease & Collins, 2018). This makes it easy to forget about the human needs and broader concerns of these individuals. It puts the organization at risk of failing to care for the well-being or long term interests of employees as valued stakeholders, instead of considering them as expendable resources. Likewise, the common practice of applying sports and game metaphors in the language of business impacts on the implicit understanding people have of the key goals and ethical guidelines that are relevant (Hamington, 2009; see also Morgan, 1986). This makes it easy to think that in business people should do 'anything to win', or to view the consequences of their decisions for workers, clients, and other stakeholders as being 'all in the game'. Yet this is the type of instrumental business culture that has been associated with the emergence of cheating, fraud, and other forms of unethical behavior in organizations (Martin & Cullen, 2006, see Chap. 8).

The persistence of such seemingly innocuous labels and widespread business practices – and the powerful messages they convey about the 'real' goals and priorities of the company – might also explain why formal instruction in business ethics so often seems ineffective (Waples et al., 2009). Providing instruction in the form of isolated courses is bound to have little effect, as long as business and legal concerns permeate all the implicit assumptions and standard approaches students are taught to use in addressing a variety of topics in management (see Box 1.4). This also explains why it is so difficult for organizations and the people working in them to behave consistently in ways that are considered 'moral' or ethically responsible, even if this is what they honestly try to do.

Box 1.4 Economic approaches to human behavior

Several Nobel prizes in economics (awarded to Herbert Simon, Daniel Kahneman, Richard Thaler, George Akerlof) highlight the added value of psychology to understand economic decision making (Akerlof & Kranton, 2010; Akerlof & Shiller, 2010). The notion that psychological mechanisms can inform economic decision making is recognized by the development of behavioral economics, economic psychology, and neuro-economics as areas of interest. For instance, studies with economic games reveal that people do lie or cheat for self-gain, without anticipating this or even admitting this is what they do (Ariely, 2013; Shalvi et al., 2015).

Despite the added value and importance attached to insights from psychology, these are not incorporated as a matter of course in the standard economic models that are so commonly used in the business world. As a result, attempts to curb undesired behavior primarily focus on economic cost-benefit thinking – for instance by reducing opportunities for self-gain. This standard remedy assumes that people make decisions about acceptable vs unacceptable behaviors on economic grounds, rather than moral grounds. Being guided by models of human behavior that only distinguish between 'rational' and 'irrational' choices, actually prompts people to consider the consequences of their decisions as 'amoral' (a domain where moral judgments are not relevant) instead of encouraging them to think of their actions as moral or immoral.

The dominant tendency of economists to consider people as utility-maximizing actors is criticized by an international movement to 'rethink economics'. It was started by students demanding a better fit of their education to economic and social realities. Analyses of university economics programs reveal that the vast majority of courses continue to rely on quantitative models of market mechanisms based on rational choices, without addressing specific sectors, contexts, or real life economic problems. Other approaches outside this 'main stream' are optional and typically take up only a small fraction of course time (Tieleman et al., 2017). Thus, even if economists do acknowledge that insights from psychology about the role of emotions, information processing biases and heuristics in decision making are seen to contribute to the prediction of human behavior, this is usually not followed through in the problem analyses and practical recommendations they make.

In sum, people generally assume that 'everyone in their right mind' is likely to agree on what is morally acceptable and what is not. Our analysis shows why this implicit assumption is false. There are many situations, particularly in a work context, where is not very clear which moral principles apply, how these might be relevant, or what these would prescribe. Moreover, organizations generally have to contend with the interests of many internal as well as external stakeholders who may prioritize the different concerns affecting their view on what is morally right. It would be too easy to think that organizational choices that do not seem ethically responsible only indicate that the people making these choices must be immoral.

1.3 Solutions: Influencing Moral Behavior in Organizations

Earlier in this chapter, we outlined three typical approaches to dealing with immoral behavior in organizations: (1) the individual difference approach: find and replace the guilty individuals, (2) the economic approach: use incentives and punishment to get people on the right track, and (3) the legal approach: develop additional rules to specify (un)acceptable behavior and increase monitoring to make sure people comply with these rules. We will now provide a more in-depth analysis to show why the assumptions about human behavior underlying these quick fixes are far too limited (see Fig. 1.3). This should clarify why we highlight the emotional and motivational impact of *social roles and identities* and the moral ideals these represent – to complement these well-known perspectives.

1.3.1 Limits of the Individual Difference Approach

Many analyses of – and solutions for – apparently immoral behavior focus on the *individuals* who do things that are unethical or illegal. These are seen as the infamous 'bad apples'. Once they are discovered and removed, the problem is solved – or so we like to believe. This approach is in line with classic views in psychology which are based on the assumption that some individuals suffer from incomplete moral development during childhood (Rest, 1986). Some people just have difficulty judging what is morally right or wrong, or are simply not motivated to act upon such judgments, according to this view (see Box 1.2). Attempts to identify the character traits and other characteristics that predispose people to immoral or criminal behavior follow this approach (e.g., Becker, 1998; Detert et al., 2008). This has led to the development of personality inventories and other tests that aim to assess people's general inclination to display empathy, honesty, or humility, or ask them to indicate the importance they attach to behaving morally (Aquino & Reed II, 2002; Ashton & Lee, 2008a).

Some of these efforts target specific sectors that are seen as particularly vulnerable in this sense, for instance because their role in society is too important, or because the temptation may be too great. For instance, specific versions of ethics education and tests for integrity and moral development have been developed for students and professionals in accounting (e.g. Christensen et al., 2016; Kidwell, 2001; Lv & Huang, 2012). Business ethics education is put forward as a solution, by examining its impact on hypothetical decision making in moral dilemmas (e.g., Borkowski & Ugras, 1998; May et al., 2014), but does this predict actual behavior in work contexts?

Many studies attest to the limitations of these individual difference approaches, such as a meta-analysis which statistically summarizes the results of 136 different studies containing data from 40,000 workers (Kish-Gephart et al., 2010). This examination of possible origins of behavior in organizations found that the work *environment* is a more decisive predictor of moral behavior than individual level characteristics (such as empathy or private endorsement of moral principles, see also Treviño et al., 2014). Other studies too have documented the power of such situational factors. These revealed that the relation between individual moral intent and moral behavior depends on organizational characteristics (Jones, 1991), and demonstrated that institutional and community contexts also impact on individual moral reasoning (Shao et al., 2008).

Yet the individual difference approach is tempting and remains widespread. When an incident comes to light, the solutions sought to prevent future problems often reflect this individual level approach. These typically advocate increased scrutiny in personnel recruitment and training, aided by integrity tests and ethics classes. Measures such as these are put in place to identify and contain the problem by 'changing the people'. However, the reality is that similar problems occur time and time again, even after intensified efforts to identify and remove 'bad apples'. Apparently, investing in the development of ever more refined instruments to avoid hiring the 'wrong' individuals or to identify – and eliminate – those who have slipped through the recruitment net, does not solve all problems. There is also a clear downside to the bad apple approach: however convenient it may seem. No matter how great the relief it can provide to assume that the problem is solved after ridding the bad apple from the organization, the truth is it usually does not work. Often, aspects of the organizational culture or climate have promoted the problems that have come to the light. If these underlying long term issues are not resolved, such problems will persist – regardless of the individuals involved.

At Boeing, for instance, months after CEO Dennis Muilenburg resigned, 'foreign object debris' was discovered inside the fuel tanks of some 737 Max aircrafts (Jolly & Rushe, 2020). These remnants of tools, rags, and metal shavings left behind by workers during the production process could cause electrical short-circuiting and fires, and should have been discovered and removed during the final inspection of the aircrafts before delivery. Of course, CEO's will not be directly involved in managing such menial tasks, but this also clarifies that simply making the CEO resign did not necessarily contribute to solving the underlying problems at Boeing.

1.3.2 Limits of the Economic Approach

In organizations, strategic and everyday decisions are made on a continual basis. This requires that the costs and benefits of different options are weighed on the basis of many kinds of information. At management level strategic decisions are made about investments, pricing, staffing, production processes, etcetera. On the work floor individuals have to enact company policies by deciding which task to do first, what to do when things take longer than intended, or whom to ask for help if vital equipment is not working. It is hard to imagine an organization surviving without relying on the processing of relevant information that guides the cost/benefit calculations which inform rational choices.

Almost every society embraces the human ideal that the individual members of these societies are prepared to find and process appropriate information. Formal education and professional training programs teach people how to weigh the costs and benefits of different outcomes to make decisions based on rational considerations. Not surprisingly, most management theories on human behavior – and the management tools that are developed to influence it – are closely aligned to this human ideal. It is increasingly recognized that there are many non-rational aspects of human behavior. Yet organizational practices based on the standard rational choice approach persist and have – sometimes unexpected – moral implications (see Box 1.4).

Rational decision making based on cost/benefit trade-offs is not always appropriate, even in a business context. Let's take the two examples cited at the outset of this chapter: automobile producer Ford was seen to weigh the costs of adapting defective fuel systems in its cars against the expenses of injuries from accidental explosions. Boeing was accused of prioritizing speed and economy of production over the installation of extra safety options and additional certification procedures. Although different accounts of these incidents exist, public outrage in both cases was inspired in particular by the economic approach to these decisions. The personal safety and well-being of customers was reduced to a business cost that was factored into the rational decision making process.

Such reluctance to estimate and negotiate about the value of human lives in monetary terms has been identified as a specific instance of a more general phenomenon. These so-called 'taboo' trade-offs pertain to all situations where economic indicators are used to evaluate the worth of societal outcomes that many consider 'priceless', such as human lives, ecological survival, or world peace (Tetlock, 2003). Research has documented that people resist making such trade-offs. Decisions made on this basis may therefore backfire. For instance, local citizens resisted when financial payment was offered to compensate for the burden of industrial projects on the community (Terwel et al., 2014). The focus on rational choices and commercial calculations is even more likely to be considered inappropriate and result in consumer backlash for companies that are seen to serve a public function, for instance in health care (McGraw et al., 2011). Indeed, such concerns often arise whenever there is public debate about the maximum costs of medical treatments claiming to cure life-threatening diseases. Attempts to estimate the economic value of saving lives during the COVID-19 pandemic – weighing the impact of measures to curb spread of the disease against loss of jobs and income – were considered inappropriate by many, as they seemed to imply a taboo trade-off (Yakusheva, 2020).

Because so many consider it bad taste or even unethical to compare such morally charged communal outcomes in terms of their monetary value, a common temptation is to somehow bring moral outcomes and business outcomes to the same level. Facilitating decision making about such unequal comparisons can be achieved either by downgrading moral goals – reducing these to business-level concerns – or by upgrading business goals, invoking higher level moral principles which supposedly guide them. This strategy is used to defuse unwelcome moral appeals, by expressing suspicion that moral concerns are merely cited as a strategy to mask more selfish interests. For instance, consumer protests against industrial innovations that might damage the natural environment, may be refuted by arguing that in truth consumers are 'mainly concerned about price increases resulting from these innovations. Here, broader moral concerns about environmental protection are dismissed by assuming these arguments are driven by lower level and selfish economic concerns. Sometimes, these suspicions are justified. Indeed organizations may seek acceptance of their decisions, by highlighting benefits that would address moral – instead of economic – concerns.

Some businesses hope to pre-empt public critique for neglecting environmental damage of their activities in this way. For instance, they may point out the public interest in retaining jobs for the local community – which is made possible by saving on expenses for environmentally responsible production methods. In this case, the decision to sacrifice the environment for economic reasons is legitimized by claiming that moral concerns instead of business concerns were decisive (Ashforth & Anand, 2003; Tetlock, 2003). Notwithstanding such resolution strategies, the fact that many people continue to think of such trade-offs as 'taboo' implies that organizations cannot afford to ignore the moral implications of their calculations and strategic decisions – if only to avoid reputational damage. These insights also clarify that preferences of workers and customers cannot always be predicted from rational choices based on cost/benefit calculations.

The influence of moral reasoning in thinking about cost/benefit analyses and financial outcomes has been documented in empirical research. Several studies have revealed that moral concerns impact on people's investment decisions (Hofmann et al., 2008; Hofmann et al., 2007). For instance, investors tend to give higher estimates of the value, and generally prefer to invest their funds in organizations that appear to display socially responsible decision making (Petersen & Vredenburg, 2009; See also Chap. 7). A similar picture emerges from more basic research on human decision making, showing that group norms and moral concerns can outweigh the value of more selfish outcomes (Andiappan & Dufour, 2018; Rosati et al., 2018). For instance, concerns about moral responsibilities can outweigh price considerations in predicting the likelihood that consumers will buy specific products (Irwin & Baron, 2001).

Treating workers (as well as customers and other stakeholders) as calculating individuals who only care about cost/benefit ratios can do more harm than good. If not managed well, pay for performance undermines intrinsic work motivation and creativity (Gerhart & Fang, 2015, see also Chap. 4 on motivation). Differences in pay levels within the same company, within work teams or between managers and production workers, can negatively influence work attitudes, performance, and turnover rates in the company (Shaw, 2014, see also Chap. 3 on leadership). Even in situations where cost/benefit calculations seem decisive – as in the international migration of nurses to more developed countries – the career choices people make are also driven by non-economic factors such as the political climate, professional development opportunities, or interpersonal relations (Dywili et al., 2013).

1.3.3 Limits of the Legal Approach

The legal perspective on coordinating behavior in organizations relies heavily on top-down thinking. In a way it is also based on a rational choice approach: rule compliance is expected because people want to avoid being punished for failing to comply. Here, the coordination of individual efforts is achieved by anticipating different courses of action people might follow and specifying the desirability of each, in ever expanding lists of company regulations, professional guidelines, and codes of conduct. Managers, compliance officers, quality monitors, or external regulators then make sure that people actually work in accordance with these guidelines. This approach requires detailed record keeping, and elaborate supervision and monitoring of activities.

A problem often encountered by external regulators is that this type of regulation invites so-called 'rule-based' (rather than 'principle-based') compliance (Arjoon, 2006; Burgemeestre et al., 2009). Offering detailed descriptions of what people should do to meet professional standards, easily tempts them to 'tick the boxes' without really thinking whether this actually leads to the intended result – often defeating the ultimate goal (see Box 1.5). Moreover, lists specifying everything that is not allowed can invite employees as well as legal experts to search for loopholes as they conclude that actions not included in the list of prohibitions must be permitted. In both cases, the individuals whose choices are being monitored are discouraged from considering which concerns gave rise to the regulations, as they focus on *what* they should do instead of *why* they should do this. Thus, they are not invited to make sure they understand what the end goal of their efforts is, or how they might work towards this goal when it is unclear how known rules might apply (Ford, 2008). Rule-based supervision may not even be feasible for innovative service-based economies, where products, markets, and procedures change too quickly to be able to anticipate their outcomes (see also Chap. 6). This makes it difficult for supervisors to ensure that formal guidelines are still relevant, and is another reason that they might better communicate about key principles rather than monitoring compliance with specific rules.

Box 1.5 Rule-based and principle-based regulation

Legal approaches to behavioral regulation rely on the definition of rules for acceptable conduct and specification of sanctions for breaking these rules. In this approach, sanctions are used as a primary tool to make people incapable of continuing unacceptable behavior (by removing them from the situation), offering justice to victims, and compensation for damage done. The key assumption is that the (threat of) punishment will influence the choices people make. When people display unacceptable behavior, this is typically tackled by adding more rules, intensifying monitoring, and raising sanctions to deter further rule breaking.

In response to bookkeeping fraud and large scandals, several legal measures were taken to counter this. In the United States, the Sarbanes-Oxley act was introduced for this purpose in 2002. This is a set of rules that specifies what companies should do to guard impartiality, transparency, accountability, truthfulness, and respect for rights ("Sarbanes-Oxley Act", 2002). These regulations specify responsibilities of executives, audit committees and auditors, sanctions for non-compliance, and a government board (the Public Company Accounting Oversight Board – PCAOB), which is overseen by the Securities and Exchange Commission (SEC). However, it has been criticized for its reliance on legal solutions for moral dilemmas – that encourage decision makers to seek loopholes - as well as for the additional bureaucracy ('red tape') it imposes on companies across the world (Sama & Shoaf, 2005).

Deviating from this 'rule-based' one-size-fits-all approach, guidelines of the European Commission, as well as regulations in the UK, Canada, Australia and New-Zealand have adopted a 'principle-based' approach. This makes it possible to specify local rules and accommodate different governance practices and national laws, without imposing a single specific set of rules. Common moral principles aim to improve corporate governance, for instance by promoting disclosure and transparency, and protecting shareholders rights. An examination of top-50 companies in New Zealand suggests that principle-based regulation can be just as effective as rule-based regulation. Compliance with key principles can just as well change the behavior of organizations and benefit firm financial performance (Reddy et al., 2010).

In practice, however, the legal approach to behavioral regulation continues to shine through. Regulators tend to apply broader principles by translating them into a large number of very specific rules organizations have to comply with. For instance, in New Zealand, the nine principles of good governance are assessed on the basis of 46 very specific criteria. The question therefore remains to what extent a 'principle-based' policy really invites legal entities to adopt a different approach in monitoring displays of desired behavior.

Enforcing top-down behavioral regulation depends on continued external monitoring. It also requires considerable resources to keep on implementing the rewards and sanctions needed to reinforce or discourage specific courses of action. In psychological theory and research, this coercive form of behavioral control is generally considered much weaker and less reliable than other known alternatives, such as the internalization of important professional values, or the voluntary adoption of model behaviors (e.g., Bausch, 2008; see also Van Steenbergen & Ellemers, 2021). This is acknowledged for instance in regulatory approaches that try to stay away from enforced rule compliance, because this does not emerge as a very helpful or even effective primary strategy (Braithwaite & Braithwaite, 2001; Desai, 2015; see also Box 8.4). Instead, such approaches aim to establish the cultural 'maturity' of organizations by assessing the extent to which rule adherence is seen as an internalized good instead of relying on external compliance (Hogan, 2008; Tyler, 2005). Indeed, even if there is no legal requirement, entrepreneurs may choose to consider their social responsibilities (Choi & Gray, 2008). Individual managers can do this, for instance, because this matches their personal values (Hemingway & Maclagan, 2004), or because they want to display awareness of their moral duty to gain trust from important stakeholders (Hosmer, 1996; Quinn & Jones, 1995).

There are drawbacks to rule enforcement within the organization too. In general, reliance on external controls easily undermines feelings of autonomy that are key to intrinsic motivation (Deci & Ryan, 2010). People tend to resent continuous surveillance and resist enforced rule compliance in organizations (McNamara & Reicher, 2019; O'Donnell et al., 2013). Experiments have found that attempts to deter people from rule breaking by threatening them with sanctions tend to spoil mutual trust. Ironically, this actually *undermines* compliance, for instance of tax payers with tax rules, or of students with plagiarism rules (Mooijman et al., 2017, 2019). In the workplace, employees have been found to show lower job satisfaction and a greater tendency to display dysfunctional behavior when they were forced to comply with behavioral norms that did not match their personal ethical opinions (Burks & Krupka, 2012). Likewise, employees who were subjected to formal controls to guide their behavior became more reluctant to share their knowledge with others in the organization (Tuan, 2012).

The limits of the legal approach are further clarified by studies attesting to the value of appealing to the power of personal engagement and internalized morals. For instance, workers developed a clearer idea on how best to behave when they understood how their actions relate to moral principles relevant to the core mission and identity of the organization (Reynolds & Ceranic, 2007; see also Turner, 1985). This also makes it more likely that they consider relevant principles instead of mindlessly applying specific rules (Neesham & Gu, 2015). A meta-analytic review summarizing results of 189 different studies additionally reveals that workers perform better when they have a voice in which goals to pursue and how to pursue them (Chamberlin et al., 2017).

1.4 Conclusion: The Three Quick Fixes Revisited

The three quick fixes all rely on *explicit* strategies organizations use to express their moral intentions – or are used by external regulators to enforce moral behavior in the organization. These are informed by standard organizational procedures and practices aiming to guide the behavior of individuals in organizations. However, results from many studies reveal that their impact on moral behavior is limited and may even backfire. More often than not, explicit moral guidelines and decisions have to be reconciled with other strategic and organizational realities – preventing people in organizations to do what is moral. This *implicit* information speaking to the moral culture and ethical climate in the organization, tends to be underestimated or even ignored. We argue that the 'hidden influence' of these situational and group mechanisms should be taken into account when attempting to understand why moral intentions do not result in moral behaviors. Attempts to address moral behavior in organizations should therefore also examine the hidden costs of standard procedures and practices – even if these occur at the implicit level. Any misalignment between explicit and implicit messages and moral guidelines can stand in the way of moral behavior – also when this is motivated by the best of intentions (see also Fig. 1.3).

In the chapters that follow we highlight the hidden costs of standard procedures used to address key concerns in organizational behavior. We focus on psychological mechanisms relating to group memberships and organizational roles, to elucidate how organizational realities members have to deal with lead them to adopt and internalize specific moral norms. Our analysis of key issues in organizational life in the following chapters is based on Social Identity Theory. This influential theory in social and organizational psychology complements standard approaches exemplified by the three quick fixes commonly used (see also Haslam, 2004, 2014). We argue that the social identities that are relevant in the workplace allow people to make sense of the situation and to reconcile explicit requests with implicit realities. This helps them to translate general moral principles into situational norms about 'right' vs. 'wrong' ways to behave in the workplace. Unfortunately, considering the situation at work in this way also makes people vulnerable. When workplace behaviors somehow seem morally 'wrong' this impacts on people's sense of who they are and where they belong, threatening their sense of identity and inclusion. In the next chapter we specify the impact of such identity threats and consider the range of strategies people use as coping responses.

In the chapters that follow, we examine how common quick fixes to address moral behavior in organizations impact on the self-views and social identities of organizational members. Each chapter demonstrates the added value of attending to people's social identities when trying to change their behavior. We reveal the hidden costs of ignoring these broader social factors for **key issues** every organization contends with. We **analyze** real life cases from this perspective by reviewing results from research to reveal when and why things go wrong. We also provide positive examples of organizations that manage to get things right, and offer practical guidelines on how to work towards practical **solutions** to achieve this. We can't offer quick fixes, unfortunately, as our analyses and examples show that long term and broader organizational efforts constitute the most effective strategy for organizations choosing to do what is moral.

Recommended Reading

Ashforth, B. E., & Anand, V. (2003). The normalization of corruption in organizations. In R. M. Kramer & B. M. Staw (Eds.), *Research in organizational behavior: An annual series of analytical essays and critical reviews* (pp. 1–52). Elsevier Science Ltd.. https://doi.org/10.1016/S0191-3085(03)25001-2

Bazerman, M. H., & Tenbrunsel, A. E. (2011). *Blind spots: Why we fail to do what's right and what to do about it*. Princeton University Press. https://doi.org/10.1515/9781400837991

Ellemers, N., & Van der Toorn, J. (2015). Groups as moral anchors. *Current Opinion in Behavioral Sciences, 6*, 189–194. https://doi.org/10.1016/j.copsyc.2015.08.018

Haidt, J. (2012). *The righteous mind: Why good people are divided by politics and religion*. Vintage.

Shalvi, S., Gino, F., Barkan, R., & Ayal, S. (2015). Self-serving justifications: Doing wrong and feeling moral. *Current Directions in Psychological Science, 24*(2), 125–130.

References

Abele, A. E., Ellemers, N., Fiske, S. T., Koch, A., & Yzerbyt, V. (2020). Navigating the social world: Toward an integrated framework for evaluating self, individuals, and groups. *Psychological Review*. Advance online publication. https://doi.org/10.1037/rev0000262

Ahmed, M. M., Chung, K. Y., & Eichenseher, J. W. (2003). Business students' perception of ethics and moral judgment: A cross-cultural study. *Journal of Business Ethics, 43*(1–2), 89–102. https://doi.org/10.1023/A:1022915316112

Akerlof, G. A., & Kranton, R. (2010). Identity economics. *The Economists' Voice, 7*(2). https://doi.org/10.2202/1553-3832.1762

Akerlof, G. A., & Shiller, R. J. (2010). *Animal spirits: How human psychology drives the economy, and why it matters for global capitalism*. Princeton University Press.

Andiappan, M., & Dufour, L. (2018). Multi-level influences on the evolution of unethical behavior amongst longshoremen in France. *Academy of Management Proceedings, 2018*(1), 10809. Briarcliff Manor, NY 10510: Academy of Management.. https://doi.org/10.5465/AMBPP.2018.10809abstract

Aquino, K., Freeman, D., Reed, A., II, Lim, V. K. G., & Felps, W. (2009). Testing a social cognitive model of moral behavior: The interactive influence of situations and moral identity centrality. *Journal of Personality and Social Psychology, 97*, 123–141. https://doi.org/10.1037/a0015406

Aquino, K., & Reed, A., II. (2002). The self-importance of moral identity. *Journal of Personality and Social Psychology, 83*(6), 1423. https://doi.org/10.1037/0022-3514.83.6.1423

Ariely, D. (2013). *The honest truth about dishonesty: How we lie to everyone – Especially ourselves*. HarperCollins.

Arjoon, S. (2006). Striking a balance between rules and principles-based approaches for effective governance: A risks-based approach. *Journal of Business Ethics, 68*, 53–82. https://doi.org/10.1007/s10551-006-9040-6

Ashforth, B. E., & Anand, V. (2003). The normalization of corruption in organizations. In R. M. Kramer & B. M. Staw (Eds.), *Research in organizational behavior: An annual series of analytical essays and critical reviews* (pp. 1–52). Elsevier Science Ltd.. https://doi.org/10.1016/S0191-3085(03)25001-2

Ashforth, B. E., Schinoff, B. S., & Brickson, S. L. (2020). "My company is friendly", "Mine's a rebel": Anthropomorphism and shifting organizational identity from "what" to "who". *Academy of Management Review, 45*, 29–57. https://doi.org/10.5465/amr.2016.0496

Ashton, M. C., & Lee, K. (2007). Empirical, theoretical, and practical advantages of the HEXACO model of personality structure. *Personality and Social Psychology Review, 11*(2), 150–166. https://doi.org/10.1177/1088868306294907

Ashton, M. C., & Lee, K. (2008a). The HEXACO model of personality structure and the importance of the H factor. *Social and Personality Psychology Compass, 2*(5), 1952–1962. https://doi.org/10.1111/j.1751-9004.2008.00134.x

Ashton, M. C., & Lee, K. (2008b). The prediction of Honesty–Humility-related criteria by the HEXACO and Five-Factor Models of personality. *Journal of Research in Personality, 42*(5), 1216–1228. https://doi.org/10.1016/j.jrp.2008.03.006

Ashton, M. C., & Lee, K. (2009). The HEXACO–60: A short measure of the major dimensions of personality. *Journal of Personality Assessment, 91*(4), 340–345. https://doi.org/10.1080/00223890902935878

Ayios, A., Jeurissen, R., Manning, P., & Spence, L. J. (2014). Social capital: A review from an ethics perspective. *Business Ethics: A European Review, 23*(1), 108–124. https://doi.org/10.1111/beer.12040

Bandura, A. (1999). Moral disengagement in the perpetration of inhumanities. *Personality and Social Psychology Review, 3*(3), 193–209. https://doi.org/10.1207/s15327957pspr0303_3

Bauman, C. W., McGraw, A. P., Bartels, D. M., & Warren, C. (2014). Revisiting external validity: Concerns about trolley problems and other sacrificial dilemmas in moral psychology. *Social and Personality Psychology Compass, 8*(9), 536–554. https://doi.org/10.1111/spc3.12131

Bausch, K. (2008). The ethics of emergence. *Systems Research and Behavioral Science, 25*(2), 271–276. https://doi.org/10.1002/sres.884

Bayer, A., & Rouse, C. E. (2016). Diversity in the economics profession: A new attack on an old problem. *Journal of Economic Perspectives, 30*(4), 221–242. https://doi.org/10.1257/jep.30.4.221

Bazerman, M. H., & Tenbrunsel, A. E. (2011). *Blind spots: Why we fail to do what's right and what to do about it*. Princeton University Press. https://doi.org/10.1515/9781400837991

Beauchamp, T. L. (2001). *Philosophical ethics: An introduction to moral philosophy*. Mcgraw-Hill.

Becker, T. E. (1998). Integrity in organizations: Beyond honesty and conscientiousness. *Academy of Management Review, 23*(1), 154–161. https://doi.org/10.5465/amr.1998.192969

Blascovich, J., & Tomaka, J. (1996). The biopsychosocial model of arousal regulation. *Advances in Experimental Social Psychology, 28*, 1–51. https://doi.org/10.1016/S0065-2601(08)60235-X

Boeing. (n.d.). *Our Values*. Boeing. Retrieved from https://www.boeing.com/principles/values.page

Böhm, B., Zollner, H., Fegert, J. M., & Liebhardt, H. (2014). Child sexual abuse in the context of the Roman Catholic Church: A review of literature from 1981–2013. *Journal of Child Sexual Abuse, 23*(6), 635–656. https://doi.org/10.1080/10538712.2014.929607

Bone, P. F., & Corey, R. J. (2000). Packaging ethics: Perceptual differences among packaging professionals, brand managers and ethically-interested consumers. *Journal of Business Ethics, 24*(3), 199–213. https://doi.org/10.1023/A:1006257523743

Borkowski, S. C., & Ugras, Y. J. (1998). Business students and ethics: A meta-analysis. *Journal of Business Ethics, 17*(11), 1117–1127. https://doi.org/10.1023/A:1005748725174

Braithwaite, V., & Braithwaite, J. (2001). An evolving compliance model for tax enforcement. In N. Shover & J. P. Wright (Eds.), *Crimes of privilege: Readings in white-collar crime*. Oxford University Press.

Brambilla, M., Sacchi, S., Pagliaro, S., & Ellemers, N. (2013). Morality and intergroup relations: Threats to safety and group image predict the desire to interact with outgroup and

ingroup members. *Journal of Experimental Social Psychology, 49*(5), 811–821. https://doi.org/10.1016/j.jesp.2013.04.005
Burgemeestre, B., Hulstijn, J., & Tan, Y. H. (2009). Rules-based versus principles-based regulators compliance. *Frontiers in Artificial Intelligence and Applications, 205*, 37–46.
Burks, S. V., & Krupka, E. L. (2012). A multimethod approach to identifying norms and normative expectations within a corporate hierarchy: Evidence from the financial services industry. *Management Science, 58*(1), 203–217. https://doi.org/10.1287/mnsc.1110.1478
Burrows, B. (1993). Essay review—The greening of business and its relationship to business ethics. *Long Range Planning, 26*(1), 130–139. https://doi.org/10.1016/0024-6301(93)90241-7
Chamberlin, M., Newton, D. W., & Lepine, J. A. (2017). A meta-analysis of voice and its promotive and prohibitive forms: Identification of key associations, distinctions, and future research directions. *Personnel Psychology, 70*(1), 11–71. https://doi.org/10.1111/peps.12185
Chirumbolo, A., & Leone, L. (2010). Personality and politics: The role of the HEXACO model of personality in predicting ideology and voting. *Personality and Individual Differences, 49*(1), 43–48. https://doi.org/10.1016/j.paid.2010.03.004
Choi, D. Y., & Gray, E. R. (2008). The venture development processes of "sustainable" entrepreneurs. *Management Research News*. https://doi.org/10.1108/01409170810892127
Christensen, A. L., Cote, J., & Latham, C. K. (2016). Insights regarding the applicability of the defining issues test to advance ethics research with accounting students: A meta-analytic review. *Journal of Business Ethics, 133*(1), 141–163. https://doi.org/10.1007/s10551-014-2349-7
Churchland, P. (2011). *Braintrust: What neuroscience tells us about morality*. Princeton University Press. https://doi.org/10.1515/9781400838080
Cloud, K. (2017, March 9). *Grocers become 'legends' as they again make '100 Best Companies To Work For' list*. The Shelby Report. Retrieved from https://www.theshelbyreport.com/2017/03/09/fortune-legends/
Cohn, A., Fehr, E., & Maréchal, M. A. (2014). Business culture and dishonesty in the banking industry. *Nature, 516*(7529), 86–89. https://doi.org/10.1038/nature13977
Deci, E. L., & Ryan, R. M. (2010). Intrinsic motivation. *The Corsini Encyclopedia of Psychology, 1–2*. https://doi.org/10.1002/9780470479216.corpsy0467
De Raad, B., Barelds, D. P., Mlačić, B., Church, A. T., Katigbak, M. S., Ostendorf, F., … Szirmák, Z. (2010). Only three personality factors are fully replicable across languages: Reply to Ashton and Lee. *Journal of Research in Personality, 44*(4), 442–445. https://doi.org/10.1016/j.jrp.2010.05.005
Derks, B., Van Veelen, R., & Handgraaf, M. (2018). Successful economists are highly masculine. *Economische Statistische Berichten, 103*(4767S), 16–19.
Desai, V. M. (2015). Under the radar: Regulatory collaborations and their selective use to facilitate organizational compliance. *Academy of Management Journal, 59*(2), 636–657. https://doi.org/10.5465/amj.2014.0943
Detert, J. R., Treviño, L. K., & Sweitzer, V. L. (2008). Moral disengagement in ethical decision making: A study of antecedents and outcomes. *Journal of Applied Psychology, 93*(2), 374. https://doi.org/10.1037/0021-9010.93.2.374
Dywili, S., Bonner, A., & O'Brien, L. (2013). Why do nurses migrate? A review of recent literature. *Journal of Nursing Management., 21*, 511–520. https://doi.org/10.1111/j.1365-2834.2011.01318.x
Edgecliffe-Johnson, A. (2018, February 27). Unilever chief admits Kraft Heinz bid forced compromises. *Financial Times*. Retrieved from https://www.ft.com/content/ea0218ce-1be0-11e8-aaca-4574d7dabfb6.
Eisenberg, N., Guthrie, I. K., Cumberland, A., Murphy, B. C., Shepard, S. A., Zhou, Q., & Carlo, G. (2002). Prosocial development in early adulthood: A longitudinal study. *Journal of Personality and Social Psychology, 82*(6), 993. https://doi.org/10.1037/0022-3514.82.6.993
Ellemers, N. (2017). *Morality and the regulation of social behavior: Groups as moral anchors*. Routledge. https://doi.org/10.4324/9781315661322

Ellemers, N. (2018). Morality and social identity. In M. van Zomeren & J. F. Dovidio (Eds.), *Oxford library of psychology* (pp. 147–158). Oxford University Press. https://doi.org/10.1093/oxfordhb/9780190247577.013.5

Ellemers, N., Kingma, L., Van de Burgt, J., & Barreto, M. (2011). Corporate social responsibility as a source of organizational morality, employee commitment and satisfaction. *Journal of Organizational Moral Psychology, 1*(2), 97–124.

Ellemers, N., & Van Nunspeet, F. (2020). Neuroscience and the social origins of moral behavior: How neural underpinnings of social categorization and conformity affect everyday moral and immoral behavior. *Current Directions in Psychological Science, 29*(5), 513–520. https://doi.org/10.1177/0963721420951584

Ellemers, N., Pagliaro, S., & Barreto, M. (2013). Morality and behavioral regulation in groups: A social identity approach. *European Review of Social Psychology, 24*(1), 160–193. https://doi.org/10.1080/10463283.2013.841490

Ellemers, N., Pagliaro, S., Barreto, M., & Leach, C. W. (2008). Is it better to be moral than smart? The effects of morality and competence norms on the decision to work at group status improvement. *Journal of Personality and Social Psychology, 95*(6), 1397. https://doi.org/10.1037/a0012628

Ellemers, N., & Van den Bos, K. (2012). Morality in groups: On the social: Regulatory functions of right and wrong. *Social and Personality Psychology Compass, 6*, 878–889. https://doi.org/10.1111/spc3.12001

Ellemers, N., & Van der Toorn, J. (2015). Groups as moral anchors. *Current Opinion in Behavioral Sciences, 6*, 189–194. https://doi.org/10.1016/j.copsyc.2015.08.018

Ellemers, N., Van der Toorn, J., Paunov, Y., & Van Leeuwen, T. (2019). The psychology of morality: A review and analysis of empirical studies published from 1940 through 2017. *Personality and Social Psychology Review, 23*(4), 332–366. https://doi.org/10.1177/1088868318811759

Fiske, A. P., & Rai, T. S. (2014). *Virtuous violence: Hurting and killing to create, sustain, end, and honor social relationships*. Cambridge University Press. https://doi.org/10.1017/CBO9781316104668

Ford, C. L. (2008). New governance, compliance, and principles-based securities regulation. *American Business Law Journal, 45*(1), 1–60. https://doi.org/10.1111/j.1744-1714.2008.00050.x

Gerhart, B., & Fang, M. (2015). Pay, intrinsic motivation, extrinsic motivation, performance, and creativity in the workplace: Revisiting long-held beliefs. *Annual Review of Organizational Psychology and Organizational Behavior, 2*, 489–521. https://doi.org/10.1146/annurev-orgpsych-032414-111418

Gert, B., & Gert, J. (2020, September 21). The definition of morality. *The Stanford Encyclopedia of Philosophy*. Retrieved from https://plato.stanford.edu/entries/morality-definition/.

Giner-Sorolla, R. (2012). *Judging passions: Moral emotion in persons and groups*. Psychology Press. https://doi.org/10.4324/9780203123874

Gioia, D. A. (1992). Pinto fires and personal ethics: A script analysis of missed opportunities. *Journal of Business Ethics, 11*, 379–389. https://doi.org/10.1007/BF00870550

Goff, P. (2017, November 7). Tax rogues like Bono are harming the world's poorest people. *The Guardian*. Retrieved from https://www.theguardian.com/commentisfree/2017/nov/07/tax-bono-harming-world-poorest-glastonbury-avoidance-paradise-papers.

Goldberg, L. R. (1990). An alternative" description of personality": The big-five factor structure. *Journal of Personality and Social Psychology, 59*(6), 1216. https://doi.org/10.1037/0022-3514.59.6.1216

Goodwin, G. P. (2015). Moral character in person perception. *Current Directions in Psychological Science, 24*(1), 38–44. https://doi.org/10.1177/0963721414550709

Graham, J. (2014). Morality beyond the lab. *Science, 345*(6202), 1242–1242. https://doi.org/10.1126/science.1259500

Graham, J., & Haidt, J. (2010). Beyond beliefs: Religions bind individuals into moral communities. *Personality and Social Psychology Review, 14*, 140–150. https://doi.org/10.1177/1088868309353415

Graham, J., Haidt, J., & Nosek, B. A. (2009). Liberals and conservatives rely on different sets of moral foundations. *Journal of Personality and Social Psychology, 96*, 1029–1045. https://doi.org/10.1037/a0015141

Graham, J., Nosek, B. A., Haidt, J., Iyer, R., Koleva, S., & Ditto, P. H. (2011). Mapping the moral domain. *Journal of Personality and Social Psychology, 101*, 366–385. https://doi.org/10.1037/a0021847

Greene, J. D. (2013). *Moral tribes: Emotion, reason, and the gap between us and them*. Penguin.

Greenwald, A. G., McGhee, D. E., & Schwartz, J. L. (1998). Measuring individual differences in implicit cognition: The implicit association test. *Journal of Personality and Social Psychology, 74*(6), 1464. https://doi.org/10.1037/0022-3514.74.6.1464

Greenwood, J. D. (2011). On the social dimensions of moral psychology. *Journal for the Theory of Social Behavior, 41*, 333–374. https://doi.org/10.1111/j.1468-5914.2011.00472.x

Haidt, J. (2001). The emotional dog and its rational tail: A social intuitionist approach to moral judgment. *Psychological Review, 108*(4), 814. https://doi.org/10.1037/0033-295X.108.4.814

Haidt, J. (2008). Morality. *Perspectives on Psychological Science, 3*, 65–72. https://doi.org/10.1111/j.1745-6916.2008.00063.x

Haidt, J. (2012). *The righteous mind: Why good people are divided by politics and religion*. Vintage.

Haidt, J., & Graham, J. (2007). When morality opposes justice: Conservatives have moral intuitions that liberals may not recognize. *Social Justice Research, 20*(1), 98–116. https://doi.org/10.1007/s11211-007-0034-z

Hamington, M. (2009). Business is not a game: The metaphoric fallacy. *Journal of Business Ethics, 86*(4), 473–484. https://doi.org/10.1007/s10551-008-9859-0

Harinck, F., & Ellemers, N. (2014). How values change a conflict. In C. K. W. de Dreu (Ed.), *Conflicts within and between groups: Functions, dynamics, and interventions* (pp. 19–36). Psychology Press.

Harris, E. A. (2019, May 15). The met will turn down sackler money amid fury over the opioid crisis. *Financial Times*. Retrieved from https://www.nytimes.com/2019/05/15/arts/design/met-museum-sackler-opioids.html

Haslam, S. A. (2004). *Psychology in organizations: The social identity approach*. Sage.

Haslam, S. A. (2014). Making good theory practical: Five lessons for an applied social identity approach to challenges of organizational, health, and clinical psychology. *British Journal of Social Psychology, 53*(1), 1–20. https://doi.org/10.1111/bjso.12061

Heilbrun, A., & Georges, M. (1990). The measurement of principled morality by the Kohlberg Moral Dilemma Questionnaire. *Journal of Personality Assessment, 55*, 183–194. https://doi.org/10.1207/s15327752jpa5501&2_17

Hemingway, C. A., & Maclagan, P. W. (2004). Managers' personal values as drivers of corporate social responsibility. *Journal of Business Ethics, 50*(1), 33–44. https://doi.org/10.1023/B:BUSI.0000020964.80208.c9

Hofmann, E., Hoelzl, E., & Kirchler, E. (2008). A comparison of models describing the impact of moral decision making on investment decisions. *Journal of Business Ethics, 82*(1), 171–187. https://doi.org/10.1007/s10551-007-9570-6

Hofmann, E., Meier-Pesti, K., & Kirchler, E. (2007). The decision process for ethical investment. *Journal of Financial Services Marketing, 12*(1), 4–16. https://doi.org/10.1057/palgrave.fsm.4760057

Hogan, T. J. (2008). The adaptive leadership maturity model. *Organization Development Journal, 26*(1).

Hosmer, L. T. (1996). Research notes and communications response to 'Do good ethics always make for good business?'. *Strategic Management Journal, 17*(6), 501. https://doi.org/10.1002/(SICI)1097-0266(199606)17:6<501::AID-SMJ812>3.0.CO;2-1

Irwin, J. R., & Baron, J. (2001). Response mode effects and moral values. *Organizational Behavior and Human Decision Processes, 84*(2), 177–197. https://doi.org/10.1006/obhd.2000.2920

Jolly, J., & Rushe, D. (2020, February 19). Boeing 737 Max: Debris found in fuel tanks of grounded planes. *The Guardian*. Retrieved from https://www.theguardian.com/business/2020/feb/19/boeing-737-max-debris-found-in-fuel-tanks-of-grounded-planes

Jones, T. M. (1991). Ethical decision making by individuals in organizations: An issue-contingent model. *Academy of Management Review, 16*(2), 366–395. https://doi.org/10.5465/amr.1991.4278958

Jones, T. M., Felps, W., & Bigley, G. A. (2007). Ethical theory and stakeholder-related decisions: The role of stakeholder culture. *Academy of Management Review, 32*(1), 137–155. https://doi.org/10.5465/amr.2007.23463924

Kidwell, L. A. (2001). Student honor codes as a tool for teaching professional ethics. *Journal of Business Ethics, 29*(1–2), 45–49. https://doi.org/10.1023/A:1006442925586

Kish-Gephart, J. J., Harrison, D. A., & Treviño, L. K. (2010). Bad apples, bad cases, and bad barrels: Meta-analytic evidence about sources of unethical decisions at work. *Journal of Applied Psychology, 95*, 1–31. https://doi.org/10.1037/a0017103

Kohlberg, L. (1971). *From is to ought: How to commit the naturalistic fallacy and get away with it in the study of moral development*. Academic. https://doi.org/10.1016/B978-0-12-498640-4.50011-1

Kohlberg, L. (1978). Revisions in the theory and practice of moral development. *New Directions for Child and Adolescent Development, 1978*(2), 83–87. https://doi.org/10.1002/cd.23219780207

Kouchaki, M., & Smith, I. H. (2020). Building an ethical career. *Harvard Business Review, 98*(1), 135–139.

Kouzakova, M., Harinck, F., Ellemers, N., & Scheepers, D. (2014). At the heart of a conflict: Cardiovascular and self-regulation responses to value versus resource conflicts. *Social Psychological and Personality Science, 5*(1), 35–42. https://doi.org/10.1177/1948550613486673

Leach, C. W., Bilali, R., & Pagliaro, S. (2015). Groups and morality. In M. Mikulincer, P. R. Shaver, J. F. Dovidio, & J. A. Simpson (Eds.), *APA handbooks in psychology. APA handbook of personality and social psychology* (Group processes) (Vol. 2, pp. 123–149). American Psychological Association. https://doi.org/10.1037/14342-005

López-Pérez, B., Howells, L., & Gummerum, M. (2017). Cruel to be kind: Factors underlying altruistic efforts to worsen another person's mood. *Psychological Science, 28*(7), 862–871. https://doi.org/10.1177/0956797617696312

Lv, W., & Huang, Y. (2012). How workplace accounting experience and gender effect ethical judgment. *Social Behavior and Personality, 40*(9), 1477–1483. https://doi.org/10.2224/sbp.2012.40.9.1477

Manz, C. C., Anand, V., Joshi, M., & Manz, K. P. (2008). Emerging paradoxes in executive leadership: A theoretical interpretation of the tensions between corruption and virtuous values. *The Leadership Quarterly, 19*(3), 385–392. https://doi.org/10.1016/j.leaqua.2008.03.009

Martin, K. D., & Cullen, J. B. (2006). Continuities and extensions of ethical climate theory: A meta-analytic review. *Journal of Business Ethics, 69*, 175–194. https://doi.org/10.1007/s10551-006-9084-7

Martin, S. R., Kish-Gephart, J. J., & Detert, J. R. (2014). Blind forces: Ethical infrastructures and moral disengagement in organizations. *Organizational Psychology Review, 4*(4), 295–325. https://doi-org.proxy.library.uu.nl/10.1177/2041386613518576.

May, D. R., Luth, M. T., & Schwoerer, C. E. (2014). The influence of business ethics education on moral efficacy, moral meaningfulness, and moral courage: A quasi-experimental study. *Journal of Business Ethics, 124*(1), 67–80. https://doi.org/10.1007/s10551-013-1860-6

Mazar, N., Amir, O., & Ariely, D. (2008). The dishonesty of honest people: A theory of self-concept maintenance. *Journal of Marketing Research, 45*(6), 633–644. https://doi.org/10.1509/jmkr.45.6.633

McCrae, R. R., & Costa, P. T., Jr. (1987). Validation of the five-factor model of personality across instruments and observers. *Journal of Personality and Social Psychology, 52*(1), 81–90. https://doi.org/10.1037/0022-3514.52.1.81

McCrae, R. R., & Costa, P. T., Jr. (1996). Toward a new generation of personality theories: Theoretical contexts for the five-factor model. In J. S. Wiggins (Ed.), *The five-factor model of personality: Theoretical perspectives* (pp. 51–87). Guilford Press.

McGraw, A. P., Schwartz, J. A., & Tetlock, P. E. (2011). From the commercial to the communal: Reframing taboo trade-offs in religious and pharmaceutical marketing. *Journal of Consumer Research, 39*(1), 157–173. https://doi.org/10.1086/662070

McNamara, M. E., & Reicher, S. D. (2019). The context-variable self and autonomy: Exploring surveillance experience,(mis) recognition, and action at airport security checkpoints. *Frontiers in Psychology, 10*, 2258. https://doi.org/10.3389/fpsyg.2019.02258

Mease, J. J., & Collins, B. L. (2018). Asset, liability, possibility: Metaphors of human difference and the business case for diversity. *Equality, Diversity and Inclusion: An International Journal, 37*(7), 664–682. https://doi.org/10.1108/EDI-05-2017-0114

Mill, J. S. (1861/1962). Utilitarianism. In M. Warnock (Ed.), *Utilitarianism and other writings* (pp. 251–321). Penguin Books.

Monin, B., Sawyer, P. J., & Marquez, M. J. (2008). The rejection of moral rebels: Resenting those who do the right thing. *Journal of Personality and Social Psychology, 95*(1), 76. https://doi.org/10.1037/0022-3514.95.1.76

Mooijman, M., Van Dijk, W. W., Van Dijk, E., & Ellemers, N. (2017). On sanction-goal justifications: How and why deterrence justifications undermine rule compliance. *Journal of Personality and Social Psychology, 112*(4), 577. https://doi.org/10.1037/pspi0000084

Mooijman, M., Van Dijk, W. W., Van Dijk, E., & Ellemers, N. (2019). Leader power, power stability, and interpersonal trust. *Organizational Behavior and Human Decision Processes, 152*, 1–10. https://doi.org/10.1016/j.obhdp.2019.03.009

Moore, C. (2008). Moral disengagement in processes of organizational corruption. *Journal of Business Ethics, 80*(1), 129–139. https://doi.org/10.1007/s10551-007-9447-8

Moore, C., Detert, J. R., Treviño, L. K., Baker, V. L., & Mayer, D. M. (2012). Why employees do bad things: Moral disengagement and unethical organizational behavior. *Personnel Psychology, 65*(1), 1–48. https://doi.org/10.1111/j.1744-6570.2011.01237.x

Moore, C., & Gino, F. (2013). Ethically adrift: How others pull our moral compass from true North, and how we can fix it. *Research in Organizational Behavior, 33*, 53–77. https://doi.org/10.1016/j.riob.2013.08.001

Moore, D. A., Tetlock, P. E., Tanlu, L., & Bazerman, M. H. (2006). Conflicts of interest and the case of auditor independence: Moral seduction and strategic issue cycling. *Academy of Management Review, 31*(1), 10–29. https://doi.org/10.5465/amr.2006.19379621

Morgan, G. (1986). *Images of organization*. Sage.

Morris, T. (1997). *If Aristotle ran General Motors: The new soul of business*. Henry Holdt.

Mullen, E., & Skitka, L. J. (2006). Exploring the psychological underpinnings of the moral mandate effect: Motivated reasoning, group differentiation, or anger? *Journal of Personality and Social Psychology, 90*(4), 629. https://doi.org/10.1037/0022-3514.90.4.629

Neesham, C., & Gu, J. (2015). Strengthening moral judgment: A moral identity-based leverage strategy in business ethics education. *Journal of Business Ethics, 131*(3), 527–534. https://doi.org/10.1007/s10551-014-2483-2

Nietzsche, F. W. (1894). *Jenseits von Gut und Böse: Vorspiel einer Philosophie der Zukunft* (Vol. 1).

O'Donnell, A. T., Ryan, M. K., & Jetten, J. (2013). The hidden costs of surveillance for performance and helping behaviour. *Group Processes & Intergroup Relations, 16*(2), 246–256. https://doi.org/10.1177/1368430212453629

O'Neill, S. (2018, February 9). Oxfam in Haiti: 'It was like a Caligula orgy with prostitutes in Oxfam T-shirts'. *The Times*. Retrieved from https://www.thetimes.co.uk/article/oxfam-in-haiti-it-was-like-a-caligula-orgy-with-prostitutes-in-oxfam-t-shirts-p32wlk0rp

Ormiston, M. E., & Wong, E. M. (2013). License to ill: The effects of corporate social responsibility and CEO moral identity on corporate social irresponsibility. *Personnel Psychology, 66*(4), 861–893. https://doi.org/10.1111/peps.12029

Padnick, S. (2012, June 22). What everybody gets wrong about Jekyll and Hyde. *TorCom*. Retrieved from https://www.tor.com/2012/06/22/what-everybody-gets-wrong-about-jekyll-and-hyde/

Pagliaro, S., Brambilla, M., Sacchi, S., D'Angelo, M., & Ellemers, N. (2013). Initial impressions determine behaviours: Morality predicts the willingness to help newcomers. *Journal of Business Ethics, 117*(1), 37–44. https://doi.org/10.1007/s10551-012-1508-y

Pagliaro, S., Ellemers, N., & Barreto, M. (2011). Sharing moral values: Anticipated ingroup respect as a determinant of adherence to morality-based (but not competence-based) group norms. *Personality and Social Psychology Bulletin, 37*(8), 1117–1129. https://doi.org/10.1177/0146167211406906

Pagliaro, S., Ellemers, N., Barreto, M., & Di Cesare, C. (2016). Once dishonest, always dishonest? The impact of perceived pervasiveness of moral evaluations of the self on motivation to restore a moral reputation. *Frontiers in Psychology, 7*, 586. https://doi.org/10.3389/fpsyg.2016.00586

Painter-Morland, M., & Slegers, R. (2018). Strengthening "giving voice to values" in business schools by reconsidering the "invisible hand" metaphor. *Journal of Business Ethics, 147*(4), 807–819. https://doi.org/10.1007/s10551-017-3506-6

Parker, M. (2018, April 27). Why we should bulldoze the business school. *The Guardian*. Retrieved from https://www.theguardian.com/news/2018/apr/27/bulldoze-the-business-school

Paulhus, D. L., & Williams, K. M. (2002). The dark triad of personality: Narcissism, Machiavellianism, and psychopathy. *Journal of Research in Personality, 36*(6), 556–563. https://doi.org/10.1016/S0092-6566(02)00505-6

Petersen, H. L., & Vredenburg, H. (2009). Morals or economics? Institutional investor preferences for corporate social responsibility. *Journal of Business Ethics, 90*(1), 1. https://doi.org/10.1007/s10551-009-0030-3

Pieters, J. (2019, September 26). Police whistleblower on racism, bullying placed on leave. *NL Times*. Retrieved from https://nltimes.nl/2019/09/26/police-whistleblower-racism-bullying-placed-leave

Public Prosecutor Placed under Stricter Supervision Interior. (2020, February 17). Retrieved from https://www.world-today-news.com/public-prosecutor-placed-under-stricter-supervision-interior/

Quinn, D. P., & Jones, T. M. (1995). An agent morality view of business policy. *Academy of Management Review, 20*(1), 22–42. https://doi.org/10.5465/amr.1995.9503271989

Rai, T. S., & Fiske, A. P. (2011). Moral psychology is relationship regulation: Moral motives for unity, hierarchy, equality, and proportionality. *Psychological Review, 118*(1), 57. https://doi.org/10.1037/a0021867

Reddy, K., Locke, S., & Scrimgeour, F. (2010). The efficacy of principle-based corporate governance practices and firm financial performance. *International Journal of Managerial Finance, 6*(3). https://doi.org/10.1108/17439131011056224

Reed, A., II, & Aquino, K. F. (2003). Moral identity and the expanding circle of moral regard towards outgroups. *Journal of Personality and Social Psychology, 84*, 1270–1286. https://doi.org/10.1037/0022-3514.84.6.1270

Rehn, A. (2008). Speaking out: On meta-ideology and moralization: A Prolegomena to a critique of management studies. *Organization, 15*(4), 598–609. https://doi.org/10.1177/1350508408091009

Rest, J. R. (1986). *Moral development: Advances in research and theory*. Praeger.

Reynolds, S. J., & Ceranic, T. L. (2007). The effects of moral judgment and moral identity on moral behavior: An empirical examination of the moral individual. *Journal of Applied Psychology, 92*(6), 1610. https://doi.org/10.1037/0021-9010.92.6.1610

Rosati, A. G., Di Nicola, L. M., & Buckholtz, J. W. (2018). Chimpanzee cooperation is fast and independent from self-control. *Psychological Science, 29*(11), 1832–1845. https://doi.org/10.1177/0956797618800042

Sama, L. M., & Shoaf, V. (2005). Reconciling rules and principles: An ethics-based approach to corporate governance. *Journal of Business Ethics, 58*, 177–185. https://doi.org/10.1007/s10551-005-1402-y

Sarbanes-Oxley Act. (2002). *The Sarbanes-Oxley Act*, [Online]. Retrieved from https://www.govinfo.gov/content/pkg/PLAW-107publ204/html/PLAW-107publ204.htm

Schwartz, S. H. (1992). Universals in the content and structure of values: Theoretical advances and empirical tests in 20 countries. In M. Zanna (Ed.), *Advances in experimental social psychology* (pp. 1–65). Academic. https://doi.org/10.1016/S0065-2601(08)60281-6

Seery, M. D. (2013). The biopsychosocial model of challenge and threat: Using the heart to measure the mind. *Social and Personality Psychology Compass, 7*(9), 637–653. https://doi.org/10.1111/spc3.12052

Sezer, O., Gino, F., & Bazerman, M. H. (2015). Ethical blind spots: Explaining unintentional unethical behaviour. *Current Opinion in Psychology, 6*, 77–81. https://doi.org/10.1016/j.copsyc.2015.03.030

Shalvi, S., Gino, F., Barkan, R., & Ayal, S. (2015). Self-serving justifications: Doing wrong and feeling moral. *Current Directions in Psychological Science, 24*(2), 125–130. https://doi.org/10.1177/0963721414553264

Shao, R., Aquino, K., & Freeman, D. (2008). Beyond moral reasoning: A review of moral identity research and its implications for business ethics. *Business Ethics Quarterly, 18*(4), 513–540. https://doi.org/10.5840/beq200818436

Shaw, J. D. (2014). Pay dispersion. *Annual Review of Organizational Psychology and Organizational Behavior, 1*, 521–544. https://doi.org/10.1146/annurev-orgpsych-031413-091253

Skitka, L. (2010). The psychology of moral conviction. *Social and Personality Psychology Compass, 4*(4), 267–281. https://doi.org/10.1111/j.1751-9004.2010.00254.x

Skitka, L. J., Bauman, C. W., & Mullen, E. (2008). Morality and justice: An expanded theoretical perspective and empirical review. *Advances in Group Processes, 25*, 1–27. https://doi.org/10.1016/S0882-6145(08)25001-0

Skitka, L. J., Bauman, C. W., & Sargis, E. G. (2005). Moral conviction: Another contributor to attitude strength or something more? *Journal of Personality and Social Psychology, 88*(6), 895. https://doi.org/10.1037/0022-3514.88.6.895

Skitka, L. J., & Mullen, E. (2002). The dark side of moral conviction. *Analyses of Social Issues and Public Policy, 2*(1), 35–41. https://doi.org/10.1111/j.1530-2415.2002.00024.x

Smit, J. (2019). *The great fight: The solitary conviction of Paul Polman*. Prometheus.

Smith, I. H., Aquino, K., Koleva, S., & Graham, J. (2014). The moral ties that bind… even to out-groups: The interactive effect of moral identity and the binding moral foundations. *Psychological Science, 25*(8), 1554–1562. https://doi.org/10.1177/0956797614534450

Soltani, B. (2014). The anatomy of corporate fraud: A comparative analysis of high profile American and European corporate schandals. *Journal of Business Ethics, 120*, 251–274. https://doi.org/10.1007/s10551-013-1660-z

Spiller, C., Pio, E., Erakovic, L., & Henare, M. (2011). Wise up: Creating organizational wisdom through an ethic of Kaitiakitanga. *Journal of Business Ethics, 104*(2), 223–235. https://doi.org/10.1007/s10551-011-0905-y

Stachowicz-Stanusch, A., Mangia, G., Caldarelli, A., & Amann, W. (2017). *Organizational social irresponsibility: Tools and theoretical insights*. Information Age Publishing.

Ståhl, T., & Ellemers, N. (2016). Ironic effects of moral motivation: Why working toward a moral goal reduces subsequent perspective taking. *Social Cognition, 34*(2), 133–148. https://doi.org/10.1521/soco.2016.34.2.133

Statista Research Department. (2020, April 28). Boeing – year-end workforce 2002–2019. *Statista*. Retrieved from https://www.statista.com/statistics/268992/change-in-employment-figures-from-boeing/

Terwel, B. W., Ter Mors, E., & Koudenburg, F. A. (2014). Effects of consultations with local residents in the process of deciding about host community compensation measures. *Energy Procedia, 63*, 7116–7118. https://doi.org/10.1016/j.egypro.2014.11.746

Tetlock, P. E. (2003). Thinking the unthinkable: Sacred values and taboo cognitions. *Trends in Cognitive Sciences, 7*(7), 320–324. https://doi.org/10.1016/S1364-6613(03)00135-9

Tieleman, J., De Muijnck, S., Kavelaars, M., & Ostermeijer, F. (2017). *Thinking like an economist? A quantitative analysis of economics bachelor curricula in the Netherlands*. Rethinking Economics NL.

Transparency International. (2020, January). *Corruption perceptions index*. Transparency International. Retrieved from https://www.transparency.org/files/content/pages/2019_CPI_Report_EN.pdf

Treviño, L. K., Den Nieuwenboer, N. A., & Kish-Gephart, J. J. (2014). (Un) ethical behavior in organizations. *Annual Review of Psychology, 65*, 635–660. https://doi.org/10.1146/annurev-psych-113011-143745

Treviño, L. K., & McCabe, D. (1994). Meta-learning about business ethics: Building honorable business school communities. *Journal of Business Ethics, 13*(6), 405–416. https://doi.org/10.1007/BF00881449

Treviño, L. K., & Victor, B. (1992). Peer reporting of unethical behavior: A social context perspective. *Academy of Management Journal, 35*(1), 38–64. https://doi.org/10.2307/256472

Tuan, L. T. (2012). Corporate social responsibility, leadership, and brand equity in healthcare service. *Social Responsibility Journal, 8*(3). https://doi.org/10.1108/17471111211247929

Turner, J. C. (1985). Social categorization and the self-concept: A social cognitive theory of group behavior. In E. J. Lawler (Ed.), *Advances in group processes* (pp. 77–122). JAI Press.

Tyler, T. R. (2005). Promoting employee policy adherence and rule following in work settings the value of self-regulatory approaches. *Brooklyn Law Review, 70*(4), 1287–1312.

Van der Lee, R., Ellemers, N., Scheepers, D., & Rutjens, B. T. (2017). In or out? How the perceived morality (vs. competence) of prospective group members affects acceptance and rejection. *European Journal of Social Psychology, 47*(6), 748–762. https://doi.org/10.1002/ejsp.2269

Van Nunspeet, F., Ellemers, N., & Derks, B. (2015). Reducing implicit bias: How moral motivation helps people refrain from making "automatic" prejudiced associations. *Translational Issues in Psychological Science, 1*(4), 382. https://doi.org/10.1093/scan/nss118

Van Nunspeet, F., Ellemers, N., Derks, B., & Nieuwenhuis, S. (2014). Moral concerns increase attention and response monitoring during IAT performance: ERP evidence. *Social Cognitive and Affective Neuroscience, 9*(2), 141–149. https://doi.org/10.1093/scan/nss118

Van Prooijen, A. M., & Ellemers, N. (2014). Does it pay to be moral? How indicators of morality and competence enhance organizational and work team attractiveness. *British Journal of Management, 26*(2), 225–236. https://doi.org/10.1177/001872679204500201

Van Prooijen, A. M., & Ellemers, N. (2015). Does it pay to be moral? How indicators of morality and competence enhance organizational and work team attractiveness. *British Journal of Management, 26*(2), 225–236. https://doi.org/10.1111/1467-8551.12055

Van Prooijen, A. M., Ellemers, N., Van Der Lee, R., & Scheepers, D. T. (2018). What seems attractive may not always work well: Evaluative and cardiovascular responses to morality and competence levels in decision-making teams. *Group Processes & Intergroup Relations, 21*(1), 73–87. https://doi.org/10.1177/1368430216653814

Van Steenbergen, E. F.. & Ellemers, N. (2021). The Social and Organizational Psychology of Compliance: How organizational culture impacts on (un)ethical behavior. In: D.D. Sokol & B. Van Rooij (Eds). Cambridge Handbook of Compliance (pp. 626–638). Cambridge University Press.

Waples, E. P., Antes, A. L., Murphy, S. T., Connelly, S., & Mumford, M. D. (2009). A meta-analytic investigation of business ethics instruction. *Journal of Business Ethics, 87*(1), 133–151. https://doi.org/10.1007/s10551-008-9875-0

Yakusheva, O. (2020, July 9). Is the COVID-19 pandemic cure really worse than the disease? Here's what our research found. *The Conversation*. Retrieved from https://theconversation.com/is-the-covid-19-pandemic-cure-really-worse-than-the-disease-heres-what-our-research-found-141700

Chapter 2
Social Identity at Work

Abstract The **key issues** highlighted in this chapter are that organizations in which people work also define who they are and what they stand for. Company logos, mission statements, and mottos all seek to capture and communicate this sense of identity within the organization and to external stakeholders. Unfortunately, efforts to mobilize people towards shared goals in this way can give rise to moral hazards, if other -equally important- goals are neglected as a result. For instance, when innovation is pursued at the expense of safety. We **analyze** how insights from Social Identity Theory elucidate the understanding of moral behavior in the workplace. Social groups and shared identities help people decide where to belong, how to behave, and whether to be proud of themselves. This explains why considering moral flaws in organizational practices is emotionally costly: It implies a threat to the identity of individuals working in these organizations. People can manage these threats by *thinking* differently about the situation. They can categorize those criticizing their behavior as outsiders, emphasize different performance criteria, or

N. Ellemers, D. de Gilder, *The Moral Organization: Key Issues, Analyses, and Solutions*, https://doi.org/10.1007/978-3-030-84175-1_2

focus on the things they did well. These strategies that people typically use as **solutions** when their identity is under threat allow us to understand when and why people are tempted to ignore or justify moral hazards in the workplace – instead of resolving them. Recognizing the hidden costs of such attempts to manage moral identities in organizations is a necessary first step to achieve moral improvement.

2.1 Key Issues: The Power of Social Identities

Moral standards delineate forms of acceptable vs unacceptable behavior that allow people to work and live together (see also Box 1.1). This definition clearly highlights the *social* nature of moral behavior, which cannot be fully understood by addressing individual differences, economic cost/benefit analyses or rule enforcement alone. In this chapter, we analyze the social mechanisms that drive moral choices, to complement prior accounts of moral behavior in organizations (offered for instance in Bisel, 2017; Comer & Vega, 2015; Muhr et al., 2010; Orts & Smith, 2017). We draw upon insights from *Social Identity Theory* (Tajfel, 1978; Tajfel & Turner, 1979; Turner et al., 1987), which explains how groups and group memberships impact on individual perceptions of appropriate conduct. Considering the moral norms individuals subscribe to in relation to their self-views as part of a team, profession, unit, or organization, offers a different understanding of their moral behavior in the workplace.

Granted, the importance of groups and social outcomes has been acknowledged in existing views on management and organizational behavior. For instance, Adam Smith, 'the father of economics', is quoted as proposing that wealth is not a valued outcome in its own right, but that '*we seek wealth to obtain distinction and esteem*' (see Brennan & Pettit, 2004, page 7). Others too have argued that selfishness may not be the primary motive driving human behavior in organizations (Davis et al., 1997; Ghoshal, 2005). They advocate that corporations should be seen as *moral agents* bearing a responsibility for the common good, long term outcomes, and ethical issues (Burrows, 1993; Moore, 1999; O'Brien, 2009; Tsui, 2016; West, 2016).

Yet a full consideration of how striving for group-based worth and esteem drives human motivation and social behavior is unique to Social Identity Theory (Tajfel, 1978; Tajfel & Turner, 1979; Turner, 1985; Turner et al., 1987). This social psychological theory emphasizes *social* incentives and *emotional* ties to a professional group, work team, or organization as important drivers of individual behaviors (Ellemers & De Gilder, 2020; see also Box 2.1). It complements rational choice models that dominate economic and legal approaches to management and organizational behavior, by clarifying how social groups and inclusion concerns in the workplace impact on a range of relevant behaviors in organizations (Ashforth & Mael, 1989; Haslam, 2004; Haslam et al., 2011; Hogg & Terry, 2000).

Box 2.1 The individual and the group

There are multiple ways in which individuals can be connected to groups, such as their work-team or the organization. Being *similar* in needs and interests can prompt people to join forces, for instance to create attractive work conditions. Being *dependent* on each other can induce mutual helping, allowing people to divide tasks and coordinate their efforts. *Liking* others in the group can forge friendship ties, and make it enjoyable to spend time together – also outside work. All these factors can also make people more inclined to be open to the opinions and views of their co-workers, and make them relevant sources of information and social influence. In such cases, people will be able to consider the *self as part of the group* of people they work with.

Social Identity Theory goes one step further, in specifying situations in which people can come to see the *group as part of the self*. If this is the case, then the needs, interests and preferences of the group are no longer external to the self. Instead, emotional ties cause people to experience concerns, achievements, and opinions of the group as if they were their own. Even when they are not technically part of the group people can pledge symbolic ties with groups that are subjectively important for them. This is the case for sports fans when they experience strong emotions at the successes and failures of the team – like these are their own. When a group becomes part of one's social identity, it becomes a source of internalized meaning and sense of self. This is a much stronger and more persistent force that binds people together than their similarity, interdependence, or liking.

However, the reverse can also be the case: even when people know they are part of the group and depend on other group members for important outcomes, recognize their similarities, and like other group members, this does not necessarily imply that the group is a source of identification for them. Studies of professional groups illustrate the difference between more externalized (interdependence, similarity, liking) versus more internalized group ties (self-definition, identification), for instance among police officers or academic scientists (Van Veelen & Derks, 2020; Veldman et al., 2017). In both cases, the occupational status and formal ties to their work-team and the organization are identical for men and women. However, the highly masculine image of these professions makes it less easy for female professionals to identify with their work-team and the organization. The difficulties women reported in tying their self-views to their occupation, impacted on their work outcomes. Lack of identification with the highly masculine image of their profession was associated with lower work satisfaction, more work stress, and higher turnover intentions.

Standard approaches to management tend to see esteem and other social outcomes as 'luxury goods' that can be safely ignored (Ghoshal & Moran, 1996; Rocha & Ghoshal, 2006). Presumably, these only become relevant once more mundane needs have been met (Maslow, 1943). However, the social identity approach argues that social outcomes represent basic concerns in organizational behavior, that are always relevant and impact all workers (see also Haslam, 2004). Accordingly, studies clearly reveal that workers at the lowest levels (cleaners, garbage collectors, sex industry workers) find it just as important as the elite to be able to think of their work as a source of dignity and social esteem (Ashforth & Kreiner, 1999; Lamont, 2000, 2002, see also Chap. 4). In fact, social inclusion and identification with others in the workplace has been found to benefit fulfillment of 'lower level' needs for physical health and mental well-being, rather than vice versa (Steffens et al., 2017).

In this chapter we connect observations of organizational behavior with insights from psychology that explain how people relate to social groups and how they define their social identities. First, we will explain how this perspective allows us to understand the impact of moral concerns on the behavior and self-views of people in the workplace. Then, we use the explanatory framework offered by Social Identity Theory to organize common responses people use to manage different types of moral hazards, as they hope to protect their social identities and self-views from the threat of appearing immoral.

2.1.1 The Organizations People Work for Also Define Who they Are

Organizations are structures designed to allow individuals to work together towards collaborative goals. If this is done well, people in the workplace do not view themselves just in terms of their individual skills or specific role in the organization. They can feel that they 'are' the organization, making this part of how they think of themselves and define their social identity. This phenomenon is well-documented, and widely used in management theories and practices (Ashforth & Mael, 1989; Ellemers et al., 2004; Haslam, Postmes, & Ellemers, 2003; Hogg & Terry, 2000; Whetten & Foreman, 2014). Company uniforms, on-boarding programs, and social activities are all used to benefit the formation of a shared identity around features that are central, enduring, and distinctive (Gioia et al., 2013). In turn, this can help direct individual efforts towards common goals, and explains how individual achievements relate to organizational outcomes. In general, such feelings of 'oneness' with the organization have been found to motivate individuals to exert themselves beyond their prescribed duties as they go the extra mile to contribute to achieving organizational goals (De Gilder & Ellemers, 2017; Ellemers et al., 2004; Ellemers & Haslam, 2011; Haslam & Ellemers, 2005, 2011).

In their purpose or mission statements many organizations build on such notions by stating 'who we are' or 'what we stand for'. For instance, at automobile rental company Avis the motto is: "we try harder". Such statements convey a sense of unity by specifying important outcomes and values for the organization. This communicates to organizational members how they are supposed to act in their organizational roles, how they can contribute to achieving valued outcomes, and what they need to do to be included and respected in the workplace. Some companies offer these instructions quite literally, for instance at Proctor & Gamble noting not only that "we improve the lives of customers" but also specifying what employees are supposed to do and to avoid to achieve this goal (Procter & Gamble, n.d.).

To those outside the organization, such statements indicate what they can expect in terms of products, services, and priorities, and how these differ from their competitors. Some of these claims are quite specific about important priorities, and clearly indicate what clients can expect. Ikea says: "we offer a wide range of well-designed, functional home-furnishing products at prices so low that as many people as possible will be able to afford them". Others are quite abstract and perhaps even vague, leaving it up to employees as well as customers to imagine what they are supposed to do or what they can expect. Like Virgin Airways, which states: "we embrace the human spirit and let it fly". Retail chain Walmart is much more straightforward. It simply promises "we save people money".

2.1.2 The Moral Hazards of Aligning People Towards Shared Goals

In general, communicating in this way what the organization considers important helps to align individual efforts. This facilitates the achievement of joint goals – rather than having each individual pursuing their personal preferences. These potential benefits of binding individuals to a joint mission, and creating a sense of 'we-ness' in the workplace are well-known, and many books have been written on how best to achieve this (e.g., Browning & Kanaga, 2007; Hakala-Ausperk, 2013; Logan et al., 2008; Morgan, 2017; Sinek, 2011). For instance, concrete and specific goals such as at Ikea more clearly reveal what employees should do and what they should avoid than more abstract and vague mission statements like the one at Virgin Airways (see also Chap. 4)

However, less attention is often paid to the possible drawbacks of engaging and uniting people in this way – even if this may be the flipside of the positive outcomes sought. Indeed, highlighting specific goals easily suggests that all other goals must be less important. At Walmart, the aim of saving money might therefore be pursued by compromising on product safety or service quality, even if this is not what Walmart would expect its suppliers or employees to do. Likewise, when members of the organization are expected to privilege the interests of some stakeholders this might make them less attentive to the interests of other stakeholders. At P&G for instance, focusing on how to improve the lives of customers, may cause product developers to disregard the depletion of natural resources or environmental damage resulting from their products. Employees who know they are expected to go the extra mile for the company may be tempted to sacrifice their personal health and well-being in the process. This could easily happen for those who try harder at Avis by working overtime and skipping breaks.

Thus, building connections between organizational members, and strengthening their ties with the organization and its key goals is not just a convenient way to coordinate individual efforts. Focusing on the achievement of the distinct mission of the organization easily causes employees to neglect the interests of other stakeholders, to ignore critical comments of outsiders, or to discard concerns about long term outcomes, including their own. Even the goal of the organization and its members to do something 'good', may thus result in choices and practices that seem morally flawed – at least to outsiders. In this sense then, the specification of shared goals to unite organizational members and align their efforts also has *moral* implications, and potentially introduces moral hazards. In further chapters (Chaps. 4 and 8) we will elaborate on the possible downside of the overcommitment to organizational goals, as well as misplaced loyalty to others in the organization (Moore & Gino, 2013; see also Conroy et al., 2017). For now, we mainly wish to point out that everything organizations do to invigorate organizational members to work towards particular goals becomes incorporated in the shared identity of its workers and, hence, guides their attitudes and behavior – for better or for worse (see also Steffens et al., 2017).

Some people ignore this downside, claiming that multiple goals and stakeholder interests can be served simultaneously. Who is to say that Walmart cannot offer high quality at competitive prices? And perhaps Avis goes out of its way to protect the health and well-being of its employees, helping them to recover and try harder every time. Indeed, organizational guidelines may incorporate many different goals that employees are expected to realize. In fact, simply expanding the list of important goals is what often happens when the moral hazards of organizational priorities come to light. Revising safety instructions, specifying quality standards, updating the description of targets and incentives, or adding quality managers and compliance officers are all used as 'quick fixes' to address such concerns and to safeguard the organization against future problems. In theory, all these measures may allow organizations to engage people towards key organizational goals, without suffering from the moral hazards of doing this. However, as indicated in Chap. 1, there are limits to what such quick fixes can achieve, particularly when multiple different goals are not compatible with each other, or when moral guidelines do not match core features that characterize the organization and the identity of its members.

The net result often is that there is some 'paper version' of the ideal situation – which does not provide a realistic guideline for everyday behavior. People know this, sometimes because they are explicitly told, for instance to ignore safety guidelines or quality standards that seem cumbersome and impractical. Sometimes they realize that in practice, some goals and achievements (sales volumes) are more likely to be highlighted and rewarded than others (customer satisfaction). Indeed, simply adding top-down guidelines is no guarantee that day-to-day practices are adapted at every organizational level: Perhaps the different concerns identified by top-management do not seem equally pressing to all line managers. Perhaps the hazards involved are not equally visible for all organizational members. Or perhaps the basic tasks to 'tick off' customers or clients, keep to budget, or even stay in business may take priority over loftier mission statements more often than would be desirable. Yet these daily experiences and workplace habits define the implicit 'moral culture' in the workplace – which can overrule more formal and explicit moral guidelines (Ashforth et al., 2020, see also Fig. 1.1). Of course, it is possible to change common procedures and organizational practices. But such transformations are notoriously difficult and time-consuming: The key function of organizational identities and cultures is to provide a sense of stability and continuity in the organization, despite turnover of personnel and changing circumstances (Deal & Kennedy, 1982; Kotter & Heskett, 1992; Schneider & Barbera, 2014; Whetten & Foreman, 2014).

2.1.3 Groups Impact on Individual Thoughts, Feelings and Behaviors

The goal of professional pledges, team building exercises and organizational mission statements is to make people think of themselves and others not as separate individuals, but as interchangeable members of a particular professional group, work team, or organization (Ashforth & Mael, 1989; Ashforth et al., 2020). This allows them to experience a sense of connection and mutual understanding that stems from the acknowledgment of being in the same profession or working for the same company – without depending on interpersonal familiarity or friendship ties. We all have acquaintances or family members who boast about the financial successes ("*We doubled our profits*"), new products ("*We invented new medication for this illness*"), or solutions provided ("*We are carbon neutral*") by the organization they work for. They do this, even if their own direct contribution to such core business results was modest – because they work in the canteen, install new computers, or clean the building. Nevertheless, shared goals, achievements, and values may come to be seen as typical group characteristics that define people's self-views, and feelings of esteem in the workplace.

Unfortunately, this shared sense of identity also makes people vulnerable, causing individual employees to feel personally threatened or damaged in case of organizational failures (Ashforth et al., 2020; Haslam & Ellemers, 2011; Haslam, Van Knippenberg, et al., 2003). Members of the organization can feel ashamed and embarrassed when it turns out that customers were cheated to realize profit increase, steep pricing prevents patients to benefit from the new medication that was developed, or when labor rights were violated to reduce the carbon footprint of the company. When such events come to light, these can threaten the self-views and identities of individuals working at these organizations, causing them to feel 'guilty by association' (e.g., Branscombe & Doosje, 2004; Doosje et al., 2006; Dutton & Dukerich, 1991). Again, they can experience such identity threat even when their own efforts in the canteen, the computer department, or in building maintenance had nothing to do with these events.

Taking pride in the unique contribution or innovative mission of the organization can help distract from the discomfort of guilt and shame when considering the moral implications of organizational achievements. This strategy to manage their identity can make organizational members blind to potential concerns (e.g. due to industry regulations or safety issues), or deaf to those who raise these concerns (e.g., external stakeholders), and generally reduces the likelihood that action will be taken to instigate some form of change. Thus, group-level mechanisms not only cause achievements as well as failures of the group (or team, unit, organization) to be experienced as personal achievements or failures. Groups and social identities also induce people to follow and defend choices made by the group as if they were personal choices (Ashforth & Schinoff, 2016; Turner, 1985; Turner et al., 1987). Behaving in ways that are approved and valued by the group allows individuals to secure inclusion and respect, and affirms their self-views as valued group members (Smith et al., 1998; Tyler, 1999; Tyler & Blader, 2000, 2003). These concerns about inclusion and shared identity – and the social outcomes these imply – are so powerful, that people can come to internalize group norms as defining their self-views (Ellemers & Jetten, 2013; Ellemers et al., 1999a). In fact, identity concerns often overrule 'rational choices' that would serve more obviously selfish motives (Fukuyama, 2018).

All these things are especially true in the moral domain, as moral guidelines indicate what a good and proper member of a particular group, community or organization should do or strive to avoid (Beauchamp, 2001; Brandt & Reyna, 2011; Gert, 1988, 2012; Giner-Sorolla, 2012; Killen et al., 2006; Leach et al., 2015). Accordingly, those who behave in line with these guidelines will be included and respected as good group members, those who don't will be devalued, excluded, or expelled from the group (Ellemers, 2017; Fry, 2006; Tooby & Cosmides, 2010). These social punishments are imposed for behavior that falls short of moral ideals, as this is seen to reveal the 'true nature' of people's moral standards, even without firm evidence of bad intentions (Clark et al., 2015; Pagliaro et al., 2016). As a result, people experience significantly more physical and emotional stress and see less improvement opportunities when their moral judgments and good intentions are called into question than when they consider deficiencies in in other domains – such as their competence. Research consistently reveals that greater cognitive, emotional and social costs are associated with moral failure of the self or other ingroup members than with competence failures (Fig. 2.1; see also Abele et al., 2020). Thus, in terms of their social effects, transgressions of moral rules tend to be very costly, making people particularly wary of breaking moral norms (see also Bicchieri, 2017). This is why we cannot understand moral behavior in the workplace without considering its social origins as well as its social outcomes. These contribute to the paradox of morality: the more people are motivated to do what is morally right, the more they run the risk of being blind to their moral failures (see also Ellemers, 2017, 2018).

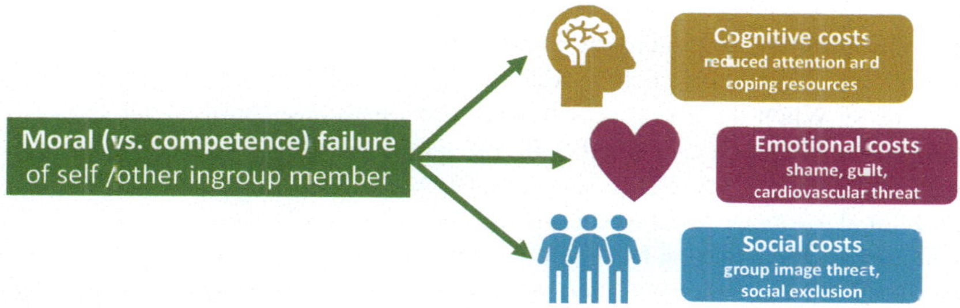

Fig. 2.1 The costs of moral inadequacy. Summarizes results from many published studies. These reveal that people suffer negative cognitive, emotional, and social outcomes, when they are confronted with moral failures of themselves or other ingroup members. (Brambilla et al., 2013; Kouzakova et al., 2014; Ståhl & Ellemers, 2016; Van der Lee et al., 2016; Van der Lee et al., 2017; Van der Toorn et al., 2015)

2.2 Analysis: Key Concerns People Have in the Workplace

The previous section highlighted the importance of group memberships and shared identities for understanding moral behavior in organizations. This revealed that group-level choices and outcomes can make people proud and contribute to a positive social identity. However, what happens in the group also makes people vulnerable. On the one hand, achievements and norms that characterize the group, influence – and possibly compromise – the moral choices made by individuals who seek to belong. On the other hand, moral failures of other group members reflect upon the group and are a source of identity threat – even for members who can in no way be held accountable. Both these types of concerns prompt people to defend, repair, or improve their positive identity.

In this section we analyze the mechanisms people use to define themselves in relation to others. This allows them to give meaning to social situations, to establish a positive identity, and to respond to identity threat (Tajfel, 1978; Tajfel & Turner, 1979; Turner, 1985; Turner et al., 1987 see also: Ellemers, 2010; Ellemers & Haslam, 2011; Ellemers & De Gilder, 2020). Social categorization indicates how people cluster individuals into groups and where they place themselves, to answer the question '*Where do I belong*'? Social comparison is the process through which the distinctive characteristics of the group are defined by comparing the group to other groups. This helps answer the question '*How should I behave*'? Social identification captures the process through which group-level features and achievements reflect upon individual group members, to answer the question '*Can I be proud of myself*'? Addressing these basic concerns people have in the workplace clarifies the psychological mechanisms that can contribute to a sense of identity threat, but also explains how these can be used strategically to alleviate this sense of threat (see Box 2.2).

Box 2.2 Identity management strategies

People can maintain a positive identity by thinking well of the groups they belong to. When the group is criticized, this raises a sense of social identity threat, which can be countered with a range of 'identity management strategies' (Ellemers, 1993; Ellemers et al., 1999a, 2002). It is not so easy for an individual to change what the group does or stands for. Yet it is possible to feel better about the situation by redefining one's *thoughts* about the group (while the threat is maintained), without necessarily taking any concrete *actions* (to eliminate the threat - see also Petriglieri, 2011).

An example is the Catholic Church where many priests had sexually abused children placed in their care (Boorstein, 2020). Even believers who did not have anything to do with this felt ashamed or guilty at having their institution become morally stained. Yet those who identified most strongly with the church were most likely to disbelieve accusers while protecting the accused (Minto et al., 2016). This strategy helps to maintain the positive identity of the group they value so deeply. Below, we characterize different types of identity management strategies that can be employed.

Recategorization: change group boundaries. A first way to deflect threat is to redefine who is 'really' included in the group. Recategorizing those who cause discomfort makes their actions seem less self-relevant. This can be done in different ways. Derogating victims (they are after monetary compensation) makes it less obvious that they deserve protection and care from the group. Denouncing the messenger (they just want to discredit the church) makes it easier to consider them as sensation seekers whose views can be safely ignored. Portraying the perpetrators as 'black sheep' who do not truly represent core values of the group (these are not 'real' priests) can help salvage the group's identity by mentally excluding them from the group (Marques & Paez, 1994).

Social creativity: redefine priorities. Group members may downplay the importance of the misbehavior as not representing what the church stands for. Instead they can focus on other things they value about their group and that contribute to a positive identity. Church members may cite voluntary work Catholics have done on behalf of third world countries, efforts to help the poor, or community services offered by the local church. While this does not deny the occurrence of child abuse, it makes these events seem less important as a source of group identity and self-definition.

Social compensation: focus on what goes well. Even when acknowledging the problems of child abuse as well as the fact that the clergy was aware and covered up these problems, believers can emphasize what was learned from this experience. For instance, they can point to measures that were eventually taken to punish perpetrators, reforms made by Pope Francis, refer to many parishes where these things never happened, or point to communities where similar problems were handled "even worse".

Social mobility: distance self from group. The damage to the group's identity can seem so severe that the only option people see is to disconnect the self from the group. For instance, believers may focus on their personal religious experience but no longer think of themselves as part of the broader institution. Some may formally terminate their membership of the church putting an end to their participation in all joint activities. Obviously this is a painful and consequential decision that alters people's sense of who they are and what they stand for, and can damage important social network, friendship and family ties.

Social change: improve behavior of the group. People who care deeply about the future of the group, may be highly motivated to take the problems that have emerged as a reason to reform the institution. Instead of leaving, they want the group to improve. Calling for change can be a lonely undertaking. Other group members who favor different identity management strategies, may even question the loyalty of such 'troublemakers'. Success in using this strategy requires collective action, where many people work together to bring about change – without giving up too quickly. In the case of the Catholic Church, the courage of many victims telling their story (e.g, "The Story Behind the 'Spotlight' Movie,", n.d.) eventually forced the church to adopt new guidelines admonishing senior clergy to contact the police when accusations are made, and declaring them negligent if they don't (Povoledo, 2020; "Vatican Issues New Manual,", 2020).

2.2.1 Where Do I Belong?

People use shared group memberships and distinctions between different groups (e.g., IT experts vs HR experts) as a way to define and give meaning to others they encounter in the workplace. Of course, the same individual can be categorized in different ways: an IT expert can also be a man or a woman, young or old, work at the main office or at a local branch, be a recent hire, or about to leave the organization.

This reveals that groups and their members should not be considered as fixed or static entities. Instead, the process of *social categorization* allows people to actively place individuals into different categories emphasizing some group memberships rather than others. They do this depending on what the situation calls for (this requires technical expertise I don't have) or on their personal needs (I think this course is only for new hires; Oakes, 1987; Tajfel, 1974). The decision 'which hat to wear', allows them to cluster others and themselves according to features that they find important at that moment (Ashforth & Johnson, 2001). This may cause people for instance to highlight distinct professional skills (e.g., knowledge of local clients) while ignoring other differences or similarities (such as gender or age) that seem less relevant in that situation. These social categorizations do not just sort people into groups. They also infuse the situation with meaning. Attributes that are seen to characterize the group are associated with individual group members by overestimating differences between categories while neglecting differences within categories. Research shows this literally alters perceptions of reality in the brain (Oakes et al., 1994; see also Ellemers, 2016; Ellemers & Van Nunspeet, 2020; Cikara et al., 2017; Xiao et al., 2016). For instance, merely assigning people to mixed-race task teams was found to reduce automatic racial biases (Cikara & Van Bavel, 2014).

The category boundaries that people draw in this way are also relevant for the moral choices they make and the way they behave towards others. Can someone be trusted to help, or are they out for themselves? Who is deserving of care, and whose needs can be ignored? Judgments such as these do not just reflect properties of specific individuals, but also depend on how they are categorized within or between organizations. How people view and engage with the concerns, actions and outcomes of others crucially depends on whether they are seen as part of the 'ingroup' (the same profession, work team, or organization), or the 'outgroup' (representing another profession, team or organization). Research shows that viewing people through an 'ingroup' or 'outgroup' lens has far-reaching implications, even if people are judging the same individuals in both cases. In general, people are more inclined to place trust in the moral intentions of ingroup than outgroup members. They are more likely to attend to their needs and concerns, and more willing to include these individuals in their 'circle of care' (Ellemers et al., 2019: see also Turner et al., 1987; Turner et al., 1994; Oakes et al., 1994).

An important consequence is that those placed in the outgroup seem less relevant for the self. The mere act of considering people as outgroup members can makes their intentions seem more suspect, their concerns seem less valid, their needs less pressing, and their outcomes less important. Thus, social categorizations not only help people to define who they are and where they belong, but also allow them to redraw group boundaries between themselves and others as a way to fend off moral threat and protect their positive identity.

2.2.2 *How Should I Behave?*

Once they have decided how to categorize individuals in a particular situation, people ask themselves what this means (Turner, 1985). Which behavioral guidelines define the members of this group, what are their key achievements, how will they show their good intentions, and how is this different from other groups? The answers to these questions are determined through the process of *social comparison*, which people use to discover the likely properties that help to distinguish different groups and their members from others.

An example of how people compare and define different groups and their characteristic behaviors is the way they translate general moral principles into group-defining behavioral norms. In a particular company, caring for others might be considered a key defining value. However, in work unit A the duty of care is seen to imply that employees should always show loyalty to the team, while work unit B emphasizes the importance of prioritizing client needs. In seeking inclusion and respect, these group-specific interpretations offer better guidance for appropriate behavior than the more generic admonition to extend care. As a result, employees in unit A might cover for each other's rule transgressions or moral failures at the expense of client interests. In unit B team members would challenge decisions made by co-workers when they feel that client interests are not well served. Yet members of both work units may be convinced that what they do is in line with company policy and morally right. Our social identity analysis clarifies that this may not just be a way to pledge one's loyalty to the group, nor does this necessarily imply the individuals give up their personal moral principles as a result of group pressures (see also Spears, 2021). Instead, within the group context, individuals may truly come to consider such behavioral guidelines as self-defining. Thus, they *internalize* the choices made in their own work team to be appropriate and may consider these morally superior compared to the choices made by other teams.

Unfortunately, much of the research in moral psychology does not address these issues. This work aims to capture general preferences that hold across different situations It relies on hypothetical scenarios about unspecified individuals presented to them as 'raceless, genderless strangers' (Hester & Gray, 2020). Yet studies that do address specific groups and situations show that people's moral judgments and the choices they make differ depending on whether behavioral guidelines are provided by ingroup members or outgroup members. In general, people are quite sensitive to judgments of other ingroup members indicating the moral thing to do. They are willing to adapt their behavior to such guidelines, anticipating that this will earn them respect in the group. They are much less likely to adjust their choices to accommodate the judgments of outgroup members. This was demonstrated in a study where specific recommendations about how to make community improvements were made either by ingroup members (people from the same region) or outgroup members (people living elsewhere). The results revealed that people adapted their own choices aligning these with what the ingroup considered moral, while they ignored *identical* recommendations when these were voiced by outgroup members (Ellemers et al., 2008; Pagliaro et al., 2011). Again, the greater attention for ingroup than outgroup recommendations is not just what people indicate when explicitly asked. It is also evident from responses beyond their control. For instance measures of brain activity revealed that people are more concerned about making erroneous moral judgments when these are tested in front of an ingroup member rather than an outgroup member (Ellemers & Van Nunspeet, 2020; Van Nunspeet et al., 2015).

2.2.3 Can I Be Proud of Myself?

Once individuals have decided which categories are important and how the behaviors of ingroup members compare to those of outgroup members, they need to establish how the group and its characteristic achievements and behaviors reflect upon the self. This final question refers to the process of *social identification* through which people define their own place in the landscape of social groups. Categorizing people as IT or HR experts not only determines whether *others* should be seen as 'ingroup' or 'outgroup' members, this also has implications for how people see *themselves*. For instance, someone working in HR might not only wonder whether they are included and respected within the HR department, but would also be concerned whether HR professionals as a group are seen to do a good job in keeping with company guidelines.

Thus when considering whether they should be proud or ashamed of themselves, people don't only have their own choices and achievements to consider, but also those of the group. For instance, people express concern that dishonesty of fellow nationals may reflect badly on their own social standing (Brambilla et al., 2013). Research reveals that these identity concerns are not just about the calculation of risks. They reflect self-involvement with the group at a relatively direct and emotional level. For instance, experimental studies show that when other members of their work-team confess their personal moral failures, research participants show the same psychophysiological threat profiles (stress indicated in their blood pressure and heart rate changes) as when they consider their own moral failures (Van der Lee et al., submitted).

The process of social identification thus highlights that the group can be a source of resilience as well as a source of vulnerability when group outcomes impact on people's felt emotions and sense of self. However, it also clarifies that this is not an automatic or predictable outcome of objective group memberships – delineating which individuals depend on each other for important outcomes and monetary rewards. In itself, someone's awareness that they belong to a particular organization or work team does not imply that this defines their subjective sense of belongingness or who they are. Some categories and group memberships seem more self-defining than others, and shine through in many situations. For instance, some may boast their political orientation or remind others of their sexual preferences wherever they are, while others take pains to conceal these features when they think this is irrelevant or inappropriate in the workplace.

Situational factors too may remind people of which group memberships or loyalties are at stake. The same people who highlight professional standards to criticize sloppy work of other work units may still be motivated to defend their organization against complaints from clients. To outsiders, these behaviors may seem inconsistent, but from a social identity perspective it makes perfect sense: as the situation changes, people's identity concerns change too (for overviews see: Ellemers, 2017; Ellemers & Haslam, 2011; Ellemers & Jetten, 2013; Ellemers & De Gilder, 2020).

Thus, social identification refers to the extent to which people let decisions and choices of other group members impact on their own sense of social worth and value. For some, the group's successes and failures can feel like their own because they consider the group as a core part of their identity. For others, the group's successes and failures may seem less relevant as they distance their self-views from the group.

In sum, our social identity analysis reveals when and why concerns about moral failures of others in the organization can threaten people's self-views, and can come to represent a source of social identity threat. It also clarifies that people can cope with such identity threats in different ways. They can recategorize others, limiting the circle of people to whom they should display loyalty and care, to alleviate concerns about their unfair treatment (Reed II & Aquino, 2003). Shifting the social comparisons they make allows people to selectively focus on those contexts and features that make them and their fellow group members look good. Resisting identification with those who do not seem to adhere to the same moral standards as they do, allows people to seek inclusion and respect in groups that are more likely to validate their own moral choices (see also Ellemers, 2017). People can use all of these identity management strategies when their moral identity is under threat (Ellemers, 1993; Tajfel & Turner, 1979; see also Box 2.2). In the next section we explain how the solutions people typically seek to manage moral hazards may alleviate feelings of shame and guilt. However, many strategic responses that help to protect and enhance a positive sense of self and identity also condone and justify the status quo, and discourage people from working towards moral change and improvement.

2.3 Solutions: Managing Moral Hazards in Organizations

In Chap. 1 we summarized research revealing the 'paradox of morality': On the one hand, people generally are generally motivated to do what is moral. On the other hand, this only makes it more painful and difficult for them to acknowledge and confront moral failures. Engaging with moral critique is not easier when moral identities and moral failures are considered at the group level. When they can, people protect themselves from such moral threats. Research shows that work team members are generally unwilling to include, collaborate with, or help individuals who prioritize high performance over honest behavior (Van der Lee et al., 2017; Van Prooijen & Ellemers, 2015). For instance, school teachers were more reluctant to help a new principal when his profile indicated low honesty and reliability rather than low competence and professional ability (Pagliaro et al., 2013).

Once the moral worth of the self or the group is called into question, this raises social identity threat (Aquino & Reed II, 2002). People are no longer secure about their acceptability as a good member of the social community as they are unsure whether they can still be proud of their professional team or organization. In the moral domain such identity concerns cause guilt and shame. These are specific socially learned (secondary) 'moral emotions' that are seen as 'self-condemning'

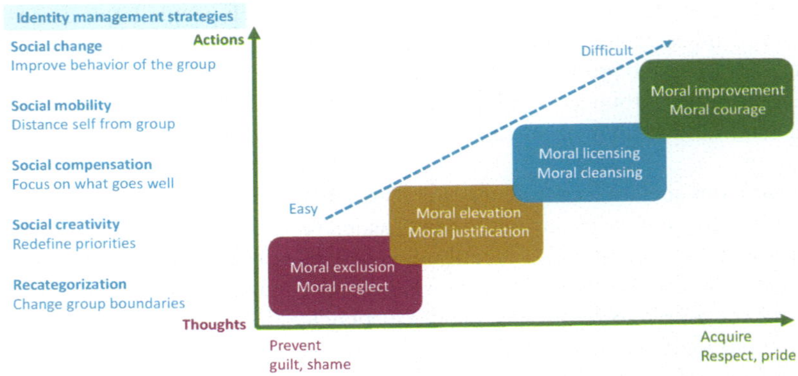

Fig. 2.2 Identity management in the moral domain. Indicates how different strategies people commonly use to manage social identity threats (listed on the left) can be mapped on to the range of self-protective phenomena known from research on moral psychology (in the graph). These strategies are ordered from 'easy' solutions to prevent guilt and shame by changing one's thoughts about the situation, to more 'difficult' solutions where people take action to acquire respect and pride

(Giner-Sorolla, 2012; Leach, 2017; Tangney & Dearing, 2002). Other than more 'basic' emotions (such as anger at disadvantage or fear about insecure outcomes) feelings of guilt and shame are activated when people's actions are not consistent with their self-views, and regulate their self-esteem (Tracy & Robins, 2004).

Research into the psychology of morality thus shows that people find it painful to consider shortcomings in their moral character, making it especially difficult to cope with moral emotions (Branscombe & Doosje, 2004). It also reveals their reluctance to strive for moral improvement compared to other types of self-improvement goals (Sun & Goodwin, 2019). Recategorizing others as outgroup members, changing the social comparisons they make, or selectively focusing on positive aspects of their identity allow people to alleviate feelings of moral inadequacy and to mitigate feelings of guilt and shame (see Fig. 2.2). Just thinking differently about the same situation can be enough to protect and restore moral self-views (Anand et al., 2004; Ellemers, 2017; Ellemers et al., 2019). However, this discourages people from engaging in the more difficult and challenging actions needed to work towards moral change and moral improvement, even if this would offer new sources of pride and respect that contribute to a positive identity (see Box 2.3).

Box 2.3 Ethical choices or window dressing?

Some of the changes companies make to become more socially responsible will not obviously have the intended effect. From their actions it is not clear how far they are willing to go in making structural changes for the benefit of society. Do these changes indicate a shift of strategic priorities, or mainly represent a communication strategy aiming at damage control? We consider some examples below.

Philip Morris International (PMI), one of the largest tobacco companies in the world, has announced the decision to work towards a 'Smoke-Free Future'. The stated aim is to shift towards the manufacturing of smoke free products such as e-cigarettes, which will eventually replace all cigarettes as a less harmful alternative to smoking. PMI deployed this campaign claiming the desire to "act responsibly towards society" (Philip Morris International, n.d.).

However, in the US alone, e-cigarettes have been linked to 6 deaths and more than 450 hospitalizations (Doward, 2019). It is therefore doubtful whether the shift of PMI towards e-cigarettes will really benefit society. Moreover, PMI has been legally accused of misleading the public and manipulating public policy with regard to the consequences of their products (Tobacco Control Legal Consortium, 2006). Critics have therefore characterized this campaign as a smart business strategy responding to the public criticism of the WHO and the declining turnover of tobacco in the world (Foley, 2019).

Shell is another large company that has tried to rebrand itself. In April 2019, Shell promised to invest $300 million in natural ecosystems over the next three years in order to act on global climate change (Shell, 2019). This seems a large amount of money but only represents a small proportion of Shell's annual income (Shell, 2018). In fact, although Shell has publicly declared agreement with the net zero carbon target by 2050, in line with the Paris climate agreement, it has withheld actual support (Ambrose, 2019). The company has therefore been accused of "greenwashing" (Watson, 2016) – making symbolic investments in natural ecosystems to divert public attention from ongoing initiatives to extract gas and oil (Monbiot, 2019).

Not only companies, but also government policies can be suspected of ethical window dressing to mask activities that harm the public interest. A case in point is the Dutch State that appears very strict in issuing licenses to gamble. There are many rules about gambling – allegedly motivated by the desire to prevent gambling addiction. Nonetheless, the regulation and enforcement of these rules also affords the Dutch State a national monopoly on land-based gambling. Holland Casino is a state-owned chain of fourteen casinos that represent an important source of income for the state. In fact, when it became apparent that a revenue of over €800 million is made each year in offshore online gambling, the government tried to pass a law to make this illegal. The dangers of gambling addition were cited as the main concern, even though it was obvious that allowing people to gamble online would also reduce profits from gambling for the Dutch State (Miller, 2019).

In the final section of this chapter we connect research in moral psychology with insights on social identity and identity management, to offer a new understanding of common responses shown in organizations contending with moral issues (see Box 2.4). The different solutions that allow people to cope with moral hazards can be

Box 2.4 The psychology of morality

Research in psychology has documented a range of different phenomena relating to morality. These characterize the self-reflective nature of moral judgments and the general desire to do what is morally right. Here we consider them as relatively 'easy' vs more 'difficult' solutions to moral concerns, mapping them on to different strategies people can use to deal with threats to their social identity.

Moral neglect. The easiest way to deflect the moral implications of one's actions is to simply refrain from considering them, indicating *moral neglect* (Bandura, 1999). Lack of concern for the moral acceptability of one's actions can be the result of social norms (Moore & Gino, 2013). Ignoring moral responsibility for the outcomes of one's actions may be implied in one's professional mission (e.g., to enhance product consumption, Mick, 2007).

Moral exclusion. People can deny fair treatment to others by redrawing group boundaries to achieve their *moral exclusion.* Placing victims of their actions outside their circle of care allows people to consider themselves as more deserving, and makes it easier to belittle, marginalize, exclude, or even dehumanize others (Haslam, 2006; Leets, 2001).

Moral justification. Even when acknowledging the morally questionable outcomes of one's actions, people can engage in *moral justification.* This implies that they redefine the meaning of these actions to make them seem more acceptable. For instance, citing morally praiseworthy causes (e.g., loyalty to the organization, commitment to customer requests) as valid priorities, may seem to justify deviation from rules of conduct (Bandura, 1999; Moore & Gino, 2013).

Moral elevation. When acknowledging that their moral choices can be improved, people may already find solace by considering the morally righteous actions of others. In theory the 'warm glow' of *moral elevation* might inspire people to follow suit. However, especially when these others are ingroup members, it is tempting to bask in their reflected glory and feel morally elevated without actually changing one's own behavior (Algoe & Haidt, 2009; Haidt, 2000).

Moral licensing. Once people have displayed moral behavior, feelings of *moral licensing* can reduce their motivation to maintain equally high moral standards in their future behavior. Considering prior evidence to reassure themselves and others of their good intentions, seemingly reduces the need to keep behaving in a morally righteous way, and makes it tempting to cut corners now and then (Monin & Miller, 2001; Simbrunner & Schlegelmilch, 2017).

Moral cleansing. After violating moral standards, people can try to redeem themselves as they engage in *moral cleansing* to restore their moral self-views. A practical option to compensate for one's 'moral debt' is to offer restitution to those suffering from one's actions. However, people may also try to clear their conscience by doing something that is totally unrelated to the damage done (donating to charity after cheating in a game), or through purely symbolic acts of cleansing (engaging in religious rituals) to reaffirm their self-views of being a good and moral person (West & Zhong, 2015).

Moral courage. People who display moral strength in promoting the accomplishment of moral goals, even in the face of opposition, display *moral courage*. This can be done by prioritizing moral choices to address ethical challenges. It can also be exemplified by the courageous decision whistle-blowers make to speak up against actions that seem morally wrong (Sekerka et al., 2009).

Moral improvement. To achieve *moral improvement* it is necessary to reduce defensiveness in acknowledging moral failures. To be able to improve one's moral behavior it is necessary to overcome feeelings of self-blame and self-condemnation. Acting in line with one's moral values can benefit self-forgiveness (Leach, 2017; Woodyatt et al., 2017).

mapped on to the range of strategies people use to manage threats to their social identity (Ellemers, 1993; Ellemers et al., 1999a). This helps us specify the nature and likely impact of concrete organizational behaviors aiming to address moral issues in the workplace (see also Anand et al., 2004; Bandura, 1999).

Distinguishing between the types of identity management strategies that are known (see Box 2.2), helps to understand that there are *different ways* in which people can respond when their moral identity is under threat. An important distinction we highlight here is that some 'easy' strategies focus on adapting the way people *think* about the situation, but do not really effect any behavioral change. In fact, the quick relief this offers to feelings of guilt and moral inadequacy can discourage them from engaging in more 'difficult' responses that would actually make them *do* something to achieve the type of moral improvement that is likely to have a long term impact, and can make them feel proud and respected (see Fig. 2.3).

2.3.1 (Re)defining the Context

As briefly indicated in Chap. 1, perhaps the easiest solution to address moral threat is by denying that moral concerns are relevant, for instance by claiming that one's organizational task performance is amoral (see also Anand et al., 2004). If the only concerns to consider are whether actions are within the law and make good business sense, people show *moral neglect* or *moral ignorance* (Bandura, 1999). This is possible by recategorizing people in such a way that rule adherence can be seen as a task for 'outgroup members'. Deciding that this is the job of an external regulator or an internal compliance department, allows those in the 'ingroup' to focus on

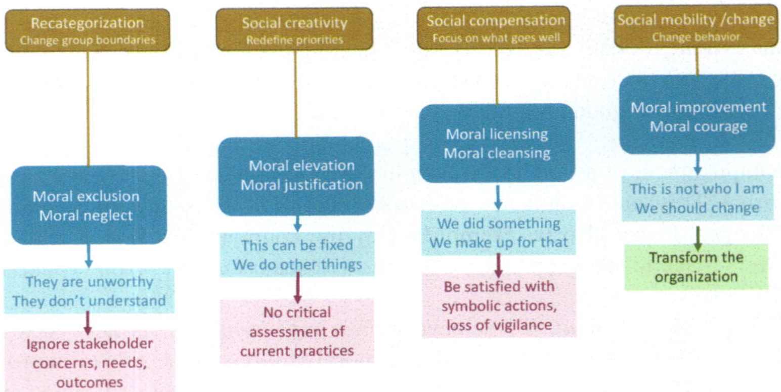

Fig. 2.3 How easy solutions introduce new moral hazards. Characterizes different strategies that are commonly used to manage moral identity threat, and explains why these introduce additional moral hazards unless the organization is transformed

efficiency issues or other performance targets. A classic example would be a situation in which people blindly follow orders and shift moral responsibility for their actions onto those who decide on the overall strategy and issue the orders (see also Box 3.1). However, as we know from the classic studies on obedience to authority (Milgram, 1974; Reicher & Haslam, 2012), this 'easy' strategy is not fully effective, as relegating moral responsibility to others not always prevents people from feeling guilt and shame for their actions.

Another way of absolving the self from moral concerns by redrawing group boundaries is by denying full ingroup membership to those who break the rules. Some organizations do this by relying on a 'fixer': scapegoating one person who does what it takes for others to be successful. This allows the rest of the ingroup to shun responsibility by avoiding direct involvement in morally questionable actions. Once these actions are challenged they can quickly expose or remove the 'fixer' as a rotten apple who doesn't really belong. This seems to have been the role played by Kweku Adoboli, a trader at Swiss bank UBS. He served a prison sentence, after being convicted for using the bank's money in unauthorized transactions. Yet, for many years he received rewards and bonuses for the millions in revenue he realized for the bank in this way. His colleagues said that everyone knew that he was the man to turn to if you had screwed up: "We didn't know how he did it, but we didn't want to know", they said (Fortado, 2015). Does this truly absolve others in the company from being complicit in what he did, or was it a convenient strategy to curb moral hazards?

A similar practice can be found in professional ice hockey teams. In ice hockey competitions teams can benefit from displaying aggression against the opponent, even if this is formally not allowed. Many teams therefore relegate this task to an 'enforcer': a player specializing in prohibited acts of fighting. A study of a professional ice hockey team results over the playing season revealed the importance of this role for the team. It showed that the team's performance particularly suffered when the 'enforcer' was injured (Stuart & Moore, 2017). Here too the question is whether individual 'enforcers' are to be blamed for breaking rules of fair play, or whether the team implicitly invites and approves of such behavior to optimize its performance – while keeping the hands of 'core team members' clean. In some cases at least, practices like this represent willful acts of moral ignorance or moral neglect. Of course, organizations would formally deny or denounce engagement of its members in activities that are questionable or prohibited. In reality, however, many instances of morally dubious conduct are informally known by colleagues and condoned or even encouraged by leaders. Assigning this role to specific individuals sets them up as a fall guy that can be removed to allow others in the organization to avoid reputational damage.

Once people are confronted with the moral implications of their actions and cannot deny their responsibility for them, they can still engage in *moral exclusion* to alleviate guilt and shame. Here too group boundaries are redrawn – in this case to curb the circle of care by categorizing those who suffer from their business strategy as outgroup members. This allows people to believe these individuals are not part of the community of those who merit their loyalty or fair treatment (Anand et al., 2004). For instance, business leaders can decide that they are good and caring people, but argue that temporary workers are not real members of the organization, and hence fall outside their responsibility. Likewise, they can decide that, in general, they feel for the plight of others but cannot be expected to check whether their suppliers offer humane work conditions. Deciding to consider these as outgroup members, alleviates people from feeling accountable for questionable practices that might occur in their supply chain.

Studies show that people can come to see others they place outside their circle of care as lesser humans, unworthy of moral consideration (Bandura et al., 1975; Haslam, 2006). In fact, such individuals or groups may not even register as real humans in their brain (Harris & Fiske, 2006; see also Ellemers, 2012). The often-cited habit of Goldman Sachs bankers to refer to overly trusting clients as 'Muppets' would be a case in point (Smith, 2012). Thus, recategorizing specific stakeholder groups as outgroups, is a moral exclusion strategy that allows members of the organization to think well of their own moral behavior, while neglecting the harm done to stakeholders.

2.3.2 *Emphasizing Good Intentions*

Even when people acknowledge the moral implications of their actions and the relevance this has for their identity, it still does not mean they are motivated to change their behavior in order to improve the moral self (see also Sun & Goodwin, 2019). Instead, they can try to salvage their moral stature by emphasizing their good intentions in a different way. Regardless of whether or not the outcomes were beneficial, people's efforts to show that at least they meant well, allow them to continue to think of the self as morally sound. First we consider how people can shift the social comparisons they make, as a form of social creativity that (re)defines the meaning and relevance of morally questionable behavior.

Focusing on how they pursue different and superior moral priorities or higher goals that outweigh the moral costs that were made, can offer a form of *moral justification* (Anand et al., 2004; Bandura, 1999). People in organizations thus creatively search for and invoke different types of efforts and dimensions of achievement to claim their behavior is moral after all. While cutting corners with safety guidelines, they might highlight the efforts made to fight for survival of the organization, to protect the interests of shareholders, or to honor commitments made to suppliers or clients. These can all be offered as socially worthy or even as moral purposes that justify practices that would otherwise seem harmful, unfair, or even illegal. Other than in the case of moral neglect or moral exclusion, those who do this might be aware and even take responsibility for the harm they did. However, they would claim they chose the lesser of two evils, and were protecting key moral values that are central to them (Skitka, 2002; Skitka & Mullen, 2002).

For instance, organizational leaders might defend the use of sweatshops by arguing they gave priority to providing employment and income to those doing this work over considerations concerning human rights and well-being. Sometimes goals or job titles are clothed in euphemistic language (e.g., referring to bribery as 'gaining local support') to convey the moral gains of the preferred choice (Anand et al., 2004). As long as such strategic justification of common practices is not challenged, members of the organization might even convince themselves and each other that they are truly trying to do what is morally right. While this may alleviate feelings of guilt and shame about 'collateral damage' of their choices, it also reduces the chances that people actively search for improvement opportunities.

Redeeming the sense of self as a moral person can also be achieved by seeking *moral elevation*. This terms refers to the fact that people can feel uplifted, touched, and inspired when they witness others displaying acts of virtue (Algoe & Haidt, 2009; Diessner et al., 2013; Haidt, 2000). When being reprimanded about environmental damage done by a company in their sector, people may point to some small startup organization aiming to reduce this, for instance by cleaning up the 'plastic soup' in the ocean. More often than not, such initiatives or individuals are unlikely to be effective and doesn't even remotely compensate for damage done. Nevertheless, people like to approve, endorse and publicize such initiatives, simply to convince themselves and others that they do care, and change might be possible. Research has documented that merely sharing stories of good practice examples can benefit physical and psychological well-being, generating a 'warm glow' which literally makes people feel better about themselves (Piper et al., 2015; Silvers & Haidt, 2008).

Some studies suggest this might prompt people to start acting in ways that attest to their general willingness to be helpful and altruistic, and may perhaps inspire them to become a better person (Aquino et al., 2011; Schnall & Roper, 2012). Yet reviews of research reveal that moral elevation mainly seems to offer a form of *emotion* regulation that is psychologically reassuring, without being clearly related to specific intentions (for instance, to change one's own environmentally damaging behavior). Thus, we consider moral elevation as a relatively 'easy' short term strategy to alleviate guilt and shame, without having clear long term effects for changes in one's own moral behavior (Moreton et al., 2019; Pohling & Diessner, 2016;

Schnall et al., 2010). We see this as another instance of social creativity, allowing people to feel good about themselves despite their moral failures, while ignoring the need to change their own behavior.

Finally, people may offer evidence of their good intentions by doing something that is morally good to offset moral concerns about other decisions they have made. This is a form of social compensation that has been documented in research on moral licensing, and moral cleansing. *Moral licensing* is the term used to indicate that people feel less concerned about their moral behavior when they have already shown their good moral intentions (Miller & Effron, 2010; Merritt et al., 2010; Monin & Miller, 2001; for overviews see: Blanken et al., 2015; Simbrunner & Schlegelmilch, 2017). Once people can boast some prior moral achievement, they may become less attentive and concerned about applying the same moral standards to future actions. The feeling that it is possible to relax one's moral conscience has been observed even after relatively minor actions attesting to good faith. For instance, after taking discarded glass to the bottle bank for recycling, people feel less guilty about taking a plane for a skiing trip – even though the environmental damage of the plane ride obviously outweighs the benefits of recycling bottles.

Moral cleansing is the phenomenon that people try to compensate prior moral failures and show their good intentions by doing something that seems obviously moral (West & Zhong, 2015). For instance, after being confronted with their efforts to dodge tax laws, people may try to salvage their moral self-views by donating money to charity – like some of the wealthy individuals identified in Chap. 1. Even if this is a symbolic act that touches upon a totally different domain – and might be quite ineffectual to repair damage done, people feel less bad about prior moral lapses when doing something that seems morally right (Gino et al., 2015; West & Zhong, 2015). Such licensing or cleansing effects can even occur vicariously, as a special form of moral elevation. In this case, evidence of morally upright behavior displayed by *other* members of the group reassures individuals of their own moral stature – if only by association. For instance, identifying strongly with another company employee who offered a job to an ethnic minority member made people less vigilant in preventing bias when they evaluated candidates for other jobs (Kouchaki, 2011). Thus, the awareness that others in the company are doing something that is morally right can be enough to make people less alert for the possibility that their own behavior may fall short of moral guidelines.

In organizations, different forms of moral licensing and moral cleansing can be observed. In this context, we consider all acts of 'good faith' that are peripheral to the core mission and strategy of the organization. Donating to charity or highlighting contributions to the community, are examples of relatively minor and symbolic acts communicating moral intentions displayed by the self or other members of the organization. This can be felt as providing compensation and offering reassurance that one is morally good after all, without changing key elements of organizational procedures or strategies that can be seen as morally questionable. Even Amazon CEO Jeff Bezos' 10 billion dollar investment in the 'Bezos Earth Plan' to support initiatives aiming to combat climate change can be seen in this light. Indeed, at the same time that Bezos announced his decision, the 'Amazon Employees for Climate

Justice' pointed out the inconsistency between this initiative and other decisions made by their CEO. Thousands of employees petitioned against the core aspects of the Amazon business strategy which allow the company to make money by placing unnecessary strain on the environment. They urged the company to invest in transportation of ordered goods by electric trucks instead of using trucks running on diesel, and requested their founder to stop donating money to climate change deniers. As long as these business choices seemed inconsistent with the pledge to save the climate, it rang false for Amazon's employees.

2.3.3 Improving the Situation

At some point, individuals may decide they are no longer willing to go along with organizational practices that they see as morally flawed (Mullen & Monin, 2016). Organizational members who communicate that the things they are expected to do feel morally wrong, engage in a form of social mobility as they separate their own moral identity from the organization (also denoted as 'identity exit', Petriglieri, 2011). It may be motivated by the hope to alert others to these moral concerns and convince them that change is needed. Unfortunately, this is not how such comments tend to be received. Expressing dissatisfaction about moral choices of the organization is often seen as a form of disloyalty. Individuals who do this may be accused of trying to 'save their own skin' by exposing and condemning the moral choices others in the organization make. Such actions tend to be repaid with disrespect and exclusion instead of inspiring others to do the same (Ellemers & Jetten, 2013).

This is what often happens to whistleblowers (Glazer & Glazer, 1989; Kohn, 2015). They can be seen as individuals at the forefront of moral change, who show *moral courage* by being the first to call out morally questionable behavior (Gahl, 1984). It can be seen as a form of moral leadership where people take action in going beyond compliance to achieve moral goals (Sekerka et al., 2009). However, people taking on such roles run the risk of being isolated, undermined and discredited by others who may still consider the moral hazards that are exposed as acceptable cost of doing business or the inevitable collateral damage of other priorities (Comer & Vega, 2015). For instance, American football player Colin Kaepernick was fired by the San Francisco 49ers, because of his protest against police brutality and racial injustice in American society. Despite his sporting qualities he could not secure a transfer to another team as long as he was 'taking the knee' instead of standing up for the national anthem played before each game.

Displays of moral courage reveal that practices that many have come to see as inevitable can also be rejected or changed. Vegetarians or 'teetotalers' for instance, expose that refusing consumption of meat or alcohol is a choice others might also make. Thus, the personal choices of these individuals not only reflect their own principles. They also hold up a mirror to others, by demonstrating that it is possible to apply different and perhaps more rigorous moral standards. Research reveals that such people are usually not welcomed as a source of self-reflection, nor are they commonly seen as an inspiration for self-improvement. Instead of being recognized as the moral leaders they might be, they often face distrust because their motives are seen as selfish. Studies examining such individuals show that they tend to be disliked and put down as 'holier than thou' or 'moral do-gooders' (Jordan & Monin, 2008; Monin et al., 2008). Even if their concerns are genuine and valid, they are often being met with hostility and denial.

Sometimes such individual efforts at exposing or improving practices that seem morally problematic only increase the organization's attempts to cover up problems – by blaming the whistleblower for making trouble – instead of addressing the issues they expose (see also Chap. 8). Again, this parallels the effect of social mobility that are documented in prior research: individuals who move away from the group to improve their own identity do not necessarily help others to improve and can even discourage group level change (see also Ellemers & Van Laar, 2010).

Only after all these temptations to take the 'easy way out' of the moral minefield have been overcome, is it possible to move towards *moral improvement* (see also Fig. 1.3). This requires collective action where organizations and the people working in them jointly acknowledge the moral shortcomings in their past behavior, and confront and overcome the guilt and shame this causes (Giner-Sorolla, 2012; Leach, 2017; Leach & Cidam, 2015). Changing the moral behavior of the organization may imply that strategic priorities have to be redefined (e.g., placing the reduction of environmental damage before the maximization of profit), that standard procedures have to be adapted (e.g., to develop a more diverse set of indicators to assess employee potential and performance), and that organizations have the courage to start making such changes regardless of what the competition does.

Realizing moral improvement is not about making a quick win. On the contrary, it is likely to incur costly, cumbersome, and time-consuming business transformations. It requires for instance that production is no longer relegated to countries where labor is cheap, that farmers are offered fair prices that allow them to reduce the usage of herbicides, or that more time and resources are spent on quality control of products. Of course, this is a daunting prospect. No wonder that many organizations and their members are satisfied with some of the easier solutions. Once moral relief is found it may be difficult to work up the courage to examine what else has to be done. Perhaps it just seems unrealistic to move to the next level every time a small improvement is made. The choice to pursue moral improvement that has a real impact on society requires commitment and persistence in changing business priorities, transforming the organizational culture, and accepting the implications of doing this. If successful, such a long term project will make people in the organization feel respected and proud of what they stand for, in a way that is acknowledged and valued by regulators, customers and investors.

2.4 Conclusion: Red Flags to Look Out for

In Chap. 1 we have seen that it is not so easy for organizations and the people in them to do what is moral – even if this is what they honestly try to do. The complex and multi-faceted nature of many situations at work makes it difficult to decide on a course of action that is morally superior. Consequences of different decisions may not be clear ahead of time. Different moral principles prescribe different actions. Extending care, fairness or loyalty to some (e.g, one's colleagues or family members) might impose harm, unfairness or disloyalty to others (e.g., one's customers or members of the broader community; Kogut & Zander, 1996; Ramarajan, 2014). This is why abstract moral standards that individuals endorse do not suffice to decide on the moral responsibility of their day-to-day behaviors. Other indicators are needed to act as 'red flags', for situations that are likely to introduce moral hazards.

The theoretical framework presented in this second chapter clarifies that the organizations people work in can come to define how they see themselves and how others see them. We have shown that the type of skills individuals develop, the professional choices they make, and the efforts they display, do not just reflect their personal character and moral convictions. These are also driven by the *social* goals of securing inclusion and respect from the groups that are subjectively important to them, and the desire to be proud of these groups. This explains why situational considerations -and the social identities that seem relevant to them- should be taken into account: These can prompt people to deviate from their individual moral principles. It also explains why people's behavior in the workplace may seem hard to predict or even 'irrational'. The choices individuals make are not fully captured by organizational procedures focusing on individual skill sets, material incentives or sanctioned regulations. People also refer to organizational groups and identities to decide which moral norms can offer them guidance. On the one hand, this helps them limit the range of individuals that fall within their circle of moral responsibility (Boegershausen et al., 2015). On the other hand, it means that questions raised about the moral implications of organizational decisions and actions are felt as critique on one's own moral stature – raising shame and guilt.

This analysis explains that people are quite sensitive to others who criticize their morals and very careful to protect their moral reputation. Because it is so painful to be confronted with one's moral failures, it is very difficult to persuade people to acknowledge these and pledge moral improvement. Instead, the emotional and physiological stress they experience at being criticized for their morals tempt them to deny their moral failures, find justifications for moral lapses, and ignore critique from outgroup members. The different strategies people use to address social identity threats help them cope with such moral critique. By redrawing group boundaries, creatively shifting social comparisons, and adapting their sense of identity, people can manage moral hazards. However, the studies we reviewed in this chapter reveal that such strategies to *think* differently about the situation mostly help to reduce *feelings* of moral inadequacy. At the same time, they do very little to convince people that they have to change their *behavior*. Being able to recognize such identity management strategies as forms of emotional relief that can impede behavioral change, makes it possible to accept the moral intentions of organizational members, while highlighting which additional steps need to be taken to achieve moral improvement. Recurring statements that characterize each of these easier strategies, can function as 'red flags' indicating that further efforts are needed to work towards moral improvement (see Box 2.5).

Box 2.5 Red flags for organizations

The desire to alleviate feelings of guilt and shame by invoking identity management strategies is wide-spread. Some of these responses seem quite constructive, but actually qualify as 'easy' solutions that do not address the root of the issue. When the use of such identity management strategies prevents the organization from engaging with more long-term and difficult solutions, this is a source of moral hazard. Below, we offer some statements that exemplify 'easy solutions', and can be seen as red flags.

Moral neglect

- As long as we act within the law, we have no reason to worry.
- It is just smart to do it this way.
- If we play this right they can't touch us – the law isn't entirely clear on this.

Moral exclusion

- They can say no if they don't like it.
- They are responsible adults, it's their decision.
- They are overreacting, these snowflakes just can't stand anything.

Moral justification

- Those are the costs of doing business – we are a commercial enterprise after all
- If we don't do this, someone else will.
- Loyalty is valued here above all else.

Moral elevation

- Here is an uplifting example, let's invite them for a talk at our event!
- There is someone at HR who has been doing this, we should put them on our website!
- One of our competitors is doing this well, so clearly the sector is taking responsibility!

Moral licensing

- We appointed someone to look out for that – they will tell us if there is a problem.
- We have introduced a code of conduct, so we should be ok.
- We have already invested a lot in sustainable energy, shouldn't that be enough?

Moral cleansing

- Why don't we make a donation to the community?
- Let's sponsor a networking activity for ethnic minority employees.
- We can use our team building activity to support a good cause.

The 'quick fixes' identified in Chap. 1 (changing people, incentives, or rules) also qualify as ways to communicate concerns about the moral identity of the organization. However, their effects will be limited if the organization fails to address core features of the strategy or procedures that continue to invite moral hazards. These are root causes of moral issues that imply that similar concerns will recur time and again, unless further changes are made. In the chapters that follow we analyze how common organizational practices and quick fixes that are often used can stand in the way of moral improvement. When organizational members recategorize others to exclude them from moral considerations, creatively redefine the situation to justify questionable moral choices, or focus on efforts made to display good intentions, this helps them cope with the identity threat of being seen as immoral, but also introduces new moral hazards.

Thus, paradoxically, the consequence of the strong motivation to be seen as moral by the self and by others makes it difficult to take action that may help confront and overcome moral shortcomings. Managing feelings of discomfort by neglecting the moral implications of organizational choices, providing some moral justification for priorities selected, finding a way to demonstrate good intentions, or discrediting those who expose moral concerns, are all relatively easy but short term strategies. These do not really resolve issues that are raised and make it all the more likely that internal and external stakeholders will continue to question choices that are made until a more satisfactory response is visible.

Throughout the chapters that follow we will demonstrate that many organizations mainly adapt the way they *think* about their moral conduct. Each time we will show the downsides of denying moral responsibility for adverse outcomes or investing effort in displays of good intentions, instead of attempting to achieve actual moral improvement. Thus, the chapters that follow elucidate that many of the strategies people use in *response* to the moral threat they experience, sustain moral blind spots and *introduce* further moral hazards. We consider these suboptimal solutions not because they only offer temporary relief, but because superficial attempts to address moral hazards can – and often do – make matters worse. Recognizing the 'red flags' that characterize these pitfalls, allows organizations to take more effective action.

Recommended Reading

Aquino, K., & Reed, A., II. (2002). The self-importance of moral identity. *Journal of Personality and Social Psychology, 83*(6), 1423. https://doi.org/10.1037/0022-3514.83.6.1423

De Gilder, D., & Ellemers, N. (2017). The social psychology of organizations. In L. Steg, K. Keizer, & B. Buunk (Eds.), *Applied social psychology* (pp. 298–318). Cambridge University Press.

Ellemers, N., & Van Nunspeet, F. (2020). Neuroscience and the social origins of (im)moral behavior: How neural underpinnings of social categorization and conformity affect every day (im)moral behavior. *Current Directions in Psychological Science, 29*, 513–520. https://doi.org/10.1177/0963721420951584

Haslam, S. A. (2004). *Psychology in organizations: The social identity approach*. Sage.

Leach, C. W. (2017). Understanding shame and guilt. In *Handbook of the psychology of self-forgiveness* (pp. 17–28). Springer. https://doi.org/10.1007/978-3-319-60573-9_2

References

Abele, A., Ellemers, N., Fiske, S., Koch, A., & Yzerbyt, V. (2020). *Navigating the social world: Shared horizontal and vertical evaluative dimensions*. Under Review.

Algoe, S. B., & Haidt, J. (2009). Witnessing excellence in action: The 'other-praising'emotions of elevation, gratitude, and admiration. *The Journal of Positive Psychology, 4*(2), 105–127. https://doi.org/10.1080/17439760802650519

Ambrose, J. (2019, June 20). *UK's big energy firms accused of failing to tackle climate crisis*. Retrieved from https://www.theguardian.com/environment/2019/jun/20/uks-big-energy-firms-accused-of-failing-to-tackle-climate-crisis

Anand, V., Ashforth, B. E., & Joshi, M. (2004). Business as usual: The acceptance and perpetuation of corruption in organizations. *Academy of Management Perspectives, 18*(2), 39–53. https://doi.org/10.5465/ame.2004.13837437

Aquino, K., & Reed, A., II. (2002). The self-importance of moral identity. *Journal of Personality and Social Psychology, 83*(6), 1423. https://doi.org/10.1037/0022-3514.83.6.1423

Aquino, K., McFerran, B., & Laven, M. (2011). Moral identity and the experience of moral elevation in response to acts of uncommon goodness. *Journal of Personality and Social Psychology, 100*(4), 703. https://doi.org/10.1037/a0022540

Ashforth, B. E., & Johnson, S. A. (2001). Which hat to wear? The relative salience of multiple identities in organizational contexts. In M. A. Hogg & D. J. Terry (Eds.), *Social identity processes in organizational contexts* (pp. 31–48). Psychology Press.

Ashforth, B. E., & Kreiner, G. E. (1999). "How can you do it?": Dirty work and the challenge of constructing a positive identity. *Academy of Management Review, 24*(3), 413–434. https://doi.org/10.5465/amr.1999.2202129

Ashforth, B. E., & Mael, F. (1989). Social identity theory and the organization. *Academy of Management Review, 14*(1), 20–39. https://doi.org/10.5465/amr.1989.4278999

Ashforth, B. E., & Schinoff, B. S. (2016). Identity under construction: How individuals come to define themselves in organizations. *Annual Review of Organizational Psychology and Organizational Behavior, 3*, 111–137. https://doi.org/10.1146/annurev-orgpsych-041015-062322

Ashforth, B. E., Schinoff, B. S., & Brickson, S. L. (2020). "My company is friendly", "Mine's a rebel": Anthropomorphism and shifting organizational identity from "what" to "who". *Academy of Management Review, 45*, 29–57. https://doi.org/10.5465/amr.2016.0496

Bandura, A. (1999). Moral disengagement in the perpetration of inhumanities. *Personality and Social Psychology Review, 3*, 193–209. https://doi.org/10.1207/s15327957pspr0303_3

Bandura, A., Underwood, B., & Fromson, M. E. (1975). Disinhibition of aggression through diffusion of responsibility and dehumanization of victims. *Journal of Research in Personality, 9*(4), 253–269. https://doi.org/10.1016/0092-6566(75)90001-X

Beauchamp, T. L. (2001). *Philosophical ethics: An introduction to moral philosophy*. Mcgraw-Hill.

Bicchieri, C. (2017). *Norms in the wild: How to diagnose, measure, and change social norms*. Oxford University Press. https://doi.org/10.1093/acprof:oso/9780190622046.001.0001

Bisel, R. S. (2017). *Organizational moral learning: A communication approach*. Routledge. https://doi.org/10.4324/9781315652252

Blanken, I., Van de Ven, N., & Zeelenberg, M. (2015). A meta-analytic review of moral licensing. *Personality and Social Psychology Bulletin, 41*(4), 540–558 https://doi.org/10.1177/0146167215572134

Boegershausen, J., Aquino, K., & Reed, A., II. (2015). Moral identity. *Current Opinion in Psychology, 6*, 162–166. https://doi.org/10.1016/j.copsyc.2015.07.017

Boorstein, M. (2020, June 26). Scandals, compensation programs lead Catholic clergy sex abuse complaints to quadruple in 2019. *The Washington Post*. Retrieved from: https://www.washingtonpost.com/religion/2020/06/26/scandals-compensation-programs-lead-catholic-clergy-sex-abuse-complaints-quadruple-2019/

Brambilla, M., Sacchi, S., Pagliaro, S., & Ellemers, N. (2013). Morality and intergroup relations: Threats to safety and group image predict the desire to interact with outgroup and

ingroup members. *Journal of Experimental Social Psychology, 49*(5), 811–821. https://doi.org/10.1016/j.jesp.2013.04.005
Brandt, M. J., & Reyna, C. (2011). The chain of being: A hierarchy of morality. *Perspectives on Psychological Science, 6*(5), 428–446. https://doi.org/10.1177/1745691611414587
Branscombe, N. R., & Doosje, B. J. (Eds.). (2004). *Collective guilt: International perspectives.* Cambridge University Press. https://doi.org/10.1017/CBO9781139106931
Brennan, G., & Pettit, P. (2004). *The economy of esteem.* Oxford University Press. https://doi.org/10.1093/0199246483.001.0001
Browning, H., & Kanaga, K. (2007). *Maintaining Team Performance by Center for Creative Leadership Staff.* Center for Creative Leadership.
Burrows, B. (1993). Essay review—The greening of business and its relationship to business ethics. *Long Range Planning, 26*(1), 130–139. https://doi.org/10.1016/0024-6301(93)90241-7
Cikara, M., & Van Bavel, J. J. (2014). The neuroscience of intergroup relations: An integrative review. *Perspectives on Psychological Science, 9*(3), 245–274. https://doi.org/10.1177/1745691614527464
Cikara, M., Van Bavel, J. J., Ingbretsen, Z. A., & Lau, T. (2017). Decoding "us" and "them": Neural representations of generalized group concepts. *Journal of Experimental Psychology: General, 146*(5), 621. https://doi.org/10.1037/xge0000287
Clark, C. J., Chen, E. E., & Ditto, P. H. (2015). Moral coherence processes: Constructing culpability and consequences. *Current Opinion in Psychology, 6*, 123–128. https://doi.org/10.1016/j.copsyc.2015.07.016
Comer, D. R., & Vega, G. (2015). Moral courage in organizations: Doing the right thing at work. *ME Sharpe*. https://doi.org/10.4324/9781315702285.
Conroy, S., Henle, C. A., Shore, L., & Stelman, S. (2017). Where there is light, there is dark: A review of the detrimental outcomes of high organizational identification. *Journal of Organizational Behavior, 38*(2), 184–203. https://doi.org/10.1002/job.2164
Davis, J. H., Schoorman, F. D., & Donaldson, L. (1997). Toward a stewardship theory of management. *Academy of Management Review, 22*(1), 20–47. https://doi.org/10.5465/amr.1997.9707180258
Deal, T. E., & Kennedy, A. A. (1982). *Corporate cultures: The rites and rituals of corporate life.* Penguin. https://doi.org/10.1016/0007-6813(83)90092-7
De Gilder, D., & Ellemers, N. (2017). The social psychology of organizations. In L. Steg, K. Keizer, & B. Buunk (Eds.), *Applied social psychology* (pp. 298–318). Cambridge University Press.
Diessner, R., Iyer, R., Smith, M. M., & Haidt, J. (2013). Who engages with moral beauty? *Journal of Moral Education, 42*(2), 139–163. https://doi.org/10.1080/03057240.2013.785941
Doosje, B. E., Branscombe, N. R., Spears, R., & Manstead, A. S. (2006). Antecedents and consequences of group-based guilt: The effects of ingroup identification. *Group Processes & Intergroup Relations, 9*(3), 325–338. https://doi.org/10.1177/1368430206064637
Doward, J. (2019, September 15). *After six deaths in the US and bans around the world – is vaping safe?* Retrieved from https://www.theguardian.com/society/2019/sep/15/how-safe-is-vaping-e-cigarettes-deaths-bans
Dutton, J. E., & Dukerich, J. M. (1991). Keeping an eye on the mirror: Image and identity in organizational adaptation. *Academy of Management Journal, 34*(3), 517–554. https://doi.org/10.2307/256405
Ellemers, N. (1993). The influence of socio-structural variables on identity management strategies. *European Review of Social Psychology, 4*(1), 27–57. https://doi.org/10.1080/14792779343000013
Ellemers, N. (2010). Social identity theory. In J. M. Levine & M. A. Hogg (Eds.), *Encyclopedia of group processes and intergroup relations* (pp. 797–801). Sage.
Ellemers, N. (2012). The group self. *Science, 336*(6083), 848–852. https://doi.org/10.1126/science.1220987
Ellemers, N. (2016). Back to the future: How today's neurocognitive techniques substantiate predictions made 50 years ago. *Psychological Inquiry, 27*(4), 290–293. https://doi.org/10.1080/1047840X.2016.1215210

Ellemers, N. (2017). *Morality and the regulation of social behavior: Groups as moral anchors*. Routledge. https://doi.org/10.4324/9781315661322

Ellemers, N. (2018). Morality and social identity. In M. Van Zomeren & J. F. Dovidio (Eds.), *The Oxford handbook of the human essence* (pp. 147–158). Oxford Library of Psychology. https://doi.org/10.1093/oxfordhb/9780190247577.013.5

Ellemers, N., & De Gilder, D. (2020). Categorization and identity as motivational principles in intergroup relations. Social Psychology: Handbook of Basic Principles (pp 452-472). Third edition. P. Van Lange, E.T. Higgins, & A. Kruglanski (Eds.) New York: Guilford Press.

Ellemers, N., De Gilder, D., & Haslam, S. A. (2004). Motivating individuals and groups at work: A social identity perspective on leadership and group performance. *Academy of Management Review, 29*(3), 459–478. https://doi.org/10.5465/amr.2004.13670967

Ellemers, N., & Haslam, S. A. (2011). Social identity theory. In P. van Lange, A. Kruglanski, & T. Higgins (Eds.), *Handbook of theories of social psychology* (pp. 379–398). Sage. https://doi.org/10.4135/9781446249222.n45

Ellemers, N., & Jetten, J. (2013). The many ways to be marginal in a group. *Personality and Social Psychology Review, 17*, 3–21. https://doi.org/10.1177/1088868312453086

Ellemers, N., Pagliaro, S., Barreto, M., & Leach, C. W. (2008). Is it better to be moral than smart? The effects of morality and competence norms on the decision to work at group status improvement. *Journal of Personality and Social Psychology, 95*(6), 1397. https://doi.org/10.1037/a0012628

Ellemers, N., Spears, R., & Doosje, B. (Eds.). (1999a). *Social identity: Context, commitment, content*. Basil Blackwell.

Ellemers, N., Spears, R., & Doosje, B. (2002). Self and social identity. *Annual Review of Psychology, 53*, 161–186. https://doi.org/10.1146/annurev.psych.53.100901.135228

Ellemers, N., Van der Toorn, J., Paunov, Y., & Van Leeuwen, T. (2019). The psychology of morality: A review and analysis of empirical studies published from 1940 through 2017. *Personality and Social Psychology Review, 23*(4), 332–366. https://doi.org/10.1177/1088868318811759

Ellemers, N., & Van Laar, C. (2010). Individual mobility: The opportunities and challenges members of devalued groups encounter when trying to avoid group-based discrimination. In J. F. Dovidio, M. Hewstone, P. Glick, & V. Esses (Eds.), *Handbook of prejudice, stereotyping, and discrimintation* (pp. 561–576). Sage. https://doi.org/10.4135/9781446200919.n34

Ellemers, N., & Van Nunspeet, F. (2020). Neuroscience and the social origins of moral behavior: How neural underpinnings of social categorization and conformity affect everyday moral and immoral behavior. *Current Directions in Psychological Science, 0963721420951584*. https://doi.org/10.1177/0963721420951584

Foley, K. E. (2019 July 26). *The world's largest tobacco company's anti-smoking campaign relies on smokers*. Retrieved from https://qz.com/1674309/philip-morris-internationals-unsmoke-campaign-relies-on-smokers/.

Fortado, L. (2015, October 22). Kweku Adoboli: A rogue trader's tale. *Financial Times*. Retrieved from https://www.ft.com/content/0fa0b42a-783a-11e5-a95a-27d368e1ddf7

Fry, D. P. (2006). Reciprocity: The foundation stone of morality. In M. Killen & J. G. Smetana (Eds.), *Handbook of moral development* (pp. 399–422). Erlbaum.

Fukuyama, F. (2018). *Identity: The demand for dignity and the politics of resentment*. Farrar, Straus and Giroux.

Gahl, L. L. (1984). Moral courage: The essence of leadership. *Presidential Studies Quarterly, 14*(1), 43–52.

Gert, B. (1988). The law of nature as the moral law. *Hobbes Studies, 1*(1), 26–44. https://doi.org/10.1163/187502588X00033

Gert, B. (2012). Neuroscience and morality. *Hastings Center Report, 42*(3), 22–28. https://doi.org/10.1002/hast.36

Ghoshal, S. (2005). Bad management theories are destroying good management practices. *Academy of Management Learning & Education, 4*(1), 75–91. https://doi.org/10.5465/amle.2005.16132558

Ghoshal, S., & Moran, P. (1996). Bad for practice: A critique of the transaction cost theory. *Academy of Management Review, 21*(1), 13–47. https://doi.org/10.5465/amr.1996.9602161563

Giner-Sorolla, R. (2012). *Judging passions: Moral emotion in persons and groups*. Psychology Press. https://doi.org/10.4324/9780203123874
Gino, F., Kouchaki, M., & Galinsky, A. D. (2015). The moral virtue of authenticity: How inauthenticity produces feelings of immorality and impurity. *Psychological Science, 26*(7), 983–996. https://doi.org/10.1177/0956797615575277
Gioia, D. A., Patvardhan, S. D., Hamilton, A. L., & Corley, K. G. (2013). Organizational identity formation and change. *The Academy of Management Annals, 7*(1), 123–193. https://doi.org/10.5465/19416520.2013.762225
Glazer, M. P., & Glazer, P. M. (1989). *The whistleblowers*. Basic Books.
Haidt, J. (2000). The positive emotion of elevation. *Prevention and Treatment, 3*(1). https://doi.org/10.1037/1522-3736.3.1.33c
Hakala-Ausperk, C. (2013). *Build a great team: One year to success*. American Library Association.
Harris, L. T., & Fiske, S. T. (2006). Dehumanizing the lowest of the low: Neuroimaging responses to extreme out-groups. *Psychological Science, 17*(10), 847–853. https://doi.org/10.1111/j.1467-9280.2006.01793.x
Haslam, A., Van Knippenberg, D., Platow, M., & Ellemers, N. (2003). *Social identity at work: Developing theory for organizational practice*. Psychology Press.
Haslam, N. (2006). Dehumanization: An integrative review. *Personality and Social Psychology Review, 10*(3), 252–264. https://doi.org/10.1207/s15327957pspr1003_4
Haslam, S. A. (2004). *Psychology in organizations: The social identity approach*. Sage.
Haslam, S. A., & Ellemers, N. (2005). Social identity in industrial and organizational psychology: Concepts, controversies and contributions. *International Review of Industrial and Organizational Psychology, 20*(1), 39–118. https://doi.org/10.1002/0470029307.ch2
Haslam, S. A., & Ellemers, N. (2011). Identity processes in organizations. In *Handbook of identity theory and research* (pp. 715–744). Springer. https://doi.org/10.1007/978-1-4419-7988-9_30
Haslam, S. A., Postmes, T., & Ellemers, N. (2003). More than a metaphor: Organizational identity makes organizational life possible. *British Journal of Management, 14*(4), 357–369. https://doi.org/10.1111/j.1467-8551.2003.00384.x
Haslam, S. A., Reicher, S. D., & Platow, M. J. (2011). *The new psychology of leadership: Identity, influence and power*. Psychology Press. https://doi.org/10.4324/9780203833896
Hester, N., & Gray, K. (2020). The moral psychology of raceless, genderless strangers. *Perspectives on Psychological Science, 15*(2), 216–230. https://doi.org/10.1177/1745691619885840
Hogg, M. A., & Terry, D. I. (2000). Social identity and self-categorization processes in organizational contexts. *Academy of Management Review, 25*(1), 121–140. https://doi.org/10.5465/amr.2000.2791606
Jordan, A. H., & Monin, B. (2008). From sucker to saint: Moralization in response to self-threat. *Psychological Science, 19*(8), 809–815. https://doi.org/10.1111/j.1467-9280.2008.02161.x
Killen, M., Margie, N. G., & Sinno, S. (2006). Morality in the context of intergroup relationships. In M. Killen & J. G. Smetana (Eds.), *Handbook of moral development* (pp. 155–183). Erlbaum. https://doi.org/10.4324/9781410615336
Kogut, B., & Zander, U. (1996). What firms do? Coordination, identity, and learning. *Organization Science, 7*(5), 502–518. https://doi.org/10.1287/orsc.7.5.502
Kohn, S. M. (2015). For the greater good: The moral courage of whistleblowers. In *Moral courage in organizations: Doing the right thing at work* (pp. 84–98). Routledge.
Kotter, J. P., & Heskett, J. L. (1992). *Corporate culture and performance*. Free Press.
Kouchaki, M. (2011). Vicarious moral licensing: The influence of others' past moral actions on moral behavior. *Journal of Personality and Social Psychology, 101*(4), 702. https://doi.org/10.1037/a0024552
Kouzakova, M., Harinck, F., Ellemers, N., & Scheepers, D. (2014). At the heart of a conflict: Cardiovascular and self-regulation responses to value versus resource conflicts. *Social Psychological and Personality Science, 5*(1), 35–42. https://doi.org/10.1177/1948550613486673
Lamont, M. (2000). *The dignity of working men: Morality and the boundaries of race, class, and immigration*. Russell Sage Foundation.

Lamont, M. (2002). Working men's imagined communities: The boundaries of race, immigration, and poverty in France and the United States. In U. Hedetoft & M. Hjort (Eds.), *The postmodern self: Imagining and belonging* (pp. 178–197). University of Minnesota Press.

Leach, C. W. (2017). Understanding shame and guilt. In *Handbook of the psychology of self-forgiveness* (pp. 17–28). Springer. https://doi.org/10.1007/978-3-319-60573-9_2

Leach, C. W., Bilali, R., & Pagliaro, S. (2015). Groups and morality. In M. Mikulincer, P. R. Shaver, J. F. Dovidio, & J. A. Simpson (Eds.), *APA handbooks in psychology. APA handbook of personality and social psychology* (Group processes) (Vol. 2, pp. 123–149). American Psychological Association. https://doi.org/10.1037/14342-005

Leach, C. W., & Cidam, A. (2015). When is shame linked to constructive approach orientation? A meta-analysis. *Journal of Personality and Social Psychology, 109*(6), 983. https://doi.org/10.1037/pspa0000037

Leets, L. (2001). Interrupting the cycle of moral exclusion: A communication contribution to social justice research. *Journal of Applied Social Psychology, 31*(9), 1859–1891. https://doi.org/10.1111/j.1559-1816.2001.tb00208.x

Logan, D., King, J., & Fischer-Wright, H. (2008). Corporate tribes: The heart of effective leadership. *Leader to Leader, 2008*(49), 25–30. https://doi.org/10.1002/ltl.290

Marques, J. M., & Paez, D. (1994). The 'Black Sheep Effect': Social categorization, rejection of ingroup deviates, and perception of group variability. *European Review of Social Psychology, 5*(1), 37–68. https://doi.org/10.1080/14792779543000011

Maslow, A. H. (1943). A theory of human motivation. *Psychological Review, 50*(4), 370. https://doi.org/10.1037/h0054346

Merritt, A. C., Effron, D. A., & Monin, B. (2010). Moral self-licensing: When being good frees us to be bad. *Social and Personality Psychology Compass, 4*(5), 344–357. https://doi.org/10.1111/j.1751-9004.2010.00263.x

Milgram, S. (1974). *Obedience to authority: An experimental view*. Harpercollins.

Miller, D. T., & Effron, D. A. (2010). Psychological license: When it is needed and how it functions. In M. P. Zanna & J. M. Olson (Eds.), *Advances in experimental social psychology 43* (pp. 117–158). Academic. https://doi.org/10.1016/S0065-2601(10)43003-8

Miller, G. (2019, February 21). *The current absurdity of the Dutch online gambling law*. Retrieved from https://europeangaming.eu/portal/compliance-updates/2019/02/21/39350/the-current-absurdity-of-the-dutch-online-gambling-law/.

Monbiot, G. (2019, June 26). Shell is not a green saviour. *It's a planetary death machine*. Retrieved from https://www.theguardian.com/commentisfree/2019/jun/26/shell-not-green-saviour-death-machine-greenwash-oil-gas

Mick, D. G. (2007). The end(s) of marketing and the neglect of moral responsibility by the American marketing association. *Journal of Public Policy and Marketing, 26*(2), 289–292. https://doi.org/10.1509/jppm.26.2.289

Minto, K., Hornsey, M. J., Gillespie, N., Healy, K., & Jetten, J. (2016). A social identity approach to understanding responses to child sexual abuse allegations. *PLoS One, 11*(4), 1–15. https://doi.org/10.1371/journal.pone.0153205

Monin, B., & Miller, D. T. (2001). Moral credentials and the expression of prejudice. *Journal of Personality and Social Psychology, 81*(1), 33. https://doi.org/10.1037/0022-3514.81.1.33

Monin, B., Sawyer, P. J., & Marquez, M. J. (2008). The rejection of moral rebels: Resenting those who do the right thing. *Journal of Personality and Social Psychology, 95*(1), 76. https://doi.org/10.1037/0022-3514.95.1.76

Moore, C., & Gino, F. (2013). Ethically adrift: How others pull our moral compass from true North, and how we can fix it. *Research in Organizational Behavior, 33*, 53–77. https://doi.org/10.1016/j.riob.2013.08.001

Moore, G. (1999). Corporate moral agency: Review and implications. *Journal of Business Ethics, 21*(4), 329–343. https://doi.org/10.1023/A:1006020214228

Moreton, S. G., Arena, A., Hornsey, M. J., Crimston, C. R., & Tiliopoulos, N. (2019). Elevating nature: Moral elevation increases feelings of connectedness to nature. *Journal of Environmental Psychology, 65*, 101332. https://doi.org/10.1016/j.jenvp.2019.101332

Morgan, J. (2017). *The employee experience advantage: How to win the war for talent by giving employees the workspaces they want, the tools they need, and a culture they can celebrate*. Wiley.

Muhr, S., Sørensen, B. M., & Vallentin, S. (Eds.). (2010). *Ethics and organizational practice: Questioning the moral foundations of management*. Edward Elgar. https://doi.org/10.4337/9781849805414

Mullen, E., & Monin, B. (2016). Consistency versus licensing effects of past moral behavior. *Annual Review of Psychology, 67*, 363–385. https://doi.org/10.1146/annurev-psych-010213-115120

Oakes, P. J. (1987). The salience of social categories. In J. C. Turner, M. A. Hogg, P. J. Oakes, S. D. Reicher, & M. S. Wetherell (Eds.), *Rediscovering the social group* (pp. 117–141). Blackwell.

Oakes, P. J., Haslam, S. A., & Turner, J. C. (1994). *Stereotyping and social reality*. Blackwell.

O'Brien, R. (2009). Global ethics: Beyond local leadership. *Journal of International Business Ethics, 2*(1).

Orts, E. W., & Smith, N. C. (2017). *The moral responsibility of firms*. Oxford University Press. https://doi.org/10.1093/oso/9780198738534.001.0001

Pagliaro, S., Brambilla, M., Sacchi, S., D'Angelo, M., & Ellemers, N. (2013). Initial impressions determine behaviours: Morality predicts the willingness to help newcomers. *Journal of Business Ethics, 117*(1), 37–44. https://doi.org/10.1007/s10551-012-1508-y

Pagliaro, S., Ellemers, N., & Barreto, M. (2011). Sharing moral values: Anticipated ingroup respect as a determinant of adherence to morality-based (but not competence-based) group norms. *Personality and Social Psychology Bulletin, 37*(8), 1117–1129. https://doi.org/10.1177/0146167211406906

Pagliaro, S., Ellemers, N., Barreto, M., & Di Cesare, C. (2016). Once dishonest, always dishonest? The impact of perceived pervasiveness of moral evaluations of the self on motivation to restore a moral reputation. *Frontiers in Psychology, 7*, 586. https://doi.org/10.3389/fpsyg.2016.00586

Petriglieri, J. L. (2011). Under threat: Responses to and the consequences of threats to individuals' identities. *Academy of Management Review, 36*(4), 641–662. https://doi.org/10.5465/amr.2009.0087

Philip Morris International. (n.d.). *Delivering a smoke-free future*. Retrieved from https://www.pmi.com/our-transformation/delivering-a-smoke-free-future

Piper, W. T., Saslow, L. R., & Saturn, S. R. (2015). Autonomic and prefrontal events during moral elevation. *Biological Psychology, 108*, 51–55. https://doi.org/10.1016/j.biopsycho.2015.03.004

Pohling, R., & Diessner, R. (2016). Moral elevation and moral beauty: A review of the empirical literature. *Review of General Psychology, 20*(4), 412–425. https://doi.org/10.1037/gpr0000089

Povoledo, E. (2020, July 16). Vatican tells bishops to report sex abuse to police (but doesn't require it). *New York Times*. https://www.nytimes.com/2020/07/16/world/europe/vatican-new-sex-abuse-rules.html

Procter & Gamble. (n.d.). *Policies & practices: Purpose, values & principles*. Retrieved from https://us.pg.com/policies-and-practices/purpose-values-and-principles/

Ramarajan, L. (2014). Past, present and future research on multiple identities: Toward an intrapersonal network approach. *The Academy of Management Annals, 8*(1), 589–659. https://doi.org/10.5465/19416520.2014.912379

Reed, A., II, & Aquino, K. F. (2003). Moral identity and the expanding circle of moral regard toward out-groups. *Journal of Personality and Social Psychology, 84*(6), 1270. https://doi.org/10.1037/0022-3514.84.6.1270

Reicher, S., & Haslam, S. A. (2012). Obedience: Revisiting Milgram's obedience studies. In J. R. Smith & S. A. Haslam (Eds.), *Social psychology: Revisiting the classic studies* (pp. 106–125). Sage.

Rocha, H. O., & Ghoshal, S. (2006). Beyond self-interest revisited. *Journal of Management Studies, 43*(3), 585–619. https://doi.org/10.1111/j.1467-6486.2006.00603.x

Schnall, S., & Roper, J. (2012). Elevation puts moral values into action. *Social Psychological and Personality Science, 3*(3), 373–378. https://doi.org/10.1177/1948550611423595

Schnall, S., Roper, J., & Fessler, D. M. (2010). Elevation leads to altruistic behavior. *Psychological Science, 21*(3), 315–320. https://doi.org/10.1177/0956797609359882
Schneider, B., & Barbera, K. (2014). *The handbook of organizational climate and culture: Antecedents, consequences, and practice*. Oxford University Press. https://doi.org/10.1093/oxfordhb/9780199860715.001.0001
Sekerka, L. E., Bagozzi, R. P., & Charnigo, R. (2009). Facing ethical challenges in the workplace: Conceptualizing and measuring professional moral courage. *Journal of Business Ethics, 89*, 565–579. https://doi.org/10.1007/s10551-008-0017-5
Shell. (2018). *Annual report 2018: Selected financial data*. https://reports.shell.com/annual-report/2018/strategic-report/summary-of-results/selected-financial-data.php
Shell. (2019 April 8). *Shell invests in nature as part of broad drive to tackle CO2 emissions*. Retrieved from https://www.shell.com/media/news-and-media-releases/2019/shell-invests-in-nature-to-tackle-co2-emissions.html
Silvers, J. A., & Haidt, J. (2008). Moral elevation can induce nursing. *Emotion, 8*(2), 291. https://doi.org/10.1037/1528-3542.8.2.291
Simbrunner, P., & Schlegelmilch, B. B. (2017). Moral licensing: A culture-moderated meta-analysis. *Management Review Quarterly, 67*, 201–225. https://doi.org/10.1007/s11301-017-0128-0
Sinek, S. (2011). *Start with why. How great leaders inspire everyone to take action*. Penguin Books Ltd.
Skitka, L. J. (2002). Do the means always justify the ends, or do the ends sometimes justify the means? A value protection model of justice reasoning. *Personality and Social Psychology Bulletin, 28*(5), 588–597. https://doi.org/10.1177/0146167202288003
Skitka, L. J., & Mullen, E. (2002). The dark side of moral conviction. *Analyses of Social Issues and Public Policy, 2*(1), 35–41. https://doi.org/10.1111/j.1530-2415.2002.00024.x
Smith, G. (2012, March 14). Why I Am Leaving Goldman Sachs. *The New York Times*. Retrieved from https://www.nytimes.com/2012/03/14/opinion/why-i-am-leaving-goldman-sachs.html?auth=login-google
Smith, H. J., Tyler, T. R., Huo, Y. J., Ortiz, D. J., & Lind, E. A. (1998) The self-relevant implications of the group-value model: Group membership, self-worth, and treatment quality. *Journal of Experimental Social Psychology, 34*(5), 470–493. https://doi.org/10.1006/jesp.1998.1360
Spears, R. (2021). Social influence and group identity. *Annual Review of Psychology, 72*. https://doi.org/10.1146/annurev-psych-070620-111818
Ståhl, T., & Ellemers, N. (2016). Ironic effects of moral motivation: Why working toward a moral goal reduces subsequent perspective taking. *Social Cognition, 34*(2), 133–148. https://doi.org/10.1521/soco.2016.34.2.133
Steffens, N. K., Haslam, S. A , Schuh, S. C., Jetten, J., & Van Dick, R. (2017). A meta-analytic review of social identification and health in organizational contexts. *Personality and Social Psychology Review, 21*(4), 303–335. https://doi.org/10.1177/1088868316656701
Stuart, H. C., & Moore, C. (2017). Shady characters: The implications of illicit organizational roles for resilient team performance. *Academy of Management Journal, 60*(5), 1963–1985. https://doi.org/10.5465/amj.2014.0512
Sun, J., & Goodwin, G. (2019). Do people want to be more moral? *PsyArXiv*. https://doi.org/10.31234/osf.io/9gux6
Tajfel, H. (1974). Social identity and intergroup behaviour. *Information (International Social Science Council), 13*(2), 65–93. https://doi.org/10.1177/053901847401300204
Tajfel, H. (1978). Social categorization, social identity and social comparison. In H. Tajfel (Ed.), *Differentiation between social groups: Studies in the social psychology of intergroup relations* (pp. 61–76). Academic.
Tajfel, H., & Turner, J. C. (1979). An integrative theory of social conflict. In W. Austin & S. Worchel (Eds.), *The social psychology of intergroup relations* (pp. 7–24). Brooks/Cole.
Tangney, J. P., & Dearing, R. L. (2002). Gender differences in morality. In R. F. Bornstein & J. M. Masling (Eds.), *Empirical studies in psychoanalytic theories* (The psychodynamics of gender and gender role) (Vol. 10, pp. 251–269). American Psychological Association. https://doi.org/10.1037/10450-007

The Story Behind the 'Spotlight' Movie. (n.d.). Retrieved December 20, 2020, from https://www.easybib.com/mla8-format/website-citation/new

Tobacco Control Legal Consortium. (2006). *The verdict is in: Findings from United States v. Philip Morris, the hazards of smoking*. Retrieved from https://www.publichealthlawcenter.org/sites/default/files/resources/tclc-verdict-is-in.pdf. https://doi.org/10.2139/ssrn.1004323.

Tooby, J., & Cosmides, L. (2010). Groups in mind: The coalitional roots of war and morality. In H. Hogh-Olesen (Ed.), *Human morality and sociality* (pp. 191–234). Palgrave Macmillan. https://doi.org/10.1007/978-1-137-05001-4_8

Tracy, J. L., & Robins, R. W. (2004). Putting the self into self-conscious emotions: A theoretical model. *Psychological Inquiry, 15*(2), 103–125. https://doi.org/10.1207/s15327965pli1502_01

Tsui, A. (2016). Reflections on the so-called value-free ideal: A call for responsible science in the business schools. *Cross Cultural & Strategic Management, 23*(1), 4–28. https://doi.org/10.1108/CCSM-08-2015-0101

Turner, J. C. (1985). Social categorization and the self-concept: A social cognitive theory of group behavior. In E. J. Lawler (Ed.), *Advances in group processes* (pp. 77–122). JAI Press.

Turner, J. C., Hogg, M. A., Oakes, P. J., Reicher, S. D., & Wetherell, M. S. (1987). *Rediscovering the social group: A self-categorization theory*. Basil Blackwell.

Turner, J. C., Oakes, P. J., Haslam, S. A., & McGarty, C. (1994). Self and collective: Cognition and social context. *Personality and Social Psychology Bulletin, 20*, 454–463. https://doi.org/10.1177/0146167294205002

Tyler, T. R. (1999). Why people cooperate with organizations: An identity-based perspective. *Research in Organizational Behavior, 21*, 201–246.

Tyler, T. R., & Blader, S. L. (2000). *Cooperation in groups*. Psychol. Press.

Tyler, T. R., & Blader, S. L. (2003). The group engagement model: Procedural justice, social identity, and cooperative behavior. *Personality and Social Psychology Review, 7*(4), 349–361. https://doi.org/10.1207/S15327957PSPR0704_07

Van der Lee, R., Ellemers, N., & Scheepers, D. (2016). Mastering moral misery: Emotional and coping responses to intragroup morality (vs. competence) evaluations. *Cognition and Emotion, 30*(1), 51–65. https://doi.org/10.1080/02699931.2015.1050357

Van der Lee, R., Ellemers, N., & Scheepers, D. (submitted). *Fysio studie immoreel gedrag zelf vs. ander*.

Van der Lee, R., Ellemers, N., Scheepers, D., & Rutjens, B. T. (2017). In or out? How the perceived morality (vs. competence) of prospective group members affects acceptance and rejection. *European Journal of Social Psychology, 47*(6), 748–762. https://doi.org/10.1002/ejsp.2269

Van der Toorn, J., Ellemers, N., & Doosje, B. (2015). The threat of moral transgression: The impact of group membership and moral opportunity. *European Journal of Social Psychology, 45*(5), 609–622. https://doi.org/10.1002/ejsp.2119

Van Nunspeet, F., Derks, B., Ellemers, N., & Nieuwenhuis, S. (2015). Moral impression management: Evaluation by an in-group member during a moral IAT affects perceptual attention and conflict and response monitoring. *Social Psychological and Personality Science, 6*(2), 183–192. https://doi.org/10.1177/1948550614548076

Van Prooijen, A. M., & Ellemers, N. (2015). Does it pay to be moral? How indicators of morality and competence enhance organizational and work team attractiveness. *British Journal of Management, 26*(2), 225–236. https://doi.org/10.1111/1467-8551.12055

Van Veelen, R., & Derks, B. (2020, November 8). *Academics as Superheroes: Female academics' lack of fit with the masculine stereotype of success limits their career advancement*. https://doi.org/10.31234/osf.io/c3k56.

Vatican Issues New Manual on Reporting Sex Abuse of Minors. (2020, July 16). Retrieved from https://www.dw.com/en/vatican-sex-abuse-minors/a-54207971

Veldman, J., Meeussen, L., Van Laar, C., & Phalet, K. (2017). Women (do not) belong here: Gender-work identity conflict among female police officers. *Frontiers in Psychology*. https://doi.org/10.3389/fpsyg.2017.00130

Watson, B. (2016, August 20). *The troubling evolution of corporate greenwashing*. Retrieved from https://www.theguardian.com/sustainable-business/2016/aug/20/greenwashing-environmentalism-lies-companies

West, A. (2016). Applying metaethical and normative claims of moral relativism to (shareholder and stakeholder) models of corporate governance. *Journal of Business Ethics, 135*(2), 199–215. https://doi.org/10.1007/s10551-014-2453-8

West, C., & Zhong, C. B. (2015). Moral cleansing. *Current Opinion in Psychology, 6*, 221–225. https://doi.org/10.1016/j.copsyc.2015.09.022

Whetten, D., & Foreman, P. (2014). An organizational identity lens for organizational climate scholarship. In B. Schneider & K. M. Barbera (Eds.), *The Oxford handbook of organizational climate and culture* (pp. 1–25). Oxford University Press. Retrieved from http://www.oxfordhandbooks.com/view/10.1093/oxfordhb/9780199860715.001.0001/oxfordhb-9780199860715-e-023.

Woodyatt, L., Wenzel, M., & Ferber, M. (2017). Two pathways to self-forgiveness: A hedonic path via self-compassion and a eudaimonic path via the reaffirmation of violated values. *British Journal of Social Psychology, 56*(3), 515–536. https://doi.org/10.1111/bjso.12194

Xiao, Y. J., Coppin, G., & Van Bavel, J. J. (2016). Perceiving the world through group-colored glasses: A perceptual model of intergroup relations. *Psychological Inquiry, 27*(4), 255–274. https://doi.org/10.1080/1047840X.2016.1199221

Chapter 3
Moral Leadership

Abstract Leaders are seen to embody the vision and goals of the organization, by their subordinates as well as outsiders. The **key issues** addressed in this chapter indicate how leaders – who define the tone at the top – set the standard for moral behavior in organizations. Unfortunately, it is not easy to specify the characteristics of a moral leader: many great leaders have done praiseworthy as well as shameful things. Situational factors can invite neglect of moral concerns, even for leaders with a strong moral identity. Our **analysis** highlights the impact of social contexts and organizational identities on displays of ethical leadership. We show how common organizational practices that set leaders apart from their subordinates can introduce a range of moral hazards. Placing leaders on a pedestal conveys a sense of entitlement causing them to devalue concerns that detract from their own achievements. Assigning leaders control over others makes them less mindful of the needs of followers. Inducing fear of losing their privileged position causes leaders to justify their own decisions, while resisting input from others. The research reviewed in this chapter points to **solutions** organizations can adopt. Avoiding conditions that

N. Ellemers, D. de Gilder, *The Moral Organization: Key Issues, Analyses, and Solutions*, https://doi.org/10.1007/978-3-030-84175-1_3

invite moral disengagement, moral exclusion, and moral justification reduces the emergence of unethical behavior among leaders and their followers. Building a shared identity defined by trust, loyalty, and responsibility among people working at different levels in the organization points the way towards moral leadership.

3.1 Key Issues: The Tone at the Top

There is a distinct fascination with leaders and leadership, in organizations and in daily life. Any media outlet will report on political or business leaders pretty much every day, in both positive and negative ways. People seek out leaders as role models and sources of inspiration, turning themselves into willing followers rather than compliant subordinates. When leaders display exemplary moral behavior they can inspire their followers to do the same. But by the same token, leaders who lie, cheat, or misbehave in other ways can also inspire others to follow suit (Brown & Treviño, 2014; Den Hartog, 2015). The advantages and disadvantages of such inspirational, or charismatic, leadership are described abundantly in every textbook on organizational behavior (e.g., Bass & Riggio, 2006; Waldman & O'Reilly, 2019; Yukl, 2013; Yukl & Van Fleet, 1992). Any attempt to understand moral behavior in organizations should therefore start with an assessment of the 'tone at the top' (see also Box 3.1).

Box 3.1 Is obedience the root of evil?
Organizations typically appoint individuals who are assigned power and authority over others. Those placed in such leadership roles are expected to make sure that subordinates comply with important guidelines and show at least some degree of obedience to their line managers. Might this be the root of the problem? If people in organizations simply do as they are told, is their obedience a key cause of immoral behavior?

Obedience to authority is a classical theme in social psychology. Many are familiar with the notorious 'Milgram studies'. This was a series of studies in which people were prompted to punish others by administering increasingly strong electrical shocks for wrong answers in a so-called learning experiment. Research participants (in the role of 'teacher') were led to believe the shocks they delivered as sanctions were painful and potentially even life-threatening. In reality, the equipment they used was not connected. They were misled by actors, participating in the role of 'learners'. Upon receipt of their 'punishment' they appeared to suffer, protested loudly that they did not want to continue, or in the end even ceased to respond - suggesting they were unconscious or worse.

What most people remember from these studies is that they reveal the dangers of obedience. Apparently, research participants went along with the request to harm innocent others, simply because someone in a position of authority (the experimenter leading the study) told them to do so (Milgram,

1965, 1974). Clear evidence, or so it would seem, of the 'banality of evil' (Arendt, 1963), in a period where the atrocities of the second world war were still the moral checkpoint to many of Milgram's contemporaries. Also today, 50 years later, people who learn about these studies are shocked by the seemingly immoral behavior of the participants – perhaps also of the experimenter. The distress many suffer when first viewing the video recordings of the original Milgram studies relates to the seemingly 'blind' obedience that is revealed. This undermines the notion that humans are generally willing to extend care to others, avoid unnecessary harm, and take responsibility for their own actions. Instead, it suggests that average people in mundane circumstances are prepared to cause severe damage to others if only a person of authority tells them to.

A closer look reveals a different conclusion. Far from being sensationalist, the original Milgram studies were based on a diligent research program. Many variations in experimental set-ups were compared, to pinpoint the *circumstances* under which obedience to authority increased or decreased. This revealed for instance that obedience was greatly decreased, or even absent, when the experimenter did not wear a lab coat, or offered audio instructions from another room. Placing the 'learner' in the same room as the 'teacher' also greatly reduced the willingness to inflict 'punishment'. In reality then, this research program mainly demonstrates how relatively small and seemingly irrelevant changes in a situation can have a dramatic impact on people's attitudes and behaviors. Recent efforts to replicate this research (with slightly adapted procedures to avoid too much emotional strain on research participants), revealed quite similar results (Burger, 2009; Haslam et al., 2015).

This attests to the fact that – also today - people can end up in situations where they go along with requests that seem clearly unethical to others. At the same time, recent studies unambiguously show that obedience to authority is not as 'blind' as many suspect. For instance, more authoritarian prompts (e.g., 'it is absolutely essential that you continue') resulted in lower compliance levels. Further research on people who comply with unethical requests in organizations, for instance to perpetuate corruption, also indicates that this cannot be simply attributed to blind obedience. Instead, other factors are instrumental such as high levels of identification with the misbehaving organization. This suggests that feelings of engagement with the perpetrators (rather than the victims) allow people to support unethical behavior. They do this not because they follow orders, but because they believe the authority is right (Haslam & Reicher, 2012, 2017; Haslam et al., 2016).

Studies on leadership do not only look at leaders and powerholders. In fact, leader behaviors and their consequences cannot be separated from their impact on the subordinates and followers placed under their guidance. This work has revealed that leadership can have positive consequences for employees and organizations

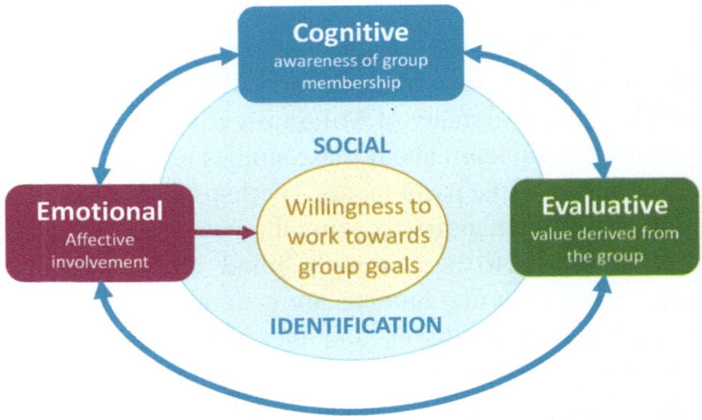

Fig. 3.1 How to inspire followers. Shows that social identification is defined by cognitive, evaluative, as well as emotional processes. Results from multiple studies show that the willingness to work towards group goals benefits more from affective involvement in the group, than from awareness of group membership or value derived from the group. (Ellemers et al., 1999; Haslam et al., 2003; Ouwerkerk et al., 1999)

when leaders allow employees to understand what they have to do and feel respected for their contributions to the organization (Ellemers, De Gilder, & Haslam, 2004; Haslam et al., 2011). Such inspirational leadership allows followers to see themselves as part of a larger whole, affording them with a sense of value and emotional involvement that enhances their willingness to work towards shared goals (Mathieu & Zajac, 1990; Meyer & Allen, 1997; see Fig. 3.1). Leaders who manage to do this well, reduce employee turnover as well as improving task performance and broader displays of effort towards organizational goals ('organizational citizenship behaviors'; Podsakoff et al., 2009).

However, research has just as well documented the existence of failing leadership and its negative implications for employees and organizations. For instance, when leaders engage in a callous and manipulative interaction style, this usually has negative consequences for the well-being and work attitudes of subordinates. Meta-analytic study reviews show that negative leader behavior towards employees causes distress. It is associated with displays of reactance and counterproductive work behavior by subordinates (e.g., O'Boyle Jr. et al., 2012), and is bad for employee health (Steffens, Yang, et al., 2018). The occurrence of such deficient leadership behavior is usually seen to stem from flaws in the individual dispositions of those leaders, such as their greed, overconfidence, need for power, or 'corporate psychopathy' (Haynes et al., 2015; Hogan & Hogan, 2014; Linstead et al., 2014; Mathieu et al., 2014). This has prompted efforts to examine whether an assessment of the so-called 'dark triad' of personality traits (narcissism, Machiavellianism, psychopathy) can be used to predict the emergence of dysfunctional leadership behaviors (Furnham et al., 2013; Furtner et al., 2017).

Obviously, it makes sense for organizations to avoid promoting individuals into leadership positions who score highly on any of the three 'dark triad' of personality aspects. Instead, they seek out individuals who exhibit tendencies that may contribute to moral leadership, such as fairness, honesty or altruism. However, in line with our social identity analysis, we highlight that aversive and unethical leadership is not simply contained in the personality traits of the individual in question, but can just as easily be encouraged and invited by organizational practices. In this chapter, we examine the impact of situational characteristics (rather than personality) that contribute to ethically questionable leadership behaviors (see also Brown & Treviño, 2006; Den Hartog, 2015). In doing this we highlight that unethical leader behavior is not defined solely by engagement in fraud or financial transgressions, but extends to the unwillingness to behave civilly and responsibly towards subordinates and other stakeholders. We reveal the hidden costs of the way organizations typically set leaders apart from their followers, and show how this can unwittingly invite unethical behavior among leaders and their followers. Understanding how these mechanisms work can help to avoid them from occurring.

The analysis we offer points to workplace circumstances that introduce foreseeable moral hazards. We note common organizational practices that invite unethical leadership behavior while allowing leaders to protect themselves from the threat of seeing this as immoral. As explained in Chap. 2, using moral disengagement, moral exclusion, or moral justification as identity management strategies prevents leaders from critically assessing or improving their moral behavior, and impacts on the moral climate in the organization.

3.1.1 *Heroes or Villains?*

Effective leaders influence others to enhance their contribution towards the realization of group goals (Haslam et al., 2011). This suggests there is great value in recruiting and appointing the right leaders, and organizations accordingly spend a great deal of time and money to find individuals who possess exemplary capabilities, in line with the individual difference approach as a quick fix to address organizational issues, as detailed in Chap. 1. Headhunting and recruitment agencies try to find and select individuals who are competent, decisive, and can inspire others while weeding out those who show aversive leadership characteristics, such as the traits included in the 'dark triad' described above. Selecting the best leaders seems even more important in view of the notion that others in the organization will comply with their authority.

Yet despite all these efforts to find the best leaders, CEO turnover has been rising during the past 20 years. This is an important conclusion from an examination of long-term leadership trends at 2500 large companies across the world. This analysis further found that company leaders are increasingly forced to resign due to ethical lapses. In 2018, scandals and misconduct involving fraud, bribery, insider trading, environmental damages, inflated CVs or sexual indiscretions were cited more often as the primary reason for forced CEO resignations than disappointing financial performance (Karlsson et al., 2019). Apparently it is not self-evident that individuals who are selected for their leadership qualities and business successes also behave decently (see also Box 3.2).

Box 3.2 Jeff Bezos' fall from grace

For many years, the founder of internet retail store Amazon, Jeff Bezos, was considered one of the best performing CEOs in the world. In 2014 he came first in the top 100 annually compiled by the Harvard Business Review, particularly receiving praise for his long-term vision (Ignatius, 2014). He went on to figure prominently in each subsequent edition (De Torres, 2019). However, in 2019 Bezos was conspicuously absent from this list despite his company's comfortable financial position (De Torres, 2019). Why did he fall off his pedestal? It's his way of doing business, the Harvard Business Review said. Questions surrounding the company's working conditions, personnel policies, personal data privacy guarantees and infringements of competition rules made Bezos tumble out of the CEO top 100 (De Torres, 2019). His financial success simply cannot make up for it.

It cannot not have come as a surprise to him. From 2015 these criteria have been explicitly included when composing the list. Apart from financial performance the Harvard Business Review now judges a CEO on his environmental, social and governance credentials (Fombrun, 2015). In the final edition the so-called ESG parameters made up 30% of the total criteria and that is likely to increase in future (De Torres, 2019). This is not a crusade by the Harvard Business Review, its makers say, but simply the recognition of a social trend and the needs of investors. Recent research has shown that investors, as well as employees and customers, are looking beyond the financial figures. They want to know what a company's social performance is like.

Of course Bezos knows this. His own workers have told him often enough. He even was one of the CEOs of US multinationals (Business Roundtable, 2019) who issued a statement on the subject (Bezos, 2020; see also Chap. 7). It said that companies must not only aim at satisfying their shareholders but that they have a duty to consider the interests of other stakeholders, such as employees, customers, suppliers and communities affected by their activities (Business Roundtable, 2019). Bezos' problem is that he offers little evidence of following through on these good intentions by transforming his way of doing business. Pursuing financial results above all else no longer is the hallmark of excellence in business leadership.

History seems to suggest that ethical compromises are an inevitable part of leadership: perhaps great leaders were only able to achieve great things because they ruthlessly used any available means to pursue their goals. Indeed, many military leaders, political leaders, and leading entrepreneurs are revered and despised, often simultaneously, because of what they have done and how they did it. An example is Napoleon Bonaparte, the self-proclaimed emperor of France, whose life history and achievements still speak to the imagination of many. He was banished from mainland France twice after catastrophic defeats in his Russian campaign and, after his return to power, at the battle of Waterloo. Despite these defeats, the loss of life among his own troops, the atrocities his armies committed, the art thefts he ordered – prominently visible in Paris in the 'Place de la Concorde' and in the Louvre museum — Napoleon is still acknowledged as a brilliant strategist and conqueror. His body lies in an exquisite tomb in the most central spot of the historic Dôme des Invalides building in Paris, surrounded by many other French heroes, attracting millions of visitors every year.

Over time, however, there may be a change of perspective, causing events that were long seen as important achievements to be seen as shameful episodes in history. The Black Lives Matter movement led people across the world to reconsider the status of national heroes. In the USA and the UK statues of Christopher Columbus, Edward Colston, and General Lee were damaged or removed due to increased awareness that these leaders were only able to contribute to national prosperity and power by blatantly disregarding human rights, and sacrificing innocent lives. The inconsistent behaviors and multiple faces of many historical leaders show that it is not so simple to separate the heroes from the villains. Even the actions of Nobel peace prize winners are not beyond moral critique (Ellis-Petersen, 2018).

Of course it is a giant leap from discussing historical atrocities to debating immoral behavior in organizations. However, these examples illustrate that well-known historical leaders are very similar to the business leaders we discussed in Chap. 1. They cannot be seen as unidimensional characters who are either all good or all bad. Nor is their general ability to care for others, pursue fairness or be honest, predictive of how they will behave in all the facets of their leadership role. Each of the leaders we discussed here can be admired for some of their actions and achievements, while being criticized for others. Some leaders strive for admirable goals, but use morally questionable means to achieve them. Others may have the best of intentions but suffer from moral lapses. They may truly repent and try to repair and compensate for their moral failures. Who is to say which leader is more ethical? This points to limitations of the individual difference approach as a quick fix to select 'morally superior' leaders. Indeed, we find it more appropriate to highlight the morality or immorality of specific decisions and behaviors and what caused people to behave in this way – than simply to conclude that some individuals are moral while others are not (see also Ellemers, 2017).

3.1.2 Championing High Performance

A second quick fix that is often used to make leaders focus on organizational outcomes instead of pursuing more selfish concerns, is to make their remuneration and rewards contingent on the success of the organization. Unfortunately, there are severe limitations to this approach.

The variable rewards in leaders' compensation packages invite decisions that maximize those rewards – even if this may not be in the best interest of the organization. This was identified as a factor contributing to the global financial crisis of 2008 that culminated in the fall of Lehmann brothers. In retrospect, it became clear that the reward systems in many companies, but specifically in banks, had promoted business strategies that represented irresponsible risks. Financial rewards for leaders mainly depended on short term company profits and share prices. So the achievement of short term profit and high share prices became a goal in itself – disregarding customer interests and long term viability of this strategy. This is a classic pitfall already identified in 1975 (see also Box 3.3).

Box 3.3 On the folly of rewarding A while hoping for B

It is by no means a new insight that reward systems can have undesirable outcomes. Already 45 years ago, this was noted in a classic paper titled "on the folly of rewarding A, while hoping for B" (Kerr, 1975). We quote this title here in honor of an insight that may seem obvious, but is often ignored. The analysis made in 1975 details many kinds of reward systems that fail to achieve their goal - or even backfire – a phenomenon known today as a system of 'perverse incentives'. The pitfall is that team leaders, organizations, or regulators often declare specific outcomes ('quality', 'customer interests', 'compliance') to be important - or even assign them as mandatory - in the hope that this will guide people's efforts. However, it is unlikely that these goals will be pursued very vigorously as long as all rewards and incentives steer people in another direction. Time and again, the result is that people can hope for B as long as they like, but if 'A' is the only thing that is rewarded, then 'A' is what they will get.

Let us consider some examples. In general, almost every company develops strategies to remain profitable and competitive in the long term (goal 'B'). However, when leaders and employees are only evaluated on the basis of short term profits or results (reward 'A'), long term goals will inevitably seem less relevant - especially for those who are only appointed for a fixed number of years. Another example is the formal obligation for organizations to communicate correctly and adequately with all their stakeholders (goal 'B'). However, when leadership bonuses are assigned on the basis of shareholder value (reward 'A'), external communication is likely to prioritize information that optimizes share prices on the stock market. Not-for-profit organizations are just as well subject to the consequences of perverse incentives. Public universities, for instance, are expected to promote the general level of education in their country (goal 'B'). However, in assigning budgets they are rewarded for the number of graduates they 'deliver' (reward 'A'). This will motivate universities to do exactly what is rewarded: hand out more degrees. This does not necessarily result in a better educated population.

When the focus on outcomes that are rewarded drives people in organizations to cut corners in achieving the desired performance, this raises moral issues. Companies that decide to adapt external communications to push up share prices may end up hiding important risks or ignoring production problems. Universities that need to turn out a fixed number of graduates to 'earn' their budget, may experience pressure to become less strict in maintaining high standards for students pursuing a degree. Sometimes perverse incentives elicit pre-meditated fraud. For instance at ENRON where management deliberately presented inaccurate performance figures to inflate the stock prices on which their bonuses were based (e.g., Eichenwald, 2002). Another example is Volkswagen. In the notorious 'dieselgate' affair it was revealed that the automobile manufacturer had developed a special device to allow millions of vehicles to pass emission tests, while actual emissions were about 40 times higher (Ewing, 2017; Van Rooij & Fine, 2018),

In general, efforts to achieve outcome 'A' that is rewarded cause people in organizations to assign less priority to intended goal 'B'. Many would argue that moral issues are not relevant to the development of rewards and incentives systems – considering this process as 'amoral'. Nevertheless, they should take note that the rewards and incentives they provide influence the goals people prioritize, and impact on the achievement of desired outcomes. For this reason, even amoral decisions may not be unproblematic, as they may still harm organizations and society in the long run.

In many cases, efforts to obtain rewards might be classified as morally neutral – also known as 'amoral' – behaviors. Yet, there are clear indications that variable reward systems can and do seduce leaders to do whatever it takes to get the bonus they covet – even if this implies they have to engage in unethical, or illegal activities (see also Chap. 8). Researcher Kees Cools revealed this by retrospectively comparing large companies where leaders were known to have been fraudulent (such as Enron, or Parmalat) with similar companies without a record of bookkeeping fraud (see also Eichenwald, 2002). This comparison made it possible to test and exclude different explanations for the occurrence of fraud. The emergence of fraud could not be traced to differences between companies in their governance structure or leadership competency. However, clear differences were found in the performance incentives they used: CEO bonuses were 3–8 times larger in fraudulent companies than in non-fraudulent companies. Further, in fraudulent companies these bonuses were tied to unrealistic performance targets as CEOs were incentivized to achieve twice the growth rate that was reported by non-fraudulent companies that were similar to them (Cools, 2009). Together, these results suggest that incentive structures which hold out the prospect of extremely high bonuses for impossibly high performance targets tempt CEOs to do 'whatever it takes' to show the intended results, even if this implies they have to commit fraud.

An additional risk of relying on rewards and performance incentives as a primary way to guide workplace behavior is that it may not attract and promote those with the 'best' motives. Championing those who are driven by monetary rewards may not attract and reward the most valuable leaders. This was revealed, for instance, in a study on the remuneration of auditors. Their response to compensation incentives, such as profit sharing and variable pay, was found to depend on their work motivation. Profit sharing and variable pay only benefited the work of individuals with a low drive to perform well. However, for those who were intrinsically motivated, adding these external incentives made them less careful in achieving their assigned goals and negatively impacted the quality of their performance (Van Brenk, 2018). Relying on incentives to steer behavioral choices may thus invite norm violations and selfish behavior. This leadership strategy celebrates and promotes individuals who achieve set targets, regardless of whether this actually benefits broader organizational goals (see also Stamkou & Van Kleef, 2014).

Not only CEOS have been found to violate moral standards to achieve performance targets. Other leaders do this too and such behavior is often motivated by more than just financial gain. Gymnastics coaches for instance, have a record of bullying female athletes to improve their performance, even resulting in widespread abuse and sexual harassment (Macur, 2020). In the Netherlands a coach admitted he saw the young pupils placed under his guidance merely as objects he could use to achieve his own performance goals of winning sports medals (Marcelis, 2020). The impact of external rewards and incentives on inviting desired leadership behaviors thus fully depends on whether the outcomes that are being valued and rewarded accurately reflect the different types of concerns that are important for the organization. Well-known cases of fraud as well as more systematic research summarized in this chapter clearly reveal that such systems are limited in their ability to safeguard public expectations about the moral responsibility of organizations, especially as they tend to run behind in reflecting changing notions of good leadership.

3.1.3 Underestimating the Power of Situations

The examples summarized above illustrate that leaders often have to perform multiple functions, combining different types of efforts and achievements which are not necessarily easy to reconcile. Keeping leaders on the straight and narrow by reminding them of formal requirements and procedures is the third quick fix that is often used. However, this ignores the power of social roles and situational forces that trigger and reinforce some behaviors rather than others.

Contemporary approaches to leadership emphasize that leaders have to deal with different situations, and that coincidental circumstances impact on how they reconcile opposite requirements and adapt to changing circumstances (Brown & Treviño, 2006; Den Hartog, 2015; Haslam et al., 2011). Of course, leaders and the principles they work by usually do have an impact, if only because they have the power to make decisions and can enforce compliance. However, in evaluating organizational choices and outcomes people tend to attach too much weight to leader decisions, while paying too little attention to aspects of the situation that led to these results (Meindl, 1995; Meindl et al., 1985).

Common perceptions of what leaders are able to do on their own, almost endow them with magical qualities. However, as indicated before, examples of leaders who performed well in one situation but badly in others abound. Highly publicized leadership transfers exemplify the reliance on individual leaders to make the right decisions. After being welcomed as superstars, a forced retreat is often their fate. Their judgments and choices which seemed infallible, may not meet the requirements of another setting, or the reverse: From zero to hero. Rex Tillerson, previously successful as CEO, will not be remembered as a great secretary of state of the USA. The success of Dutch IT company Centrics quickly disappeared once its founder Gerard Sanderink started acting on the advice of his new girlfriend, prompting his best managers to leave the company for its competitor (Kunst, 2019; Van Gils, 2020). These are not exceptional cases. In general, the successes and failures of leaders – in terms of their financial as well as ethical performance – largely depend on others they work with. Indeed, critical comments from subordinates – or lack thereof – are broadly recognized as a key factor in the prevention or emergence of suboptimal leader decision making and irresponsible risk taking (Janis, 1972; see also Postmes et al., 2001). In large companies in particular, leaders have to rely on the expert information, sincerity, and professional judgments of those around them to be able to do their job well.

The ability of leaders to stick to prescribed guidelines or follow through on their good intentions, thus crucially depends on the situations they encounter. There is very little they can achieve on their own, without a network of people that supports them or the efforts of subordinates who are willing to follow their lead. This has been recognized in scholarly theories of leadership (e.g., Deckard, 2009; Hughes et al., 1998; Yukl, 2011). Yet in practice, people tend to expect far too much from leaders, as if a single individual can redeem an entire organization. Some argue, for instance, that the presence of a female leader should benefit ethical decision making in politics or in organizations. Christine Lagarde famously stated that the financial crisis could have been prevented if only Lehman brothers had been Lehman sisters. Likewise when evaluating responses to the COVID-19 pandemic journalists speculated that countries led by female politicians were more successful in guarding public health. However, studies comparing the leadership of women and men mainly reveal that organizations invite, reward, and promote particular types of leadership behaviors, bringing these out in women and in men (see Box 3.4). In reality then, even when they are strongly committed to do what is moral, leaders are simply human beings who have to work within the limitations of the situations they encounter, and whose actions and decisions are partly shaped by the people around them.

Box 3.4 Are women more moral leaders than men? (it's the situation, dummy!)

The assumption that women are more responsible and moral leaders than men is voiced quite regularly. The quick lockdowns imposed at the start of the COVID-19 pandemic in New Zealand and Germany under the leadership of Jacinda Ardern and Angela Merkel are seen as exemplary for a more general tendency for female leaders to be more empathic and risk averse (Garikipati & Kambhampati, 2020).

European Central Bank President Christine Lagarde also thinks female leaders embody unique advantages. She has declared more than once that if only Lehman Brothers had been Lehman Sisters the world would be a better place (If it was Lehman sisters it would have been a different world, 2018). Business results show that social (non-financial) issues move up the corporate agenda when more women join the board (Bernardi & Threadgill, 2010; Shoham et al., 2017). It would be tempting to assume that men and women have 'innately' different leadership qualities and goals. However, research suggests this is not simply because 'how men and women are' but rather stems from differences in upbringing and social roles.

An overview of hundreds of studies reveals that men and women actually show very similar competencies and ambitions. No systematic differences are found in their leadership style, ethical behavior, the importance they attach to success and prestige versus caring for others, or their ability to understand the feelings of others (Hyde, 2014). Extensive research on male and female leadership mainly reveals that female leaders as seen as slightly more democratic (Eagly, 2012; Eagly & Johnson, 1990; Eagly et al., 2003; Eagly et al., 1995; Eagly et al., 1992). However, in men as well as women, behavioral styles and even differences in the production of hormones such as oxytocin and testosterone are influenced by social roles and organizational assignments (Fine, 2017; Van Anders, Steiger, & Goldey, 2015).

However, the stereotype that women are more empathic while men are more competitive, raises the expectation that women will take more responsibility for the well-being of their co-workers and family members, while men will be more ambitious and productive. As a result, professional women generally have to overcome more challenges (Ellemers, 2018), and tend to be offered less attractive leadership positions than men. For instance, women rather than men are invited to lead the company at times when future prospects are insecure (Ryan & Haslam, 2005). Additionally, women rather than men are offered leadership positions where little support and few resources are available, putting them on a 'glass cliff' (Rink et al., 2013).

The career experiences of male and female professionals further reveal that senior female professionals feel less supported in pursuing their ambitions than male professionals do (Faniko et al., 2020). Some female leaders compensate for these conditions by emphasizing how they are different from other women. Explicitly distancing themselves from the gender stereotype can also cause them to underestimate the ambitions of other women (Derks et al., 2016; Ellemers, Van den Heuvel, et al., 2004).

Thus, research does not reveal that women generally make more socially aware and morally responsible leaders. Instead, common views about the 'innate' differences between women and men mask the ways in which stereotypical expectations and situational restrictions bring out and reward different responses in women and men.

In this section, we have shown that common approaches to ethical leadership are bound to fail, mainly because they rely too much on the notion that leaders are highly influential individuals with extraordinary characteristics. Recognizing that leadership is a social process highlights that situational features and pressures from others determine the choices leaders make and the impact this has on their followers (Ellemers, Van den Heuvel, et al., 2004; Haslam et al., 2011). In the next section we will consider the status, power, and authority leaders typically receive to fulfill their special role in the organization. Unfortunately, by setting leaders apart from those they are supposed to lead, these common practices reduce the likelihood that leaders mind the concerns of their followers, and undermine the potential to engage and inspire them. We review research to reveal the hidden forces that expose leaders to predictable moral hazards.

3.2 Analysis: Moral Hazards of Setting Leaders Apart

Leaders have a special position in organizations, in the sense that they have several identities at the same time (Ashforth & Johnson, 2001). As leaders of their team or unit, they can be seen as representing the group they are leading. Standing up for the group and its interests, and communicating (in words and deeds) how it is special and different from other groups allows subordinates to see the leader as 'one of us', and makes them more inclined to follow (Haslam et al., 2011).

However, their special position also sets leaders apart from their subordinates. It is easy for leaders to consider their team as outgroup members, in terms of their roles and responsibilities as well as their remuneration, career prospects, and visibility in the organization (Kipnis, 1972). Indeed, an alternative option is to categorize themselves as representatives of management, an ingroup defined by its position in the organizational hierarchy. In terms of education, professional skills, and career prospects, other leaders may be a more relevant source of self-definition than subordinates in one's own team. Having these intertwined identities – offering the possibility to draw group boundaries in different ways – creates a dilemma for team leaders as well as for top management.

In general, organizations tend to emphasize the special status, power, and authority people might acquire as a way to entice them to take on the additional responsibilities and stresses of leadership. Indeed, these distinctive features and benefits of a leadership position contribute to a positive identity as a valued member of the organization. The downside of this common practice is that it sets leaders apart from their team in their own eyes as well as those of others. To the extent that this makes leaders seem less prototypical members of the team they are leading, it reduces the likelihood that team members accept their guidance. For instance, subordinates are less willing to comply with rules imposed by such leaders – especially when it seems their special position exempts leaders from following the same rules (Haslam et al., 2011; Postmes et al., 2001; Steffens, Yang, et al., 2018).

Fig. 3.2 The dangers of setting leaders apart. Specifies the psychological implications of common practices to position leaders as different from their followers, to illustrate the moral hazards these leadership practices introduce

In this section we consider how common organizational practices that set leaders apart from their teams may introduce different types of moral hazards (see Fig. 3.2). These can trigger unethical leadership behaviors, while offering easy strategies to alleviate concerns leaders may have about their moral responsibilities. Our analysis highlights that the way leaders are typically placed and treated impacts on their moral behavior – because it affects the way leaders perceive their own identity in relation to others inside and outside the organization. Setting leaders apart from those whose interests they should represent limits the circle of people to whom care is extended, who appear to deserve fair treatment, or should receive displays of loyalty. In this section, we reveal the psychological mechanisms through which organizations may enhance the risk of inducing morally questionable behavior among leaders and their followers.

3.2.1 The Risk of the Pedestal

Reward systems in organizations not only offer monetary acknowledgment of high performance, but typically assign substantially higher pay levels to those in positions of leadership. This is motivated by the greater demands of such positions in terms of responsibilities, time investment, and risk of failure. In commercial businesses in particular, this can result in huge pay gaps between leaders and regular employees. Data suggest that, on average, those in top-leadership positions in the US are paid 278 times more than their employees (Rushe, 2019). Even in times of economic prosperity, the difference in rewards received by leaders and their subordinates has only increased. One analysis revealed that the compensation for CEOs increased by more than a 1000% between 1978 and 2018. This stands in sharp contrast to the situation of regular employees who only received a 11.9% salary increase during the same period (Mishel & Wolfe, 2019). Ignoring the question whether this is fair payment for contributions made to the organization, amounts to moral neglect and invites unethical leadership, as we will explain below.

Without quibbling about exact numbers or the fact that not every leader is a CEO, large pay gaps between leaders and their subordinates are common across the globe. In many cases pay gaps have increased to such an extent that it is difficult if not impossible to see this as an accurate reflection of actual differences in responsibilities, effort or merit. In fact, compensation packages are often composed in such a way that risky decisions yield high rewards for individual managers when this leads to success. However, more often than not these decision makers don't suffer personal consequences in case of failure, except when they are forced to resign, for instance because they have broken the law. This became painfully clear during the global financial crisis of 2008, when governments tried to preserve financial stability by supporting 'too-big-to-fail' banks with tax payers' money. The irony was that this made it all the more tempting for the largest banks to develop new high-risk initiatives, safe in the knowledge that the state would come to their rescue if things were to get out of hand.

Scientific studies too, suggest that the monetary compensation of leaders mainly signals their perceived importance for the company instead of reflecting the quality of their achievements. In fact, long-term trends analyses reveal that sudden increases in CEO pay levels relate to requirements for public disclosure of such information – rather than the pressures of a competitive market for high achieving managers (Van Veen & Wittek, 2016). Unreasonably large income differences are a cause of considerable concern in the public debate. Income inequality relates to lower well-being in countries across the globe (De Neve & Powdthavee, 2016). Instead of low overall wages, unfair *differences* in people's incomes are increasingly seen as a cause for political division and social unrest (Piketty, 2018).

Our current concern is that, within organizations, such income differences also set leaders apart. Communicating that leaders and subordinates belong to different categories of people where different fairness rules apply invites moral neglect. In the Netherlands, care workers were outraged when they discovered that hospital leaders were awarded substantial rewards for their efforts during the COVID-19 pandemic (Archyde, 2020). At the same time legitimate requests for appropriate pay and work conditions on the work floor were not met ("Cabinet Firm on Structural Pay Rise", 2020). In general, studies reveal that high CEO pay levels make it less likely that people identify with a CEO and undermine perceived leadership and charisma (Steffens, Haslam, et al., 2018; see also Peters et al., 2019). Here, we argue that the process of setting leaders apart by affording them high pay – as a marker of their special role – also has implications for the way leaders view their own contributions to the organization and how they behave towards their subordinates.

An example of how this might come about can be seen in a televised interview of Rijkman Groenink, former CEO of ABN/AMRO, an international, too-big-to-fail bank based in the Netherlands. Months after being bailed out by the state, Groenink was forced to resign (Reuters, 2007). It did not prevent him from accepting the huge financial benefits that had been promised to him as a reward for his achievements ("ABN Amro CEO to get €26m", 2007). When the interviewer challenged him to explain the reason for such high rewards in the face of failing leadership Groenink became visibly distressed. He defended himself by arguing that this shouldn't be seen as a sign of greed, as others had determined this was a fitting reward for his exceptional contribution and superior performance (NTR, 2013).

A similar example relates to the case of ING, already mentioned in Chap. 1. Here public outrage prevented CEO Ralf Hamers from receiving a pay rise of 50 percent (Arnold, 2018a). Hamers expressed frustration and surprise about this resistance, indicating that this compensation would still be quite modest in comparison with the earnings listed by CEOs of other internationally operating banks. Apparently, Hamers was happy to assume that being in charge of a large bank placed him in the category of professionals that are entitled to receive such high rewards. He failed to take into account that rewarding his leadership so amply might seem inappropriate in view of the costs of settlements made by the bank to avert legal charges for the facilitation of criminal money laundering (Arnold, 2018b; NLtimes., 2018).

Having the fairness of one's high rewards challenged, constitutes a threat to people's moral identity. The negative emotions this raises, can be alleviated through moral neglect: refusing to acknowledge the moral implications of disproportionate high pay. Claiming that the rewards received accurately reflect one's exceptional skills and efforts instills a sense of entitlement. Simply discarding fairness concerns is a well-documented strategy to manage identity threat, and is often used by those with high societal status. Feelings of discomfort about their privileged position in society can be assuaged by highlighting exceptional achievements to explain their good fortune and high income. Even those born to privilege (e.g., royalty) tend to emphasize personal sacrifices made and efforts invested, helping them to deflect uncomfortable thoughts about unfair outcomes. In this way, people can reassure themselves and others that their riches and privilege represent a fitting reward for their superior deservingness and merit (Ellemers & Van Laar, 2010; Jost, 2020; Jost et al., 2004; Van der Toorn & Jost, 2014).

The high rewards received by those in leadership positions, then, do not only reflect the importance of their contributions to the organization. Receiving extremely high rewards also invites leaders to think of themselves as uniquely talented and deserving individuals whose outcomes cannot be compared with those of regular employees (Gemmill & Oakley, 1992). However, highlighting exceptional achievement makes it more difficult to engage with the concerns of those they are supposed to lead. Indeed, studies have documented that in a competitive context, groups that have less favorable outcomes are seen as less deserving and mainly elicit contempt, instead of pity (Caprariello et al., 2009). The experience of contempt for others, in turn, invites further derogation of their needs that can induce corruption (Fischer & Giner-Sorolla, 2016; Rosenblatt, 2012). The dangers of this state of mind are clearly documented. A program of research revealed that the experience of contempt for subordinates makes it less likely that leaders act in line with their moral identity. The contempt and dehumanization that characterize moral exclusion and neglect of subordinates' needs, make it more likely that leaders display self-serving, abusive, and otherwise unethical leadership behaviors (Sanders et al., 2013, 2015; Sanders et al., 2018).

Governing bodies are becoming increasingly aware of the potentially damaging effects that high CEO rewards may have. Regulators apply this knowledge by developing bureaucratic and costly control mechanisms, such as inspections and increased legal regulation, to counter the danger that high rewards come to represent perverse incentives. Paradoxically, this does not lead to the realization that the root of the problem is not addressed: Any system that amplifies differences in rewards between leaders and their subordinates can become a source of moral hazard when it places leaders on a pedestal.

3.2.2 *Having Control Over Others*

A key characteristic of leaders in organizations is that their position implies they have formal power over others. For instance, leaders are expected to assign tasks to their subordinates, offer guidance in how to perform these tasks, and evaluate the outcomes. In itself, the use of such formal authority in exercising one's assigned role does not necessarily have moral implications. However, power can be wielded in many different ways (French & Raven, 1959). Some like to enforce the behavior they expect to see, continually reminding subordinates 'who is boss', failing to listen to their concerns, and threatening to punish those who don't do as they are told. However, this coercive approach has a particularly bad press. It also has the highest chance of eliciting open reactance, or inviting more hidden forms of non-compliance, for instance when subordinates simply reduce their efforts or engage in subtle forms of sabotage (Mooijman & Graham, 2018; Mooijman et al., 2015). Current insights generally agree that it is unwise for leaders to rely on such coercive power use, despite its formal legitimacy.

Indeed, other forms of power use are much more common and, in principle, more benevolent. Yet power differences in organizations have psychological and behavioral consequences that may be detrimental for leaders and their subordinates, for the organization, and for society as a whole (see also Chaps. 6 and 7). Here, we consider the *psychological* consequences of placing people in a position of power (Galinsky et al., 2015; Tost, 2015). We argue that this is another factor that sets leaders apart from their subordinates and so represents a source of moral hazard.

Psychological theories of power build on the central notion that the (perceived) ability to impact the outcomes of others (through rewards and punishments), gives people control over those who depend on them (Fiske, 1993a; Haslam et al., 2011). Many programs of research have revealed that merely having such control over the situation changes people's thoughts, feelings, and behaviors (Guinote, 2007; Keltner et al., 2003; Magee & Smith, 2013; see also Kipnis, 1972). This is visible also in indicators people cannot control, such as their brain activity, as well as heart rate and blood pressure changes (Guinote, 2017; Scheepers et al., 2012). These studies reveal that being placed in a position of control (vs. lacking control) shifts the way people attend to and process information, and impacts on the stress they experience.

One well-documented implication is that those who are in control are more likely to see the abstract big picture in information that is provided, rather than focusing on concrete details (Smith & Trope, 2006). Indeed, being in control of the situation (rather than depending on others) also makes it less necessary to build a detailed impression of the concerns, needs, and motives of other individuals. Hence, having power brings out the 'cognitive miser' in all of us. Relying on quick and dirty – but possibly inaccurate and unfair – judgments of others, invites their moral exclusion (Fiske, 1993b; Fiske & Goodwin, 1994; See also Kahneman, 2011).

Research demonstrates how having a position of power affects information processing during decision making tasks. One example is a study where research participants had to evaluate different job applicants in a selection procedure. Here people who were given the power to make hiring decisions were inclined to make their decisions relatively quickly, as they relied on stereotypes instead of carefully processing the available information (Goodwin et al., 2000). The study found they favored white (Caucasian) job applicants over ethnic minority (Hispanic) job applicants, even when both candidates had identical CVs (for other examples, see Chap. 5). The results of this study not only show that simply placing people in a position of power leads them to perceive and process information differently (see Box 3.5). It also makes clear that this can have moral implications when it leads to neglect of responsibility for other people's outcomes. Research further shows that people are more likely to notice and remember unfair behavior when it is displayed by those with powerful positions. Being dependent on such leaders, elicits negative emotions and makes people fear future interactions (Barreto et al., 2010).

Box 3.5 The benefits of doing experimental research

In this book we often refer to results from scientific research. We indicate different research methods and designs by distinguishing 'experimental' studies from 'field' studies. In experimental designs researchers manipulate specific conditions to isolate and examine the impact of specific situational aspects on people's responses. Important advantages of experimental approaches are, first, that these unambiguously clarify the causal direction of relations: manipulating X leads to the observation of Y. Second, isolating specific conditions (while keeping constant everything else) makes it possible to exclude various alternative explanations that may complicate the interpretation of real life observations.

For instance, controlling who is assigned the powerful role in the situation and who is made dependent makes it possible to see what happens once people are placed in a position of power.

Controlling the information and assignments people receive allows for a careful comparison of whether the judgments and decisions people make differ, depending on the position in which they were placed – instead of anything else. Further, individuals participating in such studies are typically assigned their powerful or powerless position by chance. This allows researchers to rule out that the behavior displayed by the powerful individuals in the study emerged because their personality predisposed them for a leadership role, or because they earned this position due to their superior ability and prior performance.

Studies using this type of methodology generally show that ordinary people, on average, are inclined to process information and behave differently as soon as they are placed in a powerful position. The experimental method makes it possible to conclude this is due to the role they are assigned in the organization rather than pre-existing individual differences. In practice, many will recognize this, as colleagues or friends who are promoted at work often display a marked change in perspective and adopt a different style of behavior quickly after taking up their new role.

Despite the advantage of offering researchers control over what to examine and clarity about the process they observe, experiments are often criticized or misunderstood. Practitioners may be tempted to suspect that the obviously artificial nature of such methods does not sufficiently resemble real life to offer useful information. They tend to place more confidence in studies of actual business cases. In this context it is important to note that each method of research has its own strengths and weaknesses. Most programs of research therefore never rely on a single methodology, but combine different approaches. The conclusions in this book are also based on the combination of different types of evidence, as we refer to scientific experiments as well as business analyses.

Experiments offer 'proof of principle' by isolating the 'active ingredients' that cause specific effects. In some cases, such insights rely on non-deliberate responses that can only be captured in highly artificial situations - such as the emergence of physiological stress, or performance on experimental tasks. Adding features that would make the situation more realistic may actually be irrelevant and distract from factors that really make a difference: even if the experimental version of the phenomenon 'looks different, it might 'work' the same. Observations of actual cases in organizations try to infer what happens by documenting which behaviors and statements go together in practice. This method offers more recognition and face validity. However, there is more ambiguity about what causes what, making it more difficult to anticipate the impact of specific interventions.

A method in which strengths of both approaches can be combined is a field experiment: where people in practice allow researchers to expose them to specific treatments and monitor how this impacts their responses. Determining experimentally who receives which treatment, and monitoring people's responses while controlling for the influence of other possible explanations in a real life situation is notoriously challenging. It requires high trust and cooperation between researchers and practitioners, a long-term commitment, and patience in waiting for results. No wonder such field experiments are relatively rare.

Additional studies further document the mechanisms by which leaders' position of power and control can invite them to exclude others from their moral concerns. In general, placing people in a position of power makes them more inclined to focus on their own perspective on the situation, and on the achievement of selfish goals rather than taking the perspective of others into account and addressing their needs and concerns (Galinsky et al., 2015). Indeed, the experience of contempt for subordinates and its negative impact on ethical leadership behaviors, which we have noted before, was found to intensify as leaders had more power (Sanders et al., 2013, 2015; Sanders et al., 2018).

Being in a position of power focuses people on their own goals and concerns rather than those of others. It makes them over-confident in their decision making (See et al., 2011), reluctant to listen to advice from others (Tost et al., 2012), and willing to take irresponsible risks (Whitson et al., 2013). Placing people in control over others invites them to exclude these individuals from their moral concerns and to consider them as lesser humans. A study where leaders were assigned such control to achieve set goals found that this caused them to prioritize goal achievement over the moral permissibility of the means they used. In fact, leaders in this case were prepared to justify unethical decision making as offering them a way to do what was expected (Hoyt et al., 2013).

Does this imply that power always corrupts? Not necessarily, as we shall see. In fact, acquiring a powerful position also offers possibilities to bring about change and moral improvement. Whether leaders act upon such benefits of their position depends on the circumstances. Indeed, in the job application study already discussed (Goodwin et al., 2000), some participants were made aware that they would have to justify their decisions at the end of the session. This highlighted the responsibility associated with their position and the employment decisions they made. This seemingly minor change in the situation was found to reduce the occurrence of racial bias in hiring decisions. We will elaborate on this and other circumstances that may contribute to displays of moral leadership despite power differences in Sect. 3.3 of this chapter.

3.2.3 Being Lonely at the Top

A third moral hazard is introduced by the high status assigned to positions of leadership, and the fear of status loss. As indicated above, being promoted to a position of leadership tends to be seen as proof of the special skill, ability, and effort of some individuals in the workplace. High rewards, control over one's outcomes and those of others highlight the value the organization attaches to this achievement. Other status markers include more symbolic indicators of the importance of the role, such as the location and size of the office, the size of the department and available budget, the assignment of personal assistants and support services, or the quality of the lunch service and coffee. The 'career ladder' that people are supposed to climb during their working life clearly reflects the notion that striving for a high-status position is a normal aspect of organizational life. Although aspired by many, few will reach the top rank.

Making leadership attractive in this way, introduces the risk that people covet such positions for the status this will afford them instead of fully considering the content of the tasks and the extent of responsibilities involved (see also Steffens & Haslam, 2020). Highlighting that such positions offer the opportunity to realize personal goals, was found to attract individuals who are more concerned with the pursuit of gains and achievements than with the prevention of failures and avoidance of risks (Sassenberg et al., 2012). Another study revealed that when people are invited to compete for high-status positions, their intentions to behave unethically increased, and actually resulted in more unethical behavior (Vriend et al., 2016). The competitive up-or-out systems favored by many organizations have been found to facilitate adversarial, politicized and authoritarian leadership with low tolerance for deviance (Hoel & Salin, 2002). All these things contribute to attracting, rewarding, and retaining as leaders those who are willing to do whatever it takes to get ahead without minding ethical concerns (see also Chap. 8).

Once the attractive leadership position has been achieved, the pressure doesn't stop. On the contrary, having high status, particularly in competitive systems, will often raise concerns about the possibility of losing this privilege. Confronting people with the uncertainty of their high status has been found to result in stress and lowers interpersonal trust (Mooijman et al., 2019; Scheepers & Ellemers, 2018). In fact, the nature and extent of heart rate and blood pressure changes observed among individuals who consider the possibility of losing their position of privilege, are comparable to the stresses experienced by those who cannot escape the lower ranks (Scheepers & Ellemers, 2005, 2018; Scheepers et al., 2009; Scheepers et al., 2015). Thus, the threat of losing high status elicits efforts to justify the status quo – this is another 'easy' strategy to retain current outcomes and practices while avoiding the more difficult question whether this is morally appropriate.

Thus, the decisions and actions of many leaders not only reflect their best judgment, but are also driven by emotions and the desire to protect their high status. Even when others dare to question or criticize their decisions for being irresponsible or morally questionable, the first reflex of many leaders is to deflect such critique and resist the notion that they did something wrong (see also Janis, 1972; Selart, 2010). Admitting to failing judgment – or even asking others for guidance and advice – might seem tantamount to declaring oneself unfit to lead. The blame for apparent failures can be averted by pointing to faults of others or citing external factors beyond one's control. It is hard to find football coaches who will say their team lost because it was not well prepared, let alone that their tactical plan was wrong. References to limited budget, misguided referee decisions or even pointing the finger at players for not executing tactical instructions all are proposed as more likely explanations. Similarly, CEOs often refer to difficult market situations, increased competition, tax laws, or other external causes, when organizational performance is lackluster or when highly publicized acquisitions fail. They are, however, quick to claim credit for successes which they invariably ascribe to their superior strategic choices. These are all self-serving attributions that help them protect their position of privilege, regardless of the soundness of their judgment (Heider, 1958; Kelley & Michela, 1980; Martinko et al., 2007).

These defensive strategies and justifications for faulty decision making are not without cost. The identity threat leaders experience when they feel unsure about their own leadership and moral judgments may prompt them to engage in abusive behavior, simply to hide their own uncertainty and frustration (Fast & Chen, 2009; Tedeschi & Felson, 1994). This is also a risk factor for independent professionals who have high status due to their specific expertise which is guarded by professional licenses (doctors, lawyers, scientists, accountants). Of course, the core task of these professionals is to care for and act in the best interests of those calling on their services, and many are bound by legal pledges and codes of conduct to do so. Yet cases of unethical decision making or abusive behavior are rarely confronted – even when this is observed by colleagues. The 'professional respect' extended in acknowledgment of their special expertise and the independence of their judgment, is often cited as a reason. In these cases, protecting the high status of the profession as defining their shared identity is prioritized over the protection of clients, patients, and other dependents (see also Box 2.2).

The term abusive leadership is used to refer to sustained displays of petty tyranny and hostile verbal and nonverbal behaviors towards subordinates, such as systematic shouting, intimidation, humiliation, or the refusal to acknowledge their presence (Tepper, 2000). Even if such incidents tend to remain underreported, abusive leadership behaviors appear to be quite common, especially in high pressure performance contexts. For instance, when the International Bar Association polled thousands of lawyers in 135 different countries, 30–55% of respondents said they had experienced abusive behaviors and misconduct at the office. In over 60% of cases the culprits were those in a position of leadership, while these only constitute a small minority of all the individuals in the organization (Pender, 2019). Mistreatment of employees is not reserved for legal professionals working towards high profits, but can occur in any high-pressure environment where competition for high status is fierce. The well-respected Wellcome Sanger research institute on genomics and genetics in Cambridge attracted a lot of negative publicity in 2018 when its scientists complained about the behavior of senior management, including the director. Leadership was accused of bullying, pressurizing employees into leaving the institute at short notice, and failing to follow due process when grievances were raised (Marsh & Devlin, 2018).

Such behavior may seem justified in life-or-death crisis situations, or when it is crucial that things are done exactly as prescribed. Yet, even in military or medical contexts, being exposed to abusive leader interactions does more harm than good (e.g., Fors Brandebo et al., 2016). Such behavior is usually not even related to goal achievement, but simply emerges because supervisors have come to believe that this is an acceptable way of venting their own frustrations (Tepper, 2000). It goes without saying that being exposed to unfair and abusive leadership behaviors damages the well-being and long-term health of employees, as well as company morale. For instance, it has detrimental effects on the quality of workplace attitudes and interactions, hampering creativity, flexibility, and helpfulness (Porath & Erez, 2007), and is associated with high aggression, absenteeism, and turnover among employees (Brockner et al., 1993; Melwani & Barsade, 2011; Schmitt & Dörfel, 1999; see also Chap. 4). These adverse effects extend beyond the employees who are directly targeted by abusive behaviors. For instance, observing that business supervisors display abusive behavior towards customers, spoils the moral climate in the organization, and prompts employees with a high moral identity to resign (Greenbaum et al., 2013).

Again, the core of our argument is that common organizational practices can unwittingly bring out and sustain such behavior, by always highlighting the unique position and high status of leaders. Emphasizing their special privileges induces a preoccupation with the maintenance of high status instead of reflection on the just treatment of others (Johnson et al., 2012; Opotow, 1995). Without reconsidering the conditions under which leaders are expected to perform their tasks, there is little point in simply pressing them to demonstrate awareness of ethical issues (see also Fig. 1.3). In fact this may even backfire. Requesting that leaders monitor the ethicality of their decisions without providing the conditions that allow them to do so can only result in mental fatigue and cognitive depletion (Ståhl & Ellemers, 2016). After leaders display such efforts to demonstrate their good moral intentions they are actually more likely to show abusive behavior towards subordinates (Lin et al., 2016). Again, these studies show why it is naïve to prescribe moral behavior as a desired outcome without adapting organizational practices that continually invite moral lapses.

3.3 Solutions: Fostering Moral Leadership

When leaders are set apart — or set themselves apart — from the group they are leading, they face an uphill battle to get the support of their subordinates or followers. This is true even if their aim is to curb corruption, or to pursue other forms of change that serve moral goals. Emphasizing the distinct identity of leaders to symbolize how they stand out from their subordinates also exaggerates how different their attitudes, morals, and ideas are. This makes it hard to lead as well as to follow. The formal authority of leaders and the basic compliance that is expected is not enough to win people over to commit to shared goals – even when this is clearly the right thing to do.

A case in point is the Amsterdam fire brigade, where teams on call 24/7 were known for many years to use time and resources at the fire station for their personal benefit. Those who voiced the unease they felt about the unethical nature of these common practices were bullied, threatened with physical violence, and excluded from communal meals. A valiant attempt of the municipality to appoint a strong leader to curb this behavior failed miserably. Many circumstances may have contributed to this. But one of the key factors at play was that the firefighters did not see this leader as 'one of us', and did not trust him to stand up for their needs. Being a former policeman caused him to be seen as an outsider, who was unfamiliar with the special concerns and challenges faced by firefighters. This was exacerbated by his taking office at a location outside the fire station, as well as his tough approach to transgressions. His outsider status made the moral appeals voiced by this leader fall on deaf ears. In the process of pressing for changes that would enhance the competence as well as the morality of the squad, he was forced to resign — because he was so clearly an outsider (Kakissis, 2019).

In the preceding section we have highlighted the moral hazards of common leadership practices. The mechanisms that set leaders apart from others in the organization contribute to the emergence of moral neglect, moral exclusion, and moral justification. The research evidence we presented reveals how these 'easy' identity management strategies help leaders to salvage their moral identity while undermining the likelihood that they truly take into account the needs and concerns of others within and outside the organization. In this final section we offer the counterpoint, as we focus on how organizations can empower leaders to engage their followers. Research evidence shows this depends on the creation of conditions that allow leaders to build a shared identity, extend trust to others, and show awareness of their responsibilities. Narrowing the gap between leaders and their followers offers a more sustainable approach towards moral improvement, by guarding against leadership behaviors that undermine moral standards and decisions that jeopardize the moral identity of the organization.

3.3.1 Engaging Support Through Shared Identity

Whether they like it or not, leaders and their behaviors are scrutinized by many: their behavior is seen to reflect what others in the organization are like, and how a good member of the organization is expected to behave. Are customers, employees, or community members to be treated as important stakeholders, or should their needs and outcomes be ignored? What are the norms in this organization: should everyone look out only for themselves, or do we care for each other? And how to consider incidents of fraud, deception, or misbehavior – is this to be seen as collateral damage of smart business conduct, or a cause to reconsider what the organization stands for? (Reicher et al., 2006). The answers leaders provide to such questions – and demonstrate in their own behavior – communicate a form of guidance that easily overrules more formal policy statements. When leaders are seen as prototypical of their team, they are even more likely to be a source of identification and to impact on the work-related efforts of their subordinates (Barreto & Hogg, 2017; Hirst et al., 2009; Steffens et al., 2020). Support for such leaders seems quite resilient: even when they do not achieve difficult goals they can retain loyalty, as long as they are seen as representing the key concerns and needs of their subordinates (Giessner & Van Knippenberg, 2008).

With regard to our purpose to explain moral behavior in organizations, we have noted that there is nothing inherently moral or immoral about leading people: history makes all too clear that leaders can entice their followers to commit acts of cruelty, crimes and other immoral behavior, just as leaders can stimulate benevolence, creativity, civility and other types of positive behavior (Den Hartog, 2015; Smith & Overbeck, 2014). The social identity perspective on leadership suggests that identical processes are at the basis of leader-follower relations in both cases.

Indeed, as noted before, research shows that power in itself does not corrupt: it all depends on additional circumstances which determine how leaders experience their position in the organization and how they construe their role (Foulk et al., 2020; Sassenberg et al., 2014).

In examining this process, we have highlighted the psychological mechanisms that impact leaders at every organizational level. Indeed, the highly visible behavior of CEOs – as role models of success – sets the stage for the broader ethical climate that develops in the workplace. Exemplary behavior of top management cascades through the organization, as it tends to be emulated by lower level team leaders, who in turn impact on the behavior of their subordinates (Brown & Treviño, 2014; Schaubroeck et al., 2012, see also Chap. 8). Research has documented these trickle-down effects by establishing that ethical behavior at top management level related to ethical leadership among team leaders, which in turn predicted the occurrence of citizenship behavior versus deviance of team members (Mayer et al., 2009). However, this is also true when top management behaves unethically, with the same mechanisms causing subordinates to copy transgressions (Garratt, 2003). When subordinates see that leaders are not being punished for setting bad examples, this may contribute to an unethical climate in the organization as a whole (Bauman et al., 2016). A first point to note is therefore that organizations cannot afford to make exceptions: maintaining high moral standards is only possible when even those in top management are held responsible for their actions and visibly suffer the consequences of moral transgressions.

As indicated in Chap. 2, the willingness of individuals to work towards shared goals depends on how well these capture important aspects of their social identity. The likelihood that people exert themselves on behalf of the organization is not implied by the cognitive awareness that their personal fate depends on the organization. Nor can it be bought by simply trading their input for favorable outcomes that are highly valued. Instead, the ability of individuals to feel emotionally included and involved in the organization is decisive for their willingness to direct their efforts towards the achievement of key organizational goals (Ellemers, Van den Heuvel, et al., 2004; see also Fig. 3.1). Being able to subscribe to the moral values exemplified by the organization and being able to approve of the moral behavior of its representatives is a key determinant of such felt involvement (Van Prooijen & Ellemers, 2015). Thus, the ability to engage people towards displaying moral behavior in the organization, also depends on the extent to which leaders exemplify the ethical guidelines that they expect their subordinates to follow – in their own interactions and decisions. The behavioral integrity of leaders indicates the apparent alignment of their words with their deeds and can be captured for instance in the Ethical Leadership Scale (Brown et al., 2005). The extent to which leaders enact their moral principles is strongly related to the positive attitudes and work commitment of subordinates, a meta-analysis revealed (Davis & Rothstein, 2006). In fact, behavioral integrity of leaders has stronger effects on employee trust, in-role task performance and citizenship behavior than other concerns that might be relevant – such as violations of employee expectations (i.e., a breach of psychological contract; Simons et al., 2015).

This is not to say that people mindlessly copy what leaders do. In fact, a study revealed that members of the organization do not necessarily model their own behavior on that displayed by those who are seen as highly competent and successful in the organization. Instead, only leaders who realize such achievements while being seen as models of moral behavior are considered examples to follow (Peters et al., 2018). Nevertheless, attending to such leader behavior can inspire others in the organization towards moral improvement (Pohling & Diessner, 2016; Schnall & Cannon, 2012). Leaders who show fairness, self-sacrifice, and moral courage in how they approach others, are seen as morally elevating by their subordinates. This causes subordinates to be more prosocial in how they approach others, to display more citizenship behavior towards the organization, and to follow ethical guidelines (Vianello et al., 2010; see also Perlmutter, 2012). In sum, subordinates will only follow appeals to do what is moral when these seem authentic. In this sense, those aiming to lead others face the same challenges as parents raising children: they are less likely to do what you say, than to do what you do. Thus, a second point to attend to is whether leaders are 'allowed' to enact organizational guidelines, or are forced to violate the moral norms they should set for others – due to time pressure, impossible targets, or conflicting assignments.

Building a strong, shared identity can also protect leaders against the hazards of moral neglect and moral exclusion of others. This was demonstrated in a research program which established the impact of situational frames and circumstances on leader behavior. The way supervisors acted towards their subordinates was found to depend on the way they thought of their position of leadership. These situational effects were observed independently of the quality of interpersonal relations between supervisors and their subordinates, and regardless of overall leader dispositions to care for others. Across the board, conditions that reminded leaders of the identity they shared with followers made them feel more responsible for the achievement of collective (rather than selfish) goals and oriented them towards the protection of shared interests (Scholl, Sassenberg, et al., 2018). Further, leaders who were invited to focus on the outcomes and perspective of others displayed more responsibility and concern for other people's needs and interests (Scholl et al., 2017). Thus, explicitly encouraging leaders to consider others can prevent moral disengagement and moral exclusion. It allows leaders to enact shared goals and defend moral values, which also makes it easier for subordinates to identify with them and follow their lead.

Highlighting identities leaders share with others in the workplace – instead of emphasizing their special status – is a very concrete example of how such a mind state can be activated. The impact of such reminders has been documented in the context of family roles and responsibilities (see also Chap. 7). For instance, experimental research revealed that when men are addressed in their role of fathers they are more inclined to support measures for fair treatment of women and minorities in the workplace (Park & Banchefsky, 2018). Likewise, it seems that those who raise daughters are more aware of the shared identity of men and women, making them more sensitive to diversity issues and fair treatment within their own company. A study that examined leaders of large US companies found that when CEOs had daughters, the social performance of their company was 9% above the median. The greater concern of these companies for social issues remained after controlling for a number of alternative explanations, and was not only visible in diversity measures, but also in broader socially responsible activities relating to the environment and employee relations. The authors suggested that these CEOs views of what is important in their leadership were also 'shaped by their daughters' (Cronqvist & Yu, 2017).

3.3.2 *Earning Loyalty by Extending Trust*

Of course, there are many ways to induce loyal behavior among followers. Creating special ties by exchanging favors with specific individuals or groups might seem a tempting way to buy support, but is a hallmark of corruption. Yet this is a strategy not only followed by politicians to garner support from voters. It is also known to be used by leaders in organizations as a way to secure their position of power and control over others. Indeed, several studies (Haslam & Platow, 2001) have shown that leaders who favor members of their own team actually receive more support than those who treat different groups equally, as well as leaders who favor other groups.

However, to the extent that such favors are extended for instrumental motives and concerns about one's own position, this strategy is unlikely to truly motivate or inspire moral behavior in followers. Indeed, in the studies just mentioned, leaders were expected to show equal treatment of all groups, and so received low fairness ratings, even from those supporting them (Haslam & Platow, 2001). And although such 'divide and rule' tactics may buy cooperation from followers, it also fuels competition between individuals and groups who are supposed to collaborate, which can poison the work climate and undermine the achievement of organizational goals (Ellemers, Van den Heuvel, et al., 2004; see also Chap. 8). Instead, leaders can *earn* loyalty – instead of buying it – by truly attending to the needs of others and treating them fairly. Indeed, employees who feel they are treated fairly by their leaders generally display more ethical behavior themselves. This was a key conclusion emerging from a meta-analysis summarizing results obtained from 134 samples examining 54,920 people working in different types of businesses across the world (Bedi et al., 2016).

Over time, the experience of being 'on the same team' shapes interpretations of leadership behaviors – and is a stronger source of support from subordinates than simply doing what makes them happy. This was demonstrated in a program of research in which research participants were confronted with a supervisor who frequently overruled the decisions they had made. In general, people did not appreciate the lack of approval of their supervisor for the input they had provided. Yet they accepted or even expected receiving corrections from a supervisor who was more competent than they were. Further, subordinates were more likely to interpret the behavior of the leader as being driven by legitimate concerns when they considered the supervisor as an ingroup member rather than an outgroup member. This interpretation of unpleasant supervisor behavior, colored by their shared identity,

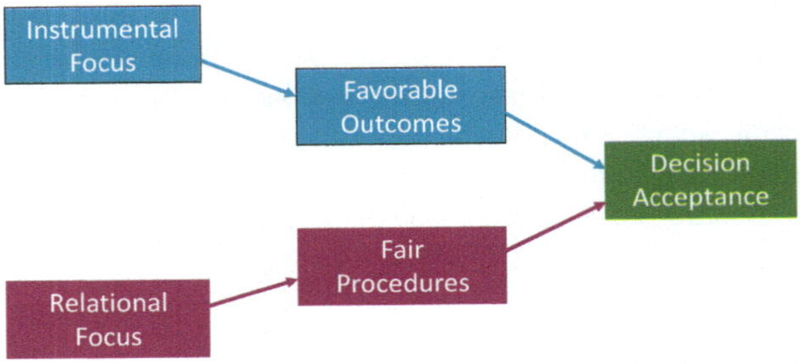

Fig. 3.3 Accepting procedures and outcomes. Summarizes results from a program of research. When authorities emphasize costs and benefits in an instrumental approach, people accept decisions that yield them favorable outcomes. When authorities attend to good relations, people accept decisions where fair procedures were followed – even when the outcomes are not favorable for them. (Ståhl et al., 2008a)

actually predicted the willingness of subordinates to continue engaging with the task, and even to help the supervisor by complying with a request to do additional work (Bruins et al., 1999; Ellemers et al., 1998).

Other research programs also support the notion that responses to leadership do not depend on the favorability of subordinate outcomes but on the perceived motives and values driving leader behaviors (Folger & Cropanzano, 1998; Lind & Tyler, 1988). Indeed, when relational concerns were highlighted in the interactions between leaders and followers, followers focused on the nature of the procedure that was followed. As long as leaders acted fairly and in line with relevant guidelines, subordinates accepted their decisions, even if these were unfavorable for them personally. However, when the interaction between leaders and followers was characterized by a focus on instrumental aspects, followers focused on the outcomes they received and were only inclined to support leaders when this was beneficial to them (Ståhl et al., 2006, 2008b; see also Fig. 3.3).

This process too, cascades through different levels of the organization. It is difficult for team leaders to stand up for the interests of their team, and extend fair treatment when they are continually reminded of the precariousness of their own special position in the organization. This can tempt them, for instance, to take personal credit for the achievements and efforts of their subordinates. While this may seem to fortify their own value in the eyes of those above them, it undermines their ability to lead others. This was clearly demonstrated in a series of studies in which some leaders properly acknowledged and rewarded subordinates for their contributions, while others took personal credit for the performance of their subordinates. Here, subordinates were unwilling to continue investing time and effort when they did not receive the credit that was their due (Rodgers et al., 2013). Importantly, alleviating feelings of status threat by offering them support and stability allows leaders to address concerns other than their own. Only when feeling secure about their own position, leaders feel able to trust subordinates to do as they are told, which actually increases the chances of subordinate rule compliance (Mooijman et al., 2017, 2019; Tyler, 1997).

3.3.3 Balancing Opportunities with Responsibilities

Moral leaders are those who use their special position not only as an opportunity to achieve personal goals but also by taking responsibility for enacting and promoting important organizational principles and moral values in their day-to-day behavior. Sometimes this requires moral courage, and the willingness to jeopardize their own status and position in the organization. For instance, when leaders speak up to condemn unethical behavior of their subordinates, peers, or even superiors. Supporting such displays of moral courage or moral entrepreneurship can be a highly effective way to change existing moral norms in the organization and realize moral improvement (Hornung, 2010; Kaptein, 2019; Yurtsever, 2003).

Leaders who take responsibility for behaving fairly and ethically have been found to increase the chances of their subordinates voicing contributions and concerns about moral implications of organizational practices because they feel it is safe to do so (Hu et al., 2018; Schaubroeck et al., 2012). Ultimately, this only benefits the organization. Indeed, when displays of ethical leadership encourage subordinates to identify with their leader, employees are more likely to speak up about issues that attract their concern. These internal whistleblowers can help the organization to address ethical problems before they get out of hand (Zhang et al., 2016). Listening and taking action to resolve these problems often curbs further escalation and external complaints about problems preventing reputational damage for the organization (Anvari et al., 2019; see also the section on whistleblowers in Chap. 8).

As indicated before, awareness of broader responsibilities can be induced at the organizational level by emphasizing the identities leaders share with their subordinates, and inviting them to take into account the needs and concerns of others before contemplating their own actions. Rewarding a focus on joint outcomes and the needs of others supports leaders who aim to serve the organization, instead of those who use the organization for the achievement of selfish goals (Liden et al., 2014). On the one hand, enhancing awareness of leader responsibilities makes positions of leadership seem less attractive, and induces stress (Sassenberg et al., 2012; Scholl, Sassenberg, et al., 2018). Yet research has also shown this has benefits for the moral performance and effectiveness of leaders. Experiments reveal that reminding leaders of the responsibilities attached to their special position allows them to value and accept advice they receive from experts, peers, and subordinates (De Wit et al., 2017). Further, when they feel accountable to the group for achieving shared goals they adapt their strategy to what is best for the group, instead of acting in line with personal preferences (Scheepers et al., 2013).

In sum, highlighting collective goals and responsibilities – instead of personal advantages – of leadership positions will help leaders benefit from the input and observations of others. This should also fuel their moral courage to act in line with the values and purpose of the organization, and enhances the likelihood that they will be able to create a moral legacy.

3.4 Conclusion: Building a Shared Identity

In this chapter we have identified common organizational practices that treat leaders as individuals with special qualities and abilities. Considering the different ways in which organizations set their leaders apart from others, clarifies the moral hazards this raises. Research evidence demonstrates how standard approaches to leadership can invite moral disengagement, moral exclusion and moral justification that induce and sustain unethical behaviors in leaders and undermine the ability of leaders to inspire moral behavior in their followers.

Large differences in pay levels and compensation packages introduce a sense of superiority and entitlement. This invites neglect of the moral implications of unequal pay and only raises contempt of those who earn less. Assigning people authority and control over the situation makes them less mindful of the characteristics and needs of others who depend on them. Excluding subordinates from the circle of people who merit moral consideration increases the risk of unfair treatment. Celebrating their high status places leaders in a position where they fear loss of privilege. This makes them inclined to justify their own decisions, and can tempt them to engage in abusive behavior to protect their position, instead of being open to feedback and input from others.

In general, then, treating individuals in positions of leadership as special members of the organization in all these ways, diminishes their ability to identify with the needs of their subordinates. It makes them less concerned about the moral implications of their decisions, less mindful of the outcomes of others, and reduces their willingness to engage with ideas and concerns voiced by their subordinates. These are all moral hazards that invite and sustain unethical leadership behaviors.

To allow leaders to act in line with key moral principles, organizational practices should continually remind leaders of the identity they share with others, monitor fair treatment of subordinates, and sanction hostility and abuse. Furthermore, because of the trickle-down effects of the tone at the top, it is unrealistic to aim for moral leadership in the organization unless top management curbs selfish concerns for ever-increasing rewards, shows courage by inviting and acting upon critique from subordinates, and behaves civilly towards all organizational members.

It may seem that we are painting a bleak picture of leadership. However, the focus of this book is on the emergence of moral failures in organizations, and the high incidence of bigger and smaller scandals clearly reveals the far-reaching consequences when this happens — for organizations involved and for society as a whole. Our analysis reveals the pitfalls of common leadership practices but also shows how leaders may be induced to refrain from displaying immoral behavior while at the same time maintaining positive relationships with their subordinates as they collectively strive for the achievement of organizational goals.

Recommended Reading

Den Hartog, D. N. (2015). Ethical leadership. *Annual Review of Organizational Psychology and Organizational Behavior, 2*, 409–434.

Ellemers, N., De Gilder, D., & Haslam, S. A. (2004). Motivating individuals and groups at work: A social identity perspective on leadership and group performance. *Academy of Management Review, 29*(3), 459–478. https://doi.org/10.5465/amr.2004.13670967
Haslam, S. A., Reicher, S. D., & Platow, M. J. (2011). *The new psychology of leadership: Identity, influence and power*. Psychology Press. https://doi.org/10.4324/9780203833896
Sassenberg, K., Ellemers, N., Scheepers, D., & Scholl, A. (2014). "Power corrupts" revisited: The role of construal of power as opportunity or responsibility. In J. W. Van Prooijen & P. A. M. Van Lange (Eds.), *Power, politics, and paranoia: Why people are suspicious of their leaders* (pp. 73–87). Cambridge University Press. https://doi.org/10.1017/CBO9781139565417.007
Steffens, N. K., Munt, K. A., Van Knippenberg, D., Platow, M. J., & Haslam, S. A. (in press). Advancing the social identity theory of leadership: A meta-analytic review of leader group prototypicality. *Organizational Psychology Review, 2041386620962569.*

References

ABN Amro CEO to get €26m. (2007, October 12). ABN Amro CEO to get €26m golden handshake. *Dutch News*. Retrieved from https://www.dutchnews.nl/news/2007/10/abn_amro_ceo_to_get_26m_golden/
Anvari, F., Wenzel, M., Woodyatt, L., & Haslam, S. A. (2019). The social psychology of whistle-blowing: An integrated model. *Organizational Psychology Review, 9*(1), 41–67. https://doi.org/10.1177/2041386619849085
Archyde. (2020, August 8). Healthcare personnel work themselves to the fullest while their managers appropriate a nice 'corona bonus' – De Daily Standaard. *Archyde*. Retrieved from https://www.archyde.com/healthcare-personnel-work-themselves-to-the-fullest-while-their-managers-appropriate-a-nice-corona-bonus-de-daily-standaard/
Arendt, H. (1963). *A report on the banality of evil*. Faber.
Arnold, M. (2018a, March 13). ING drops 50% pay rise for CEO after political uproar. *Financial Times*. Retrieved from https://www.ft.com/content/14bb9a6e-26b7-11e8-b27e-cc62a39d57a0
Arnold, M. (2018b, September 4). ING to pay €775m in money laundering case. *Financial Times*. Retrieved from https://www.ft.com/content/f3e64e3e-b02b-11e8-99ca-68cf89602132
Ashforth, B. E., & Johnson, S. A. (2001). Which hat to wear? The relative salience of multiple identities in organizational contexts. In M. A. Hogg & D. J. Terry (Eds.), *Social identity processes in organizational contexts* (pp. 31–48). Psychology Press.
Barreto, M., Ellemers, N., & Fiske, S. T. (2010). "What did you say, and who do you think you are?" How power differences affect emotional reactions to prejudice. *Journal of Social Issues, 66*(3), 477–492. https://doi.org/10.1111/j.1540-4560.2010.01657.x
Barreto, N. B., & Hogg, M. A. (2017). Evaluation of and support for group prototypical leaders: A meta-analysis of twenty years of empirical research. *Social Influence 12*(1), 41–55. https://doi.org/10.1080/15534510.2017.1316771
Bass, B. M., & Riggio, R. E. (2006). *Transformational leadership*. Psychology Press. https://doi.org/10.4324/9781410617095
Bauman, C. W., Tost, L. P., & Ong, M. (2016). Blame the shepherd not the sheep: Imitating higher-ranking transgressors mitigates punishment for unethical behavior. *Organizational Behavior and Human Decision Processes, 137*, 123–141. https://doi.org/10.1016/j.obhdp.2016.08.006
Bedi, A., Alpaslan, C. M., & Green, S. (2016). A meta-analytic review of ethical leadership outcomes and moderators. *Journal of Business Ethics, 139*(3), 517–536. https://doi.org/10.1007/s10551-015-2625-1
Bernardi, R. A., & Threadgill, V. T. (2010). Women directors and corporate social responsibility. *EJBO Electronic Journal of Business Ethics and Organization Studies, 15*(2), 15–21.
Bezos, J. [@jeffbezos]. (2020, February 17). Today, I'm thrilled to announce I am launching the Bezos Earth Fund. Climate change is the biggest threat to our planet. I want to

work alongside others both to amplify known ways and to explore new ways of fighting the devastating… [Instagram photo]. Retrieved from https://www.instagram.com/p/B8rWKFnnQ5c/?utm_source=ig_embed

Brandebo, F. M., Nilsson, S., & Larsson, G. (2016). Leadership: Is bad stronger than good? *Leadership & Organization Development Journal, 37*(6), 690–710. https://doi.org/10.1108/LODJ-09-2014-0191

Brockner, J., Wiesenfeld, B. M., Reed, T., Grover, S., & Martin, C. (1993). Interactive effect of job content and context on the reactions of layoff survivors. *Journal of Personality and Social Psychology, 64*(2), 187. https://doi.org/10.1037/0022-3514.64.2.187

Brown, M. E., & Treviño, L. K. (2006). Ethical leadership: A review and future directions. *The Leadership Quarterly, 17*(6), 595–616. https://doi.org/10.1016/j.leaqua.2006.10.004

Brown, M. E., & Treviño, L. K. (2014). Do role models matter? An investigation of role modeling as an antecedent of perceived ethical leadership. *Journal of Business Ethics, 122*(4), 587–598. https://doi.org/10.1007/s10551-013-1769-0

Brown, M. E., Treviño, L. K., & Harrison, D. A. (2005). Ethical leadership: A social learning perspective for construct development and testing. *Organizational Behavior and Human Decision Processes, 97*(2), 117–134. https://doi.org/10.1016/j.obhdp.2005.03.002

Bruins, J., Ellemers, N., & De Gilder, D. (1999). Power use and differential competence as determinant of subordinates'evaluation and behavioural responses in simulated organizations. *European Journal of Social Psychology, 29*, 843–870. https://doi.org/10.1002/(SICI)1099-0992(199911)29:7<843::AID-EJSP959>3.0.CO;2-5

Burger, J. M. (2009). Replicating Milgram: Would people still obey today? *American Psychologist, 64*(1), 1. https://doi.org/10.1037/a0010932

Business Roundtable. (2019, August 19). Business roundtable redefines the purpose of a corporation to promote 'an economy that serves all Americans'. *Business Roundtable*. Retrieved from https://www.businessroundtable.org/business-roundtable-redefines-the-purpose-of-a-corporation-to-promote-an-economy-that-serves-all-americans#:~:text=Aug%2019%2C%202019&text=WASHINGTON%20%E2%80%93%20Business%20Roundtable%20today%20announced,%2C%20suppliers%2C%20communities%20and%20shareholders.

Cabinet Firm on Structural Pay Rise. (2020, August 19). Cabinet firm on structural pay rise for nurses: There is no more money. *Dutch News*. Retrieved from https://www.dutchnews.nl/news/2020/08/cabinet-firm-on-structural-pay-rise-for-nurses-there-is-no-more-money/

Caprariello, P. A., Cuddy, A. J., & Fiske, S. T. (2009). Social structure shapes cultural stereotypes and emotions: A causal test of the stereotype content model. *Group Processes & Intergroup Relations, 12*(2), 147–155. https://doi.org/10.1177/1368430208101053

Cools, K. (2009). *Controle is goed, vertrouwen nog beter. Over bestuurders en corporate governance*. Stichting Management Studies / Van Gorcum.

Cronqvist, H., & Yu, F. (2017). Shaped by their daughters: Executives, female socialization, and corporate social responsibility. *Journal of Financial Economics, 126*(3), 543–562. https://doi.org/10.1016/j.jfineco.2017.09.003

Davis, A. L., & Rothstein, H. R. (2006). The effects of the perceived behavioral integrity of managers on employee attitudes: A meta-analysis. *Journal of Business Ethics, 67*(4), 407–419. https://doi.org/10.1007/s10551-006-9034-4

Deckard, G. J. (2009). Contingency theories of leadership. *Organizational behavior in health care, 2*, 191–208.

De Neve, J-E., & Powdthavee, N. (2016, January 12). Income inequality makes whole countries less happy. *Harvard Business Review*. Retrieved from https://hbr.org/2016/01/income-inequality-makes-whole-countries-less-happy

Den Hartog, D. N. (2015). Ethical leadership. *Annual Review of Organizational Psychology and Organizational Behavior, 2*, 409–434. https://doi.org/10.1146/annurev-orgpsych-032414-111237

Derks, B., Van Laar, C., & Ellemers, N. (2016). The Queen Bee Phenomenon: Why women leaders distance themselves from junior women. *The Leadership Quarterly, 27*, 456–469. https://doi.org/10.1016/j.leaqua.2015.12.007

De Torres, C. (2019). The best-performing CEOs in the world, 2019. *Harvard Business Review, 97*(6), 45. Retrieved from https://hbr.org/2019/11/the-best-performing-ceos-in-the-world-2019#the-best-performing-ceos-in-the-world-2019

De Wit, F. R., Scheepers, D., Ellemers, N., Sassenberg, K., & Scholl, A. (2017). Whether power holders construe their power as responsibility or opportunity influences their tendency to take advice from others. *Journal of Organizational Behavior, 38*(7), 923–949. https://doi.org/10.1002/job.2171

Eagly, A. (2012). Behavior: Meta-analytic studies of social psychological research. *The Development of Sex Differences and Similarities in Behavior, 73*, 421. https://doi.org/10.1007/978-94-011-1709-8_25

Eagly, A. H., & Johnson, B. T. (1990). Gender and leadership style: A meta-analysis. *Psychological Bulletin, 108*(2), 233. https://doi.org/10.1037/0033-2909.108.2.233

Eagly, A. H., Johannesen-Schmidt, M. C., & Van Engen, M. L. (2003). Transformational, transactional, and laissez-faire leadership styles: A meta-analysis comparing women and men. *Psychological Bulletin, 129*(4), 569. https://doi.org/10.1037/0033-2909.129.4.569

Eagly, A. H., Karau, S. J., & Makhijani, M. G. (1995). Gender and the effectiveness of leaders: A meta-analysis. *Psychological Bulletin, 117*(1), 125. https://doi.org/10.1037/0033-2909.117.1.125

Eagly, A. H., Makhijani, M. G., & Klonsky, B. G. (1992). Gender and the evaluation of leaders: A meta-analysis. *Psychological Bulletin, 111*(1), 3. https://doi.org/10.1037/0033-2909.111.1.3

Eichenwald, K. (2002, September 23). The findings against Enron. *The New York Times*. Retrieved from https://www.nytimes.com/2002/09/23/business/the-findings-against-enron.html

Ellemers, N. (2017). *Morality and the regulation of social behavior: Groups as moral anchors*. Routledge. https://doi.org/10.4324/9781315661322

Ellemers, N. (2018). Gender stereotypes. *Annual Review of Psychology, 69*, 275–298. https://doi.org/10.1146/annurev-psych-122216-011719

Ellemers, N., De Gilder, D., & Haslam, S. A. (2004). Motivating individuals and groups at work: A social identity perspective on leadership and group performance. *Academy of Management Review, 29*(3), 459–478. https://doi.org/10.5465/amr.2004.13670967

Ellemers, N., Kortekaas, P., & Ouwerkerk, J. W. (1999). Self-categorisation, commitment to the group and group self-esteem as related but distinct aspects of social identity. *European Journal of Social Psychology, 29*(2–3), 371–389. https://doi.org/10.1002/(SICI)1099-0992(199903/05)29:2/3<371::AID-EJSP932>3.0.CO;2-U

Ellemers, N., Van den Heuvel, H., De Gilder, D., Maass, A., & Bonvini, A. (2004). The underrepresentation of women in science: Differential commitment or the Queen-bee syndrome? *British Journal of Social Psychology, 43*, 315–338. https://doi.org/10.1348/0144666042037999

Ellemers, N., & Van Laar, C. (2010). Individual mobility: The opportunities and challenges members of devalued groups encounter when trying to avoid group-based discrimination. In J. F. Dovidio, M. Hewstone, P. Glick, & V. Esses (Eds.), *Handbook of prejudice, stereotyping, and discrimintation* (pp. 561–576). Sage. https://doi.org/10.4135/9781446200919.n34

Ellemers, N., Van Rijswijk, W., Bruins, J., & De Gilder, D. (1998). Group commitment as a moderator of attributional and behavioural responses to power use. *European Journal of Social Psychology, 28*, 555–573. https://doi.org/10.1002/(SICI)1099-0992(199807/08)28:4<555::AID-EJSP879>3.0.CO;2-W

Ellis-Petersen, H. (2018, November 23). From peace icon to pariah: Aung San Suu Kyi's fall from grace. *The Guardian*. Retrieved from https://www.theguardian.com/world/2018/nov/23/aung-san-suu-kyi-fall-from-grace-myanmar

Ewing, J. (2017). *Faster, higher, farther: The Volkswagen scandal*. Norton.

Faniko, K., Ellemers, N., & Derks, B. (2020). The Queen Bee phenomenon in Academia 15 years after: Does it still exist, and if so, why? *British Journal of Social Psychology, e12408*. https://doi.org/10.1111/bjso.12408

Fast, N. J., & Chen, S. (2009). When the boss feels inadequate: Power, incompetence, and aggression. *Psychological Science, 20*(11), 1406–1413. https://doi.org/10.1111/j.1467-9280.2009.02452.x

Fine, C. (2017). *Testosterone Rex: Myths of sex, science, and society*. WW Norton & Company.

Fischer, A., & Giner-Sorolla, R. (2016). Contempt: Derogating others while keeping calm. *Emotion Review, 8*(4), 346–357. https://doi.org/10.1177/1754073915610439
Fiske, S. T. (1993a). Controlling other people: The impact of power on stereotyping. *American Psychologist, 48*(6), 621. https://doi.org/10.1037/0003-066X.48.6.621
Fiske, S. T. (1993b). Social cognition and social perception. *Annual Review of Psychology, 44*(1), 155–194. https://doi.org/10.1146/annurev.ps.44.020193.001103
Fiske, S. T., & Goodwin, S. A. (1994). Social cognition research and small group research, a West Side Story or …. *Small Group Research, 25*, 147–171. https://doi.org/10.1177/1046496494252001
Folger, R. G., & Cropanzano, R. (1998). *Organizational justice and human resource management* (Vol. 7). Sage.
Fombrun, C. (2015, February 6). How do you rank the world's best CEOs? *Business Harvard Review*. Retrieved from https://hbr.org/2015/02/how-do-you-rank-the-worlds-best-ceos?registration=success
Foulk, T. A., Chighizola, N., & Chen, G. (2020). Power corrupts (or does it?): An examination of the boundary conditions of the antisocial effects of experienced power. *Social and Personality Psychology Compass, 14*(4), e12524. https://doi.org/10.1111/spc3.12524
French, J., & Raven, B. (1959). The bases of social power in Cartwright. *Studies in Social Power*, 150–167.
Furnham, A., Richards, S. C., & Paulhus, D. L. (2013). The Dark Triad of personality: A 10 year review. *Social and Personality Psychology Compass, 7*(3), 199–216. https://doi.org/10.1111/spc3.12018
Furtner, M. R., Maran, T., & Rauthmann, J. F. (2017). Dark leadership: The role of leaders' dark triad personality traits. In M. Clark & C. Gruber (Eds.), *Leader development deconstructed* (pp. 75–99). Springer. https://doi.org/10.1007/978-3-319-64740-1_4
Galinsky, A. D., Rucker, D. D., & Magee, J. C. (2015). Power: Past findings, present considerations, and future directions. In M. Mikulincer & P. R. Shaver (Eds.), *APA handbook of personality and social psychology* (pp. 421–460). American Psychological Association. https://doi.org/10.1016/j.obhdp.2019.03.009
Garikipati, S., & Kambhampati, U. (2020). Leading the fight against the pandemic: Does gender 'really' matter? *SSRN*. https://doi.org/10.2139/ssrn.3617953
Garratt, B. (2003). *The fish rots from the head: The crisis in our boardrooms: Developing the crucial skills of the competent director*. Profile Books.
Gemmill, G., & Oakley, J. (1992). Leadership: an alienating social myth? *Human Relations, 45*(2), 113–129.
Giessner, S. R., & Van Knippenberg, D. (2008). "License to fail": Goal definition, leader group prototypicality, and perceptions of leadership effectiveness after leader failure. *Organizational Behavior and Human Decision Processes, 105*(1), 14–35. https://doi.org/10.1016/j.obhdp.2007.04.002
Goodwin, S. A., Gubin, A., Fiske, S. T., & Yzerbyt, V. Y. (2000). Power can bias impression processes: Stereotyping subordinates by default and by design. *Group Processes & Intergroup Relations, 3*(3), 227–256. https://doi.org/10.1177/1368430200003003001
Greenbaum, R. L., Mawritz, M. B., Mayer, D. M., & Priesemuth, M. (2013). To act out, to withdraw, or to constructively resist? Employee reactions to supervisor abuse of customers and the moderating role of employee moral identity. *Human Relations, 66*(7), 925–950. https://doi.org/10.1177/0018726713482992
Guinote, A. (2007). Power and goal pursuit. *Personality and Social Psychology Bulletin, 33*(8), 1076–1087. https://doi.org/10.1177/0146167207301011
Guinote, A. (2017). How power affects people: Activating, wanting, and goal seeking. *Annual Review of Psychology, 68*, 353–381. https://doi.org/10.1146/annurev-psych-010416-044153
Haslam, S. A., & Platow, M. J. (2001). The link between leadership and followership: How affirming social identity translates vision into action. *Personality and Social Psychology Bulletin, 27*(11), 1469–1479. https://doi.org/10.1177/01461672012711008
Haslam, S. A., & Reicher, S. D. (2012). Contesting the "nature" of conformity: What Milgram and Zimbardo's studies really show. *PLoS Biology, 10*(11), e1001426. https://doi.org/10.1371/journal.pbio.1001426

Haslam, S. A., & Reicher, S. D. (2017). 50 years of "obedience to authority": From blind conformity to engaged followership. *Annual Review of Law and Social Science, 13*, 59–78. https://doi.org/10.1146/annurev-lawsocsci-110316-113710

Haslam, S. A., Reicher, S. D., & Birney, M. E. (2016). Questioning authority: New perspectives on Milgram's 'obedience' research and its implications for intergroup relations. *Current Opinion in Psychology, 11*, 6–9. https://doi.org/10.1016/j.copsyc.2016.03.007

Haslam, S. A., Reicher, S. D., & Millard, K. (2015). Shock treatment: Using immersive digital realism to restage and re-examine Milgram's 'Obedience to Authority'research. *PLoS One, 10*(3), e109015. https://doi.org/10.1371/journal.pone.0109015

Haslam, S. A., Reicher, S. D., & Platow, M. J. (2011). *The new psychology of leadership: Identity, influence and power*. Psychology Press. https://doi.org/10.4324/9780203833896

Haslam, A., Van Knippenberg, D., Platow, M., & Ellemers, N. (2003). *Social identity at work: Developing theory for organizational practice*. Psychology Press.

Haynes, K. T., Hitt, M. A., & Campbell, J. T. (2015). The dark side of leadership: Towards a mid-range theory of hubris and greed in entrepreneurial contexts. *Journal of Management Studies, 52*(4), 479–505. https://doi.org/10.1111/joms.12127

Heider, F. (1958). *The psychology of interpersonal relations*. Lawrence Erlbaum. https://doi.org/10.1037/10628-000

Hirst, G., Van Dick, R., & Van Knippenberg, D. (2009). A social identity perspective on leadership and employee creativity. *Journal of Organizational Behavior: The International Journal of Industrial, Occupational and Organizational Psychology and Behavior, 30*(7), 963–982. https://doi.org/10.1002/job.600

Hoel, H., & Salin, D. (2002). Organisational antecedents of workplace bullying. In D. Einarsen, D. Zapf, & C. L. Cooper (Eds.), *Bullying and emotional abuse in the workplace* (pp. 221–236). CRC Press.

Hogan, R. T., & Hogan, J. C. (2014). U.S. Patent Application No. 13/673,175.

Hornung, S. (2010). Alienation matters: Validity and utility of Etzioni's theory of commitment in explaining prosocial organizational behavior. *Social Behavior and Personality, 38*(8), 1081–1095. https://doi.org/10.2224/sbp.2010.38.8.1081

Hoyt, C. L., Price, T. L., & Poatsy, L. (2013). The social role theory of unethical leadership. *The Leadership Quarterly, 24*(5), 712–723. https://doi.org/10.1016/j.leaqua.2013.07.001

Hu, Y., Zhu, L., Zhou, M., Li, J., Maguire, P., Sun, H., & Wang, D. (2018). Exploring the influence of ethical leadership on voice behavior: How leader-member exchange, psychological safety and psychological empowerment influence employees' willingness to speak out. *Frontiers in Psychology, 9*, 1718. https://doi.org/10.3389/fpsyg.2018.01718

Hughes, R. L., Ginnett, R. C., & Curphy, G. J. (1998). Contingency theories of leadership. In *Leading organizations: Perspectives for a new era* (pp. 141–157).

Hyde, J. S. (2014). Gender similarities and differences. *Annual Review of Psychology, 65*, 373–398. https://doi.org/10.1146/annurev-psych-010213-115057

If it was Lehman sisters it would have been a different world. (2018, September 5). The Guardian. Retrieved from: https://www.theguardian.com/business/2018/sep/05/if-it-was-lehman-sisters-it-would-be-a-different-world-christine-lagarde

Ignatius, A. (2014). The best-performing CEOs in the world. *Harvard Business Review, 92*(11), 16. Retrieved from https://hbr.org/2013/01/the-worlds-top-ceo

Janis, I. L. (1972). *Victims of group think*. Houghton Mifflin.

Johnson, R. E., Venus, M., Lanaj, K., Mao, C., & Chang, C. H. (2012). Leader identity as an antecedent of the frequency and consistency of transformational, consideration, and abusive leadership behaviors. *Journal of Applied Psychology, 97*(6), 1262. https://doi.org/10.1037/a0029043

Jost, J. T. (2020). *A theory of system justification*. Harvard University Press. https://doi.org/10.2307/j.ctv13qfw6w

Jost, J. T., Banaji, M. R., & Nosek, B. A. (2004). A decade of system justification theory: Accumulated evidence of conscious and unconscious bolstering of the status quo. *Political Psychology, 25*(6), 881–919. https://doi.org/10.1111/j.1467-9221.2004.00402.x

Kahneman, D. (2011). *Thinking, fast and slow*. Allen Lane.

Kakissis, J. (Reporter). (2019, September 27). *This American Life 684: Burn It Down* [Podcast transcript]. Retrieved from https://www.thisamericanlife.org/684/transcript

Kaptein, M. (2019). The moral entrepreneur: A new component of ethical leadership. *Journal of Business Ethics, 156*(4), 1135–1150. https://doi.org/10.1007/s10551-017-3641-0

Karlsson, P. O., Turner, M., & Gassmann, P. (2019). Succeeding the long-serving legend in the corner office. Strategy +. *Business, 15*.

Kelley, H., & Michela, J. (1980). Attribution theory and research. *Annual Review of Psychology, 31*, 457–501. https://doi.org/10.1146/annurev.ps.31.020180.002325

Keltner, D., Gruenfeld, D. H., & Anderson, C. (2003). Power, approach, and inhibition. *Psychological Review, 110*(2), 265. https://doi.org/10.1037/0033-295X.110.2.265

Kerr, S. (1975). On the folly of rewarding A, while hoping for B. *Academy of Management Journal, 18*(4), 769–783. https://doi.org/10.5465/255378

Kipnis, D. (1972). Does power corrupt? *Journal of Personality and Social Psychology, 24*(1), 33. https://doi.org/10.1037/h0033390

Kunst, A. (2019, December 25). Hoe de top van Gerard Sanderinks IT-bedrijf Centric leeg loopt. *Tubantia*. https://www.tubantia.nl/enschede/hoe-de-top-van-gerard-sanderinks-it-bedrijf-centric-leeg-loopt~af29ee20/?referrer=https%3A%2F%2Fwww.google.com%2F

Liden, R. C., Wayne, S. J., Liao, C., & Meuser, J. D. (2014). Servant leadership and serving culture: Influence on individual and unit performance. *Academy of Management Journal, 57*(5), 1434–1452. https://doi.org/10.5465/amj.2013.0034

Lin, S. H. J., Ma, J., & Johnson, R. E. (2016). When ethical leader behavior breaks bad: How ethical leader behavior can turn abusive via ego depletion and moral licensing. *Journal of Applied Psychology, 101*(6), 815. https://doi.org/10.1037/apl0000098

Lind, E. A., & Tyler, T. R. (1988). *The psychology of procedural justice*. Plenum Press. https://doi.org/10.1007/978-1-4899-2115-4

Linstead, S., Maréchal, G., & Griffin, R. W. (2014). Theorizing and researching the dark side of organization. *Organization Studies, 35*(2), 165–188. https://doi.org/10.1177/0170840613515402

Macur, J. (2020, August 3). Gymnasts Worldwide Push back on Their Sport's Culture of Abuse. *The New York Times*. Retrieved from https://www.nytimes.com/2020/08/03/sports/olympics/gymnastics-abuse-athlete-a.html.

Magee, J. C., & Smith, P. K. (2013). The social distance theory of power. *Personality and Social Psychology Review, 17*(2), 158–186. https://doi.org/10.1177/1088868312472732

Marcelis, F. I. (2020, July 25). Top gymnastics coach acknowledges history of abuse, mistreatment. *NL Times*. Retrieved from https://nltimes.nl/2020/07/25/top-gymnastics-coach-acknowledges-history-abuse-mistreatment

Marsh, S., & Devlin, H. (2018, August 29). Bosses at leading UK science institute accused of bullying staff. *The Guardian*. Retrieved from https://www.theguardian.com/science/2018/aug/29/wellcome-sanger-institute-bosses-accused-bullying-staff

Martinko, M. J., Harvey, P., & Douglas, S. C. (2007). The role, function, and contribution of attribution theory to leadership: A review. *The Leadership Quarterly, 18*(6), 561–585. https://doi.org/10.1016/j.leaqua.2007.09.004

Mathieu, C., Neumann, C. S., Hare, R. D., & Babiak, P. (2014). A dark side of leadership: Corporate psychopathy and its influence on employee well-being and job satisfaction. *Personality and Individual Differences, 59*, 83–88. https://doi.org/10.1016/j.paid.2013.11.010

Mathieu, J. E., & Zajac, D. M. (1990). A review and meta-analysis of the antecedents, correlates, and consequences of organizational commitment. *Psychological Bulletin, 108*(2), 171. https://doi.org/10.1037/0033-2909.108.2.171

Mayer, D. M., Kuenzi, M., Greenbaum, R., Bardes, M., & Salvador, R. B. (2009). How low does ethical leadership flow? Test of a trickle-down model. *Organizational Behavior and Human Decision Processes, 108*(1), 1–13. https://doi.org/10.1016/j.obhdp.2008.04.002

Meindl, J. R. (1995). The romance of leadership as a follower-centric theory: A social constructionist approach. *The Leadership Quarterly, 6*(3), 329–341. https://doi.org/10.1016/1048-9843(95)90012-8

Meindl, J. R., Ehrlich, S. B., & Dukerich, J. M. (1985). The romance of leadership. *Administrative Science Quarterly, 30*(1), 78–102. https://doi.org/10.2307/2392813

Melwani, S., & Barsade, S. G. (2011). Held in contempt: The psychological, interpersonal, and performance consequences of contempt in a work context. *Journal of Personality and Social Psychology, 101*(3), 503. https://doi.org/10.1037/a0023492

Meyer, J. P., & Allen, N. J. (1997). *Commitment in the workplace: Theory, research, and application*. Sage.

Milgram, S. (1965). Some conditions of obedience and disobedience to authority. *Human Relations, 18*(1), 57–76. https://doi.org/10.1177/001872676501800105

Milgram, S. (1974). *Obedience to authority: An experimental view*. Harpercollins.

Mishel, L., & Wolfe, J. (2019, August 14). CEO compensation has grown 940% since 1978. *Economic Policy Institute*. Retrieved from https://www.epi.org/publication/ceo-compensation-2018/

Mooijman, M., & Graham, J. (2018). Unjust punishment in organizations. *Research in Organizational Behavior, 38*, 95–106. https://doi.org/10.1016/j.riob.2018.10.001

Mooijman, M., Van Dijk, W. W., Ellemers, N., & Van Dijk, E. (2015). Why leaders punish: A power perspective. *Journal of Personality and Social Psychology, 109*(1), 75. https://doi.org/10.1037/pspi0000021

Mooijman, M., Van Dijk, W. W., Van Dijk, E., & Ellemers, N. (2017). On sanction-goal justifications: How and why deterrence justifications undermine rule compliance. *Journal of Personality and Social Psychology, 112*(4), 577. https://doi.org/10.1037/pspi0000084

Mooijman, M., Van Dijk, W. W., Van Dijk, E., & Ellemers, N. (2019) Leader power, power stability, and interpersonal trust. *Organizational Behavior and Human Decision Processes, 152*, 1–10. https://doi.org/10.1016/j.obhdp.2019.03.009

NLtimes. (2018, March 8). Politicians furious about ING boss's massive pay raise. *NLtimes*. Retrieved from https://nltimes.nl/2018/03/08/politicians-furious-ing-bosss-massive-pay-raise

NTR. (2013, August 8). Het slijk der aarde [video]. *NTR*. Retrieved from https://www.ntr.nl/Kijken-in-de-Ziel/55/detail/Kijken-in-de-ziel-Topondernemers-afl-3/NPS_1215990#content

O'Boyle, E. H., Jr., Forsyth, D. R., Banks, G. C., & McDaniel, M. A. (2012). A meta-analysis of the Dark Triad and work behavior: A social exchange perspective. *Journal of Applied Psychology, 97*(3), 557–579. https://doi.org/10.1037/a0025679

Opotow, S. (1995). Drawing the line: Social categorization, moral exclusion, and the scope of justice. In B. Bunker & J. Rubin (Eds.), *Conflict, cooperation, and justice: Essays inspired by the work of Morton Deutsch* (pp. 347–369). Jossey-Bass.

Ouwerkerk, J. W., Ellemers, N., & De Gilder, D. (1999). Group commitment and individual effort in experimental and organizational contexts. In N. Ellemers, R. Spears, & B. Doosje (Eds.), *Social identity: Context, commitment, content* (pp. 184–204). Blackwell.

Park, B., & Banchefsky, S. (2018). Leveraging the social role of dad to change gender stereotypes of men. *Personality and Social Psychology Bulletin, 44*(9), 1380–1394. https://doi.org/10.1177/0146167218768794

Pender, K. (2019, May). Us too? Bullying and sexual harassment in the legal profession. *International Bar Association*. Retrieved from https://www.ibanet.org/bullying-and-sexual-harassment.aspx.

Perlmutter, L. S. (2012). *Transformational leadership and the development of moral elevation and trust* (Doctoral dissertation, University of British Columbia).

Peters, K., Fonseca, M. A., Haslam, S. A., Steffens, N. K., & Quiggin, J. (2019). Fat cats and thin followers: Excessive CEO pay may reduce ability to lead. In J. Jetten & K. Peters (Eds.), *The social psychology of inequality* (pp. 21–34). Springer. https://doi.org/10.1007/978-3-030-28856-3_2

Peters, K., Steffens, N. K., & Morgenroth, T. (2018). Superstars are not necessarily role models: Morality perceptions moderate the impact of competence perceptions on supervisor role modeling. *European Journal of Social Psychology, 48*(6), 725–746. https://doi.org/10.1002/ejsp.2372

Piketty, T. (2018). Brahmin left vs merchant right: Rising inequality and the changing structure of political conflict. *WID: World Working Paper*, 7.

Podsakoff, N. P., Whiting, S. W., Podsakoff, P. M., & Blume, B. D. (2009). Individual- and organizational-level consequences of organizational citizenship behaviors: A meta-analysis. *Journal of Applied Psychology, 94*(1), 122–141. https://doi.org/10.1037/a0013079

Pohling, R., & Diessner, R. (2016). Moral elevation and moral beauty: A review of the empirical literature. *Review of General Psychology, 20*(4), 412–425. https://doi.org/10.1037/gpr0000089

Porath, C. L., & Erez, A. (2007). Does rudeness really matter? The effects of rudeness on task performance and helpfulness. *Academy of Management Journal, 50*(5), 1181–1197. https://doi.org/10.2307/20159919

Postmes, T., Spears, R., & Cihangir, S. (2001). Quality of decision making and group norms. *Journal of Personality and Social Psychology, 80*(6), 918. https://doi.org/10.1037/0022-3514.80.6.918

Reicher, S., Cassidy, C., Wolpert, I., Hopkins, N., & Levine, M. (2006). Saving Bulgaria's Jews: An analysis of social identity and the mobilisation of social solidarity. *European Journal of Social Psychology, 36*(1), 49–72. https://doi.org/10.1002/ejsp.291

Reuters. (2007, May 17). ABN Amro CEO won't step down: Report. *CNBC*. Retrieved from https://www.cnbc.com/2007/05/17/abn-amro-ceo-wont-step-down-report.html

Rink, F., Ryan, M. K., & Stoker, J. I. (2013). Social resources at a time of crisis: How gender stereotypes inform gendered leader evaluations. *European Journal of Social Psychology, 43*(5), 381–392. https://doi.org/10.1002/ejsp.1954

Rodgers, M. S., Sauer, S. J., & Proell, C. A. (2013). The lion's share: The impact of credit expectations and credit allocations on commitment to leaders. *The Leadership Quarterly, 24*(1), 80–93. https://doi.org/10.1016/j.leaqua.2012.08.003

Rosenblatt, V. (2012). Hierarchies, power inequalities, and organizational corruption. *Journal of Business Ethics, 111*(2), 237–251. https://doi.org/10.1007/s10551-012-1204-y

Rushe, D. (2019, August 14). Top US bosses earn 278 times more than their employees. *The Guardian*. Retrieved from https://www.theguardian.com/us-news/2019/aug/14/ceo-worker-pay-gap

Ryan, M. K., & Haslam, S. A. (2005). The glass cliff: Evidence that women are over-represented in precarious leadership positions. *British Journal of Management, 16*(2), 81–90. https://doi.org/10.1111/j.1467-8551.2005.00433.x

Sanders, S., Wisse, B. M., & Van Yperen, N. W. (2013). Contemptuous leaders: Power exacerbates contempt's negative impact on leaders' people orientation. *Academy of Management Proceedings, 2013*(1), 14477. https://doi.org/10.5465/ambpp.2013.14477abstract

Sanders, S., Wisse, B. M., & Van Yperen, N. W. (2015). Holding others in contempt: The moderating role of power in the relationship between leaders' contempt and their behavior vis-à-vis employees. *Business Ethics Quarterly, 25*(2), 213–241. https://doi.org/10.1017/beq.2015.14

Sanders, S., Wisse, B. M., Van Yperen, N. W., & Rus, D. (2018). On ethically solvent leaders: The roles of pride and moral identity in predicting leader ethical behavior. *Journal of Business Ethics, 150*(3), 631–645. https://doi.org/10.1007/s10551-016-3180-0

Sassenberg, K., Ellemers, N., & Scheepers, D. (2012). The attraction of social power: The influence of construing power as opportunity versus responsibility. *Journal of Experimental Social Psychology, 48*(2), 550–555. https://doi.org/10.1016/j.jesp.2011.11.008

Sassenberg, K., Ellemers, N., Scheepers, D., & Scholl, A. (2014). "Power corrupts" revisited: The role of construal of power as opportunity or responsibility. In J. W. Van Prooijen & P. A. M. Van Lange (Eds.), *Power, politics, and paranoia: Why people are suspicious of their leaders* (pp. 73–87). Cambridge University Press. https://doi.org/10.1017/CBO9781139565417.007

Schaubroeck, J. M., Hannah, S. T., Avolio, B. J., Kozlowski, S. W., Lord, R. G., Treviño, L. K., … Peng, A. C. (2012). Embedding ethical leadership within and across organization levels. *Academy of Management Journal, 55*(5), 1053–1078. https://doi.org/10.5465/amj.2011.0064

Scheepers, D., De Wit, F., Ellemers, N., & Sassenberg, K. (2012). Social power makes the heart work more efficiently: Evidence from cardiovascular markers of challenge and threat. *Journal of Experimental Social Psychology, 48*(1), 371–374. https://doi.org/10.1016/j.jesp.2011.06.014

Scheepers, D., & Ellemers, N. (2005). When the pressure is up: The assessment of social identity threat in low and high status groups. *Journal of Experimental Social Psychology, 41*, 192–200. https://doi.org/10.1016/j.jesp.2004.06.002

Scheepers, D., & Ellemers, N. (2018). Stress and the stability of social systems: A review of neurophysiological research. *European Review of Social Psychology, 29*(1), 340–376. https://doi.org/10.1080/10463283.2018.1543149

Scheepers, D., Ellemers, N., & Sassenberg, K. (2013). Power in group contexts: The influence of group status on promotion and prevention decision making. *British Journal of Social Psychology, 52*(2), 238–254. https://doi.org/10.1111/j.2044-8309.2011.02063.x

Scheepers, D., Ellemers, N., & Sintemaartensdijk, N. (2009). Suffering from the possibility of status loss: Physiological responses to social identity threat in high status groups. *European Journal of Social Psychology, 39*(6), 1075–1092. https://doi.org/10.1002/ejsp.609

Scheepers, D., Röell, C., & Ellemers, N. (2015). Unstable power threatens the powerful and challenges the powerless: Evidence from cardiovascular markers of motivation. *Frontiers in Psychology, 6*, 720. https://doi.org/10.3389/fpsyg.2015.00720

Schmitt, M., & Dörfel, M. (1999). Procedural injustice at work, justice sensitivity, job satisfaction and psychosomatic well-being. *European Journal of Social Psychology, 29*(4), 443–453. https://doi.org/10.1002/(SICI)1099-0992(199906)29:4<443::AID-EJSP935>3.0.CO;2-C

Schnall, S., & Cannon, P. R. (2012). The clean conscience at work: Emotions, intuitions and morality. *Journal of Management, Spirituality & Religion, 9*(4), 295–315. https://doi.org/10.1080/14766086.2012.742749

Scholl, A., Sassenberg, K., Ellemers, N., Scheepers, D., & De Wit, F. (2018). Highly identified power-holders feel responsible: The interplay between social identification and social power within groups. *British Journal of Social Psychology, 57*(1), 112–129. https://doi.org/10.1111/bjso.12225

Scholl, A., Sassenberg, K., Scheepers, D., Ellemers, N., & De Wit, F. (2017). A matter of focus: Power-holders feel more responsible after adopting a cognitive other-focus, rather than a self-focus. *British Journal of Social Psychology, 56*(1), 89–102. https://doi.org/10.1111/bjso.12177

See, K. E., Morrison, E. W., Rothman, N. B., & Soll, J. B. (2011). The detrimental effects of power on confidence, advice taking, and accuracy. *Organizational Behavior and Human Decision Processes, 116*(2), 272–285. https://doi.org/10.1016/j.obhdp.2011.07.006

Selart, M. (2010). *A leadership perspective on decision making*. Cappelen Academic Publishers.

Shoham, A., Almor, T., Lee, S. M., & Ahammad, M. F. (2017). Encouraging environmental sustainability through gender: A micro-foundational approach using linguistic gender marking. *Journal of Organizational Behavior, 38*(9), 1356–1379. https://doi.org/10.1002/job.2188

Simons, T., Leroy, H., Collewaert, V., & Masschelein, S. (2015). How leader alignment of words and deeds affects followers: A meta-analysis of behavioral integrity research. *Journal of Business Ethics, 132*(4), 831–844. https://doi.org/10.1007/s10551-014-2332-3

Smith, P. K., & Overbeck, J. R. (2014). The leaders' rosy halo: Why do we give powerholders the benefit of the doubt. In J. W. Van Prooijen & P. A. M. Van Lange (Eds.), *Power, politics, and paranoia: Why people are suspicious of their leaders* (pp. 53–71). Cambridge University Press.

Smith, P. K., & Trope, Y. (2006). You focus on the forest when you're in charge of the trees: Power priming and abstract information processing. *Journal of Personality and Social Psychology, 90*(4), 578. https://doi.org/10.1037/0022-3514.90.4.578

Ståhl, T., & Ellemers, N. (2016). Ironic effects of moral motivation: Why working toward a moral goal reduces subsequent perspective taking. *Social Cognition, 34*(2), 133–148. https://doi.org/10.1521/soco.2016.34.2.133

Ståhl, T., Vermunt, R., & Ellemers, N. (2006). Friend or foe? Ingroup identification moderates reactions to outgroup members' allocation behavior. *European Journal of Social Psychology, 36*(6), 877–885. https://doi.org/10.1002/ejsp.327

Ståhl, T., Vermunt, R., & Ellemers, N. (2008a). For love or money? How activation of relational versus instrumental concerns affects reactions to decision-making procedures. *Journal of Experimental Social Psychology, 44*(1), 80–94. https://doi.org/10.1016/j.jesp.2007.02.004

Ståhl, T., Vermunt, R., & Ellemers, N. (2008b). Reactions to outgroup authorities' decisions: The role of expected bias, procedural fairness and outcome favorability. *Group Processes & Intergroup Relations, 11*(3), 281–299. https://doi.org/10.1177/1368430208090643

Stamkou, E., & Van Kleef, G. A. (2014). Do we give power to the right people? When and how norm violators rise to the top. In J. W. Van Prooijen & P. A. M. Van Lange (Eds.), *Power, politics, and paranoia: Why people are suspicious of their leaders* (pp. 33–52). Cambridge University Press. https://doi.org/10.1017/CBO9781139565417.005

Steffens, N. K., & Haslam, S. A. (2020). The narcissistic appeal of leadership theories. *American Psychologist*. https://doi.org/10.1037/amp0000738

Steffens, N. K., Haslam, S. A., Peters, K., & Quiggin, J. (2018). Identity economics meets identity leadership: Exploring the consequences of elevated CEO pay. *The Leadership Quarterly*. https://doi.org/10.1016/j.leaqua.2018.10.001.

Steffens, N. K., Munt, K. A., Van Knippenberg, D., Platow, M. J., & Haslam, S. A. (2020). Advancing the social identity theory of leadership: A meta-analytic review of leader group prototypicality. *Organizational Psychology Review*, 2041386620962569.

Steffens, N. K., Yang, J., Jetten, J., Haslam, S. A., & Lipponen, J. (2018). The unfolding impact of leader identity entrepreneurship on burnout, work engagement, and turnover intentions. *Journal of Occupational Health Psychology, 23*(3), 373. https://doi.org/10.1037/ocp0000090

Tedeschi, J. T., & Felson, R. B. (1994). *Violence, aggression, and coercive actions*. American Psychological Association. https://doi.org/10.1037/10160-000

Tepper, B. J. (2000). Consequences of abusive supervision. *Academy of Management Journal, 43*(2), 178–190. https://doi.org/10.2307/1556375

Tost, L. P. (2015). When, why, and how do powerholders "feel the power"? Examining the links between structural and psychological power and reviving the connection between power and responsibility. *Research in Organizational Behavior, 35*, 29–56. https://doi.org/10.1016/j.riob.2015.10.004

Tost, L. P., Gino, F., & Larrick, R. P. (2012). Power, competitiveness, and advice taking: Why the powerful don't listen. *Organizational Behavior and Human Decision Processes, 117*(1), 53–65. https://doi.org/10.1016/j.obhdp.2011.10.001

Tyler, T. R. (1997). The psychology of legitimacy: A relational perspective on voluntary deference to authorities. *Personality and Social Psychology Review, 1*(4), 323–345. https://doi.org/10.1207/s15327957pspr0104_4

Van Anders, S. M., Steiger, J., & Goldey, K. L. (2015). Effects of gendered behavior on testosterone in women and men. Proceedings of the National Academy of Sciences, 112(45), 13805–13810.

Van Brenk, H. (2018). *Beloningsprikkels en persoonlijkheidseigenschappen: Drie studies naar de gezamenlijke effecten hiervan op oordeels- en besluitvorming van accountants* (PhD thesis). Nijenrode University, Breukelen, The Netherlands.

Van der Toorn, J., & Jost, J. T. (2014). Twenty years of system justification theory: Introduction to the special issue on "ideology and system justification processes". *Group Processes & Intergroup Relations, 17*(4), 413–419. https://doi.org/10.1177/1368430214531509

Van Gils, S. (2020, September 23). Gerard Sanderink van Strukton knokt door met ex in elfde rechtszaak. *Het Financiële Dagblad*. https://fd.nl/achtergrond/1357847/gerard-sanderink-van-strukton-knokt-door-met-ex-in-elfde-rechtszaak.

Van Prooijen, A. M., & Ellemers, N. (2015). Does it pay to be moral? How indicators of morality and competence enhance organizational and work team attractiveness. *British Journal of Management, 26*(2), 225–236. https://doi.org/10.1111/1467-8551.12055

Van Rooij, B., & Fine, A. (2018). Toxic corporate culture: Assessing organizational processes of deviancy. *Administrative Sciences, 8*(3), 23. https://doi.org/10.3390/admsci8030023

Van Veen, K., & Wittek, R. (2016). Relational signaling and the rise of CEO compensation. "... It's not just about money, it is about what the money says...". *Long Range Planning, 49*(4), 477–490. https://doi.org/10.1016/j.lrp.2015.12.009

Vianello, M., Galliani, E. M., & Haidt, J. (2010). Elevation at work: The effects of leaders' moral excellence. *The Journal of Positive Psychology, 5*(5), 390–411. https://doi.org/10.1080/17439760.2010.516764

Vriend, T., Jordan, J., & Janssen, O. (2016). Reaching the top and avoiding the bottom: How ranking motivates unethical intentions and behavior. *Organizational Behavior and Human Decision Processes, 137*, 142–155. https://doi.org/10.1016/j.obhdp.2016.09.003

Waldman, D. A., & O'Reilly, C. (2019). *Leadership for organizations*. SAGE Publications.

Whitson, J. A., Liljenquist, K. A., Galinsky, A. D., Magee, J. C., Gruenfeld, D. H., & Cadena, B. (2013). The blind leading: Power reduces awareness of constraints. *Journal of Experimental Social Psychology, 49*(3), 579–582. https://doi.org/10.1016/j.jesp.2012.10.009

Yukl, G. (2011). Contingency theories of effective leadership. *The SAGE Handbook of Leadership, 24*(1), 286–298.

Yukl, G. (2013). *Leadership in organizations*. Prentice Hall.

Yukl, G., & Van Fleet, D. (1992). *Theory and research on leadership in organizations* (Vol. 13, pp. 14–19). Consulting Psychologists Journal.

Yurtsever, G. (2003). Measuring the moral entrepreneurial personality. *Social Behavior and Personality, 31*(1), 1–12. https://doi.org/10.2224/sbp.2003.31.1.1

Zhang, F. W., Liao, J. Q., & Yuan, J. M. (2016). Ethical leadership and whistleblowing: Collective moral potency and personal identification as mediators. *Social Behavior and Personality, 44*(7), 1223–1231. https://doi.org/10.2224/sbp.2016.44.7.1223

Chapter 4
Motivating Moral Choices

Abstract The procedures organizations commonly use as they try to motivate employees to perform well can discourage them from making morally responsible choices in their interactions with colleagues and clients. **Key issues** addressed here highlight the unfortunate side effects of emphasizing monetary outcomes, building a distinct identity, and incentivizing performance targets. These motivational strategies are meant to focus people's efforts and enhance task achievement. However, they can also invite unethical and morally irresponsible behavior. **Our analysis** builds on research evidence revealing the hidden costs of these common motivational practices – for task performance as well as organizational morality. We highlight how lack of attention for workplace conduct may undermine perceptions of fairness and justice in different ways, and introduces various moral hazards. **Solutions** relate to the importance of treating employees with respect, and confronting misbehavior – instead of condoning or ignoring this. Communicating and enacting the moral values that define their shared identity, and treating employees as valued members of the organization offers a sense of purpose that benefits task performance as well as rule compliance.

N. Ellemers, D. de Gilder, *The Moral Organization: Key Issues, Analyses, and Solutions*, https://doi.org/10.1007/978-3-030-84175-1_4

4.1 Key Issues: Morality and Motivation

Attempts to understand or guide human behavior in organizations place motivation front and center. Motivating individuals is deservedly seen as a key factor in reaching organizational goals, and many theories explain (specific aspects of) human motivation. The key aim of most of these approaches is on promoting efficient task completion and inviting other forms of pro-organizational behavior. However, efforts of scientists and managers alike to understand what drives human conduct in the workplace are also informed by their awareness of a dark side to how people behave in organizations. Despite insights offered by motivation theories and the range of tools and approaches used to align individual choices with organizational goals, anti-organizational behavior occurs quite frequently and seems impossible to eradicate. Some of these behaviors are obviously illegal and immoral such as stealing money, equipment or other valuable resources from the organization, which directly damage its outcomes. Other practices may seem less harmful at first sight, such as exchanging favors with clients, prioritizing assignments of family members, or sharing confidential company information with friends. Nevertheless, these are all forms of corruption. Once discovered, these likely cause long-term reputational damage to the organization as a whole, and may attract high fines as well as increased – and time-consuming – monitoring by regulatory authorities. Further, seemingly innocent practices such as slacking, tardiness or addressing personal issues during work hours may not be illegal, but can be seen to violate organizational moral guidelines and undermine workplace morale. Each of the above behaviors may also indirectly hurt the organization, as these affect team spirit, absenteeism and turnover.

Organizations typically try to prevent and root out such negative employee behaviors, and the three quick fixes to deal with immoral behavior in organizations, identified in Chap. 1, are commonly used to this effect. Depending on the severity of the transgression, individual employees may be sacked or even legally prosecuted after discovery, to remove the culprit and set an example for others (individual difference approach). Efforts to steer individual employees are usually implemented through reward and punishment systems that attempt to nudge them into the organizationally desired behavior (economic approach). New employees are often asked to present a certificate of good conduct or to sign pledges that they will comply with specific organizational rules and procedures (legal approach). Ideally, these practices clearly communicate what employees are (not) supposed to do, and offer transparency and fairness in applying equal rules to all organizational members. However, in larger organizations in particular, this typically leads to quite complex and bureaucratic systems, adorned to regulate budget expenditures, expense claims, client contracts, leave allowances, etcetera. Uncovering transgressions typically invites the development of ever more elaborate and stricter rules, with more time-consuming instructions and controls, which detract from primary tasks and easily frustrate the achievement of key organizational goals.

These well-meant attempts to manage and control individual behavior make sense. They constitute inevitable features of any professional organization, and should help curb and redress intentional misbehavior. Nevertheless, the examples already shared in prior chapters suggests that anti-organizational, and even immoral behavior is widespread might never be fully eradicated. Here we offer an alternative view that complements standard approaches by addressing workplace motivation as a social process. We first explain how common ways to motivate individual workers unwittingly impact on the way they define their identity in relation to the organization. In the first section of this chapter, we highlight how monetary rewards, professional guidelines and performance targets implicitly convey the distinct identity of organizational members and define key values characterizing such identities. In the second section, we specify how the motivational tools that neglect social relations and workplace conduct introduce different types of moral hazards and invite morally irresponsible behavior – despite formal regulations. In the third section we examine how speaking to people's workplace identities by affirming their inclusion and respect, sanctioning misbehavior, and taking pride in moral values allows them to make morally responsible choices.

In doing this, we build on the insights into moral leadership, discussed in Chap. 3. Self-evidently, leaders and managers are key players in determining motivation at work. These are the ones who decide on work conditions, reward systems, task goals and characteristics, and define important rules and regulations as well as sanctioning those breaking them. In addition, however, it is worth considering the everyday interactions and conduct among colleagues and team members. These help shape the way people consider and define their tasks, roles, and position in the workplace and constitute an important source of social influence. It is through these daily social interactions that people come to define their shared identity and position in the organization, which can either fortify or undermine their resolution and ability to make moral choices.

4.1.1 Money, Money, Money: It's a Rich Man's World

Classic approaches to work motivation are based on the notion that people are rational agents who generally strive for the optimization of their personal outcomes. Current analyses generally reveal that these agentic approaches to human nature -considering individuals as 'economic men' who are motivated by extrinsic, short term, and individualistic outcomes – may not be correct. Over the years, organizational scientists have therefore developed alternative views of human motivation, that highlight the importance of more intrinsic, self-actualizing, long term, and collective motives, for instance in theories on organizational stewardship (Davis et al., 1997; see Fig. 4.1: Agency vs stewardship approaches to motivation). Still, agentic 'economic man' approaches permeate the implicit assumptions and motivational practices in many organizations. The obvious result of this assumption is that offering personal gains seems the best way to motivate people to exert themselves on behalf of the company.

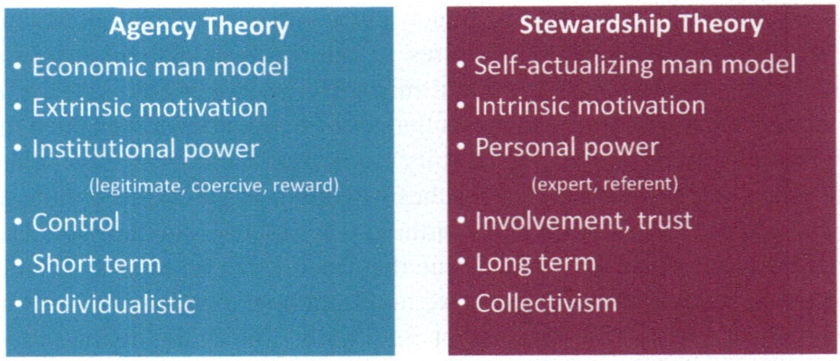

Fig. 4.1 Agency and stewardship. Summarizes characteristic features of two approaches to motivation. The implicit assumptions about human nature that guide Agency Theory and Stewardship Theory give rise to fundamentally different motivational systems. (Davis et al., 1997)

Those who work hard are rewarded with higher pay and more career opportunities, and receiving these rewards will keep people happy and motivated – or so it would seem. The occurrence of morally questionable behavior, when people lie, steal, or cheat to maximize their rewards, then seems an inevitable downside of this naturally selfish outlook people have in the workplace, which can only be curbed with stricter rules and costly sanctions.

Despite the wide-spread nature of this approach to individual motivation, there is little evidence for its validity (Ellemers et al., 2004). In fact, scientific studies as well as business analyses consistently reveal something else. The motivation, engagement and productivity of people in the workplace mainly relates to the nature of their daily activities and social rewards rather than selfish gains and monetary outcomes. For instance an 'experience survey' carried out among over 23,000 employees in 45 countries revealed that employees felt motivated for their job when they received feedback to acknowledge their task contributions, had some autonomy and voice in making decisions about their activities and work-life balance, and experienced good relations with their co-workers and the organization (IBM & Globoforce, 2017). Similar results emerge from scientific studies into the key determinants of motivation and satisfaction in the workplace (e.g., Grant & Berg, 2010; Parmar et al., 2019).

In fact, such social outcomes may overrule the importance of monetary rewards. This is the conclusion from an analysis that compared thousands of company reviews to capture the factors that determine individual workplace experiences in the United States. Possible predictors included individually rewarding factors such as daily tasks, compensation, and growth opportunities as well as broader characteristics of the work environment, such as the culture and reputation of the company and the relation with co-workers. The number one 'happy job' emerging from this analysis was the job of Teaching Assistant – a lowly paid position that people experience as highly engaging. The number one 'unhappy job', was Accountant – despite its high pay (Careerbliss, 2018). This too converges with results from scientific studies revealing that earning more money does not necessarily make people more satisfied or engaged with their job. Indeed, employees who are psychologically committed and engaged to their work team and organization are more likely to display efforts that benefit the organization than those who are bound by more selfish concerns (Mathieu & Zajac, 1990; Allen & Meyer, 1990; see also Ellemers et al., 1998).

Thus, there is little evidence that appealing to selfish outcomes is the best way to engage and motivate employees. In fact, focusing on personal monetary rewards and company earnings is not without cost. When high earnings define the status and identity of the company, this also communicates what individuals need to do to be valued and successful in that context. If making money at any cost is advertised as a hallmark of success, it is this motivation strategy – rather than the 'naturally selfish' outlook of employees – that invites immoral behavior. This seemed to have been the case, for instance at Stratton Oakmont, a stock trading company pushing employees to mislead rich customers to earn high profits as an explicit business strategy. Although hundreds of stock brokers participated in this scheme, it would seem inadequate to simply assume that they were all driven by selfishness alone. From what is known about the motivational strategies that were used, ruthlessness in cheating clients was set as an explicit norm in this company, and quite some effort was made to persuade brokers to engage with this norm (see Box 4.1: The wolf of Wall Street). Thus, the company identity rather than individual selfish tendencies would encourage employees to display their professional ability by cheating clients, as this is what was requested from them. In this case, showing loyalty to the company by executing the recommended business strategy would invite morally questionable behavior instead of preventing it.

Box 4.1: The Wolf of Wall Street

Jordan Belfort is better known as the 'Wolf of Wall Street'. He started his stock broker firm Stratton Oakmont with the explicit goal of making money by deceiving potential investors. The firm used a scheme called 'pump and dump'. First, investors were aggressively approached with 'a golden tip' to buy small caps with dubious value ('penny stocks'), and relatively little trading activity. In reality, prices of these shares were artificially inflated ('pumped') in this way, until a price level was reached where the operators of the scheme would sell ('dump') their own overvalued shares. This is how these stockbrokers made large profits while investors lost their money, as share prices inevitably collapsed after the 'dump'. At the height of the firm's 'success' more than 1000 stock brokers were enticed to participate in this scam.

During 'motivational meetings', one hundred dollar bills were ripped before their eyes – indicating that such 'peanuts' were only fit for losers. Instead, the firm expected them to have their eyes on bigger prizes. Ideally, they would be trapping 'whales' in this way: large investors who were cajoled into incurring equally large losses – to the benefit of the firm and its brokers. High on drugs and high on money, there was a buzz in the broker room as brokers encouraged each other to make money, not minding the inappropriateness of their scheme. Group meetings and memorable events such as these became part of the folklore in the company. This convinced brokers that it would be ok to sell worthless shares to their customers as long as this allowed them to amass riches for themselves. In fact, while Belfort was first characterized as the 'wolf of Wall Street' in a critical publication about his business strategy in Forbes Magazine, this nickname became a source of pride in the company, celebrating the signature ruthlessness displayed in making money (Belfort, 2007; Gray, 2013; Leonard, 2008; Solomon, 2013).

In this company then, making 'big' and 'quick' money was more than just a valued outcome or incentive. Instead, it was presented as the essence of its unique business strategy that characterized the identity of those executing it. In fact, the stories recounted by former employees, suggest they identified strongly with their organization and its dubious practices, at least for a while. The fact that this was immoral or even illegal did not count. Within the company the reputations and standing of individuals were defined only in terms of the money they made. Thus, from a social identity perspective, the brokers were willing to engage in such behavior because this was what Stratton Oakmont was about. The company had socialized them to measure the value of their professional efforts only by the money they earned and the wealth they displayed by spending their earnings on cars, prostitutes, and other high profile expenditures.

These practices are not outdated. In Australia, Jeffrey Revell-Reade was sentenced to jail on 6 June 2014, for using similar methods. He made millions by selling worthless stocks in teak wood, CO_2 emission rights, or Australian wine to customers across the world. The media referred to him as 'the Wolf of Wimbledon' because his business plan and motivation scheme so resembled the practices at Stratton Oakmont. In fact, former employees recount how managers would stick hundred dollar bills on the whiteboard in the morning, assigning these to the person who made the first sale of the day. Regulators have noticed increasing activity of these and similar boiler room fraud schemes during the COVID-19 pandemic. In the summer of 2020, the Netherlands Financial Market Authority even tried to combat this growing problem by writing letters of warning to thousands of rich entrepreneurs whose names they found on the 'sucker lists' used by these organizations for cold calling customers (Dutch News, 2020).

Of course Stratton Oakmont is an extreme case. It received much attention because of its spectacular downfall that was widely publicized in a book and movie. However, detailed accounts of this and similar cases do clarify the dangers of what can happen when professional status, success, and company identity are defined by money, and money alone. In fact, experimental studies reveal that only making people think about money before they start to work on a task is sufficient to increase the number of individuals who cheat and results in higher levels of cheating on the task (Gino & Mogilner, 2014). When monetary outcomes are the only thing that matters, this invites moral disengagement, as moral concerns are made to seem irrelevant to the success of the organization and people in it. In Chap. 8 we consider how such moral neglect may come to define the ethical climate in the organization (see also Umphress & Bingham, 2011).

In sum, instead of revealing that people are 'naturally selfish' research evidence demonstrates how selfish behavior may result from the dedication to organizational goals. Organizations that recruit, reward, and promote people by emphasizing and relying on monetary gains and other personal rewards, unwittingly select, create, and retain employees who come to believe that displaying selfish behavior is the best way to show their loyalty and fit to the company.

4.1.2 Living in a Bubble: Protecting One's Distinct Identity

Some researchers note that low identification with the organization is a cause for concern, as this may tempt individuals to direct unethical or criminal behavior towards the organization itself (Vadera & Pratt, 2013). Indeed, this should be the greatest concern when unethical behavior stems from purely selfish motives. Here, we also note the dangers of high identification (already discussed in Chap. 2). Employees who identify most strongly with the organization are those most susceptible to the risk of uncritically going along with organizational guidelines. They will defend common professional practices even when this results in conduct that seems undesirable from a societal point of view. Sometimes, they are even actively groomed to do this. Isolating people from their former life and social interactions once they enter a particular profession or industry, also prevents them from questioning the appropriateness of its practices (see also Box 4.2: Living in a bubble).

Box 4.2: Living in a Bubble

In her book 'liquidated' anthropologist Karen Ho recounts her personal experiences working at a large Wall Street investment bank (Ho, 2009). Her story convincingly illustrates how these companies deliberately and carefully groom financial professionals, by seeking out high performing ivy league students on campus, and socializing them in the major financial companies.

Straight out of college, professionals in their early twenties are offered impossibly high rewards and career prospects that can set them up for life, in some of the most successful companies in the world. These privileges and high rewards place them in a bubble, which is reinforced in multiple ways. Young recruits are quickly taught what is a fitting way to speak, dress, and behave, and are expected to show extreme dedication to their work – under the implicit and sometimes very explicit threat of being laid off when they do not meet set standards. The side effect is that no time is left for socializing with family and friends, isolating these individuals from their former social network.

Only months after they graduate these young bankers end up in a world where they only interact with colleagues who experience the exact same situation. The sheer lack of interaction and knowledge of what life on the outside is like prevents them from testing their worldviews and experiences against those of people outside their network. This also discourages these young professionals from comparing their work conditions with those in other sectors, and quickly makes their high income, long working hours, and work ethics seem normal.

Similar observations have been recorded by Joris Luyendijk, a Dutch anthropologist who over a number of years interviewed professionals in finance working in the London City. In his book 'swimming with sharks' he notes how quickly individuals adapt to the social and ethical norms that characterize their work in these companies. His conclusion is that displays of selfishness and cynicism result from situational pressures instead of reflecting individual character flaws. In support, he records family members and partners noting the enormous changes their loved ones went through after they started to work in finance. For instance, in an interview about his book he recounts how a 'perfectly normal and friendly' individual changes into a ruthless professional as soon as she walks into the bank – aiming to fire people, with pregnant women going first (Luyendijk, 2015)

This is not to say that financial institutions only bring out the worst in people, or that they all fuel competitiveness and selfish behavior. In fact, after the financial crisis many financial institutions and their regulators have invested in emphasizing long term stability and the protection of client interests and other stakeholders (see also Chaps. 7 and 8). And, as we note throughout this book, similar issues have been identified in other sectors too. What these examples do show is when and how organizational and professional standards of acceptable behavior can overrule people's personal moral principles.

Such 'overcommitment' to the organization and its representatives can entice individuals to disregard the moral implications of their choices, causing them to engage in immoral or illegal behavior (Blader et al., 2017; Conroy et al., 2017). Professional identities and pro-organizational motives can drive this behavior, for instance when employees try to protect the organization's outcomes or reputation (Leavitt & Sluss, 2015), even when this implies condoning or participating in unethical or unlawful behavior (Pulfrey & Butera, 2013; Pulfrey et al., 2018; Umphress et al., 2010).

Likewise, people who identify strongly with a subgroup within their organization, (i.e., their work team or professional ingroup), are more prone to lie to protect the reputation of this group, and can damage the organization and its long term interests (Leavitt & Sluss, 2015). For instance, over-identifiers are likely to look the other way when supervisors display abusive behavior rather than challenging them (Decoster et al., 2013).

Such behavior can have far-reaching effects with life-and-death consequences, as was revealed in a study interviewing team members who were working on an urban infrastructure project. When the project team realized they were about to miss the deadline to deliver the tunnel that had to be completed, those who felt their professional identity was under threat were most inclined to be untruthful. In fact they collectively tried to hide unsuccessful – and even dangerous – results of tunnel repair works to avoid interference from others outside the project team (Van Os et al., 2015). A study of medical errors likewise revealed that physicians and nurses showed defensive responses prioritizing protection of their professional identity, instead of learning from errors made (Van Os et al., 2015). In both cases, obviously this would jeopardize the health and safety of citizens and patients relying on the quality of professional services provided.

Identifying strongly with one's work team or organization, and living in a bubble that emphasizes the distinct identity and professional norms of this group, are key social forces that can allow individuals to 'normalize' corruption (Ashforth & Anand, 2003). Indeed, viewing that someone cheated on an experimental task to gain a higher reward caused research participants to cheat as well, especially when the cheater was seen as an ingroup member (Gino et al., 2009). When such unethical behavior is seen as typical for the ingroup, displays of unethical behavior increase even further – as exemplified by the case of Stratton Oakmont (Box 4.1; O'Fallon & Butterfield, 2012).

Separating one's work identity (e.g., as a ruthless financial professional) from non-work identities (e.g., as a caring father), allows for moral disengagement from such questionable practices. In fact, when their non-work identities are salient (e.g., among friends) individuals may publicly support broadly shared social norms about the undesirability of corruption (for instance in sports competitions). However, when their work identity is salient these same individuals may rationalize their own behavior that would be characterized as corrupt according to broadly shared social norms (e.g., paying fees to intermediaries who allow them to do business abroad; Ashforth & Anand, 2003). Likewise, shifting loyalties and adherence to guidelines that define specific professional identities also allow employees to justify – even systematic – theft from their organization's resources. The same individuals who have no objection against the proverbial stealing of office supplies or coffee cups (downplaying their organizational identity) might never consider appropriating even the slightest possession owned by co-workers (because they highlight their team identity; see also Greenberg, 1990a). The general recommendation to admonish people to care for others as a way to prevent immoral behavior clearly would not be effective in this case. In fact, these examples show how extending care for others can become a source of corruption – with the mafia as the most well-known example.

Viewed from the outside, these behavioral shifts may seem irrational – apparently indicating a lack of consistent moral standards. To ingroup members, it can makes perfect sense. Citing team loyalties allows people to rationalize and explain their own behavior – to themselves as well as others (Ashforth & Anand, 2003). Thus, placing employees in a bubble may seem an innocent way to introduce them to professional norms and offer them a sense of belonging (see also Chap. 2). However, the danger is that this invites them to justify and accept displays of questionable behavior in themselves and others like them.

The identity threat of being confronted with external societal ethical standards that disapprove of one's professional behavior can be relieved in this way. Highlighting group norms and the desire to show group loyalty as legitimizing forces would attest to one's intentions to do what is morally right (Ashforth & Anand, 2003). Protecting one's work team or organization from such critique can also cause members of the organizations to see competitors, regulators, or other outsiders as enemies whose critical observations can only harm the organization (Campbell & Göritz, 2014). Experimental research reveals that people generally are less responsive to criticism about the moral behavior of their group when this is delivered by outgroup members rather than ingroup members (Esposo et al., 2013). For instance identical concerns about lack of diversity tolerance in Australia, were dismissed while the source of these messages was derogated when these were voiced by foreigners rather than fellow nationals (Hornsey & Imani, 2004). Likewise, when the Dutch were morally criticized for doing less well than the Germans in combating climate change, or welcoming migrants, they expressed annoyance and irritation at the Germans, instead of being motivated towards self-improvement (Taüber & Van Zomeren, 2013; see also Petriglieri, 2011, and Chap. 6).

In sum, as indicated in Chap. 2, when moral concerns are experienced as a threat to one's social identity, expression of such concerns can invite people to rationalize their immoral behavior instead of changing it (Ashforth & Anand, 2003; Shalvi et al., 2015; Shu et al., 2011). They may justify themselves by suggesting other people are more immoral than they are (Barkan et al., 2012), or even blame those who suffer from their behavior (Bandura, 1999), rather than considering how they might improve. Research evidence further suggests that people are less inclined to attend to or mentally encode the details of their errors and transgressions when these have moral implications – indicating moral neglect. This literally makes it more difficult for them to remember what they did wrong or how this came about, and makes it more likely they will make similar transgressions in future situations (Kouchaki & Gino, 2016).

4.1.3 Targets as Incentives: Irresistible Temptations

Targets and incentives are commonly used to direct the efforts of individual workers towards organizational goals, and can make them persist despite difficulties they encounter (Pinder, 1998; see also Ellemers et al., 2004). However, over the years, multiple scandals have come to light, in which such performance targets were seen to invite immoral acts, as employees felt compelled to do 'anything for success' (Box 4.3: The dangers of high performance targets). Research on corruption clearly supports the notion that situational factors – rather than individual shortcomings – are an important cause of such behavior (Ashforth & Anand, 2003; Coleman, 1988; Greve et al., 2010).

Box 4.3: The Dangers of High Performance Targets

Performance targets had led employees of the Commonwealth Bank of Australia to sell inappropriate credit card insurances to 64000 customers, a legal investigation revealed (Knaus, 2018). Formally, these customers were not eligible for the credit they received because they were unemployed at the time. Sales representatives of this biggest bank in the country also put other vulnerable customers at risk. For instance the performance incentives mortgage brokers received encouraged them to write large loans. While this inflated their volume-based commissions, it also unnecessarily increased monthly interest payments, putting customers at risk at being unable to pay off the loan (Hutchens & Knaus, 2018).

Similar problems came to light at Wells Fargo Bank in the United States. Here the slogan 'eight is great' symbolizes the performance target that was imposed on sales representatives and customer relations managers. This slogan was used to motivate employees to sell multiple (ideally eight) Wells Fargo products to their customers. Many of them, struggling to support a family on \$12 or \$15 an hour, saw no other option than complying with these performance demands to avoid being fired. Some worked off the clock to make their quotas, others cut corners, even if this didn't serve customer needs or was clearly inappropriate. Their efforts gained the bank millions of dollars in fees (An Examination of Wells Fargo's unauthorized account, 2016; McGrath, 2016).

When this practice was exposed, it turned out that employees had ordered credit cards for customers without their consent, created fraudulent deposit accounts, and kept on charging clients for these services even after they died. Furthermore, they forced unnecessary insurances on clients and created accounts for homeless people, just to satisfy performance quotas. Ultimately, Wells employees issued more than 500.000 unauthorized credit cards and opened more than 1.5 million unauthorized deposit accounts between 2011 to mid-2016 —possibly even going back to 2009. Although the high performance targets succeeded in influencing employee behaviors, the result was clearly undesirable.

Of course, leaders have an important role to play in this process, as they are the ones setting specific targets, and can punish or reward subordinates depending on their results (see also Chap. 3 and Box 3.3 On the folly of rewarding A while hoping for B). Further, leaders can either fuel or prevent the emergence of a competitive climate that is characterized by rivalry and performance pressures, regardless of the nature or content of targets that are set (see also Chap. 8). Indeed, in some of the cases documented here, the perverse effects of set targets apparently were fully taken into account when admonishing employees to do as they were told – regardless of whether this might harm their clients as well as themselves.

Notwithstanding these leadership influences, it is relevant to consider how the specification of performance targets in itself changes the way people view and interpret the situation, and can invite immoral behavior. This common practice used to motivate people in organizations is informed by insights revealing that setting specific goals allows people to focus their attention on what is relevant for these goals and can enhance their motivation to overcome difficulties in reaching them ('goal setting theory'; Latham & Pinder, 2005; Locke & Latham, 1984). Indeed, the performance gains of doing this have been well documented (for an overview, see Locke & Latham, 2002). However, setting high goals only enhances people's efforts when they think they will be able to improve their performance (see also Ouwerkerk et al., 2000). Further, the same mechanisms that allow people to focus on the achievement of set goals, also prompt them to neglect alternative concerns. Striving for success can even tempt them to ignore important guidelines they should take into account, for instance to guard their personal safety.

For instance, an experiment revealed that people were more inclined to lie about their performance when specific goals were set than when they were simply told to 'do their best' (Schweitzer et al., 2004). In fact, the temptation to overstate task achievements was particularly strong for those who had just missed their set targets. In this case, the impact of goal setting could be separated from the lure of monetary rewards. The researchers showed that untruthful performance statements were made irrespective of whether or not participants were promised a tangible reward for meeting set targets. Thus, the awareness of working towards a specific goal was sufficient to have this corrupting effect (Schweitzer et al., 2004).

Thus, as we have seen with the dark and bright sides of team and organizational identification, the benefit of goal setting – enhancing focus on a specific outcome as well as the motivation to realize it – may just as well introduce a pitfall at the same time. The psychological explanation for this is relatively straightforward, and in line with claims of goal setting theory. Because people's cognitive resources are limited, they may simply attend less to alternative concerns, such as the morality of their behavior, when completely focusing on reaching their goals (Barsky, 2008). Unfortunately, people are quite optimistic about their ability to focus on multiple concerns at the same time. Hence, failing to attend to important guidelines when focusing on specific performance goals represents a form of moral neglect that people usually don't anticipate (Ariely, 2013).

In addition to these cognitive effects, goal setting also introduces motivational concerns, relating to the desire to demonstrate the performance that is specified.

Meeting goals that are set allows individuals to reassure themselves and others that they are proper professionals and valid members of their team or organization. These social rewards invite individuals to prioritize goal achievement over alternative concerns that might call into question the morality of their choices and efforts. The fact that they do what is requested of them alleviates identity threat by justifying unethical practices, instead of challenging them (Bandura, 1999; Gino, 2015; Shalvi et al., 2015). Even when people are not aware this is what they are doing, evidence from multiple studies documents the pervasiveness of such situational effects. Merely imposing performance targets or setting achievement goals introduces small changes in the situation that prompt people to loosen their moral standards, and invites unethical behavior (Ordóñez & Welsh, 2015).

It is important to acknowledge these limits and unintended side effects of goal setting – as well as motivational practices relying on these insights. The research reviewed here clearly documents the possible downside associated with the cognitive and motivational effects of working towards set goals. Those who specify performance goals may hope to guard against detrimental effects by minding key boundary conditions and adhering to appropriate guidelines in defining what should be achieved. A popular approach for doing this is to make goals 'SMART' (Specific, Measurable, Attainable, Realistic and Time-specific). However, this crucially requires incorporating employee concerns and their estimated abilities to complete the task specified within the constraints provided – instead of simply imposing managerial ambitions, as often is the case (see also Haslam, 2004). Clearly, enforcing the achievement of unrealistically high targets by threatening to fire those who fail to meet them is a recipe for problems. In fact, imposing unattainable targets only raises stress and defeats its purpose by lowering performance (Huber, 1985). This practice actually neglects key insights of goal setting theory, which reveals that increased efforts and performance gains only emerge for goals that are challenging but realistic. When goals seem unattainable, people simply give up trying (Drach-Zahavy & Erez, 2002; Mikulincer, 1989) turn to less ambitious goals (Ilies & Judge, 2005), or – if the stakes are sufficiently high – do 'whatever it takes' to achieve the desired outcome, as we have seen above.

In many large organizations, performance targets and goal setting are connected to pay-for-performance plans. While these remain quite common, there is convincing evidence of their potentially negative consequences. First, focusing people on the achievement of extrinsic goals is based on agentic conceptions of human motivation (see Fig. 4.1), that are known to undermine intrinsic motivation to perform the task well (e.g., Pearce, 1987). Further, tying rewards to performance is easier for quantitative targets (e.g., sales volumes) than for qualitative performance aspects (e.g., quality of service). This pushes people towards greater efficiency in achieving what can be measured, even if this does not accurately capture the added value of their activities. Even artists, scientists, or doctors are expected to offer quantitative evidence to document their productivity, as a way to externally control and reward their performance. While this is intended to enhance efficiency and transparency, it actually causes widespread attempts to 'work the system' because stated guidelines do not capture the essence of their professional skill, added value, or intrinsic motivation to do a good job. Introducing rivalry by making such systems competitive, further raises envy that results in sabotage of co-workers and other forms of unethical behavior (Duffy et al., 2012; Ellemers, 2021; Kilduff et al., 2012). In fact, the agentic approach of such competitive systems makes people assume that others will cheat to get a higher reward, which tempts them to engage in cheating themselves (Tzini & Jain, 2018; see also the section on performance pressures in Chap. 8). Real life examples show that the common use of competitive pay-for-performance plans can have severe consequences, as it invites workers to take irresponsible risks with their own health and safety and jeopardize the lives of others (see Box 4.4: Uber-sensitivity to rewards).

Box 4.4: Uber-Sensitivity to Rewards

Accidents caused by Uber-drivers resulted in the deaths of three pedestrians, and one cyclist, and left a nine-year-old girl badly injured. This all happened in the city of Amsterdam, within a time span of less than 2 months. These events prompted the Dutch road safety organization to request a ban on Uber, for allowing young, inexperienced drivers with a recently acquired driving license to service clients (Challans, 2019).

Interviews with Uber drivers additionally revealed how company policies and performance incentives elicit reckless driving (Kruyswijk, 2019). With the low earnings offered, drivers frequently work for 60–70 h a week, often driving around 12 h on a single day. Of course this doesn't absolve drivers from their individual responsibility to drive safely – for their own benefit, as well as to protect customers and other road users. Yet it is clear that there are obvious risks associated with the reward system implemented by the Uber platform.

The competition for lucrative rides prompts drivers to monitor the uber-app closely. When a section on the map 'turns red', this indicates a 'surge' – the expectation that many cars are likely to be needed in that area on short notice. When a '2.0' appears, double rates apply. A '30+' promises a lucrative ride of 30 or more minutes. Each of these announcements invites the driver to speed towards the appointed place to avoid missing out on probably the most attractive rides of the day. These conditions are very different from the way regular taxi drivers work in Amsterdam. In taxi companies drivers have regulated shifts, make rides by prior bookings, pick up customers from specific addresses, or wait their turn at taxi stands.

Uber drivers admit they know what they do is potentially dangerous: "You are getting reckless"; "The night is the jungle. That's when you step on the gas". Moreover, when avoiding to speed causes the client to cancel the ride "you will get a bad track record", drivers fear. Despite all these perverse incentives, Uber deflects moral responsibility for the risky driving behavior it invites. The company emphasizes that Uber only provides an online platform for information sharing that drivers can join without being considered as company employees.

While maintaining the claim that the company cannot be held responsible, after the surge of accidents in Amsterdam Uber raised the minimum age of new drivers, and implemented additional requirements for driving experience and road safety training. In the media this was characterized as a 'quick fix' to relieve public pressure. Journalists emphasized that the root of the problem is not addressed: "that the conditions offered by Uber prompt too many (young) drivers chase too many (cheap) fares for too many hours" (Challans, 2019).

Having company leadership ignoring their role in the well-being and safety of Uber drivers amounts to moral neglect. Deflecting responsibility by pointing to their status as platform instead of an employer is as easy form of moral justification. Claiming to resolve the issue just by increasing the minimum requirements for drivers is a superficial response that qualifies as a form of moral cleansing. As long as Uber is unwilling to reconsider the potentially perverse impact of its incentive systems, moral improvement is not in sight.

Even valiant attempts to quantify and include more qualitative and fuzzy performance aspects in what is rewarded can do more harm than good. Again, this may only tempt organizations to equate qualitative judgments of creativity, novelty, or added value with the quantitative indicators that are available to them. Subjective judgments of quality are known to invite bias or even corruption, especially when stakes are high, as we know from sports (Maennig, 2005). Systematically taking such measures may actually defeat the purpose. For instance, bombarding customers with evaluation requests only raises annoyance and can even deter them from seeking repeat service. In general, such human judgments are less accurate than they seem, and known to be 'polluted' by peripheral and irrelevant concerns. For instance, quality of teaching is commonly assessed with quantitative student evaluations, and this can have far-reaching implications for teacher's monetary rewards and career prospects. Yet experiments show that an identical online teaching experience can be evaluated differently depending on irrelevant circumstances such as teacher gender (MacNell et al., 2015, see Chap. 5). For all these reasons, such performance plans rarely achieve what was intended while often enhancing immoral or illegal behavior out of frustration with the system (e.g., Stout, 2014).

All in all, the targets and incentives so commonly used to motivate people, prompt them to focus on the attainment of only those goals that are rewarded by the organization. Being subjected to such a system demonstrably alters the way people perceive the situation. This modifies their motivated efforts, even regardless of the rewards at stake. Research clearly reveals the hidden costs involved: Individuals are more likely to prioritize quantifiable, individual targets over other outcomes, and are tempted do anything for success. At the same time, their focus on target attainment causes them to lose sight of broader organizational and social concerns that define the moral implications of their behavior.

4.2 Analysis: The Hidden Costs of Ignoring Workplace Conduct

The appeal of goal setting, task design, and reward systems to foster employee motivation is conceivable: the organization can actually *do* something and thereby cause something to happen. It is based on cause-effect thinking that works too, as it does change employee responses, as we have seen in the prior section. Isn't this wat organizations are all about? Here we address the hidden costs of ignoring the way organization members are being treated in this process. Even if this invokes so called 'soft skills' and not so easy to pinpoint interaction styles, hard evidence attests to the profound effects of workplace conduct on the attitudes and behaviors of people in the organization. In fact, this speaks to another recurring theme in this book, namely that actions speak louder than words. As a result, there is little use in trying to motivate people towards more moral behavior while exposing them – or allowing them to be exposed – to unjust, disrespectful, or incivil workplace treatment (see also Fig. 4.2: Moral hazards of workplace conduct).

In this section, we build on theory and research separating different types of fairness and justice (Blader & Tyler, 2009; Greenberg, 1990a; Tyler, 2013; Tyler & Blader, 2003; see also Chap. 3; Fig. 3.2, Accepting procedures and outcomes). Common sense conceptions of justice tend to focus on the fair distribution of *outcomes*. Indeed, people tend to compare their own contributions and outcomes with the contributions of others. However, this doesn't necessarily imply that every organizational member is expected to receive equal benefits. Unequal outcome distributions may seem quite legitimate when these accurately represent different efforts and achievements, or accommodate different needs and limitations (cf. Adams, 1965). When comparing one's own contributions with those of others, it may seem quite fair that those who perform better receive higher pay. Judgments and concerns such as these – focusing on how fairly outcomes are distributed among members of the organization – speak to the experience of *distributive* justice.

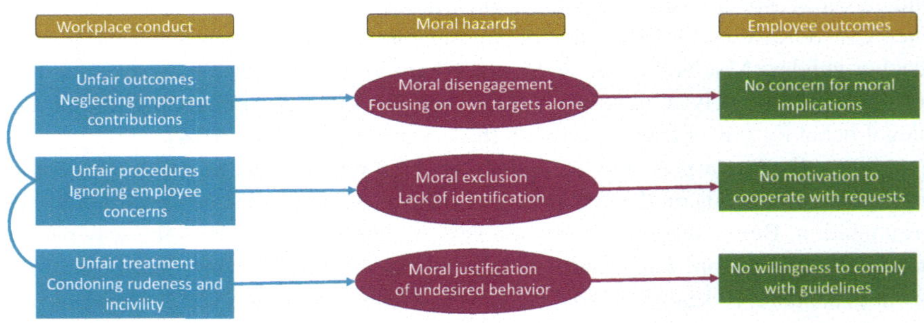

Fig. 4.2 The moral hazards of workplace conduct. Identifies how different forms of undesirable workplace conduct carry moral hazards, as these induce employee responses that can damage the organization

In addition, notions of fair treatment may incorporate the rules and procedures of the organization. Which standards are used to assign different outcomes to different people, who gets a say in this process, and how are final decisions made? Concerns that refer to the transparent establishment and fair execution of such procedures indicate the experience of *procedural* justice, that is relatively independent of the fairness of the distribution that results.

Finally, perceptions of *interactional* justice in the organization depend on the quality of the way individuals or groups are treated by relevant others in the organization, for instance the dignity and respect extended in verbal and non-verbal communications (for an overview see Rupp et al., 2017; Schermerhorn, 2013). All three forms of justice refer to subjective experiences and perceptions, instead of reflecting objective organizational features. This implies that some may react strongly to what they perceive as injustices, whereas others or outside observers could view the situation as completely fair. When (groups of) people disagree about the severity of perceived injustices, this makes it difficult to understand why others react so strongly 'over nothing' or, mutatis mutandis, why others remains passive despite 'obvious' unfairness. Such uncomfortable disagreements can be 'resolved' by deciding that those with diverging views represent an outgroup perspective that can be dismissed. This easily starts a cycle of derogatory attitudes and behaviors that results in moral neglect.

The distinction between these types of justice is relevant because each relates to specific attitudes and behaviors that impact moral behavior in organizations (Aquino, 1995). Extreme responses aiming to harm the organization, such as sabotage or other acts of retaliation and revenge, may only emerge when people feel all three justice principles have been violated (Ambrose et al., 2002; Skarlicki & Folger, 1997). In principle, positive procedural or interactional experiences (for instance at the team level) may help people cope with an unfair distribution of outcomes in the organization. In practice, however, allowing any of these forms of unfair treatment is socially costly and introduces moral hazards because they each contribute to different forms of non-compliance. Even when these remain unnoticed, such responses to experiences of unfairness can severely damage the outcomes or reputation of the organization. For instance, seemingly innocent practices such as 'cyberloafing' (personal use of email and the internet at work) can introduce digital security risks when people access sites that are not approved (Lim, 2002). Paradoxically, organizational attempts to invoke the three quick fixes to prevent unauthorized behaviors by blaming individuals, threatening with sanctions, or increasing regulation will backfire when these convey lack of trust and are seen as unfair instead of motivating employees to make moral choices.

4.2.1 Highlighting Individual Results Invites Moral Neglect

The key goal of organizations is to coordinate and combine the efforts of individual workers, in order to realize outcomes that could not be achieved otherwise. This core mission to facilitate interpersonal coordination in the collaboration of joint goals, is not well-aligned with attempts to offer fair distribution of rewards to individual employees. Working in teams on collective assignments makes it more difficult for individuals to display their added value, and makes it more challenging for others to adequately perceive and value their unique contributions. In retrospect, it may not be visible who suffered the transaction costs of coordination and balancing individual workloads, who reminded others of impending deadlines, who came up with an action plan or who made sure that interpersonal tensions did not escalate. More often than not, tasks and responsibilities such as these are not formally assigned or rewarded but taken for granted, yet these are crucial ingredients of collaborative success.

This is an important reason that many workers – like many students – dislike group assignments, as these make it possible for some to shirk their responsibility and benefit from the contributions of others. This phenomenon is known as 'social loafing': the reduction in motivation and effort when individuals work collectively compared with when they work individually or coactively pool their individual efforts (Karau & Williams, 1993; p. 681). The awareness that all team members are rewarded equally for joint outcomes, despite their diverging contributions, can indeed solicit such free rider behavior. The standard remedy is to make individuals accountable for their personal contribution, and sanction them if they defect from their duties (Tenbrunsel & Messick, 1999).

However, free riding is not a standard response to group assignments, and there may be quite legitimate reasons for team members to reduce or step up their contributions. For instance, those with less experience may refrain from speaking up because they feel they have little to contribute (Karau & Williams, 1993). Likewise, more experienced or highly competent individuals may increase their effort to get the task done, compensating for others especially when the task is meaningful to them (Williams & Karau, 1991). Further, displays of social loafing do not emerge as soon as people start working together in a group, but are most likely to arise over time, prompted by feelings of unfairness about decision-making processes that impact the group (Price et al., 2006).

Accordingly, simply increasing accountability for the achievement of individual results may do more harm than good. In fact, it only introduces further transaction costs in monitoring, comparing, and rewarding the performance of individual team members. At the same time, this undermines collective responsibilities instead of affirming them, and discourages individuals from supporting or helping each other (see also Ellemers et al., 2004). Indeed, this was found to be the case in a study conducted among employees of a large bank (Ellemers et al., 1998). Here, individuals who focused on how their efforts might contribute to their personal visibility and career development were most likely to abuse time and resources from the organization for their own purposes. By contrast, those who felt strongly committed to their team were more motivated to contribute to the team performance and actually were seen by their supervisors as investing more effort in doing this.

Thus, the main challenge in securing fair distribution of outcomes is whether such broader contributions to joint success are accurately specified, and rewarded.

Are those who achieve their targets before the deadline seen as more valuable than those who developed new solutions, or spent extra time on quality control? Are women naturally gifted to manage team relations, or do they invest additional effort doing this – and is this recognized and rewarded? What was the role of support staff: did they work overtime to secure timely completion, despite receiving their assignments too late? Unfortunately, such crucial investments and contributions to joint successes often remain unnoted. Making people accountable for their individual contributions alone may prevent free riding, but also reduces the likelihood that they are willing to make such broader investments helping each other to optimize team and organizational performance.

This asymmetry in how different efforts and contributions are accounted for and valued reflects a more general tendency in commercial enterprises and private companies as well as not-for-profit organizations, such as public service organizations and NGOs. The achievement of visible gains and positive outcomes is more often highlighted and rewarded than the prevention of problems and reduction of risks. Yet, both are crucial for long term success (Beudeker et al., 2013). Indeed, a recurring frustration of those charged with compliance issues or quality control is that the indispensability of their tasks and assignments only becomes visible when problems arise. More often than not, their crucial contributions remain unnoticed and undervalued, as their efforts made sure that 'nothing went wrong' (see also Chap. 6).

In sum, making people individually accountable for their contributions is a motivation strategy that is not morally neutral. It discourages individuals from feeling responsible for how their actions impact on others in their team or organization, resulting in moral neglect. Deferring rule compliance and quality control to the responsibility of specific officers, further allows individuals to take credit for visible successes without being forced to consider whether they actually realized these achievements on their own. Making people accountable for their own contributions alone neglects the possibility that their actions and choices also impact other people's options and outcomes. Limiting people's responsibility to their own tasks, without specifying or evaluating broader moral implications of their choices, presents a clear source of moral hazard.

4.2.2 Injustice Conveys Moral Exclusion

In Chap. 3 we have already noted that people might be quite willing to accept unequal outcomes, as long as the procedures and interactions leading to these outcomes are seen as fair and just (see Fig. 3.2). However, when people feel they are treated unfairly, they are tempted to even the balance by showing unfair behavior too. This was observed in a study where the organization was compelled to lower employee wages to deal with a temporary setback Greenberg (1990b). After employee wages were reduced, more goods disappeared from the organization's stocks, suffering from theft by employees. Apparently they saw this as fair compensation for their loss of income. However, this study also allowed for the rare opportunity to compare responses in three plants that implemented these changes differently. This revealed the strengths of procedural justice: at one of the plants personnel was carefully informed about the reasons for introducing a temporary change of rewards. This procedure largely prevented employees from appropriating organizational goods, even though they suffered the same wage cuts (Greenberg, 1990b).

When employees and their concerns are taken seriously before decisions that affect them are made, this contributes to a sense of fairness. Most people are sufficiently realistic to see that it is impossible to have exactly what they want, as decision makers have to contend with multiple concerns and wishes. Of course, it is impractical or even unrealistic to have all individual voices heard. Accordingly, people are quite willing to trust that fair decisions are made and are motivated to act accordingly, when they know that the interests of their group are represented and acknowledged (Terwel et al., 2010). Thus, faithful attempts to involve and include different constituents and perspectives, with efforts being made to explain why and how decisions were made, can instill a sense of procedural justice. This allows people to commit to the resulting guidelines and be motivated to follow them (Ståhl et al., 2008; Van Prooijen et al., 2005). However, many decision makers think this all takes too much time and will only complicate the decision process. Many of them too feel embarrassed to engage in a conversation that can only reveal the unfairness of decisions made. And of course there always are those who fail to consider others and their outcomes, because they just don't think or truly don't care.

Failing to engage in fair procedures by allowing people voice in decisions that affect them, introduces moral hazards as it makes people feel excluded and ignored. Not listening to their valid concerns, neglecting employee interests and perspectives, and not being bothered to carefully explain what was decided and why, all contribute to these feelings. Ignoring employee concerns may alleviate feelings of identity threat among decision makers, as they morally exclude them from fair treatment. To employees, however, this implicitly communicates the message that they are not seen as worthy of consideration and not particularly valued as members of the organization (Tyler, 2013; Tyler & Blader, 2003). Studies show the costs of moral exclusion by denying fair process to employees. The feelings of injustice that result have been found to reduce the motivation to perform well and invites misbehavior and retaliation (Skarlicki & Folger, 1997).

Experimental studies reveal the psychological mechanisms that are involved. A popular paradigm to examine this, uses a computer ball tossing game called 'cyberball', where animated figures pass the ball between them. In some conditions the research participant – who represents one of the players – never receives the ball. This has turned out to be a deeply aversive experience. Also in this virtual reality, and even after being made aware they are playing against the computer, the experience of being excluded and ignored causes social pain (Zadro et al., 2004). In fact, neuroimaging studies, used to capture brain activity during the task, revealed that the social exclusion experience activated the same brain areas that are known to be associated with the experience of physical pain (Eisenberger et al., 2003). A meta-analysis summarizing results of 120 cyberball studies confirmed that the impact of being excluded by others is large and robust, occurring irrespective of gender, age group or country of residence (Hartgerink et al., 2015).

The documented effects of such treatment go beyond experimental observations. In the workplace, social exclusion experiences that raise anxiety and physiological arousal are found to increase displays of unethical and selfish behavior (Kouchaki & Desai, 2015; Kouchaki & Wareham, 2015). Those who feel socially excluded decrease their identification with the organization, and reduce organizational citizenship behavior (Wu et al., 2016a). Not being acknowledged by supervisors also reduces employee creativity (Kwan et al., 2018) and invites counterproductive work behaviors that violate codes of conduct in the organization (Hitlan & Noel, 2009; see also Hitlan et al., 2006). Even anticipating that this may happen can promote unethical behavior, for instance when employees start awarding favors to others in their work team to make sure they are at least seen and included there (Thau et al., 2015).

4.2.3 Incivility Breeds Non-compliance

Rude behavior and incivility in interpersonal conduct expresses lack of interactional fairness. Verbal and nonverbal acts that are rude and condescending violate workplace norms of respectful interaction (Cortina et al., 2001; Ferris et al., 2017). This includes routine slights and indignities without overt malice, such as not using people's names, calling them stupid or dumb, teasing them inappropriately, or interrupting and silencing them. While these may appear mundane and even harmless experiences, an overview of 15 years of scientific research documents how severely this impacts on the well-being, motivation, and performance of many employees. Exposure to incivil workplace behavior has been found to distract people from task performance as it depletes mental, emotional, and social resources. It is a clear source of interpersonal injustice that causes distress and negative affect, and leads to emotional withdrawal (Cortina et al., 2017).

Studies reveal that almost all employees are exposed to such behavior (Pearson et al., 2005). A program spanning many years of research examining tens of thousands of workers in different job types and industries reported that 98% are routinely insulted, belittled or blamed for outcomes beyond their control. Half of those examined in 2011 said this happened at least once a week. Managers are estimated to spend more than ten per cent of their time in resolving conflicts that ensue (Porath & Pearson, 2013). Research clearly reveals 'the price of incivility', by showing that such behavior dramatically increases every negative employee behavior one can think of (Cortina et al., 2017; Pearson et al., 2000). Those who suffer rude treatment are unable to focus on their tasks or feel morally justified to refrain from trying to meet organizational expectations. Creativity, performance and team spirit decline, and a substantial proportion of employees examined indicates that they intentionally reduce the quality of their work. Some employees take out their frustrations on customers, but even if it is not directed towards them, customers turn away when they perceive that members of the organization behave rudely towards each other (Porath et al., 2011). Allowing employees to be exposed to such routine slights and indignities thus is very costly for organizations, and undermines more formal attempts intended to motivate employees towards rule adherence and moral behavior.

The drama is compounded because evidence suggests that employees who are most dedicated to the organization are the ones most affected by incivility. Highly committed and highly conscientious workers experience more negative affect, show higher rates of burnout and are more likely to leave the organization due to incivility (Kabat-Farr et al., 2016; Taylor et al., 2014). Incivility erodes trust in the organization, and elicits stress and role ambiguity (Hauge et al., 2011; Miner-Rubino & Reed, 2010), Thus, workplace incivility raises counterproductive work behavior, particularly among employees who are highly involved in their jobs (Welbourne & Sariol, 2017).

More severe and deliberate displays of interpersonal misbehavior, such as bullying and harassment in the workplace have similar effects even if these occur less frequently (Hershcovis, 2011). At the same time, research in different industries reveals that motivational systems characterized by performance rivalry and competition for insecure jobs frustrate people and contribute to the emergence of bullying and aggressive behavior in the workplace (De Cuyper et al., 2009; Fox & Spector, 1999). In fact, a business survey estimates that in the United States alone more than 60 million workers suffer or witness such obviously harmful behavior in their jobs (see also the section on abusive leadership in Chap. 3). Even if the damaging and performance degrading effects of these workplace aggressions should be clear, 70–75 per cent of employers deny, discount, or rationalize such behavior, and fail to take appropriate action (Namie, 2014, 2017). Research evidence suggests that such organizational conditions and passive leadership responses to misbehavior – communicating lack of interpersonal justice – contribute to further workplace aggression and acts of revenge, in a vicious circle of escalating incivility (Aquino et al., 2006; Hershcovis et al., 2007; Samnani & Singh, 2016).

In this section we have argued that the impact of motivation and reward systems will be limited, as long as employees are not treated fairly. Making people accountable for their own results only, ignoring their views and concerns in establishing rules and procedures, and allowing them to be treated rudely, all erode the motivation to do what is expected from them and invite unethical behavior. Current employment relations only contribute to such effects (see also Chap. 6). Routinely terminating contracts at the drop of a hat, even by email – escorting people outside the building with their boxed-up possessions within an hour – ever increasing efficiency pressures and relying on part-time employees, agency workers and zero-hour contract employees all communicate to employees that they are not very highly valued. This is an obvious source of identity threat that prevents them from engaging with the organization and its goals. Trying to improve moral behavior in organizations while ignoring workplace conduct is like trying to prevent theft by locking the front door, while keeping the back door wide open.

4.3 Solutions: Getting People to Do the Right Thing

In the previous section we have argued that experiencing unfair treatment discourages employees because this makes them feel excluded and devalued as members of the organization. This insight also reveals what can be done to motivate employees to comply with organizational guidelines.

Offering some variety and autonomy in daily tasks – instead of pushing for efficient goal achievement – has been found to reduce rule breaking (Derfler-Rozin et al., 2016). Affording respectful treatment and clarifying how they add value to the organization, further allows employees to feel worthy members of an organization they can be proud of (Blader & Yu, 2017). This contributes to the positive identity of employees, engaging them to work towards organizational goals and to comply with important regulations.

The pride and esteem that can be derived from the organization also depend on what the organization stands for (Foreman & Parent, 2008; Pratt & Foreman, 2000; Whetten, 2006). Here, organizational scientists distinguish the reputation of organizations in the eyes of outsiders from employee Perceptions of External organizational Prestige (PEP; Bergami & Bagozzi, 2000; Carmeli & Freund, 2002). Outsiders will tend consider product and service characteristics or economic success as appropriate indicators of the reputation of the organization. However, employees tend to highlight social and human factors as characterizing key aspects of the identity of the organization that determine its external prestige (Carmeli, 2005; Carmeli et al., 2006; see also Box 4.5: The New York Port Authority caring for the homeless). Further, the organizational prestige that is perceived by employees predicts their level of identification with the organization, and their willingness to engage with its goals (Smidts et al., 2001). Conversely, low levels of perceived organizational prestige relate to deviant workplace behavior. This was shown in a study in the hospitality industry examining employees at five-star hotels in Turkey, who were more inclined to steal or damage hotel property, arrange personal issues during work hours, or display inappropriate interpersonal conduct as they thought less favorably of the organization's external prestige (Tuna et al., 2016). Thus, the harmful effects of moral transgressions or inappropriate conduct in the organization on task motivation and rule compliance are compounded when this is seen to impact negatively on employee perceptions of external organizational prestige.

Box 4.5: New York Port Authority Caring for the Homeless
A classic study examining the New York Port Authority (NYPA; Dutton & Dukerich, 1991) reveals how an organization can be affected when its morality is suddenly questioned. The long term effort of the researchers to monitor the organization for many months clarified that strong employee identification with the organization can have positive as well as negative effects (cf. Conroy et al., 2017).

The researchers documented the changing perspectives on unsolicited problems the NYPA encountered with homeless people using the NYPA facilities. The strong identification of NYPA employees with their organization, caused them to go along with the organization's stance that the homeless created safety and hygiene risks for their clients. Employees executed company policy by chasing away homeless people who sought refuge at the NYPA facilities. With this response they behaved as good organizational citizens, accepting the justification that dealing with the homeless was not a task for the NYPA. When their actions raised criticism from news outlets reporting about NYPA's harsh treatment of the homeless, it represented a threat to their identity as members of the organization.

At first, employees tried to salvage the external prestige of their company by fending off responsibility. They highlighted that the organization's clients did not include the homeless, and emphasized that media representatives were outsiders who didn't understand this. Emphasizing the outgroup status of victims as well as critics of the company policy, made it easier to question their motives, and derogate their concerns as an identity management strategy (cf., Esposo et al., 2013; Petriglieri, 2011, see also Box 2.2). Excluding the needs of the homeless from their moral responsibility allowed employees to neglect their plight. However, as a long term strategy this proved ineffective.

Over time, these defensive responses to the critique leveled at their organization could not be maintained. Gradually, it became evident that simply chasing away the homeless from the NYPA facilities was not very effective: there was no other institution that addressed these problems, and nowhere else they could turn to. On a daily basis, employees were confronted with the fact that the organizational policy they supported was not very effective. They were criticized by outsiders, and felt ashamed of their role. Mounting concerns expressed in the media shifted the public perception of the issue. Despite the policy endorsed by the NYPA, the organization was now seen as being responsible for the problem, which was defined as a moral issue.

In the end, this prompted the NYPA to accept that action was needed. They initiated the provision of alternative shelters for the homeless, in cooperation with other institutions. The strong sense of identification that initially led employees to defend and execute the harsh policy, now caused them to support the organization in its opposite approach. While they first shunned responsibility for the outcomes of the homeless, they now took pride in the fact that the NYPA was able to 'get things done' when something had to be done and nobody was doing it. The burden of having the homeless rely on them was turned into a source of positive distinctiveness that was seen to restore the perceived external prestige of the organization they so strongly identified with. Once the organization had taken moral responsibility for addressing the issue, and was prepared to improve on initial solutions, this reinforced the sense of pride and identity of its employees.

This study not only offers an example of how 'easy' solutions to evade the problem (through moral exclusion or moral justification) only offer short-term relief and may even backfire. It also illustrates the benefits of policy changes that represent moral improvement – for employees and the organization.

Concerns about such reputational damages threaten the moral identity of the organization, often prompting efforts to justify or deny problems, instead of addressing them (see also Chap. 7). In fact, concerns about the moral appropriateness of intervening in problems are often cited as a reason not to address them. For instance, targets of incivility may be silenced by labeling their protests against rude treatment as lacking civility (Cortina et al., 2017). The desire to guard against inappropriate or unfounded accusations is often cited to discourage victims of harassment from filing formal complaints. Similar tactics – discrediting those who question organizational practices – are often used to suppress unpopular or minority opinions, even when these represent valid moral concerns (Cramwinckel et al., 2015; Shaw, 2015). This makes it unsafe to speak up about problems noticed or to express divergent views, suppressing diversity of thought and stifling innovation (Calabrese, 2015; Scott, 2015). Yet such defensive responses typically only offer temporary relief, or only make problems worse. As we will elaborate in Chap. 8, problems cannot be resolved before they are acknowledged and identified. Embracing the 'positive deviance' of individuals who show moral courage is a first step. Allowing them to act as pathbreakers and elevate others towards organizational moral improvement makes it possible for organizations to build a distinct and positive reputation in a competitive situation, and can be a source of organizational pride (Chang et al., 2015; see also Ellemers & Jetten, 2013).

4.3.1 Affirming Inclusion and Respect

In 2012, employees and their unions organized the longest strike since 1933 in The Netherlands. Across the country, cleaners were on strike, demanding a pay rise. Only when rubbish and dirt accumulated in offices, trains and streets, did people notice how important their work was. The banners the cleaners carried while walking the picket line revealed their frustration at being routinely ignored and devalued, and stated the root of their concerns: "we want respect" (Heijnen & Verdonschot, 2018).

Indeed, the need for respect is ubiquitous. Individuals want to feel accepted, valued, and well regarded by their group (Blader & Yu, 2017). Experiencing respect is an important predictor of positive behavior by group members. Group members who feel respected identify more strongly with their (in)group and are more likely to exert themselves to contribute to the group's performance (Sleebos et al., 2006a). This also occurs at the team level and can even have life-and-death consequences for the quality of their collaboration. This was established for instance in a study of the Dutch military on an international peace keeping mission. Professional soldiers in military teams who felt included and valued by their teammates reported a more positive team identity and were more willing to invest in their team. Further, teams where this was the case were rated more positively by their supervisor in terms of combat readiness (Ellemers et al., 2013).

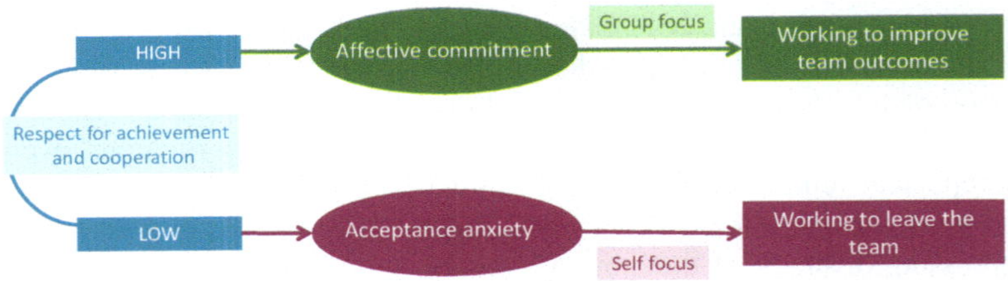

Fig. 4.3 Communicating (dis)respect. Summarizes results from a program of research showing how high vs low respect from other group or work team members elicits different emotional and behavioral responses. In both cases, people may display increased effort, but the nature and direction of these efforts only benefits the team when it is based on high respect. (Sleebos et al., 2006a, 2006b, 2007)

This may seem to contradict common views that offering people comfort and reassurance about their standing and inclusion can only make them lazy and complacent. Many people believe that making people insecure about their standing and inclusion will motivate them to prove themselves. However, these beliefs are unfounded. Results from research reveal that denying people respect mainly lowers their sense of belonging, and undermines their self-esteem. The lack of belonging that ensues is known to invite harmful instead of helpful interpersonal behavior (Thau et al., 2007) and can elicit aggression (DeBono & Muraven, 2014). It is true that lack of clarity about their position in the group can cause people to step up their efforts to show they are worthy members. However, when these efforts are not rewarded after an initiation or socialization phase, people typically give up or turn away from the group (Ellemers & Jetten, 2013). Indeed, while otuward displays of individual effort may appear quite similar, the psychological process underlying this behavior is very different for the respected and disrespected individuals (see Fig. 4.3: Communicating (dis)respect). Respected individuals exert themselves because they feel committed to the group and wish to contribute to group performance. However, those who are not respected focus on more selfish goals: they report low commitment and only invest in improving their opportunities to move away – in the hope of being valued elsewhere (Sleebos et al., 2006b). Thus, evidence from multiple studies suggests that the best way to engage and motivate employees is to affirm their inclusion as valued group members by affording them fair and respectful treatment.

4.3.2 *Confronting Misbehavior*

Obviously, we concur that the 'moral character' of individuals relates to their unethical behavior (Kim & Cohen, 2015). At the same time, it is known that permissive situations are more likely than personality characteristics to trigger immoral behavior in organizations, such as corruption (Coleman, 1988). Observing others in the organization is an important source of social learning. When someone suffers unfair or inappropriate treatment, this also impacts on their coworkers (Cortina et al., 2017; O'Reilly & Aquino, 2011). They may display performance loss, or 'payback' the perpetrator as they sympathize and identify with the targets of such behavior (Porath & Erez, 2009; Reich & Hershcovis, 2015; Wesselmann et al., 2009). For instance, permanent employees indicated being distressed because temporary workers were appointed to do identical jobs with a worse contract (Davis-Blake et al., 2003; Pearce, 1993).

When minor offenses and breaches of fair and civil conduct are not explicitly confronted or discouraged, this sets a standard where such behaviors are incorporated as acceptable or even distinctive forms of conduct for members of the organization (Ashforth & Anand, 2003). The larger the number of coworkers displaying such actions, the greater its impact on others who observe and 'learn' this is how to behave (Robinson et al., 2014). It is extremely difficult for individual employees, let alone for newcomers, to question the moral appropriateness of such behaviors. Before long, critics are seen as troublemakers who are out to discredit co-workers, and only threaten and undermine the positive identity of the organization in this way. Especially activists for change, who show moral courage by being the first to highlight the morally questionable nature of common practices, can count on derogatory responses from fellow ingroup members (for an overview, see Cramwinckel et al., 2015; see also Chap. 8, in the section on whistleblowers). The easiest response is for members of the organization to engage in some form of moral justification by creating a narrative that emphasizes the moral appropriateness of common forms of conduct in defense of such critique. However, addressing the identity threat experienced by re-directing their *thoughts* about current practices deters individuals from taking *action* towards moral improvement and further normalizes inappropriate conduct (Becker, 2012; see also Chap. 2).

The likelihood that such morally questionable norms develop is just as strong for employees of businesses as for public service organizations. Misplaced loyalty is known to perpetuate corruption in all manner of organizations, ranging from blatantly criminal organizations such as the mafia, and their vigorously enforced 'omerta' to those who should protect against such misbehavior, such as the police. Experimental studies have revealed that even honest people are tempted to benefit from the dishonesty of others in their team (Gross et al., 2018), and more easily lie to help others whom they see as having been treated unfairly (Leib et al., 2019). Indeed, processes such as these also explain the long standing persistence of misconduct and sexual abuse of children by priests of the Catholic church (see also Box 2.2). Especially those who identified strongly with the church were found to be skeptical about the accuracy of the experiences reported. They dealt with the identity threat they experienced by discrediting and derogating targets and witnesses of misbehavior, in spite of objective evidence suggesting high likelihood that their testimonies were truthful (Minto et al., 2016; see also Chap. 5). This is not surprising in view of our analysis of how people typically deal with threats to their moral identity.

Fortunately, observation and social learning works both ways. Observing moral behavior by others is likely to increase the observer's own moral behavior (Eskine et al., 2013; Van de Vyver & Abrams, 2015). Systematically exposing employees to courteous treatment when providing them feedback, specifying norms of acceptable and unacceptable interaction in the workplace, and even training people in displays of civility can all improve the quality of social interactions, and offer an anchor for appropriate behavior (Andersson & Pearson, 1999). Once it is clear what behavioral standards are, these are more likely to be maintained on the work floor. In fact, while people tend to perceive workplace gossip as undesirable work behavior that damages others, the threat of reputational damage and social exclusion also is a powerful tool work groups can use to exchange information about ambiguous situations and to keep norms of positive behavior (Beersma et al., 2019; Giardini & Wittek, 2019; see also Spears, 2021). Indeed, violations of group norms have been found to elicit gossip, motivated by prosocial concerns and the desire to protect the group (Beersma & Van Kleef, 2012; Feinberg et al., 2012). Accordingly, the threat of gossip has been found to induce people to share scarce resources, and to benefit cooperation (Piazza & Bering, 2008; Wu et al., 2016b). This can be an important way to redress unfair cooperation in work teams resulting from free riders who try to profit from the efforts of others. Indeed, research found that gossiping about free riders can help to secure that cooperation is maintained (Dores Cruz et al., 2019).

Norms for respectful treatment and civil conduct thus are set and maintained by valuing those who exemplify civil conduct and holding to account those who don't. Indeed, researchers found that people appreciate organizations that are responsive in appropriately dealing with harassment complaints – rather than dismissing these. In fact, such responsive action was found to alleviate concerns about the fact that misconduct occurred in the organization in the first place. This benefited the reputation of the organization almost to the same level as was found for an organization where no complaints about misconduct were made (Does et al., 2018). Thus, the cold feet many organizations have in confronting conduct issues – for fear or damaging their reputation by calling attention to such occurrences – are misplaced. Instead, exemplifying fairness, respect, civility and inclusion in employee treatment generally enhance employee motivation and benefit the moral choices they make (see also Chap. 8 on ethical work climates).

4.3.3 Taking Pride in Shared Moral Values

Organizations generally seem aware of the importance of communicating about shared values that indicate the broader purpose of their activities and define their common identity. However, in practice they don't seem to prioritize this. In 2016, a business survey conducted among thousands of employees and business leaders representing a broad range of industries in the US revealed a substantial gap between what motivates employees and what companies offer to them. Employees see the purpose of the organization as an important source of engagement and personal fulfillment that offers meaning to their daily activities, provides them with a sense of community, and energizes them to work towards company impact. Indeed, almost eighty percent of business leaders consider the purpose of the organization as a key contributor to its distinct reputation and commercial success. Ironically however, only about a third indicate they use this as a guideline in their decision making or even communicate about their purpose with employees. (PricewaterhouseCoopers, 2016).

The benefits of successfully defining and enacting shared organizational values are well-documented in the management literature. The highest performing and 'visionary' companies are those that build systems and develop practices to support employees in taking responsibility for acting in line with key organizational values. When company ideals allow people in the organization to know who they are and what they stand for this has been found to drive their efforts and benefits the long term success of the company – also financially (Collins & Porras, 1995, 1996). Indeed, studies find that employee well-being, motivation, productivity, and citizenship are more strongly related to everyday experiences indicating the meaning of their work than to the money they can earn (Grant & Berg, 2010; Parmar et al., 2019). These concerns are all the more important in times of crisis – such as the challenges faced by organizations during and after the COVID-19 pandemic. An examination of the impact of financial crisis of 2008 on the life choices of adolescents and young adults, revealed that the recession that followed only prompted them to be less focused on making money or buying things, while it increased their concern for non-material values such as wellbeing of others and the environment (Park et al., 2014). Of course, uncertainty about the continuity of one's job, for instance due to a merger or other enforced change, may lower identification with the organization and undermine cooperation (Lupina-Wegener et al., 2014; Van Vuuren et al., 2010). Yet having a strong identity and working towards shared values and ideals, while communicating truthfully about impending changes can offer a source of purpose and continuity that binds and motivates employees – despite such changes (Bartels et al., 2006; Bartels et al., 2009; Collins & Porras, 1995, 1996; see also Chap. 6).

The COVID-19 pandemic forced many organizations to redefine their meaning and function in society. A study examined this by asking almost 2000 CEOs of companies in different industries around the world to indicate the purpose of their business. In response to this question, three quarters offered some information about the nature of their products and services. However, 95 percent failed to indicate *why* their company offers these things, three quarters did not explain *how* they aimed to achieve key goals, and half did not specify *who* should benefit from their efforts (Michaelson et al., 2020). Not knowing why or for whom they are doing their job makes it difficult if not impossible for employees to be motivated. Not knowing how they are supposed to work makes it impossible to do this well or to define correct ethical conduct and appropriate moral choices in the workplace. This not only demotivates people but also undermines their sense of shared identity, prevents them from taking pride in their behavior, and invites anti-social behavior (Aquino & Douglas, 2003). Thus, clearly communicating about key values – as well as their concrete implications for everyday work practices – is essential. This can help maintain motivation and engagement even among employees who might lose their job due to changes faced by the organization (Gopinath & Becker, 2000).

Being able to take pride in key values and knowing why and for whom they are doing their work has been found to benefit even those working in jobs that seem quite unattractive to outsiders (Ashforth & Kreiner, 1999). Such 'dirty work' encompasses jobs involving activities that are physically, socially or morally tainted, such as garbage collector, shoe shiner, tabloid reporter or prostitute (cf., Hughes, 1951). While the people performing such jobs are generally aware of the stigma associated with their work, they still seem quite able to see this as a source of positive identity and moral value (Ashforth & Kreiner, 1999). Some people do this by pointing to jobs that are even worse ("boning in a slaughterhouse, now that really is an awful job"). However, mostly they do acknowledge negative aspects of their job but also creatively reframe and label their activities to define their identity in a positive sense. Tabloid reporters claim to help celebrities by providing them free publicity. Shoe shiners proudly tell how they offered the finishing touch that helped their clients get hired. Garbage collectors boast about keeping the streets free of vermin, and prostitutes explain how they combat loneliness and offer comfort to single men. By highlighting the nature of the problems they solve or calling out the beneficiaries of their services in this way, the key values and positive identity offered even by the most humble jobs can become a source of pride and motivation.

4.4 Conclusion: Working Towards a Common Purpose

Offering monetary rewards, providing people with a distinct professional identity, and setting performance targets are classical motivation techniques that have proven effects on behavior. Unfortunately, the behavior that ensues is not always what is expected and desired. Holding employees only accountable for their own performance tempts them to neglect the moral implications of their choices and discourages them from taking responsibility for broader organizational goals. Ignoring employee input and concerns excludes them from fair treatment and undermines cooperation with important guidelines. Condoning incivility in the workplace communicates lack of care for employee wellbeing and invites noncompliance. The risk that people lie, cheat, or sabotage the organization in retaliation is increased when they feel treated unfairly in multiple ways. Fortunately, research also shows that individual employees may be quite resilient to seemingly adverse jobs, work conditions and unpleasant social exchanges (for instance with customers). They can remain motivated and engaged to work towards organizational goals, as long as they feel respected as valued members of the organization, and can be proud of its mission and purpose.

The research reviewed here also makes clear that focusing organization members on their shared identity will not automatically resolve these problems. Despite all its positive consequences, there also is a downside. In extreme cases, team loyalty and organizational commitment can result in unproductive competition, lack of regard for important rules, or reluctance to share important information. Overcommitment to the achievement of organizational results can degenerate into extreme or even illegal actions that will actually damage the organization once discovered. In fact, a strong sense of shared identity can lead those within the organization to dismiss external critics who 'just don't understand', or to simply shrug away such moral concerns, as an identity management strategy. In sum, misplaced loyalty and over-commitment preclude a critical assessment of common organizational practices, allowing for the persistence of morally questionable behavior. If these practices continue to reward A while hoping for B, this is bound to be ineffective. Motivating employees to make moral choices is only possible when people who make such choices are respected and rewarded.

Recommended Reading

Conroy, S., Henle, C. A., Shore, L., & Stelman, S. (2017). Where there is light, there is dark: A review of the detrimental outcomes of high organizational identification. *Journal of Organizational Behavior, 38*(2), 184–203. https://doi.org/10.1002/job.2164

Cortina, L. M., Kabat-Farr, D., Magley, V. J., & Nelson, K. (2017). Researching rudeness: The past, present, and future of the science of incivility. *Journal of Occupational Health Psychology, 22*(3), 299–313.

Gino, F., Ayal, S., & Ariely, D. (2009). Contagion and differentiation in unethical behavior: The effect of one bad apple on the barrel. *Psychological Science, 20*(3), 393–398. https://doi.org/10.1111/j.1467-9280.2009.02306.x

Skarlicki, D. P., & Folger, R. (1997). Retaliation in the workplace: The roles of distributive, procedural, and interactional justice. *Journal of Applied Psychology, 82*(3), 434–443. https://doi.org/10.1037/0021-9010.82.3.434

Tyler, T. R. (2013). *Why people cooperate: The role of social motivations*. Princeton University Press.

References

Adams, J. S. (1965). Inequity in social exchange. In L. Berkowitz (Ed.), *Advances in experimental social psychology* (pp. 267–299). Academic. https://doi.org/10.1016/S0065-2601(08)60108-2

Allen, N. J., & Meyer, J. P. (1990). The measurement and antecedents of affective, continuance and normative commitment to the organization. *Journal of Occupational Psychology, 63*(1), 1–18. https://doi.org/10.1111/j.2044-8325.1990.tb00506.x

Ambrose, M. L., Seabright, M. A., & Schminke, M. (2002). Sabotage in the workplace: The role of organizational injustice. *Organizational Behavior and Human Decision Processes, 89*, 947–965. https://doi.org/10.1016/S0749-5978(02)00037-7

An Examination of Wells Fargo's unauthorized account and the regulatory response. (2016). *Relations* (Serial 114-510). U.S. Government Publishing Office, 114th Cong

Andersson, L. M., & Pearson, C. M. (1999). Tit for tat? The spiraling effect of incivility in the workplace. *Academy of Management Review, 24*, 452–471. https://doi.org/10.5465/amr.1999.2202131

Aquino, K. (1995). Relationships among pay inequity, perceptions of procedural justice, and organizational citizenship. *Employee Responsibilities and Rights Journal, 8*(1), 21–33. https://doi.org/10.1007/BF02621253

Aquino, K., & Douglas, S. (2003). Identity threat and antisocial behavior in organizations: The moderating effects of individual differences, aggressive modeling, and hierarchical status. *Organizational Behavior and Human Decision Processes, 90*(1), 195–208. https://doi.org/10.1016/S0749-5978(02)00517-4

Aquino, K., Tripp, T. M., & Bies, R. J. (2006). Getting even or moving on? Power, procedural justice, and types of offense as predictors of revenge, forgiveness, reconciliation, and avoidance in organizations. *Journal of Applied Psychology, 91*(3), 653. https://doi.org/10.1037/0021-9010.91.3.653

Ariely, D. (2013). *The honest truth about dishonesty: How we lie to everyone – Especially ourselves*. HarperCollins.

Ashforth, B. E., & Anand, V. (2003). The normalization of corruption in organizations. In R. M. Kramer & B. M. Staw (Eds.), *Research in organizational behavior: An annual series of analytical essays and critical reviews* (pp. 1–52). Elsevier Science Ltd.. https://doi.org/10.1016/S0191-3085(03)25001-2

Ashforth, B. E., & Kreiner, G. E. (1999). "How can you do it?": Dirty work and the challenge of constructing a positive identity. *Academy of Management Review, 24*(3), 413–434. https://doi.org/10.5465/amr.1999.2202129

Bandura, A. (1999). Moral disengagement in the perpetration of inhumanities. *Personality and Social Psychology Review, 3*(3), 193–209. https://doi.org/10.1207/s15327957pspr0303_3

Barkan, R., Ayal, S., Gino, F., & Ariely, D. (2012). The pot calling the kettle black: Distancing response to ethical dissonance. *Journal of Experimental Psychology: General, 141*(4), 757. https://doi.org/10.1037/a0027588

Barsky, A. (2008). Understanding the ethical cost of organizational goal-setting: A review and theory development. *Journal of Business Ethics, 81*(1), 63–81. https://doi.org/10.1007/s10551-007-9481-6

Bartels, J., Douwes, R., De Jong, M., & Pruyn, A. (2006). Organizational identification during a merger: Determinants of employees' expected identification with the new organization. *British Journal of Management, 17*(S1), S49–S67. https://doi.org/10.1111/j.1467-8551.2006.00478.x

Bartels, J., Pruyn, A., & De Jong, M. (2009). Employee identification before and after an internal merger: A longitudinal analysis. *Journal of Occupational and Organizational Psychology, 82*(1), 113–128. https://doi.org/10.1348/096317908X283770

Becker, J. C. (2012). The system-stabilizing role of identity management strategies: Social creativity can undermine collective action for social change. *Journal of Personality and Social Psychology, 103*(4), 647. https://doi.org/10.1037/a0029240

Beersma, B., & Van Kleef, G. A. (2012). Why people gossip: An empirical analysis of social motives, antecedents, and consequences. *Journal of Applied Social Psychology, 42*(11), 2640–2670. https://doi.org/10.1111/j.1559-1816.2012.00956.x

Beersma, B., Van Kleef, G. A., & Dijkstra, M. T. (2019). Antecedents and consequences of gossip in work groups. In F. Giardini & R. Wittek (Eds.), *The Oxford handbook of gossip and reputation* (pp. 417–434). Oxford University Press. https://doi.org/10.1093/oxfordhb/9780190494087.013.22

Belfort, J. (2007). *The wolf of wall street*. Bantam Books.

Bergami, M., & Bagozzi, R. P. (2000). Self-categorization, affective commitment and group self-esteem as distinct aspects of social identity in the organization. *British Journal of Social Psychology, 39*(4), 555–577. https://doi.org/10.1348/014466600164633

Beudeker, D., Rink, F., Ellemers, N., & Blonk, R. (2013). Initiatiefrijk en functie-inhoudelijk presteren. De regulatiestrategieën van leiders in relatie tot het functioneren van medewerkers. *Gedrag en Organisatie, 26*, 277–292.

Blader, S. L., & Tyler, T. R. (2009). Testing and extending the group engagement model: Linkages between social identity, procedural justice, economic outcomes, and extrarole behavior. *Journal of Applied Psychology, 94*(2), 445. https://doi.org/10.1037/a0013935

Blader, S. L., & Yu, S. (2017). Are status and respect different or two sides of the same coin? *Academy of Management Annals, 11*(2), 800–824. https://doi.org/10.5465/annals.2015.0150

Blader, S. L., Patil, S., & Packer, D. J. (2017). Organizational identification and workplace behavior: More than meets the eye. *Research in Organizational Behavior, 37*, 19–34. https://doi.org/10.1016/j.riob.2017.09.001

Calabrese, A. (2015). Liberalism's disease: Civility above justice. *European Journal of Communication, 30*, 539–553. https://doi.org/10.1177/0267323115595306

Campbell, J. L., & Göritz, A. S. (2014). Culture corrupts! A qualitative study of organizational culture in corrupt organizations. *Journal of Business Ethics, 120*(3), 291–311. https://doi.org/10.1007/s10551-013-1665-7

Careerbliss. (2018, April 27). Unhappiest jobs of 2018. *CareerBliss*. Retrieved from https://www.careerbliss.com/blog/the-careerbliss-happiest-and-unhappiest-jobs-of-2018/

Carmeli, A. (2005). The relationship between organizational culture and withdrawal intentions and behavior. *International Journal of Manpower, 26*(2), 177–196. https://doi.org/10.1108/01437720510597667

Carmeli, A., & Freund, A. (2002). The relationship between work and workplace attitudes and perceived external prestige. *Corporate Reputation Review, 5*(1), 51–68. https://doi.org/10.1057/palgrave.crr.1540164

Carmeli, A., Meitar, R., & Weisberg, J. (2006). Self-leadership skills and innovative behavior at work. *International Journal of Manpower, 27*(1). https://doi.org/10.1108/01437720610652853

Challans, K., (2019, January 23). *(Update) Uber-drivers in Amsterdam kill 4 road users in six weeks: Road safety organization demands Uber ban*. Retrieved from: https://www.taxiintelligence.com/update-uber-drivers-in-amsterdam-kill-4-road-users-in-six-weeks-road-safety-organization-demands-uber-ban/

Chang, J. W., Turan, N., & Chow, R. M. (2015). A desire for deviance: The influence of leader normativeness and inter-group competition on group member support. *Journal of Experimental Social Psychology, 56*, 36–49. https://doi.org/10.1016/j.jesp.2014.08.006

Coleman, J. S. (1988). Social capital in the creation of human capital. *American Journal of Sociology, 94*, S95–S120. https://doi.org/10.1086/228943

Collins, J. C., & Porras, J. I. (1995). Built to last. *Soundview Executive Book Summaries*, 17–12.

Collins, J. C., & Porras, J. I. (1996). Building your company's vision. *Harvard Business Review, 74*(5), 65.

Conroy, S., Henle, C. A., Shore, L., & Stelman, S. (2017). Where there is light, there is dark: A review of the detrimental outcomes of high organizational identification. *Journal of Organizational Behavior, 38*(2), 184–203. https://doi.org/10.1002/job.2164

Cortina, L. M., Magley, V. J., Williams, J. H., & Langhout, R. D. (2001). Incivility in the workplace: Incidence and impact. *Journal of Occupational Health Psychology, 6*(1), 64. https://doi.org/10.1037/1076-8998.6.1.64

Cortina, L. M., Kabat-Farr, D., Magley, V. J., & Nelson, K. (2017). Researching rudeness: The past, present, and future of the science of incivility. *Journal of Occupational Health Psychology, 22*(3), 299–313. https://doi.org/10.1037/ocp0000089

Cramwinckel, F. M., Van den Bos, K., & Van Dijk, E. (2015). Reactions to morally motivated deviance. *Current Opinion in Psychology, 6*, 150–156. https://doi.org/10.1016/j.copsyc.2015.08.007

Davis, J. H., Schoorman, F. D., & Donaldson, L. (1997). Toward a stewardship theory of management. *Academy of Management Review, 22*(1), 20–47. https://doi.org/10.5465/amr.1997.9707180258

Davis-Blake, A., Broschak, J. P., & George, E. (2003). Happy together? How using nonstandard workers affects exit, voice, and loyalty among standard employees. *Academy of Management Journal, 46*(4), 475–485. https://doi.org/10.2307/30040639

De Cuyper, N., Baillien, E., & De Witte, H. (2009). Job insecurity, perceived employability and targets' and perpetrators' experiences of workplace bullying. *Work & Stress, 23*(3), 206–224. https://doi.org/10.1080/02678370903257578

DeBono, A., & Muraven, M. (2014). Rejection perceptions: Feeling disrespected leads to greater aggression than feeling disliked. *Journal of Experimental Social Psychology, 55*, 43–52. https://doi.org/10.1016/j.jesp.2014.05.014

Decoster, S., Camps, J., Stouten, J., Vandevyvere, L., & Tripp, T. M. (2013). Standing by your organization: The impact of organizational identification and abusive supervision on followers' perceived cohesion and tendency to gossip. *Journal of Business Ethics, 118*(3), 623–634. https://doi.org/10.1007/s10551-012-1612-z

Derfler-Rozin, R., Moore, C., & Staats, B. R. (2016). Reducing organizational rule breaking through task variety: How task design supports deliberative thinking. *Organization Science, 27*(6), 1361–1379. https://doi.org/10.1287/orsc.2016.1094

Does, S., Gundemir, S., & Shih, M. (2018, June 11). *Research: How sexual harassment affects a company's public image.* Retrieved from https://hbr.org/2018/06/research-how-sexual-harassment-affects-a-companys-public-image

Dores Cruz, T. D., Beersma, B., Dijkstra, M., & Bechtoldt, M. N. (2019). The bright and dark side of gossip for cooperation in groups. *Frontiers in Psychology, 10*, 1374. https://doi.org/10.3389/fpsyg.2019.01374

Drach-Zahavy, A., & Erez, M. (2002). Challenge versus threat effects on the goal–performance relationship. *Organizational Behavior and Human Decision Processes, 88*(2), 667–682. https://doi.org/10.1016/S0749-5978(02)00004-3

Duffy, M. K., Scott, K. L., Shaw, J. D., Tepper, B. J., & Aquino, K. (2012). A social context model of envy and social undermining. *Academy of Management Journal, 55*, 643–666. https://doi.org/10.5465/amj.2009.0804

Dutch News. (2020, August 13). *2,500 potential investors are warned they are on boiler room 'sucker list'.* Retrieved from https://www.dutchnews.nl/news/2020/08/2500-potential-investors-are-warned-they-are-on-boiler-room-sucker-list/

Dutton, J. E., & Dukerich, J. M. (1991). Keeping an eye on the mirror: Image and identity in organizational adaptation. *Academy of Management Journal, 34*(3), 517–554. https://doi.org/10.2307/256405

Eisenberger, N. I., Lieberman, M. D., & Williams, K. D. (2003). Does rejection hurt? An fMRI study of social exclusion. *Science, 302*(5643), 290–292. https://doi.org/10.1126/science.1089134

Ellemers, N. (2021). Science as collaborative knowledge generation. *British Journal of Social Psychology, 60*(1), 1–28. https://doi.org/10.1111/bjso.12430

Ellemers, N., & Jetten, J. (2013). The many ways to be marginal in a group. *Personality and Social Psychology Review, 17*, 3–21. https://doi.org/10.1177/1088868312453086

Ellemers, N., De Gilder, D., & Van den Heuvel, H. (1998). Career-oriented versus team-oriented commitment and behavior at work. *Journal of Applied Psychology, 83*, 717–730. https://doi.org/10.1037/0021-9010.83.5.717

Ellemers, N., De Gilder, D., & Haslam, S. A. (2004). Motivating individuals and groups at work: A social identity perspective on leadership and group performance. *Academy of Management Review, 29*(3), 459–478. https://doi.org/10.5465/amr.2004.13670967

Ellemers, N., Sleebos, E., Stam, D., & De Gilder, D. (2013). Feeling included and valued: How perceived respect affects positive team identity and willingness to invest in the team. *British Journal of Management, 24*(1), 21–37. https://doi.org/10.1111/j.1467-8551.2011.00784.x

Eskine, K. J., Novreske, A., & Richards, M. (2013). Moral contagion effects in everyday interpersonal encounters. *Journal of Experimental Social Psychology, 49*(5), 947–950. https://doi.org/10.1016/j.jesp.2013.04.009

Esposo, S. R., Hornsey, M. J., & Spoor, J. R. (2013). Shooting the messenger: Outsiders critical of your group are rejected regardless of argument quality. *British Journal of Social Psychology, 52*(2), 386–395. https://doi.org/10.1111/bjso.12024

Feinberg, M., Willer, R., Stellar, J., & Keltner, D. (2012). The virtues of gossip: Reputational information sharing as prosocial behavior. *Journal of Personality and Social Psychology, 102*(5), 1015. https://doi.org/10.1037/a0026650

Ferris, D. L., Chen, M., & Lim, S. (2017). Comparing and contrasting workplace ostracism and incivility. *Annual Review of Organizational Psychology and Organizational Behavior, 4*, 315–338. https://doi.org/10.1146/annurev-orgpsych-032516-113223

Foreman, P. O., & Parent, M. M. (2008). The process of organizational identity construction in iterative organizations. *Corporate Reputation Review, 11*(3), 222–244. https://doi.org/10.1057/crr.2008.23

Fox, S., & Spector, P. E. (1999) A model of work frustration–aggression. *Journal of Organizational Behavior, 20*(6), 915–931. https://doi.org/10.1002/(SICI)1099-1379(199911)20:6<915::AID-JOB918>3.0.CO;2-6

Giardini, F., & Wittek, R. (2019). Gossip, reputation, and sustainable cooperation. In F. Giardini & R. Wittek (Eds.), *The Oxford handbook of gossip and reputation* (pp. 23–46). Oxford University Press. https://doi.org/10.1093/oxfordhb/9780190494087.013.2

Gino, F. (2015). Understanding ordinary unethical behavior: Why people who value morality act immorally. *Current Opinion in Behavioral Sciences, 3*, 107–111. https://doi.org/10.1016/j.cobeha.2015.03.001

Gino, F., & Mogilner, C. (2014). Time, money, and morality. *Psychological Science, 25*(2), 414–421. https://doi.org/10.1177/0956797613506438

Gino, F., Ayal, S., & Ariely, D. (2009). Contagion and differentiation in unethical behavior: The effect of one bad apple on the barrel. *Psychological Science, 20*(3), 393–398. https://doi.org/10.1111/j.1467-9280.2009.02306.x

Gopinath, C., & Becker, T. E. (2000). Communication, procedural justice, and employee attitudes: Relationships under conditions of divestiture. *Journal of Management, 26*(1), 63–83. https://doi.org/10.1177/014920630002600107

Grant, A. M., & Berg, J. (2010). Prosocial motivation at work: When, why, and how making a difference makes a difference. In K. Cameron & G. Spreitzer (Eds.), *The Oxford handbook of positive organizational scholarship* (pp. 28–44). Oxford University Press.

Gray, G. (2013, November 22). The wolf of wall street can't sleep. *New York*. Retrieved from https://nymag.com/news/features/jordan-belfort-2013-12/index1.html

Greenberg, J. (1990a). Organizational justice: Yesterday, today, and tomorrow. *Journal of Management, 16*(2), 399–432. https://doi.org/10.1177/014920639001600208

Greenberg, J. (1990b). Employee theft as a reaction to underpayment inequity: The hidden cost of pay cuts. *Journal of Applied Psychology, 75*(5), 561–568. https://doi.org/10.1037/0021-9010.75.5.561

Greve, H. R., Palmer, D., & Pozner, J. E. (2010). Organizations gone wild: The causes, processes, and consequences of organizational misconduct. *The Academy of Management Annals, 4*(1), 53–107. https://doi.org/10.5465/19416521003654186

Gross, J., Leib, M., Offerman, T., & Shalvi, S. (2018). Ethical free riding: When honest people find dishonest partners. *Psychological Science, 29*(12), 1956–1968. https://doi.org/10.1177/0956797618796480

Hartgerink, C. H., Van Beest, I., Wicherts, J. M., & Williams, K. D. (2015). The ordinal effects of ostracism: A meta-analysis of 120 Cyberball studies. *PLoS One, 10*(5), e0127002. https://doi.org/10.1371/journal.pone.0127002

Haslam, S. A. (2004). *Psychology in organizations: The social identity approach*. Sage.

Hauge, L. J., Skogstad, A., & Einarsen, S. (2011). Role stressors and exposure to workplace bullying: Causes or consequences of what and why? *European Journal of Work and Organizational Psychology, 20*(5), 610–630. https://doi.org/10.1080/1359432X.2010.482264

Heijnen, H., (Producer) & Verdonschot, L. (Director). (2018). *2Doc: Het Schoonmakersparlement* [Documentary]. Netherlands: BNN-VARA

Hershcovis, M. S. (2011). "Incivility, social undermining, bullying… oh my!": A call to reconcile constructs within workplace aggression research. *Journal of Organizational Behavior, 32*(3), 499–519. https://doi.org/10.1002/job.689

Hershcovis, M. S., Turner, N., Barling, J., Arnold, K. A., Dupré, K. E., Inness, M., & Sivanathan, N. (2007). Predicting workplace aggression: A meta-analysis. *Journal of Applied Psychology, 92*(1), 228. https://doi.org/10.1037/0021-9010.92.1.228

Hitlan, R. T., & Noel, J. (2009). The influence of workplace exclusion and personality on counterproductive work behaviours: An interactionist perspective. *European Journal of Work and Organizational Psychology, 18*(4), 477–502. https://doi.org/10.1080/13594320903025028

Hitlan, R. T., Kelly, K. M., Schepman, S., Schneider, K. T., & Zárate, M. A. (2006). Language exclusion and the consequences of perceived ostracism in the workplace. *Group Dynamics: Theory, Research, and Practice, 10*(1), 56. https://doi.org/10.1037/1089-2699.10.1.56
Ho, K. (2009). *Liquidated: An ethnography of wall street.* Duke University Press. https://doi.org/10.1215/9780822391371
Hornsey, M. J., & Imani, A. (2004). Criticizing groups from the inside and the outside: An identity perspective on the intergroup sensitivity effect. *Personality and Social Psychology Bulletin, 30*(3), 365–383. https://doi.org/10.1177/0146167203261295
Huber, V. L. (1985). Effects of task difficulty, goal setting, and strategy on performance of a heuristic task. *Journal of Applied Psychology, 70*(3), 492–504. https://doi.org/10.1037/0021-9010.70.3.492
Hughes, E. C. (1951). Work and the self. In I. J. H. Rohrer & M. Sherif (Eds.), *Social psychology at the crossroads: The University of Oklahoma lectures in social psychology* (pp. 313–323).
Hutchens, G., & Knaus, C. (2018, November 19). CBA admits wrongly selling insurance to 60,000 unemployed customers. *The Guardian.* Retrieved from https://www.theguardian.com/australia-news/2018/nov/19/cba-admits-wrongly-selling-insurance-to-60000-unemployed-customers
IBM Corporation & Globoforce Limited. (2017). The Employee Experience Index around the globe: How countries measure up and create human workplaces. *IBM Corporation & Globoforce Limited.* Retrieved from http://www.globoforce.com/wp-content/uploads/2017/09/The-Employee-Experience-Index-Around-the-Globe.pdf
Ilies, R., & Judge, T. A. (2005). Goal regulation across time: The effects of feedback and affect. *Journal of Applied Psychology, 90*(3), 453. https://doi.org/10.1037/0021-9010.90.3.453
Kabat-Farr, D., Cortina, L. M., & Marchiondo, L. A. (2016). The emotional aftermath of incivility: Anger, guilt, and the role of organizational commitment. *International Journal of Stress Management, 25*(2), 109.
Karau, S. J., & Williams, K. D. (1993). Social loafing: A meta-analytic review and theoretical integration. *Journal of Personality and Social Psychology, 65*(4), 681. https://doi.org/10.1037/0022-3514.65.4.681
Kilduff, G., Galinsky, A. D., Gallo, E., & Reade, J. J. (2012, June). Whatever it takes: Rivalry and unethical behavior. In *Intl. Association for Conflict Management, IACM 25th Annual Conference*. IACM 25th Annual Conference, Spier, South-Africa. https://doi.org/10.2139/ssrn.2084845
Kim, Y., & Cohen, T. R. (2015). Moral character and workplace deviance: Recent research and current trends. *Current Opinion in Psychology, 6*, 134–138. https://doi.org/10.1016/j.copsyc.2015.08.002
Knaus, C. (2018, November 19). CBA chief struggles to explain 'significant failings' of insurance products – as it happened. *The Guardian.* Retrieved from https://www.theguardian.com/australia-news/live/2018/nov/19/banking-chiefs-face-royal-commission-commonwealth-live
Kouchaki, M., & Desai, S. D. (2015). Anxious, threatened, and also unethical: How anxiety makes individuals feel threatened and commit unethical acts. *Journal of Applied Psychology, 100*(2), 360–375. https://doi.org/10.1037/a0037796
Kouchaki, M., & Gino, F. (2016). Memories of unethical actions become obfuscated over time. *Proceedings of the National Academy of Sciences., 113*(22), 6166–6171. https://doi.org/10.1073/pnas.1523586113
Kouchaki, M., & Wareham, J. (2015). Excluded and behaving unethically: Social exclusion, physiological responses, and unethical behavior. *Journal of Applied Psychology, 100*(2), 547. https://doi.org/10.1037/a0038034
Kruyswijk, M. (2019, January 19). Drie Uberchauffeurs over overuren en ongelukken. *Het Parool.* Retrieved from: https://www.parool.nl/nieuws/drie-uberchauffeurs-over-overuren-en-ongelukken~b81f0559/
Kwan, H. K., Zhang, X., Liu, J., & Lee, C. (2018). Workplace ostracism and employee creativity: An integrative approach incorporating pragmatic and engagement roles. *Journal of Applied Psychology, 103*(12), 1358. https://doi.org/10.1037/apl0000320

Latham, G. P., & Pinder, C. C. (2005). Work motivation theory and research at the dawn of the twenty-first century. *Annual Review Psychology, 56*, 485–516. https://doi.org/10.1146/annurev.psych.55.090902.142105

Leavitt, K., & Sluss, D. M. (2015). Lying for who we are: An identity-based model of workplace dishonesty. *Academy of Management Review, 40*, 587–610. https://doi.org/10.5465/amr.2013.0167

Leib, M., Moran, S., & Shalvi, S. (2019). Dishonest helping and harming after (un) fair treatment. *Judgment and Decision making, 14*(4), 423–439.

Leonard, T. (2008. February 25). Jordan Belfort: Confessions of the Wolf of Wall Street. *The Daily Telegraph*. Retrieved from https://www.telegraph.co.uk/news/features/3635727/Jordan-Belfort-Confessions-of-the-Wolf-of-Wall-Street.html

Lim, V. K. (2002). The IT way of loafing on the job: Cyberloafing, neutralizing and organizational justice. *Journal of Organizational Behavior: The International Journal of Industrial, Occupational and Organizational Psychology and Behavior, 23*(5), 675–694. https://doi.org/10.1002/job.161

Locke, E. A., & Latham, G. P. (1984). *Goal setting: A motivational technique that works*. Prentice Hall.

Locke, E. A., & Latham, G. P. (2002). Building a practically useful theory of goal setting and task motivation: A 35-year odyssey. *American Psychologist, 57*(9), 705. https://doi.org/10.1037/0003-066X.57.9.705

Lupina-Wegener, A., Drzensky, F., Ullrich, J., & Van Dick, R. (2014). Focusing on the bright tomorrow? A longitudinal study of organizational identification and projected continuity in a corporate merger. *British Journal of Social Psychology, 53*(4), 752–772. https://doi.org/10.1111/bjso.12056

Luyendijk, J. (2015). *Swimming with sharks: My journey into the world of the bankers* (Vol. 4). Guardian Faber Publishing.

MacNell, L., Driscoll, A., & Hunt, A. N. (2015). What's in a name: Exposing gender bias in student ratings of teaching. *Innovative Higher Education, 40*(4), 291–303. https://doi.org/10.1007/s10755-014-9313-4

Maennig, W. (2005). Corruption in international sports and sport management: Forms, tendencies, extent and countermeasures. *European Sport Management Quartely, 5*(2), 187–225. https://doi.org/10.1080/16184740500188821

Mathieu, J. E., & Zajac, D. M. (1990). A review and meta-analysis of the antecedents, correlates, and consequences of organizational commitment. *Psychological Bulletin, 108*(2), 171. https://doi.org/10.1037/0033-2909.108.2.171

McGrath, M. (2016, September 23). How the Wells Fargo phony account scandal sunk John Stumpf. *Forbes*. Retrieved from https://www.forbes.com/sites/maggiemcgrath/2016/09/23/the-9-most-important-things-you-need-to-know-about-the-well-fargo-fiasco/?sh=17b2e703bdc4

Michaelson, C., Lepisto, D. A., & Pratt, M. G. (2020). *Why corporate purpose statements often miss their mark*. Strategy + Business. Retrieved from https://www.strategy-business.com/article/Why-corporate-purpose-statements-often-miss-their-mark?gko=e6d01

Mikulincer, M. (1989). Cognitive interference and learned helplessness: The effects of off-task cognitions on performance following unsolvable problems. *Journal of Personality and Social Psychology, 57*(1), 129. https://doi.org/10.1037/0022-3514.57.1.129

Miner-Rubino, K., & Reed, W. D. (2010). Testing a moderated mediational model of workgroup incivility: The roles of organizational trust and group regard. *Journal of Applied Social Psychology, 40*, 3148–3168. https://doi.org/10.1111/j.1559-1816.2010.00695.x

Minto, K., Hornsey, M. J., Gillespie, N., Healy, K., & Jetten, J. (2016). A social identity approach to understanding responses to child sexual abuse allegations. *PLoS One, 11*(4), 1–15. https://doi.org/10.1371/journal.pone.0153205

Namie, G. (2014). *2014 WBI U.S. workplace bullying survey*. Workplace Bullying Institute. Retrieved from https://workplacebullying.org/research-wbi/

Namie, G. (2017). *2017 WBI U.S. workplace bullying survey*. Workplace Bullying Institute. Retrieved from https://workplacebullying.org/research-wbi/

O'Fallon, M. J., & Butterfield, K. D. (2012). The influence of unethical peer behavior on observers' unethical behavior: A social cognitive perspective. *Journal of Business Ethics, 109*(2), 117–131. https://doi.org/10.1007/s10551-011-1111-7

O'Reilly, J., & Aquino, K. (2011). A model of third parties' morally motivated responses to mistreatment in organizations. *Academy of Management Review, 36*(3), 526–543. https://doi.org/10.5465/AMR.2011.61031810

Ordóñez, L. D., & Welsh, D. T. (2015). Immoral goals: How goal setting may lead to unethical behavior. *Current Opinion in Psychology, 6*, 93–96. https://doi.org/10.1016/j.copsyc.2015.06.001

Ouwerkerk, J. W., De Gilder, D., & De Vries, N. K. (2000). When the going gets tough, the tough get going: Social identification and individual effort in intergroup competition. *Personality and Social Psychology Bulletin, 26*(12), 1550–1559. https://doi.org/10.1177/01461672002612009

Park, H., Twenge, J. M., & Greenfield, P. M. (2014). The great recession: Implications for adolescent values and behavior. *Social Psychological and Personality Science, 5*(3), 310–318. https://doi.org/10.1177/1948550613495419

Parmar, B. L., Keevil, A., & Wicks, A. C. (2019). People and profits: The impact of corporate objectives on employees' need satisfaction at work. *Journal of Business Ethics, 154*(1), 13–33. https://doi.org/10.1007/s10551-017-3487-5

Pearce, J. L. (1987). Making sense of volunteer motivation: The sufficiency of justification hypothesis. In R. M. Steers & L. W. Porter (Eds.), *Motivation and work behavior* (pp. 545–554). Prentice Hall.

Pearce, J. L. (1993). Toward an organizational behavior of contract laborers: Their psychological involvement and effects on employee co-workers. *Academy of Management Journal, 36*, 1082–1096. https://doi.org/10.5465/256646

Pearson, C. M., Andersson, L. M., & Porath, C. L. (2000). Assessing and attacking workplace incivility. *Organizational Dynamics, 29*(2), 123–137. https://doi.org/10.1016/S0090-2616(00)00019-X

Pearson, C. M., Andersson, L. M., & Porath, C. L. (2005). On the nature, consequences and remedies of workplace incivility: No time for "nice"? Think again. *Academy of Management Review, 19*(1), 7–18. https://doi.org/10.5465/ame.2005.15841946

Petriglieri, J. L. (2011). Under threat: Responses to and the consequences of threats to individuals' identities. *Academy of Management Review, 36*(4), 641–662. https://doi.org/10.5465/AMR.2011.65554645

Piazza, J., & Bering, J. M. (2008). Concerns about reputation via gossip promote generous allocations in an economic game. *Evolution and Human Behavior, 29*(3), 172–178. https://doi.org/10.1016/j.evolhumbehav.2007.12.002

Pinder, C. C. (1998). *Work motivation in organizational behavior*. Prentice-Hall.

Porath, C. L., & Erez, A. (2009). Overlooked but not untouched: How rudeness reduces onlookers' performance on routine and creative tasks. *Organizational Behavior and Human Decision Processes, 109*(1), 29–44. https://doi.org/10.1016/j.obhdp.2009.01.003

Porath, C., & Pearson, C. (2013). The price of incivility. *Harvard Business Review, 91*(1–2), 114–121.

Porath, C., MacInnis, D., & Folkes, V. S. (2011). It's unfair: Why customers who merely observe an uncivil employee abandon the company. *Journal of Service Research, 14*(3), 302–317. https://doi.org/10.1177/1094670511404393

Pratt, M. G., & Foreman, P. O. (2000). The beauty of and barriers to organizational theories of identity. *Academy of Management Review, 25*(1), 141–143. https://doi.org/10.5465/amr.2000.27711650

Price, K. H., Harrison, D. A., & Gavin, J. H. (2006). Withholding inputs in team contexts: Member composition, interaction processes, evaluation structure, and social loafing. *Journal of Applied Psychology, 91*(6), 1375. https://doi.org/10.1037/0021-9010.91.6.1375

PricewaterhouseCoopers. (2016). Putting purpose to work: A study of purpose in the workplace. *PricewaterhouseCoopers*. Retrieved from https://www.pwc.com/us/en/about-us/corporate-responsibility/assets/pwc-putting-purpose-to-work-purpose-survey-report.pdf

Pulfrey, C., & Butera, F. (2013). Why neoliberal values of self-enhancement lead to cheating in higher education: A motivational account. *Psychological Science, 24*(11), 2153–2162. https://doi.org/10.1177/0956797613487221

Pulfrey, C., Durussel, K., & Butera, F. (2018). The good cheat: Benevolence and the justification of collective cheating. *Journal of Educational Psychology, 110*(6), 764–784. https://doi.org/10.1037/edu0000247

Reich, T. C., & Hershcovis, M. S. (2015). Observing workplace incivility. *Journal of Applied Psychology, 100*(1), 203. https://doi.org/10.1037/a0036464

Robinson, S. L., Wang, W., & Kiewitz, C. (2014). Coworkers behaving badly: The impact of coworker deviant behavior upon individual employees. *Annual Review of Organizational Psychology and Organizational Behavior, 1*, 123–143. https://doi.org/10.1146/annurev-orgpsych-031413-091225

Rupp, D. E., Shapiro, D. L., Folger, R., Skarlicki, D. P., & Shao, R. (2017). A critical analysis of the conceptualization and measurement of organizational justice: Is it time for reassessment? *Academy of Management Annals, 11*(2), 919–959. https://doi.org/10.5465/annals.2014.0051

Samnani, A. K., & Singh, P. (2016). Workplace bullying: Considering the interaction between individual and work environment. *Journal of Business Ethics, 139*(3), 537–549. https://doi.org/10.1007/s10551-015-2553-x

Schermerhorn, J. R. (2013). *Exploring management*. John Wiley & Sons.

Schweitzer, M. E., Ordóñez, L., & Douma, B. (2004). Goal setting as a motivator of unethical behavior. *Academy of Management Journal, 47*(3), 422–432. https://doi.org/10.2307/20159591

Scott, J. W. (2015). The new thought police: Why are campus administrators invoking civility to silence critical speech? *The Nation*. https://www.thenation.com/article/new-thought-police/

Shalvi, S., Gino, F., Barkan, R., & Ayal, S. (2015). Self-serving justifications: Doing wrong and feeling moral. *Current Directions in Psychological Science, 24*(2), 125–130. https://doi.org/10.1177/0963721414553264

Shaw, J. D. (2015). Pay dispersion, sorting, and organizational performance. *Academy of Management Discoveries, 1*(2), 165–179. https://doi.org/10.5465/amd.2014.0045

Shu, L. L., Gino, F., & Bazerman, M. H. (2011). Dishonest deed, clear conscience: When cheating leads to moral disengagement and motivated forgetting. *Personality and Social Psychology Bulletin, 37*(3), 330–349. https://doi.org/10.1177/0146167211398138

Skarlicki, D. P., & Folger, R. (1997). Retaliation in the workplace: The roles of distributive, procedural, and interactional justice. *Journal of Applied Psychology, 82*(3), 434–443. https://doi.org/10.1037/0021-9010.82.3.434

Sleebos, E., Ellemers, N., & De Gilder, D. (2006a). The carrot and the stick: Affective commitment and acceptance anxiety as motives for discretionary group efforts by respected and disrespected group members. *Personality and Social Psychology Bulletin, 32*(2), 244–255. https://doi.org/10.1177/0146167205282147

Sleebos, E., Ellemers, N., & De Gilder, D. (2006b). The paradox of the disrespected: Disrespected group members' engagement in group-serving efforts. *Journal of Experimental Social Psychology, 42*(4), 413–427. https://doi.org/10.1016/j.jesp.2005.06.002

Sleebos, E., Ellemers, N., & De Gilder, D. (2007). Explaining the motivational forces of (dis)Respect: How self-focused and group-focused concerns can result in the display of group-serving efforts. *Gruppe. Interaktion. Organisation. Zeitschrift Für Angewandte Organisationspsychologie (GIO), 38*(3), 327–342. https://doi.org/10.1007/s11612-007-0028-1

Smidts, A., Pruyn, A. T. H., & Van Riel, C. B. (2001). The impact of employee communication and perceived external prestige on organizational identification. *Academy of Management Journal, 44*(5), 1051–1062. https://doi.org/10.5465/3069448

Solomon, B. (2013, December 28). Meet the real 'Wolf of Wall Street' in Forbes' original takedown of Jordan Belfort. *Forbes*. Retrieved from https://www.forbes.com/sites/briansolomon/2013/12/28/meet-the-real-wolf-of-wall-street-in-forbes-original-takedown-of-jordan-belfort/?sh=346d56c15e06

Spears, R. (2021). Social influence and group identity. *Annual Review of Psychology, 72*, 367–390. https://doi.org/10.1146/annurev-psych-070620-111818

Ståhl, T., Vermunt, R., & Ellemers, N. (2008). Reactions to outgroup authorities' decisions: The role of expected bias, procedural fairness and outcome favorability. *Group Processes & Intergroup Relations, 11*(3), 281–299. https://doi.org/10.1177/1368430208090643

Stout, L. A. (2014). Killing conscience: The unintended behavioral consequences of 'pay for performance'. *Journal of Corporation Law, 39*, 525–546.

Taüber, S., & Van Zomeren, M. (2013). Outrage towards whom? Threats to moral group status impede striving to improve via out-group-directed outrage. *European Journal of Social Psychology, 43*(2), 149–159. https://doi.org/10.1002/ejsp.1930

Taylor, S. G., Bedeian, A. G., Cole, M. S., & Zhang, Z. (2014). Developing and testing a dynamic model of workplace incivility change. *Journal of Management, 43*(3), 645–670. https://doi.org/10.1177/0149206314535432

Tenbrunsel, A. E., & Messick, D. M. (1999). Sanctioning systems, decision frames, and cooperation. *Administrative Science Quarterly, 44*(4), 684–707. https://doi.org/10.2307/2667052

Terwel, B. W., Harinck, F., Ellemers, N., & Daamen, D. D. (2010). How organizational motives and communications affect public trust in organizations: The case of carbon dioxide capture and storage. *Journal of Environmental Psychology, 29*(2), 290–299. https://doi.org/10.1016/j.jenvp.2008.11.004

Thau, S., Aquino, K., & Poortvliet, P. M. (2007). Self-defeating behaviors in organizations: The relationship between thwarted belonging and interpersonal work behaviors. *Journal of Applied Psychology, 92*(3), 840. https://doi.org/10.1037/0021-9010.92.3.840

Thau, S., Derfler-Rozin, R., Pitesa, M., Mitchell, M. S., & Pillutla, M. M. (2015). Unethical for the sake of the group: Risk of social exclusion and pro-group unethical behavior. *Journal of Applied Psychology, 100*(1), 98. https://doi.org/10.1037/a0036708

Tuna, M., Ghazzawi, I., Yesiltas, M., Tuna, A. A., & Arslan, S. (2016). The effects of the perceived external prestige of the organization on employee deviant workplace behavior. *International Journal of Contemporary Hospitality Management, 28*(2), 366–396. https://doi.org/10.1108/IJCHM-04-2014-0182

Tyler, T. R. (2013). *Why people cooperate: The role of social motivations*. Princeton University Press.

Tyler, T. R., & Blader, S. L. (2003). The group engagement model: Procedural justice, social identity, and cooperative behavior. *Personality and Social Psychology Review, 7*(4), 349–361. https://doi.org/10.1207/S15327957PSPR0704_07

Tzini, K., & Jain, K. (2018). Unethical behavior under relative performance evaluation: Evidence and remedy. *Human Resource Management, 57*(6), 1399–1413. https://doi.org/10.1002/hrm.21913

Umphress, E. E., & Bingham, J. B. (2011). When employees do bad things for good reasons: Examining unethical pro-organizational behaviors. *Organization Science, 22*(3), 621–640. https://doi.org/10.1287/orsc.1100.0559

Umphress, E. E., Bingham, J. B., & Mitchell, M. S. (2010). Unethical behavior in the name of the company: The moderating effect of organizational identification and positive reciprocity beliefs on unethical pro-organizational behavior. *Journal of Applied Psychology, 95*(4), 769–780. https://doi.org/10.1037/a0019214

Vadera, A. K., & Pratt, M. G. (2013). Love, hate, ambivalence, or indifference? A conceptual examination of workplace crimes and organizational identification. *Organization Science, 24*(1), 172–188. https://doi.org/10.1287/orsc.1110.0714

Van de Vyver, J., & Abrams, D. (2015). Testing the prosocial effectiveness of the prototypical moral emotions: Elevation increases benevolent behaviors and outrage increases justice behaviors. *Journal of Experimental Social Psychology, 58*, 23–33. https://doi.org/10.1016/j.jesp.2014.12.005

Van Os, A., De Gilder, D., Van Dyck, C., & Groenewegen, P. (2015). Responses to professional identity threat. *Journal of Health Organization and Management, 29*(7), 1011–1028. https://doi.org/10.1108/JHOM-12-2013-0273

Van Prooijen, J. W., Van den Bos, K., & Wilke, H. A. (2005). Procedural justice and intragroup status: Knowing where we stand in a group enhances reactions to procedures. *Journal of Experimental Social Psychology, 41*(6), 664–676. https://doi.org/10.1016/j.jesp.2004.12.003

Van Vuuren, M., Beelen, P., & De Jong, M. D. (2010). Speaking of dominance, status differences, and identification: Making sense of a merger. *Journal of Occupational and Organizational Psychology, 83*(3), 627–643. https://doi.org/10.1348/096317909X463661

Welbourne, J. L., & Sariol, A. M. (2017). When does incivility lead to counterproductive work behavior? Roles of job involvement, task interdependence, and gender. *Journal of Occupational Health Psychology, 22*, 194–206. https://doi.org/10.1037/ocp0000029

Wesselmann, E. D., Bagg, D., & Williams, K. D. (2009). "I feel your pain": The effects of observing ostracism on the ostracism detection system. *Journal of Experimental Social Psychology, 45*(6), 1308–1311. https://doi.org/10.1016/j.jesp.2009.08.003

Whetten, D. A. (2006). Albert and Whetten revisited: Strengthening the concept of organizational identity. *Journal of Management Inquiry, 15*(3), 219–234. https://doi.org/10.1177/1056492606291200

Williams, K. D., & Karau, S. J. (1991). Social loafing and social compensation: The effects of expectations of co-worker performance. *Journal of Personality and Social Psychology, 61*(4), 570. https://doi.org/10.1037/0022-3514.61.4.570

Wu, J., Balliet, D., & Van Lange, P. A. (2016a). Reputation management: Why and how gossip enhances generosity. *Evolution and Human Behavior, 37*(3), 193–201. https://doi.org/10.1016/j.evolhumbehav.2015.11.001

Wu, C. H., Liu, J., Kwan, H. K., & Lee, C. (2016b). Why and when workplace ostracism inhibits organizational citizenship behaviors: An organizational identification perspective. *Journal of Applied Psychology, 101*(3), 362. https://doi.org/10.1037/apl0000063

Zadro, L., Williams, K. D., & Richardson, R. (2004). How low can you go? Ostracism by a computer is sufficient to lower self-reported levels of belonging, control, self-esteem, and meaningful existence. *Journal of Experimental Social Psychology, 40*(4), 560–567. https://doi.org/10.1016/j.jesp.2003.11.006

Chapter 5
Diversity and Inclusion

Abstract The **key issues** in this chapter address concerns often voiced by opponents of diversity targets in organizations. They see such policies as unfair, valuing employee demographics rather than individual merit. Common organizational practices for employee recruitment, selection and development aim to assess professional standards and skills in a neutral fashion. However, our **analysis** reveals that people are often rewarded and selected for identity-defining characteristics, that are unrelated to merit. Diversity programs can alleviate such concerns and attest to good intentions, but are a source of moral licensing when these are ineffective. Ignoring that identical contributions are more difficult to realize for members of some groups than for others indicates moral neglect. Expecting all employees to behave alike deprives those who are different from fair treatment – implying their moral exclusion. These strategies reinforce the belief that the organization only rewards excellence, but undermine the ability of those who are different to perform

N. Ellemers, D. de Gilder, *The Moral Organization: Key Issues, Analyses, and Solutions*, https://doi.org/10.1007/978-3-030-84175-1_5

well. **Solutions** acknowledge hidden influences that jeopardize fair treatment, and recognize different types of contributions. Preventing that people who are different either adapt to the majority or leave the organization requires inclusive leadership. Looking beyond numbers allows for different ways of belonging, where fair treatment also implies the willingness to make changes that realize inclusion for all in a diverse organization.

5.1 Reconciling Fairness and Excellence

Organizations generally try to do what is considered morally right by aiming to offer fair employment for everyone. In hiring and firing personnel they focus on individual merit alone, and excellence is the only criterion for promotion – at least that is the aim. Nowadays, many companies subscribe to the goal of becoming more diverse and engage different means available to them to achieve this. How come then, that so many organizations still employ very few women and ethnic minority members at the highest job levels? Does it mean that they are less qualified? And if so, would it be worth pursuing diversity at the expense of excellence? Or are organizations deceiving themselves by assuming the skills they seek – and the standards they use to test these – treat everyone fairly? Providing answers to these questions is not that straightforward (see also Nishii et al., 2018).

What we do know, is that organizations often think that 'doing something' must be better than doing nothing, and tend to copy each other's 'best practices'. However, the measures introduced in this way mostly are 'best guesses' that are rarely evaluated, often raise resistance and are quickly abandoned (Dobbin & Kalev, 2016; Kalev et al., 2006; see also Box 5.1: KPN struggling with diversity targets). Scientists lament this approach, where diversity policies are introduced without taking note of available evidence. Such policies are strewn with pitfalls that are difficult to avoid (Moss-Racusin et al., 2014). Studies reveal that such programs can also harm rather than help those who are supposed to benefit from them. Appointing female leaders through a special talent program for women easily raises suspicion about their true abilities. Offering extra mentoring and support to ethnic minority workers can undermine confidence in their own learning ability and lowers self-esteem (see Barreto & Ellemers, 2015; Kaiser et al., 2013; Swim & Stangor, 1998 for overviews).

Box 5.1: Struggling with Diversity – The Case of KPN Telecom
In 2009 Dutch telecom KPN took firm measures to achieve its target of 30% female representation in positions. After many years of well-intentioned attempts to recruit and promote women the company decided that time alone would not take of this. were explicitly required to propose female candidates for every leadership vacancy. They even faced a reduction of their bonus when failing to do so. Yet, only a few years later, the company terminated these measures, even though the target figure for female leadership still was not met. When asked about the reasons for this decision (De Jong, 2014), diversity leader Jasper Rynders was quoted to say: "*We were hoping for who would add, due to their gender, important, insights and qualities to the business process.*" He felt these of gender were not realized, however: "*Some of them resembled in their behavior and qualities very much the men who were already there, including their shortcomings.*" Thus, the fact that the few women who successfully climbed the organizational ladder seemed to contribute very similar skills and as the men making up the majority in positions of , was seen to call into question the added of employee diversity. Further, the policy was said to be considered unfair by "*well-educated multicultural men*" in the company, who had complained that focused on women only.

Adapting their diversity in this way did not help: KPN was unable to reach the desired levels of gender and ethnic diversity in senior year after year. This prompted CEO Maximo Ibarra to reintroduce the target of 30% women in top echelons in 2018, together with the obligation to shortlist at least 50% female candidates for vacancies in upper level management positions (Bremmer, 2018). Implementing these and quota seemed a last resort – it hadn't been effective before and privileged women over other minority groups in the company. Clearly the company didn't really know what would be the best way to meet its diversity .

The added value of 'doing something' may not be obvious to those experiencing the results in practice either. James Damore lost his job at Google because he challenged the company's diversity policy for what he perceived was a lack of supporting evidence (Wong, 2018). It probably does not contribute to the acceptance of diversity policies when merely questioning the rationale or impact of diversity programs is seen as an act of obstruction that can have such dire consequences. These policies are based on good intentions and seem sympathetic from a moral perspective, but given the reliance on 'best guesses' at what might work it is no wonder that many attempts at increasing diversity in organizations turn out to be ineffective (Dobbin & Kalev, 2019; Dover et al., 2016; 2020a).

In this chapter we assess pitfalls organizations often encounter when aiming to enhance organizational diversity. Attempts to increase policy support by focusing on individual merit, promoting the business gains of diversity, or implementing rules to prevent discrimination are common strategies, that can easily backfire. We consider each of these three standard approaches, as well as their limitations as 'quick fixes'. We then illustrate different types of identity threats typically raised by diversity policies, to reveal the unintended and adverse effects these may have. We show how the introduction of diversity programs may invite *moral licensing* that prevents further changes in the organization. We explain why ignoring different backgrounds and cultural identities amounts to *moral neglect*. And we highlight that expecting everyone to be the same amounts to *moral exclusion* of those with a different identity (see Box 2.4, for explanations of these terms). These strategies all protect people in organizations from the threat of acknowledging that current personnel practices may be unfair, but also prevent them from considering further changes that may be needed to make diversity policies more effective (see also Fig. 2.3). We conclude by outlining how organizations can offer groups of employees different pathways towards acceptance as full members of the organization, without having to give up who they are.

5.1.1 Defining Professional Standards

The dominant view in many organizations is that they would welcome more women, cultural minorities, gay and lesbian workers, people with disabilities or other underrepresented groups in their ranks. However they are reluctant to 'lower their professional standards' that would enable them to do so. This view relies on the individual difference approach discussed in Chap. 1, and the assumption that the only thing being assessed is individual merit. Indeed, many HR departments invest heavily in specifying appropriate criteria and procedures allowing them to reliably establish these differences. The general assumption therefore is that current procedures for evaluating and selecting the potential and performance of individuals are fair, and allow the organization to objectively assess and compare the excellence and achievements of specific individuals. This way of thinking almost inevitably leads to the conclusion that a lack of diversity in the organization can only mean that some people just don't 'have what it takes'. The assumption is that those who do not succeed must somehow be less skilled, less qualified or less deserving (see also Box 5.2: Denial of discrimination). It also informs the types of solutions that are typically sought to increase diversity: To avoid having to lower the standards, attempts to include different people in the organization focus on ways to 'fix' these individuals, with extra training, mentoring, or other types of additional support.

Box 5.2: Denial of Discrimination
Declaring that is undesirable does not eliminate its existence. Assuming that the decision to introduce a policy guarantees for everyone is naïve. In fact, it can have the opposite effect.

We know from countless studies (many of which are referenced in this chapter) that humans are limited in their ability to process information fully and accurately. In practice, people often rely on a variety of mental shortcuts and heuristics that color their judgment in forming impressions of others. Pledging to evaluate alone does not resolve these mental . Hence, relying on to treat everyone the same way introduces the of blinding people to the biased that persist (Ellemers & Barreto, 2009, 2015).

Where do these biases come from, and how are they sustained? People form expectations about the abilities and preferences of themselves and others on the basis of what they see around them. When it is clearly visible how few women and ethnic succeed in securing a position of , the conclusion seems to be that apparently women and do not 'have what it takes' to become a leader. Emphasizing once again that everyone is treated equally doesn't help – it only makes this worse.

Insisting that everyone is judged in the same way and receives the same , only leaves one conclusion when people fail: there must be something wrong with them. Apparently they are not smart enough, not ambitious enough, or make the wrong life choices to be successful. This view ignores the well-documented reality that there are many difficulties that members of minority groups have to – merely due to the fact that there are so few of them in these positions. These include the lack of organizational support, absence of mentors and role models, lack of understanding for their needs and experiences or outright .

Overlooking more biases and additional hurdles is referred to as ' of '. This is a form of in its own right as it justifies existing that are designed to match the needs of the majority, while ignoring minority concerns. It prevents the organization from reconsidering the of its and for a more diverse population of employees, as it maintains the notion that the organization is , but these individuals are inadequate.

But is this view valid? Are organizations and the people working in them really able to judge all individuals fairly, without being distracted by group-level features that should be irrelevant? Perhaps this is not as easy as it seems, as we have already noted in Chap. 3 (Goodwin et al., 2000). The following experience illustrates this too.

Donald McCloskey was a well-respected and widely published Professor of economics at the University of Chicago. At age 53 he decided to change gender

(McCloskey, 1999). In the process of transitioning into Deirdre, Professor McCloskey noted: "*I've just started to get the treatment that women get. When I was the sole woman in a group of a half-dozen economists and I made a point, no one took notice. A few minutes later, George made exactly the same point, and the men said: that's a great point, George!*" Another anecdote recounts Deirdre overhearing two people evaluating her presentation at a scientific conference. While they admitted Deirdre was a decent economist, they agreed that the work of her brother Donald was much better. Of course this work was produced by the same person – the only difference being that the author's name on the publication predated the gender transition.

The professional experiences of adult transgender persons offer a rare opportunity to separate evaluations of individual merit and the objective quality of contributions from responses to their appearance and categorization as a man or a woman. While such personal stories only provide anecdotal evidence, they coincide with results of more rigorous scientific studies investigating the same questions. The main conclusion is consistent but disconcerting. The objective products and 'real' merits of individuals, such as the ideas they come up with, the achievement records they build up, or the interactions they have with others, are perceived differently, depending on their group identity. For instance, the same resumé or architectural design received a more positive evaluation when it was signed with the name of a man rather than a woman (e.g., Moss-Racusin et al., 2014; Proudfoot et al., 2015). The realization that this can be the case has led to the practice of 'blind auditioning'. Some orchestras have adopted this procedure to assess the quality of candidates' musical performance without being distracted by knowledge of their gender or ethnicity. A study of 11 US symphony orchestras examining over 7000 individuals in over 300 auditions found that allowing women to audition behind a screen increased their probability of being selected by 50 per cent (Goldin & Rouse, 2000). This again shows how difficult it is for people to evaluate individual skills and abilities without being distracted by irrelevant identity features.

Another example of how stereotypical expectations may prevent an objective consideration of individual merit was documented in a study examining government decisions to grant venture capital. The analysis of comments made in evaluating different funding requests revealed that exactly the same properties that were seen as positive in men, were interpreted negatively in female applicants. For instance, youth was seen as indicating 'promise' in male candidates but counted as a mark of 'inexperience' in female candidates. Likewise, expressions of caution by male candidates were found to be 'sensible', while female candidates expressing similar caution were dismissed as 'not sufficiently daring'. In their joint decision making about candidates, evaluators also tended to discuss the education of male candidates, while dwelling on the appearance of female candidates. In view of these judgments, it should not come as a surprise that male candidates were more likely to have their funding requests accepted, and that men who were successful received almost twice as much money as women did. Yet when asked to comment on their judgments, the evaluators making the decisions were fully convinced they had been rating merit alone. In fact, they explicitly declared not to have favored either male or female applicants (Malmström et al., 2017).

The dominant individual difference approach neglects this and related evidence, and continues to attribute all evaluative judgments to the qualities of the individuals in question. Why would this be the case? It can be explained by the paradox of morality. Acknowledging that current evaluation procedures are unfair, or that merit judgments may be biased, would threaten the identity of the organization and people working in it, and undermine their self-views of being fair and moral. As we have seen in Chap. 2, research reveals that such threats typically invite a tendency to highlight one's good moral intentions. However, the cognitive effort made to reassure the self and others that fair judgments are made can actually enhance the likelihood that biased decisions continue to reoccur. This was demonstrated in a study showing that after having selected a highly qualified minority candidate (a Latino applicant) people were more likely to show an unwarranted preference for a (white) majority candidate in subsequent selection decisions (Monin & Miller, 2001). Such moral licensing effects can even emerge vicariously. Observing *another* member of their majority group behave in a non-prejudicial way boosted research participants' moral self-views. The ironic effect was that relieving the threat to their moral identity gave them a false sense of security and actually reduced their own vigilance against bias. In fact, research participants were *more* likely to discriminate against a minority candidate in their own selection decisions after being reassured of the ingroup's moral stature in this way (Kouchaki, 2011; see also Zhong et al., 2009).

5.1.2 *Managing Different Skills and Perspectives*

The wide-spread reluctance to acknowledge that unfair treatment persists, can lead advocates of diversity to present it primarily as a business case, instead of a moral case. Focusing on the added value of having a more diverse workforce, should clarify why this is important and prompt people into action to make this happen, or so they think. Thus, simply emphasizing the economic benefits of increased diversity is often seen as a quick fix to get organizational members to recruit, welcome, and collaborate effectively with a diverse selection of co-workers.

This view is based on evidence indicating that employee diversity can raise a range of favorable outcomes. Diversity can benefit product and service innovation, attract a broader range of clients, and increase community support. These are all benefits of diversity that contribute to company profitability (e.g., Woolley et al., 2015). Indeed, a survey of over 20,000 firms in 91 countries found companies with more women in positions of leadership performed better financially (Noland et al., 2016). A meta-analysis of 146 different studies examining 612 effect sizes, further demonstrated that employee diversity is related to a more innovative performance, particularly of complex tasks (Van Dijk et al., 2012). Likewise, over a period of 15 years, female representation in top management of Standard and Poor 1500 firms was related to more innovation (Dezso & Ross, 2012). The stock market seems to place even more value on ethnic diversity than on gender diversity on company boards (Ntim, 2015).

Only emphasizing these business benefits of diversity allows for *moral neglect*. It focuses the discussion on the economic gains the organization expects from becoming more diverse. Considering this as a *moral choice* people want to make would be a fundamentally different approach, which implies that diversity should be pursued despite the difficulties or costs that are incurred, even when business outcomes are uncertain (Fine et al., 2020). Yet this is more in line with research evidence showing that the beneficial effects of diversity for employees on the work floor are not so clear. In fact, reviews of many studies show there is no one-to-one relation between employee diversity and individual and team performance, or organizational success (Guillaume et al., 2012; see also Van Knippenberg & Schippers, 2007). Rather than the demographics of the individuals involved, the crucial factor explaining the added value of diversity is whether the situation allows them to bring more different views to the table – not whether they have a different gender, age, or skin color. In fact, research shows that the relationship between employee diversity and team performance is indirect, and depends on whether demographic differences lead people to contribute different views, approaches and knowledge to the team (see Fig. 5.1: How diversity works). In line with this analysis, business benefits seem related to *functional* differences rather than demographic differences. For instance, companies with more functionally diverse management teams were found to hold product portfolios that contain more products that are new to market or employ novel technologies compared to companies with homogeneous top management teams. This was found to benefit the capital market performance of more diverse firms, which was visible in the key indicator investors use for this purpose (Tobin's q; see Talke et al., 2011).

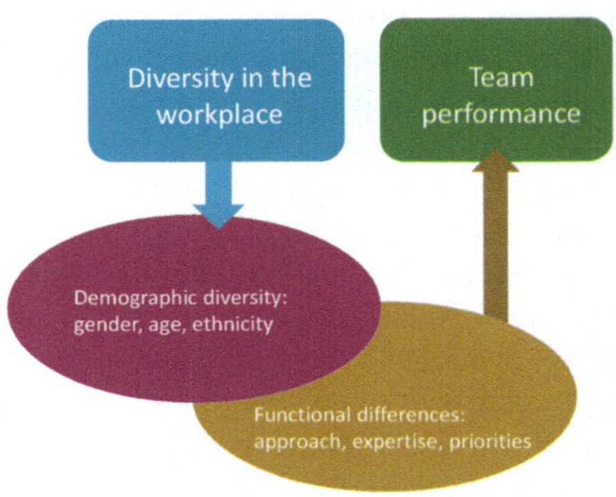

Fig. 5.1 How diversity works. Illustrates that there is no direct relation between workplace diversity and team performance. Efforts to increase demographic diversity will not benefit team performance unless people are encouraged to express functional differences in the way they approach the task, introduce a broader range of expertise, or identify different priorities. (Adapted from: Ellemers and Rink (2016))

In theory, people with different cultural and demographic backgrounds can bring diverging perspectives and experiences to the table. In practice, however, it may be quite challenging and time consuming to understand, value, or benefit from people with different cultural backgrounds, professional skills, or work styles. It is not self-evident that these different visions are actually acknowledged and discussed. In some cases being confronted with such differences only raises conflict and misunderstanding which undermine joint performance rather than enhance it. This can make it quite difficult to benefit from diversity, and sometimes it is quite legitimate to see this as a hurdle. For instance, among professionals handling life-or-death emergency situations which require immediate trust and blind coordination, for instance in the police force, the fire brigade, or healthcare. Promising employees that diversity will only bring them benefits raises false expectations. It ignores the responsibility of the organization to monitor whether work conditions actually allow for curiosity and experimentation rather than requiring high speed and efficiency (see also Ellemers & Rink, 2005; Rink & Ellemers, 2008, 2010a).

Moreover, it is by no means self-evident that individuals with different backgrounds will really and pro-actively introduce diverging views or task solutions. In general, the mere awareness of being in a numerical minority can cause individuals to infer that their unique contributions are unlikely to be valued by the people they collaborate with (Derks et al., 2009). This is not just the fruit of their imagination: abundant research evidence shows that minority workers tend to receive less encouragement and support, and are offered fewer career opportunities, even if they show identical dedication and performance (e.g., Williams & Dempsey, 2018, see also Box 5.3: The career experiences of men and women). Another counterforce is that majority workers are quick to feel *their* efforts are disregarded when the success of the organization is portrayed as depending on increasing diversity. This raises insecurity about their own position and their continued value for the organization – again introducing identity threat. Experiments comparing people who collaborate under different conditions show this makes existing team members ignore the novel perspectives offered by newcomers, while they invest in establishing the continued worth of their own contributions (Rink & Ellemers, 2009, 2010b).

In sum, results of many studies reveal how difficult it is to reap business benefits from diversity. In fact, substantial costs may have to be incurred to do this. Further, not all organizations benefit from a broader range or insights or aim to increase creativity. In fact, for some tasks (production security, crisis prevention) efficiency or standardization is more important than diversity of perspectives. If the business case is the only reason to engage with diversity goals, people are likely to be discouraged or disappointed when the benefits that were promised do not materialize or are not that clear (Eagly, 2016).

Box 5.3: The Career Experiences of Women

The diverging career experiences of men and women -despite equal investment and performance- plausibly explain why women consistently report lower well-being at work. This is the pattern that emerges from a meta-analysis comparing life satisfaction and job satisfaction. The comparison of hundreds of studies investigating many thousands of respondents established that women who reported being equally satisfied with their lives still indicated less work satisfaction than men. Further, observed gender differences in work satisfaction (not life satisfaction) were related to national levels of gender inequality. This suggests that differential opportunities and outcomes for men and women result in lesser satisfaction of women with the way they are treated in the workplace in particular (Batz-Barbarich et al., 2018).

Studies among many professional groups additionally reveal that women are more likely than men to experience harassment or other forms of misbehavior in the workplace. For instance a survey of the International Bar Association Report examining thousands of lawyers in over one hundred countries found that one in three men and one in two women report experiencing misbehavior at work (Pender, 2019). The impact of such experiences can be far-reaching. Analysing the results from 88 studies examining over 70,000 working women made it possible to systematically examine the impact of different types of potentially harmful events. The researchers assessed whether incidents of misbeavior were related to gender or sexuality, and whether they represented the general organizational climate or should be seen as isolated experiences (Sojo et al., 2016). Further, the researchers were able to rule out alternative explanations that might explain lower well-being of women at work, such as general job stress (e.g., due to overload or lack of autonomy), and the dominance of men in the workplace.

After correcting for all these variables, the researchers found that the well-being of women at work suffers as much from frequent exposure to adverse experiences that may seem relatively innocent (e.g., repeated questions about one's competence, affordance of less pay or professional opportunities) as from rarer but more intense experiences (e.g., sexual coercion; Sojo et al., 2016). Indeed the mental and physical health implications that were reported relate to the pervasiveness -not the intensity- of repeated exposure to behaviors indicating that contributions of women are generally devalued at work. The damage adds up when this is communicated by different co-workers and repeated over time. Frequently experienced slights seem more normatively accepted and are more difficult to avoid than more extreme but less common forms of misbehavior. This makes their impact pervasive and undermines the ability of women to thrive in the workplace.

5.1.3 Good Intentions Are Not Enough

If it turns out that it is not so easy for the organization to realize the ambition of becoming more diverse, managers or external regulators may be tempted to enforce diversity rules and targets as they hope for a quick fix (Dobbin & Kalev, 2016). However, as long as people continue to believe that differences in career success only stem from differences in merit (the individual difference approach) such enforcement attempts can backfire too. Quota and other top-down regulations meant to increase diversity lead people to distrust the capabilities of those who are under-represented, and perceive their success as stemming only from preferential treatment (Dobbin & Kalev, 2016). Of course many minority members then elect to pass through 'regular' selection procedures rather than benefit from affirmative action policies (Dover et al., 2020b; Kaiser et al., 2013).

The perceived unfairness of diversity measures may also cause resentment, loss of motivation, and performance impairment among majority group members. This was clearly demonstrated in a series of studies in which majority members (in this case white men) considered applying for a job at a particular company. When the description of the company explicitly mentioned its commitment to diversity, study participants expressed more concern about being treated unfairly than when diversity goals were not mentioned. Their heart-rate and blood-pressure changes revealed that the prospect of applying for a job at a company that supported diversity goals raised maladaptive physical stress. In fact, the white male research participants actually performed worse when interviewing for a job in a company that explicitly subscribed to diversity goals (Dover et al., 2016).

In general, the pattern seems to be that the stricter the policies proposed, the less likely they are to be supported. Even those who should benefit from such policies tend to resist them, and indicate that they prefer showing their skill in a regular competition (e.g., Faniko et al., 2012). Although they are meant to level the playing field, policies and formal regulations to enforce increases in employee diversity raise the suspicion of reverse discrimination. This feels unfair to majority workers, and undermines the perceived suitability of minority candidates, even if they are clearly qualified (Kaiser et al., 2013). In practice, such measures can therefore do more harm than good. Indeed, they are often abandoned quickly without explicitly documenting why they failed (see Box 5.1: KPN struggling with diversity targets).

The widespread reluctance to adapt existing procedure in the hope of achieving more diversity can be explained by research evidence on 'just world beliefs'. This is the general conviction that everyone gets what they deserve and therefore people deserve what they get. This motivation is so strong, that people are found to ignore concrete evidence of unequal treatment when it is available (Ellemers & Van Laar, 2010; Cuddy et al., 2015; Handley et al., 2015; Ridgeway, 2001; Van der Lee & Ellemers, 2015; Zhu et al., 2016). People are more likely to consider the possibility that others are being treated unfairly, when they observe disrespectful interpersonal treatment rather than inconsistent use of evaluation procedures or inequality in assignment of wages (O'Reilly et al., 2016).

The persistence of just world beliefs has not only been documented among those who benefit from current procedures (usually majority members, for instance white men) but also among those who suffer from them (cultural minorities and women). In general, people tend to blame victims rather than perpetrators in cases of biased judgement: surely they must have done something wrong to deserve this (Kaiser & Miller, 2001, 2003). In fact, majority as well as minority members tend to devalue and dislike those who complain, even if it is obvious their treatment was unfair (Kaiser & Miller, 2004; see also Barreto & Ellemers, 2002). Any problems encountered are attributed to oversensitivity or shortcomings of those who experience them, especially when these seem to occur incidentally rather than structurally (Garcia et al., 2010; Stroebe et al., 2011). Likewise, people are disinclined to acknowledge that procedures are biased unless they personally suffer from them (Stroebe et al., 2009). Research has revealed that the motivation to believe that selection procedures are fair is so strong that exposing individuals to information revealing that members of their group are not judged fairly only increases their anxiety and stress (Schmitt & Branscombe, 2001; Stroebe et al., 2009).

This research illustrates why it is unlikely that representatives of the organization will accurately perceive that their judgments may be biased. It is equally unlikely that individuals who are disadvantaged by these procedures can be relied on to point out instances of unfair treatment when these occur. These joint efforts to ignore evidence of bias – even when it is clearly present – explain why so many individuals and organizations resist diversity regulations: They continue to believe that pledging their good intentions suffices to secure fair judgments.

In this section we have seen that just world beliefs make people reluctant to accept the possibility that current procedures for the selection and evaluation of individuals in organizations might be unfair. This prevents feelings of identity threat, but makes it difficult to believe that additional steps may need to be taken. The three quick fixes provide organizations with a false sense of security about their ability to offer fair treatment to all. Ironically, this makes them blind for the disadvantage that some still encounter, and actually reduces their tolerance for those legitimately indicating that unfair treatment in hiring, promotion, or wage affordance persists (Kaiser et al., 2013).

5.2 Analysis: Fitting in or Opting Out

The paradox of morality thus prevents people from following through on changes that are needed to enhance the fairness of current systems for the selection and evaluation of personnel. As a result, building a more diverse population of employees seems an impossible assignment to many. Diversity representatives or organizations asking for input from scientists often comment: "*We have already tried so many things, but nothing seems to work*" (Ellemers et al., 2019). In this section we consider how social identity mechanisms contribute to understanding the further implications of these difficulties – as well as viable ways of addressing them. In doing this we consider employee diversity, based on *gender differences, cultural differences,* and differences in *sexual orientation*. In addition to demonstrating the unique challenges that emerge in each case, we will identify the common mechanisms which connect them, and which are characterized by the *moral justification* of the difficulties they face in the organization, *moral neglect* of their diverging experiences, and *moral exclusion* of their distinct identity (see also Fig. 2.3). Identifying the identity management strategies that allow people to believe that current practices are fair, makes it possible to understand why it is so difficult to increase employee diversity and inclusion, and elucidates how these difficulties can be overcome.

5.2.1 Does Everyone Have Equal Returns on Investment?

As briefly indicated at the outset of this chapter, the effects of gender stereotypical expectations on performance judgments have been documented time and again. Although predominance of the individual difference approach makes it difficult to imagine this is the case, women tend to be judged against a broader range of criteria than men, and generally have to offer more proof of their ability (Moscatelli et al., 2020; Van den Brink & Benschop, 2012; Williams & Dempsey, 2018). Even when their objective performance is the same, female professionals are generally seen as less creative, less intelligent, less dedicated, and generally less competent than men (see also Box 5.4: Gender similarities and differences). In the scientific literature this is documented as the phenomenon of shifting standards – conveying that people actually employ different criteria when they judge members of different groups (Biernat & Manis, 1994). In more popular accounts it is known as 'prove-it-again' bias – highlighting that members of minority groups have to offer more evidence of their abilities than majority group members before it is considered convincing (Williams & Dempsey, 2018).

Some of the studies revealing these patterns examine actual work behaviors among large numbers of individuals, while controlling for objective performance differences between male and female workers. Other studies use experimental designs, in which judges evaluate the merits of exactly the same product design, computer code, CV, work plan, or on-line interaction, while being led to believe it was produced by either a man or a woman (for overviews, see Ellemers, 2018b; Williams & Dempsey, 2018). A famous example is the study where identical job applications were more likely to result in a job offer and rewarded with higher pay when the application had been signed by 'John' instead of 'Jennifer' (Moss-Racusin et al., 2014). In fact, female excellence that does not match the stereotype can even be penalized. This was revealed when a female mathematics major with a resume indicating high grades was three times less likely to be called back than a male

Box 5.4: Gender Similarities and Differences

Over the years, many studies have been conducted to capture the differential qualities, motivation and performance of male and female workers. Generally, meta-analyses statistically assessing the evidence accumulated in this way (e.g., Eagly, 2012), do not yield convincing evidence for such generic gender differences. A compelling example is a review of meta-analyses, summarizing "*mountains of research*" derived from hundreds of studies investigating millions of men and women for psychological gender differences (Hyde, 2014, p. 392).

The outcome of this review is that overall differences between men and women are statistically small or trivial (effect sizes *d* between 0.10 and 0.20) for a range of general qualities we value in work contexts and tend to consider as 'typical' for men or women. These include mathematical ability, verbal ability, conscientiousness, gregariousness, relational aggression, tentative speech, leadership effectiveness, self-esteem and academic self-concept. Moderate to large gender differences (effect sizes *d* between 0.50 and 0.80) were found in other abilities and preferences – which are less relevant for many work assignments, such as interest in things vs people, sensation seeking, and propensity to display physical aggression.

Most importantly, however, this review concluded, first, that there is considerable variation among individual men and women in terms of all of these properties, and second, that most of the differences in behavior and preferences displayed by men and women could be traced to cultural differences, social role expectations, and differences in the experiences and training they were exposed to (Hyde, 2014; see also Eagly & Wood, 2013; Ellemers, 2018a; Fine, 2013) For instance, gender differences in 3D mental rotation ability that emerged could be traced at least partially to the different games boys and girls typically play. Indeed, when women were offered the opportunity to play a computer game in which they could train this ability for ten hours, they achieved the same level of spatial skills as men did (Uttal et al., 2013).

applicant. (Quadlin, 2018). Although the number of studies examining evaluations of cultural minority members with such methodologies is smaller, these generally reveal similar effects. For instance, in the Netherlands Mohammed is less likely to receive callback than Mark after submitting exactly the same motivation and credentials in applying for a vacant job (Andriessen et al., 2010; Blommaert, Coenders, & van Tubergen, 2014a, 2014b; Gras & Bovenkerk, 1999).

All this evidence shows that group-based stereotypes and expectations guide the way people select, interpret, and recall available facts. People seldomly realize that this is what they do. Nevertheless, it even influences the way individuals remember and consider their own achievements (*self-stereotyping*, Turner et al., 1987; Turner et al., 1994). For instance, a study showed that men and women who endorsed gender stereotypes inaccurately recalled their own school grades: Men overestimated their past performance in mathematics. Women in this study recalled lower grades for maths than they had actually achieved, while overestimating their arts and language grades (Chatard et al., 2007).

Even though many women participate in the labor force these days, their needs and perspectives tend to be neglected in very basic ways. Workplaces at remote locations without nearby shops, schools, or childcare make it more difficult to combine work with family responsibilities. Work stations, uniforms and protective suits that are designed for the physique of men offer suboptimal fit, protection, and ergonomics for female workers. Temperature settings in offices and placement of toilets often ignore female body temperature and biological functions; Criado-Perez, 2019; see also Nishii, 2012). Such inconveniences are compounded when multiple minority group memberships intersect. An illustration of how this can impede individual well-being and work performance on an everyday basis can be found in the book and movie '*Hidden figures*', portraying a group of African American female scientists participating in NASA's race to space in the 1950s. Being made to feel irrelevant by having to work under conditions that literally ignore one's physical and practical needs, constitutes a form of *moral exclusion*. This inevitably affects the self-confidence, long term motivation, and professional ambition of those whose concerns are not taken into account, and undermines the chances for individuals to succeed.

Differences also emerge in the way the day-to-day efforts and achievements of men and women at work are perceived and evaluated. This was demonstrated in a large scale effort to compare the early career experiences of over a thousand male and female graduates with a university degree in Science, Technology, Engineering and Mathematics (STEM). Census data revealed that -despite having completed the same qualifications and being employed in comparable jobs- women received substantially lower wages (Buffington et al., 2016). A similar pattern emerged from a meta-analysis, statistically summarizing the results of 30 years of research, sampling 95,882 performance evaluations and 378,850 reward allocations of male and female workers. The study revealed a systematic difference in the way the performances of men and women were evaluated which could not be explained from differences in occupation, industry, or job level (Joshi et al., 2015; see also Roberson et al., 2007). Additionally, there were robust differences in rewards received by men and women, including salary, bonuses or promotions. Even if males were also seen to show a superior performance, this could not explain the observed gender difference in rewards received: Reward differences were *fourteen times larger* than the performance differences that were perceived (Joshi et al., 2015).

Other indicators too reveal that women generally receive less return on the investment in their professional achievements than men. This has been consistently established for the careers of male and female scientists, where the number and impact of publications is generally seen as an objective mark of quality. This allows researchers to correct for these objective performance indicators as well as other potentially relevant individual differences (relating to age, family status, discipline, or place of work). Yet studies systematically find that female scientists are less likely to receive grants to support their work at early career stages, even if the quality of their research plans is rated equally favorably (Van der Lee & Ellemers, 2015; Witteman et al., 2019). Young female scientists are less likely to receive a permanent contract with the same publication records (Wyer et al., 2013). Senior female scholars are less likely to receive prestigious honors and awards at later career stages, despite equal achievement (Ma et al., 2019).

Such gender gaps in payment and employment outcomes are often attributed to presumed behavioral differences, such as a lack of assertiveness and negotiation skills allegedly displayed by women. This exemplifies the *moral justification* sought in explaining gender disparities by highlighting the importance of individual behaviors instead of scrutinizing whether men and women are treated equally. In reality, there is no convincing evidence that the lower outcomes of women merely reflect their own shortcomings. Instead, studies reveal that the same 'best practice' negotiation behaviors used successfully by male negotiators are not appreciated in female negotiators, and can even have adverse effects when displayed by them (Kulik & Olekalns, 2012; see also Stuhlmacher & Walters, 1999; Wade, 2001). The notion that gender pay-gaps emerge because 'women don't ask' was refuted in this way. A study of men and women employed at Dutch universities demonstrated that female scientists are more likely than male scientists to initiate a negotiation about work conditions including pay. However, women experience less willingness in the organization than men to discuss these conditions, and were less likely to have their requests accommodated (Hidden Pay Differences in Academia, 2019; Van Veelen & Derks, 2019a, 2019b).

What can women do in response to such treatment? More often than not, female professionals buy into explanations that attribute unfavorable outcomes to their personal failures. This is understandable. Isolated personal experiences offer no reliable record of how others in the organization are treated. Individual employees typically do not have access to organizational-level information that might reveal a systematic gender bias in career evaluations (Crosby et al., 2013; Stroebe et al., 2011). In the end, the moral justifications offered may seem plausible, especially in organizations that pledge commitment to diversity. However, accepting the claim that unequal outcomes only reflect differences in individual merit imply they only have themselves to blame. Being led to believe that lack of success can only indicate their lack of ability causes some to give up and 'opt out' – further supporting the notion that women are less motivated and ambitious by nature (See Fig. 5.2: Fitting in or opting out).

Those who persist have to invest additional effort into displaying their professional ability and career motivation against the odds. While receiving little support for their ambitions from the organization, they prioritize their career over relational commitments and family planning, display extreme ambition and competitiveness, and generally start behaving like 'one of the boys' (Ellemers, 2014). Studies reveal that this is a strategy some women adopt in the course of their career as they try to demonstrate their willingness and ability to behave like a 'good' member of organizations in which contributions of women tend to be devalued (Derks et al., 2011; Ellemers et al., 2012; Ellemers et al., 2004; Faniko et al., 2016; Faniko et al., 2017;

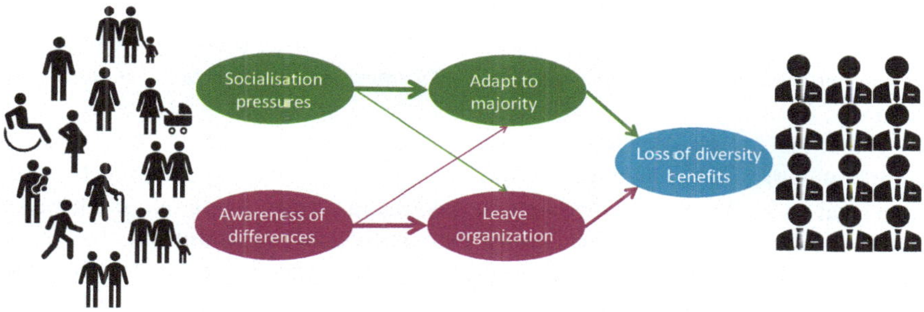

Fig. 5.2 Fitting in or opting out. Illustrates that attracting different types of workers does not necessarily result in diversity benefits. As long as models of success and high performance are defined by majority characteristics, minority representatives will either adapt to the majority to fit in, or leave the organization as they opt out. In both cases, the potential of benefiting from their different insights, viewpoints of approaches is lost. (Adapted from: Ellemers and Rink (2016))

Sheppard & Aquino, 2017). However, this doesn't help the organization become more diverse. In fact, research shows that the tendency of successful females to emulate organizational models of success by displaying their masculinity persists, despite increasing numbers of women present in the organization (Faniko et al., 2020). Unfortunately, once junior women become aware of the ways in which female leaders differ from them, this only lowers their own leadership confidence and career ambitions (Asgari et al., 2012). Further, the advantage women might offer by introducing a different perspective is lost when they start acting like men in order to fit in. This is probably what women did to achieve a position of leadership at KPN Telecom – resulting in the complaint that they had adopted the behavior of their male colleagues, including their shortcomings (see Box 5.1: KPN struggling with diversity targets).

Lack of support for the success of women may also be shown by male subordinates who have been found to have difficulty accepting female leaders (Arvate et al., 2018; Vial et al., 2018). They indicate feeling threatened and competitive as a result of female leaders' displays of ambition and assertiveness, and devalue the leadership ability of their female superiors. These negative responses can be alleviated when female leaders enact their position in a more stereotypically feminine way, for instance by focusing on efficient project management (Netchaeva et al., 2015). The price female leaders pay when developing such strategies to be accepted by their subordinates, is that they have less opportunity to demonstrate their ability to command leadership skills that would enhance their career opportunities, such as vision and boldness (Rink et al., 2013b; Ryan et al., 2016; Ryan & Haslam, 2007). Accordingly, it has been noted that female professionals have to walk a tightrope. On the one hand they have to display agency and ambition to accommodate career requirements. On the other hand they have to appear warm and likeable, to avoid violating gender stereotypical expectations. Comedian Sarah Cooper captures the sometimes absurd consequences of these dual requirements in a series of cartoons. These clearly reveal the difficulties women often face in their attempts to *'be successful without hurting men's feelings'* (Cooper, 2018; see also Williams & Dempsey, 2018).

In sum, there is ample evidence that men and women are likely to be *treated* differently at work – even when they show identical performance and display the same behavioral style. Women who respond to this treatment by 'opting out' confirm the stereotypical view that women simply less motivated and ambitious than men. Those who manage to fit in by adopting typically masculine behaviors reinforce the conviction that the organization 'has nothing against women'. Either way, this only contributes to the notion that career opportunities depend on individual merit alone, offering moral justification of current practices while allowing unfair treatment of women to persist (see also Faniko et al., 2020). In fact, the few who are successful tend to be held up to others in evidence that the organization offers equal advancement opportunities for all. This further legitimizes practices that actually disadvantage women (Ellemers, 2001).

5.2.2 Is It About What You Do or Where You Come From?

Members of cultural minorities likewise contend with the fact that others tend to underestimate their competence and professional ability. Social categorization and stereotypical expectations based on their group memberships cause people to hold minority workers to higher standards, or to ascribe their high achievement to luck, instead of skill (Roberson et al., 2007). Accordingly, they are expected to offer more evidence of appropriate qualifications than would be the case for majority group members, just like the 'prove-it-again' bias faced by women. For instance, labor statistics reveal that even when showing the same educational performance and professional qualifications, migrant workers are at greater risk of remaining unemployed at every job level (Jongen et al., 2019; Osborne, 2019). In general, research consistently shows that workers' cultural or ethnic identities elicit differential ratings that cannot be explained by actual performance differences. This evidence includes experimental investigations where reports of identical work behaviors and career credentials are rated differently depending on the alleged identity of the individual in question (Mohammed or Mark). Converging results are obtained in field studies. Here indicators of the actual ability, experience, and performance of workers are statistically controlled in tests revealing that evaluations of individual potential and achievement are influenced by group-based identities (Roberson et al., 2007).

In addition to this general reluctance to place confidence in their professional abilities, members of cultural minority groups have additional hurdles to overcome. These relate to the actual or perceived incompatibility of their cultural and work identities (see Box 5.5: The path of greatest resistance). At a practical level this may be very obvious. For instance, women who wear a face-covering niqaab are less able to communicate nonverbally, and physical labor may be more challenging for practicing Muslims during Ramadan. In addition, there may be less obvious differences between cultural groups, regarding, for instance, the implicit norms, interaction rules, or leadership styles they are familiar with. Such differences are more difficult to anticipate or address, while they are equally likely to make cultural minority members seem unsuitable workers, and can make them feel out of place.

Box 5.5: The Path of Greatest Resistance

Neil de Grasse Tyson was nine years old when he first visited the Hayden Planetarium in New York. He was so excited about what he saw that he decided then and there that he wanted to become an astronomer. He succeeded in doing this, and eventually became the director of the Hayden Planetarium, as well as a well-known public scientist. But to achieve his life's ambition, he had to "*walk the 'path of greatest resistance*", so he recounts. Every time he stated his goal when a teacher or other adult asked what he wanted to be when he grew up, they looked at the African American boy and said: "*Why? Don't you want to become an athlete?*".

When considering the education and work experiences members of different cultural groups, there is overwhelming evidence that they too are not evaluated and treated on the basis of their individual merit alone. As in the case of men and women, the stereotypes indicating what members of different cultural groups are expected to be like -and prescribing their appropriate life and career choices- influence the way we judge individuals. In fact, the above quote from Neil de Grasse Tyson's personal experiences was prompted by a question from the audience at a scientific symposium asking why there were so few women in the field. When the other (white male) panel members didn't know what to say, Neil de Grasse Tyson drew the parallel between gender minorities and cultural/ethnic minorities when he answered: "*I have never been a woman, but I've been black all my life*" (Truth Seeker, 2015).

Research also shows that the differential treatment and implicit bias that affect cultural minorities in the workplace resemble the experiences of professional women. Formal impediments preventing them from pursuing their personal career choices are few or absent. However in both cases they have to walk the path of greatest resistance to realize their ambitions.

There are known differences between people growing up in different regions or cultural groups, causing them to have different *conceptions of self* (Markus & Conner, 2014). Cultural minority members in the Western world often come from so-called *collectivistic* cultures that benefit the development of an *interdependent* conception of self. Individuals growing up in such cultures (e.g., in East-Asia, or Africa), typically attach a high degree of importance to the maintenance of good relations with others. They are keenly aware of common roots and similarities, and have been taught to adjust the expression of their individual views and ambitions to their social rank (Markus & Conner, 2014). This doesn't naturally match the systems and procedures most organizations originating in the Western world use to incentivize, assess and reward workers. These were developed in so-called *individualistic* cultures (Hofstede, 2001; Markus & Kitayama, 1991) that assume people have *independent* conceptions of self. This implies that workers are treated as separate individuals, who are driven by personal desires and choices. A key assumption is that people feel free to voice their ideas and express their views, for instance to show their contribution to the team or to influence others. The implications this can have in the workplace are illustrated by a study in a multinational company. American employees felt motivated by instructions that emphasized their autonomy and independence. However, calling upon professional obligations proved a more effective strategy to motivate Indian employees (Tripathi et al., 2018).

Likewise, there may be differences between people raised in so-called 'dignity' vs. 'honor' cultures (for reviews, see, e.g., Cohen et al., 2007; Hamamura & Heine, 2008; Triandis, 1994; Vandello & Cohen, 2003). Dignity cultures typically develop when people feel secure about their civil rights and the protection they receive from formal authorities. This allows them to feel entitled to their own freedom and opinions as internal sources of self-worth (Kim & Cohen, 2010; Leung & Cohen, 2011). Honor cultures emerge in communities where formal rights and authorities are less accessible, making the safety of individuals dependent on their ability to recruit protection from powerful others (e.g., around the Mediterranean, in South and Middle America; see Harinck et al., 2013; Rodriguez Mosquera, 2013). These cultural experiences impact on the ways in which people express differences of opinion and resolve conflicts (Harinck et al., 2013). In honor cultures, conflicts easily escalate and are difficult to reconcile. This can make individuals who have grown up in such a culture quite reluctant to engage in milder forms of disagreement, no matter how minor. Instead of speaking up in dissent or confronting diverging opinions, research found they prefer to avoid or walk away from potentially conflictual interactions – as they fear irreversible escalation (Harinck et al., 2013). This may make it challenging to do well in a place of work where people are expected to speak up in dissent, for instance to generate new ideas or to offer their unique expertise in joint decision making.

In general, such cultural differences may make people's cultural identity seem incompatible with their work identity, and can make them feel out of place. Organizations in individualist countries (such as Western Europe and North America) generally expect their employees to speak up for themselves, and reveal their ambition, to signal their professional suitability and high potential. Majority workers in the organization may not realize how difficult and stressful this is for ethnic minority workers, as the cultural differences giving rise to these feelings are not very obvious. Yet having to deal with these multiple identities can easily make people feel out of place. Failing to notice that standard procedures closely map on to the expectations of some – while neglecting the experiences of others is a form of *moral ignorance*. It prevents the organization from acknowledging that the behavior they invite and reward may be culturally specific. Hence, lack of fairness in employee treatment is likely to persist – while differential career success is attributed to performance deficits of cultural minorities.

Here too, the pattern typically observed is that individuals who find it hard to adjust will 'opt out', while others learn to behave in ways that the organization expects from them. There are clear personal costs associated with both options. For instance Hindustani workers in the Netherlands were found to 'fit in', by emphasizing their assertiveness as a strategy towards professional success (Derks et al., 2015). However, adapting to what is required in the workplace – instead of being allowed to 'be oneself' – is emotionally challenging and cognitively effortful. Adjusting one's behavior to majority requirements disconnects minority workers from their family and cultural network, who in turn feel rejected, making them reluctant to provide support (Derks et al., 2015; Van Laar et al., 2014; Van Laar et al., 2013). The incompatibility of cultural and professional identities and their behavioral styles is acknowledged in different countries. Those who try to reconcile these dual requirements are indicated with derogatory terms used for individuals who are black on the outside but 'act white'. In the USA the term '*Oreos*' is used for African Americans; 'coconut' or 'bounty-bar' refers to European professionals originating from the Caribbean. The price of renouncing one's cultural background and ethnic heritage in order to fit in at work may seem impossibly high. This contributes to the difficulty that many organizations experience in recruiting, retaining, and promoting minority representatives.

In sum, the discrepancy between cultural identities and social networks at home and at work is a source of emotional strain and deprives cultural minority members of important sources for guidance and support. Yet it is easy to forget that talented individuals may be held back in their professional careers for lacking the social resources that come so naturally to others (DiTomaso, 2013; Gladwell, 2010). Neglecting these 'invisible' boundaries minorities face allows organizations to maintain the conviction they offer equal opportunities to all. However, persisting in such moral ignorance prevents the organization from adapting work conditions or performance requirements that are culture-specific. Here too, expecting individuals to fit in or opt out deprives the organization from the opportunity to become more diverse. Regardless of which of these two 'solutions' minority members choose, the net result is a homogeneous organization where only those who resemble the majority workers will remain.

5.2.3 Should You Hide Who You Are at Work?

When the ban on homosexuality in the US military was lifted by the Clinton administration in 1993, the new policy required that military personnel adopt a 'don't ask – don't tell' strategy regarding their sexual orientation (Borch, 2010; Department of

Defense, 1993). Openly admitting to being homosexual might undermine the cohesion of military units and reduce combat effectiveness, or so the Joint Chiefs of Staff feared. Gay rights lawyers argued that this policy did not secure equal treatment of gay, lesbian or bisexual military personnel. For instance, they were not allowed to visit gay bars near military bases, have sex with each other, or (plan to) get married. It was judged as an unconstitutional restriction of their civil rights, in a court of law (Log Cabin Republicans v. United States, 2010). Only when the policy was abolished in 2010 by the Obama administration were gay, lesbian and bisexual persons openly allowed to join the US army, navy, or air-force (DADT Repeal Act, 2010).

This example speaks to a source of diversity that is often seen as relatively unproblematic, because sexual preferences that make individuals stand out are 'concealable'. Indeed, some stigmatized identities that would easily taint the perceived potential of individuals to perform well and might undermine their acceptance in the workplace, are not immediately visible to others. Examples are a history of mental illness, previous detention, chronic diseases, or an LGBT identity. At first consideration, such minority identities seem relatively easy to contend with, as employees can simply choose not to reveal them in order to 'pass' at work (Clair et al., 2005). In fact, this is an advice they often receive. The general expectation thus is that concealing their stigmatized identity will help them be treated like any other worker and reduce the risk of being discriminated. This was the idea guiding the US Military 'don't ask, don't tell' policy. Research shows such advice may be misguided. It deprives those who are different from the right to fair treatment, unless they hide who they really are. It represents a form of *moral exclusion* that allows the organization to ignore the needs of those who are different, simply by discouraging them from revealing their true identity.

Studies show how unreasonable this is, and attest to the cognitive and emotional burden of carrying an important secret such as this (Quinn & Chaudoir, 2009). Preventing others on a day-to-day basis from finding out about their sexual orientation, a history of mental illness, shameful family connections or other concealable stigmas requires people to continually monitor what they reveal to others about their personal lives. They cannot speak about their significant others, and have to adapt accounts of their free time activities. The cognitive attention that is needed to filter out the acceptable from the unacceptable information wears people out. The reluctance to share personal events and experiences, to keep secret large and important parts of one's life, makes these individuals seem socially inept or unfriendly, research shows (Newheiser & Barreto, 2014; Newheiser et al., 2015). This makes it more difficult to build trust or to form meaningful relations with colleagues at work. Ironically then, the advice to conceal rather than reveal some hidden form of stigma at work is likely to induce social isolation of those who can't speak about their differences – instead of fostering the cohesion that was hoped for (Barreto & Ellemers, 2015; Ellemers & Barreto, 2006).

In addition to these cognitive implications that affect the quality of social interactions at work, the act of concealing a stigmatized identity places an emotional burden on workers and diminishes their work performance. Studies document they experience shame and guilt, forego social support from others, and fail to benefit from special provisions provided to accommodate their needs for fear of revealing themselves (Marks et al., 2018). As a result, individuals who hide a stigmatized identity at work report lower self-confidence and work motivation as well as decreased mental and physical health (Barreto & Ellemers, 2015; Newheiser & Barreto, 2014; Newheiser et al., 2015). Some of the studies documenting these findings used experimental designs, allowing researchers to systematically compare the impact when individuals are prompted to hide or to reveal a stigmatized identity. Participants in such experiments typically anticipate to be better off when they hide their true identity. However, the results of these studies show that those who reveal their true identity to their co-workers actually feel more accepted and included for who they are. Hence, paradoxically, allowing workers to state their sexual orientation at work might be more beneficial to their well-being, commitment and work performance than ignoring such differences in the workplace (Clair et al., 2005; Cramwinckel et al., 2018; Griffith & Hebl, 2002; Ragins et al., 2007; see also Gino et al., 2015; Van der Toorn, 2019).

When employees feel unable to reveal their true identity at work – because this would preclude them from being accepted – they do not only suffer personally. They are also likely to harm their colleagues and put the organization at risk by displaying unethical behavior, studies reveal Ebrahimi et al., 2019; Kouchaki, 2019). The physiological arousal and stress caused by social exclusion was found to be the driver of such unethical behavior (Kouchaki & Wareham, 2015). Prompting people to think of the incompatibility of work and non-work identities made them feel less authentic and made them more likely to cheat when reporting on their own performance in an experimental task. A cross-industry workplace survey confirmed that employees who indicated incompatibility between work and non-work identities felt they could not reveal their true identity at work. Workplace misconduct reports of their supervisors (e.g., reporting false business expense reports, being mean to a co-worker) revealed these workers were more likely to behave in ways that violate ethical norms for financial or social behavior (Ebrahimi et al., 2019; Kouchaki, 2019).

In sum, our analysis reveals why identities that are usually visible (gender) less visible (ethnicity, culture), and concealable (mental illness, sexual preference) may seem incompatible with existing views on what characterizes a 'good' member of the organization. Individuals who represent such a minority may feel compelled to compensate, change, or hide who they really are in order to be accepted in the workplace. Across different cases, research evidence shows the costs of doing this for the individuals as well as the organizations involved. Some individuals adapt as best as they can: They try to renounce, disprove, or deny the features that set them apart from other members of the organization. These attempts to fit in are detrimental to their well-being and work satisfaction, and undermine their task performance and professional ambition. Others give up and opt out, causing the organization to lose out on their unique contribution and undermining confidence in the organization's ability to become more diverse. Either way, maintaining the homogeneity among individuals in the organization reduces the likelihood of identifying work conditions or performance criteria that may put those who are different at a disadvantage. Thus, offering one-size-for-all employee solutions may seem to communicate that all are considered equal, and alleviate moral concerns. In reality, it introduces moral justifications for unfair treatment, invites moral ignorance of special needs, and allows for moral exclusion of those who are different. All these strategies can sustain the notion that the organization supports diversity, while preventing further consideration of ways to accommodate different groups of workers.

5.3 Solutions: Striving for Acceptance and Belonging

The desire to increase the diversity of employees is often translated into the ambition to increase the *number* of individuals coming from underrepresented groups (e.g., Madera et al., 2018). Granted, numerical targets can help retain diversity as a legitimate business priority which deserves management attention and resources (Dobbin & Kalev, 2016). Over time, the visible presence and success of different types of workers in all functions and at all levels of the organization can broaden people's perceptions of potential and merit, and reduce (implicit) bias (Vuletich & Payne, 2019). However, even when organizations begin to pursue this goal, the evidence reviewed in prior sections of this chapter reveals that people are highly motivated to believe that everyone receives fair treatment in the workplace. Thus, they run the risk of being quickly reassured this is the case – even by symbolic pledges to diversity goals that may be ineffective or counterproductive. At the same time, stricter measures seem unfair and are generally being shunned, preventing further policy changes.

Our analysis in the prior section revealed the pitfalls of diversity initiatives that focus on recruiting different groups of workers without securing their full acceptance and inclusion into the organization. The message is that they can be present, but they can't be different. Expecting minority workers to 'fit in' or 'opt out' without critically considering system-level factors that force all workers into the same mold is unlikely to be effective. Indeed, even organizations that make considerable efforts to recruit minority members into their workforce and talent programs often see them underrepresented at higher job levels, and overrepresented in their 'regretted losses'.

Successfully addressing these issues is only possible after accepting that current practices may not be fair, as they result in diverging experiences of minority and majority workers. This includes the day-to-day experiences that communicate incompatible expectations (e.g. for female leaders), imply the absence of informal support (e.g., for cultural minorities), or induce fears about revealing one's true identity (e.g., for gay, lesbian and bisexual workers). In this final section we outline how to truly embrace individuals who are different, why it is important to reconsider criteria for 'good' organizational members, and how to overcome difficulties associated with increasing organizational diversity. These are all concrete steps towards redefining the moral identity of the organization as a place where a broad range of individuals should be able to expect fair treatment and full inclusion.

5.3.1 *Fair Treatment Despite Inequality*

Who is included in the organization and its 'circle of care'? Offering 'one size fits all' procedures might seem fair, but can be dysfunctional or even unreasonable when this excludes those who are different. The consequences of neglecting diverging circumstances and physical variations go beyond the ill-fitting uniforms or lack of sanitary facilities we already discussed (Criado-Perez, 2019). Some 'standard practices' can make it impossible for people to display their individual ability, and damage the health and well-being of those who try to accommodate them. What to think of women who are requested to interview for a job or research grant days before or after giving birth because all candidates are held to the same evaluation schedule?

Are they to be considered outgroup members whose own responsibility it is to resolve their 'special needs' emerging from personal life choices? Or should they be seen as ingroup members who can rely on the organization to prevent factors beyond their control from becoming impossible hurdles in realizing their professional ambitions? This calls for a deliberate reconsideration of which forms of standardization can help to secure fair treatment for all, and which ones unwittingly communicate to organizational members who are different that they are excluded from fair treatment.

Companies struggle when trying to balance fair treatment with obvious individual differences. Sometimes they go overboard in focusing on these differences, for instance when using gender-specific requirements to define high performance. A classic case is that of Ann Hopkins, a female consultant at PriceWaterhouse Coopers. Despite her outstanding performance record and success in attracting clients, her application to be made partner was rejected. She was told this decision was made because her appearance and demeanor were not sufficiently feminine. She received the advice to improve her career opportunities by wearing more soft-hued clothes, putting on some lipstick, and attending 'charm school'. When Ann Hopkins contested this decision, the court ruled that she had been rejected for failing to act in line with gender stereotypes instead of being evaluated for her business performance (Fiske et al., 1991; Hopkins, 1996). More recent examples include women who object to gender-specific notions of appropriate business attire, forcing them to wear make-up, skirts, or high heels at work, even if they would prefer not to do so (Carbado et al., 2006). This way of addressing men and women seems to account for their physical differences. However, when it imposes additional requirements for some that are not applied to others it implies unfair treatment that can be dysfunctional for their well-being and ability to perform well.

The situation is complicated: it may be equally unfair to apply the exact same standards to all organizational members. This can happen for instance when career development trajectories are only offered to individuals in specific age groups. Young parents may suffer from this when they request to delay further career opportunities by a few years. They may find themselves removed from the list of high potentials merely by falling outside the age group targeted for talent development programs. Yet their request does not necessarily imply they are less ambitious, but just that they have to accommodate the practicalities of competing family and work demands in the 'rush hour of life'. In a similar vein, many organizations assume that employees in more advanced age groups will not be interested in further training opportunities or (digital) upskilling. Yet when individuals who might wish to develop such skills are not invited to do so they can feel 'written off', even if they still have 10–20 working years ahead of them. In principle, using 'standard' criteria to identify target groups for selection and promotion may seem to offer equal treatment to all. However, this can be extremely unfair when such convenient proxies do not accurately capture the performance and potential that is sought.

What will help is critically reconsidering 'standard' procedures and revising them where needed. This includes going beyond relatively abstract notions of the qualities that are sought. Specifying at a more practical and specific level which skills are needed and how people might attest to these skills should not imply a lowering of standards, but might broaden the ways in which people can qualify. This also prevents evaluators from inferring individual skills from stereotypical expectations based on people's group memberships. When recruiting for a job where social relations management is important female candidates would seem to be most likely to qualify, making it easy to overlook suitable male candidates (Davison & Burke, 2000; Ryan & Haslam, 2007; Rink et al., 2013a). Actually specifying and testing for these skills reduces the risk of relying on such unfounded assumptions.

Encouraging people to call out and confront 'standard' practices and procedures that are more welcoming for some than for others -instead of simply accepting that discrimination persists- is an important step in this procedure (Britton, 2017; Jaurique et al., 2019; Maranto & Griffin, 2010). Stating the willingness to recognize and acknowledge biased treatment when it occurs in itself can already empower and motivate minority members to show a superior performance, experiments show (Cihangir et al., 2014). Having majority workers acknowledge the different experiences of minority groups in the workplace may even be more effective than having such issues flagged only by those suffering from them. Indeed, a review of relevant research shows that when men acknowledge that women may suffer from sexism in the workplace, this is generally seen as a legitimate observation. When women make such complaints they are more likely to be suspected of selfish motives that can be easily dismissed (Drury & Kaiser, 2014). Likewise, an experimental study showed the positive impact of having men point out that women were treated unfairly in a job interview. Having men speak out on their behalf empowered female candidates to retain their self-confidence. This allowed them to show a superior performance on an IQ test used in the selection procedure, and encouraged them to critically comment on the way they were treated. Female candidates did not display such assertive behavior when the suspicion of gender bias was only called out by other women (Cihangir et al., 2014).

More generally, majority acknowledgment and support for the plight of the minority communicates their inclusion in the ingroup of organizational members and is a way of taking action in its own right. Examples are 'he-for-she' initiatives, or organizations correcting pay differences to qualify for equal pay certification. Some feel the commitment of men to protecting professional women from workplace harassment is the primary gain that came out from the wide sharing of #MeToo experiences. Women who had already resigned suffering harassment would be an inevitable aspect of their professional lives felt empowered by these expressions of support. The support many white employees and managers extended to the Black Lives Matter movement can be viewed in the same way. In general, having majority members explicitly recognize and take a stance against unfair treatment of minority groups at work can be a key factor in communicating their status as ingroup members in the organization who have the right to having such issues uncovered and resolved. Thus, the first thing organizations can do is to acknowledge and accurately specify the diverging needs, experiences and realities of individual employees. This makes it possible to examine whether traditional indicators of talent or potential might offer inaccurate or unreliable information in specific cases. Actively searching for the possibility of unfair procedures, instead of trying to justify or ignore this may happen is another way to reveal commitment to inclusion and equal treatment of all.

5.3.2 *Allowing for Different Ways of Belonging*

Including more different people in the organization also calls for a reconsideration of what the organization is and what it stands for. Perhaps a broader set of behaviors should come to be seen as characterizing organizational members? Might there be multiple ways to display loyalty to the organization and commitment to its goals? Truly including a more diverse range of individuals often implies acknowledging a broader range of features to accurately represent and encompass the common identity of organizational members.

The ambition to transform into a more diverse organization requires that different types of workers are included and valued them as important contributors to the organization (Rink et al., 2013a). Actively managing differences between employees is the key to achieving this. This doesn't stop at policies implemented at the top management levels or formal procedures offered by HR. In addition, it is important that team leaders highlight and explain the added value of different perspectives, approaches and life experiences. The degree to which such 'inclusive' team leadership was displayed on a day-to-day basis was found to predict whether or not members of ethnically/culturally diverse work teams in the public sector felt that they were accepted and included (Ashikali et al., 2020). Experimental research, manipulating and comparing responses to different messages and team instructions, reveals how this can be done (Rink & Ellemers, 2007a, 2010a). Explaining ahead of time the functionality of a diversity of inputs for joint task achievement helps to anticipate and manage differences that come to the fore. Once made explicit, this prevents confusion, alleviates concerns about the value of diverging contributions, and allows the team to form a shared identity which includes their differences (Rink & Ellemers, 2007b, 2007c). A study in the oil and gas industry revealed that the different inputs offered by members of multi-disciplinary teams allowed for team learning and improved team performance – provided that a sense of joint identity could be retained (Van Der Vegt & Bunderson, 2005).

Another important way in which organizations can allow different types of employees to belong without requesting that they give up other parts of their identity is by facilitating the combination of work and family roles – for men and for women. Too often, these two types of roles are seen as incompatible. The professional ambition and suitability of female workers is systematically perceived as being lower after they have children, regardless of how they respond to this life transition. This is a robust phenomenon, often indicated as the 'motherhood penalty'. It emerges from studies comparing the actual career experiences of men and women before and after they have children. But it is also found in experiments aimed at comparing how people evaluate identical credentials of men and women with or without children. (Correll et al., 2007; Cuddy et al., 2004; Fuegen et al., 2004; Heilman & Okimoto, 2008). Likewise, research suggests that fathers are devalued when they reduce their working hours or pause their career to care for their family (Ellemers, 2018a; Riggs, 1997). In other words, those who indicate they take their family responsibilities seriously run the risk of being seen as less suitable workers.

However, no support for this inference is found in studies examining the actual performance of men and women who combine work and family roles (Van Steenbergen et al., 2009). A large program of research in a multinational financial services organization revealed that these two types of responsibilities need not conflict. This research combined different types of methods and measures, including interviews, observations, and surveys of thousands of employees over several years. Assessments included self-stated job satisfaction and career motivation, the absence and performance records that were kept by the company, and indicators of employee physical health (cholesterol level, performance on a physical stamina test, body mass index). Regardless of their objective family status and childcare arrangements, male and female employees who felt they were supported by the organization in combining their work and family roles proved to be happier, healthier and more productive workers (Van Steenbergen & Ellemers, 2009a, 2009b). A series of experiments revealed that the feelings of support that lead to such facilitation effects emerge when team leaders communicate about the combination of work and family roles as a challenging opportunity for personal enrichment and growth. Addressing and managing these challenges was found to be more productive than treating family roles merely as a source of conflict that detracts from work performance and commitment (Van Steenbergen et al., 2008).

5.3.3 *Acknowledging the Costs and Benefits of Diversity*

A final step organizations can take to become more inclusive is to be very specific on why it might be important to invest in employee diversity. Considering this goal as having value in its own right goes beyond approaches that treat employee diversity purely as a business case. It may be more productive to not just consider what is to be gained from having a more diverse workforce but also to contemplate how the degree of diversity (or lack of it) speaks to the way the organization wants to define itself in its own eyes and the eyes of important stakeholders. Accommodating diverging needs, and transforming long-standing practices to be able to do so makes it obvious that there are costs as well as benefits to increasing employee diversity. Yet it seems that many organizations that claim to be aiming for more diversity are unwilling to incur such costs. In truth, they would be better advised then to abandon their diversity ambitions.

Studies attest to the futility of hiring people with different backgrounds without considering efforts that might be made to make them feel at home in the organization. This was revealed in a study of college educated Muslim women employed at different organizations in the Netherlands. The employers' acknowledgment of their multiple identities (e.g., by offering Halal food in the canteen, or allowing them to align their holidays with important religious days) benefited the work motivation, career ambition, and organizational commitment of these women. Employers that were unwilling to make these adaptations – expecting Muslim employees to fit in by ignoring their distinct identity – only undermined the positive work attitudes of minority workers, and ironically made them more reluctant to adapt their behavior to organizational requirements – for instance by refusing to take off their headscarf (Van Laar et al., 2013). Other studies too show that organizational values and a work climate which communicate acceptance and inclusion of different groups of workers can reduce bias, allowing them to collaborate more productively (Roberson et al., 2007). The goal then is to create a climate where diversity is seen as a valued outcome in its own right. This allows dissimilar workers to feel they all belong, without having to give up or hide who they really are (Jansen et al., 2015, 2017; Jansen et al., 2014; Şahin et al., 2019).

Instead, the business case for diversity that is so often cited tends to focus on the recruitment of different groups of people mainly to enhance the success of the organization in reaching standard business goals, such as access to broader client populations, improved creativity and product ranges, and increased profits. However, as we have seen, the evidence for the impact of employee diversity on these traditional indicators of team and organizational performance is mixed and depends on conditions such as the quality of team leadership. When looking at outcomes that are less closely related to the business performance of the organization, a review of many studies shows that diversity can and does often have added value for the quality of the governance and decision making and the well-being of employees (Fine et al., 2020).

Fig. 5.3 The importance of inclusion. Summarizes results from a large study revealing that important work-related outcomes do not depend on 'surface level' dissimilarity of employees (i.e., differences in gender, age, ethnicity). The key factor in obtaining beneficial results is a work climate that offers social inclusion for all, despite 'deep level' differences (i.e., in skills or approaches to the task). (Adapted from: Şahin et al. (2019))

Importantly, research shows that subjective feelings of inclusion – rather than the existence of objective differences – are crucial to elicit positive work attitudes. This was revealed, for instance, in a study investigating a broad sample of individuals employed at different levels and job types in a large organization. Countering common expectations, visible differences relating to 'surface level' characteristics such as gender, age or skin color were not decisive for their experiences or for work-related outcomes. Instead, the extent to which the work climate in the organization allowed all to feel included despite more 'deep level' differences in experiences and perspectives was decisive. This predicted a range of outcomes that are important for employees and for the organization, such as their job satisfaction, stress and turnover intentions, career commitment and advancement motivation (see Fig. 5.3: the importance of inclusion; Şahin et al., 2019).

5.4 Conclusion: Beyond Numbers

The benefit of diversity for team and organizational performance is not in having on board workers with different demographics per se. The added value of diversity lies in the openness of the organization to different perspectives, experiences, and sources of expertise workers can bring to the table (see also Chap. 6). The organization's persistence in defining and testing merit with standard procedures that were developed through experiences with the majority group may alleviate concerns about fairness by engaging in moral justification of current practices, moral licensing by expressing good intentions, and moral exclusion by accepting those who are different only when they decide to fit in. However, organizations that do this run the risk of selecting and rewarding workers who may *seem* different (in terms of gender, cultural background) but do not feel free to *act* differently from the norm set by the majority. This will erode their positive attitudes towards the organization and prevents the organization from actually acknowledging the needs of different types of workers. Confronting the painful conclusion that good intentions do not necessarily result in fair practices is necessary to be able to truly accommodate and include different groups of workers and to benefit from their differences.

Recommended Reading

Dobbin, F., & Kalev, A. (2016). Why diversity programs fail. *Harvard Business Review, 94*(7), 14.

Dover, T. L., Kaiser, C. R., & Major, B. (2020). Mixed signals: The unintended effects of diversity initiatives. *Social Issues and Policy Review, 14*(*1*), 152–181. https://doi.org/10.1111/sipr.12059

Ellemers, N., & Barreto, M. (2015). Modern discrimination: How perpetrators and targets interactively perpetuate social disadvantage. *Current Opinion in Behavioral Sciences, 3*, 142–146.

Markus, H. R., & Conner, A. (2014). *Clash!: How to thrive in a multicultural world*. Penguin.

Williams, J. C., & Dempsey, R. (2018). *What works for women at work: Four patterns working women need to know*. NYU Press.

References

Andriessen, I., Nievers, E., Faulk, L., & Dagevos, J. (2010). Liever Mark dan Mohammed? *Sociaal en Cultureel Planbureau.*

Arvate, P. R., Galilea, G. W., & Todescat, I. (2018). The queen bee: A myth? The effect of top-level female leadership on subordinate females. *The Leadership Quarterly, 29*(5), 533–548. https://doi.org/10.1016/j.leaqua.2018.03.002

Asgari, S., Dasgupta, N., & Stout, J. G. (2012). When do counter stereotypic ingroup members inspire versus deflate? The effect of successful professional women on young women's leadership self-concept. *Personality and Social Psychology Bulletin, 38*(3), 370–383. https://doi.org/10.1177/0146167211431968

Ashikali, T., Groeneveld, S., & Kuipers, B. (2020). The role of inclusive leadership in supporting an inclusive climate in diverse public sector teams. *Review of Public Personnel Administration*. https://doi.org/10.1177/0734371X19899722

Barreto, M., & Ellemers, N. (2002). The impact of respect versus neglect of self-identities on identification and group loyalty. *Personality and Social Psychology Bulletin, 28*(5), 629–639. https://doi.org/10.1177/0146167202288007

Barreto, M., & Ellemers, N. (2015). Detecting and experiencing prejudice: New answers to old questions. In M. O. James & P. Z. Mark (Eds.), *Advances in experimental social psychology* (pp. 139–219). Academic. https://doi.org/10.1016/bs.aesp.2015.02.001

Batz-Barbarich, C., Tay, L., Kuykendall, L., & Cheung, H. K. (2018). A meta-analysis of gender differences in subjective well-being: Estimating effect sizes and associations with gender inequality. *Psychological Science, 29*(9), 1491–1503. https://doi.org/10.1177/0956797618774796

Biernat, M., & Manis, M. (1994). Shifting standards and stereotype-based judgments. *Journal of Personality and Social Psychology, 66*(1), 5. https://doi.org/10.1037/0022-3514.66.1.5

Blommaert, L., Coenders, M., & van Tubergen, F. (2014a). Discrimination of Arabic-named applicants in the Netherlands: An internet-based field experiment examining different phases in online recruitment procedures. *Social Forces, 92*(3), 957–982. https://doi.org/10.1093/sf/sot124

Blommaert, L., Coenders, M., & van Tubergen, F. (2014b). Ethnic discrimination in recruitment and decision makers' features: Evidence from laboratory experiment and survey data using a student sample. *Social Indicators Research, 116*(3), 731–754. https://doi.org/10.1007/s11205-013-0329-4

Borch, F. L. (2010). The history of "Don't Ask, Don't Tell" in the army: How we got to it and why it is what it is. *Military Law Review, 203*, 189–206.

Bremmer, D. (2018, June 21). KPN voert vrouwenquotum opnieuw in. *AD*. Retrieved from: https://www.ad.nl/economie/kpn-voert-vrouwenquotum-opnieuw-in~acf16eb4/

Britton, D. M. (2017). Beyond the chilly climate: The salience of gender in women's academic careers. *Gender & Society, 31*(1), 5–27. https://doi.org/10.1177/0891243216681494

Buffington, C., Cerf, B., Jones, C., & Weinberg, B. A. (2016). STEM training and early career outcomes of female and male graduate students: Evidence from UMETRICS data linked to the 2010 census. *American Economic Review, 106*(5), 333–338. https://doi.org/10.1257/aer.p20161124

Carbado, D. W., Gulati, G. M., & Ramachandran, G. (2006). Makeup and women at work. *Harvard Civil Rights-Civil Liberties Law Review (CR-CL)*, 06-01.

Chatard, A., Guimond, S., & Selimbegovic, L. (2007). "How good are you in math?" The effect of gender stereotypes on students' recollection of their school marks. *Journal of Experimental Social Psychology, 43*(6), 1017–1024. https://doi.org/10.1016/j.jesp.2006.10.024

Cihangir, S., Barreto, M., & Ellemers, N. (2014). Men as allies against sexism: The positive effects of a suggestion of sexism by male (vs. female) sources. *SAGE Open, 4*(2). https://doi.org/10.1177/2158244014539168

Clair, J. A., Beatty, J. E., & MacLean, T. L. (2005). Out of sight but not out of mind: Managing invisible social identities in the workplace. *The Academy of Management Review, 30*, 78–95. https://doi.org/10.5465/amr.2005.15281431

Cohen, D., Hoshino-Browne, E., & Leung, A. K.-Y. (2007). Culture and the structure of personal experience: Insider and outsider phenomenologies of the self and social world. In M. Zanna (Ed.), *Advances in experimental social psychology* (pp. 1–67). Academic. https://doi.org/10.1016/S0065-2601(06)39001-6

Cooper, S. (2018). *How to be successful without hurting men's feelings: Non-threatening leadership strategies for women*. Random House.

Correll, S. J., Benard, S., & Paik, I. (2007). Getting a job: Is there a motherhood penalty? *American Journal of Sociology, 112*(5), 1297–1338. https://doi.org/10.1086/511799

Cramwinckel, F. M., Scheepers, D. T., & Van der Toorn, J. (2018). Interventions to reduce blatant and subtle sexual orientation-and gender identity prejudice (SOGIP): Current knowledge and future directions. *Social Issues and Policy Review, 12*(1), 183–217. https://doi.org/10.1111/sipr.12044

Criado-Perez, C. (2019). *Invisible women: Data bias in a world designed for men*. Abrams.

Crosby, F. J., Sabattini, L., & Aizawa, M. (2013). Affirmative action and gender equality. In M. K. Ryan & N. R. Branscombe (Eds.), *The SAGE handbook of gender and psychology* (pp. 484–499). SAGE. https://doi.org/10.4135/9781446269930.n29

Cuddy, A. J., Fiske, S. T., & Glick, P. (2004). When professionals become mothers, warmth doesn't cut the ice. *Journal of Social Issues, 60*(4), 701–718. https://doi.org/10.1111/j.0022-4537.2004.00381.x

Cuddy, A. J., Wolf, E. B., Glick, P., Crotty, S., Chong, J., & Norton, M. I. (2015). Men as cultural ideals: cultural values moderate gender stereotype content. *Journal of Personality and Social Psychology, 109*(4), 622. https://doi.org/10.1037/pspi0000027

Davison, H. K., & Burke, M. J. (2000). Sex discrimination in simulated employment contexts: A meta-analytic investigation. *Journal of Vocational Behavior, 56*, 225–248. https://doi.org/10.1006/jvbe.1999.1711

De Jong, J. (2014, September 25). Telecomvrouw bokst op tegen allochtone man. *Intermediair.* Retrieved from: https://www.intermediair.nl/emancipatie-en-diversiteit/

vrouwen-op-de-arbeidsmarkt/telecomvrouw-bokst-op-tegen-allochtone-man?referrer=https%3A%2F%2Fwww.google.com%2F

Department of Defense. (1993). *Defense directive: Qualification standards for enlistment, appointment, and induction (1304 26)*. Department of Defense. Retrieved from https://www.biotech.law.lsu.edu/blaw/dodd/corres/html2/d130426x.htm

Derks, B., Van Laar, C., & Ellemers, N. (2009). Working for the self or working for the group: How self-versus group affirmation affects collective behavior in low-status groups. *Journal of Personality and Social Psychology, 96*(1), 183. https://doi.org/10.1037/a0013068

Derks, B., Ellemers, N., Van Laar, C., & De Groot, K. (2011). Do sexist organizational cultures create the Queen Bee? *British Journal of Social Psychology, 50*(3), 519–535. https://doi.org/10.1348/014466610X525280

Derks, B., Van Laar, C., Ellemers, N., & Raghoe, G. (2015). Extending the Queen Bee Effect: How Hindustani workers cope with disadvantage by distancing the self from the group. *Journal of Social Issues, 71*, 476–496. https://doi.org/10.1111/josi.12124

Dezso, C. L., & Ross, D. G. (2012). Does female representation in top management improve firm performance? A panel data investigation. *Strategic Management Journal, 33*(9), 1072–1089. https://doi.org/10.1002/smj.1955

DiTomaso, N. (2013). *The American non-dilemma: Racial inequality without racism*. Russell Sage.

Dobbin, F., & Kalev, A. (2016). Why diversity programs fail. *Harvard Business Review, 94*(7), 14.

Dobbin, F., & Kalev, A. (2019). The promise and peril of sexual harassment programs. *Proceedings of the National Academy of Sciences, 116*(25), 12255–12260. https://doi.org/10.1073/pnas.1818477116

Don't Ask. (2010). Don't tell repeal act of 2010, Pub. L. No. 111-321, 124 Stat. 3515. Retrieved from www.gpo.gov/fdsys/pkg/PLAW.../pdf/PLAW-111publ321.pdf

Dover, T. L., Major, B., & Kaiser, C. R. (2016). Members of high-status groups are threatened by pro-diversity organizational messages. *Journal of Experimental Social Psychology, 62*, 58–67. https://doi.org/10.1016/j.jesp.2015.10.006

Dover, T. L., Kaiser, C. R., & Major, B. (2020a). Mixed signals: The unintended effects of diversity initiatives. *Social Issues and Policy Review, 14*(1), 152–181. https://doi.org/10.1111/sipr.12059

Dover, T. L., Major, B., & Kaiser, C. R. (2020b). Cardiovascular, behavioral, and psychological responses to organizational prodiversity messages among racial/ethnic minorities. *Group Processes and Intergroup Relations*. https://doi.org/10.1177/1368430220944222

Drury, B. J., & Kaiser, C. R. (2014). Allies against sexism: The role of men in confronting sexism. *Journal of Social Issues, 70*(4), 637–652. https://doi.org/10.1111/josi.12083

Eagly, A. H. (2012). Behavior: Meta-analytic studies of social psychological research. *The Development of Sex Differences and Similarities in Behavior, 73*, 421. https://doi.org/10.1007/978-94-011-1709-8_25

Eagly, A. H. (2016). When passionate advocates meet research on diversity, does the honest broker stand a chance?: Erratum. *Journal of Social Issues, 72*(2), 413. https://doi.org/10.1111/josi.12173

Eagly, A. H., & Wood, W. (2013). The nature–nurture debates: 25 years of challenges in understanding the psychology of gender. *Perspectives on Psychological Science, 8*(3), 340–357. https://doi.org/10.1177/1745691613484767

Ebrahimi, M., Kouchaki, M., & Patrick, V. M. (2019). Juggling work and home selves: Low identity integration feels less authentic and increases unethicality. *Organizational Behavior and Human Decision Processes, 158*, 101–111. https://doi.org/10.1016/j.obhdp.2019.02.005

Ellemers, N. (2001). Individual upward mobility and the perceived legitimacy of intergroup relations. In J. T. Jost & B. Major (Eds.), *The psychology of legitimacy: Emerging perspectives on ideology, justice, and intergroup relations* (pp. 205–222). Cambridge University Press.

Ellemers, N. (2014). Women at work: How organizational features impact career development. *Policy Insights From the Behavioral and Brain Sciences, 1*(1), 46–54. https://doi.org/10.1177/2372732214549327

Ellemers, N. (2018a). Gender stereotypes. *Annual Review of Psychology, 69*, 275–298. https://doi.org/10.1146/annurev-psych-122216-011719

Ellemers, N. (2018b). Morality and social identity. In M. van Zomeren & J. F. Dovidio (Eds.), *Oxford library of psychology. The Oxford handbook of the human essence* (pp. 147–158). Oxford University Press. https://doi.org/10.1093/oxfordhb/9780190247577.013.5

Ellemers, N., & Barreto, M. (2006). Categorization in everyday life: The effects of positive and negative categorizations on emotions and self-views. *European Journal of Social Psychology, 36*(6), 931–942. https://doi.org/10.1002/ejsp.333

Ellemers, N., & Barreto, M. (2009). Collective action in modern times: How modern expressions of prejudice prevent collective action. *Journal of Social Issues, 65*, 749–768. https://doi.org/10.1111/j.1540-4560.2009.01621.x

Ellemers, N., & Barreto, M. (2015). Modern discrimination: How perpetrators and targets interactively perpetuate social disadvantage. *Current Opinion in Behavioral Sciences, 3*, 142–146. https://doi.org/10.1016/j.cobeha.2015.04.001

Ellemers, N., & Rink, F. (2005). Identity in work groups: The beneficial and detrimental consequences of multiple identities and group norms for collaboration and group performance. *Advances in Group Processes, 22*(1), 1–41. https://doi.org/10.1016/S0882-6145(05)22001-5

Ellemers, N., & Rink, F. (2016). Diversity in work groups. *Current Opinion in Psychology, 11*, 49–53. https://doi.org/10.1016/j.copsyc.2016.06.001

Ellemers, N., & Van Laar, C. (2010). Individual mobility: The opportunities and challenges members of devalued groups encounter when trying to avoid group-based discrimination. In J. F. Dovidio, M. Hewstone, P. Glick, & V. Esses (Eds.), *Handbook of prejudice, stereotyping, and discrimintation* (pp. 561–576). Sage. https://doi.org/10.4135/9781446200919.n34

Ellemers, N., Van den Heuvel, H., De Gilder, D., Maass, A., & Bonvini, A. (2004). The underrepresentation of women in science: Differential commitment or the Queen-bee syndrome? *British Journal of Social Psychology, 43*, 315–338. https://doi.org/10.1348/0144666042037999

Ellemers, N., Rink, F., Derks, B., & Ryan, M. (2012). Women in high places: When and why promoting women into top positions can harm them individually or as a group (and how to prevent this). *Research in Organizational Behavior, 32*, 163–187. https://doi.org/10.1016/j.riob.2012.10.003

Ellemers, N., Van der Toorn, J., Paunov, Y., & Van Leeuwen, T. (2019). The psychology of morality: A review and analysis of empirical studies published from 1940 through 2017. *Personality and Social Psychology Review, 23*(4), 332–366. https://doi.org/10.1177/1088868318811759

Faniko, K., Lorenzi-Cioldi, F., Buschini, F., & Chatard, A. (2012). The influence of education on attitudes toward affirmative action: The role of the policy's strength. *Journal of Applied Social Psychology, 42*(2), 387–413. https://doi.org/10.1111/j.1559-1816.2011.00892.x

Faniko, K., Ellemers, N., & Derks, B. (2016). Queen Bees and Alpha Males: Are successful women more competitive than successful men? *European Journal of Social Psychology, 46*(7), 903–913. https://doi.org/10.1002/ejsp.2198

Faniko, K., Ellemers, N., Derks, B., & Lorenzi-Cioldi, F. (2017). Nothing changes, really: Why women who break through the glass ceiling end up reinforcing it. *Personality and Social Psychology Bulletin, 43*(5), 638–651. https://doi.org/10.1177/0146167217695551

Faniko, K., Ellemers, N., & Derks, B. (2020). The Queen Bee phenomenon in Academia 15 years after: Does it still exist, and if so, why? *British Journal of Social Psychology, 60*(2), e12408. https://doi.org/10.1111/bjso.12408

Fine, C. (2013). Neurosexism in functional neuroimaging: from scanner to pseudo-science to psyche. *The SAGE Handbook of Gender and Psychology*, 45–60.

Fine, C., Sojo, V., & Lawford-Smith, H. (2020). Why does workplace gender diversity matter? Justice, organizational benefits, and policy. *Social Issues and Policy Review, 14*(1), 36–72. https://doi.org/10.1111/sipr.12064

Fiske, S. T., Bersoff, D. N., Borgida, E., Deaux, K., & Heilman, M. E. (1991). Social science research on trial: Use of sex stereotyping research in Price Waterhouse v. Hopkins. *American Psychologist, 46*(10), 1049. https://doi.org/10.1037/0003-066X.46.10.1049

Fuegen, K., Biernat, M., Haines, E., & Deaux, K. (2004). Mothers and fathers in the workplace: How gender and parental status influence judgments of job-related competence. *Journal of Social Issues, 60*(4), 737–754. https://doi.org/10.1111/j.0022-4537.2004.00383.x

Garcia, D., Schmitt, M. T., Branscombe, N. R., & Ellemers, N. (2010). Women's reactions to ingroup members who protest discriminatory treatment: The importance of beliefs about inequality and response appropriateness. *European Journal of Social Psychology, 40*, 733–745. https://doi.org/10.1002/ejsp.644

Gino, F., Kouchaki, M., & Galinsky, A. D. (2015). The moral virtue of authenticity: How inauthenticity produces feelings of immorality and impurity. *Psychological Science, 26*(7), 983–996. https://doi.org/10.1177/0956797615575277

Gladwell, M. (2010, September 27). Small change: Why the revolution will not be tweeted. *The New Yorker*. Retrieved from https://www.newyorker.com/magazine/2010/10/04/small-change-malcolm-gladwell

Goldin, C., & Rouse, C. (2000). Orchestrating impartiality: The impact of "blind" auditions on female musicians. *American Economic Review, 90*(4), 715–741. https://doi.org/10.1257/aer.90.4.715

Goodwin, S. A., Gubin, A., Fiske, S. T., & Yzerbyt, V. Y. (2000). Power can bias impression processes: Stereotyping subordinates by default and by design. *Group Processes & Intergroup Relations, 3*(3), 227–256. https://doi.org/10.1177/1368430200003003001

Gras, M., & Bovenkerk, F. (1999). Migrants and ethnic minorities in the Netherlands: Discrimination in access to employment. In J. Wrench, A. Rea, & N. Ouali (Eds.), *Migrants, ethnic minorities and the labour market. Migration, minorities and citizenship*. Palgrave Macmillan. https://doi.org/10.1007/978-1-349-27615-8_6

Griffith, K. H., & Hebl, M. R. (2002). The disclosure dilemma for gay men and lesbians: "Coming out" at work. *Journal of Applied Psychology, 87*(6), 1191. https://doi.org/10.1037/0021-9010.87.6.1191

Guillaume, Y. R. F., Brodbeck, F. C., & Riketta, M. (2012). Surface and deep-level dissimilarity effects on social integration and individual effectiveness related outcomes in work groups: A meta-analytic integration. *Journal of Occupational and Organizational Psychology, 85*, 80–115. https://doi.org/10.1111/j.2044-8325.2010.02005.x

Hamamura, T., & Heine, S. (2008). The role of self-criticism in self-improvement and face maintenance among Japanese. In E. C. Chang (Ed.), *Self-criticism and self-enhancement: Theory, research, and clinical implications* (pp. 105–122). https://doi.org/10.1037/11624-007

Handley, I. M., Brown, E. R., Moss-Racusin, C. A., & Smith, J. L. (2015). Quality of evidence revealing subtle gender biases in science is in the eye of the beholder. *Proceedings of the National Academy of Sciences, 112*(43), 13201–13206. https://doi.org/10.1073/pnas.1510649112

Harinck, S., Shafa, S., Ellemers, N., & Beersma, B. (2013). The good news about honor culture: The preference for cooperative conflict management in the absence of insult. *Negotiation and Conflict Management Research, 6*, 67–78. https://doi.org/10.1111/ncmr.12007

Heilman, M. E., & Okimoto, T. G. (2008). Motherhood: A potential source of bias in employment decisions. *Journal of Applied Psychology, 93*(1), 189. https://doi.org/10.1037/0021-9010.93.1.189

Hidden Pay Differences in Academia. (2019, March 25). Hidden pay differences in academia: Female scientists do ask, but don't get. *Utrecht University*. Retrieved from https://www.uu.nl/en/news/hidden-pay-differences-in-academia-female-scientists-do-ask-but-dont-get

Hofstede, G. (2001). *Culture's consequences: Comparing values, behaviours, institutions and organizations across nations*. Beverly Hills.

Hopkins, A. B. (1996). *So ordered: Making partner the hard way*. University of Massachusetts Press.

Hyde, J. S. (2014). Gender similarities and differences. *Annual Review of Psychology, 65*, 373–398. https://doi.org/10.1146/annurev-psych-010213-115057

Jansen, W. S., Otten, S., Van der Zee, K. I., & Jans, L. (2014). Inclusion: Conceptualization and measurement. *European Journal of Social Psychology, 44*(4), 370–385. https://doi.org/10.1002/ejsp.2011

Jansen, W. S., Otten, S., & Van der Zee, K. I. (2015). Being part of diversity: The effects of an all-inclusive multicultural diversity approach on majority members' perceived inclusion and support for organizational diversity efforts. *Group Processes & Intergroup Relations, 18*(6), 817–832. https://doi.org/10.1177/1368430214566892

Jansen, W. S., Otten, S., & Van der Zee, K. I. (2017). Being different at work: How gender dissimilarity relates to social inclusion and absenteeism. *Group Processes & Intergroup Relations, 20*(6), 879–893. https://doi.org/10.1177/1368430215625783
Jaurique, A., Ryan, D. A., Smith, H. J., & Paolucci-Callahan, M. (2019). Observing discrimination: Implications for group-based respect and organizational morality. *Social Issues and Policy Review, 13*(1), 125–153. https://doi.org/10.1111/sipr.12050
Jongen, E. L. W., Bolhaar, J., Elk, R. V., Koot, P., & Vuuren, D. V. (2019). Inkomensongelijkheid naar migratieachtergrond. *CPB Policy Brief, 15*.
Joshi, A., Son, J., & Roh, H. (2015). When can women close the gap? A meta-analytic test of sex differences in performance and rewards. *Academy of Management Journal, 58*(5), 1516–1545. https://doi.org/10.5465/amj.2013.0721
Kaiser, C. R., & Miller, C. T. (2001). Stop complaining! The social costs of making attributions to discrimination. *Personality and Social Psychology Bulletin, 27*(2), 254–263. https://doi.org/10.1177/0146167201272010
Kaiser, C. R., & Miller, C. T. (2003). Derogating the victim: The interpersonal consequences of blaming events on discrimination. *Group Processes & Intergroup Relations, 6*(3), 227–237. https://doi.org/10.1177/13684302030063001
Kaiser, C. R., & Miller, C. T. (2004). A stress and coping perspective on confronting sexism. *Psychology of Women Quarterly, 28*(2), 168–178. https://doi.org/10.1111/j.1471-6402.2004.00133.x
Kaiser, C. R., Major, B., Jurcevic, I., Dover, T. L., Brady, L. M., & Shapiro, J. R. (2013). Presumed fair: Ironic effects of organizational diversity structures. *Journal of Personality and Social Psychology, 104*(3), 504. https://doi.org/10.1037/a0030838
Kalev, A., Dobbin, F., & Kelly, E. (2006). Best practices or best guesses? Assessing the efficacy of corporate affirmative action and diversity policies. *American Sociological Review, 71*(4), 589–617. https://doi.org/10.1177/000312240607100404
Kim, Y., & Cohen, D. (2010). Information, perspective, and judgments about the self in face and dignity cultures. *Personality and Social Psychology Bulletin, 36*, 537–550. https://doi.org/10.1177/0146167210362398
Kouchaki, M. (2011). Vicarious moral licensing: The influence of others' past moral actions on moral behavior. *Journal of Personality and Social Psychology, 101*(4), 702. https://doi.org/10.1037/a0024552
Kouchaki, M. (2019). Why authentic workplaces are more ethical. *Harvard Business Review*. Retrieved from https://hbr.org/2019/06/why-authentic-workplaces-are-more-ethical
Kouchaki, M., & Wareham, J. (2015). Excluded and behaving unethically: Social exclusion, physiological responses, and unethical behavior. *Journal of Applied Psychology, 100*(2), 547. https://doi.org/10.1037/a0038034
Kulik, C. T., & Olekalns, M. (2012). Negotiating the gender divide: Lessons from the negotiation and organizational behavior literatures. *Journal of Management, 38*(4), 1387–1415. https://doi.org/10.1177/0149206311431307
Leung, A. K. Y., & Cohen, D. (2011). Within- and between-culture variation: Individual differences and the cultural logics of honor, face, and dignity cultures. *Journal of Personality and Social Psychology, 100*(3), 507–526. https://doi.org/10.1037/a0022151
Log Cabin Republicans v. United States. (2010). 716 F. Supp. 2d 88, C.D. Cal. Retrieved from https://www.casetext.com/case/log-cabin-republicans-v-us-3
Ma, Y., Oliveira, D. F., Woodruff, T. K., & Uzzi, B. (2019). Women who win prizes get less money and prestige. *Nature*. https://doi.org/10.1038/d41586-019-00091-3
Madera, J. M., Dawson, M., & Neal, J. A. (2018). Why investing in diversity management matters: Organizational attraction and person–organization fit. *Journal of Hospitality & Tourism Research, 42*(6), 931–959. https://doi.org/10.1177/1096348016654973
Malmström, M., Johansson, J., & Wincent, J. (2017). Gender stereotypes and venture support decisions: How governmental venture capitalists socially construct entrepreneurs' potential. *Entrepreneurship Theory and Practice, 41*(5), 833–860. https://doi.org/10.1111/etap.12275
Maranto, C. L., & Griffin, A. E. (2010). The antecedents of a 'chilly climate' for women faculty in higher education. *Human Relations, 64*(2), 139–159. https://doi.org/10.1177/0018726710377932

Marks, K., McCarthy, S., Matthewson, T., Mullan, L., & Jovic, M. (2018). Research into the low visibility and engagement of same-sex attracted women in the workplace: Where are all the women? *PricewaterhouseCoopers*. Retrieved from http://www.prideinhealth.com.au/wp-content/uploads/2020/03/PID_where-are-all-the-women-aug18_optimised.pdf

Markus, H. R., & Conner, A. (2014). *Clash!: How to thrive in a multicultural world*. Penguin.

Markus, H. R., & Kitayama, S. (1991). Culture and the self: Implications for cognition, emotion, and motivation. *Psychological Review, 98*(2), 224. https://doi.org/10.1037/0033-295X.98.2.224

McCloskey, D. N. (1999). From donald to deirdre: How a man became a woman — and what it says about identity. *Excerpt from Deirdre McCloskey's Crossing, A Memoir*. Retrieved from https://www.deirdremccloskey.com/gender/dee.php

Monin, B., & Miller, D. T. (2001). Moral credentials and the expression of prejudice. *Journal of Personality and Social Psychology, 81*(1), 33. https://doi.org/10.1037/0022-3514.81.1.33

Moscatelli, S., Menegatti, M., Ellemers, N., Mariani, M.G., & Rubini, M. (2020). Men should be competent, women should have it all: Multiple criteria in the evaluation of female candidates. *Sex Roles, 83*, 269–288. https://doi.org/10.1007/s11199-019-01111-2

Moss-Racusin, C. A., Van der Toorn, J., Dovidio, J. F., Brescoll, V. L., Graham, M. J., & Handelsman, J. (2014). Scientific diversity interventions. *Science, 343*(6171), 615–616. https://doi.org/10.1126/science.1245936

Netchaeva, E., Kouchaki, M., & Sheppard, L. D. (2015). A man's (precarious) place: Men's experienced threat and self-assertive reactions to female superiors. *Personality and Social Psychology Bulletin, 41*(9), 1247–1259. https://doi.org/10.1177/0146167215593491

Newheiser, A. K., & Barreto, M. (2014). Hidden costs of hiding stigma: Ironic interpersonal consequences of concealing a stigmatized identity in social interactions. *Journal of Experimental Social Psychology, 52*, 58–70. https://doi.org/10.1016/j.jesp.2014.01.002

Newheiser, A. K., Barreto, M., Ellemers, N., Derks, B., & Scheepers, D. (2015). Regulatory focus moderates the social performance of individuals who conceal a stigmatized identity. *British Journal of Social Psychology, 54*, 787–797. https://doi.org/10.1111/bjso.12107

Nishii, L. H. (2012). The benefits of climate for inclusion for gender-diverse groups. *Academy of Management Journal, 56*(6), 1754–1774. https://doi.org/10.5465/amj.2009.0823

Nishii, L. H., Khattab, J., Shemla, M., & Paluch, R. M. (2018). A multi-level process model forunderstanding diversity practice effectiveness. *Academy of Management Annals, 12*(1), 37–82. https://doi.org/10.5465/annals.2016.0044

Noland, M., Moran, T., & Kotschwar, B. R. (2016). Is gender diversity profitable? Evidence from a global survey. *Peterson Institute for International Economics Working Paper, 16*(3). https://doi.org/10.2139/ssrn.2729348

Ntim, C. G. (2015). Board diversity and organizational valuation: Unravelling the effects of ethnicity and gender. *Journal of Management & Governance, 19*(1), 167–195. https://doi.org/10.1007/s10997-013-9283-4

O'Reilly, J., Aquino, K., & Skarlicki, D. (2016). The lives of others: Third parties' responses to others' injustice. *Journal of Applied Psychology, 101*(2), 171–189. https://doi.org/10.1037/apl0000040

Osborne, J. (2019). The impact of migration on earnings inequality, *Working Papers, 19*(5), Federal Reserve Bank of Boston, Boston, MA.

Pender, K. (2019). Us Too? Bullying and sexual harassment in the legal profession. *International Bar Association*. https://www.ibanet.org/bullying-and-sexual-harassment.aspx

Proudfoot, D., Kay, A. C., & Koval, C. Z. (2015). A gender bias in the attribution of creativity: Archival and experimental evidence for the perceived association between masculinity and creative thinking. *Psychological Science, 26*(11), 1751–1761. https://doi.org/10.1177/0956797615598739

Quadlin, N. (2018). The mark of a woman's record: Gender and academic performance in hiring. *American Sociological Review, 83*(2), 331–360. https://doi.org/10.1177/0003122418762291

Quinn, D. M., & Chaudoir, S. R. (2009). Living with a concealable stigmatized identity: The impact of anticipated stigma, centrality, salience, and cultural stigma on psychological distress and health. *Journal of Personality and Social Psychology, 97*, 634–651. https://doi.org/10.1037/a0015815

Ragins, B. R., Singh, R., & Cornwell, J. M. (2007). Making the invisible visible: Fear and disclosure of sexual orientation at work. *Journal of Applied Psychology, 92*, 1103–1118. https://doi.org/10.1037/0021-9010.92.4.1103

Ridgeway, C. L. (2001). Gender, status, and leadership. *Journal of Social Issues, 57*(4), 637–655. https://doi.org/10.1111/0022-4537.00233

Riggs, J. M. (1997). Mandates for mothers and fathers: Perceptions of breadwinners and care givers. *Sex Roles, 37*(7–8), 565–580. https://doi.org/10.1023/A:1025611119822

Rink, F., & Ellemers, N. (2007a). The role of expectancies in accepting task-related diversity: Do disappointment and lack of commitment stem from actual differences or violated expectations? *Personality and Social Psychology Bulletin, 33*, 842–854. https://doi.org/10.1177/0146167207301016

Rink, F., & Ellemers, N. (2007b). Defining the common feature: Task-related differences as the basis for dyadic identity. *British Journal of Social Psychology, 46*, 499–515. https://doi.org/10.1348/014466606X154872

Rink, F., & Ellemers, N. (2007c). Diversity as a source of common identity: Towards a social identity framework for studying the effects of diversity in organizations. *British Journal of Management, 18*(1), 17–27. https://doi.org/10.1111/j.1467-8551.2007.00523.x

Rink, F., & Ellemers, N. (2008). Diversity, newcomers, and team innovation: The importance of a common identity. *Diversity and Groups: Research on Managing Groups and Teams, 11*, 221–243. https://doi.org/10.1016/S1534-0856(08)11010-6

Rink, F., & Ellemers, N. (2009). Temporary versus permanent group membership: How the future prospects of newcomers affect newcomer acceptance and newcomer influence. *Personality and Social Psychology Bulletin, 35*(6), 764–775. https://doi.org/10.1177/0146167209333177

Rink, F., & Ellemers, N. (2010a). Benefiting from deep-level diversity: How congruence between knowledge and decision rules improves team decision making and team perceptions. *Group Processes & Intergroup Relations, 13*(3), 345–359. https://doi.org/10.1177/1368430209344866

Rink, F., & Ellemers, N. (2010b). From current state to desired future: How compositional changes affect dissent and innovation in work groups. *Rebels in Groups: Dissent, Deviance, Difference and Defiance*, 54–72. https://doi.org/10.1002/9781444390841.ch4

Rink, F., Kane, A. A., Ellemers, N., & Van der Vegt, G. (2013a). Team receptivity to newcomers: Five decades of evidence and future research themes. *Academy of Management Annals, 7*(1), 247–293. https://doi.org/10.5465/19416520.2013.766405

Rink, F., Ryan, M. K., & Stoker, J. I. (2013b). Social resources at a time of crisis: How gender stereotypes inform gendered leader evaluations. *European Journal of Social Psychology, 43*(5), 381–392. https://doi.org/10.1002/ejsp.1954

Roberson, L., Galvin, B. M., & Charles, A. C. (2007). When group identities matter: Bias in performance appraisal. *The Academy of Management Annals, 1*(1), 617–650. https://doi.org/10.5465/078559818

Rodriguez Mosquera, P. M. (2013). In the name of honor: On virtue, reputation and violence. *Group Processes and Intergroup Relations, 16*(3), 271–278. https://doi.org/10.1177/1368430212472590

Ryan, M. K., & Haslam, S. A. (2007). The glass cliff: Exploring the dynamics surrounding the appointment of women to precarious leadership positions. *Academy of Management Review, 32*(2), 549–572. https://doi.org/10.5465/amr.2007.24351856

Ryan, M. K., Haslam, S. A., Morgenroth, T., Rink, F., Stoker, J., & Peters, K. (2016). Getting on top of the glass cliff: Reviewing a decade of evidence, explanations, and impact. *The Leadership Quarterly, 27*(3), 446–455. https://doi.org/10.1016/j.leaqua.2015.10.008

Şahin, O., Van der Toorn, J., Jansen, W. S., Boezeman, E. J., & Ellemers, N. (2019). Looking beyond our similarities: How perceived (in) visible dissimilarity relates to feelings of inclusion at work. *Frontiers in Psychology, 10*, 575. https://doi.org/10.3389/fpsyg.2019.00575

Schmitt, M. T., & Branscombe, N. R. (2001). The good, the bad, and the manly: Threats to one's prototypicality and evaluations of fellow in-group members. *Journal of Experimental Social Psychology, 37*(6), 510–517. https://doi.org/10.1006/jesp.2001.1476

Sheppard, L. D., & Aquino, K. (2017). Sisters at arms: A theory of female same-sex conflict and its problematization in organizations. *Journal of Management, 43*(3), 691–715. https://doi.org/10.1177/0149206314539348

Sojo, V. E., Wood, R. E., & Genat, A. E. (2016). Harmful workplace experiences and women's occupational well-being: A meta-analysis. *Psychology of Women Quarterly, 40*(1), 10–40. https://doi.org/10.1177/0361684315599346

Stroebe, K. E., Ellemers, N., Barreto, M., & Mummendey, A. (2009). For better or for worse: The congruence of personal and group outcomes on targets' responses to discrimination. *European Journal of Social Psychology, 39*, 576–591. https://doi.org/10.1002/ejsp.557

Stroebe, K. E., Dovidio, J. F., Barreto, M., Ellemers, N., & John, M. S. (2011). Is the world a just place? Countering the negative consequences of pervasive discrimination by affirming the world as just. *British Journal of Social Psychology, 50*, 484–500. https://doi.org/10.1348/014466610X523057

Stuhlmacher, A. F., & Walters, A. E. (1999). Gender differences in negotiation outcome: A meta-analysis. *Personnel Psychology, 52*(3), 653–677. https://doi.org/10.1111/j.1744-6570.1999.tb00175.x

Swim, J. K., & Stangor, C. (1998). *Prejudice: The target's perspective*. Elsevier.

Talke, K., Salomo, S., & Kock, A. (2011). Top management team diversity and strategic innovation orientation: The relationship and consequences for innovativeness and performance. *Journal of Product Innovation Management, 28*(6), 819–832. https://doi.org/10.1111/j.1540-5885.2011.00851.x

Triandis, H. C. (1994). *Culture and social behavior*. McGraw-Hill.

Tripathi, R., Cervone, D., & Savani, K. (2018). Are the motivational effects of autonomy-supportive conditions universal? Contrasting results among Indians and Americans. *Personality and Social Psychology Bulletin, 44*(9), 1287–1301. https://doi.org/10.1177/0146167218764663

Truth Seeker. (2015, July 8). *Neil Tyson on being a woman and black in science* [Video]. YouTube. Retrieved from https://www.youtube.com/watch?v=q5S7QD9dryI

Turner, J. C., Hogg, M. A., Oakes, P. J., Reicher, S. D., & Wetherell, M. S. (1987). *Rediscovering the social group: A self-categorization theory*. Basil Blackwell.

Turner, J. C., Oakes, P. J., Haslam, S. A., & McGarty, C. (1994). Self and collective: Cognition and social context. *Personality and Social Psychology Bulletin, 20*, 454–463. https://doi.org/10.1177/0146167294205002

Uttal, D. H., Meadow, N. G., Tipton, E., Hand, L. L., Alden, A. R., Warren, C., & Newcombe, N. S. (2013). The malleability of spatial skills: A meta-analysis of training studies. *Psychological Bulletin, 139*(2), 352. https://doi.org/10.1037/a0028446

Van den Brink, M., & Benschop, Y. (2012). Gender practices in the construction of academic excellence: Sheep with five legs. *Organization, 19*(4), 507–524. https://doi.org/10.1177/1350508411414293

Van der Lee, R., & Ellemers, N. (2015). Gender contributes to personal research funding success in The Netherlands. *Proceedings of the National Academy of Sciences, 112*(40), 12349–12353. https://doi.org/10.1073/pnas.1510159112

Van der Toorn, J. (2019). Toward an inclusive workplace: Sexual orientation and gender identity at work. *Gedrag & Organisatie, 32*(3), 162–180.

Van Der Vegt, G. S., & Bunderson, J. S. (2005). Learning and performance in multidisciplinary teams: The importance of collective team identification. *The Academy of Management Journal, 48*(3), 532–547. https://doi.org/10.2307/20159674

Van Dijk, H., Van Engen, M. L., & Van Knippenberg, D. (2012). Defying conventional wisdom: A meta-analytical examination of the differences between demographic and job-related diversity relationships with performance. *Organizational Behavior and Human Decision Processes, 119*(1), 38–53. https://doi.org/10.1016/j.obhdp.2012.06.003

Van Knippenberg, D., & Schippers, M. C. (2007). Work group diversity. *Annual Review Psychology, 58*, 515–541. https://doi.org/10.1146/annurev.psych.58.110405.085546

Van Laar, C., Derks, B., & Ellemers, N. (2013). Motivation for education and work in young Muslim women: The importance of value for ingroup domains. *Basic and Applied Social Psychology, 35*(1), 64–74. https://doi.org/10.1080/01973533.2012.746609

Van Laar, C., Bleeker, D., Ellemers, N., & Meijer, E. (2014). Ingroup and outgroup support for upward mobility: Divergent responses to ingroup identification in low status groups. *European Journal of Social Psychology, 44*, 563–577. https://doi.org/10.1002/ejsp.2046

Van Steenbergen, E. F., & Ellemers, N. (2009a). Feeling committed to work: How specific forms of work-commitment predict work behavior and performance over time. *Human Performance, 22*(5), 410–431. https://doi.org/10.1080/08959280903248385

Van Steenbergen, E. F., & Ellemers, N. (2009b). Is managing the work–family interface worthwhile? Benefits for employee health and performance. *Journal of Organizational Behavior, 30*(5), 617–642. https://doi.org/10.1002/job.569

Van Steenbergen, E. F., Ellemers, N., Haslam, S. A., & Urlings, F. (2008). There is nothing either good or bad but thinking makes it so: Informational support and cognitive appraisal of the work-family interface. *Journal of Occupational and Organizational Psychology, 81*(3), 349–367. https://doi.org/10.1348/096317908X312669

Van Steenbergen, E. F., Ellemers, N., & Mooijaart, A. (2009). How family supportive work environments and work supportive home environments can reduce work-family conflict and enhance facilitation. *Handbook of Families & Work: Interdisciplinary Perspectives*, 79–104.

Van Veelen, R., & Derks, B. (2019a). *Double trouble: How being outnumbered ánd negatively stereotyped negatively affect career outcomes of women in STEM*. Paper presented at 19th European Congress of Work and Organizational Psychology 2019, Turin, Italy. https://doi.org/10.3389/fpsyg.2019.00150.

Van Veelen, R., & Derks, B. (2019b). Verborgen verschillen in werktaken, hulpbronnen en onderhandelingen over arbeidsvoorwaarden tussen vrouwelijke en mannelijke wetenschappers in Nederland: Onderzoek uitgevoerd in opdracht van het Landelijk Netwerk Vrouwelijke Hoogleraren. *LNVH*.

Vandello, J. A., & Cohen, D. (2003). Male honor and female fidelity: Implicit cultural scripts that perpetuate domestic violence. *Journal of Personality and Social Psychology, 84*, 997–1010. https://doi.org/10.1037/0022-3514.84.5.997

Vial, A. C., Brescoll, V. L., Napier, J. L., Dovidio, J. F., & Tyler, T. R. (2018). Differential support for female supervisors among men and women. *Journal of Applied Psychology, 103*(2), 215–227. https://doi.org/10.1037/apl0000258

Vuletich, H. A., & Payne, B. K. (2019). Stability and change in implicit bias. *Psychological Science, 30*(6), 854–862. https://doi.org/10.1177/0956797619844270

Wade, M. E. (2001). Women and salary negotiation: The costs of self-advocacy. *Psychology of Women Quarterly, 25*(1), 65–76. https://doi.org/10.1111/1471-6402.00008

Williams, J. C., & Dempsey, R. (2018). *What works for women at work: Four patterns working women need to know*. NYU Press.

Witteman, H. O., Hendricks, M., Straus, S., & Tannenbaum, C. (2019). Are gender gaps due to evaluations of the applicant or the science? A natural experiment at a national funding agency. *The Lancet, 393*(10171), 531–540. https://doi.org/10.1016/S0140-6736(18)32611-4

Wong, J. C. (2018, February 22). Ex-engineer sues Google, saying he was fired for condemning diversity memo. *The Guardian*. Retrieved from https://www.theguardian.com/technology/2018/feb/21/google-lawsuit-tim-chevalier-diversity-james-damore

Woolley, A. W., Aggarwal, I., & Malone, T. W. (2015). Collective intelligence and group performance. *Current Directions in Psychological Science, 24*(6), 420–424. https://doi.org/10.1177/0963721415599543

Wyer, M., Barbercheck, M., Cookmeyer, D., Ozturk, H., & Wayne, M. (2013). *Women, science, and technology: A reader in feminist science studies*. Routledge. https://doi.org/10.4324/9780203427415

Zhong, C. B., Liljenquist, K., & Cain, D. M. (2009). Moral self-regulation: Licensing and compensation. In D. De Cremer (Ed.), *Psychological perspectives on ethical behavior and decision making* (pp. 75–89). Information Age Publishing.

Zhu, L. L., Aquino, K., & Vadera, A. K. (2016). What makes professors appear credible: The effect of demographic characteristics and ideological beliefs. *Journal of Applied Psychology, 101*(6), 862–880. https://doi.org/10.1037/apl0000095

Chapter 6
The Human Factor in Organizational Change

Abstract The **key issues** in this chapter all relate to the risk that organizational change and innovation deplete human resources. Using quick fixes to adopt new forms of employment, new ways of working, or new products and services, impact on the identity and inclusion of people in organizations. It makes those who express valid concerns about the timeliness, feasibility, or risks of such changes seem less central to the key focus and mission of the organization. Our **analysis** reveals the moral hazards of addressing organizational change purely as a strategic business problem. Relying on flexible employment ignores employee needs. Awarding the highest prestige to those who develop new ideas devalues those who are responsible for the feasibility and safety of proposed changes. The use of moral exclusion,

---

The original version of this chapter was revised. The correction to this chapter is available at https://doi.org/10.1007/978-3-030-84175-1_9

N. Ellemers, D. de Gilder, *The Moral Organization: Key Issues, Analyses, and Solutions*, https://doi.org/10.1007/978-3-030-84175-1_6

moral neglect and moral justification as identity management strategies allow organizations to dismiss valid concerns as stemming from 'resistance to change'. Research reveals that this reduces the likelihood that vital information is shared, and diminishes the ability of the organization to make morally responsible decisions. We propose **solutions** that mitigate the moral hazards of organizational change, by more explicitly taking into account the human factor. The success of mergers and acquisitions is enhanced when culture clashes are anticipated and resolved. Attracting newcomers will add more value when they are encouraged to collaborate with old hands. Creating mutual trust and respect between those who develop new ideas and those who are able to recognize high quality, feasible, and safe options protects the organization from introducing new strategies, products, and services that turn out to be morally irresponsible. Ensuring that multiple viewpoints are included and valued as defining the identity of the organization prevents moral hazards and benefits responsible adaptation.

6.1 Key Issues: Stagnation Means Decline?

There is no dispute that adaptation and change are essential to the long-term survival of almost any organization. Continually updating, improving, and developing new products, services, and procedures is indispensable when it comes to catering for changing client populations or customer demands. It helps to sustain competitive advantage, and is generally needed to keep up with global developments (Birkinshaw et al., 2017; Tidd & Bessant, 2018). This realization easily leads to the assumption that any form of change is, by definition, superior to continuing business as usual. *Stagnation means decline* is frequently offered as the primary reason to introduce change – and to dismiss those who question the need for doing this.

Not every change is an improvement, however, and some introduce moral hazards. Changes can have moral implications when people and products are labeled outdated and discarded before viable alternatives are available, while legitimate concerns not to do so are dismissed as resulting from 'resistance to change'. Some companies go to market before fully testing the quality of new services or the safety of innovative products – which happened at Boeing, at the cost of hundreds of human lives (see Chap. 1). The eagerness to keep up with market changes can also tempt organizations to implement new ways of working and (digital) solutions that harm the well-being of their employees, turn out not to be legally admissible, or undermine the continuity of customer services in ways that were not anticipated (Morgan, 2019). Clearly moral hazards are incurred by companies and managers who embrace new solutions before critically assessing whether proposed changes offer the best way to address urgent problems. Yet when large companies are asked about far-reaching business transformations, for instance to 'go digital', more than half (55%) indicate the main reason for doing this is 'because other businesses do this', a 2019 Vlerick Business School study revealed (FD, 2019; see also Box 6.1: Fear Of Missing Out on FinTech – haste makes waste).

Box 6.1: Fear of Missing out on FinTech – Haste Makes Waste

In 2020, the Dutch bank ING completed the acquisition of Payvision, an omni-channel payment platform for e-commerce, that was started in 2018 by taking a 75% share in this company (ING, 2018). The takeover was supposed to strengthen ING's footprint in FinTech and e-commerce for business customers. Instead it ended up as a great embarrassment to ING.

FinTech is a contraction of the English words financial and technology. The term refers to a range of innovative financial products and services, mostly developed by technology-driven start-ups. These all aim to simplify and accelerate the way people handle money, usually by cutting out the role of intermediaries, such as banks. Fintech is therefore an uncomfortable concept for traditional banks: they see their core business model challenged but are ill-prepared to adopt the 'revolutionary' financial concepts that are changing the traditional ecosystem of finance. At the moment banks still are a main force in servicing business and personal finances. However, in order to stay relevant, they have to adapt to these new developments (Geer, 2017; Ginsel et al., 2019).

The ambition to safeguard its position in the industry led ING bank to invest in innovation. Taking over Payvision seemed a smart move: it promised to offer the exact technology that would be right for ING (ING, 2018). However, in its eagerness to participate in new developments, the bank overlooked an important feature characterizing the start-up. Payvision catered for many customers who were excluded from the regular banking circuit because of the questionable nature of their business activities. Payvision did not just include 'adult entertainment' companies in its customer base – for instance in the porn and gambling industry. It was also accused of facilitating the transfer of stolen money.

The European Funds Recovery Initiative filed a claim against the company now owned by ING for repayment of substantial commissions it had received from financial scams that robbed victims in Serbia and Bulgaria of their entire life savings. One of the accused was Gal Barak, also known as 'the wolf of Sofia'. He was convicted for prison sentence in Austria for his activities in international cybercrime involving illegal online trading (Hinchliffe, 2020). In fact, Payvision had been on the radar of the American money laundering watchdog FinCEN for many years.

Once the full extent of their acquisition became apparent, ING sold more than half of Payvision. This effort to repair its image as a clean bank, resulted in the loss of 350 million euros. Eventually ING also decided to cut off the most profitable portfolio, the porn customers. For the symbolic amount of one euro it was transferred back to a former owner of Payvision ('Takeover of Porn and Gambling Customers is a Great Embarrassment to ING', 2020). The supposedly strategic acquisition was meant to gain ING a competitive advantage. Instead, the Fear Of Missing Out cost the bank dearly in its image as well as its capital.

In this chapter we emphasize that organizations run the risk of depleting their human resources in pursuing change. This makes it more difficult to show moral responsibility in efforts to stay ahead of the competition and keep up with market developments. The process of social innovation allows for the *reconciliation* of tested knowledge and procedures with novel insights and developments. If this is successful, individuals and departments who develop 'out-of-the box' ideas collaborate with those who can examine the safety and security of new solutions. However, these people and their organizational roles represent diverging achievements and requirements, which are not naturally compatible and tend not to be equally valued. Highlighting the importance of continuous innovation depicts those who represent change as central to the identity of the organization. By comparison, those who guard viability and safety of new developments seem more peripheral and hence dispensable. Such implicit messages introduce moral hazards when individuals who guard against irresponsible risks and unsafe solutions are devalued or ignored.

We first consider the three quick fixes introduced in Chap. 1 as common strategies that guide organizational change. Replacing employees is easier than engaging with doubts they express about the feasibility of impending changes, and curbs moral responsibility for their needs. Highlighting and rewarding creativity as a key organizational asset tempts people to ignore moral concerns in developing new ideas. Prioritizing the release of new products and services as the focal outcome, may seem to justify neglect of procedural guidelines relating to safety and security. The research we review in this chapter clarifies that these common strategies to achieve organizational change overlook the importance of the human factor. Studies show that this reduces the likelihood that vital information is shared, and introduces moral hazards. We then specify how insight in the group-level mechanisms and identity concerns that people have can be engaged in a more constructive way. Defining individuals who represent change as well as those who represent continuity as equally important but complementary allows organizations to take moral responsibility in realizing adaptive change.

6.1.1 Different Generations of Workers Have Similar Needs

Replacing personnel and hiring employees with different expertise is seen as a quick and easy solution that can benefit organizational adaptation and change (Anderson et al., 2004; Argote & Ingram, 2000; De Dreu & West, 2001; Guimerà et al., 2005). This resonates with the individual difference approach as a quick fix to change behavior in organizations. These ambitions are often cited as an important reason for organizations to limit the commitments they make to their workers, arguing this should facilitate their adaptation to changing circumstances. Former in-house activities are increasingly outsourced, so that staff can be reduced. Flextime or seasonal workers are called in only when needed, even if the very same people who were discarded as employees are hired back only days or weeks later as 'independent contractors' for specific projects. This exemplifies the on-demand recruitment of skills – without considering the needs of the people who contribute these skills – that characterizes the 'gig economy'.

Some argue that this business strategy is preferred by the younger generations of workers. The assumption is that 'Generation X' or 'Millennials' attach less value to employment security or long-term career prospects than prior generations. We note that scientific evidence does not support these claims (Costanza & Finkelstein, 2015). Differences between generations that are observed in the media rather stem from transitions to other age groups or life stages, as people's employment needs typically shift across the life span (Mayr & Freund, 2020). Millennials and young people comprising 'Generation Z' do acknowledge that temporary assignments and the gig economy offer them flexibility and can improve work-life balance. However, they also express concern that companies only use these employment options to reduce costs and weaken employee rights. Growing up in an age of "unbridled disruption" makes these young people feel unsettled about their future. They embrace technology, but are also well aware of its disadvantages when expressing concern about risks for data security, privacy and fraud. In general, they prefer businesses to take more social responsibility, also in offering better prospects for employment and income security (Deloitte, 2020). In this sense, then, the attitudes of the younger generation are not very different from broader population samples across the world, who expect employers to take responsibility for social issues, including employment security (Edelman., 2019; see also Chap. 7).

The failure to offer some basic employment and income security can have severe consequences, also at the societal level. In the United States, for instance, hourly workers who live from paycheck to paycheck cannot afford to stay at home even when they are ill. During the COVID-19 pandemic, they continued going to work even when suspecting they were contaminated with the virus. This not only jeopardized their own well-being and recovery but also contributed to the spread of the disease. For instance, in residential care homes for the elderly many deaths might have been avoided with better employment conditions (CBS, 2020; Gollan, 2020).

Being ready to discard employees, exchanging them for people with different expertise, and continually introducing 'fresh blood' would seem to facilitate adaptive innovation. Perhaps companies that follow this strategy expect it will keep people motivated and 'on their toes' for fear of being made redundant (see also Ellemers & Jetten, 2013). Some companies actively fuel such fears. Here, we highlight the hidden costs to using employee turnover and minimizing commitments to employees as a quick fix to achieve change. These costs not only emerge at the individual level, but impact the functioning of work teams and organizations (see Fig. 6.1: The hidden costs of flexible employment). Paradoxically, these may undermine the organization's potential for change instead of increasing its adaptability. Failing to offer employees long-term prospects, refusing to show loyalty when business slows down or markets change, implicitly communicates a lack of confidence in their adaptability, and signals they are less valued organizational members. The research we review in this chapter reveals that this process prevents employees from identifying with the organization. It precludes them from fully understanding its mission and client base, and actually discourages them from making an effort to update their skills. In fact, studies suggests that the sense of being devalued impedes the willingness to collaborate with others in the organization. Frustrations about

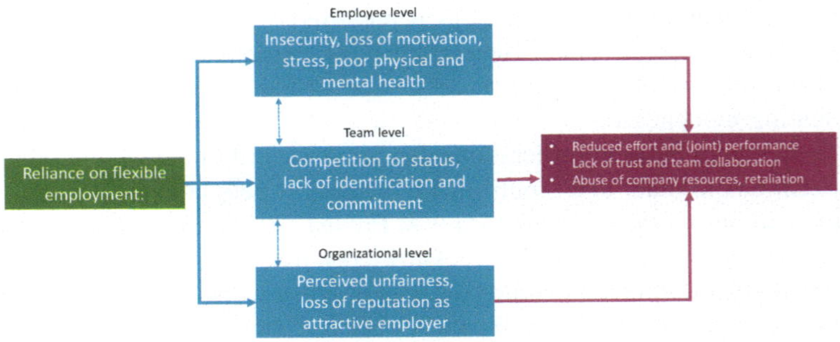

Fig. 6.1 Hidden costs of flexible employment. Illustrates how the reliance on flexible employment impacts psychological mechanisms at different organizational levels, and introduces important costs for the organization

lack of commitment from the organization may even tempt employees to retaliate by abusing organizational resources for personal gain. In the end, this introduces moral hazards and makes it less likely that they truly add value or facilitate change.

6.1.2 New Solutions Have Unanticipated Outcomes

Changes in business models, production methods or services that are prompted by external developments and requirements are often morally charged. These include increased regulation (stricter quality standards), evolving stakeholder concerns (about animal testing, chemicals, human rights, climate change), or market changes (concerns about responsible food production, depletion of natural oil reserves; see also Chap. 7). The more disruptive these changes are, the more difficult it is to anticipate whether novel solutions will not raise new and additional regulatory, stakeholder, or market concerns. When making strategic decisions about realities that might emerge in the future, organizations therefore cannot rely on existing knowledge of legal restrictions, established risks, or known mitigation strategies to prevent such problems.

Yet the choices they make often have moral implications. Facebook experienced public outrage after selling its user data to Cambridge Analytics, due to breaches of data protection guidelines (Patterson, 2020). Google was challenged for the algorithms they used for personnel selection – optimizing for the characteristics of current employees resulted in built-in biases against underrepresented groups (Dattner et al., 2019). At Apple software developers made it possible for voice recognition facility SIRI to record personal conversations and connect these to user data. Even though it was intended to improve customers' experiences, this feature was condemned as a violation of privacy regulations (Hern, 2020). The inability of all parties involved in these examples to anticipate and regulate these hazards illustrate the limits of relying on the legal approach as a quick fix to secure adherence to moral standards through innovations and strategic organizational changes (see Box 6.2: Kodak: from film to pharmaceuticals).

Box 6.2: Kodak: From Film to Pharmaceuticals

After being founded by George Eastman in 1888, Kodak film company grew to become one of the biggest players in the photographic industry, employing more than 145,000 people at its peak. Now the legendary film company is characterized as a 'fallen giant'. The increasing use of digital photography by the general public as well as professional filmmakers and photographers forced the company to shift its activities to printing for professional companies. This couldn't prevent the company from having to file for bankruptcy protection in 2012 ("Coronavirus: Camera Firm Kodak turns to Drugs to Fight Virus", 2020).

It all changed in the summer of 2020, when the COVID-19 pandemic disrupted international supply chains. The resulting shortage of active pharmaceutical ingredients in the USA, raised calls for the domestic production of generic medicines. These events prompted Kodak to announce the repurposing of two existing US production facilities. Supported by a $765 million Federal loan, the company stated the ambition to produce up to 25% of the domestic need for non-biological generic farmaceuticals. In the process, the company promised to create up to 1500 new jobs. Questions were raised about the conditions under which the loan was awarded, about the ability of the company to deliver on its promises, and about the choice of pharmaceuticals (such as Chloroquine) that would be produced (Blankenship, 2020).

Nevertheless, when news of the deal was made public Kodak's share price skyrocketed from $2.62 to $43.45 per share. Clearly investors considered the willingness of the company to adapt to changing market needs a smart move. However, Kodak's plans to relaunch its production of pharmaceuticals were quickly put on hold. The Securities and Exchange Commission decided to investigate the fact that company executives bought millions of stock options, while conducting secret negotiations about the Federal loan (Warmbrodt, 2020). A premature leak of the deal to the media, implies that legal options for insider trading convictions are reduced. Regardless of the outcome, production plans will not proceed until the investigation is closed (Carosa, 2020). So far, only the company's executives profited from the decision to start producing pharmaceuticals.

In fact, this was not the first time Kodak ventured into the drug industry. Already in 1988 the company acquired the Sterling Drug company, hoping to benefit from its extensive experience in the production of chemical compounds. At the time, the state also offered an incentive package of over $100 million to protect local employment for 1300 people. Notwithstanding promises made, only a year later the research and manufacturing facilities at this site were closed down, resulting in massive loss of jobs (Rulison, 2020).

So how should we view Kodak? As a company that is willing and able to do make radical changes as a way to survive? Or as a business that repeatedly appropriated public money and violated employee expectations? In both cases, the move from film to pharmaceuticals seems to be driven by the ambitions of executives to benefit from government support as much as by the desire to keep up with market changes.

Regulators too find it challenging to take responsibility for monitoring the ethical and legal consequences of new technologies, ideas, and processes – that often are unprecedented. The less certain people are about the relation between their actions and the impact these have, the more problematic this responsibility is. In general, companies as well as regulators can only take on such responsibilities when their professionals can adhere to established standards of excellence, and can exercise relative autonomy in deciding whether or not strategic decisions are ethically acceptable (Pandza & Ellwood, 2013). By definition, however, there are no established standards for new developments. Further, most organizations are quite reluctant to afford discretion to make such decisions to their professionals.

The frequent occurrence of unprecedented changes makes reliance on regulation to prevent that innovations and strategy changes result in ethical breaches extremely difficult. Digitalization and the introduction of 'smart' technologies, such as cars without drivers, robots for healthcare, algorithms for personnel selection, genetic modification for more efficient food production, or the use of drones for surveillance all have quite disruptive effects. Organizations and their employees may therefore not fully envision the ethical implications of their decisions. Further, existing regulations may not apply and appropriate certification guidelines still have to be developed. Examples such as this show why relying on legal guidelines and (external) regulation may be of limited use as a quick fix to ensure that the implications of product and service innovations are morally acceptable.

6.1.3 The Human Factor Is Key to Successful Adaptation

The adaptive potential of organizations is generally seen to depend on specific characteristics that indicate their agility, and on strategic decisions, for instance to invest in the development of new technologies. Indeed, from an economic perspective, investing in new facilities and technologies would seem the key to successful adaptation. However, simply investing more money in the development of new technologies, services, or products does not necessarily enhance innovative company performance. For instance on the list of 'most innovative companies in the world' between 2002 and 2017 'top innovators' were not the companies that made the highest investments in Research and Development activities (Jaruzelski et al., 2018). Instead, these were all companies that aligned innovation projects with the needs of their end-users and their overall business strategy. Companies that were able to recruit company-wide support to integrate competing requirements were seen as the most innovative ones and also outperformed their industry peers in terms of financial success (Jaruzelski et al., 2018).

More generally, research results offer no convincing evidence for the common view that specific characteristics of the organization – such as its size or the sector in which it operates – are the decisive factor for successful adaptation to changing demands (Andriopoulos & Lewis, 2009; Damanpour, 1991; Hage, 1999). For instance, a meta-analysis examining 10,538 study results obtained from 52 different samples found no advantage in this respect for smaller companies, high tech firms, or the invention of new products (Sarooghi et al., 2015). Instead, studies highlight the decisive role of micro-level mechanisms relating to communication and people management – as often neglected factors in this regard (Ghoshal & Bartlett, 1997; see also West & Farr, 1989).

This human factor turned out to be an impediment to successful adaptation at Finnish company Nokia. The company was market leader in first generation mobile phones because of its reliable products that offered good value for money. But when Apple launched the first iPhone in 2007, Nokia quickly lost market share. This seemed unnecessary because of its healthy finances, and investments in product development, including the know-how to create a touch-screen. However, the company did not benefit from its new technological and software features that would allow it to keep up with new competitors. They key hurdle was that knowledge about these innovations was *not shared* with other departments and was not included in strategic decision making (Cord, 2014; Heikkinen, 2010; Nykänen & Salminen, 2014; Peltonen, 2019).

Different indicators thus point to the conclusion that there is no quick fix in pushing for change by acquiring new technology, developing new products, or even buying up other companies to introduce different insights and skills. Approaching change purely as a strategic business decision makes it easy to neglect important stakeholders and their interests, and introduces safety risks and other moral hazards. Whether and how organizations actually benefit from these opportunities for change crucially depends on the *human factor*. This includes the willingness of the organization to invest in developing new ways of working, to help newcomers forge relationships with more experienced workers, and to support different groups of professionals in sharing their knowledge with each other (Kane et al., 2019; Nahapiet & Ghoshal, 1998; Tsai & Ghoshal, 1998). For organizational adaptation to be successful, changes in human behavior are required. Benefiting from technical developments requires 'social innovation' (Anderson et al., 2014; West & Farr, 1989). In the next section we consider common organizational approaches to this human factor, and highlight the moral hazards that tend to be introduced in this way.

6.2 Analysis: The Moral Hazards of Workplace Disruptions

Organizational structures are designed to help people define their specific task in the organization – be it product development, quality control, budget specification, or project management. This allows them to focus on their own specific responsibilities, without being distracted by alternative requirements. Distinguishing between specific organizational concerns and functions in this way is generally seen as a way to secure that a range of different – and seemingly incompatible – goals are met. However, it can also introduce a lack of clarity about the key mission and identity of the organization especially during times of disruptive change. For instance, after the global financial crisis of 2008, regulators required banks to separate managerial responsibility for sales of new products from accountability for compliance and product quality. This was seen as an important step towards mitigating the risks of account managers recommending risky financial products to customers, just to meet their sales targets. However, in practice this did not resolve the moral dilemmas that emerge in customer relations. Instead, it only resulted in stressing out lower level employees because performance targets set by their sales manager were incompatible with the demand for more careful client selection communicated by their quality manager.

Research evidence highlights that assigning the task of quality control to a specific department or officer may even introduce a false sense of security. It is a way to separate these concerns from the core business and day-to-day practices, making others in the company less attentive to quality concerns and risks associated with the new products they develop. An examination of financial derivatives offered by 157 large US banks between 1995 and 2010 for instance, revealed a pattern that is akin to the moral licensing effects of appointing diversity officers, that we have noted in Chap. 5. In this case, banks that appointed Chief Risk Officers (CRO's) were also the ones that developed the most complex new financial derivatives (Pernell et al., 2017). These findings suggest that outsourcing quality control to the assigned risk officer made trading desk managers less concerned about developing and selling potentially risky products. The researchers characterize this sense of false safety as an example of moral licensing, where appointing a CRO allowed organizations to maximize financial returns instead of eliminating risks. Containing responsibility for the quality of products to specific departments or officers, separates it from the ambition to offer new financial products or to compete for customers in the market. This implicitly communicates that product quality is not seen as a key performance feature that defines the success of the organization in reaching its goals.

In this analysis section we elucidate how the focus on innovation and change impacts upon the identity of the organization and its members. A likely consequence is that the importance of prior knowledge and existing expertise is neglected – and that individuals representing these insights are ignored. We specify how common organizational approaches convey implicit messages about which people, roles, and tasks are valued in the organization – and which are devalued. In keeping with the paradox of morality, endorsing such messages can alleviate feelings of identity threat people may experience due concerns about the moral appropriateness of their decisions. These identity management strategies prevent people from fully considering the moral implications of their choices and priorities, and stand in the way of addressing moral concerns that are raised by their actions. Below, we present results from research that highlights the moral hazards that are likely to ensue.

6.2.1 Moral Exclusion in Employment Relations

Temporary, flexible, and gig employment are seen as securing the continuous introduction of 'fresh blood' to benefit the adaptability and innovative potential of the organization. Indeed, studies have documented that the introduction of newcomers into existing task groups can increase the number of unique ideas that they develop, as well as general team creativity (Choi & Thompson, 2005; Nemeth & Ormiston, 2007) and innovative outcomes (Perretti & Negro, 2007). However, it is not self-evident that this happens. Introducing new members into existing work teams can be time consuming, and disruptive (Baer et al., 2010; McGrath et al., 2000). If not managed well, frequent changes in the composition of work teams can undermine a sense of commitment to joint goals, and threaten feelings of security that are needed to be able to accommodate new insights and skills offered by newcomers. Ongoing changes in the composition of work teams prevent incoming team members as well as longstanding employees from feeling fully respected and included. This is a source of identity threat that undermines their motivation and ability to work well together (Ellemers & Rink, 2005; Rink & Ellemers, 2008).

Research evidence consistently reveals that employees usually prefer to have more long-term prospects and job security. They suffer in different ways when this is not forthcoming (e.g., Veenstra et al., 2004; Von Hippel et al., 1997). Hidden costs of reliance on flexible employment, can emerge at the level of the employee, the work team, and the organization (see Fig. 6.1). Temporary work and insecurity about job continuity is associated with increased stress and burnout rates, reduced well-being, self-reported somatic complaints and overall poor health (De Witte et al., 2016; Zeytinoglu et al., 2004). People who work in insecure jobs generally have less long-term career success (De Cuyper et al., 2011), and may even become alienated from the regular labor market (Feldman et al., 1994; Kalleberg et al., 2000; McLean Parks & Kidder, 1994).

The absence of long-term prospects is not only costly for individual employees, but also for their employers (McLean Parks & Kidder, 1994). Some proffer a cynical view on the risk of absenteeism due to stress, burnout, and loss of mental or physical health (Darr & Johns, 2008). Instead of noting these as downsides of hiring people for specific tasks, they argue that temporary employment is the best solution for the organization to avoid such employee costs. However, there is convincing evidence that reliance on temporary contracts is just as costly, if not more so. Temporary employment prevents workers from identifying with the long-term mission and success of the organization. This is a serious hazard when the organization's employment strategy implicitly communicates lack of concern for their income security or overall well-being. When the organization fails to reciprocate and reward the efforts invested by employees by refusing steady employment, they see this as unfair and feel morally excluded. Such violations of the 'psychological contract' where organizations don't offer the employment rewards that were implicitly promised occur quite regularly (Robinson & Rousseau, 1994). Research shows such breaches undermine employee enthusiasm and engagement, and reduce efforts extended towards organizational effectiveness (Beard & Edwards, 1995; De Gilder, 2003).

Thus, organizations suffer when their reliance on flexible work and temporary contracts fails to instill a sense of shared identity in employees. A study documented this in a chain of 270 US retail stores among over 7000 employees and 3000 temps (Eldor & Cappelli, 2020). In the company, agency temps were seen as lower status workers, who are less well trained, screened, and instructed, and work under less favorable conditions. Four years of data, including attitude surveys, financial performance, and secret shopper ratings of sales personnel in the store revealed the cost of implicit messages communicated by relying on such lower status workers as a matter of course. The decision to place agency temps at core functions in frontline sales lowered the perceived status of the company and reduced the willingness of regular employees to identify with their workplace. In turn, this lowered the work performance of regular employees on such key indicators as service quality and sales volume. Importantly, adverse effects of reduced company status and identification occurred independently of more instrumental concerns employees might have about their own career prospects. That is, statistical analyses revealed the key role of decreased organizational identification due to the reliance on agency temps, even after correcting for the negative impact of people being insecure about their job.

Other studies have revealed similar patterns, attesting to the downside of temporary work for the identity of the organization. For instance, one study showed that permanent workers come to see their organization as less trustworthy when they observe that many of their colleagues are only offered temporary employment (Pearce, 1993). Additionally, relationships between permanent and temporary staff often suffer from the introduction of such perceived unfairness. For instance, temporary employees have been found to show resentment towards permanent staff, whom they suspect of having to work less hard under more favorable labor conditions (Kossek et al., 1997).

Some organizations allude to the possibility of more steady employment as a long-term vision, hoping this will guard against the downsides of insecure jobs. Surely, the chances of earning such a 'reward' should only make people work harder to prove their worth? Indeed, as long as temporary employees perceive the acquisition of steady employment as a realistic prospect, they might be willing to invest in the organization and develop a sense of identification (Marler et al., 2002; McDonald & Makin, 2000; Veenstra et al., 2004; Von Hippel, 2006). However, research evidence also shows that there is a limit to the efforts people are willing to invest to be more securely included in the team or organization (Ellemers & Jetten, 2013; Ellemers et al., 2013; Sleebos et al., 2006a, 2006b). As it becomes evident that the organization is not really willing to extend more long-term commitments, workers will find it increasingly difficult to engage with their job, to care about the organization's interests, or to identify with its goals and mission. What is the use of continuing to invest in a relationship with an organization or co-workers when it is clear your efforts and interests are not valued?

When flexible employment is not just a form of probation but a core organizational strategy to accelerate new developments, at some point people will give up and stop trying. Research shows they are then more inclined to devote their efforts to other activities that might benefit their personal well-being, development, and career goals – even abusing organizational resources in the process (see also Chap. 4). Flexible, temporary, and gig employment can be quite legitimate and may even be indispensable when dealing with sudden peaks in customer demand, one-time projects, or seasonal production. But using flexible employment as a standard business strategy to maximally curb organizational responsibility for the human labor that is hired, implies lack of care for the long-term interests of individual workers. Not considering them as people whose interests and outcomes matter communicates that they are morally excluded (Anand et al., 2004).

Such moral exclusion may seem to relieve the organization and its decision makers from feeling responsible for the uncertain fates of these individuals (see Chap. 2). But neglecting the preferences and interests of workers as a matter of course by only offering flexible employment conveys lack of concern for their outcomes. As we have seen in Chap. 4, such disrespectful treatment is known to prevent concern with long-term organizational outcomes, damages the positive image of the organization, and reduces the willingness of individuals to identify with its leaders, or to psychologically commit to its goals (Ellemers et al., 2004; Graen & Scandura, 1987; Tyler & Blader, 2000; see also Ashford et al., 1989; Barnett & Miner, 1992; Broschak & Davis-Blake, 2006; Pearce, 1998; Uzzi & Barsness, 1998). Especially employees who feel they have invested 'the best years of their lives' in the company, or incurred occupational illnesses will consider the neglect of their long-term commitment aversive. The perceived unfairness of such treatment can invite forms of misbehavior that damage the organization including sabotage, appropriation of company resources, sharing of confidential information and other forms of 'organizational retaliation' (Skarlicki & Folger, 1997). When those who are laid off see this as a breach of the 'psychological contract' they think they have with the organization, this may carry over into lack of trust in a new employer (Kim & Choi, 2010). While excluding these employees from the organization's circle of care may seem to relieve the organization from taking moral responsibility for their outcomes, the costs of this identity management strategy might fully outweigh its anticipated benefits.

The negative effects of job insecurity for work satisfaction and somatic health can only be avoided when people voluntarily opt for temporary employment (Ellingson et al., 1998; Isaksson & Bellaagh, 2002). As noted above, however, even among younger generations of workers, employee preferences for such flexibility may be less wide-spread than many employers conveniently think. In reality, being known for failing to offer long-term prospects can actually make it highly challenging for the organization to attract, motivate and retain young talents or key specialists when new expertise is sought (see also Chap. 7).

6.2.2 *Moral Justification in Celebrating Creativity*

Organizations often strive to develop creative innovations, to be the first to capture market potential with novel solutions, or to get customers to quickly replace prior versions of their products. Commercial enterprises as well as public service organizations – and scientific research institutions – commonly invite and celebrate the development of new products and different solutions. However, this strategy has implications for the perceived identity of the organization as well as the people working there, introducing another source of moral hazard.

Studies and experiments into the psychology of creative thinking reveal there may be a dark side to encouraging creativity. For instance, some of this research clearly shows that organizations where creativity is highlighted as a rare quality, induces a sense of entitlement that invites cheating. Supervisors reported more unethical workplace behavior for subordinates who considered themselves exceptionally creative (Vincent & Kouchaki, 2016). Further, seeking exposure to multiple contexts and moral rule systems may boost creativity, but can also result in a sense of 'moral relativism' implying that people also become less motivated to take seriously or comply with any particular set of rules (Lu et al., 2017). Indeed, one study found that prompting people to think creatively caused them to be creative in the moral domain as well, as they reasoned that dishonest behavior might be permissible in pursuit of this important goal (Gino & Ariely, 2012). Thus, different studies and observations show that encouraging and celebrating creative thinking can also tempt people to think creatively about important rules and guidelines, even to the extent that they think cheating is justified.

Always highlighting the benefits of 'new and improved' solutions as defining the success of the organization calls into question the value and continued relevance of past achievements and current guidelines – and of the individuals responsible for them. Focusing on the added value of new and different services, products, and ideas, neglects the work needed to carefully test for safety, quality, or even the actual feasibility and novelty of these inventions (see Box 6.3, Theranos – too good to be true). This is one of the moral hazards of defining creative roles as inherently superior and more central to the mission of the organization than monitoring the safety and viability of these solutions. Affording more status to the people performing in creative roles and attaching more value to their contributions threatens the esteem for and identity of organizational members responsible for compliance and quality control, while at the same time offering moral justification for neglecting their concerns or ignoring their recommendations.

Box 6.3: Theranos – Too Good to Be True

Theranos was a high tech company founded by Stanford dropout Elizabeth Holmes. She was able to inspire and commit experienced business people (such as Rupert Murdoch, the Walton family), jaded politicians (such as Henry Kissinger, George Shultz) and well-connected private investors (such as Carlos Slim) to support her vision (see also Asher-Shapiro, 2019). The ambition was to develop the technology to offer quick, inexpensive, and non-invasive medical diagnoses for a number of diseases by analyzing only one drop of blood on-site.

The company developed a production site in Silicon Valley, and hired many hardware and software developers to create innovative solutions to realize the promises that were made. However, Theranos started selling its products before procedures were tested or approved by regulators, and medical experts maintained it was simply not possible to achieve what was promised. Yet, the initiative successfully attracted billions of dollars as startup capital, and persuaded US pharmacy store chain Walgreens to offer the 'disruptive' but non-existent service to customers at their stores (Carreyrou, 2018).

Analyses emphasize that even former employees of the company voiced their doubts and concerns about the feasibility of the project to responsible managers time and again. However, the pressure to deliver, the ambition to disrupt the industry and the strong belief that medical problems could be overcome through innovative high-tech solutions made investors, and clients, politicians and managers deaf to such concerns. In the end, inevitably everything fell apart, revealing large scale deception of all stakeholders: patients, jobs and investors, when the company went bankrupt (see Gibney et al., 2019).

Focusing on creative solutions as the key outcome to be achieved generally overlooks the fact that – by definition – creative processes are unpredictable, often taking up extra time and resources that were not planned for. Even at the level of very simple cognitive tasks, a robust observation is that people suffer from so-called 'speed-accuracy-trade-offs', where emphasizing fast responses invites mistakes while more careful work inevitably takes up more time (e.g., Liesefeld et al., 2015). This is especially true when adapting procedures, developing different solutions or designing new products: expecting people to do this quickly deprives them from the opportunity to try out different options or learn from mistakes. A more careful and precise approach would make it possible to develop high quality and fool-proof outcomes, but takes more time.

A comparison of thousands of companies in many different countries revealed that organizations typically adopt one of these strategies. Some organizations invite the development of creative solutions and innovative ideas by investing in high-risk projects. Others incentivize research and development activities with a focus on long-term implications and compliance issues (Almor et al., 2019). For instance, a 20 year longitudinal study revealed an overall trade-off between patenting activity in product development and ISO 9000 quality program certification in paint and photography industries. Companies boasting higher rates of creative product development were less likely to have quality certification, and vice versa (Benner & Tushman, 2002). These results highlight that focusing on the importance of new discoveries and creative solutions implicitly communicates that potentially adverse outcomes in terms of quality and safety are relatively less important.

The moral hazards of this approach became clearly visible when leading medical journal 'The Lancet' had to withdraw a study it had published on the effectiveness of Cholorquine as a possible treatment for patients with COVID-19. Only after the scientific community expressed concerns about the reliability of the reported data, did the journal conclude that it could not verify the actual existence of these data or check the accuracy of the analyses that had been reported (Mehra et al., 2020). This is not the only example where huge incentives and high rewards of being the first going to market with remedies for medical conditions induce healthcare companies to adopt and prepare commercial use of their products before their quality is verified in peer review (see also Box 6.4, Healthcare unicorns). These cases clearly illustrate the moral hazards of celebrating creativity as the key ingredient of organizational success.

Box 6.4: Healthcare Unicorns

In the business world, privately owned startup companies that have an estimated value of over $1 Billion are called 'Unicorns'. The name indicates the mythical status of such a company, rendering it as desirable and difficult to find as the famous fantasy animal. Until about ten years ago, this label seemed appropriate: such a company would be as rare as a unicorn: an investment one could only dream of. During the past years, unicorns have been sprouting like mushrooms: in December 2020, 511 such companies were known, 68% of which were listed since 2018. These include 26 'decacorns' (worth over $10 Billion), and even one 'hectocorn' (worth over $100 Billion; CB insights, 2020a, December 22).

The enormous size and impact of such companies implies these can have disruptive impact. Not only on its own investors, employees, or clients, but also on local, national, and even global markets and economies. Yet, unlike publicly listed companies, their private ownership implies that these companies fall under national regulatory regimes in which there typically is no legal obligation to disclose vital information about their business (Fan, 2016; Tarver, 2020).

This concern is particularly pressing in the healthcare sector, where 42 unicorns were listed in the summer of 2020 – doubling the number of the previous year (CB insights, 2020b, May 28). These companies not only consist of digital platforms to sell health-related products, but also include start-ups that propose disruptive therapeutics and health-care devices, develop 'revolutionary' new drugs, or sell tools for the detection and diagnosis of potentially life-threatening diseases such as cancer. In addition to concerns about financial stability, such public health claims also raise questions about the scientific basis documenting the effectiveness of these 'revolutionary' new products. As long as these companies remain private, however, there is no obligation to reveal such information.

Researchers have attempted to link the activities of 47 healthcare unicorns to the scientific literature. They argue that patent registration does not require the same level of documentation as scientific publication. Further, data submitted to the US Food and Drug Administration (FDA) as well as reasons for rejection remain confidential (Cristea et al., 2019). Therefore, the researchers used the criterion of peer-review as a minimum threshold for the transparency, accountability and credibility of underlying principles in the scientific community. Their main conclusion is that much of the evidence supporting the claims of healthcare unicorns is collected in stealth: the innovative healthcare solutions they sell are not subjected to scientific scrutiny.

The conclusion is based on the following findings: First, the number of peer-reviewed articles published by healthcare start-ups is extremely low. Even the most highly valued healthcare unicorns had published only very few or even no scientific papers. The highly cited publications that were found mostly document early phase pre-clinical research, which does not offer conclusive evidence for the effectiveness of new treatments. Finally, only in very few cases did company websites indicate the involvement of influential scientists as founders, leaders, or members of a scientific advisory board (Cristea et al., 2019). In sum, the 'revolutionary' healthcare innovations that are promised to customers and attract such enormous investments have no foundation in tested scientific insights.

6.2.3 *Moral Neglect of Prioritizing Novelty*

Adaptability is often seen as an individual difference variable, associated with specific personality traits (being open to new experiences) or demographics (being educated, being young). These are seen to indicate the flexibility vs rigidity of particular workers and explain their (un)willingness to adapt to changing organizational requirements. However, such assumptions ignore the power of situations. In fact, research demonstrates that the same individuals may either resist or embrace change, depending on how they are treated by the company. It all relates to how the proposed changes speak to the way they think of themselves and affect their role in the organization. In the end, openness vs resistance to change is prompted by the implications of proposed changes for the way people perform their professional duties as well as their prospects of remaining included and valued as organizational members.

Psychological theory and research generally distinguish between two different types of motivation in task motivation and goal achievement ('regulatory focus theory'; Higgins, 1997, 1998; Molden et al., 2008; see Fig. 6.2; Promotion and prevention goals). The term '*promotion focus*' is used to indicate an emphasis on the realization of desired endstates and the achievement of ideals. In a state of promotion people typically pursue happiness by trying to gain positive outcomes. The term '*prevention focus*' refers to the pre-occupation with avoiding negative outcomes and meeting important obligations. People in a state of prevention aim to

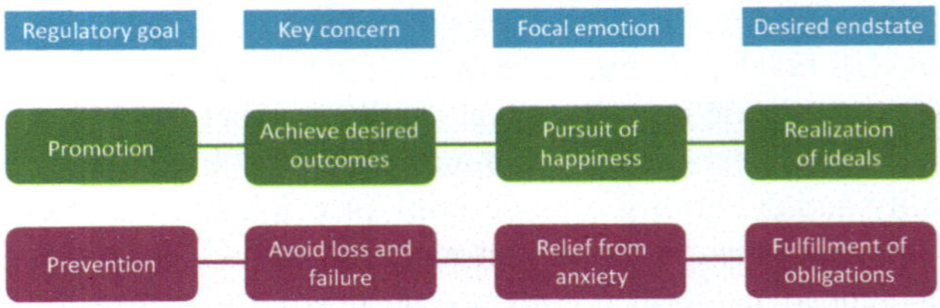

Fig. 6.2 Promotion and prevention goals. Summarizes the main differences between promotion and prevention goals, in terms of the key concern that is highlighted, the focal emotions that are addressed and the endstates that are desired

relieve the tension they experience when considering the possibility of loss or failure (Brockner & Higgins, 2001; Higgins et al., 2001; Higgins et al., 1997).

Surely everyone can think of examples among their own acquaintances or friends of the prototypical daring entrepreneur, in contrast with the rule-abiding civil servant. People often assume these two states of mind refer to stable differences between individuals, reflecting character traits that were formed during childhood and persist through the life-course. However, research clearly reveals that certain roles, assignments, or situations can activate a focus on promotion or a focus on prevention – regardless of more stable individual differences (Higgins et al., 2001). The daring entrepreneur may also be an overprotective parent or display hypervigilance about healthy food choices, while the rule-abiding civil servant may surprise you with tales about thrill-seeking sports activities or travels to faraway destinations that many see as risky.

Organizational roles, assignments or incentive structures can cause individuals or work teams to adopt a focus on promotion or on prevention. Experimental research shows that emphasizing promotion goals by offering work teams specific mottos ('if there is a will, there will be a way') induces them to come up with more creative and 'out-of-the-box' solutions. However, this also made them more lenient and liberal in accepting solutions that did not meet stated requirements. Conversely, when prevention goals were highlighted ('an ounce of prevention is worth a pound of cure'), team members were more inclined to reject solutions. Unfortunately, this also led them to reject solutions that were objectively acceptable (Faddegon et al., 2009; Faddegon et al., 2008). These study results clarify that there is not a single best way of approaching work related problems or task assignments. In both cases team members performed sub-optimally: prioritizing productivity and creativity led them to propose and accept incorrect solutions; prioritizing security and avoidance of failure lowered performance rates and prompted the rejection of correct solutions. For individuals as well as organizations, *both* types of orientation complement each other and are needed to function well. This is why it is important to secure a balance between the two – even though they do not naturally go together.

Prioritizing novelty and change also impacts upon the types of organizational roles and contributions that are valued and are seen as defining the organization's identity. For instance in tech startups, which often are highly coveted employers. The energy of creating something new tends to be captured in the sense of working together in realizing a joint vision – often at an unconventional location where opportunities to play, work out, eat, and relax are offered alongside attractive spaces for solo and teamwork. When nobody has prior experience and all are new to the company, everyone's contributions are valued, and people with different types of skills and abilities can only improve and advance as they go along. However, at some point in the growth of a small startup company standard business facilities relating to accounting, HR, customer services or logistics are needed too. Over time, these more standard departments tend to become separated from product development, or are even outsourced to external parties. The creative work to develop new products is typically seen as defining the core business and identity of the company. People doing this work are afforded high visibility, high status, and the best possible work conditions. However, departments responsible for administrative and service roles are often housed at less attractive locations, work under less favorable conditions, and are generally given to understand their efforts are less valued and less important for company success.

A case in point is Booking.com, the holiday accommodation website. During the initial startup phase all company workers shared the same location. New recruits starting out in support jobs would be assigned more challenging and creative tasks as they gained more experience. All were part of the excitement about their innovative mission that strengthened their shared identity. It all changed when customer services were relegated to a building outside the center of Amsterdam. Those working in this service center were suddenly offered less attractive lunch options, less pay, and less management support. At the same time, they were subjected to higher performance targets and longer working hours than before. These changes not only resulted in more sick-leave and burnout among those working at the customer service center, but also raised unease among the computer programmers who remained at the city center location. They felt that the company did not fairly attend to all its responsibilities. In fact, they joined forces in a works council to communicate their view that the work practices that had evolved failed to represent the shared values of the company they signed up for (Rengers et al., 2020). Similar developments were observed at other major Tech companies. For instance, at Amazon the highly visible and well-paid website designers expressed concern about the unfair employment conditions and lack of personal safety of warehouse workers preparing the shipments that were ordered online. Tech workers and programmers participated in – and sometimes led – the protests against the way the company treated its warehouse workers, when increased sales of the online store during the COVID-19 crisis intensified these problems and further damaged the image of the company (Paul, 2020; see also Chap. 7).

These are just two examples. Both companies suffered from focusing on their mission of new product development as representing the distinct identity of the company. This approach did not benefit work that needed to be done to secure continuity of their services and optimize customer satisfaction. The dangers of prioritizing some types of solutions over others are well-known and have been documented as a key pitfall in strategic decision making (Harrison, 1987; Janis, 1972; Nutt & Wilson, 2010). When novelty and change are seen as key defining features of the company it is easy to prioritize resources and budgets for the development of new products and ideas while neglecting to provide facilities to monitor continuity and compliance. These implicit (or sometimes quite explicit!) messages about the value of different organizational tasks and team roles define the perceived image of the organization as change oriented instead of conservative. At the same time, ignoring key organizational outcomes that seem less central to this identity discourage those working at these tasks, damages the image of the organization, and is likely to introduce moral hazards.

Defining the identity of the organization in terms of its ability to create novelty and change prompts employees to be less focused on procedures to ensure public safety or prevent financial risks. Even when such concerns are expressed they are likely to be ignored, because the prevention goals they represent are seen as less strategically important for the success of the organization. In fact, such expert judgments are often dismissed as simply communicating aversion to change of these individuals. The counterpoint of this observation is that preventing problems and reducing chances of failure are not at all beyond the scope of innovative industries – it is just that these risks are often underestimated or neglected. Indeed, media analyses of company scandals often reveal that people inside the company had been aware of and warned against impending problems at an early stage – to no effect. This suggests that many (socially) costly innovation failures could have been avoided if only companies had paid more attention to balancing their focus on novelty and change with the desire to prevent engagement with morally questionable options (see also Chap. 8, in the section on whistle blowers).

6.3 Solutions: Mutual Trust for Responsible Adaptation

The work reviewed in the prior sections of this chapter reveals that the reluctance to embrace innovation and change may constitute a healthy response to a one-sided focus on temporary employment, the celebration of creativity, and the prioritization of novelty over safety. The moral dangers of these common strategies emerge because they implicitly communicate lack of appreciation for the professional expertise and relevant knowledge networks of existing members of the organization, or for the trust they have built with external stakeholders (Hage, 1999). Discarding specialized skills and information time and again makes the organization vulnerable to moral hazards when new solutions are proposed, as it disregards employees with knowledge about relevant risks.

Research evidence clearly reveals pitfalls to look out for, and what can be done to circumvent them. Importantly, it counters common expectations about lack of appropriate knowledge and information as the main cause of work-related problems. This conclusion emerged for instance from a study among medical residents in the USA that examined 70 hospital incidents (Sutcliffe et al., 2004). A closer analysis revealed that the observed failures in communication and patient management did not reflect lack of available knowledge. Instead, these all related to *social* factors, such as hierarchical differences, role conflict, or lack of balance in interpersonal power, which prevented people from *acting* upon the information they had. Thus, even if the knowledge and expertise needed are present in the organization, in itself this doesn't imply that these inputs are taken into account or even heard.

Similar conclusions emerge from studies examining decisive factors that predict innovative team or organizational performance. This was observed, for instance, in the functioning of different business units in a large multinational electronics company. Here, work units could exchange key resources to foster product innovation. However, the likelihood that such exchanges were actually made crucially depended on social factors and trust between workers from different units (Tsai & Ghoshal, 1998). This is similar to the pattern found in negotiations, where the ability to reach key turning points also depends on perceiving good faith in the other party ('affective trust'), instead of reliance on the accuracy of their insights ('cognitive trust'; Olekalns & Smith, 2005).

An in-depth analysis of the network ties of 153 employees at two different firms likewise pointed to the importance of interpersonal trust in understanding the way they work together in project teams. The researchers distinguished between people's trust in the task abilities, interpersonal benevolence, and integrity of their co-workers (Shazi et al., 2015). This study revealed that employees did not just approach co-workers because of the unique insights or knowledge they had to offer, but because of their perceived benevolence and integrity. In fact, when co-workers were seen to be lacking in integrity, their ability seemed irrelevant (see also Chap. 1). This combination of skills could even function as a negative selection criterion, where people actively avoid interactions with co-workers whom they see as competent but untrustworthy. The importance of mutual trust in building productive collaborations between co-workers was further substantiated in a meta-analysis, drawing together results from 112 studies examining 7763 task teams (De Jong et al., 2016). This analysis concluded that trust among team members was more decisive for the team's performance than professional abilities, past achievements, or trust in team leadership.

These research results clarify that the innovative power of people working together does not simply depend on the novelty or diversity of available insights and knowledge. Importantly, the potential for social innovation is determined by their willingness to work together, to benefit from differences between them, and to learn from errors that are initially made. This only happens when they feel they can trust each other's benevolent and sincere intentions. In this final section we take a closer look at how the use of identity management strategies can prevent the development of mutual trust and cooperation. Avoiding the moral hazards introduced in this way is possible, provided that organizations make an effort to value and include the efforts of those who guard against irresponsible risks as well as those who represent innovative change.

6.3.1 Transforming Through Mergers and Acquisitions

In general, a sense of shared purpose and common identity is a key condition for facilitating mutual trust and fostering productive working relations. As noted before, it is notoriously difficult to secure a common identity through organizational disruption and change. This has been well-documented in the case of corporate acquisitions and mergers. Such strategic decisions are often initiated as a way to extend existing expertise, promising a benefit from the combination of different sources of knowledge and professional networks (Ellis et al., 2009). However, three out of four mergers fail to yield these anticipated benefits, even when the combination of resources, product knowledge and customer relations should have offered an obvious source of competitive advantage (Marks & Mirvis, 2001). In fact, business analysts see human factors and incompatibility between company cultures as the root cause of such failures (Bradt, 2015). One example is acquisition in 2017 of the Whole Foods grocery store chain by online retail company Amazon. Whole Foods CEO John Mackey said the merger had resulted from "love at first sight". Yet efficiency changes implemented by Amazon after the merger mainly frustrated customers and depressed Whole Foods employees (Gelfand et al., 2018). In a merger, the main challenge is to prevent moral exclusion of those representing 'the other organization'. Showing concern for their needs and appreciation for their knowledge and abilities makes it more likely that the individuals involved actually share their knowledge and experience in a process of social innovation.

Despite considerable resources being invested in catalyzing such synergies, a key factor identifying merger success versus failure is the (lack of) management attention for incompatibility of company identities (Das et al., 2011). Perceived incompatibility of company identities is especially problematic when trying to realize added value by integrating 'rule making' with 'rule breaking' organizations. 'Rule making' organizations typically focus on efficiency and rule standardization, and have 'tight' organizational cultures. 'Rule breaking' organizations are characterized by creativity and personal freedom, and have 'loose' organizational cultures (Gelfand, 2018). An obvious way for large and traditional 'rule making' organizations (such as multinationals) to become more change oriented and innovative is to take over smaller startup companies with a 'rule breaking' approach (such as digital startups).

However, transforming the organization through such an acquisition is not self-evident. A study of over 4500 international mergers from 32 different countries between 1989 and 2013 highlighted differences between 'rule making' versus 'rule breaking' organizations as a recurring problem (Gelfand et al., 2018). After correcting for other possible explanatory factors, the (in)compatibility between these two types of pre-merger identities and day-to-day practices was decisive for merger success, measured in return on assets in the years after the merger (Gelfand et al., 2018). In this process, it is crucial to avoid the experience of identity threat. If constituents feel undervalued, they will focus on defending their unique and separate identity. Such defensive responses make it less likely that they will find new ways of thinking of their joint mission that would allow them to productively work together (see also Van Leeuwen et al., 2003). Indeed, research shows that lack of concern for social tensions and insufficient management of integration problems is an important reason that mergers and acquisitions often don't deliver the added value that was hoped for (Meglio et al., 2015).

When employees of the pre-merger company with unique expertise or coveted technology feel out of place after the merger, they will seek employment elsewhere. Likewise, the focus on new product development or digitalization can frustrate employees of the pre-merger company. Their contribution of longstanding customer relations or regulatory experience seems to be devalued. In both cases the most cherished experts often are the first to leave. Awareness of this risk has led some multinationals to retain smaller companies as separate organizational entities instead of trying to merge them with the larger organization, sometimes even keeping the acquisition secret. However, this defeats the purpose of achieving social innovation that benefits from the combination of human abilities and informational assets (see also Box 6.5, Ben & Jerry's 'secret' acquisition).

Box 6.5: Ben and Jerry's 'Secret' Acquisition

Unilever, a multinational consumer products company, bought ice cream manufacturer Ben and Jerry's in 2000. Despite its small size and modest client base, Ben and Jerry's was an attractive acquisition. It embodied the values and priorities that exemplified the future vision Unilever had embraced in formulating its new business strategy. When this acquisition was finalized, both parties agreed to a deal in which Unilever would not reduce jobs, nor would it alter Ben & Jerry's production process or social mission. In fact, Unilever committed to donating 7,5 percent of Ben & Jerry's profits to foundations, minority-owned businesses, and poor neighborhoods. In return, the owners of Ben & Jerry's pledged to help Unilever achieve its social and environmental goals (Hays, 2000).

Despite offering a perfect match with the social and environmental mission Unilever had embraced, the multinational company was careful not to advertise this acquisition too widely in the media. The Unilever brand was not communicated in the way Ben and Jerry's products were packaged or marketed. Instead, Unilever carefully maintained the impression that Ben and Jerry's was a separate small brand. Presumably, this also helped to prevent people from noticing that its other brands were not as innovative or didn't meet the same responsibility and sustainability targets.

Other multinationals too, such as Nestlé taking over Wildscape or Danone acquiring Stok Cold Brew-coffee, do not advertise their ownership of small brands. The dilemma these large companies face is how to best include and benefit from their acquisitions of these brand products and activities. On the one hand, these small companies embody innovative ways of doing business that could enhance the socially responsible image of the multinational. On the other hand, emphasizing these high standards and ambitions may also call into question the moral appropriateness of business practices and lack of change in the rest of the company.

Realizing the added value of additional opportunities and resources represented by organizational mergers crucially depends on the success of creating a common identity (see also Giessner et al., 2011). Only when 'rule makers' and 'rule breakers' trust and benefit from each other's insights and skills will both be able to contribute to the ability of the organization to develop innovations and to do this responsibly. Unfortunately, this key precondition for social innovation is not always anticipated or actively managed. Standard attempts to prevent 'merger failures' tend to secure *material* outcomes for employees, for instance relating to job continuity and pay levels. However, research reveals that such measures only address part of the concerns employees are likely to have (Ullrich et al., 2005; Van Dick et al., 2006). Studies of actual mergers documented the importance of catering for *social* needs, such as belonging and respect. In fact, the likelihood that managers and employees were able to realize anticipated synergies depended on how well their feelings of identity threat were managed.

Results from other studies in organizations – as well as experiments with mergers of ad-hoc work teams – lead to similar conclusions. Across the board, the likelihood that employees are committed to their new role in the merged organization depends on whether they perceive their pre-merger identity is properly acknowledged and valued (Giessner et al., 2011; Terry, 2001, 2003; Van Dick et al., 2004; Van Knippenberg & Van Leeuwen, 2001; see also Bartels et al., 2006; Bartels et al., 2009). Only when this is the case, will the merged organization be able to reap the benefits of combining the diverging strengths and skills that motivated the merger in the first place. In the merged organization it is therefore important to explicitly highlight the added value of 'rule makers' in guarding against irresponsible risks, while also acknowledging the creative contributions of 'rule breakers'.

Survey data of Korean companies that had been taken over or had acquired other companies in different types of industry revealed the importance of offering such social support. In this study, employees who felt they still had access to management support and resources for creative work and experienced the merger as an opportunity, saw the transformation as a boost to their creativity. However, those who considered themselves cut off from such support and experienced the merger as a threat found their creativity to be reduced by the merger (Zhou et al., 2008).

The likelihood that social innovation can be achieved through mergers and acquisitions depends on the ability of management to define and build a shared identity. Ideally, the shared identity includes and values the pre-merger entity that represents creative 'rule breaking' skills and practices as well as the pre-merger company that is known for responsible 'rule making' and safety maintenance. The success of this endeavor is not defined by rational considerations alone, as demonstrated in the research reviewed above. Instead, a crucial factor is the success of the merged organization in defining and supporting a shared goal and mission, in which each constituent can be trusted to play its unique and valued role. Highlighting the importance of creative work, while also noting and valuing those who are responsible for safety regulation and risk management, benefits the mutual learning that prevents moral hazards.

In sum, social innovation is only possible when those who represent continuity and those who represent change are both secure about the perceived worth of their contributions. This makes it possible to trust and benefit from each other's insights, without entering a competition for whose ideas and solutions are the 'best'. In particular when 'rule making' and 'rule breaking' work teams and organizational units are merged, there are important differences to overcome. Handling this successfully requires management to attend to the human factor and invest in the explicit articulation of how the *combination* of these different perspectives and ways of working will help achieve joint goals. We will now consider how this can be fostered in daily interactions, by examining the integration of newcomers and old hands in work-teams.

6.3.2 Benefiting from Newcomers and Old Hands

As is the case with mergers and acquisitions, a crucial factor when introducing newcomers to existing work teams, is whether individuals manage to share their knowledge and adopt a different perspective to collaborate towards shared goals (see also Hoever et al., 2012). A review of 52 studies on the acceptance of newcomers in organizations reveals how difficult it is to do this well (Rink et al., 2013). Emphasizing the added value of newcomers and their insights and skills implicitly devalues existing employees and their concerns. Highlighting newcomer contributions can make longstanding employees insecure about their own position in the team, and easily fosters competition and hostility between 'newcomers' and 'old hands'. These instances of identity threat impede the willingness of both parties to reflect upon the appropriateness of current practices, to benefit from new insights they encounter, or to engage with the other at the interpersonal level. Offering clarity and security about the positions and roles of newcomers and old hands facilitates social innovation and helps to avoid moral hazards.

Responsible adaptation requires that valid concerns are accommodated when incoming experts introduce novel perspectives. Such concerns have been raised for instance about the replacement of human labor with technological solutions or transferring tasks to robots. A review of 42 studies investigating acceptance of robots in production industry and service sectors reveals that workers generally do see the benefits of such innovations, and are open to implementing them. At the same time, their experience is that these also introduce new difficulties, such as reduced human contact, and unnecessary reliance on technology (Savela et al., 2018). Further, employees find it more difficult to identify with their work team when collaborating with robots rather than humans (Savela et al., 2019). Such discomfort about a lack of a common identity is also reported by customers when interacting with service robots designed to resemble humans (Mende et al., 2019). Engaging with these difficulties to resolve them makes it more likely that important technological innovations can be followed through. Dismissing such concerns – and devaluing the insights and expertise of the individuals voicing them – will only increase the chances of following through on innovations that may prove to be too risky or turn out to be morally unacceptable.

There is no dispute that introduction of newcomers, tech experts or robots can enhance the knowledge base of the organization and benefit innovation. However, whether these assets can be used in morally responsible ways also depends on whether new knowledge is successfully shared with existing members who can evaluate how it might contribute to the achievement of organizational goals (Kogut & Zander, 2003; March, 1991; Miller, 1994; Miner, 1994; Zander & Kogut, 1995). In general, however, people find it notoriously difficult to deal with different viewpoints and dissent (Jetten & Hornsey, 2014), and this is a common source of distrust and miscommunication (Coupland et al., 1991).

Encouraging people to share and benefit from diverging insights therefore requires great care. Opinion differences can lead to intellectual debate. Diverging interests can be negotiated to a compromise. But a productive working relationship can only be maintained when those who contribute different insights or dissenting opinions are not suspected of being incompetent, or even worse, of being disloyal (Halevy et al., 2015; Jehn et al., 1999). Unfortunately, the very fact that a newcomer is seen as representing a group with different professional expertise (tech skills), or introduces different concerns (customer interests) can undermine the impact of the information they contribute, due to suspicion and mistrust about their true motives (Hornsey & Imani, 2004). Standard solutions to prevent such difficulties include socialization and onboarding programs offered to newcomers. Training newcomers to adhere to existing standards should increase trust in their abilities and intentions, and can build a sense of common identity and purpose. However, research shows such introduction programs also make incoming team members less inclined to bring to the table different insights or critical knowledge they may have – for fear of standing out (Rink et al., 2013). Without sharing their different insights or unique information, however, old hands cannot benefit from their added value (Gruenfeld et al., 2000).

Extending mutual trust and confidence is even more challenging when the educational background or prior commitments of newcomers seem to prioritize different *moral values*. Unfortunately, this feeling is easily triggered when individuals with different professional identities are expected to work together. In general, people tend to see their own moral position as universally valid and objectively true. Being exposed to others who represent a different type of expertise is likely to confront different value priorities. For instance, new team members may advocate the development of technical solutions rather than addressing human concerns, or emphasize the importance of efficiency rather than high quality. The identity threat introduced in this way jeopardizes moral self-views and can be resolved by morally excluding them. This process can result in the dismissal of valid solutions, merely because the people presenting them are not trusted. For instance, an experiment revealed that suggestions to devote more time to patient care instead of office work were evaluated more negatively when these were voiced by incoming colleagues who only had 3 weeks of work experience, rather than by co-workers with 18 years of experience (Hornsey et al., 2007).

When allowing newcomers to introduce diverging concerns care should therefore be taken to prevent that this is seen to question the validity of one's own professional values and moral priorities. Once disagreements are seen to stem from diverging values they seem absolute and insurmountable, offering no middle ground or room for compromise. Research reveals this elicits emotional and physiological threat. It makes people less inclined to find a productive solution (Kouzakova et al., 2012; Kouzakova et al., 2014), and tempts them to see their opponents as lesser humans (Skitka & Mullen, 2002). This can invite and justify aggression against them (Skitka et al., 2015). Known techniques for peaceful conflict resolution are not effective in such cases (Harinck & Ellemers, 2014).

Anticipating and actively preventing such concerns reduces the danger that the arrival of newcomers only introduces unproductive conflict (O'Connor et al., 1993). Explicitly communicating positive expectations about the contributions of newcomers can help create a shared identity where they are respected by other ingroup members (Chen, 2005; Renger et al., 2019). This makes it more likely that they speak up to voice their ideas, and enhances the likelihood that others will recognize the value of their proposals (Kane et al., 2005). However, it is just as important to prevent the emergence of identity threat among existing team members caused by fears of position loss (Scheepers & Ellemers, 2005). If not managed well, highlighting the unique experiences and novel expertise represented by newcomers easily signals a lack of appreciation for the past contributions and loyalty displays of existing team members (Hage, 1999). If this is the case, it can only result in loss of motivation and commitment on all sides. Offering everyone clarity and security about their own position in the team allows them to work towards the achievement of joint goals (Ilgen & Sheppard, 2001; see also Ellemers et al., 1998). In fact, reassuring existing team members about their own value and position can prevent old hands from defending their own ideas, and makes them more attentive and accepting of valuable contributions offered by newcomers (Rink & Ellemers, 2015).

Introducing newcomers easily raises identity threats that invite moral exclusion and destructive conflict (Jehn et al., 1999). Benefiting from dissent between newcomers and old hands is only possible after explicitly establishing that all team members subscribe to the 'right' values and are needed to achieve shared goals. Research shows the added value of explicitly providing advance explanations about the different contributions to be expected and why these are needed (Rink & Ellemers, 2007a, 2007b, 2011). This makes it possible to focus the discussion on the issue and task at hand, without questioning the competence or integrity of the individuals involved (Ellemers et al., 2020). If this is done well, people become more willing to engage with someone who is critical of their solution (such as a legal expert). It benefits information sharing, improves the quality of team outcomes, and helps prevent morally questionable decision making (Nemeth & Rogers, 1996). Importantly, this effect is most clearly visible when the disagreement is authentic; explicitly assigning someone the role of devil's advocate to foster debate was found to be much less effective (Nemeth et al., 2001a, 2001b).

6.3.3 Reconciling Continuity and Change

We have argued that responsible adaptation requires that novel insights and ideas are not introduced before testing them against existing knowledge of important risks and procedures. Of course, changes in organizations usually involve competence enhancement (acquisition of new skills) as well as competence destruction (removal of those with outdated skills). As indicated in prior sections of this chapter, this prompts many organizations to accelerate the acquisition of new skills by first identifying and removing people with skills and competencies that are no longer needed. However, research reveals that focusing mainly on the destruction of competencies that are no longer needed (usually for efficiency reasons) tends to be more difficult and less successful than achieving change by also building on and extending existing competences (Gatignon et al., 2002). One reason for this is that it is not always easy to anticipate exactly which skills and experiences have become obsolete, and how these can be replaced by other types of expertise. People who are aware of customer history, who are able to compare specifics of new with previous solutions, or remember the steps that need to be followed to implement production changes, can be sorely missed.

A truly innovative company is characterized not by its ability to show a one-time disruptive transformation, but by its general adaptability to continually changing circumstances – even without knowing what these may require. The key to successful adaptation, researchers therefore agree, is to find a way to continually *reconcile* past successes and existing capabilities with demands of new products and markets instead of replacing one with the other (Smith & Tushman, 2005; see Fig. 6.3: Successful innovation). As should be clear by now, it is not self-evident that this happens, and it takes special care to manage this process well (He & Wong, 2004). A first requirement is that businesses acknowledge the tension between different aspects of success: through optimal use of existing knowledge and skills ('exploitation'), and through the development and trying out of new knowledge and skills ('exploration'). Both activities are needed, and have to be balanced for responsible adaptation (Andriopoulos & Lewis, 2009; O'Reilly & Tushman, 2004).

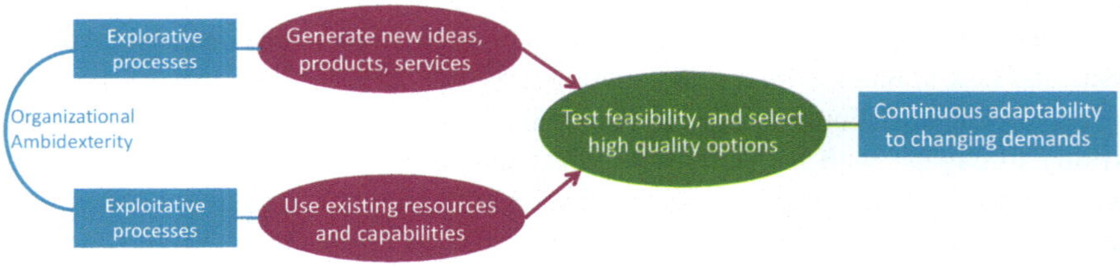

Fig. 6.3 Successful innovation. Highlights that organizational adaptability to changing demands depends on whether the development of new ideas, products, and services benefits from existing resources and capabilities. Social mechanisms determine whether efforts are made to test the feasibility of different options and select those with the highest potential

Organizing such forms of integrative collaboration implies placing trust in the experience and good judgment of the people on the work floor. Decentralized organizational structures allow professionals to communicate directly and effectively with each other to mobilize and integrate all available skills and knowledge. The recommendations on how to allow people to benefit from diverging insights – and the pitfalls to avoid – resemble the guidelines on creating feelings of inclusion despite employee diversity (see also Chap. 5; Ellemers & Rink, 2016; Guillaume et al., 2012; Rink & Ellemers, 2008, 2010). This enables them to work out solutions to competing demands, for instance in project teams. Doing this successfully requires the creation of complex assignments and team tasks that *include* quality control and production scheduling – instead of separating these for efficiency reasons and management control. If done well, this allows for more flexibility and customization, as well as maintenance and exploitation of existing capabilities on the work floor (Hage, 1999).

The continued ability of companies to attract and retain people with different types of experience, professional skills and expertise is key in this process. Embedding these in a structure that recruits and combines their different inputs and efforts allows for the rapid solution of complex problems, and is associated with company survival through change (Hage, 1999). Companies that manage to do this well show a high level of 'ambidexterity', that allows them to increase their flexibility and productivity (Damanpour, 1991). The organization's ability to build on existing resources and capabilities as well as adapting to varying circumstances, enables a process of continuous adaptation and responsible renewal. A review of many studies aiming to identify conditions that foster innovation, highlights the added value of supportive human resource practices in achieving this (Colakoglu et al., 2019). Organizations that care for the needs of employees induce high employee involvement, commitment and trust, which benefits effective information exchange, and skills development. These studies consistently reveal that intrinsic interest and empowerment of employees – rather than employment flexibility or monetary incentives – are key factors in achieving the ambidexterity that fosters responsible innovation (Colakoglu et al., 2019). Organizations that do this well not only manage to be truly innovative, but are also more likely to be successful in the long run (Almor et al., 2019; Hage, 1999; Junni et al., 2013; O'Reilly & Tushman, 2004).

To achieve this, organizations also have to be 'culturally ambidextrous', in facilitating the collaboration between 'rule breakers' and 'rule makers' (Gelfand, 2018; Gelfand et al., 2018). Managers and employees charged with quality monitoring and production continuity might focus on prevention goals. Even if this does not represent their chronic outlook in life, the prospect of production or quality failures easily makes them concerned about relinquishing control. In a similar vein, managers and employees hired for creative product development and innovation are continually prompted to address promotion goals, and might fear loss of autonomy. Communicating clearly that both performance aspects and concerns are valid and need to be met, allows people to understand how their different skills and expertise can complement each other, contribute to the achievement of joint goals, and even define their shared identity (Rink & Ellemers, 2007b, 2007c). This should help alleviate the feelings of threat that make them reluctant to embrace change.

6.4 Conclusion: Reliability Anchors Innovation

The business examples and research reviewed in this chapter demonstrate some of the hidden costs of the three quick fixes often used to push for change. Relying on flexible employment communicates moral exclusion that invites noncompliance and misbehavior. Celebrating creativity contributes to irresponsible risk taking when it devalues those who monitor security and continuity. Prioritizing novelty as a valued outcome in its own right invites misbehavior or even fraud when this tempts people to do anything for success. In general, requesting that people change the way they need to do their job is not only about the specific skills they do or do not have. It also disrupts their sense of who they are and raises concerns about whether they (still) belong in the organization.

Instead, we recommend to maintain an equilibrium between novelty and safety concerns by attending to the human factor in organizational change. Organizations can achieve this by explicitly noting the value of different individuals and departments for the organization. This makes it more likely that they *share* their knowledge and resources and *trust* each other in pursuing similar goals and values (Ghoshal & Bartlett, 1997; Nahapiet & Ghoshal, 1998). Doing this requires active interventions to avoid that task roles, organizational structures, and power differences prevent people from adequately communicating their expertise when this is relevant or share their knowledge when it is needed (Sutcliffe et al., 2004). Clearly defining the continuity as well as the changes in the status and identity of different departments, roles, and people in the organization, is a key factor to secure collaboration and knowledge sharing. In general, explicitly valuing and combining promotion and prevention goals, and ensuring that 'rule breakers' work together constructively with 'rule makers' will benefit such ongoing knowledge sharing. Realizing social innovation in this way will allow the organization to show continuous and responsible adaptation to changing circumstances, markets and clients.

Recommended Reading

Ellemers, N., & Rink, F. (2016). Diversity in work groups. *Current Opinion in Psychology, 11*, 49–53. https://doi.org/10.1016/j.copsyc.2016.06.001

Gelfand, M. J. (2018). *Rule makers, rule breakers: How tight and loose cultures wire our world.* Scribner.

Higgins, E. T. (1998). Regulatory focus as a motivational principle. In M. E. Zanna (Ed.), *Advances in experimental social psychology* (pp. 1–46). Academic Press. https://doi.org/10.1016/S0065-2601(08)60381-0

Jetten, J., & Hornsey, M. J. (2014). Deviance and dissent in groups. *Annual Review of Psychology, 65*, 461–485. https://doi.org/10.1146/annurev-psych-010213-115151

Kane, A. A., Argote, L., & Levine, J. M. (2005). Knowledge transfer between groups via personnel rotation: Effects of social identity and knowledge quality. *Organizational Behavior and Human Decision Processes, 96*(1), 56–71. https://doi.org/10.1016/j.obhdp.2004.09.002

References

Almor, T., Bazel-Shoham, O., & Lee, S. M. (2019). The dual effect of board gender diversity on R&D investments. *Long Range Planning, 101884*. https://doi.org/10.1016/j.lrp.2019.05.004

Anand, V., Ashforth, B. E., & Joshi, M. (2004). Business as usual: The acceptance and perpetuation of corruption in organizations. *Academy of Management Perspectives, 18*(2), 39–53. https://doi.org/10.5465/ame.2004.13837437

Anderson, N., De Dreu, C. K., & Nijstad, B. A. (2004). The routinization of innovation research: A constructively critical review of the state-of-the-science. *Journal of Organizational Behavior, 25*(2), 147–173. https://doi.org/10.1002/job.236

Anderson, N., Potočnik, K., & Zhou, J. (2014). Innovation and creativity in organizations: A state-of-the-science review, prospective commentary, and guiding framework. *Journal of Management, 40*(5), 1297–1333. https://doi.org/10.1177/0149206314527128

Andriopoulos, C., & Lewis, M. W. (2009). Exploitation-exploration tensions and organizational ambidexterity: Managing paradoxes of innovation. *Organization Science, 20*(4), 696–717. https://doi.org/10.1287/orsc.1080.0406

Argote, L., & Ingram, P. (2000). Knowledge transfer: A basis for competitive advantage in firms. *Organizational Behavior and Human Decision Processes, 82*(1), 150–169. https://doi.org/10.1006/obhd.2000.2893

Asher-Shapiro, A. (2019, March 29). What the Theranos documentary misses. *The New Republic*. Retrieved from https://newrepublic.com/article/153419/theranos-documentary-misses

Ashford, S. J., Lee, C., & Bobko, P. (1989). Content, cause, and consequences of job insecurity: A theory-based measure and substantive test. *Academy of Management Journal, 32*(4), 803–829. https://doi.org/10.2307/256569

Baer, M., Leenders, R. T. A., Oldham, G. R., & Vadera, A. K. (2010). Win or lose the battle for creativity: The power and perils of intergroup competition. *Academy of Management Journal, 53*(4), 827–845. https://doi.org/10.5465/amj.2010.52814611

Barnett, W. P., & Miner, A. S. (1992). Standing on the shoulders of others: Career interdependence in job mobility. *Administrative Science Quarterly*, 262–281. https://doi.org/10.2307/2393224

Bartels, J., Douwes, R., De Jong, M., & Pruyn, A. (2006). Organizational identification during a merger: Determinants of employees' expected identification with the new organization. *British Journal of Management, 17*(1), S49–S67. https://doi.org/10.1111/j.1467-8551.2006.00478.x

Bartels, J., Pruyn, A., & De Jong, M. (2009). Employee identification before and after an internal merger: A longitudinal analysis. *Journal of Occupational and Organizational Psychology, 82*(1), 113–128. https://doi.org/10.1348/096317908X283770

Beard, K. M., & Edwards, J. R. (1995). Employees at risk: Contingent work and the psychological experience of contingent workers. *Journal of Organizational Behavior, 1986-1998*, 109.

Benner, M. J., & Tushman, M. (2002). Process management and technological innovation: A longitudinal study of the photography and paint industries. *Administrative Science Quarterly, 47*(4), 676–707. https://doi.org/10.2307/3094913

Birkinshaw, J., Ambos, T. C., & Bouquet, C. (2017). Boundary spanning activities of corporate HQ executives insights from a longitudinal study. *Journal of Management Studies, 54*(4), 422–454. https://doi.org/10.1111/joms.12260

Blankenship, K. (2020, July 29). Camera maker Kodak dives into drug manufacturing with $765M federal loan. *Fierce Pharma*. Retrieved from https://www.fiercepharma.com/manufacturing/camera-maker-kodak-dives-into-drug-manufacturing-765m-federal-loan

Bradt, G. (2015, January 27). 83% of mergers fail – leverage a 100-day action plan for success instead. *Forbes*. Retrieved from https://www.forbes.com/sites/georgebradt/2015/01/27/83-mergers-fail-leverage-a-100-day-value-acceleration-plan-for-success-instead/#601d23f75b86

Brockner, J., & Higgins, E. T. (2001). Regulatory focus theory: Implications for the study of emotions at work. *Organizational Behavior and Human Decision Processes, 86*(1), 35–66. https://doi.org/10.1006/obhd.2001.2972

Broschak, J. P., & Davis-Blake, A. (2006). Mixing standard work and nonstandard deals: The consequences of heterogeneity in employment arrangements. *Academy of Management Journal, 49*(2), 371–393. https://doi.org/10.5465/amj.2006.20786085

Carosa, C. (2020, August 16). How a PR error might absolve Kodak of insider trading charges. *Forbes*. Retrieved from: https://www.forbes.com/sites/chriscarosa/2020/08/16/how-a-pr-error-might-absolve-kodak-of-insider-trading-charges/?sh=289243565919

Carreyrou, J. (2018). *Bad blood: Secrets and lies in a Silicon Valley startup*. Knopf.

CB insights (2020a, December 22). *$1B+ Market map: The world's 500+ Unicorn companies in one infographic*. Retrieved from: https://www.cbinsights.com/research/unicorn-startup-market-map/

CB insights (2020b, May 28). Mapping healthcare unicorns around the world. *Research Briefs* https://www.cbinsights.com/research/healthcare-unicorns-q1-20/

CBS. (2020, March 19). Even with coronavirus threat, some hourly workers would go to work sick: "I can't afford to miss a day". *CBS News*. Retrieved from https://www.cbsnews.com/news/coronavirus-us-hourly-workers-paid-sick-leave/

Chen, G. (2005). Newcomer adaptation in teams: Multilevel antecedents and outcomes. *Academy of Management Journal, 48*(1), 101–116. https://doi.org/10.5465/amj.2005.15993147

Choi, H. S., & Thompson, L. (2005). Old wine in a new bottle: Impact of membership change on group creativity. *Organizational Behavior and Human Decision Processes, 98*(2), 121–132. https://doi.org/10.1016/j.obhdp.2005.06.003

Colakoglu, S. S., Erhardt, N., Pougnet-Rozan, S., & Martin-Rios, C. (2019). Reviewing creativity and innovation research through the strategic HRM lens. In M. R. Buckley, A. R. Wheeler, J. E. Baur, & J. R. B. Halbesleben (Eds.), *Research in personnel and human resources management* (Vol. 37, pp. 227–271). Emerald Publishing Limited. https://doi.org/10.1108/S0742-730120190000037007

Cord, D. J. (2014). *The decline and fall of Nokia*. Schildts & Söderströms.

Coronavirus: Camera firm Kodak turns to drugs to fight virus. (2020, July 29). *BBC*. Retrieved from https://www.bbc.com/news/business-53563601

Costanza, D. P., & Finkelstein, L. M. (2015). Generationally based differences in the workplace: Is there a there there? *Industrial and Organizational Psychology, 8*(3), 308. https://doi.org/10.1017/iop.2015.15

Coupland, N., Giles, H., & Wiemann, J. M. (1991). *"Miscommunication" and problematic talk*. Sage.

Cristea, I. A., Cahan, E. M., & Ioannidis, J. P. (2019). Stealth research: Lack of peer-reviewed evidence from healthcare unicorns. *European Journal of Clinical Investigation, 49*(4), e13072–e13078. https://doi.org/10.1111/eci.13072

Damanpour, F. (1991). Organizational innovation: A meta-analysis of effects of determinants and moderators. *Academy of Management Journal, 34*(3), 555–590. https://doi.org/10.5465/256406

Darr, W., & Johns, G. (2008). Work strain, health, and absenteeism: A meta-analysis. *Journal of Occupational Health Psychology, 13*(4), 293. https://doi.org/10.1037/a0012639

Das, A., Chon, G., & Cimilluca, D. (2011). M&A began to pick up in 2010. *The Private Equity Analyst*.

Dattner, B., Chamorro-Premuzic, T., Buchband, R., & Schettler, L. (2019, April 25). The legal and ethical implications of using AI in hiring. *Harvard Business Review, 25*.

De Cuyper, N., De Witte, H., & Van Emmerik, H. (2011). Temporary employment: Costs and benefits for (the careers of) employees and organizations. *Career Development International, 16*(2), 104–113. https://doi.org/10.1108/13620431111115587

De Dreu, C. K. W., & West, M. A. (2001). Minority dissent and team innovation: The importance of participation in decision making. *Journal of Applied Psychology, 86*(6), 1191–1201. https://doi.org/10.1037/0021-9010.86.6.1191

De Gilder, D. (2003). Commitment, trust and work behaviour. *Personnel Review, 32*(2), 588–604. https://doi.org/10.1108/00483480310488351

De Jong, B. A., Dirks, K. T., & Gillespie, N. (2016). Trust and team performance: A meta-analysis of main effects, moderators, and covariates. *Journal of Applied Psychology, 101*(8), 1134–1150. https://doi.org/10.1037/apl0000110

Deloitte. (2020, January). The deloitte global millennial survey 2020. *Deloitte*. Retrieved from https://www2.deloitte.com/global/en/pages/about-deloitte/articles/millennialsurvey.html

De Witte, H., Pienaar, J., & De Cuyper, N. (2016). Review of 30 years of longitudinal studies on the association between job insecurity and health and well-being: Is there causal evidence? *Australian Psychologist, 51*(1), 18–31. https://doi.org/10.1111/ap.12176

Edelman. (2019). Edelman trust barometer global report 2019. *Edelman*. Retrieved from https://www.edelman.com/sites/g/files/aatuss191/files/2019-02/2019_Edelman_Trust_Barometer_Global_Report.pdf

Eldor, L., & Cappelli, P. (2020). Agency temps hurts business performance: An integrated indirect model. *Academy of Management Journal*. https://doi.org/10.5465/amj.2019.0392

Ellemers, N., De Gilder, D., & Haslam, S. A. (2004). Motivating individuals and groups at work: A social identity perspective on leadership and group performance. *Academy of Management Review, 29*(3), 459–478. https://doi.org/10.5465/amr.2004.13670967

Ellemers, N., De Gilder, D., & Van den Heuvel, H. (1998). Career-oriented versus team-oriented commitment and behavior at work. *Journal of Applied Psychology, 83*, 717–730. https://doi.org/10.1037/0021-9010.83 5.717

Ellemers, N., Fiske, S. T., Abele, A. E., Koch, A., & Yzerbyt, V. (2020). Adversarial alignment enables competing models to engage in cooperative theory building toward cumulative science. *Proceedings of the National Academy of Sciences, 117*(14), 7561–7567. https://doi.org/10.1073/pnas.1906720117

Ellemers, N., & Jetten, J. (2013). The many ways to be marginal in a group. *Personality and Social Psychology Review, 17*, 3–21. https://doi.org/10.1177/1088868312453086

Ellemers, N., & Rink, F. (2005). Identity in work groups: The beneficial and detrimental consequences of multiple identities and group norms for collaboration and group performance. *Advances in Group Processes, 22*(1), 1–41. https://doi.org/10.1016/S0882-6145(05)22001-5

Ellemers, N., & Rink, F. (2016). Diversity in work groups. *Current Opinion in Psychology, 11*, 49–53. https://doi.org/10.1016/j.copsyc.2016.06.001

Ellemers, N., Sleebos, E., Stam, D., & De Gilder, D. (2013). Feeling included and valued: How perceived respect affects positive team identity and willingness to invest in the team. *British Journal of Management, 24*(1), 21–37. https://doi.org/10.1111/j.1467-8551.2011.00784.x

Ellingson, J. E., Gruys, M. L., & Sackett, P. R. (1998). Factors related to the satisfaction and performance of temporary employees. *Journal of Applied Psychology, 83*(6), 913. https://doi.org/10.1037/0021-9010.83.6.913

Ellis, K. M., Reus, T. H., & Lamont, B. T. (2009). The effects of procedural and informational justice in the integration of related acquisitions. *Strategic Management Journal, 30*(2), 137–161. https://doi.org/10.1002/smj.728

Faddegon, K., Ellemers, N., & Scheepers, D. (2009). Eager to be the best, or vigilant no to be the worst: The emergence of regulatory focus in disjunctive and conjunctive group tasks. *Group Processes and Intergroup Relations, 12*, 653–671. https://doi.org/10.1177/1368430209339922

Faddegon, K., Scheepers, D., & Ellemers, N. (2008). If we have the will, there will be a way: Regulatory focus as a group identity. *European Journal of Social Psychology, 38*(5), 880–895. https://doi.org/10.1002/ejsp.483

Fan, J. S. (2016). Regulating unicorns: Disclosure and the new private economy. *Boston College Law Review, 57*, 583–642.

FD. (2019, June 21). Digitalisering raakt de kern. *FD*. Retrieved from https://fd.nl/specials/1305134/digitalisering-raakt-de-kern

Feldman, D. C., Doerpinghaus, H. I., & Turnley, W. H. (1994). Managing temporary workers: A permanent HRM challenge. *Organizational Dynamics, 23*, 49–63. https://doi.org/10.1016/0090-2616(94)90068-X

Gatignon, H., Tushman, M. L., Smith, W., & Anderson, P. (2002). A structural approach to assessing innovation: Construct development of innovation locus, type, and characteristics. *Management Science, 48*(9), 1103–1122. https://doi.org/10.1287/mnsc.48.9.1103.174

Geer, D. (2017, October 8). 4 ways FinTech is changing global finance. *The Next Web.* Retrieved from https://thenextweb.com/contributors/2017/10/08/4-ways-fin-tech-changing-global-finance/

Gelfand, M. J. (2018). *Rule makers, rule breakers: How tight and loose cultures wire our world.* Scribner.

Gelfand, M., Gordon, S., Li, C., Choi, V., & Prokopowicz, P. (2018). *One reason mergers fail: The two cultures aren't compatible.* Harvard Business Review. Retrieved from https://hbr.org/2018/10/one-reason-mergers-fail-the-two-cultures-arent-compatible

Ghoshal, S., & Bartlett, C. A. (1997). *The individualized corporation: A fundamentally new approach to management; great companies are defined by purpose, process, and people.* HarperCollins.

Gibney, A., Deeter, J., & Edeiken, E. (Producers), & Gibney, A. (Director). (2019). *The inventor: Out for blood in Silicon Valley* [Video file]. Retrieved from https://www.hbo.com/documentaries/the-inventor-out-for-blood-in-silicon-valley

Giessner, S. R., Ullrich, J., & Van Dick, R. (2011). Social identity and corporate mergers. *Social and Personality Psychology Compass, 5*(6), 333–345. https://doi.org/10.1111/j.1751-9004.2011.00357.x

Gino, F., & Ariely, D. (2012). The dark side of creativity: Original thinkers can be more dishonest. *Journal of Personality and Social Psychology, 102*(3), 445. https://doi.org/10.1037/a0026406

Ginsel, D., Bos, M., Pippo, G., & Pytkowska, J. (2019). *The Fintech market in the Netherlands: The current state of the fintech sector and its potential to contribute to financial inclusion and health.* Microfinance Centre. Retrieved from http://mfc.org.pl/wp-content/uploads/2020/03/NETHERLANDS_FINTECH-CASE-STUDY_FEB2020.pdf

Gollan, J. (2020, March 6). As coronavirus spreads, caregivers in elder care facilities fear they can't afford to call in sick. *Reveal News.* Retrieved from https://www.revealnews.org/article/as-coronavirus-spreads-caregivers-in-elder-care-facilities-fear-they-cant-afford-to-call-in-sick/

Graen, G. B., & Scandura, T. A. (1987). Toward a psychology of dyadic organizing. In L. L. Cummings & B. M. Staw (Eds.), *Research in organizational behavior* (pp. 175–208). JAI.

Gruenfeld, D. H., Martorana, P. V., & Fan, E. T. (2000). What do groups learn from their worldliest members? Direct and indirect influence in dynamic teams. *Organizational Behavior and Human Decision Processes, 82*(1), 45–59. https://doi.org/10.1006/obhd.2000.2886

Guillaume, Y. R. F., Brodbeck, F. C., & Riketta, M. (2012). Surface and deep-level dissimilarity effects on social integration and individual effectiveness related outcomes in work groups: A meta-analytic integration. *Journal of Occupational and Organizational Psychology, 85*, 80–115. https://doi.org/10.1111/j.2044-8325.2010.02005.x

Guimerà, R., Uzzi, B., Spiro, J., & Amaral, L. A. N. (2005). Team assembly mechanisms determine collaboration network structure and team performance. *Science, 308*(5722), 697–702. https://doi.org/10.1126/science.1106340

Hage, J. T. (1999). Organizational innovation and organizational change. *Annual Review of Sociology, 25*, 597–622. https://doi.org/10.1146/annurev.soc.25.1.597

Halevy, N., Kreps, T. A., Weisel, O., & Goldenberg, A. (2015). Morality in intergroup conflict. *Current Opinion in Psychology, 6*, 10–14. https://doi.org/10.1016/j.copsyc.2015.03.006

Harinck, F., & Ellemers, N. (2014). How values change a conflict. In C. K. W. de Dreu (Ed.), *Conflicts within and between groups: Functions, dynamics, and interventions* (pp. 19–36). Psychology Press.

Harrison, F. E. (1987). *The managerial decision-making process.* Houghton Mifflin.

Hays, C. L. (2000, April 13). Ben & Jerry's to Unilever, with attitude. *The New York Times.* Retrieved from https://www.nytimes.com/2000/04/13/business/ben-jerry-s-to-unilever-with-attitude.html

He, Z. L., & Wong, P. K. (2004). Exploration vs. exploitation: An empirical test of the ambidexterity hypothesis. *Organization Science, 15*(4), 481–494. https://doi.org/10.1287/orsc.1040.0078

Heikkinen, M.-P. (2010, October 8). Knock, knock, Nokia's heavy fall. *Kuukausiliite*. Retrieved from https://www.hs.fi/english/article/Knock+Knock+Nokias+Heavy+Fall/1135260596609/

Hern, A. (2020, May 20). Apple whistleblower goes public over 'lack of action'. *The Guardian*. Retrieved from https://www.theguardian.com/technology/2020/may/20/apple-whistleblower-goes-public-over-lack-of-action

Higgins, E. T. (1997). Beyond pleasure and pain. *American Psychologist, 52*, 1280–1300. https://doi.org/10.1037/0003-066X.52.12.1280

Higgins, E. T. (1998). Regulatory focus as a motivational principle. In M. E. Zanna (Ed.), *Advances in experimental social psychology* (pp. 1–46). Academic. https://doi.org/10.1016/S0065-2601(08)60381-0

Higgins, E. T., Friedman, R. S., Harlow, R. E., Idson, L. C., Ayduk, O. N., & Taylor, A. (2001). Achievement orientations from subjective histories of success: Promotion pride versus prevention pride. *European Journal of Social Psychology, 31*, 3–23. https://doi.org/10.1002/ejsp.27

Higgins, E. T., Shah, J., & Friedman, R. (1997). Emotional responses to goal attainment: Strength of regulatory focus as moderator. *Journal of Personality and Social Psychology, 72*(3), 515. https://doi.org/10.1037/0022-3514.72.3.515

Hinchliffe, R. (2020, November 10). ING subsidiary Payvision accused of pushing €131.2m in fraudulent payments. *FinTech Futures*. Retrieved from: https://www.fintechfutures.com/2020/11/ing-subsidiary-payvision-accused-of-pushing-e131m-in-fraudulent-payments/

Hoever, I. J., Van Knippenberg, D., Van Ginkel, W. P., & Barkema, H. G. (2012). Fostering team creativity: Perspective taking as key to unlocking diversity's potential. *Journal of Applied Psychology, 97*(5), 982. https://doi.org/10.1037/a0029159

Hornsey, M. J., Grice, T., Jetten, J., Paulsen, N., & Callan, V. (2007). Group-directed criticisms and recommendations for change: Why newcomers arouse more resistance than old-Timers. *Personality and Social Psychology Bulletin, 33*, 1036–1048. https://doi.org/10.1177/0146167203010029

Hornsey, M. J., & Imani, A. (2004). Criticizing groups from the inside and the outside: An identity perspective on the intergroup sensitivity effect. *Personality and Social Psychology Bulletin, 30*(3), 365–383. https://doi.org/10.1177/0146167203261295

Ilgen, D. R., & Sheppard, L. (2001). Motivation in work teams. *Work Motivation in the Context of a Globalizing Economy*, 169–179.

ING. (2018, March 13). ING completes acquisition of majority stake in Payvision. *ING*. Retrieved from https://www.ing.com/Newsroom/News/Press-releases/ING-completes-acquisition-of-majority-stake-in-Payvision.htm

Isaksson, K. S., & Bellaagh, K. (2002). Health problems and quitting among female "temps". *European Journal of Work and Organizational Psychology, 11*(1), 27–45. https://doi.org/10.1080/13594320143000744

Janis, I. L. (1972). *Victims of group think*. Houghton Mifflin.

Jaruzelski, B., Chwalik, R., & Goehle, B. (2018, October 30). What the top innovators get right. *Strategy & Business*. Retrieved from https://www.strategy-business.com/feature/What-the-Top-Innovators-Get-Right?gko=bdbc7

Jehn, K. A., Northcraft, G. B., & Neale, M. A. (1999). Why differences make a difference: A field study of diversity, conflict and performance in workgroups. *Administrative Science Quarterly, 44*(4), 741–763. https://doi.org/10.2307/2667054

Jetten, J., & Hornsey, M. J. (2014). Deviance and dissent in groups. *Annual Review of Psychology, 65*, 461–485. https://doi.org/10.1146/annurev-psych-010213-115151

Junni, P., Sarala, R., Taras, V., & Tarba, S. (2013). Organizational ambidexterity and performance: A meta-analysis. *Academy of Management Perspectives, 27*(4), 299–312. https://doi.org/10.5465/amp.2012.0015

Kalleberg, A. L., Reskin, B. F., & Hudson, K. (2000). Bad jobs in America: Standard and nonstandard employment relations and job quality in the United States. *American Sociological Review*, 256–278 https://doi.org/10.2307/2657440

Kane, A. A., Argote, L., & Levine, J. M. (2005). Knowledge transfer between groups via personnel rotation: Effects of social identity and knowledge quality. *Organizational Behavior and Human Decision Processes, 96*(1), 56–71. https://doi.org/10.1016/j.obhdp.2004.09.002

Kane, G. C., Nguyen Phillips, A., Copulsky, J. R., & Andrus, G. R. (2019). The technological fallacy: How people are the real key to digital transformation. *Management on the Cutting Edge*. https://doi.org/10.7551/mitpress/11661.001.0001

Kim, M. S., & Choi, J. N. (2010). Layoff victim's employment relationship with a new employer in Korea: Effects of unmet tenure expectations on trust and psychological contract. *The International Journal of Human Resource Management, 21*(5), 781–798. https://doi.org/10.1080/09585191003658938

Kogut, B., & Zander, U. (2003). Knowledge of the firm and the evolutionary theory of the multinational corporation. *Journal of International Business Studies, 34*(6), 516–529. https://doi.org/10.1057/palgrave.jibs.8400058

Kossek, E. E., Huber-Yoder, M., Castellino, D. R., & Lerner, J. V. (1997). The working poor: Locked out of careers and the organizational mainstream? *Academy of Management Executive, 11*, 75–91. https://doi.org/10.5465/ame.1997.9707100661

Kouzakova, M., Ellemers, N., Harinck, F., & Scheepers, D. (2012). The implications of value conflict: How disagreement on values affects self-involvement and perceived common ground. *Personality and Social Psychology Bulletin, 38*, 798–807. https://doi.org/10.1177/0146167211436320

Kouzakova, M., Harinck, F., Ellemers, N., & Scheepers, D. (2014). At the heart of a conflict: Cardiovascular and self-regulation responses to value versus resource conflicts. *Social Psychological and Personality Science, 5*(1), 35–42. https://doi.org/10.1177/1948550613486673

Liesefeld, H. R., Fu, X., & Zimmer, H. D. (2015). Fast and careless or careful and slow? Apparent holistic processing in mental rotation is explained by speed-accuracy trade-offs. *Journal of Experimental Psychology: Learning, Memory, and Cognition, 41*(4), 1140. https://doi.org/10.1037/xlm0000081

Lu, J. G., Quoidbach, J., Gino, F., Chakroff, A., Maddux, W. W., & Galinsky, A. D. (2017). The dark side of going abroad: How broad foreign experiences increase immoral behavior. *Journal of Personality and Social Psychology, 112*(1), 1. https://doi.org/10.1037/pspa0000068

March, J. G. (1991). Exploration and exploitation in organizational learning. *Organization Science, 2*(1), 71–87. https://doi.org/10.1287/orsc.2.1.71

Marks, M. L., & Mirvis, P. H. (2001). Making mergers and acquisitions work: Strategic and psychological preparation. *Academy of Management Perspectives, 15*(2), 80–92. https://doi.org/10.5465/ame.2001.4614947

Marler, J. H., Barringer, M. W., & Milkovich, G. T. (2002). Boundaryless and traditional contingent employees: Worlds apart. *Journal of Organizational Behaviour, 23*, 425–453. https://doi.org/10.1002/job.148

Mayr, U., & Freund, A. M. (2020). Do we become more prosocial as we age, and if so, why? *Current Directions in Psychological Science*. https://doi.org/10.1177/0963721420910811

McDonald, D. J., & Makin, P. J. (2000). The psychological contract, organizational commitment and job satisfaction of temporary staff. *Leadership and Organizational Development Journal, 21*, 84–91. https://doi.org/10.1108/01437730010318174

McGrath, J. E., Arrow, H., & Berdahl, J. L. (2000). The study of groups: Past, present, and future. *Personality and Social Psychology Review, 4*(1), 95–105. https://doi.org/10.1207/S15327957PSPR0401_8

McLean Parks, J., & Kidder, D. L. (1994). "Till death us do part…" Changing work relationships in the 1990s. In C. L. Cooper & D. M. Rousseau (Eds.), *Trends in organizational behavior* (pp. 111–133). Wiley.

Meglio, O., King, D. R., & Risberg, A. (2015). Improving acquisition outcomes with contextual ambidexterity. *Human Resource Management, 54*(1), 29–43. https://doi.org/10.1002/hrm.21721

Mehra, M. R., Ruschitzka, F., & Patel, A. N. (2020, June 5). Retraction—Hydroxychloroquine or chloroquine with or without a macrolide for treatment of COVID-19: A multinational registry analysis. *The Lancet*. Retrieved from https://www.thelancet.com/journals/lancet/article/PIIS0140-6736(20)31324-6/fulltext

Mende, M., Scott, M. L., Van Doorn, J., Grewal, D., & Shanks, I. (2019). Service robots rising: How humanoid robots influence service experiences and elicit compensatory consumer responses. *Journal of Marketing Research, 56*(4), 535–556. https://doi.org/10.1177/0022243718822827

Miller, S. (1994). New discourse city: An alternative model for collaboration. In S. B. Reagan, T. Fox, & D. Bleich (Eds.), *Writing with: New directions in collaborative teaching, learning, and research* (pp. 283–300). State U of New York P.

Miner, A. S. (1994). Seeking adaptive advantage: Evolutionary theory and managerial action. *Evolutionary dynamics of organizations, 76*, 89.

Molden, D. C., Lee, A. Y., & Higgins, E. T. (2008). Motivations for promotion and prevention. In J. Y. Shah & W. L. Gardner (Eds.), *Handbook of motivation science* (pp. 169–187). Guilford Press.

Morgan, B. (2019, September 30). Companies that failed at digital transformation and what we can learn from them. *Forbes*. Retrieved from https://www.forbes.com/sites/blakemorgan/2019/09/30/companies-that-failed-at-digital-transformation-and-what-we-can-learn-from-them/#458a7122603c

Nahapiet, J., & Ghoshal, S. (1998). Social capital, intellectual capital, and the organizational advantage. *Academy of Management Review, 23*(2), 242–266. https://doi.org/10.5465/amr.1998.533225

Nemeth, C. J., Brown, K., & Rogers, J. (2001b). Devil's advocate versus authentic dissent: Stimulating quantity and quality. *European Journal of Social Psychology, 31*(6), 707–720. https://doi.org/10.1002/ejsp.58

Nemeth, C. J., Connell, J. B., Rogers, J. D., & Brown, K. S. (2001a). Improving decision making by means of dissent 1. *Journal of Applied Social Psychology, 31*(1), 48–58. https://doi.org/10.1111/j.1559-1816.2001.tb02481.x

Nemeth, C. J., & Ormiston, M. (2007). Creative idea generation: Harmony versus stimulation. *European Journal of Social Psychology, 37*(3), 524–535. https://doi.org/10.1002/ejsp.373

Nemeth, C. J., & Rogers, J. (1996). Dissent and the search for information. *British Journal of Social Psychology, 35*(1), 67–76. https://doi.org/10.1111/j.2044-8309.1996.tb01083.x

Nutt, P. C., & Wilson, D. C. (2010). *Handbook of decision making* (Vol. 6). John Wiley & Sons.

Nykänen, P., & Salminen, M. (2014, October 14). Wie of wat heeft Nokia de das omgedaan? *Project Syndicate*. Retrieved from https://www.project-syndicate.org/commentary/nokia-lessons-for-apple-and-google-by-pekka-nyk-nen-and-merina-salminen-2014-10/dutch?barrier=accesspaylog

O'Connor, K. M., Gruenfeld, D. H., & Mcgrath, J. E. (1993). The experience and effects of conflict in continuing work groups. *Small Group Research, 24*, 362–382. https://doi.org/10.1177/1046496493243005

Olekalns, M., & Smith, P. L. (2005). Moments in time: Metacognition, trust, and outcomes in dyadic negotiations. *Personality and Social Psychology Bulletin, 31*(12), 1696–1707. https://doi.org/10.1177/0146167205278306

O'Reilly, C. A., & Tushman, M. L. (2004). The ambidextrous organization. *Harvard Business Review*, 74–83.

Pandza, K., & Ellwood, P. (2013). Strategic and ethical foundations for responsible innovation. *Research Policy, 42*(5), 1112–1125. https://doi.org/10.1016/j.respol.2013.02.007

Patterson, D. (2020, July 30). Facebook data privacy scandal: A cheat sheet. *Tech Republic*. Retrieved from https://www.techrepublic.com/article/facebook-data-privacy-scandal-a-cheat-sheet/

Paul, K. (2020, April 21). Hundreds of Amazon warehouse workers to call in sick in coronavirus protest. *The Guardian*. Retrieved from https://www.theguardian.com/technology/2020/apr/20/amazon-warehouse-workers-sickout-coronavirus

Pearce, J. L. (1993). Toward an organizational behavior of contract laborers: Their psychological involvement and effects on employee co-workers. *Academy of Management Journal, 36*, 1082–1096. https://doi.org/10.2307/256646

Pearce, J. L. (1998). Job Insecurity is important, but not for the reasons you might think: The example of contingent workers. In C. L. Cooper & D. M. Rousseau (Eds.), *Trends in organization behavior* (Vol. 5, pp. 31–46). John Wiley.

Peltonen, T. (2019). Case study 4: The collapse of Nokia's mobile phone business: Wisdom and stupidity in strategic decision-making. In *Towards wise management* (pp. 163–188). Palgrave Macmillan. https://doi.org/10.1007/978-3-319-91719-1_6

Pernell, K., Jung, J., & Dobbin, F. (2017). The hazards of expert control: Chief risk officers and risky derivatives. *American Sociological Review, 82*(3), 511–541. https://doi.org/10.1177/0003122417701115

Perretti, F., & Negro, G. (2007). Mixing genres and matching people: A study in innovation and team composition in Hollywood. *Journal of Organizational Behavior, 28*(5), 563–586. https://doi.org/10.1002/job.464

Renger, D., Mommert, A., Renger, S., Miché, M., & Simon, B. (2019). Voicing one's ideas: Intragroup respect as an antecedent of assertive behavior. *Basic and Applied Social Psychology, 41*(1), 34–47. https://doi.org/10.1080/01973533.2018.1542306

Rengers, M., Bronzwaer, S., & Kooiman, J. (2020, May 15). Booking is uitgefeest. Hoe kon de reisgigant zó in problemen komen? *NRC*. Retrieved from https://www.nrc.nl/nieuws/2020/05/15/het-feestje-van-booking-is-voorbij-2-a3999859

Rink, F., & Ellemers, N. (2007a). The role of expectancies in accepting task-related diversity: Do dissapointment and lack of commitment stem from actual differences or violated expectations? *Personality and Social Psychology Bulletin, 33*, 842–845. https://doi.org/10.1177/0146167207301016

Rink, F., & Ellemers, N. (2007b). Defining the common feature: Task-related differences as the basis for dyadic identity. *British Journal of Social Psychology, 46*, 499–515. https://doi.org/10.1348/014466606X154872

Rink, F., & Ellemers, N. (2007c). Diversity as a source of common identity: Towards a social identity framework for studying the effects of diversity in organizations. *British Journal of Management, 18*(1), 17–27. https://doi.org/10.1111/j.1467-8551.2007.00523.x

Rink, F., & Ellemers, N. (2008). Diversity, newcomers, and team innovation: The importance of a common identity. In B. Mannix, M. Neale, & K. Phillips (Eds.), *Diversity & Groups. Research on managing groups and teams* (pp. 221–243). JAI Press. https://doi.org/10.1177/1368430214550339

Rink, F., & Ellemers, N. (2010). Benefiting from deep-level diversity: How congruence between knowledge and decision rules improves team decision making and team perceptions/. *Group Processes & Intergroup Relations, 13*(3), 345–359. https://doi.org/10.1177/1368430209344866

Rink, F., & Ellemers, N. (2011). From current state to desired future: How compositional changes affect dissent and innovation in work groups. In J. Jetten & M. J. Hornsey (Eds.), *Rebels in groups: Dissent, deviance, difference, and defiance* (pp. 54–72). Blackwell. https://doi.org/10.1002/9781444390841.ch4

Rink, F., & Ellemers, N. (2015). The pernicious effects of unstable work group membership: How work group changes undermine unique task contributions and newcomer acceptance. *Group Processes & Intergroup Relations, 18*(1), 6–23. https://doi.org/10.1177/1368430214550339

Rink, F., Kane, A. A., Ellemers, N., & Van der Vegt, G. (2013). Team receptivity to newcomers: Five decades of evidence and future research themes. *Academy of Management Annals, 7*(1), 247–293. https://doi.org/10.5465/19416520.2013.766405

Robinson, S. L., & Rousseau, D. M. (1994). Violating the psychological contract: Not the exception but the norm. *Journal of Organizational Behavior, 15*(3), 245–259. https://doi.org/10.1002/job.4030150306

Rulison, L. (2020, August 11). Kodak's drug business has history of letdowns, including in Capital Region. *Times Union*. Retrieved from https://www.timesunion.com/business/article/Kodak-s-drug-business-has-history-of-implosions-15475284.php

Sarooghi, H., Libaers, D., & Burkemper, A. (2015). Examining the relationship between creativity and innovation: A meta-analysis of organizational, cultural, and environmental factors. *Journal of Business Venturing, 30*(5), 714–731. https://doi.org/10.1016/j.jbusvent.2014.12.003

Savela, N., Kaakinen, M., Ellonen, N., & Oksanen, A. (2019, June 26-28). *Working with robots challenges the ingroup-outgroup boundaries: The negative effect of robot coworkers on the work team identification* [Symposium presentation]. EASP Meeting: Intergroup Communication, University of Bologna, Bologna, Italy. https://www.easp.eu/getmedia.php/_media/easp/201909/1156v0-orig.pdf

Savela, N., Turja, T., & Oksanen, A. (2018). Social acceptance of robots in different occupational fields: A systematic literature review. *International Journal of Social Robotics, 10*(4), 493–502. https://doi.org/10.1007/s12369-017-0452-5

Scheepers, D., & Ellemers, N. (2005). When the pressure is up: The assessment of social identity threat in low and high status groups. *Journal of Experimental Social Psychology, 41*(2), 192–200. https://doi.org/10.1016/j.jesp.2004.06.002

Shazi, R., Gillespie, N., & Steen, J. (2015). Trust as a predictor of innovation network ties in project teams. *International Journal of Project Management, 33*(1), 81–91. https://doi.org/10.1016/j.ijproman.2014.06.001

Skarlicki, D. P., & Folger, R. (1997). Retaliation in the workplace: The roles of distributive, procedural, and interactional justice. *Journal of Applied Psychology, 82*, 434–443. https://doi.org/10.1037/0021-9010.82.3.434

Skitka, L. J., & Mullen, E. (2002). The dark side of moral conviction. *Analyses of Social Issues and Public Policy, 2*(1), 35–41. https://doi.org/10.1111/j.1530-2415.2002.00024.x

Skitka, L. J., Washburn, A. N., & Carsel, T. S. (2015). The psychological foundations and consequences of moral conviction. *Current Opinion in Psychology, 6*, 41–44. https://doi.org/10.1016/j.copsyc.2015.03.025

Sleebos, E., Ellemers, N., & De Gilder, D. (2006a). The carrot and the stick: Affective commitment and acceptance anxiety as motives for discretionary group efforts by respected and disrespected group members. *Personality and Social Psychology Bulletin, 32*(2), 244–255. https://doi.org/10.1177/0146167205282147

Sleebos, E., Ellemers, N., & De Gilder, D. (2006b). The paradox of the disrespected: Disrespected group members' engagement in group-serving efforts. *Journal of Experimental Social Psychology, 42*(4), 413–427. https://doi.org/10.1016/j.jesp.2005.06.002

Smith, W. K., & Tushman, M. L. (2005). Managing strategic contradictions: A top management model for managing innovation streams. *Organization Science, 16*(5), 522–536. https://doi.org/10.1287/orsc.1050.0134

Sutcliffe, K. M., Lewton, E., & Rosenthal, M. M. (2004). Communication failures: An insidious contributor to medical mishaps. *Academic Medicine, 79*(2), 186–194. https://doi.org/10.1097/00001888-200402000-00019

Takeover of Porn and Gambling Customers is a Great Embarrassment to ING. (2020, November 13). *News1*. Retrieved from https://www.news1.news/2020/11/takeover-of-porn-and-gambling-customers-is-a-great-embarrassment-to-ing.html

Tarver, E. (2020, May 10). *Are private companies required to publish financial statements?* Retrieved from: https://www.investopedia.com/ask/answers/062415/private-company-required-disclose-financial-information-public.asp#:~:text=As%20the%20name%20implies%2C%20a,small%20and%20medium%2Dsized%20companies

Terry, D. J. (2001). Intergroup relations and organizational mergers. In M. A. Hogg & D. J. Terry (Eds.), *Social identity processes in organizational contexts* (pp. 229–248). Psychology Press.

Terry, D. J. (2003). A social identity perspective on organizational mergers: The role of group status, permeability and similarity. In S. A. Haslam, D. van Knippenberg, M. J. Platow, &

N. Ellemers (Eds.), *Social identity at work – Developing theory for organizational practice* (pp. 223–240). Psychology Press.
Tidd, J., & Bessant, J. R. (2018). *Managing innovation: Integrating technological, market and organizational change*. John Wiley & Sons.
Tsai, W., & Ghoshal, S. (1998). Social capital and value creation: The role of intrafirm networks. *Academy of Management Journal, 41*(4), 464–476. https://doi.org/10.2307/257085
Tyler, T. R., & Blader, S. L. (2000). *Cooperation in groups: Procedural justice, social identity, and behavioral engagement*. Taylor & Francis Group.
Ullrich, J., Wieseke, J., & Van Dick, R. (2005). Continuity and change in mergers and acquisitions: A social identity case study of a German industrial merger. *Journal of Management Studies, 42*(8), 1549–1569. https://doi.org/10.1111/j.1467-6486.2005.00556.x
Uzzi, B., & Barsness, Z. I. (1998). Contingent employment in British establishments: Organizational determinants of the use of fixed-term hires and part-time workers. *Social Forces, 76*(3), 967–1005. https://doi.org/10.1093/sf/76.3.967
Van Dick, R., Ullrich, J., & Tissington, P. (2004). *Working under a black cloud: How to sustain organizational identification after a merger*. Aston Business School.
Van Dick, R., Ullrich, J., & Tissington, P. A. (2006). Working under a black cloud: How to sustain organizational identification after a merger. *British Journal of Management, 17*(S1), 69–79. https://doi.org/10.1111/j.1467-8551.2006.00479.x
Van Knippenberg, D., & Van Leeuwen, E. (2001). Organizational identity after a merger: Sense of continuity as the key to post-merger identification. In M. A. Hogg & D. J. Terry (Eds.), *Social identity processes in organizational contexts* (pp. 249–264). Psychology Press.
Van Leeuwen, E., Van Knippenberg, D., & Ellemers, N. (2003). Continuing and changing group identities: The effects of merging on social identification and ingroup bias. *Personality and Social Psychology Bulletin, 29*, 679–690. https://doi.org/10.1177/0146167203029006001
Veenstra, K., Haslam, S. A., & Reynolds, K. J. (2004). The psychology of casualization: Evidence for the mediating roles of security, status and social identification. *British Journal of Social Psychology, 43*, 499–514. https://doi.org/10.1348/0144666042565380
Vincent, L. C., & Kouchaki, M. (2016). Creative, rare, entitled, and dishonest: How commonality of creativity in one's group decreases an individual's entitlement and dishonesty. *Academy of Management Journal, 59*(4), 1451–1473. https://doi.org/10.5465/amj.2014.1109
Von Hippel, C. D. (2006). When people would rather switch than fight: Out group favoritism among temporary employees. *Group Processes and Intergroup Relations, 9*(4), 533–546. https://doi.org/10.1177/1368430206067556
Von Hippel, C. D., Mangum, S. L., Greenberger, D. B., Heneman, R. L., & Skoglind, J. D. (1997). Temporary employment: Can organizations and employees both win? *Academy of Management Executive, 11*(1), 93–104. https://doi.org/10.5465/ame.1997.9707100662
Warmbrodt, Z. (2020, October 8). Kodak's federal loan in doubt after agency cites 'serious concerns'. *Politico*. Retrieved from: https://www.politico.com/news/2020/08/10/kodaks-federal-loan-in-doubt-after-agency-cites-serious-concerns-393085
West, M. A., & Farr, J. L. (1989). Innovation at work. *Psychological Perspectives, 4*, 15–30.
Zander, U., & Kogut, B. (1995). Knowledge and the speed of the transfer and imitation of organizational capabilities: An empirical test. *Organization Science, 6*(1), 76–92. https://doi.org/10.1287/orsc.6.1.76
Zeytinoglu, I., Lillevik, W., Seaton, B., & Moruz, J. (2004). Part-time and casual work in retail trade: Stress and other factors affecting the workplace. *Relations Industrielles/Industrial Relations, 59*(3), 516–544. https://doi.org/10.7202/010923ar
Zhou, J., Shin, S. J., & Cannella, A. A. (2008). Employee self-perceived creativity after mergers and acquisitions: Interactive effects of threat—Opportunity perception, access to resources, and support for creativity. *The Journal of Applied Behavioral Science, 44*(4), 397–421. https://doi.org/10.1177/0021886308328010

Chapter 7
Relating to Stakeholders

Abstract **Key issues** addressed in this chapter relate to the growing awareness in many organizations that displaying concern for different stakeholders and their interests is crucial, if only to secure the 'license to operate'. Here too it is tempting to fall back on quick fixes to signal good intentions. Organizations may try to communicate responsible management for instance by getting rid of questionable supply chain partners, giving money to good causes, or applying for social impact certification. Our **analysis** reveals that such efforts are likely to be ineffective when the core mission and activities of the organization ignore broader stakeholder concerns. Attempts to cleanse the reputation of the organization without reconsidering key aspects of its identity will only compound the problem. Neglecting the moral responsibility of the organization for key activities, product safety issues or environmental damage makes such communications seems insincere. Research shows this undermines the reputation of the organization as a reliable partner. **Solutions** are more effective when strategic decisions take into account different stakeholders and their concerns as relevant to the identity and mission of the organization. The will-

N. Ellemers, D. de Gilder, *The Moral Organization: Key Issues, Analyses, and Solutions*, https://doi.org/10.1007/978-3-030-84175-1_7

ingness of organizations to integrate social impact as a key outcome to pursue, signals true commitment. Research shows that the appeal of contributing to this social purpose increases employee efforts, and secures long term support from other stakeholders.

7.1 Key Issues: Stakeholder Management

Commercial enterprises as well as public organizations have to contend with different stakeholders as they consider how to satisfy the needs of their customers or clients, how to attract and retain suppliers and employees, or how to account for their activities towards investors and regulators (Crane & Ruebottom, 2011; Mitchell et al., 1997). To achieve this, organizations and their managers have long relied on 'primary' organizational assets relating to efficiency, productivity, and profitability. For many years, customers have been attracted with competitive pricing, and employees retained by offering career prospects. Regulators have been reassured by documenting rule compliance, and investors satisfied by incentivizing production efficiency and profits. In the last decades, this has started to shift.

What used to be seen as the primary social responsibility of organizations - making profit - (Friedman, 2007) is no longer seen as sufficient. Nowadays, many organizations recognize their 'secondary' responsibility for social outcomes. Granted, this can be prompted by financial concerns relating to fines, penalties, employee turnover, loss of customers (Baur & Palazzo, 2011). It can also stem from a wish to avoid increased oversight and regulation, which may even force companies to reconsider key features of the overall business model (Thomas et al., 2004). However, some organizations explicitly pledge their social purpose as a relevant outcome of their activities. They do this for instance by specifying how their strategy aims to contribute to United Nations Sustainable Development Goals, such as the reduction of global poverty and hunger, and the improvement of health and education (United Nations Sustainable Development, n.d.).

Organizations across the world increasingly consider their impact on the Environment, Social outcomes, and the quality of their Governance (ESG), and stakeholders increasingly expect them to do so. ESG benchmarks and certifications have mushroomed. These are proudly cited as organizational assets when communicating to stakeholders. Unfortunately, it is quite unclear whether these indicators actually capture ESG performance. Further, criteria defined by rating agencies seem unbalanced and offer very little guidance on how to integrate ESG performance goals in the overall organizational strategy and governance (Veenstra & Ellemers, 2020).

In times of crisis, such as the COVID-19 pandemic, priorities might be shifting. Potentially this forces organizations to focus on their financial health and continuity before all else, as it seems they cannot spare time or resources for other goals. This would seem to be suggested by an analysis of 110 publicly listed firms in Germany (the so-called HDAX firms), including large internationally operating companies such as BASF, Daimler, Deutsche Bank, and Siemens. Examination of the content of CEO statements in annual reports between 2003 and 2012 revealed that social and governance issues were less often mentioned as a relevant concern in times of economic downturn (Fehre, & Weber, 2016).

Many business leaders are certainly experiencing more pressure than before to reduce costs of labor, terminate support of community activities, or to delay the transition to more environmentally friendly production methods. Given the economic uncertainties and external threats that are bound to emerge from time to time, can organizations really afford to invest in broader social goals or should they focus on profit as the primary business outcome needed for survival and continuity?

More often than not, the situation is not that black-and-white (see also Box 7.1: Returning government support). Take Amazon Web Services: during the COVID-19 lockdown this online retailer experienced an unprecedented increase in business profits. Yet warehouse employees indicated that they had to work under conditions that prevented proper hygiene and social distancing. Notwithstanding the CEO's pledges to social responsibility (see also Box 3.2: Jeff Bezos' fall from grace), Amazon threatened to fire those who went public with these problems - instead of taking measures to guard the health and safety of its warehouse employees. Even

Box 7.1: Returning Government Support

Changing circumstances can introduce unexpected and severe threat to the continuity of primary organizational processes. This might be seen to enforce a focus on financial security above all else, as many organizations experienced during the COVID-19 pandemic. Nevertheless, some companies are quite aware that social responsibility issues do not disappear when economic prospects become uncertain, and consider the possibility that business results might suffer even more when ignoring stakeholder interests that would damage their reputation.

In the United States, for instance, several large for-profit companies such as the New York Lakers decided to return government support they received in the spring of 2020. They acknowledged that this wasn't meant for financially strong organizations such as theirs, even though they too suffered severely from the COVID-19 lockdown. In France, Louis Vuitton luxury fashion house withdrew its application for government support citing similar reasons. Allegedly this was prompted by public statements competitor Chanel had made about its decision to decline such funds, raising concerns that Louis Vuitton would be seen as the less socially responsible brand (Abboud, 2020).

Apparently, all these organizations estimated the benefits for their company and its moral reputation to be larger than the extra income they gave up – even in times of crisis. This attests to the emerging consensus that the long term future of an organization is not defined by its profitability alone, but rather requires engaging with a broader set of relevant outcomes, including stakeholder concerns. Indeed, current stakeholder demands suggest that companies can no longer afford to focus on financial business goals alone.

employees who did not personally suffer felt uncomfortable, and no longer wished to remain associated with such an uncaring employer. Office workers who publicized these issues had their contracts terminated. Software developer and Vice President Tim Bray resigned from the company in protest (Bray, 2020). Thus, neglecting the needs of its workers – even in times of obvious financial prosperity – was not without cost. Not only did the negative publicity damage the reputation of the company, Amazon also suffered a painful loss in the competitive market for high level IT specialists.

In this chapter we focus on the moral implications of different ways to engage with organizational stakeholders. In the first section, we consider the three quick fixes organizations and people within them commonly use to alleviate the reputational issues and identity threat raised by stakeholder concerns. In the second section we review studies that have examined displays of stakeholder commitment, and identify the hidden costs and moral hazards of approaching this primarily as a problem in organizational communication. In the third section we consider research evidence revealing the benefits for organizations of more fully engaging with different stakeholders and their concerns, by integrating social outcomes in their primary mission and long-term strategy as an organization that aims to do what is morally right.

7.1.1 People, Planet, Profit: What Is the Purpose?

Practitioners and organizational scholars increasingly acknowledge that being seen as socially involved and morally responsible is indispensable for organizational success and survival. Over the years, many organizations have come to the conclusion that it is not enough to focus solely on maximizing their efficiency and profits. Instead, by subscribing to the "triple-p bottom line" (People, Planet, Profit) they must express awareness of the importance of taking into account the interests of multiple parties inside and outside the company, ranging from the people who work for them to the planet they inhabit.

The general public expects organizations to acknowledge broader stakeholder concerns. These expectations clearly emerge from the annual 'trust barometer', prepared by Edelman Brand Communications after surveying opinions of large population samples located across the world. Data collected near the end of 2019 revealed an overwhelming desire for businesses to engage more with social issues. The populations surveyed perceive businesses as competent, but not very ethical. They see stakeholders - not shareholders - as key to long term business success, and place their trust in companies that embrace an all-stakeholder model. In fact, 76% of the trust placed in a business by members of the general public depends on ethical drivers, such as integrity, dependability and purpose. Business competence only accounts for 24% of public trust (Edelman, 2020). Further, three-quarters indicated they expect CEO's to lead change towards more ethical and responsible business conduct, for instance by addressing income inequality, employment security, and climate change.

Business leaders seem aware of these expectations. In 2019, the annual American Business Roundtable resulted in a statement on the purpose of a corporation, signed by 181 CEOs. These high level corporate leaders publicly committed to looking beyond profit maximization in conducting their business. In addition to creating long-term value for shareholders that provide them with capital, they pledged to invest in the compensation, education, and diversity of their employees, deliver value to their customers, deal fairly with suppliers, support the communities and protect the environment in which they work ("Business Roundtable Redefines the Purpose of a Corporation", 2019).

Yet a 2020 'spring update' of the Edelman Trust Survey mainly showed frustration and disappointment with business conduct in response to the COVID-19 pandemic. Respondents noted that most companies do not prioritize employee well-being and health, are not trying to safeguard their jobs, and will not help smaller suppliers and customers stay afloat. Further, CEOs were seen not to respond very well to the demands of the pandemic as they focused on selling their products rather than redefining the organization's purpose, or working with governments and NGOs to find solutions ("Edelman Trust Barometer Spring Update", 2020).

This discrepancy between moral ambitions and moral realities resonates with the recurring theme of this book: the wide-spread motivation to do what is moral does not necessarily induce moral decision making or guarantee ethical business conduct. This observation also points to a broader concern, as it reveals how difficult it is for organizations to incorporate and reconcile the interests of a broad range of stakeholders, whose priorities do not necessarily align. This is a core issue targeted by stakeholder theory (see Fig. 7.1: Different types of stakeholders and their concerns; see also Reynolds et al., 2006). This approach to organizational behavior highlights that protecting the interests of some will inevitably jeopardize outcomes for others. It is a difficult dilemma faced for instance by traditional industries that have to weigh securing the employment for the community against the environmental damage of their activities (see Box 7.2: Mining licenses). Even focusing on a single stakeholder group or issue does not prevent such dilemmas. For instance, some employee interest groups might advocate for job security, while others prioritize improvement of wages, or employee health and safety. Likewise, parties raising

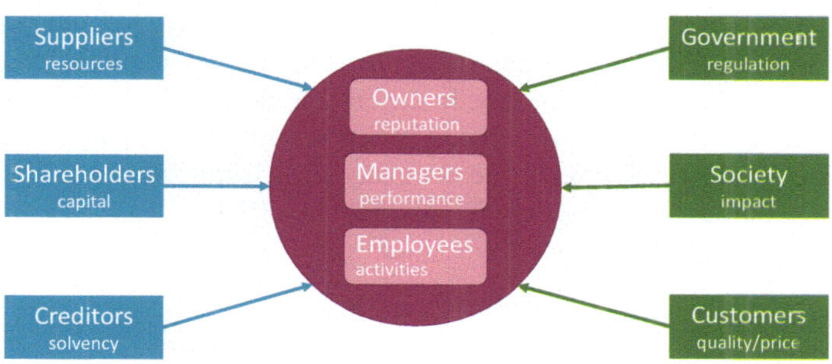

Fig. 7.1 Stakeholders and their key concerns. Identifies different types of external and internal stakeholders and the diverging concerns they represent

Box 7.2 Mining Licenses

The mining of raw materials still supports a large proportion of economic activities in the world (Wang, 2015). Coal mining and extraction of natural oil are primary examples of activities that relate to traditional production industries. However, even when the transition is made to more sustainable sources of energy, mining will not be outdated. The continuity and further development of high tech consumer and defense products also depends on the activities of mining companies. These provide the natural materials and hard to extract rare earth metals (also known as Rare Earth Elements) needed need to produce – for example – cell phones, computers, electric cars, permanent magnets or energy saving lamps (Carvalho, 2017; De Lima & Filho, 2015).

Large scale mining is different from other industries in that it cannot easily be displaced to alternative locations. The continuity of this industry crucially depends on the support of local communities where their activities are conducted. Effective community protests and legal rulings have resulted in local governments withholding support of mining activities, for instance in the Australian Hunter Valley. Permission to open a coalmine at Rocky Hill was withheld by a judge because of the damage this would do to the natural environment as well as the social fabric of the town (McGowan & Cox, 2019). To be able to continue their activities, these industries will have to find ways to protect the natural environment, benefit employees at these sites, and generally display responsible stewardship.

British-Australian mining company Rio Tinto underestimated the importance of such community support. In May 2020, two ancient rock shelters in Western Australia were blown up to expand their iron ore mine. The destruction of this sacred Aboriginal site of exceptional cultural and archeological value led to a government inquiry. Although the company initially claimed that they did not violate any legal rights, an internal investigation revealed that procedural faults had been made (Timeline: Rio Tinto's sacred indigenous caves blast scandal, 2020). In an attempt to repair relations with the local community, the company initially announced that it would cut bonuses of the responsible executives. This decision only made matters worse, as it was felt to represent a taboo trade-off (see also Chap. 1). In this way the company seemed to communicate that it considered the loss of this unique and priceless site simply as a business transaction. Apparently the problem could be resolved by letting the culprits pay. In the end ongoing protests from community stakeholders prompted the company to take further action, by forcing the responsible executives to leave the company (Rio Tinto chief Jean-Sébastien Jacques to quit over Aboriginal cave destruction, 2020).

environmental concerns may focus on different aspects, such as the scarcity of raw materials, animal welfare and protection of biodiversity, or air pollution, depending on their political orientation (see also Feinberg & Willer, 2013).
Further, merely expressing support for these goals is not enough. As we shall see later in this chapter, communicating concern for stakeholder interests may function as a form of 'moral cleansing'. Symbolic acts of stakeholder support may alleviate moral threat, but ironically also prevent a more profound reconsideration of how standard procedures and strategic decisions reflect on the moral identity of the organization. In fact, to the extent that stakeholders perceive a discrepancy between pledges communicated and ongoing organizational practices, such statements can do more harm than good.

7.1.2 *Attracting Employees, Customers, and Investors*

The potential of any organization to make a profit and create value crucially depends on its ability to attract, satisfy, and retain workers, as well as customers or clients, and private investors or public sponsors. Each of these constituents represents important stakeholders whose interests and impressions of the organization matter (see also Freudenreich et al., 2019).

There is no dispute that attracting and retaining highly qualified professionals is needed to survive and thrive in a competitive market. However, to win the 'war on talent', it is no longer sufficient to offer job security, career prospects, or fair pay as a quick fix. Increasingly, large companies have difficulty filling their talent pools as young professionals question their purpose and mission, or express reluctance to comply with work conditions they consider outdated. News headlines report that young engineers and technical experts no longer want to work for companies that damage the natural environment, such as SHELL (Leupen & Van Dijk, 2018). Financial professionals leave large investment banks to offer their services to private customers and small businesses. Legal and consultancy talents shun the up-or-out career competition towards partnership at global firms, instead seeking employment at smaller family businesses or social enterprises (see also Alonso-Almeida & Llach, 2019).

Efforts to investigate these trends more systematically, consistently reveal that people are most attracted to work that is meaningful and has a positive impact on society (Turban & Greening, 1997). To judge this, (prospective) employees look beyond formal organizational mission and strategy statements. For instance, a study examining a sample of 304 young working adults revealed that the ethical values embodied by the company for which they worked was a key factor in explaining whether they felt they fit well with the organization, and felt committed to it (Valentine et al., 2002). More generally, employees expect to find more fulfillment and work satisfaction with employers who demonstrate they attend to the interests of multiple stakeholders than with those who focus on profit maximization for the benefit of shareholders' value (Parmar et al., 2019).

Experimental studies, in which university graduates select the type of organization where they want to seek employment, make it possible to systematically compare how prospective employees value specific organizational assets. The research designs used provide an insight into whether they prioritize organizational integrity and morality, or focus on business success and career potential when comparing different employers. For instance, one option would be to work at a company that is highly profitable and can offer long term employment prospects, but isn't always fully transparent in its annual reports and makes false promises to clients. An alternative employer would offer less financial and career security, but takes pride in reporting honestly about its activities and acting reliably towards customers. When having to make trade-offs such as these in choosing where to work, research participants show a consistent preference for a workplace where people are moral - even if they seem less competent (Van Prooijen & Ellemers, 2015; Van Prooijen et al., 2018).

This research on the job preferences of graduates starting their professional careers aligns with results from studies among broader populations of employees at different career stages in a variety of industries. An examination of almost 30,000 firm-year observations from US based companies in the Standard and Poor database, found that employee engagement depended on company investments in work-life balance, health and safety rather than indicators of the firm's financial success (Flammer & Luo, 2017). Employee surveys consistently reveal that the perceived morality and integrity of the organization is a strong determinant of organizational attraction and identification, which may even outweigh its professional competence or business success (e.g., Ellemers et al., 2011; for an overview see Ellemers, 2017).

For similar reasons, organizations can no longer rely on competitive pricing as a quick fix to attract customers. Instead, they have to contend with a broader range of customer wishes and shifting client priorities. This is an important group of stakeholders that can either display loyalty or boycott products or services of specific firms. They can express their support for organizational policies and practices, or enforce change (Donaldson & Dunfee, 1999). Customer calls for moral improvement increasingly occur in the form of online protests in digital media. These can snowball very quickly to have a substantive impact on sales numbers and brand image, and are not so easy to counteract (Van den Broek et al., 2017). Research reveals that such customer actions are not just driven by selfish consumer motives (Chung & Park, 2013). Instead, these are also prompted by ethical concerns which elicit moral anger at the company, and relate to the extent to which the company is seen as acting in a socially responsible way (Harrison, 2003; Harrison et al., 2005). It was established for instance when customers objected against labor exploitation and cheap production methods at Walmart (Cronin et al., 2012). Over time, such expressions of customer preferences can improve ethical business conduct by forcing companies to reconsider the strategic choices they make. Indeed, anticipated customer concerns have been found to affect the way businesses set up their value-chain and select their own suppliers, so choices that may be seen as unethical can be avoided (Carter, 2000). Demands from sponsors can also force business owners to reconsider strategic decisions. This happened to the Boston Redskins, who for decades had been deaf to public concerns and lawsuits arguing that their name and logo of a Native American warrior were inappropriate and disparaging of this ethnic group. Owner Dan Snyder repeatedly declared his football club would "never change its name". Yet, this all changed in the summer of 2020, when main sponsors FedEx, Nike and PepsiCo, publicly threatened to remove their names and sponsorship from the club (Schad, 2020).

Examples such as this point to a more general development: indicating that a focus on financial success and monetary profits alone is no longer a quick fix to attract professional investors. In fact, institutional and private investors increasingly consider moral hazards and ethical scandals as a potential source of financial and reputational risk (Eccles & Klimenko, 2019). Most investors nowadays are reluctant to invest their capital in industries or companies that violate human rights (for instance by using child labor) contribute to violent conflict (through production of weapons) undermine health (as is the case for the tobacco industry) or pollute the environment (by producing petroleum or herbicides). Initially, these investment preferences prompted banks to set up separate investment funds specifically catering for customers who wanted to support socially responsible initiatives. However, the ever increasing demands for this type of investment have caused some financial institutions to reconsider their whole investment policy from this perspective. For instance, the Dutch Central Bank (De Nederlandsche Bank, DNB) was the first central bank to fully commit to Principles for Responsible Investment in 2019, by integrating environmental, social, and governance (ESG) concerns in *all* its investment decisions. (De Nederlandsche Bank, 2018).

Here too, we see that the ambition to make socially responsible investments - adopted as an important mission by large and important groups of investors - forces organizations to reconsider the interests of different stakeholders. In fact, taking into account broader stakeholder concerns might actually benefit company financial success. An investigation tracing developments in stock returns over 25 years revealed that inclusion of a company in the annual list of 100 'best companies to work for in America' impacted on its financial results. In subsequent years this resulted in a performance increase of 2.1% above industry benchmarks. After controlling for a range of alternative explanations for this relation, the study concludes that high employee satisfaction is an 'intangible asset', that increases company financial success because it benefits employee recruitment, retention and motivation (Edmans, 2011).

Similar observations were made by Lazard, a leading advisory firm in financial asset management. Their quarterly review concluded that ESG and sustainability-oriented funds globally outperformed conventional funds, despite the market chaos in the first quarter of 2020 due to COVID-19 (Lazard, 2020b). Accordingly, the worlds three largest Index Funds (Blackrock, Vanguard and State Street) declared their continued commitment to sustainable development, aligning their investment strategies with boards taking responsibility for ESG issues. Countering market analysts who view sustainability as a 'luxury good' which is only viable in times of prosperity, these investors consider attention for a broad range of stakeholders a company asset that helps businesses withstand macro-economic shocks (Lazard, 2020b).

The high level of support expressed for companies that indicate awareness of their broader social responsibilities continues to be an investment strategy explicitly motivated by the particular concern of this type of stakeholder: the desire to maximize financial returns. After being criticized by climate activists for failing to push for strategy changes, in 2020 Blackrock reported it had placed 244 companies 'on watch' and had voted against management of 53 companies (mostly in the energy industry) for lack of progress on climate concerns. However, the Blackrock representative also specified their concern was primarily motivated by the financial risk to the value of their investments (Harty, 2020).

Thus, employees, customers, as well as investors can – and increasingly do – expect organizations to consider broader concerns than financial profitability alone. However, as yet there is no concrete evidence that public pledges made to appeal to employees, appease customers, or attract investors, actually reflect a change in strategy that might result from a deeper reconsideration of how everyday practices and core business strategies actually impact on broader stakeholder concerns (Yang & Reeves, 2020; see also Bebchuk & Tallarita, 2020). In fact, communications about engagement in Corporate Social Responsibility (CSR) activities are often distrusted and dismissed as a superficial 'image laundering' strategy (Chopova, 2020).

7.1.3 Securing the 'License to Operate'

One way for stakeholders to make sure their perspective and concerns are taken into account, is by trying to exert legal control over the strategic decisions organizations make. We consider this as another attempt towards a 'quick fix' – which in reality might start a lengthy process in which different stakeholders battle it out for the 'license to operate' through court of law rulings.

Perhaps the best-known example involves so-called 'shareholder activism', where investors try to gain control over strategic decisions in companies whose shares they have bought. Shareholder activism is an increasing trend among investors who start 'campaigns', try to acquire board seats, and seek to replace board members, even if they only hold a minority of company shares. In theory, shareholder activists can use this control to enforce more concern for broader stakeholder concerns, as indicated above. In practice, companies are mostly targeted by such campaigns to benefit short-term shareholder dividends (Lazard, 2020a).

This approach draws on the so-called principal-agent model (Jensen & Meckling, 1976), and assumes that there is a general tendency of board members (acting as agents) to take advantage of the capital provided by investors (principals). Accordingly, activist stakeholders aim to align the interests of board members with those of financial shareholders. Assigning more power to shareholders and less power to the board of directors while tying executive pay to share price should ensure that strategic decisions are controlled by those who put up the capital which allows the company to do business (Friedman, 2007). Importantly, this approach does not necessarily take into account the interests of other stakeholders. Activist shareholders are generally feared for calling on management to sell or dismantle less profitable parts of the company, laying off staff as a cost reduction strategy, or delaying investments in environmentally friendly production methods (see also: Kolhatkar, 2018).

This happened after activist investor Elliott had acquired only 2.5 percent of the shares in French family-owned Pernod-Ricard. Elliott's management characterized the firm as a 'perennial under-performer' with weak profit margins. It urged the company to change its strategy and cut production costs in order to increase profits. When the family expressed reluctance to change its long-term value creation strategy, Elliot criticized the governance and board of the company and threatened to take over the firm so as to overrule the business decisions of the third generation of family owners (Abboud, 2018).

The concern that such short term financial gains are prioritized over more long-term interests of employees, communities, and other stakeholders has caused regulators and governments to call into question the legitimacy of the decision power claimed by activist shareholders (Crane et al., 2014). The French government expressed dismay about the prospect of the Pernod-Ricard family losing control over their company and ownership of premium spirit brands such as Ballantines Whisky, and Absolut Vodka (Abboud, 2018). The Dutch government likewise expressed alarm at attempts of US food producer Kraft-Heinz to take over Unilever, voicing concern that this would jeopardize Unilever's commitment to socially responsible business conduct (Wilming, 2017). Indeed, as a counterforce against shareholder activism, these and other governments have tried to increase legal control over organizational decision making, with reference to the desire to protect national interests of retaining employment and tax income.

Sometimes it is clear that company decisions or financial interests are opposed to the concerns of the general public. This was the case for instance, when Turing Pharmaceuticals acquired a 62-year-old drug used by AIDS patients (Daraprim), and suddenly raised the price from $13.50 to $750 per tablet (Pollack, 2015). In a similar vein, pharmaceutical company Novartis systematically bought up competitors in the production of lutetium-octreotate after its patent had run out. Once it had created a monopoly in this way, Novartis raised the price of this medication for cancer by 500% per cent (Pascoe, 2019). This prompted the Dutch minister of public health to take legal action, allowing hospital pharmacies to produce their own version to secure a low-cost alternative for their patients.

However, the national interests governments seek to protect do not necessarily align with the concerns of the general public or other types of stakeholders. This too became clear during the COVID-19 pandemic, when some countries made government financial support for businesses suffering from the lockdown contingent on pledges to transform and adapt business priorities. For instance, the Dutch government awarded billions of – essentially tax payers' – funds to Royal Dutch Airlines. Its aim was to protect the airline's key asset - providing a network of transatlantic and direct long distance flights across the world. However, government funds were made available under the condition that the company would reduce staff costs and make an effort to mitigate environmental damage, for instance by encouraging passengers to connect to final destinations within Europe by train (Dutch Government, 2020). Airline management expressed extreme dismay at this assignment to change its core business model, and labor unions were frustrated that these conditions reduced their power to negotiate employee rights (Duursma, 2020). Despite their protests, all these other stakeholders had no choice but to accept the conditions imposed by the party providing the necessary capital: the Dutch government.

This example shows that increased government control does not necessarily imply that the interests and well-being of the broader population is served. In fact, some have expressed concern that government support during the COVID-19 pandemic is wasting tax money on keeping alive zombie organizations. These organizations would not have been viable even without the pandemic, but now use tax payers' money to delay necessary restructuring or avert bankrupcy. Each country has its own examples of scandals where public interests were damaged by government organizations (see also Chap. 1). Even if government representatives are not driven by profit motives, there may be other reasons for failing their public mission and responsibility. Political priorities, reputational concerns of key officials, failing leadership, and lack of oversight can all cause these institutions to violate the interests of their clients.

In this context it is not surprising that employees or concerned citizens may also recruit the power of litigation to control organizational strategies. They may use this tool not only to protect employee rights, but also to enforce policy reform to guard public health and safety, or to protect local communities and the natural environment. A case in point is the citizens' initiative Urgenda, which initiated legal action against the Dutch State to enforce action that should mitigate climate change (see Box 7.3: Urgenda – the people against the Dutch State).

Box 7.3: Urgenda – The People Against the Dutch State

In 2013, the Urgenda Foundation joined forces with a group of 896 Dutch citizens who were concerned about . The environmental organization claimed that the national government was not making enough of an effort to reduce greenhouse gas emissions, despite its to international agreements. On this basis they began procedures against the Dutch State. The initiative started by a handful of concerned citizens eventually became a landmark legal case, known as the Urgenda case.

The first lawsuit was handled in a district court. The key argument referred to the duty of for citizens specified in Dutch civil law. This court agreed with the complaint that the government had failed to take reasonable action to protect its citizens against dangerous levels of . When the government contested this decision in the court of appeal, it was still held up. This court additionally cited the right to life specified in the European Convention of (ECHR). It ordered the government to reduce greenhouse gas emissions in keeping with international agreements (Khan, 2019). A final appeal from the state was handled by the supreme court. It was also rejected. In December 2019, the supreme court ruled that the Dutch government had violated obligations by failing to protect individuals within their jurisdiction from 'genuine and imminent' risk (Lutak, 2020).

With a substantial proportion of the Netherlands lying below sea level, the of flooding as a result of are of particular concern to this country. However, by the time the final verdict was decided, the deadline to reach the set target (25–40% reduction of greenhouse gas emissions by 2020) already was very close. One may therefore argue that it might have been better to invest time, and in the development of measures and technologies to reduce , instead of procedures. Yet the significance of this ruling is also located in the court's specification that positive obligations to protect citizens not only apply to specific individuals but can refer to members of society in general. Further, the verdict clarifies that these legal citizen rights also apply to long term affecting future generations.

This insight is what makes the Urgenda case a landmark case. In fact, the broad publicity for this initiative inspired other groups of citizens. Courts in other European states for instance in Ireland have now made similar rulings with reference to the European Convention of (Muinzer, 2019).

Actions such as these have prompted legal scholars to question who legally 'owns' a company, going beyond normative concerns about ethical behavior and moral duty in doing business (Quinn & Jones, 1995). This has caused some to characterize the dominant principal-agent approach as perpetuating the 'dangerous myth' that those who invest financial capital are the primary stakeholders whose interests should determine company strategy (Stout, 2001, 2012a). Court rulings suggest that there is no legal basis for this belief. Instead, legal regulations specify that corporations are independent legal entities that 'own' themselves, can hold properties and enter into legal contracts that regulate the rights of shareholders. Accordingly, across national legal systems in the USA, the UK and the EU, legal provisions afford the board of directors with the power to decide which group of stakeholders (customers, employees, shareholders) gets which share of residual profits (Stout, 2012; see also "Statement on Company Law", n.d.)

The examples cited here clearly demonstrate that governments, investors, clients, and the general public all can – and do – vie for control over organizational strategic choices through legal measures. However, enforcing change of specific decisions may not be the best way to improve ethical business conduct or increase the future likelihood of socially responsible decision making. Struggling for control over the organization's strategy in a court of law is time consuming, and wastes resources and goodwill that might be used for other purposes. Further, as noted in Chap. 1, enforced changes tempt company directors to do what is minimally required, ticking the boxes to avoid fines and appease regulators without actually taking into account broader stakeholder concerns.

7.2 Analysis: Addressing Reputational Concerns

In the course of 2018, social media company Facebook was publicly criticized for offering a platform that could be used by undisclosed interest groups to spread political propaganda and hate speech. The company was challenged to address these charges by improving procedures to scrutinize the identity of their customers and the content of messages that were posted. Instead, Facebook mainly invested in ways to discredit the critics – morally excluding them. With reference to the fact that well-known investor and philanthropist George Soros was an important source of the charges made against Facebook, media reporters received information raising doubt about his true motives. The information released suggested that Mr Soros had a financial interest in undermining Facebook. Only later did it become clear that this information was deliberately circulated by Definers Public Affairs, a company that had been hired by Facebook's Chief Operating Officer Sheryl Sandberg, with the explicit aim of distracting the general public from Facebook's passive attitude towards their security policies (Confessore & Rosenberg, 2018; Frenkel et al., 2018).

There are many professional agencies and commercial initiatives, such as the internationally operating "Reputation Institute" (The RepTrak Company, n.d.), that emphasize the importance and business advantages of protecting and enhancing the public reputation and perceived trustworthiness of a company. This is in line with scholarly analyses documenting the importance of company reputations, as reviewed in this chapter. Nevertheless, what is striking is that these services mostly focus on offering moral justifications for questionable business practices, targeting *communication* professionals working at those companies. This implicitly conveys that reputation management is a matter of communicating carefully and strategically about the activities and properties of the company. But is this really the case? Why would members of the general public believe such formal communications, especially when these convey an image of the organization that is not consistent with their own observations and experiences of what is actually going on or what the organization stands for?

Expanding the direct observations made by stakeholders inside the organization (see also Chap. 4), the external reputation of an organization represents the way others who are not directly involved perceive and evaluate its image. Research has documented reputational ratings by third parties as a relevant source of information about the organization, which is informed by the strategic decisions of the organization (e.g. to downsize or to merge) and predicts relevant outcomes such as stakeholder support (Lange et al., 2011). Some scholars have considered the reputation of the organization in terms of its general prominence and visibility. However, here we define organizational reputation as: "*being known for particular behaviors, concerns, and outcomes, that inform people's overall impressions of the organization's favorability and attractiveness*" (see also Lange et al., 2011). This conceptualization clarifies that in its very nature the reputation of an organization is dynamic and subjective. It does not merely come about by combining pieces of factual information in a 'bottom-up' fashion. It is just as much the result of an active 'top-down' process through which people interpret and integrate information to form a particular image of the organization (Ravasi et al., 2018).

Research has revealed that people tend to manage and form impressions of companies and other organizations as social actors, anthropomorphizing them by allocating defining features comparable to those of individuals and groups (Ashforth et al., 2020; Malone & Fiske, 2013). Insights on social impression formation specify how people tend to capture, interpret, and integrate information that helps them form an overall impression of the 'true nature' of different types of targets. This reveals that people do not simply accept and combine observations or statements they receive about the intentions and behaviors of others. Instead, they actively search for, weigh, and adjust different pieces of information to make sense of what this target is about, and how this is relevant to them (see also Abele et al., 2020). As a result, people's social identities, and how these relate to the identity of the target they try to understand also inform and motivate their judgments. These insights imply that each stakeholder views and interprets organizational communications from their own perspective. As a result, initial impressions and existing knowledge people have about the key features or core mission of an organization color the way they interpret communications they receive, and shape the resulting impression (Hornsey & Esposo, 2009; Hornsey & Imani, 2004).

In this process of sense-making, studies consistently show that people begin by trying to determine the beneficial vs. harmful *intentions* of companies as a framework to interpret information provided about their activities and achievements (Malone & Fiske, 2013; see also Brambilla et al., 2013; Goodwin, 2015). This implies that managing the reputation of an organization goes beyond monitoring the image that is portrayed in formal communications. The impact of such communications depends on pre-existing views of the organization's trustworthiness, and prior knowledge of what the organization actually values and defends. Evaluating 'who the organization is', not only depends on the goals and strategies that are explicitly communicated (what is it *saying*), but also on how it demonstrates actual care for different stakeholder concerns (what it is *showing;* Ashforth et al., 2020).

In this section we consider the hidden costs of common efforts to address reputational concerns as a communication assignment. We examine when and why such communications are perceived as indicating moral neglect, moral cleansing or moral licensing – that stand in the way of more profound moral improvement. Research shows that communications indicating how stakeholder concerns are taken into account are likely to backfire when these are not aligned with the identity of the organization and how this visibly emerges in everyday strategic, procedural and business decisions (see Fig. 7.2: Organizational reputation management).

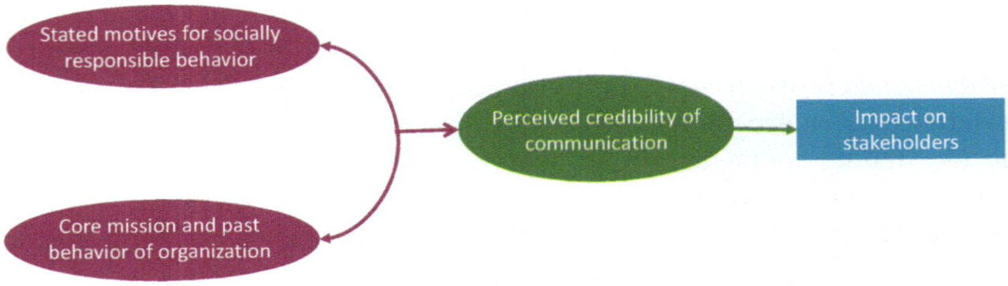

Fig. 7.2 Organizational reputation management. Summarizes results from a program of research. The impact of organizational communications on its reputation as being socially responsible depends on whether stated motives align with the core mission of the organization. (De Vries et al., 2015, 2016; Terwel et al., 2009a, 2009b, 2011)

7.2.1 What You Say and Who You Are

The credibility of organizational communications when it comes to sense-making and social connection crucially depend on their consistency when considering visible acts, and experiences with the organization (Ashforth et al., 2020). For instance, when incoming employees note that their actual work experiences do not align with prior expectations, their ability to trust and identify with the organization decreases (Smith et al., 2017).

In general, people determine such inconsistencies by comparing public statements of organizational goals, with the actual behavior displayed by organizational representatives (Chopova, 2020). These are not necessarily aligned, as was illustrated in a study investigating archival data from 49 Fortune-500 firms. The researchers found that those organizations which were found to publicly endorse socially responsible business decisions in the media were also the ones that actually treated their stakeholders less ethically in the two years following these statements (indicated by the KLD - Kinder, Lydenberg, & Domini, ratings of stakeholder treatment; Ormiston & Wong, 2013). Small startups too may pursue social goals, for instance by aiming to address environmental concerns, while failing to show social responsibility for their employees (Tiba et al., 2019), for instance, by preventing unionization (Conger & Scheiber, 2019).

Apparent failures to take into account broader stakeholder concerns may be even more damaging when these counter the key mission and formal purpose of the organization. This might explain the extreme disappointment of sponsors of Amnesty International when a staff wellbeing review revealed the long term presence of a 'toxic' work climate that undermined its credibility and jeopardized its mission as human rights organization (Avula et al., 2019). The report revealed widespread bullying, public humiliation, nepotism and other forms of power abuse, creating a 'toxic' working environment where multiple staff suicides seemed related to complaints about extreme levels of work stress (McVeigh, 2019). Likewise, public outrage resulted at the discovery that Oxfam professionals in Haiti had harassed and abused the earthquake victims they were supposed to help – without meeting visible repercussions from management (Oriti, 2019).

Realizing that even organizations with a core mission to do good in society can demonstrate ill treatment of key stakeholders only makes people more distrustful of other types of organizations. Thus, in responding to organizational communications they try to determine whether the organization is taking its social responsibility seriously or merely claims to do so for reputational reasons - thereby displaying moral neglect of broader stakeholder concerns (Chopova, 2020). A study revealed that a broad range of employees felt more committed to organizations where they felt stakeholder activities were more aligned with key strategic decisions and financial goals of the organization (Rodrigo et al., 2019).

Communicating about socially responsible initiatives that do not align with key services, brand image, or market strategy does not contribute to the moral image of the organization to enhance stakeholder support (Chopova, 2020). Instead, it only undermines perceived credibility of the company and has a negative impact on consumer attitudes and purchase intentions (Becker-Olsen et al., 2006). This was documented in studies that systematically compared the impact of different types of organizational communication. Stated actions of the organization (e.g., investing in clean production methods) that were incongruent with perceived organizational motives (e.g., of energy production companies), only undermined trust. When engagement in these same initiatives was motivated by goals that seemed consistent with the organization's key mission (i.e., by citing the economic gains of doing so) the communication was considered more honest, and increased trust in the organization (Terwel et al., 2010).

Other cues may also help to determine whether organizations actually care about the broader impact of their activities, or show moral neglect of stakeholder interests (Forehand & Grier, 2003; Yoon et al., 2006). For instance, initiatives that were seen to emerge under pressure of external demands from consumers or regulators (instead of occurring pro-actively), were regarded as selfish and profit driven choices indicating moral neglect instead of a commitment to virtuous organizational conduct (Becker-Olsen et al., 2006; Van de Ven, 2008). In fact, supply chain changes towards more socially responsible business practices (abandoning sweat shop labor for the production of clothing) were less likely to be copied by other organizations when these resulted from consumer protests instead of independent organizational decision making (Briscoe et al., 2015). In general, engaging in the 'right' behaviors for the 'wrong' reasons conveys moral neglect, and a perceived lack of true concern for broader stakeholder interests. Such strategic behaviors undermine the reputation of the organization instead of supporting it (see also Fig. 7.2: Organizational reputation management).

Likewise, organizational efforts to appear socially responsible which only focus on external stakeholders (e.g., by donating to local communities), while neglecting the needs of key internal stakeholders (employees) are seen as hypocritical and only damage employee well-being and commitment (Scheidler et al., 2019). For instance, Lush soap, a cosmetics company that boasts ethical production methods that avoid animal cruelty, apparently was less attentive to fair treatment of its manufacturing and retail employees. The company admitted to eight years of 'significant underpayment' for over 5000 employees, and pledged to compensate this by awarding millions of dollars in back pay (McGowan, 2018).

7.2.2 Apologies for Organizational Failure

The insight that stakeholders not only consider what organizations do but also *why* they do it, offers a different perspective on the way organizations respond to consumer complaints and product failures. These cannot always be avoided, and sometimes knowledge of public health issues resulting from production methods or product characteristics only becomes available over time. When viewed from a business perspective, such organizational failures are primarily seen as a source of financial liability and legal hazard that needs to be mitigated. Thus, the common legal advice and standard response is to avoid taking responsibility, and deny that problems exist (for an example see Gillam, 2017; Box 7.4: Monsanto's Roundup - 'safer than table salt'; see also Chap. 8). Indeed, some studies suggest that denial of problems can be a viable option as long as the evidence is not convincing (Fuoli et al., 2017). Yet we note that such attempts to protect the reputation of the organization can also decrease its perceived legitimacy (Ashforth & Gibbs, 1990). Whether or not this happens depends on whether stakeholders think the organization is sincere in communicating about possible problems, or is mainly concerned with reputation management through moral cleansing.

Box 7.4: Monsanto's Roundup – 'Safer Than Table Salt'
Roundup is a widely used spray-on weed killer. It is used in private gardens, sports fields and farms in the USA, as well as in many countries around the world. Its key ingredient, produced by Monsanto (currently owned by Bayer) is the chemical substance glyphosate.

Under the brand name Roundup the firm not only sells its broad-spectrum herbicide, but also markets seeds for "Roundup Ready" corn, soy, or cotton. These seeds are genetically modified to be tolerant to glyphosate, allowing famers to use Roundup without damaging their crops. This patented feature has greatly contributed to the success of Roundup. Undoubtedly it has also supported the credibility of Monsanto's claims that Roundup can be considered as an innovative and safe tool for "integrated weed management".

The company claims that "over 800 rigorous scientific studies" have shown the product is safe for humans as well as honey bees and other animal wildlife. These claims are substantiated by explaining that the product has a very high degradation rate without leaving a residue. Further, its effects are due to technology that blocks a specific enzyme pathway not found in humans or animals. On its website considering the safety of the product for human health

Monsanto portrays glyphosate to be 'at least 100 times below levels shown to have no negative effect in safety studies' (Bayer, 2020). Until recently, the company characterized the product less toxic than baking powder, table salt, or caffeine, placing it in the same category as hot tea.

Unfortunately, over the years, evidence has accumulated that this information is unsubstantiated or even false – the claim that it is safer than table salt was discontinued for that reason. Farming families and grounds keepers working with the substance are documented to suffer from health threats and frequently incur cancer. In 2015, the International Agency for Research on Cancer (IARC), which falls under the World Health Organization, convened 17 experts from 11 countries. After reviewing about 1000 studies representing all publicly available research on glyphosate at the time, they issued a report concluding that glyphosate is probably carcinogenic in humans. Exposure to the substance is associated with the emergence of non-Hodgkin Lymphoma in particular (IARC, 2016). In 2019, Roundup was banned from further use in France, and the use of glyphosate is now prohibited in many countries ("France Takes Roundup Weed-Killer Off Market", 2019).

Still the company website claims transparency. It pledges commitment to "helping farmers grow healthy crops for a growing world, while using natural resources efficiently, preserving the environment, and protecting biodiversity". Not only do such statements reveal that the company is in denial of documented problems relating to their products, it is worse than that. There is evidence that over many years Monsanto has undertaken persistent and aggressive action to discredit scientists, intimidate regulators, and to present the IARC report as an unreliable outlier. All these efforts were deliberately made to deny evidence of health damage due to its products, and to manipulate public perceptions in an effort to protect business interests (Gillam, 2017).

By 2019, court cases won by farmers in the USA have already forced the company to award hundreds of millions of dollars in damages. Thousands of further plaintiffs are lining up in the USA, and farmers in Australia and Canada are also starting to sue Monsanto. In October of 2019, the stock price of Bayer plummeted as a result of these developments. In the summer of 2020, Bayer decided to allocate over $10 billion to settle lawsuits representing claims from close to 100,000 cancer patients in the US (Burger & Bellon, 2020). Apparently the company has to acknowledge that its products are not as safe as advertised.

Typical organizational responses were examined, for instance, by content coding and rating replies to 134 customer complaint letters. When restaurants and high-tech manufacturers provided customers who had complained with an apology, the response was seen as more believable and considerate. Such responses had a more positive impact on customer satisfaction, and future intent of patronage than responses without apologies. Notably – and countering widespread beliefs and common legal advice – no negative effects were observed when the organization declared its responsibility for unfavorable customer experiences (Bolkan et al., 2010). Research further suggest that consumers are well able to separate judgments of high vs low performance from judgments about the good vs bad intentions and morality of the actors involved ('moral decoupling'; Bhattacharjee et al., 2013; see also Malone & Fiske, 2013).

Experimental research further reveals that common defensive responses (justification, excuses, denial) have a negative impact on customer perception. Indeed, those who offered a sincere apology and attempted to correct damage actually were more effective, even if engaging in such behavior was associated with the experience of guilt (Salvador et al., 2012). This is in line with our analysis in Chap. 2, indicating the need to confront feelings of shame and guilt when acknowledging one's moral failures. This points to the emotional pain of facing threats to one's moral identity, that is part of the process of moral improvement.

How to restore trust then, after organizational failure? Organizational scientists emphasize that merely signaling good intentions is not enough to repair a damaged reputation. Instead a more systemic approach is needed, in which congruence of different signals is key (Gillespie & Dietz, 2009). As indicated above, voluntary and proactive offers of apologies and reparations are a good start. Studies like the ones cited above reveal that apologizing and admitting to performance failures can help to convey good intentions. However, apologies are less effective when delayed, or not empathic (Roschk & Kaiser, 2013). Further, the effectiveness of reparation attempts crucially depends on *visible actions* that demonstrate the organization's ability, benevolence, and integrity. These can include the withdrawal of products, redefinition of strategic priorities, or the allocation of resources committed to achieve true change (Gillespie & Dietz, 2009).

The difference between symbolic and more sincere attempts at reputation management was clearly illustrated by a study of product recalls by toy companies based in the U.S.A. between 1998 and 2007 (Zavyalova et al., 2012). The researchers examined the positive vs the negative content of 37,500 media articles and blog postings about the firms involved, and related these to the actions the firm had taken, gleaned from over 5500 press releases. In all cases, product recalls resulted from external requests made by the Consumer Product Safety Committee. In the study, firm statements relating to these events were classified into those referring to *actual* solutions and changes made vs. more *symbolic* responses focusing on reputation repairs.

Among the actual solutions offered were statements made about technical changes in the production and distribution of products, announcements about customer compensation schemes, and measures taken to improve the cooperation with regulation and investigation initiatives. These included for instance the installation of free toy repair centers, or suspending the shipment of defective toys. In contrast, the symbolic responses included a variety of initiatives aimed at improving the reputation of the company that had no implications for the quality of the products it sold. These included name changes, endorsements by celebrities, charitable donations, promotions, sponsoring activities and company awards. This study revealed that communicating about actual changes made to resolve product issues attenuated the negative tone of media coverage. However, attempts to salvage the reputation of the company with positive symbolic messages, backfired and only increased negative comments in the media (Zavyalova et al., 2012).

Similar conclusions were drawn from a study conducted among 1.5 million Uber rideshare consumers in the USA (Halperin et al., 2019). During the study, all customers whose ride had arrived 10–15 minutes later than had been indicated when they booked the trip, received an apology by email. But the nature and content of the apology differed, depending on the experimental condition they were in. The researchers examined how this affected the net spending on other Uber rides in the days after the apology - after correcting for the frequency with which the customers used this service and how much they typically spent on a trip. The study revealed that the apology was more effective in retaining customer's use of the ridesharing service after a bad experience, when the company's commitment to change seemed more sincere. This was the case in the condition where the apology was accompanied by a five dollar promotional coupon. Indeed, sending out promotional coupons to random customers without being connected to a service failure did not have the same effect (Halperin et al., 2019).

This aligns with broader insights from research on the perceived morality of individuals and groups, which we reviewed in Chap. 2. Studies consistently show that displaying lack of ability is sometimes quite easily forgiven as this can be attributed to external circumstances. By comparison, lack of truthfulness and reliability are more socially costly and more difficult to compensate since these are more often seen as diagnostic of people's true intentions and future behavior (Mishina et al., 2012; Skowronski & Carlston, 1987; see also Pagliaro et al., 2016). Accordingly, some case examinations of trust repair after organizational scandals (e.g., fraud, data manipulation) distinguish between trust based on abilities vs trust based on benevolent intentions and integrity (see also Terwel et al., 2010). When making this distinction, it becomes clear that open, transparent and honest communication about performance problems and the way these were addressed speaks to good intentions. It is the best way to convey integrity and restore legitimacy (Dietz & Gillespie, 2011; Gillespie, Dietz, & Lockey, 2014; Gillespie et al., 2012). The flip side of this insight again is that problems are likely to be exacerbated when apologies and other attempts to restore trust seem insincere or inconsistent with broader organizational strategies. It raises the suspicion that the organization is dishonest and merely engages in moral cleansing as a form of reputation management instead of committing to actual moral improvement.

7.2.3 Stakeholder Initiatives as Greenwashing

Engaging in stakeholder initiatives is often seen as a reputational resource for competitive advantage (Branco & Rodrigues, 2006). Some even recommend this as a tool for reputation management ('cause related marketing'; Adkins, 2007; Brønn & Vrioni, 2001; Pringle & Thompson, 1999). To the extent that this helps to attract consumers and influences their purchasing intentions, it should also benefit the financial performance of a company (Baron, 2009; Schuler & Cording, 2006). As was also reflected in the strategies of large investors we discussed before, evidence suggests that engagement in stakeholder activities (such as employee relations, community, environment or product quality) can benefit firm value over time. This was found to be the case in a sample of 475 US firms whose primary mission would raise environmental, social or ethical concerns. Over a period of 15 years (1995–2009) even in industries focusing on the production of tobacco, gambling and alcohol, oil and nuclear energy or weapons perceived engagement in stakeholder activities was shown to relate positively to stock market firm value (Cai et al., 2012).

However, there is no one-to-one relation between external ratings of stakeholder initiatives and the socially responsible nature of other organizational activities. This allows companies to publicize investments in positive stakeholder outcomes, while neglecting the potentially harmful implications of their core mission and activities (Scalet & Kelly, 2010). As noted before, there is a multitude of rankings, certificates, and metrics to evaluate and compare such stakeholder activities, which often rely on organizational self-reports and disclosure decisions. This makes it difficult to verify or compare their actual stakeholder performance (Pope & Lim, 2020; Scheidler et al., 2019; Spiller, 2000; Wood, 1991; see also Hoekstra, 2019). In fact, this practice allows for 'rankings entrepreneurship', where organizations selectively display initiatives that would result in higher ratings without reconsidering the moral implications of their other activities (Aguilera et al., 2007; Rindova et al., 2018; see also Chap. 4).

Some companies have been accused of using stakeholder initiatives as a form of 'greenwashing'. This term is commonly used to indicate deliberate efforts of the organization to mislead external stakeholders. Communications about environmentally friendly – but often symbolic – initiatives are used to distract public attention from the environmental damage caused by other organizational activities (Delmas & Burbano, 2011). We note that greenwashing only offers one form of moral cleansing to compensate for the violation of stakeholder interests. There are many other ways in which organizations can highlight activities that would exemplify good intentions as a strategy to mask other problems. (Delmas & Burbano, 2011; Fassin, & Buelens, 2011). With increasing pressures resulting from media attention for incidents and public expectations, it is tempting to convey concern for social and environmental issues as a moral impression management strategy, even independently of the actual activities and identity of the company (Hooghiemstra, 2000).

Evidence that this happens was documented by investigating company responses to ethical concerns in 221 cases that emerged in the media between 1990 and 2005. These included a broad range of industries including food production and service, chemical production, petroleum refinery, merchandise stores, transportation, printing, and communications. Ethical concerns examined included issues relating to animal rights and the environment as well as labor conditions and racial bias (McDonnell & King, 2013). The results showed that after having been challenged for its perceived unethical behavior (by calling for a consumer boycott in the media), firms typically responded by emphasizing examples of their socially responsible behaviors. They were more likely to do this when more was at stake, for instance because the moral critique had attracted more media attention, when the initial reputation of the firm was more favorable (in Fortune magazine's ranking of most admired companies), or when it had made more claims about its socially responsible behavior before being criticized. Another study revealed that companies which grappled with product safety and environmental concerns were more likely to make donations to charitable causes (Chen et al.,, 2008).

A similar conclusion emerged from a study examining external communications of over 100,000 annual financial reports submitted to the regulator of the USA stock exchange (the Security and Exchange Commission - SEC). Firms which invested money in ethically questionable stocks associated with alcohol, tobacco and gaming, had been the object of class action lawsuits, or scored poorly on measures of corporate governance, were most likely to use ethics-related terms as a form of moral cleansing in their annual reports (Loughran et al., 2009). Similar conclusions were drawn from a case study of a public listed Scandinavia-based company, engaged in worldwide production of pulp from forests for paper manufacturing (Stora Enso). This company was found to emphasize socially responsible activities in its annual reports, apparently to compensate for disclosures about long-standing arrangements for significant tax relief (Ylönen, & Laine, 2015). Likewise, public donations wealthy individuals make to good causes have been criticized for being used to mask the fact that they are actively avoiding to pay taxes (Harrington, 2016; see also Bregman, 2017; Giridharadas, 2018). The tendency to make such donations has been found to be related to the desire for social recognition – instead of the desire to advance good causes, especially among those with low internalized moral identities (Winterich et al., 2013).

When the general public finds out, or even suspects, that stakeholder engagement only serves as a strategy for reputation management and moral cleansing or moral licensing, the image of truthfulness and trustworthiness is undermined, doing more harm than good to the company's reputation (Berens & Van Riel, 2004; Newell & Goldsmith, 2001). For instance, a study of mobile phone users revealed that repeat patronage and recommendation of a telecom provider were independent of the quality of service. Instead, their support depended on whether communicating about Christmas donations to poor children was seen as driven by moral values or by strategic concerns of the company (Vlachos et al., 2009). In general, displays of concern, benevolence and cooperation towards different stakeholders are unlikely to benefit the reputation of the company when they are seen as insincere or making promises that will not be kept (Berens & Van Riel, 2004; Gillespie et al., 2012).

In sum, when minding their concerns, stakeholders are not only interested in *what* organizations do. They also try to find out *why* they are doing it in their search for the organization's moral identity. This implies that engaging in stakeholder initiatives as a form of reputation management aimed at inducing moral cleansing or moral licensing is not effective and may even backfire. Being seen to do 'something good' does not compensate for morally questionable business conduct and being insincere about the true motives driving these choices only makes things worse.

7.3 Solutions: Taking Social Responsibility

The evidence we have reviewed so far reveals that the way different stakeholders are treated should be a key concern for many organizations (Donaldson & Preston, 1995; Driver, 2012; Jones & Wicks, 1999; Miller et al., 2012). However, the demand for responsible stewardship is not always acknowledged by company representatives who are making strategic decisions based on pragmatic and financial calculations (Davis et al., 1997). Professionals tend to underestimate the ethical and moral concerns that influence consumer evaluations of their products (Bone & Corey, 2000). For instance, college representatives tend to highlight academic achievements when raising money for their institution, assuming this is the primary information people use to decide about financial contributions. In reality, however, donations were found to suffer from moral breaches of the institution, in this case exemplified by sanctioned infractions in collegiate athletic competitions (Zavyalova et al., 2016).

Engaging in stakeholder activities as a strategy to communicate good intentions is likely to backfire when this is detached from other organizational goals (Agle et al., 1999). Stakeholder activities that are seen as indicating true concern with community welfare and other stakeholder outcomes (rather than serving as a tool for reputation management) make working adults feel more supported, more committed, and more motivated to invest in the company (Donia et al., 2017). Only initiatives that convey genuine moral concern about the impact of organizational activities on stakeholder interests allow them to identify with the organization and take pride in its mission (Schaefer et al., 2020).

How can organizations achieve this? It is true that social protest movements and stakeholder actions can lead to new insights that instigate organizational change (Rao et al., 2000). However, as noted before, the reputation of the organization does not necessarily benefit when socially responsible behavior is enforced by external pressure from customers, regulators, or activist stakeholders. Indeed, a study of 171 small and medium sized Australian machinery manufacturers found that stakeholder initiatives only benefited firm financial performance in companies which had developed a shared vision about the importance of being *proactive* in stakeholder management (Torugsa et al., 2012).

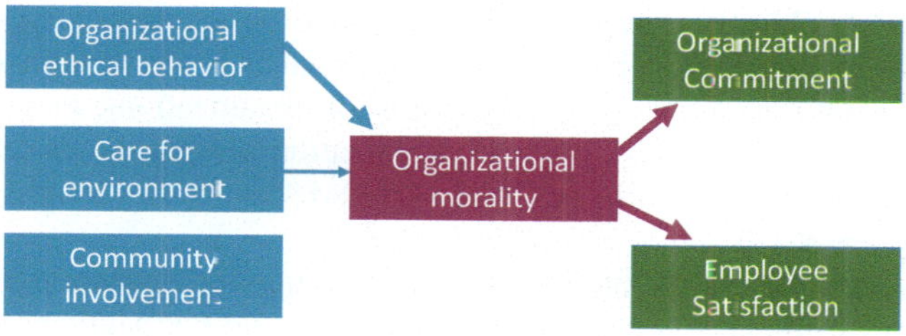

Fig. 7.3 Organizational integrity and job attitudes. Summarizes study results showing that perceptions of organizational morality – that benefit employee attitudes – primarily depend on the ethical behavior of the organization. Displays of care for the environment or engagement in community activities are much less relevant in this process. (Ellemers et al., 2011)

In line with organizational signaling theory, the impressions people form of organizations are not determined by what organizations *say*, but depend on what they *do* to communicate their moral intentions (Ashforth et al., 2020; Connelly et al., 2011). Only when making 'costly' choices - that actually have instrumental, relational, or moral implications - will this be seen to reveal the true identity of the organization (see also Shaw et al., 2003). Such costly choices are made for instance when organizations invest in ethical business conduct by being honest and transparent in offering disclosure about their activities, or prove trustworthy by avoiding to make false promises to clients. Improving the perceived morality of the organization in this way increases support from key stakeholders such as customers or employees (Chopova, 2020). In fact, employees were more inclined to perceive the organization as moral when they observed organizational actors as generally behaving in an ethically responsible way than when they witnessed more isolated CSR initiatives, for instance to protect the environment, or to offer community sponsoring (Ellemers et al., 2011; see Fig. 7.3: Organizational integrity and job attitudes). A meta-analysis summarizing the results of 65 studies accordingly showed that employees were more likely to identify, trust, and engage with organizations that offered evidence of having made economic, as well as legal, ethical, and philanthropic investments in displaying socially responsible behavior (Wang et al., 2020). The study of the New York Port Authority shows that such decisions may even restore the perceived morality an organization after it has been damaged (see also Box 4.6). In the final section of this chapter, we consider some practical guidelines that can help organizations take more social responsibility.

7.3.1 *Philanthropy as 'Costly Commitment'*

The term 'corporate philanthropy' is commonly used to indicate the practice of many organizations to invest money in community causes or to make resources and expertise available for social activities unrelated to the mission of the organization.

A review of 162 publications representing 30 years of research on corporate philanthropy reveals that this practice is generally endorsed as a way to indicate commitment to the common good, and willingness of organizations to invest in the community (Gautier & Pache, 2015). An organization which extends care and concern for stakeholder interests in this way signals its ethical awareness and moral integrity (Zlatev, 2019).

However, some also advocate the charitable giving and sponsoring of community activities as ingredients of a smart strategy to avoid tax payment while at the same time enhancing consumer attitudes and employee morale. Such strategic investments in stakeholder concerns hope to improve the moral reputation of the organization, for instance to secure government support and influence consumer choices. This view promotes raising goodwill and building up community capital to guard against reputational risks associated with core organizational activities as a form of moral licensing (Godfrey, 2005). Indeed, in line with their 'shared value approach' management gurus Michael Porter and Mark Kramer offer a step-by-step explanation of how organizations can develop a philanthropic strategy to this effect. They focus on ways to leverage efforts and infrastructures of nonprofit organizations and local communities to expand company opportunities for productivity, innovation, and growth, as key sources of competitive advantage (Porter & Kramer, 2002). Accordingly, 'corporate giving managers' of US firms that had ongoing and substantial programs of philanthropic donations reported they experienced increasing management pressure to use these donations strategically to enhance business exposure (Saiia et al., 2003).

In-depth studies have documented the strategic uses of such practices in specific cases. For instance tobacco company Philip Morris targeted donations to interest groups and policy makers, to influence their decisions in regulating marketing and sales of tobacco products (Tesler & Malone, 2008, 2010). A more systematic examination of donations made by hundreds of Fortune 500 companies over a period of ten years yielded similar conclusions. The study found that company resources were mainly used to benefit charities the CEOs were affiliated with. It documented how this furthered the personal interests of company directors, instead of increasing firm value (Masulis, & Reza, 2015). However, effectively using donations for commercial reasons is not as easy as it seems, and some companies only expect a negative impact on their financial results (De Gilder & Van Teunenbroek, 2020). For their part, community initiatives and good causes may be reluctant to associate themselves with sponsors that might taint their moral reputation and perceived integrity (Andreasen, 1996). When such concerns cause charities to publicly reject company offerings, this can cause great reputational damage, as happened to the Sackler family (see also Chap. 1).

People and organizations can have different reasons to engage in charitable giving. A review of 500 empirical studies documents a range of motives that are likely to play a role. These include other-focused motives (such as perceived need and altruism) as well as self-focused motives (to improve esteem and reputation; Bekkers & Wiepking, 2007). Thus, it is worthwhile to take a closer look at *why* organizations and people in them decide to contribute to good causes and community initiatives, what the relative strength of different motives is, and to assess whether these are reported truthfully.

In line with our conclusions regarding other types of stakeholder initiatives, the *perceived* motives for engaging in philanthropic initiatives are decisive for their impact. Again, this is not only about *what* organizations do, but also about the *way* that they do it. Strategic contributions to community activities and good causes that are meant to compensate for damaging effects of core organizational activities only raise skepticism and suspicion which are bound to backfire (Forehand & Grier, 2003). True testaments to the social responsibility and stakeholder involvement of an organization consist of investments that can be seen as 'costly' in that they are not meant to serve strategic goals of the organization. This can be realized, for instance, by delegating decisions about such initiatives to the lowest organizational levels. Here, individual employees or work teams are given the opportunity to make available work time, expertise or company resources for causes they find important. This allows them to 'give back' to the community in which they conduct their activities. Greater involvement of employees in developing, donating to and participating in community activities sponsored by their company (school renovations, recycling activities) was found to benefit the perceived social impact of these initiatives in their own eyes and the eyes of external perceivers (Raub, 2017).

Even though this type of volunteering implies that employees work on community activities in company time, it does not seem to damage the organization. A study established this by comparing employees who participated in the organizational volunteer program with non-participants (De Gilder et al., 2005). Both groups were highly committed to the organization for making such employee volunteering possible. Even non-participants - who had to compensate for volunteers who were absent from work during their activities - were supportive of the initiative. In fact, volunteers seemed highly motivated to make up for their time away from work, as they indicated increased performance and attendance. Across the board, more positive attitudes towards the program related to higher levels of organizational commitment and increased organizational citizenship behaviors. Implementing this program apparently communicated a positive social norm in the organization which benefited organizational as well as individual outcomes of the initiative (De Gilder, et al., 2005).

An examination of long term trends on corporate giving in the Netherlands indicates that this form of philanthropy is on the rise. During the period examined (1995–2018) the total value of donations made increased from an estimated 610 million Euros in 1995 to almost 2 billion Euros in 2018. Trends further reveal an increasing tendency to sponsor employee time, instead of giving away money or other resources (e.g., office equipment; De Gilder & Van Teunenbroek, 2020). Donations of employee time cover a variety of charitable causes and community initiatives, including public health, international aid, wildlife and environment, research and education, culture, and sports - often chosen by themselves. In this study, from the range of motives that could be cited, organizations consistently prioritized commitment to society and a sense of obligation to the community. More business-related motives, such as strategic concerns relating to employee engagement, reputational benefits, or customer loyalty were mentioned less often. The conclusion that these companies did not invest in stakeholder activities for reputational reasons was substantiated by the observation that only a small minority reported about these initiatives in its external communications (De Gilder & Van Teunenbroek, 2020).

In sum, notwithstanding strategic and commercial approaches to organizational philanthropy, there is sufficient evidence that many organizations engage in voluntary, intrinsically motivated and pro-active forms of philanthropy. Especially when initiated by employees, investments of time, resources, skills and advice suggest true involvement with broader social issues and qualify as indicators of 'costly commitment' to stakeholders interests. Even during the COVID-19 lockdown, many examples of charitable organizational behavior were documented, ranging from office caterers donating food supplies to the unemployed, to star restaurants having their chefs cook for the homeless, and large consultancy firms having their professionals offer free financial advice to small entrepreneurs. For similar reasons, some companies permanently allocate a fixed proportion of their profits to the support such goals. Other companies – that prefer to support public causes - happily forego options they might have to avoid paying taxes.

7.3.2 *Organizations as Families*

Family firms often get a bad press. These are typically seen as lacking professionalism, and suffering from leadership succession issues as well as other family conflicts (Xi et al., 2015). The common view is that small businesses started by the first generation and made to thrive by the second generation, will be destroyed by the third generation squandering family capital and organizational assets. Studies accordingly report mixed success of family firms (Chrisman et al., 2004), and indicate it is only possible to distinguish successful from unsuccessful family businesses after the second generation of owners (Baek & Cho, 2017).

However, the evidence indicates that family businesses actually do better than this stereotype suggests. For instance, a study examining 700,000 family-owned and not family-owned private companies, found less evidence of organizational failure in organizations with a family owner on the board (Wilson et al., 2013). Likewise, a study examining 403 companies included in the Standard & Poor 500 index revealed better performance for companies when a family founder had a board seat (Anderson & Reeb, 2003).

Family firms also have specific advantages. Family owners often focus on long-term sustainability instead of short term growth. This is due in part to their non-financial attachment to the company. Their sense of commitment and identity is also implied in the often stated ambition to nurture the company for the next generation (see also Box 7.5: Fattoria La Vialla). This may prompt family owners for instance to maintain financial independence and liquid assets allowing them to invest prior profits back into the business when needed (Arregle et al., 2007). Direct involvement of the family in the strategy and leadership of the organization appears to be positively related to its business success (Miller et al., 2014). The values and legacy of the family, and their visibility in the local community typically increase perceived responsibility for other stakeholders (Nordqvist & Jack, 2020), which is noted as a source of trust and customer loyalty (Orth & Green, 2009).

Box 7.5: Fattoria la Vialla

Fattoria La Vialla is a family run farm and wine estate in Tuscany, Italy (https://www.lavialla.it/uk/). It originated from an abandoned old farmhouse, bought in 1978 by Piero and Giuliana Lo Franco: a young couple who wanted to restore the building to live in the Italian countryside. After starting a vegetable garden, they also tried to revive the olive trees and vineyards surrounding it, to provide healthy food for the family.

What began as a family hobby, over the years turned into a large and successful agricultural business. The family gradually started acquiring and restoring other houses, replanting old orchards and reinstating fields in the area. Their consultations of local farmers to learn about traditional agricultural techniques, further developed their ideas for responsible local food production (Pisci, 2019). The philosophy was and still is to only use organic and biodynamic production methods.

Although the company grew substantially, it only produces and sells directly to private consumers. Its unique marketing strategy embodies this approach, and is part of this philosophy. Customers are treated as old family friends, and are addressed as members of the community of 'Viallini'. Several times a year customers receive a 'handwritten' letter with personal stories, including pictures of the family and their friends working the fields, and enjoying the food they produce. In this way customers are kept informed of how the crops were harvested, where new vines were planted, or why another traditional technique was reinstated. Being treated as 'family friends' also implies that customers can and do visit the farm to view the production methods, participate in the harvesting and taste the products (True Foods, 2019).

Today, the company is run by the second generation, and has over 150 employees. Through the newsletters, long-time customers know the names of the three sons, having seen the current owners grow up on the farm. They still take pride in only using organic and bio-dynamic production methods, using traditional skills and techniques, and retaining local employment. This extends to the way sheep, bees and chickens are held, how olive oil is pressed, how the crops are fertilized, and how water and waste is managed to protect the ecosystem.

Respectful treatment is also extended to employees, who are literally given a 'face' when their pictures and personal stories are included in newsletters. A recent example is the way a new employee from Africa was introduced. He was not considered as an anonymous seasonal worker, illegal migrant, or a fortune seeker. Instead, he was identified as the teacher at a village school in Burkina Faso, who was 'forced to emigrate to sustain his family'.

The new owners have also professionalized and expanded the company in many ways. Nowadays the company collaborates with academic researchers to validate their production methods and its beneficial effects on the nutritional value of their products. In recent years, they have started a family foundation to teach their methods to local farmers elsewhere. Their strategy has won the company numerous awards for its products. It was named 'international producer of the year' five times in a row at the Mundus Vini Biofach, the largest European fair for organic food and wine. It has also been identified multiple times as an example of sustainable agriculture. Clearly, business success and responsible stakeholder treatment can go hand in hand.

Paradoxically, family-owned companies often do these things without *explicitly* specifying formal rules for ethical behavior and stakeholder initiatives (Campopiano & De Massis, 2015). However, family support and positive role modeling was found to offer an important *implicit* guideline for company members to act in ethically responsible ways (Adams et al. 1996). The direct connection of the family and its name to the company implies that decisions made touch upon the moral identity of the family owners. In fact, symbolic and identity involvement of the family proves more decisive for feelings of responsibility and connection than their economic and legal ties with the company (see also Fig. 2.1). For instance, research revealed that concerns for the good family name steer family companies away from aggressive tax policies (Chen et al., 2010). Another study found that fewer incidents relating to social responsibility, stakeholder compliance or ethical behavior in family-owned businesses have been documented in companies where the brand identity was more explicitly tied to the family name (Block & Wagner, 2014). Similar observations were made across 197 large companies in eight countries with different cultural expectations and governance structures. After controlling for firm size and financial performance, this study found that stakeholders afforded more trust and respect to companies with higher levels of family ownership and family presence on the board (Deephouse & Jaskiewicz, 2013).

Family ownership and visible family involvement in the company implies that the firm is part of the family identity. The way stakeholders are treated not only reflects on the reputation of the firm, but affects the good name of the family. This offers a long-term perspective which changes strategic priorities and offers a different perspective on stakeholder concerns. In addition, family firms typically highlight their social capital as a source of strategic flexibility, innovation and business performance. This sense of 'familiness' indicates the key role assigned to social networks and human capital in relating to different types of stakeholders. This is a feature that characterizes the culture of many family organizations.

The emphasis on human relations and social networks can also benefit other types of organization (Craig et al., 2014). Research has found the distinct approach of family firms to be tied to their characteristic organizational *culture*, instead of their formal governance characteristics (Zahra et al., 2004). The personal and emotional involvement of the family was found to be more decisive for the performance of the organization than the level of entrepreneurship revealed by the owners (Madison et al.,, 2014). Indeed, other studies too suggest it is not family ownership *per se* but the concern for long term stakeholder outcomes that makes a difference – and can also be adopted by other types of companies. In a comparison of small businesses, the degree of emotional involvement and the strategic orientation of company leadership turned out to be more decisive for firm performance than family versus non-family ownership (Madison et al., 2014).

A more general insight emerging from research on family firms, then, is that a sense of identity and moral involvement with the organization induces a different perspective on the relations with key stakeholders. This work also shows that involving different perspectives and stakeholder concerns in strategic decision making and organizational practices – treating organizational stakeholders as 'family members' – can guard against morally questionable practices without undermining business success. This is an important insight that can also benefit other types of companies, as we shall explain below.

7.3.3 Social Benefit Corporations

Individuals and organizations seeking to care for broader stakeholder concerns often look to 'social impact companies' or 'social enterprises'. These firms use business skills and procedures to achieve a range of social missions, in line with Porter and Kramer's (2002) vision of shared value creation. Examples are workplace integration of problem groups through skill development and employment (Jamie Oliver: Jamie's kitchen), responsible food production and retail (Tony Chocolonely; Ben & Jerry's), or water conservation and recycling initiatives (e.g., urban mining companies that 'harvest' materials from buildings designated for demolition). Companies like this are very popular among customers and prospective employees, and are often embraced as contributors to solutions for global problems, allowing these businesses to do well by doing good.

Many of these business strategies reflect the personal ideals and values of their founders. Case studies document how they guarded their financial independence, and hired employees who shared their values in order to differentiate themselves in the marketplace as a socially responsible company while making a profit (Choi & Gray, 2008). However, in time, some of these enterprises were no longer commercially viable or were not managed well (Jamie's kitchen), while those that seemed most profitable were bought up by larger companies, shifting their stakeholder priorities (Ben & Jerry; the Body Shop). In other cases, the singular focus on specific impact concerns (the environment) blinded company leaders to other stakeholder issues (harassment of employees and customers at Starbucks). Further, such private initiatives have been criticized for highlighting issues and approaches that align with their expertise and business interests while neglecting more generic and perhaps superior long-term solutions that are less commercially interesting (Giridharadas, 2018).

A meta-analysis of 52 different studies in organizations confirms that long-term social and financial performance are not necessarily opposed, and can, in fact, sustain each other. The evidence relating financial performance to social performance does not favor one temporal sequence over the other, suggesting a self-reinforcing cycle where 'good social management' benefits 'financial slack' and vice versa (Orlitzky et al., 2003). This suggests that the ambition to engage with social goals does not necessarily undermine financial profitability and may even be financially beneficial. Yet the relation is not so strong as to suggest that improving one type of outcome will automatically also improve other types of outcomes. For practical purposes, financial and social outcomes might best be considered as separate business concerns, to be pursued as valued outcomes in their own right. It is fair to note that case studies also reveal considerable practical and organizational challenges faced by companies that try to make a profit by serving social goals. It is by no means self-evident that they succeed in achieving a measurable social impact, making a reliable profit, or scaling up from a promising start-up initiative to a firm that can really make a difference. This insight aligns with approaches that argue for normative and ethical arguments to engage with stakeholders in addition to instrumental reasons for doing so – emphasizing that one cannot be reduced to the other (Jones & Wicks, 1999).

This insight is relevant for many public interest sectors where corporations have started to take over roles that were traditionally held by (local) government. These range from infrastructures for energy, communication, and transportation to facilities for housing, childcare, education, and healthcare. However, the changes made are not without cost. The transformation from a public service to a commercial company often implies that new functions and facilities are added. While these may enhance commercial viability, they can also undermine corporate citizenship (Matten, & Crane, 2005). The diverging goals and values of different stakeholders may not align, raising leadership dilemmas that are not easily resolved (Crane et al., 2014; Smith et al., 2013).

In general, the specification of moral guidelines and ethical touchstones cannot depend on the mission of the organization, nor can it be tied to the personal values and ideals of a visionary individual or a successful entrepreneur. Instead, they should reflect carefully specified and broadly shared social norms, which can be legally negotiated, registered, monitored, and sanctioned. Developing such specific and legal guidelines defining the social purpose and social performance of organizations makes it possible to pursue social outcomes that are real, measurable, and transformative (Smith & Lewis, 2011). This allows stakeholders to raise questions about the legitimacy of procedures and activities, and to resolve ambiguity and confusion about seemingly incompatible aspects of the identity of the organization (Dacin et al., 2011).

This task has been taken up by legal experts, engaging with the wide-spread belief that corporate law requires executives to maximize (financial) shareholder value of the company above all other concerns, based on the principal-agent model discussed above. This prompted socially responsible businesses to seek legal protection from mismanagement claims that might be filed by investors when pursuing their commitment to other stakeholders. They started to formalize their social commitments by referring to themselves as 'Benefit corporations'.

Legal authorization for this business model (also indicated as social purpose cooperation, flexible purpose cooperation, or public-benefit corporation) was first obtained in Maryland USA, in 2010, and is now provided in many of the United States (Barnes, 2017). Italy was the first state in Europe to pass similar laws in 2016 (Società Benefit; "Italian Parliament Approves Benefit Corporation Legal Status", n.d.). In 2019 French law created a model for the 'enterprise à mission', which was first adopted by Danone in 2020, to align its social and environmental objectives with its purpose as set out in its Articles of Association. Calls for similar legal provisions are also made elsewhere, for instance in Australia (Cooper, 2016) and in the Netherlands. The goal of such legislation is to formalize the public purpose of the organization, resisting shareholder profit maximization as its primary legal duty that can be legally enforced. This releases such companies from the obligation to sell to the highest bidder and allows them to retain their original mission and values also after takeovers.

Such formal pledges to social impact and purpose force organizations to clearly define their role in society, by specifying their broader purpose and stating their desired legacy. The legal commitment made to the pursuit of non-financial outcomes also makes it easier for stakeholders to identify and monitor the true identity and intentions of the organization. Being able to check whether they actually do as they say makes it possible to determine whether and how the organization's initiatives and decisions align with values and identities that are important to them.

7.4 Conclusion: An Integrated Approach

This chapter focused on the importance of support from different types of stakeholders for the long term legitimacy and survival of organizations. Instead of being peripheral to the identity and core mission of the organization, employees, customers, and investors offer crucial resources and support. We reviewed research showing that demonstrating awareness and commitment to the concerns of different stakeholders is not just a matter of communicating well. The reputation of the organization is not enhanced by making pledges that seem superficial, symbolic, or peripheral to the core activities of the organization. Stakeholder initiatives will be distrusted and appear untruthful when they are used for moral cleansing or moral licensing – doing more harm than good. Only when stakeholder concerns are integrated into the key mission and purpose will they appear to be part of the true identity of the organization, and harness stakeholder loyalty and support. Some family firms already do this well. Formalizing the decision to protect stakeholders by becoming a social benefit corporation also makes it possible for other organizations.

Recommended Reading

Ashforth, B. E., Schinoff, B. S., & Brickson, S. L. (2020b). "My company is friendly", "Mine's a rebel": Anthropomorphism and shifting organizational identity from "what" to "who". *Academy of Management Review, 45*, 29–57. https://doi.org/10.5465/amr.2016.0496

De Gilder, D., Breedijk, M., & Schuyt, T. N. M. (2005b). Effects of an employee volunteering program on the work force: The ABN-AMRO case. *Journal of Business Ethics, 61*, 143–152. https://doi.org/10.1007/s10551-005-7101-x

Gillespie, N., & Dietz, G. (2009b). Trust repair after an organization-level failure. *Academy of Management Review, 34*(1), 127–145. https://doi.org/10.5465/amr.2009.35713319

Malone, C., & Fiske, S. T. (2013b). *The human brand: How we relate to people, products, and companies*. Jossey Bass.

Stout, L. A. (2012b). *The shareholder value myth: How putting shareholders first harms investors, corporations, and the public*. Berrett-Koehler Publishers. Retrieved from https://ebookcentral.proquest.com/lib/uunl/detail.action?docID=881726

References

Abboud, L. (2018, Dec 13). Pernod Ricard chief defends family firm from activist. *Financial Times*. Retrieved from https://www.ft.com/content/db3a91bc-fe4e-11e8-ac00-57a2a826423e

Abboud, L. (2020, April 7). LVMH and Kering backtrack on French state support for staff. *Financial Times*. Retrieved from https://www.ft.com/content/dc58474a-0768-41dc-9894-6100054dcd36

Abele, A. E., Ellemers, N., Fiske, S. T., Koch, A., & Yzerbyt, V. (2020). Navigating the social world: Toward an integrated framework for evaluating self, individuals, and groups. *Psychological Review*. Advance online publication. https://doi.org/10.1037/rev0000262

Adams, J. S., Taschian, A., & Shore, T. H. (1996). Ethics in family and non-family owned firms: An exploratory study. *Family Business Review, 9*(2), 157–170. https://doi.org/10.1111/j.1741-6248.1996.00157.x

Adkins, S. (2007). *Cause related marketing*. Routledge. https://doi.org/10.4324/9780080490625

Agle, B. R., Mitchell, R. K., & Sonnenfeld, J. A. (1999). Who matters to Ceos? An investigation of stakeholder attributes and salience, corporate performance, and Ceo values. *Academy of Management Journal, 42*(5), 507–525. https://doi.org/10.5465/256973

Aguilera, R. V., Rupp, D. E., Williams, C. A., & Ganapathi, J. (2007). Putting the S back in corporate social responsibility: A multilevel theory of social change in organizations. *Academy of Management Review, 32*(3), 836–863. https://doi.org/10.5465/amr.2007.25275678

Alonso-Almeida, M. D. M., & Llach, J. (2019). Socially responsible companies: Are they the best workplace for millennials? A cross-national analysis. *Corporate Social Responsibility and Environmental Management, 26*(1), 238–247. https://doi.org/10.1002/csr.1675

Anderson, R. C., & Reeb, D. M. (2003). Founding-family ownership and firm performance: Evidence from the S&P 500. *Journal of Finance, 58*, 1301–1329. https://doi.org/10.1111/1540-6261.00567

Andreasen, J. (1996). Urban tenants and community involvement. *Habitat International, 20*(3), 359–365. https://doi.org/10.1016/0197-3975(96)00015-X

Arregle, J.-L., Hitt, M. A., Sirmon, D. G., & Very, P. (2007). The development of organizational social capital: Attributes of family firms. *Journal of Management Studies, 44*, 73–95. https://doi.org/10.1111/j.1467-6486.2007.00665.x

Ashforth, B. E., & Gibbs, B. W. (1990). The double-edge of organizational legitimation. *Organization Science, 1*(2), 177–194. https://doi.org/10.1287/orsc.1.2.177

Ashforth, B. E., Schinoff, B. S., & Brickson, S. L. (2020a). "My company is friendly", "Mine's a rebel": Anthropomorphism and shifting organizational identity from "what" to "who". *Academy of Management Review, 45*, 29–57. https://doi.org/10.5465/amr.2016.0496

Avula, K., McKay, L., & Galland, S. (2019). *Amnesty International: Staff wellbeing review.* Amnesty International. Retrieved from https://www.amnesty.org/download/Documents/ORG6097632019ENGLISH.PDF

Baek, H. Y., & Cho, D. (2017). Family firm succession and performance. *Applied Economics Letters, 24*, 117–121. https://doi.org/10.1080/13504851.2016.1167822

Back at the branch: More Swedish lessons for the banking industry. (2009, May 16). *The Economist Newspaper. Retrieved.* from https://www.economist.com/special-report/2009/05/16/back-at-the-branch.

Bank Australia. (2019). *Financial Report 2019*. Retrieved from https://www.bankaust.com.au/globalassets/assets/reporting-governance%2D%2Dpolicies/corporate%2D%2Dfinancial-reports/2019/2019-financial-report.pdf

Barnes, A. (2017, Nov 29). Joining trend, WI creates new business entity: Benefit corporations. *Xconomy.* Retrieved from https://xconomy.com/wisconsin/2017/11/29/joining-trend-wi-creates-new-business-entity-benefit-corporations/

Baron, D. P. (2009). A positive theory of moral management, social pressure, and corporate social performance. *Journal of Economics & Management Strategy 18*(1), 7–43. https://doi.org/10.1111/j.1530-9134.2009.00206.x

Baur, D., & Palazzo, G. (2011). The moral legitimacy of NGOs as partners of corporations. *Business Ethics Quarterly, 21*(4), 579–604. https://doi.org/10.5840/beq201121437

Bayer. (2020). *Here are the facts about agriculture and nutrition.* Bayer. Retrieved from https://www.bayer.com/sites/default/files/2020-04/here-are-the-facts-about-agriculture-and-nutrition-brochure.pdf.

Bebchuk, L. A., & Tallarita, R. (2020). The illusory promise of stakeholder governance. Forthcoming. *Cornell Law Review*. Retrieved from http://dx.doi.org/https://doi.org/10.2139/ssrn.3544978

Becker-Olsen, K. L., Cudmore, B. A., & Hill, R. P. (2006). The impact of perceived corporate social responsibility on consumer behavior. *Journal of Business Research, 59*(1), 46–53. https://doi.org/10.1016/j.jbusres.2005.01.001

Bekkers, R., & Wiepking, P. (2007). *Understanding philanthropy: A review of 50 years of theories and research.* Paper presented at the 35th Annual Conference of the Association for Research on Nonprofit and Voluntary Action, Chicago (November 16–18).

Berens, G., & Van Riel, C. B. M. (2004). Corporate associations in the academic literature: Three main streams of thought in the reputation measurement literature. *Corporate Reputation Review, 7*(2), 161–178. https://doi.org/10.1057/palgrave.crr.1540218

Bhattacharjee, A., Berman, J. Z., & Reed, A. (2013). Tip of the hat, wag of the finger: How moral decoupling enables consumers to admire and admonish. *Journal of Consumer Research, 39*(6), 1167–1184. https://doi.org/10.1086/667786

Block, J., & Wagner, M. (2014). Ownership versus management effects on corporate social responsibility concerns in large family and founder firms. *Journal of Family Business Strategy, 5*, 339–346. https://doi.org/10.1016/j.jfbs.2014.08.005

Bolkan, S., Goodboy, A. K., & Daly, J. A. (2010). Consumer satisfaction and repatronage intentions following a business failure: The importance of perceived control with an organizational complaint. *Communication Reports, 23*(1), 14–25. https://doi.org/10.1080/08934211003598767

Bone, P. F., & Corey, R. J. (2000). Packaging ethics: Perceptual differences among packaging professionals, brand managers and ethically-interested consumers. *Journal of Business Ethics, 24*(3), 199–213. https://doi.org/10.1023/A:1006257523743

Brambilla, M., Sacchi, S., Pagliaro, S., & Ellemers, N. (2013). Morality and intergroup relations: Threats to safety and group image predict the desire to interact with outgroup and ingroup members. *Journal of Experimental Social Psychology, 49*(5), 811–821. https://doi.org/10.1016/j.jesp.2013.04.005

Branco, M. C., & Rodrigues, L. L. (2006). Corporate social responsibility and resource-based perspectives. *Journal of Business Ethics, 69*(2), 111–132. https://doi.org/10.1007/s10551-006-9071-z

Bray, T. (2020, April 29). Bye, Amazon. *Tbray*. Retrieved from https://www.tbray.org/ongoing/When/202x/2020/04/29/Leaving-Amazon

Bregman, R. (2017, March 30). No, wealth isn't created at the top. It is merely devoured there. *The Guardian*. Retrieved from https://www.theguardian.com/commentisfree/2017/mar/30/wealth-banks-google-facebook-society-economy-parasites#:~:text=3%20years%20old-,No%2C%20wealth%20isn't%20created%20at%20the%20top.,It%20is%20merely%20devoured%20there&text=This%20piece%20is%20about,on%20reflection%20%E2%80%93%20cannot%20be%20denied.

Briscoe, F., Gupta, A., & Anner, M. S. (2015). Social activism and practice diffusion: How activist tactics affect non-targeted organizations. *Administrative Science Quarterly, 60*(2), 300–332. https://doi.org/10.1177/0001839215579235

Brønn, P. S., & Vrioni, A. B. (2001). Corporate social responsibility and cause-related marketing: An overview. *International Journal of Advertising, 20*(2), 207–222. https://doi.org/10.1080/02650487.2001.11104887

Burger, L., & Bellon, (2020, June 24). Bayer to pay up to $10.9 billion to settle bulk of Roundup weedkiller cancer lawsuits. *Reuters*. Retrieved from: https://www.reuters.com/article/us-bayer-litigation-settlement-idUSKBN23V2NP

Business Roundtable Redefines the Purpose of a Corporation to Promote 'An Economy That Serves All Americans'. (2019, Aug 19). *Business Roundtable.*. Retrieved from https://www.businessroundtable.org/business-roundtable-redefines-the-purpose-of-a-corporation-to-promote-an-economy-that-serves-all-americans.

Cai, Y., Jo, H., & Pan, C. (2012). Doing well while doing bad? CSR in controversial industry sectors. *Journal of Business Ethics, 108*, 467–480. https://doi.org/10.1007/s10551-011-1103-7

Campopiano, G., & De Massis, A. (2015). Corporate social responsibility reporting: A content analysis in family and non-family firms. *Journal of Business Ethics, 129*, 511–534. https://doi.org/10.1007/s10551-014-2174-z

Carter, C. R. (2000). Ethical issues in international buyer–supplier relationships: A dyadic examination. *Journal of Operations Management, 18*(2), 191–208. https://doi.org/10.1016/S0272-6963(99)00016-9

Carvalho, F. P. (2017). Mining industry and sustainable development: Time for change. *Food and Energy Security, 6*(2), 61–77. https://doi.org/10.1002/fes3.109

Chen, J. C., Patten, D. M., & Roberts, R. W. (2008). Corporate charitable contributions: A corporate social performance or legitimacy strategy? *Journal of Business Ethics, 82*(1), 131–144. https://doi.org/10.1007/s10551-007-9567-1

Chen, S., Chen, X., Cheng, Q., & Shevlin, T. (2010). Are family firms more tax aggressive than non-family firms? *Journal of Financial Economics, 95*, 41–61. https://doi.org/10.1016/j.jfineco.2009.02.003

Choi, D. Y., & Gray, E. R. (2008). The venture development processes of "sustainable" entrepreneurs. *Management Research News, 8*(31), 558–569. https://doi.org/10.1108/01409170810892127

Chopova, T. (2020). *Doing good in business: Examining the importance of morality in business contexts*. Utrecht University: Doctoral dissertation.

Chrisman, J. J., Chua, J. H., & Litz, R. A. (2004). Comparing the agency costs of family and non-family firms: Conceptual issues and exploratory evidence. *Entrepreneurship Theory and Practice, 28*, 335–354. https://doi.org/10.1111/j.1540-6520.2004.00049.x

Chung, S., & Park, J. (2013). Effects of social and temporal distance on evaluation of corporate ambivalent behavior. *Social Behavior and Personality, 41*(7), 1219–1224. https://doi.org/10.2224/sbp.2013.41.7.1219

Confessore, N., & Rosenberg, M. (2018, Nov 29). Sheryl Sandberg asked for Soros research, Facebook acknowledges. *The New York Times*. Retrieved from https://www.nytimes.com/2018/11/29/technology/george-soros-facebook-sheryl-sandberg.html

Conger, K., & Scheiber, N. (2019, July 8). Employee activism is alive in tech. It stops short of organizing unions. *The New York Times*. Retrieved from https://www.nytimes.com/2019/07/08/technology/tech-companies-union-organizing.html

Connelly, B. L., Certo, S. T., Ireland, R. D., & Reutzel, C. R. (2011). Signaling theory: A review and assessment. *Journal of Management, 37*(1), 39–67. https://doi.org/10.1177/0149206310388419

Cooper, E. (2016, March 9). Push for benefit corporation law. *Probono Australia*. Retrieved from https://probonoaustralia.com.au/news/2016/03/623970/

Craig, J. B., Dibrell, C., & Garrett, R. (2014). Examining relationships among family influence, family culture, flexible planning systems, innovativeness and firm performance. *Journal of Family Business Strategy, 5*, 229–238. https://doi.org/10.1016/j.jfbs.2013.09.002

Crane, A., Palazzo, G., Spence, L. J., & Matten, D. (2014). Contesting the value of "creating shared value". *California Management Review, 56*(2), 130–153. https://doi.org/10.1525/cmr.2014.56.2.130

Crane, A., & Ruebottom, T. (2011). Stakeholder theory and social identity: Rethinking stakeholder identification. *Journal of Business Ethics, 102*(1), 77–87. https://doi.org/10.1007/s10551-011-1191-4

Cronin, T., Reysen, S., & Branscombe, N. R. (2012). Wal-Mart's conscientious objectors: Perceived illegitimacy, moral anger, and retaliatory consumer behavior. *Basic and Applied Social Psychology, 34*(4), 322–335. https://doi.org/10.1080/01973533.2012.693347

Dacin, M. T., Dacin, P. A., & Tracey, P. (2011). Social entrepreneurship: A critique and future directions. *Organization Science, 22*(5), 1203–1213. https://doi.org/10.1287/orsc.1100.0620

Davis, J. H., Schoorman, F. D., & Donaldson, L. (1997). Toward a stewardship theory of management. *Academy of Management Review, 22*(1), 20–47. https://doi.org/10.5465/amr.1997.9707180258

Deephouse, D. L., & Jaskiewicz, P. (2013). Do family firms have better reputations than non-family firms? An integration of socioemotional wealth and social identity theories. *Journal of Management Studies, 50*, 337–360. https://doi.org/10.1111/joms.12015

De Gilder, D., Breedijk, M., & Schuyt, T. N. M. (2005a). Effects of an employee volunteering program on the work force: The ABN-AMRO case. *Journal of Business Ethics, 61*, 143–152. https://doi.org/10.1007/s10551-005-7101-x

De Gilder, T. C., & Van Teunenbroek, C. (2020). Geven door bedrijven. In R. Bekkers, B. Gouwenberg, & T. Schuyt (Eds.), *Geven in Nederland 2020* (pp. 124–141).

De Lima, I. B., & Leal Filho, W. (Eds.). (2015). *Rare earths industry: Technological, economic, and environmental implications*. Elsevier.

Delmas, M. A., & Burbano, V. C. (2011). The drivers of greenwashing. *California Management Review, 54*(1), 64–87. https://doi.org/10.1525/cmr.2011.54.1.64

De Nederlandsche Bank. (2018). Responsible Investment Charter. *De Nederlandse Bank*. Retrieved from https://www.dnb.nl/en/binaries/DNB%20Responsible%20Investment%20Charter_tcm47-382883.pdf.

De Vries, G., Terwel, B. W., & Ellemers, N. (2016). Perceptions of manipulation and judgments of illegitimacy: Pitfalls in the use of emphasis framing when communicating about CO2 capture and storage. *Environmental Communication, 10*(2), 206–226. https://doi.org/10.1080/17524032.2015.1047884

De Vries, G., Terwel, B. W., Ellemers, N., & Daamen, D. D. (2015). Sustainability or profitability? How communicated motives for environmental policy affect public perceptions of corporate greenwashing. *Corporate Social Responsibility and Environmental Management, 22*(3), 142–154. https://doi.org/10.1002/csr.1327

Dietz, G., & Gillespie, N. (2011). *Building and restoring organizational trust*. Institute of Business Ethics.

Donaldson, T., & Dunfee, T. W. (1999). When ethics travel: The promise and peril of global business ethics. *California Management Review, 41*(4). https://doi.org/10.2307/41166009

Donaldson, T., & Preston, L. E. (1995). The stakeholder theory of the corporation: Concepts, evidence, and implications. *Academy of Management Review, 20*(1), 65–91. https://doi.org/10.5465/amr.1995.9503271992

Donia, M. B., Tetrault Sirsly, C. A., & Ronen, S. (2017). Employee attributions of corporate social responsibility as substantive or symbolic: Validation of a measure. *Applied Psychology, 66*(1), 103–142. https://doi.org/10.1111/apps.12081

Driver, C. (2012). Governance, innovation and finance. In *Sage handbook of corporate governance*. Sage Publications.

Dutch Government. (2020, June 26). Government offers financial support to KLM as a result of the corona crisis. *Government of the Netherlands*. Retrieved from https://www.government.nl/latest/news/2020/06/26/government-offers-financial-support-to-klm-as-a-result-of-the-corona-crisis

Duursma, M. (2020, July 9). Vakbonden protesteren tegen steunpakket klm bij europese commissie. *NRC.* Retrieved from https://www.nrc.nl/nieuws/2020/07/09/vakbonden-protesteren-tegen-steunpakket-klm-bij-europese-commissie-a4005454

Eccles, R. G., & Klimenko, S. (2019). The investor revolution. *Harvard Business Review.* Retrieved from https://hbr.org/2019/05/the-investor-revolution

Edelman. (2020). Edelman Trust Barometer Global Report 2020. *Edelman.* Retrieved from https://cdn2.hubspot.net/hubfs/440941/Trust%20Barometer%202020/2020%20Edelman%20Trust%20Barometer%20Global%20Report.pdf?utm_campaign=Global:%20Trust%20Barometer%202020&utm_source=Website

Edelman Trust Barometer Spring Update 2020: Trust and the COVID-19 Pandemic. (2020, May 5). Retrieved from https://www.edelman.com/research/trust-2020-spring-update

Edmans, A. (2011). Does the stock market fully value intangibles? Employee satisfaction and equity prices. *Journal of Financial Economics, 101*(3), 621–640. https://doi.org/10.1016/j.jfineco.2011.03.021

Ellemers, N. (2017). *Morality and the regulation of social behavior: Groups as moral anchors.* Routledge. https://doi.org/10.4324/9781315661322

Ellemers, N., Kingma, L., Van de Burgt, J., & Barreto, M. (2011). Corporate social responsibility as a source of organizational morality, employee commitment and satisfaction. *Journal of Organizational Moral Psychology, 1*(2), 97–124.

Fassin, Y., & Buelens, M. (2011). The hypocrisy-sincerity continuum in corporate communication and decision making: A model of corporate social responsibility and business ethics practices. *Management Decision, 49*(4), 586–600. https://doi.org/10.1108/00251741111126503

Fehre, K., & Weber, F. (2016). Challenging corporate commitment to CSR: Do CEOs keep talking about corporate social responsibility (CSR) issues in times of the global financial crisis? *Management Research Review, 39*(11), 1410–1430. https://doi.org/10.1108/MRR-03-2015-0063

Feinberg, M., & Willer, R. (2013). The moral roots of environmental attitudes. *Psychological Science, 24*(1), 56–62. https://doi.org/10.1177/0956797612449177

Flammer, C., & Luo, J. (2017). Corporate social responsibility as an employee governance tool: Evidence from a quasi-experiment. *Strategic Management Journal, 38*(2), 163–183. https://doi.org/10.1002/smj.2492

Forehand, M. R., & Grier, S. (2003). When is honesty the best policy? The effect of stated company intent on consumer skepticism. *Journal of Consumer Psychology, 13*(3), 349–356. https://doi.org/10.1207/S15327663JCP1303_15

France takes Roundup weed-killer off market after court ruling. (2019, Jan 15). *Phys Org.*. Retrieved from https://phys.org/news/2019-01-france-roundup-weed-killer-court.html.

Frenkel, S., Confessore, N., Kang, C., Rosenberg, M., & Nicas, J. (2018, Nov 14). Delay, deny and deflect: How Facebook's leaders fought through crisis. *The New York Times.* Retrieved from https://www.nytimes.com/2018/11/14/technology/facebook-data-russia-electionracism.html

Freudenreich, B., Lüdeke-Freund, F., & Schaltegger, S. (2019). A stakeholder theory perspective on business models: Value creation for sustainability. *Journal of Business Ethics*, 1–16. https://doi-org.proxy.library.uu.nl/10.1007/s10551-019-04112-z

Friedman, M. (2007). The social responsibility of business is to increase its profits. In W. C. Zimmerli, M. Holzinger, & K. Richter (Eds.), *Corporate ethics and corporate governance* (pp. 173–178). Springer. https://doi.org/10.1007/978-3-540-70818-6_14

Fuoli, M., Van de Weijer, J., & Paradis, C. (2017). Denial outperforms apology in repairing organizational trust despite strong evidence of guilt. *Public Relations Review, 43*(4), 645–660. https://doi.org/10.1016/j.pubrev.2017.07.007

Gautier, A., & Pache, A. C. (2015). Research on corporate philanthropy: A review and assessment. *Journal of Business Ethics, 126*(3), 343–369. https://doi.org/10.1007/s10551-013-1969-7

Gillam, C. (2017). *Whitewash: The story of a weed killer, cancer, and the corruption of science.* Island Press. https://doi.org/10.5822/978-1-61091-833-6

Gillespie, N., & Dietz, G. (2009a). Trust repair after an organization-level failure. *Academy of Management Review, 34*(1), 127–145. https://doi.org/10.5465/amr.2009.35713319

Gillespie, N., Dietz, G., & Lockey, S. (2014). Organizational reintegration and trust repair after an integrity violation: A case study. *Business Ethics Quarterly, 24*(3), 371–410. https://doi.org/10.5840/beq2014437

Gillespie, N., Hurley, R., Dietz, G., & Bachman, R. (2012). Restoring institutional trust after the global financial crisis: A systemic approach. In R. M. Kramer & T. L. Pittinsky (Eds.), *Restoring trust in organizations and leaders: Enduring challenges and emerging answers* (pp. 1–43). Oxford University Press. https://doi.org/10.1093/acprof:oso/9780199756087.003.0010

Giridharadas, A. (2018). *Winners take all: The elite charade of changing the world.* Vintage.

Godfrey, P. C. (2005). The relationship between corporate philanthropy and shareholder wealth: A risk management perspective. *Academy of Management Review, 30*(4), 777–798. https://doi.org/10.5465/amr.2005.18378878

Goodwin, G. P. (2015). Moral character in person perception. *Current Directions in Psychological Science, 24*(1), 38–44. https://doi.org/10.1177/0963721414550709

Halperin, B., Ho, B., List, J. A., & Muir, I. (2019). *Toward an understanding of the economics of apologies: evidence from a large-scale natural field experiment* (No. w25676). National Bureau of Economic Research. https://doi.org/10.3386/w25676

Harrington, B. (2016). *Capital without borders: Wealth managers and the one percent*. Harvard University Press. https://doi.org/10.4159/9780674973619

Harrison, R. (2003). Corporate social responsibility and the consumer movement. *Consumer Policy Review, 13*(4), 127–131.

Harrison, R., Newholm, T., & Shaw, D. (Eds.). (2005). *The ethical consumer*. Sage.

Harty, D. (2020, July 14). BlackRock voted - against management at 53 companies over climate concerns. *S&P Global.* Retrieved from https://www.spglobal.com/marketintelligence/en/news-insights/latest-news-headlines/blackrock-voted-against-management-at-53-companies-over-climate-concerns-59426142.

Hoekstra, R. (2019). *Replacing GDP by 2030: Towards a common language for the well-being and sustainability community*. Harvard University Press. https://doi.org/10.1017/9781108608558

Hooghiemstra, R. (2000). Corporate communication and impression management–new perspectives why companies engage in corporate social reporting. *Journal of Business Ethics, 27*(1–2), 55–68. https://doi.org/10.1023/A:1006400707757

Hornsey, M. J., & Esposo, S. (2009). Resistance to group criticism and recommendations for change: Lessons from the intergroup sensitivity effect. *Social and Personality Psychology Compass, 3*(3), 275–291. https://doi.org/10.1111/j.1751-9004.2009.00178.x

Hornsey, M. J., & Imani, A. (2004). Criticizing groups from the inside and the outside: An identity perspective on the intergroup sensitivity effect. *Personality and Social Psychology Bulletin, 30*(3), 365–383. https://doi.org/10.1177/0146167203261295

IARC. (2016). *Q&A on Glyphosate.* IARC. Retrieved from https://www.iarc.fr/wp-content/uploads/2018/11/QA_Glyphosate.pdf

Italian Parliament Approves Benefit Corporation Legal Status. (n.d.). Ethical Markets. Retrieved from https://www.ethicalmarkets.com/italian-parliament-approves-benefit-corporation-legal-status/.

Jensen, M. C., & Meckling, W. H. (1976). Theory of the firm: Managerial behavior, agency costs and ownership structure. *Journal of Financial Economics, 3*(4), 305–360. https://doi.org/10.1016/0304-405X(76)90026-X

Jones, T. M., & Wicks, A. C. (1999). Convergent stakeholder theory. *Academy of Management Review, 24*(2), 206–221. https://doi.org/10.5465/amr.1999.1893929

Khan, T. (2019, Sept 25). Litigation is a powerful tool for holding those responsible for the Climate crisis to account. *Time*. Retrieved from https://time.com/5686087/courtroom-climate-change-litigation/

Kolhatkar, S. (2018, Aug 20). Paul Singer, Doomsday Investor. *The New Yorker.* Retrieved from https://www.newyorker.com/magazine/2018/08/27/paul-singer-doomsday-investor#

Lange, D., Lee, P. M., & Dai, Y. (2011). Organizational reputation: A review. *Journal of Management, 37*(1), 153–184. https://doi.org/10.1177/0149206310390963

Lazard. (2020a). Lazard's 2019 annual review of Shareholder Activism. *Lazard.* Retrieved from https://www.lazard.com/perspective/lazards-2019-annual-review-of-shareholder-activism

Lazard. (2020b). Lazard's quarterly review of shareholder activism – Q1 2020. *Lazard.* Retrieved from https://www.lazard.com/perspective/lazards-quarterly-review-of-shareholder-activism-q1-2020/

Leupen, J., & Van Dijk, B. (2018, May 1). Schaars technisch talent bedankt voor een carrière bij fossiel ´vies´ Shell. *FD.* Retrieved from https://fd.nl/economie-politiek/1252018/schaars-technisch-talent-bedankt-voor-een-carriere-bij-fossiel-vies-shell

Loughran, T., McDonald, B., & Yun, H. (2009). A wolf in sheep's clothing: The use of ethics-related terms in 10-K reports. *Journal of Business Ethics, 89*(1), 39–49. https://doi.org/10.1007/s10551-008-9910-1

Lutak, O. (2020, Jan 27). The Urgenda decision: The landmark Dutch climate change case. *LeidenLawBlog.* Retrieved from: https://leidenlawblog.nl/articles/the-urgenda-decision-the-landmark-dutch-climate-change-case

Madison, K., Runyan, R. C., & Swinney, J. L. (2014). Strategic posture and performance: Revealing differences between family and nonfamily firms. *Journal of Family Business Strategy, 5*, 239–251. https://doi.org/10.1016/j.jfbs.2013.11.006

Malone, C., & Fiske, S. T. (2013a). *The human brand: How we relate to people, products, and companies*. Jossey Bass.

Masulis, R. W., & Reza, S. W. (2015). Agency problems of corporate philanthropy. *The Review of Financial Studies, 28*(2), 592–636. https://doi.org/10.1093/rfs/hhu082

Matten, D., & Crane, A. (2005). Corporate citizenship: Toward an extended theoretical conceptualization. *Academy of Management Review, 30*(1), 166–179. https://doi.org/10.5465/amr.2005.15281448

McDonnell, M. H., & King, B. (2013). Keeping up appearances: Reputational threat and impression management after social movement boycotts. *Administrative Science Quarterly, 58*(3), 387–419. https://doi.org/10.1177/0001839213500032

McGowan, M. (2018, July 17). Lush cosmetics payroll error underpaid staff by $2m. *The Guardian.* Retrieved from https://www.theguardian.com/australia-news/2018/jul/17/lush-cosmetics-payroll-error-underpaid-staff-by-2m

McGowan, M., & Cox, L. (2019, Feb 7). *Court rules out Hunter Valley coalmine on climate change grounds.*. Retrieved from https://www.theguardian.com/australia-news/2019/feb/08/court-rules-out-hunter-valley-coalmine-climate-change-rocky-hill.

McVeigh, K. (2019, Feb 6). Amnesty International has toxic working culture, report finds. *The Guardian.* Retrieved from https://www.theguardian.com/world/2019/feb/06/amnesty-international-has-toxic-working-culture-report-finds

Miller, D. T., Le Breton-Miller, I., Minichilli, A., Corbetta, G., & Pittino, D. (2014). When do non-family CEOs outperform in family firms? Agency and behavioural agency perspectives. *Journal of Management Studies, 51*, 547–572. https://doi.org/10.1111/joms.12076

Miller, T. L., Wesley, C. L., & Williams, D. E. (2012). Educating the minds of caring hearts: Comparing the views of practitioners and educators on the importance of social entrepreneurship competencies. *Academy of Management Learning & Education, 11*(3), 349–370. https://doi.org/10.5465/amle.2011.0017

Mishina, Y., Block, E. S., & Mannor, M. J. (2012). The path dependence of organizational reputation: How social judgment influences assessments of capability and character. *Strategic Management Journal, 33*(5), 459–477. https://doi.org/10.1002/smj.958

Mitchell, R. K., Agle, B. R., & Wood, D. J. (1997). Toward a theory of stakeholder identification and salience: Defining the principle of who and what really counts. *Academy of Management Review, 22*(4), 853–886. https://doi.org/10.5465/amr.1997.9711022105

Muinzer, T. L. (2019, Oct 8). A Climate of change? Taking stock of the Urgenda case with a Supreme Court ruling on the horizon. *UK Human Rights Blog*. Retrieved from https://ukhumanrightsblog.com/2019/10/08/a-climate-of-change-taking-stock-of-the-urgenda-case-with-a-supreme-court-ruling-on-the-horizon/

Newell, S. J., & Goldsmith, R. E. (2001). The development of a scale to measure perceived corporate credibility. *Journal of Business Research, 52*(3), 235–247. https://doi.org/10.1016/S0148-2963(99)00104-6

Nordqvist, M., & Jack, S. (2020). Resilience and family busines. In *In: Sweden through the crisis: How lessons from family businesses can help all facets of society to bounce back*. Stockholm School of Economics Institute for Research.

Oriti, T. (2019, June 12). Oxfam under fire over Haiti sexual misconduct and cover-up. *ABC*. Retrieved from https://www.abc.net.au/radio/programs/am/oxfam-report/11201320

Orlitzky, M., Schmidt, F. L., & Rynes, S. L. (2003). Corporate social and financial performance: A meta-analysis. *Organization Studies, 24*(3), 403–441. https://doi.org/10.1177/0170840603024003910

Ormiston, M. E., & Wong, E. M. (2013). License to ill: The effects of corporate social responsibility and CEO moral identity on corporate social irresponsibility. *Personnel Psychology, 66*(4), 861–893. https://doi.org/10.1111/peps.12029

Orth, U. R., & Green, M. T. (2009). Consumer loyalty to family versus non-family business: The roles of store image, trust and satisfaction. *Journal of Retailing and Consumer Services, 16*, 248–259. https://doi.org/10.1016/j.jretconser.2008.12.002

Pagliaro, S., Ellemers, N., Barreto, M., & Di Cesare, C. (2016). Once dishonest, always dishonest? The impact of perceived pervasiveness of moral evaluations of the self on motivation to restore a moral reputation. *Frontiers in Psychology, 7*, 586. https://doi.org/10.3389/fpsyg.2016.00586

Parmar, B. L., Keevil, A., & Wicks, A. C. (2019). People and profits: The impact of corporate objectives on employees' need satisfaction at work. *Journal of Business Ethics, 154*(1), 13–33. https://doi.org/10.1007/s10551-017-3487-5

Pascoe, R. (2019, Jan 10). Minister to 'talk to Novartis' after five-fold cancer drug price hike. *Dutch News*. Retrieved from https://www.dutchnews.nl/news/2019/01/minister-to-talk-to-novartis-after-five-fold-cancer-drug-price-hike/

Pisci, S. (2019, #6). Culinary happiness in Tuscany: Fattoria La Vialla *Wideoyster*. Retrieved from: https://magazine.wideoyster.com/en/fattoria-la-vialla/

Pollack, A. (2015, Sept 20). Drug goes from $13.50 a tablet to $750, overnight. *The New York Times*. Retrieved from https://www.nytimes.com/2015/09/21/business/a-huge-overnight-increase-in-a-drugs-price-raises-protests.html

Pope, S., & Lim, A. (2020). The governance divide in global corporate responsibility: The global structuration of reporting and certification frameworks, 1998–2017. *Organization Studies, 41*(6), 821–854. https://doi.org/10.1177/0170840619830131

Porter, M. E., & Kramer, M. R. (2002). The competitive advantage of corporate philanthropy. *Harvard Business Review, 80*(12), 56–68.

Pringle, H., & Thompson, M. (1999). *Brand spirit: How cause related marketing builds brands*. Wiley.

Quinn, D. P., & Jones, T. M. (1995). An agent morality view of business policy. *Academy of Management Review, 20*(1), 22–42. https://doi.org/10.5465/amr.1995.9503271989

Rao, H., Morrill, C., & Zald, M. N. (2000). Power plays: How social movements and collective action create new organizational forms. *Research in Organizational Behavior, 22*, 237–281. https://doi.org/10.1016/S0191-3085(00)22007-8

Raub, S. (2017). When employees walk the company talk: The importance of employee involvement in corporate philanthropy. *Human Resource Management, 56*(5), 837–850. https://doi.org/10.1002/hrm.21806

Ravasi, D., Rindova, V., Etter, M., & Cornelissen, J. (2018). The formation of organizational reputation. *Academy of Management Annals, 12*(2), 574–599. https://doi.org/10.5465/annals.2016.0124

Reynolds, S. J., Schultz, F. C., & Hekman, D. R. (2006). Stakeholder theory and managerial decision-making: Constraints and implications of balancing stakeholder interests. *Journal of Business Ethics, 64*(3), 285–301. https://doi.org/10.1007/s10551-005-5493-2

Rindova, V. P., Martins, L. L., Srinivas, S. B., & Chandler, D. (2018). The good, the bad, and the ugly of organizational rankings: A multidisciplinary review of the literature and directions for future research. *Journal of Management, 44*(6), 2175–2208. https://doi.org/10.1177/0149206317741962

Rio Tinto chief Jean-Sébastien Jacques to quit over Aboriginal cave destruction. (2020, Sept 11). *BBC News*.. Retrieved from: https://www.bbc.com/news/world-australia-54112991

Rodrigo, P., Aqueveque, C., & Duran, I. J. (2019). Do employees value strategic CSR? A tale of affective organizational commitment and its underlying mechanisms. *Business Ethics: A European Review, 28*(4), 459–475. https://doi.org/10.1111/beer.12227

Roschk, H., & Kaiser, S. (2013). The nature of an apology: An experimental study on how to apologize after a service failure. *Marketing Letters, 24*(3), 293–309. https://doi.org/10.1007/s11002-012-9218-x

Saiia, D. H., Carroll, A. B., & Buchholtz, A. K. (2003). Philanthropy as strategy: When corporate charity "begins at home". *Business & Society, 42*(2), 169–201. https://doi.org/10.1177/0007650303042002002

Salvador, R. O., Folger, R., & Priesemuth, M. (2012). Organizational apology and defense: Effects of guilt and managerial status. *Journal of Managerial Issues*, 124–139.

Scalet, S., & Kelly, T. F. (2010). CSR rating agencies: What is their global impact? *Journal of Business Ethics, 94*(1), 69–88. https://doi.org/10.1007/s10551-009-0250-6

Schad, T. (2020, July 6). What we know: The latest on mounting pressure that could prompt Washington Redskins to change team name. *USA Today*. Retrieved from https://eu.usatoday.com/story/sports/nfl/redskins/2020/07/06/washington-redskins-name-change-nfl-nike-sponsors-history/5383345002/

Schaefer, S. D., Terlutter, R., & Diehl, S. (2020). Talking about CSR matters: Employees' perception of and reaction to their company's CSR communication in four different CSR domains. *International Journal of Advertising, 39*(2), 191–212. https://doi.org/10.1080/02650487.2019.1593736

Scheidler, S., Edinger-Schons, L. M., Spanjol, J., & Wieseke, J. (2019). Scrooge posing as Mother Teresa: How hypocritical social responsibility strategies hurt employees and firms. *Journal of Business Ethics, 157*(2), 339–358. https://doi.org/10.1007/s10551-018-3788-3

Schuler, D. A., & Cording, M. (2006). A corporate social performance–corporate financial performance behavioral model for consumers. *Academy of Management Review, 31*(3), 540–558. https://doi.org/10.5465/amr.2006.21318916

Shaw, J. C., Wild, E., & Colquitt, J. A. (2003). To justify or excuse?: A meta-analytic review of the effects of explanations. *Journal of Applied Psychology, 88*(3), 444. https://doi.org/10.1037/0021-9010.88.3.444

Skowronski, J. J., & Carlston, D. E. (1987). Social judgment and social memory: The role of cue diagnosticity in negativity, positivity, and extremity biases. *Journal of Personality and Social Psychology, 52*(4), 689. https://doi.org/10.1037/0022-3514.52.4.689

Smith, D. W. (2014, May 28). *Handelsbanken: A different kind of bank.* Retrieved from https://www.wearesalt.org/the-swedish-bank-that-is-not-all-money-money-money/

Smith, L. G., Gillespie, N., Callan, V. J., Fitzsimmons, T. W., & Paulsen, N. (2017). Injunctive and descriptive logics during newcomer socialization: The impact on organizational identification, trustworthiness, and self-efficacy. *Journal of Organizational Behavior, 38*(4), 487–511. https://doi.org/10.1002/job.2131

Smith, W. K., Gonin, M., & Besharov, M. L. (2013). Managing social-business tensions: A review and research agenda for social enterprise. *Business Ethics Quarterly, 23*(3), 407–442. https://doi.org/10.5840/beq201323327

Smith, W. K., & Lewis, M. W. (2011). Toward a theory of paradox: A dynamic equilibrium model of organizing. *Academy of Management Review, 36*(2), 381–403. https://doi.org/10.5465/AMR.2011.59330958

Spiller, R. (2000). Ethical business and investment: A model for business and society. *Journal of Business Ethics, 27*(1–2), 149–160. https://doi.org/10.1023/A:1006445915026

Statement on Company Law. (n.d.). Retrieved from https://themoderncorporation.wordpress.com/company-law-memo/

Stout, L. A. (2001). Bad and not-so-bad arguments for shareholder primacy. *Southern California Law Review, 75*, 1189–1210. https://doi.org/10.2139/ssrn.331464

Stout, L. A. (2012a). *The shareholder value myth: How putting shareholders first harms investors, corporations, and the public*. Berrett-Koehler Publishers. Retrieved from https://ebookcentral.proquest.com/lib/uunl/detail.action?docID=881726.

Terwel, B., Harinck, F., Ellemers, N., & Daamen, D. L. (2009a). Competence-based and integrity-based trust as predictors of acceptance of carbon dioxide capture and storage technology (CCS). *Risk Analysis: An International Journal, 29*, 1129–1140. https://doi.org/10.1111/j.1539-6924.2009.01256.x

Terwel, B., Harinck, F., Ellemers, N., & Daamen, D. L. (2009b). How organizational motives and communications affect public trust in organizations: The case of carbon dioxide capture and storage. *Journal of Environmental Psychology, 29*, 290–299. https://doi.org/10.1016/j.jenvp.2008.11.004

Terwel, B. W., Harinck, F., Ellemers, N., & Daamen, D. D. (2010). How organizational motives and communications affect public trust in organizations: The case of carbon dioxide capture and storage. *Journal of Environmental Psychology, 29*(2), 290–299. https://doi.org/10.1016/j.jenvp.2008.11.004

Terwel, B. W., Harinck, F., Ellemers, N., & Daamen, D. D. (2011). Going beyond the properties of CO2 capture and storage (CCS) technology: How trust in stakeholders affects public acceptance of CCS. *International Journal of Greenhouse Gas Control, 5*(2), 181–188. https://doi.org/10.1016/j.ijggc.2010.10.001

Tesler, L. E., & Malone, R. E. (2008). Corporate philanthropy, lobbying, and public health policy. *American Journal of Public Health, 98*(12), 2123–2133. https://doi.org/10.2105/AJPH.2007.128231

Tesler, L. E., & Malone, R. E. (2010). "Our reach is wide by any corporate standard": How the tobacco industry helped defeat the Clinton health plan and why it matters now. *American Journal of Public Health, 100*(7), 1174–1188. https://doi.org/10.2105/AJPH.2009.179150

The RepTrak Company. (n.d.). What is your company's reputation? *RepTrak Company.* Retrieved July 22, 2020, from https://www.reptrak.com/

Thomas, T., Schermerhorn, J. R., Jr., & Dienhart, J. W. (2004). Strategic leadership of ethical behavior in business. *Academy of Management Perspectives, 18*(2), 56–66. https://doi.org/10.5465/ame.2004.13837425

Tiba, S., Van Rijnsoever, F. J., & Hekkert, M. P. (2019). Firms with benefits: A systematic review of responsible entrepreneurship and corporate social responsibility literature. *Corporate Social Responsibility and Environmental Management, 26*(2), 265–284. https://doi.org/10.1002/csr.1682

Timeline: Rio Tinto's sacred indigenous caves blast scandal. (2020, Dec 3). *Reuters.* Retrieved from: https://www.reuters.com/article/us-australia-mining-indigenous-timeline-idUSKBN28D0OC

Torugsa, N. A., O'Donohue, W., & Hecker, R. (2012). Capabilities, proactive CSR and financial performance in SMEs: Empirical evidence from an Australian manufacturing industry sector. *Journal of Business Ethics, 109*(4), 483–500. https://doi.org/10.1007/s10551-011-1141-1

True Foods (2019, April 7). *Fattoria La Vialla – brand analysis.* Retrieved from: https://www.truefoodsblog.com/brands/fattoria-la-vialla-brand-analysis_2434/

Turban, D. B., & Greening, D. W. (1997). Corporate social performance and organizational attractiveness to prospective employees. *Academy of Management Journal, 40*(3), 658–672. https://doi.org/10.2307/257057

United Nations Sustainable Development. (n.d.). About the sustainable development goals. *United Nations Sustainable Development.* Retrieved from https://www.un.org/sustainabledevelopment/sustainable-development-goals [Accessed 22 July 2020].

Valentine, S., Godkin, L., & Lucero, M. (2002). Ethical context, organizational commitment, and person-organization fit. *Journal of Business Ethics, 41*(4), 349–360. https://doi.org/10.1023/A:1021203017316

Van den Broek, T., Langley, D., & Hornig, T. (2017). The effect of online protests and firm responses on shareholder and consumer evaluation. *Journal of Business Ethics. 146*(2), 279–294. https://doi.org/10.1007/s10551-017-3653-9

Van de Ven, B. (2008). An ethical framework for the marketing of corporate social responsibility. *Journal of Business Ethics, 82*(2), 339–352. https://doi.org/10.1007/s10551-008-9890-1

Van Prooijen, A. M., & Ellemers, N. (2015). Does it pay to be moral? How indicators of morality and competence enhance organizational and work team attractiveness. *British Journal of Management, 26*(2), 225–236. https://doi.org/10.1111/1467-8551.12055

Van Prooijen, A. M., Ellemers, N., Van der Lee, R., & Scheepers, D. T. (2018). What seems attractive may not always work well: Evaluative and cardiovascular responses to morality and competence levels in decision-making teams. *Group Processes & Intergroup Relations, 21*(1), 73–87. https://doi.org/10.1177/1368430216653814

Veenstra, E., & Ellemers, N. (2020). ESG indicators as organizational performance goals: Do rating agencies encourage a holistic approach? *Sustainability, 12*(24), 10228. https://doi.org/10.3390/su122410228

Verghis, S. (2019, July 25). *Understanding the 'clean money' movement.* Retrieved from https://www.sbs.com.au/topics/article/2019/06/12/understanding-clean-money-movement%3Futm_medium%3Dpartnerships%26utm_source%3Dsbs%26utm_campaign%3Dclean%2Bmoney%26utm_content%3Dbra_pl_awa_dir_nat_q1_cm

Vlachos, P. A., Tsamakos, A., Vrechopoulos, A. P., & Avramidis, P. K. (2009). Corporate social responsibility: Attributions, loyalty, and the mediating role of trust. *Journal of the Academy of Marketing Science, 37*(2), 170–180. https://doi.org/10.1007/s11747-008-0117-x

Wang, U. (2015, Jan 5). Sustainable mining: an inherent contradiction in terms? *The Guardian.* Retrieved from https://www.theguardian.com/sustainable-business/2015/jan/05/sustainable-mining-business-poverty-environment-new-framework

Wang, Y., Xu, S., & Wang, Y. (2020). The consequences of employees' perceived corporate social responsibility: A meta-analysis. *Business Ethics: A European Review, 29*(3), 471–496. https://doi.org/10.1111/beer.12273

Wilming, M. (2017, March 28). Hostile takeovers are the dark side of capitalism. *Risk Magazine.* Retrieved from https://riskmagazine.nl/article/2016-09-08-hostile-takeovers-are-the-dark-side-of-capitalism

Wilson, N., Wright, M., & Scholes, L. (2013). Family business survival and the role of boards. *Entrepreneurship Theory and Practice, 37*, 1369–1389. https://doi.org/10.1111/etap.12071

Winterich, K. P., Mittal, V., & Aquino, K. (2013). When does recognition increase charitable behavior? Toward a moral identity-based model. *Journal of Marketing, 77*(3), 121–134. https://doi.org/10.1509/jm.11.0477

Wood, D. J. (1991). Corporate social performance revisited. *Academy of Management Review, 16*(4), 691–718. https://doi.org/10.5465/amr.1991.4279616

Xi, J., Kraus, S., Filser, M., & Kellermanns, F. W. (2015). Mapping the field of family business research: Past trends and future directions. *International Entrepreneurship and Management Journal, 11*, 113–132. https://doi.org/10.1007/s11365-013-0286-z

Yang, D., & Reeves, M. (2020, March 10). The quest for sustainable business model innovation. *BCG.* Retrieved from https://www.bcg.com/publications/2020/quest-sustainable-business-model-innovation

Ylönen, M., & Laine, M. (2015). For logistical reasons only? A case study of tax planning and corporate social responsibility reporting. *Critical Perspectives on Accounting, 33*, 5–23. https://doi.org/10.1016/j.cpa.2014.12.001

Yoon, Y., Gürhan-Canli, Z., & Schwarz, N. (2006). The effect of corporate social responsibility (CSR) activities on companies with bad reputations. *Journal of Consumer Psychology, 16*(4), 377–390. https://doi.org/10.1207/s15327663jcp1604_9

Zahra, S. A., Hayton, J. C., & Salvato, C. (2004). Entrepreneurship in family vs. non-family firms: A resource-based analysis of the effect of organizational culture. *Entrepreneurship Theory and Practice, 28*, 363–381. https://doi.org/10.1111/j.1540-6520.2004.00051.x

Zavyalova, A., Pfarrer, M. D., Reger, R. K., & Hubbard, T. D. (2016). Reputation as a benefit and a burden? How stakeholders' organizational identification affects the role of reputation following a negative event. *Academy of Management Journal, 59*(1), 253–276. https://doi.org/10.5465/amj.2013.0611

Zavyalova, A., Pfarrer, M. D., Reger, R. K., & Shapiro, D. L. (2012). Managing the message: The effects of firm actions and industry spillovers on media coverage following wrongdoing. *Academy of Management Journal, 55*(5), 1079–1101. https://doi.org/10.5465/amj.2010.0608

Zlatev, J. J. (2019). I may not agree with you, but I trust you: Caring about social issues signals integrity. *Psychological Science, 30*(6), 880–892. https://doi.org/10.1177/0956797619837948

Chapter 8
The Power of Ethical Climates

Abstract The **key issues** in this chapter address the shortcomings of common measures to prevent unethical work behavior. These specify how character traits, incentives, and opportunities influence individual decisions to commit fraud. However, this approach ignores group processes and work climate characteristics that can facilitate irresponsible decision making. Performance pressures as well as rules and sanctions that permeate many organizational practices can unintentionally invite cheating and unethical behavior. Our **analysis** highlights unintended consequences of common responses to organizational misbehavior. Relying on loyalty and care can seem to justify questionable practices. Punishing scapegoats can seem to cleanse the organization from moral problems. Morally excluding whistleblowers allows to ignore their concerns. All these strategies protect people in organizations against identity threats, but perpetuate moral hazards. **Solutions** require that people in organizations overcome shame and guilt in following through on moral intentions. An ethical work climate can be created by allowing people to learn from workplace errors, and taking pride in doing what is morally right. Making a difference is only

N. Ellemers, D. de Gilder, *The Moral Organization: Key Issues, Analyses, and Solutions*, https://doi.org/10.1007/978-3-030-84175-1_8

possible when people take moral responsibility for their actions, and prioritize moral improvement without being distracted by other goals.

8.1 Key Issues: Securing Compliance

The ethical concerns and moral dilemmas faced by individuals in the workplace highlight key issues organizations encounter in their everyday practices. Research reveals that people tend to have inflated views of their own morality, and are overly optimistic about how strongly this guides their decisions and task performance (Stellar & Willer, 2014; Tappin & McKay, 2017). For instance, in a global survey of organizational integrity almost all respondents indicate that it is important to be seen to act with integrity. Unfortunately, everyday realities are not in line with these moral ideals, as respondents also observe many breaches of ethical guidelines in their own workplace (see Box 8.1: Moral intentions versus moral behaviors). These problems only seem to have intensified in the wake of the financial difficulties caused by the COVID-19 pandemic (Gordon, 2020). This attests to the discrepancy between broadly shared *beliefs* that integrity is important and the difficulty organizations and their managers encounter when they try to *act* in line with these beliefs.

Box 8.1: Moral intentions Versus Moral Behaviors

The 'Global integrity report' published in 2020 by consultancy firm EY (forensics and integrity services) surveys a broad sample of almost 3000 individuals, representing the largest private and public organizations in a range of different countries across the world. Employees, as well as their managers, senior managers and board members were included (EY, 2020).

In the sample examined, 95% indicates it is important to demonstrate that they act with integrity. Respondents think this implies they should comply with rules, laws and regulations, and act responsibly towards colleagues, customers and suppliers. More than a third (38%) further considers behaving with integrity as implying that they 'do the right thing, even when nobody is watching'. Almost all the individuals surveyed (98%) think this benefits the organization, for instance because it improves the reputation of the organization, helps attract and retain employees and clients, reduces regulatory and legal risks, and can improve the organization's financial performance.

At the same time, almost 30% indicated being prepared to behave unethically to improve their own career or financial outcomes. About half further believe that managers in their organization would sacrifice integrity for short-term financial gain. Indeed, respondents in more senior positions indicated being more inclined than lower level employees to ignore unethical conduct in their team, mislead auditors or regulators, or to accept a bribe if this would benefit their career or income. Senior respondents are aware of such issues, and acknowledge that management does not always act with integrity. However, they also think they do address these issues and that integrity standards are improving.

The majority of employees do not see this. They fear negative consequences if they report wrongdoing, they do not believe management operates with integrity, and doubt that standards are improving. Further, about a third of employees thinks that people in senior positions and high performers are more likely to get away with unethical behavior – and a third of the managers agrees this is the case. Clearly, the moral intentions expressed do not translate into moral workplace behavior.

These observations illustrate the urgency and relevance of finding new ways of thinking about moral behavior in the workplace, and bring together a number of themes we have highlighted in this book. In this final chapter we address the different issues and concerns that influence everyday decisions people make in morally charged situations and dilemmas. We first identify the key issues that emerge from standard organizational practices. These reveal how quick fixes organizations use to prevent fraud, invite high performance, and address rule compliance, can have the unintentional effect of undermining moral choices and reducing ethical behavior. Then we review research which demonstrates how common responses to misbehavior in organizations may alleviate moral identity threats but also introduce new moral hazards. We finish by outlining how organizations can build an ethical work climate which helps employees and decision makers to do what they consider morally right, even when nobody is watching.

8.1.1 *Detecting and Preventing Fraud*

Provisions to detect and prevent breaches of integrity in organizations are modeled on early experiences with 'white-collar crime', focusing on embezzlement in particular (Sutherland (1949). This work formed the basis of defining the 'fraud triangle' (Cressey, 1973), which is embedded in accounting standards (such as ISA 240, IFAC, SAS 99, PCAOB-AU Section 316; Soltani, 2007). These standards focus on financial statement fraud, which is defined as "the intentional misrepresentation of financial statements, punishable criminally or civilly" (Shapiro, 2011, p. 61). This legal bookkeeping approach -and its underlying assumptions about deliberate human behavior- has been very influential in informing broader systems for monitoring rule compliance, and external regulation of the behavior of people in organizations.

The elements in the fraud triangle view regulatory compliance (vs. rule breaking) as resulting from the deliberate weighing of pros and cons in individual rational choices. The reasoning is that incentives (financial benefits or management pressure), opportunities (absence of or ineffective controls), and attitudes (character, personal values, rationalizations), together can invite individuals to disregard regulations applying to them (Cressey, 1973). Accordingly, this wide-spread model for prevention of unethical behavior relies on the three quick fixes we have come to know so well by now: it recommends to (a) monitor individual differences to identify bad apples, (b) adapt the cost/benefit ratio as a way to influence deliberate decisions (not) to comply with guidelines, and (c) increase regulation as key strategies to prevent rule breaking and fraud.

The fraud triangle has also been criticized for the limitations of these standard approaches (Buchholz, 2012), and the impracticality of its recommendations, for instance to reliably identify character traits (Ramamoorti, 2008), or to fully eliminate all fraud opportunities (Brody et al., 2011; Dorminey et al., 2010). Indeed, despite the continued popularity of this approach, scholars have argued that additional factors beyond these three should be taken into account (e.g. in the 'new fraud triangle', Kassem & Higson, 2012, or the 'fraud diamond', Wolfe & Hermanson, 2004), to address the broader organizational context and ethical climate in particular.

Similar conclusions emerge from post-hoc analyses of corporate scandals involving bookkeeping fraud which have come to the fore in the US (e.g., Enron, WorldCom, HealthSouth) and Europe (e.g., Parmalat, Royal Ahold, and Vivendi Universal). These point to the role of 'poor ethical climate' in these organizations at that time, in addition to external factors such as market developments, or political, legal, and regulatory laxness (Soltani, 2014). Other case studies of fraud also emphasize the influence of corporate culture on all three elements of the fraud triangle (Schuchter & Levi, 2016). Current insights on the prevention of fraud explicitly recommend including contextual factors, such as the regulatory framework, the control environment, as well as the ethical climate in the organization, and acknowledge limitations of the classic approach offered by the fraud triangle.

Considering which aspects of organizational climates may make people vulnerable to unethical decision making and fraud requires a closer examination of the implicit messages conveyed by standard procedures and organizational practices. These may have unintended consequences that undermine more deliberate and formal efforts to prevent misbehavior in organizations (see also Chap. 1 and Fig. 1.3). We will now examine common approaches to performance incentives as well as the implementation of regulation and sanctions from this perspective.

8.1.2 Performance Pressures

Competing against others is thought to benefit motivation and performance. This common notion informs many organizational performance systems (see also Chap. 4). The work results obtained by individuals within the same team are compared to decide who is promoted and who has to leave, and to assign or deny bonuses to individual team members. Champions of this approach often refer to sports competitions to support their reasoning. Indeed, in a sports context evidence suggests that performance can be enhanced through rivalry in competition. This was documented for instance in men's US Basketball, Football and Hockey National League competitions (Pike et al., 2018). Notably, this evidence pertains to *team-level* competition and outcomes. In most organizations, however, teams have to coordinate and pool their efforts, instead of competing with each other, and the dangers of ignoring this have been extensively noted in Chap. 6.

Pushing *individuals* to compete with each other is even more harmful, especially when they are supposed to perform on the same team. Studies reveal that - even in sports - interpersonal competition and performance rankings undermine cooperative thoughts, helping behaviors, and information sharing while inviting unethical behavior. These drawbacks of inducing interpersonal rivalry extend to other performance settings (Chambers & Baker, 2020; Kilduff et al., 2016; Landkammer et al., 2019). Individuals who are led to believe they perform well due to special individual qualities that are rare ('rainmakers') feel entitled to high rewards and are more likely to cheat as a way to obtain these rewards (Vincent & Kouchaki, 2016). Expressing pride at individual achievements can be seen to degrade others who are less successful and conveys lack of sensitivity for their feelings (Grandey et al., 2018). While these drawbacks of competitive systems are well-documented, their benefits for team and organizational performance are not so clear (see also Ellemers, 2021).

Competitive performance systems may well induce feelings of unfairness in co-workers who appear to invest equal effort but end up with unequal outcomes (Ambrose & Cropanzano, 2003; Moore & Gino, 2013; see also Chap. 4). The explicit use of comparisons between co-workers to decide on financial rewards or career opportunities invites envy among them (Schaubroeck & Lam, 2004; Tai et al., 2012; Vecchio, 2000, 2005). In turn, the experience of envy has been found to raise counterproductive work behaviors, for instance when employees start spreading rumors about their co-workers, or refuse to help them when needed (Cohen-Charash & Mueller, 2007; Duffy et al., 2012; Duffy et al., 2008). Accordingly, because of the importance of teamwork in almost any workplace, the focus on interpersonal competition as a standard model for performance motivation has been questioned (Heffernan, 2014). In fact, the widespread use of sports and gaming metaphors in the workplace has been identified as a source of ethical vulnerability because it portrays work assignments as a competition between rivals where any means are allowed to defeat the other competitors, and winning is the only viable option (Hamington, 2009).

Competition and high achievement goals often result in time pressure leading to physical exhaustion and lack of sleep, which in turn induce cognitive depletion and undermine the ability to perform well. For instance, a study examining factors that contribute to performance failures identified excessive workload as an important cause of medication errors among healthcare workers (Brady et al., 2009). Importantly, cognitive depletion and fatigue are also known factors to reduce the monitoring and self-regulation of moral decisions, and have been found to facilitate cheating and other forms of undesirable behavior (Barnes et al., 2011; Gino et al., 2011). The anxiety and threat associated with high performance targets have been found to induce unethical behavior, such as cheating for personal gain. At the same time, the emotional distress experienced reduces the individual memory of such behaviors (Kouchaki & Desai, 2015; Kouchaki & Gino, 2016). Further, assigning monetary primes to performance achievement makes people view their work more as a business transaction. This is another source of moral ignorance which contributes to breaches of integrity (Barsky, 2008; Kouchaki et al., 2013). Together, all these documented forces can initiate a downward spiral of self-dehumanization and unethical behavior under high performance pressure (Kouchaki et al., 2018; see also Sun & Goodwin, 2019).

These negative effects have been documented across different achievement contexts, such as the workplace. Some famous examples clearly reveal how competitive performance pressures can invite fraud and unethical behavior. For instance, sales employees at American bank Wells Fargo were found to open bank accounts and assign credit cards without these services having been requested or approved by customers. Post-hoc analyses revealed this was prompted by extreme performance pressures, threatening the employment of those who could not meet near-to-impossible sales targets (see also Box 4.3; Reckard, 2013). In other sectors too, use of performance metrics and perverse incentives are seen to invite unethical behavior. For instance the up-or-out system in academia with hypercompetition for research funding, getting published in high impact scientific journals, and jobs is seen as a threat to scientific integrity (Edwards & Roy, 2017; Ellemers, 2021; see Box 8.2: Competition in science;).

Box 8.2: Competition in Science

In scientific research, competition between individual researchers, research groups and institutions is generally seen as a driver of academic excellence. Limited time and resources for research drive individual scholars to vie with each other for academic jobs, and for grants to do research. Research leaders and university administrators envy each other for rare academic honors bestowed upon themselves or their labs. The resulting academic culture is often characterized by referring to sports metaphors, reminding researchers of the importance of 'getting there first, and urging them to do 'everything to win'.

However, this practice is not without cost. For instance, a large scale survey revealed that researchers experience the focus on competition as undermining cross-disciplinary collaboration, stifling creativity and fostering bullying and harassment in the workplace (Wellcome, 2020). Further, rewarding researchers for carving out and protecting their own territory, leads to the dispersion of knowledge instead of the accumulation of insights (Ellemers, 2013). Other negative side effects that have been documented include lack of open communication about important insights and violations of research integrity, ranging from data fabrication to the frustration of peer review (Martinson et al., 2005). No wonder the annual PhD survey conducted by *Nature* reveals increasing levels of anxiety and depression among young scholars (Woolston, 2019).

National systems aiming to reward research funding on the basis of scientific excellence (such as the UK Research Excellence Framework - REF) mainly lead researchers and institutions to prioritize activities that will earn them high ratings. Unfortunately, some of these activities are quite peripheral to the actual quality of the research that is carried out (Sivertsen, 2017). Accordingly, a comparative analysis could not establish an advantage in terms of scientific output for more competitive compared to less competitive systems for the allocation of research funds (Sandström & Van den Besselaar, 2018).

Large scale attempts to reform academic practices, such as the Open Science Framework (https://osf.io/) or the Declaration On Research Assessment (https://sfdora.org/) are also spoiled by the dominance of competitive incentives and work climates in academia. Calls for more openness and transparency, integrity and robustness, and societal impact and relevance are valid and timely. However, these new developments have caused many researchers to seek ways to outperform others on these new criteria, instead of embracing different ways of conducting science (Wilson et al., 2020).

Unfortunately, instead of fostering excellence the competitive climate in science drives out those who do not want to compete, undermines transparency and mutual trust, and frustrates cross-disciplinary collaboration. It harms the well-being and motivation of individual researchers, accumulation of insights within and across research groups, and progress in science. Far from prompting the scientific advances hoped for, these competitive exchanges stand in the way of cooperative knowledge sharing that characterizes intellectual progress (Ellemers, 2021).

The emphasis on competitive results is found to invite cheating because it focuses people on the realization of specific outcomes, irrespective of how these were obtained (Van Yperen et al., 2011). Experimental studies consistently show that fueling interpersonal rivalry in competition induces unethical behavior, as it leads people to falsely inflate their performance, or to deceive their opponent for self-gain (see also Chap. 4). External and situational pressures to compete trigger such tendencies, overruling personal moral guidelines (Kilduff & Galinsky, 2017). Studies in organizations accordingly show that unethical behavior such as lying, stealing, cheating, falsifying reports, harmful behavior towards customers, misreporting outcomes, acceptance of bribes, and other forms of corruption and fraud, are more likely to occur when employees are pushed to achieve a specific outcome (Kaptein, 2011b; Mayer et al., 2010; Peterson, 2002; Simha & Cullen, 2012).

The common practice of specifying SMART performance goals (that are Specific, Measurable, Attainable, Realistic and Time-specific) would seem to guard against such problems. Unfortunately, however, in practice people are expected to meet performance targets that are specific and measurable and should be realized within a particular time frame, such as a monthly sales volume, or customer satisfaction score. However, whether this actually is attainable or realistic – and whether the achievement of such goals even can be attributed to employee efforts rather than external circumstances - is not always taken into consideration. Accordingly, examinations in the public as well as the private sector revealed that incentivizing employees to achieve specific performance incentives made them more vulnerable to corruption, regardless of interpersonal differences in the moral norms they endorsed (Gorsira et al., 2018; Pagliaro et al., 2018). In general, external pressures to reach specific outcomes prompt people to disregard moral concerns (see also Chap. 6). For instance, managers were found to violate financial reporting standards when this would allow them to meet the earnings target that would yield their performance bonus (Carpenter & Reimers, 2005). Likewise, prompting leaders to complete performance goals set by the organization (instead of reminding them to represent ethical standards) made them more likely to engage in morally questionable decision making. Regardless of whether the goal of the organization was to make a profit (e.g., by selling cosmetics) or to do good (e.g., by helping poor families), being reminded of organizational performance goals made research participants more inclined to do whatever they could to achieve these goals, including the allocation of resources that were not meant to be used in this way (Hoyt et al., 2013; see also Chap. 4).

8.1.3 Rules and Sanctions

The implementation of additional rules and more severe sanctions captures a common response to such problems. These dominant legal and business tools are recommended by traditional approaches to organizational misbehavior and fraud. However, research shows that these are not always effective as a way to steer human behavior in organizations (Fehr & Rockenbach, 2003; Feldman, 2018; FSB, 2018; Tenbrunsel & Messick, 1999).

In fact, such attempts at behavioral control can have counterproductive effects, depending on how they are implemented (Weibel et al., 2016). When people are threatened with sanctions to deter them from undesired behaviors – even before they have given cause to doubt their integrity - they feel distrusted. It undermines their willingness to follow these rules and was actually found to reduce behavioral compliance, for instance causing workers to misreport their productivity, and citizens to show less tax compliance (Mooijman et al., 2017). Further, when external factors – such as the performance pressures discussed above – make cheating seem inevitable, people are likely to consider punishment as unjust. Indeed, this can be part of a negative spiral where sanctions are mainly used to flag differences in power and status, and only foster misconduct that invites more distrust and further punishment (Mooijman & Graham, 2018). This points to a more gradual process of ethical dissolution and ethical disengagement rather than deliberate calculations made to avoid sanctions (Jackson et al., 2013; see also Chap. 1).

Accordingly, in psychology enforced compliance is seen as the weakest form of social influence (Cialdini & Goldstein, 2004). It depends on continuous monitoring and ability to reward and sanction. In line with the fraud triangle approach, it assumes that rule transgressions are the result of individual level rational choices:

the estimated chances of getting caught and the severity of sanctions. Decades of theory development and research in psychology (e.g., Bagozzi & Lee, 2002; Kelman, 1974; McCauley, 1989) have revealed the effectiveness of this approach to control people's behavior is limited. The impact of efforts to influence individual behaviors is much larger when people understand the broader implications of their actions, and why certain guidelines are so important ('conversion'). And in order for them to act in line with important guidelines, even when nobody is watching, they have to go even further and *internalize* these rules – for instance because they have come to see them as identity-defining behavioral norms (Turner, 1991; Spears, 2021).

Thus, relying on externally imposed rules and sanctions enforces 'mere compliance', where people only do what is needed to avoid problems. This limits the impact of regulatory efforts, as it is impossible to specify all possible transgressions or to anticipate all regulatory loopholes (see also Chap. 6). Accordingly, organizational corruption has been found to relate to social norms and identity mechanisms, that are not captured in this way (Den Nieuwenboer & Kaptein, 2008a). Further, once people subscribe to formal guidelines or ethics codes, it can make them blind to the possibility that problems still emerge. The awareness that such guidelines exist can even become a source of hazard due to moral licensing (Neesham & Gu, 2015; Zhong et al., 2009). This was found to be the case in a study where employees of companies that had an ethics code were found to rate top management and supervisors, as well as their peers, subordinates and themselves as more ethical than employees in companies without such a code. At the same time, there was no clear evidence that they had cause for such beliefs. Ironically, having an ethics code in place led employees to *assume* that satisfactory solutions were found for ethical problems – even when they could not recall the content of the code that would allow them to actually evaluate this (Adams et al., 2001). In this way, outsourcing moral responsibilities to compliance monitors and external regulators can prevent people from carefully considering the broader implications of their actions (see also Chap. 1).

8.2 Analysis: Dealing with Misbehavior

Addressing the 'dark side' of behavior in organizations, then, requires a systemic approach (Conroy et al., 2017). Whether or not members of the organization engage in morally questionable behavior does not just reflect individual deviance from common moral standards (Vaughan, 1999). Instead, moral choices and priorities in the workplace also echo the apparent value everyday practices assign to different types of incentives, concerns, stakeholders and outcomes. These situational forces can cause even upstanding members of the community to become involved in corruption scandals, as they are incrementally socialized into justifying and neutralizing such behavior (Anand et al., 2004). For instance, a study of financial reports revealed that the occurrence of fraudulent statements could not be fully explained from personality features or *a priori* moral reasoning of responsible CFO's. The decision to commit fraud in financial statements also was caused by prompts from other managers - encouraging them to make the company look better in the eyes of customers and investors, or to make sure they secured a management bonus. Recommendations other managers had made, for instance to adapt income statements or to refrain from disclosing liabilities, impacted the perceived acceptability of such behavior (Uddin & Gillett, 2002).

Similar effects have been observed across a range of contexts and populations, among business people as well as public servants. Across the board, these studies document the impact of social pressures that increase vulnerability to corruption in the shape of, for instance, the acceptance of money, goods or services for preferential treatment (Pagliaro et al., 2018). The persistence of corruption and other forms of misbehavior is facilitated by a range of common strategies people use to salvage their moral identity, such as the use of euphemistic language. For instance organizational communications referred to 'a relationship' in cases of sexual abuse, or indicated clear cases of bullying as 'teasing' (Lucas & Fyke, 2014; Pornari & Wood, 2010). Such language use allows people in organizations to ignore the moral implications of their actions and neglect responsibility for harmful outcomes to the victims. They justify their morally questionable behavior by referring to higher loyalties, or highlight symbolic actions attesting to their good intentions (Bandura et al., 1996; see also Chap. 2).

Group norms that offer such narratives in the workplace form an easily accessible set of guidelines which allows individuals to disconnect common work behaviors from broader moral standards (Moore, 2015). Such specific moral norms also explain why practices that are seen as morally good in some organizations (e.g., high performance merits greater reward), can be seen as morally problematic by people in other organizations (e.g., where equal effort deserves equal pay, see also Ellemers & Van der Toorn, 2015). A study where 13 former financial executives were interviewed about their role in major cases of accounting fraud documented how people can come to embrace such specific moral norms. These individuals explained how workplace practices slowly drew them step by step onto a path that did not reflect their individual motivation (Suh et al., 2018). A cynical view may be to dismiss these narratives as a form of self-justification aimed at deflecting personal blame after the fact. Nevertheless, these retrospective accounts match converging evidence from other studies generally showing that contextual factors and social consensus gradually come to define what is seen as ethically problematic in business organizations - and what is not (Ashforth & Anand, 2003; Butterfield et al., 2000).

Due to the paradox of morality, people tend to deal with such moral conflicts and tensions by actively managing their social identities: they justify their actions and construe narratives that connect their preferred self-views to specific aspects of the organizational context. Depending on which decision they consider and who is watching, they actively choose which of multiple alternative identities to emphasize (Ashforth & Johnson, 2001). For instance, high service standards can prompt employees do everything in their power to accommodate clients. They may feel this is the moral thing to do even when it violates company regulations or legal rules. The work-related identities people have do not only direct the way they feel, think, and behave at work. People also actively seek and construct identities which offer a way to secure validation and approval from significant others for their actions in order to confirm their preferred self-views of being morally good citizens (Ashforth & Schinoff, 2016). Thus, when talking about their work achievements, employees who go beyond their mandate to help clients may decide to highlight their identity as caring professionals as moral justification - rather than considering whether their actions are in line with organizational rules or broader ethical concerns.

In this section we review research which illustrates that even well-meaning attempts to prevent and address misbehavior of individuals in organizations are unlikely to be effective - as long as the hidden influence of social norms and practices that act as a counterforce is not taken into account (see also Fig. 1.3). Here we examine three mechanisms that are not always obvious. Again, we point to the motivation of organizations to do what is moral and of people within organizations to think of themselves as moral persons. The research we review below clarifies that different strategies that may help people in organizations to manage threats to their moral identity, actually prevent them from considering more profound ways in which moral behavior in and of the organization might be improved. We address three moral hazards introduced in this way. First, we highlight that reliance on loyalty and care as sources of moral guidance may be misplaced when it prevents organizations from confronting morally questionable behavior. Second, we explain why blaming scapegoats as a form of moral cleansing can impede the ability of the organization to recognize broader issues that create a corrupting climate. Third, we elucidate that questioning the motives and loyalty of whistle blowers might help salvage the moral reputation of the organization, but also amounts to moral exclusion of those whose observations might guide the organization towards moral improvement.

8.2.1 Loyalty and Care as Moral Justifications

Individual difference approaches consider unethical behavior as stemming from the neglect of harm done to others, due shortcomings in people's ability to show empathy and altruism (see also Ellemers, 2017). According to this reasoning, it should be possible to prevent such problems by selecting and rewarding individuals who will display loyalty and care for others in the workplace. However, research shows this is a pitfall that can introduce new moral concerns. For instance, the desire to care for one's co-workers and their important outcomes, can prompt individuals to neglect the needs of key stakeholders (e.g., customers), or even to break important rules in displaying their loyalty. For instance, one study found clear evidence that extending care for others may introduce a new source of moral concern. Here, women were more inclined to be untruthful when trying to help others than when pursuing selfish goals (while men were equally deceptive in both cases; Kouchaki & Kray, 2018). Another study further revealed that in the course of time, the development of group cohesion that increased mutual loyalty and care shifted individual priorities away from formal rules and procedures (Schminke & Wells, 1999). Apparently, selecting individuals on the basis of their ability to empathize or care for others does not preclude such moral issues.

The broader implications such behaviors can have emerge from a meta-analytical review of studies conducted among a broad range of organizations located in different parts of the world Simha & Cullen, 2012). Here, some companies were characterized by an emphasis on caring for one's co-workers and clients, instead of emphasizing high performance targets. Despite the undoubtedly good intentions of the individuals involved, the study identified this as a moral hazard. The desire to extend care by prioritizing the interests and desires of clients and co-workers was associated with the occurrence of misbehavior. That is, it prompted workers to break rules in their efforts to cover up problems of co-workers or to accommodate customer preferences that were not allowed (Simha & Cullen, 2012; see Box 8.3: Instrumental and caring climates). Over time, such breaches can even result in a cycle of mutual patronage where the recipients of such favors are expected to disregard formal guidelines to express their gratitude (Wakeman & Moore, 2018).

Box 8.3: Instrumental and caring Work Climates

Researchers have attempted to specify and measure which climate aspects reinforce the willingness to act in ways that are considered morally responsible, and discourage unethical behavior and rule breaking (Kaptein, 2008; Peterson, 2002). The most well-known instrument to assess this is the Ethical Climate Questionnaire (ECQ) (Cullen et al., 1993, see also Victor & Cullen, 1988).

Different versions of this questionnaire (ranging from 36 to 6 items), and different labels of subscales and climate-types are used (Simha & Cullen, 2012). These different aspects are often reduced to three climate prototypes:

(a) An *instrumental* climate, where the primary focus is on self-interest and efficiency in achieving company profit and material outcomes,
(b) A *caring* climate, where the primary focus is on maintaining good relations with others such as co-workers or clients,
(c) A *rules* climate, where the focus is on important principles, such as personal ethics, company rules, and laws and codes.

Over the years, hundreds of studies have been conducted with (different versions of) this climate measure. A range of professional samples and organizations in many different countries have participated. For instance health care workers, police officers, accountants, manufacturing, warehouse and sales employees, middle-managers and executives (for more details see Martin & Cullen, 2006; Simha & Cullen, 2012).

Across the board, in a workplace with an instrumental climate more dysfunctional behavior is observed, such as lying stealing, falsifying reports, misreporting outcomes, acceptance of gifts and favors as bribes, physical injuries and bullying. At the same time, employees working in such a climate report lower commitment, satisfaction and well-being. A strong emphasis on rules, regulations and legal procedures only compensates for this to some extent, as it is associated with more adherence to safety standards and more willingness to signal the occurrence of rule transgressions when these occur (Martin & Cullen, 2006; Simha & Cullen, 2012; see also Ellemers, 2017).

A caring climate can elicit positive as well as negative effects, depending on other climate aspects. Caring for good relations with customers and colleagues can buffer against some of the negative effects of instrumental climates. However, a caring climate can also induce morally questionable behavior, in particular when maintaining good relations with customers and co-workers is seen as more important than rule adherence Under these conditions a caring climate caused co-workers to cover problems for each other, or prompted employees to help customers in ways that were not allowed (Martin & Cullen, 2006; Simha & Cullen, 2012).

In work teams, interpersonal closeness and friendship ties can induce ingroup favoring biases. Thus, prosocial motives can make individuals less critical of their colleagues, and more likely to cover for or forgive each other's moral lapses (Knoll & Van Dick, 2013; Kouchaki et al., 2015; Kouchaki et al., 2019). This has been found to make questionable practices seem more morally acceptable in highly cohesive work teams (Barnett & Vaicys, 2000). It becomes increasingly difficult to challenge the moral implications or correctness of such norms, even when there are valid reasons for doing so (e.g., when team expenses are discouraged by company policy). Social disapproval and embarrassment can cause people to reconsider their initial moral judgment (Warren & Smith-Crowe, 2008).

The point here is that efforts to enhance loyalty and care – that are beneficial in many ways - do not necessarily guard against moral failures. In fact high team and organizational cohesion can become a risk factor in its own right when this precludes critical consideration of shared practices. Overcommitting to organizational realities can make people resilient against moral critique from outsiders as well as critical ingroup members (see the section below on whistle blowers and Chap. 4). Failing to confront misbehavior or corruption out of misplaced loyalty implicitly communicates the norm that these practices are allowed. Over time, repeated observations of misbehavior and corruption being covered with the cloak of empathy increase the risk that organizational bystanders become involved as future perpetrators (Zyglidopoulos & Fleming, 2008).

Rather than revealing the pitfalls in addition to the benefits of interpersonal loyalty and care, this work points to the power of social identities and group norms in inviting, maintaining and even justifying morally questionable behavior in organizations (Greve et al., 2010). Loyalty to group norms can prompt individuals to take irresponsible risks (Saini & Martin, 2009) while care for team members can make questionable practices seem morally acceptable (Barnett & Vaicys, 2000). An analysis of internal email traffic at Boeing for instance revealed "group bonding techniques that crowd out any individual sense of shame" (Taylor, 2020). Loyalty to group norms can even bring people to act in ways that jeopardize their individual interests and personal well-being. For instance studies reveal that the engagement in health-damaging behaviors such as overconsumption of alcohol by students (Zhou & Heim, 2016) or the use of performance enhancing drug in sports (Strelan & Boeckmann, 2006) can be attributed to social pressures from peers and role models. Analyses such as these show that interpersonal care, prosocial behavior and loyalty to organizational goals do not preclude the involvement in morally questionable actions, and may even contribute to it by offering a form of moral justification.

Indeed, the term 'prosocial unethical work behavior' is used to indicate a broader tendency in employees to disregard formal guidelines as they attempt to 'help' the organization. Examples include misrepresentations of the truth to make the organization look good, exaggerating positive features of products to mislead clients, or withholding refunds to which customers are entitled. The occurrence of such behaviors has been examined in a range of employees working in different organizational and cultural contexts. A study in the US revealed that employees who identified strongly with the organization were more inclined to 'help' in this way, as they thought this was what a good member of the organization was expected to do (Umphress et al., 2010). Similar behaviors were observed in a study of Chinese firms, where employees ignored the moral implications of unethical decisions when they thought this would benefit the organization (Zhang et al., 2020).

These results clearly illustrate that inducing loyalty and care will not prevent the occurrence of morally questionable behavior in the workplace. When shared justifications of morally questionable practices make individuals less attentive of personal moral standards or formal guidelines it may even become an additional source of moral vulnerability.

8.2.2 *Scapegoating for Moral Cleansing*

The public exposure of incidents of fraud or unethical behavior become public is usually followed by the knee-jerk reflex of managers and regulators to identify and remove the "bad apples" – exemplifying the individual difference approach. It is a recommendation often supported by legal counsel, as it helps to pinpoint and contain the responsibility for things that went wrong to one individual, or a few people at most. Indeed public calls that "heads must roll", seem to be dealt with most effectively by quickly finding, punishing and getting rid of a plausible scapegoat. This apparently is the preferred way to communicate the faithful intentions of the organization to do what is morally right. It clearly demonstrates the willingness to take action, while at the same time absolving the rest of the organization from guilt. This was precisely how such actions were presented to the financial regulator by top executives of 'too big to fail' banks in Europe (Scholten & Ellemers, 2016). Unfortunately, this common response also offers a convenient scapegoating strategy, allowing the organization to engage in moral cleansing while ignoring the possible presence of broader underlying problems.

This practice has been documented extensively in the banking industry, in the aftermath of the financial crisis of 2008 (Scholten & Ellemers, 2016). Root cause analyses made after incidents of financial fraud were discovered tend to consist of factual narratives of 'who did what', without asking *why* they did it, or what led up to it. In fact, an annual report examining dozens of incidents within the same company even stated explicitly that these all represent isolated cases, and should not be seen as revealing broader patterns (Scholten, 2018). Even if this approach might be beneficial to assign (and deflect) legal responsibility, it also prevents more systematic or recurring issues from coming to the fore.

The objective of limiting legal accountability in this way prevents organizational learning and development. Nor is it in line with insights from research in organizational psychology, which clearly points to common work practices which can turn organizations or work teams into 'corrupting barrels' where problems emerge time after time (Kish-Gephart et al., 2010a). Similar conclusions emerged from a study examining cases of fraud in other industries, for instance at BP, Volkswagen and Wells Fargo. Here, researchers concluded that a 'toxic climate' ensues when organizational norms implicitly condone rule breaking, obstruct compliance, or advocate practices that contrast the value of rules (Van Rooij & Fine, 2018). Observations such as these have been made in different types of contexts, including commercial businesses, not-for-profit, as well as government organizations. A study comparing possible risk factors revealed that misconduct could be more reliably predicted from organizational pressure to compromise ethical standards than from individual characteristics or moral reasoning. The words and observed actions of others in the organization influenced moral choices, and had an effect regardless of stated codes of conduct and other formal compliance mechanisms (Andreoli & Lefkowitz, 2009). Another study showed that professional socialization (rather than individual moral reasoning) explained the moral choices made by tax professionals (Doyle et al., 2013).

Seemingly 'innocent' and common procedures may invite and sustain misbehavior in this way and define the moral climate (Van Steenbergen & Ellemers, 2021). These include the performance pressures and outcome inequalities discussed earlier in this chapter, as well as the way the organization commonly responds to errors made, which we will highlight later on (See Fig. 8.1: A corrupting barrels perspective). The overall impact of such organizational factors is well documented in the case of Kweku Adoboli, an investment trader who served a prison sentence for bookkeeping fraud, already mentioned in Chap. 2. Although he was publicly portrayed as "a rotten apple in an otherwise clean industry", his colleagues said that everyone knew that he simply did what was needed to earn money for the bank. In

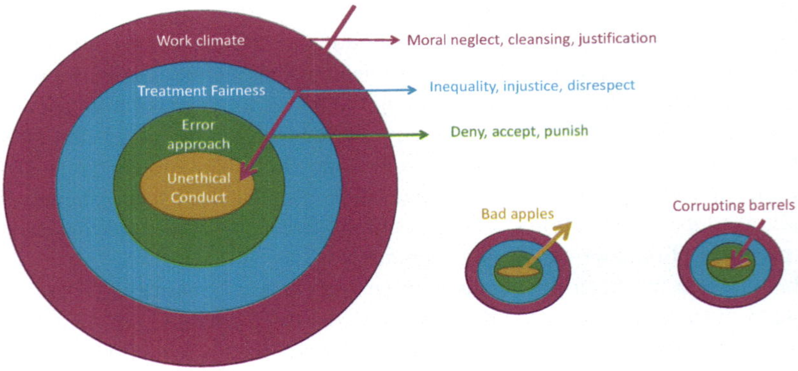

Fig. 8.1 A corrupting barrels perspective. Figure illustrates that unethical conduct can ensue from the way performance errors are handled, from unfair treatment, and from a work climate characterized by moral neglect, moral cleansing, or moral justification. 'Bad apples' will continue to emerge as long as the organizational factors that create corrupting barrels remain in place. (Adapted from: Scholten and Ellemers (2016))

fact, for years he had received large bonuses for doing exactly this (Fortado, 2015). Rewarding individuals for going against formal guidelines, and scapegoating them when things go wrong, communicates a desire for moral cleansing, instead of a commitment to learn and improve. This is why blaming individuals for alleged character flaws without addressing the broader systemic issues is bound to be ineffective (Scholten & Ellemers, 2016; Van Steenbergen & Ellemers, 2021). In fact, twenty years after completing his jail sentence for concealing illegal trades that brought down Barings Bank in 1995, Nick Leeson, 'the most notorious rogue in banking' has a lucrative business giving talks about the continuation of shady practices to financial professionals across the world (Carroll, 2019).

8.2.3 Moral Exclusion of Whistleblowers

It will not come as a surprise that organizations tend to respond defensively to public outrage and regulatory pressures when incidents come to the fore. The general public and regulators tend to be seen as outsiders. They can be derogated as being unlikely to fully understand all the difficulties encountered by those inside the organization. Further, outsiders are often accused of being motivated by the desire to damage the reputation of the organization, instead of helping it to improve. Because insiders are more aware of strategic concerns and broader organizational goals, it might be more effective when they highlight ethical issues (Hornsey & Imani, 2004). After all, insiders can be expected to understand how current routines can be adapted to prevent further problems (Briscoe & Gupta, 2016). Yet even then, ambiguity about their motives and defensive responses may remain (Van Dyne et al., 2003).

People realize that their moral critique is unlikely to be welcomed, and that their motives might be questioned. They are generally reluctant to express ethical concerns for fear of jeopardizing their position in the group. The willingness of ingroup members to call into question the appropriateness of common group behaviors is enhanced when they feel more securely included in the group and the group is more important to them (Ellemers & Jetten, 2013; Masson & Fritsche, 2019). Thus on the one hand, noting that common modes of conduct may be harmful or violate important guidelines is a source of identity threat that causes psychological discomfort - especially for those who strongly identify with the organization (Dahling & Gutworth, 2017). On the other hand, these are the individuals who are most likely to express disapproval of such practices - despite the social costs of doing so (Henik, 2008; Packer & Chasteen, 2010).

Again, this shows there is no one-to-one relation between the loyalty experienced by organizational members, the behavior they display, and the implications this has for the moral behavior of the organization: it all depends on the moral climate and behavioral norms in the organization. In the prior section we highlighted that high levels of loyalty may be 'bad' when this leads organizational members to comply with morally questionable organizational norms and cover up organizational misbehavior. Here we note that concern for the team and loyalty to the organization can be 'good' and benefit moral behavior, when it prompts people to speak up and voice their dissent with morally questionable practices – instead of looking away or disengaging the self from the organization (Packer, 2008). Indeed, such loyal and constructive deviance generally stems from the desire for moral improvement, rather than aiming to discredit the group (Ellemers & Jetten, 2013; Masson & Fritsche, 2019). A survey of over 5000 members of the US adult working population employed across different industries, offers support for these conclusions. Here respondents indicated that they would speak up about any wrongdoing in the company to their management, in the hope that local or senior management would try to resolve the problem (Kaptein, 2011a).

Unfortunately, sincere intentions to help the organization improve in this way are rarely recognized. As we have seen in Chap. 6, organizational members who call out risks and identify possible failures tend to be seen as troublemakers who frustrate the achievement of organizational goals. As a result, members of the organization who voice concern about the appropriateness of common organizational practices are often ignored, dismissed, or discredited. They stand accused of self-promotion and wanting to damage the organization. An examination of the personal consequences experienced by those who identify fraud, breaches of procedure, or other forms of misbehavior, reveals that most suffer severe negative consequences from their actions. These include negative performance evaluations, closer monitoring by supervisors, critique and avoidance from co-workers, dismissal or mandatory retirement, and being prevented from getting another job in their field through blacklisting (Miceli & Near, 1989; Near & Miceli, 2008, 2016a; Wolfe et al., 2014). The personal and professional costs of going down this path are extreme. Whistleblowers have been known to lose their livelihood, friends, spouses, and homes, despite being proven right - sometimes only many years later.

These observations resonate with research findings reviewed before (see Chap. 1) which show that people generally resent and downgrade others who point out transgressions of moral guidelines. Their courage to call out and criticize organizational practices is seen to expose a lack of moral vigilance in others (Cramwinckel et al., 2013; Monin et al., 2008). In general, being reminded of one's moral failures is painful. It implies an identity threat that raises defensive responses (Täuber & Van Zomeren, 2012). Avoiding or rejecting 'moral do-gooders' offers an easier way to cope with critique than using it as input for self-improvement (Jordan & Monin, 2008; Monin, 2007). Responding to uncertainty about the group's moral behavior by denigrating ingroup members who dare to call out problems or criticize group norms might seem a viable strategy to protect the group's moral identity. However, morally excluding such individuals as 'black sheep' does not do justice to their sincere attempts to lead the way towards moral improvement (Eidelman & Biernat, 2003; Marques et al., 2001; Pinto et al., 2010; Rullo et al., 2019).

In the process of legally containing and averting responsibility for misbehavior in the workplace, those who express concern about behavioral transgressions tend to be cautioned to keep silent as a show of loyalty (Dungan et al., 2015; Dungan et al., 2019). Knowing that those who voice concerns tend to be the most committed members of the organization clarifies the degree of psychological pressure this implies. Silencing whistleblowers in this way may even be part of a top-down organizational strategy (Morrison & Milliken, 2000). Indeed, valid complaints about workplace bullying and sexual harassment tend to have more severe consequences for complainants than for perpetrators. In fact, retaliating against whistleblowers is a documented cause of further workplace bullying (Bjørkelo & Matthiesen, 2011). Even when codes of conduct are clearly violated, a common response is to press victims and bystanders into signing Non-Disclosure Agreements (NDAs), allowing misbehavior to continue. The wide-spread practice of silencing victims and witnesses of misbehavior makes it more difficult for them to discover they are not alone and seek support from each other (see also Chap. 5). Further, giving priority to the protection of perpetrators as a source of organizational liability is cited as an important reason for the failure of programs initiated to curb sexual harassment (Dobbin & Kalev, 2019; Tenbrunsel et al., 2019).

When calls for action are ignored in this way, the concerns raised are not resolved (Pinder & Harlos, 2001). This leaves complainants with no other option than to escalate their concerns to the next level every time they are not heard. The decision to blow the whistle by informing external regulators or going to the media to expose organizational misbehavior is usually a strategy of last resort, after multiple attempts to instigate behavioral improvement have fallen on deaf ears (Anvari et al., 2019). The desperate decision to 'wash dirty laundry in public' is often mistakenly interpreted as a lack of care for the reputation of the organization. Adding insult to injury, whistleblowers tend to be morally excluded because many organizations fail to see them as loyal members of the organization and refuse to address their concerns. This not only harms whistleblowers in many ways, but also damages organizations.

In sum, the identity management strategies people commonly use stand in the way of moral improvement in organizations. Representatives of the organization can refer to loyalty to their co-workers or care for the organization to justify morally questionable decisions. They can blame and remove specific individuals, as a scapegoating strategy for moral cleansing. And they can exclude whistleblowers from their moral concerns by questioning their motives. All these strategies allow people in organizations to think more positively about what has happened in the past, but do not help them improve their moral behavior in the future. In the next section we will indicate what might be done to transform the ethical climate in the organization, as a strategy towards moral improvement.

8.3 Solutions: The Power of Ethical Climates

Some argue that increasing trends towards cheating and other violations of common moral standards are a sign of contemporary economic pressures and cultural shifts, encouraging people to do 'anything' to get ahead – regardless of their moral beliefs and convictions (Callahan, 2004; Jackson et al., 2019). Notwithstanding such broader societal developments, meta-analytical findings summarizing the results of many studies indicate that unethical decisions in the workplace are influenced by organizational level factors (Kish-Gephart et al., 2010a). Here we consider the organizational culture and work climate – offering shared notions of how 'things are done around here' - as key determinants of which behaviors are considered morally (un)acceptable (Deal & Kennedy, 1982; Schein, 1996).

As argued throughout this book, implicit assumptions and unwritten rules are more likely to determine day-to-day decision making and common work practices than formal directives or assigned goals (see also Schein, 1996). In words often ascribed to management guru Peter Drucker: "*culture eats strategy for breakfast*" (although whether and when he actually said this is disputed, see "Culture Eats Strategy for Breakfast,", 2017). Our social identity analysis further clarifies how such 'unwritten rules' of what 'everybody here does' may come to signify what seems unique and special for a work team or organization and its members – as a *descriptive* norm. Over time, this may evolve into a more morally charged guideline prescribing 'the right thing to do' - an *injunctive* norm. Such evolved notions of morally appropriate behavior indicate how people should behave in order to be included as a loyal team member or to be seen as a true representative of the organization (Eriksson et al., 2015). To the extent that informal narratives specify how to work in practice with official procedures, they communicate the actual priority of specific rules and regulations. This is how implicit guidelines come to define the ethical climate on the work floor (see also Schneider et al., 2013).

These social normative processes can cause employees to ignore cumbersome reporting guidelines or safety procedures, because 'everyone says', this is how a real professional should behave (Ellemers, 2017; Haslam & Reicher, 2012). Accordingly, research has revealed social networks and social contagion as key sources of unethical behavior (Brass et al., 1998; Slingerland, 2018). This happened for instance when business students saw that other students were cheating, or received help they were not supposed to receive. Observing such models made students see this as the behavior which characterized their discipline. Emulating this behavior seemed the best way to express their identity and self-involvement with others in their profession (O'Fallon & Butterfield, 2012). Indeed, when unethical behavior seems normative for organizational members (in the Mafia and other criminal organizations, see also Box 4.1), identification with the organization can be sufficient reason to endorse and support misconduct (Homan et al., in press).

The importance of organizational cultures and work climates in defining how professionals should behave explains how morally questionable behaviors can become normalized in the organization (Ashforth & Anand, 2003). It also implies that efforts to prevent corruption, fraud and misbehavior should take into account the implicit influence of institutional logic, allocation of resources, and support from social actors (Misangyi et al., 2008). Indeed, oversight bodies increasingly recognize the added value of including insights into the impact of organizational cultures and climates when monitoring and guarding work behavior. In the financial sector, regulators have started to incorporate these elements in their supervisory efforts (see also Box 8.4 Regulating behavior and culture). In the context of these developments, knowledge from the behavioral sciences is used to specify the characteristics of an ethical organizational climate, and monitor whether these are present (Van Steenbergen et al., 2019a). In the final sections of this book, we note the key issues that should benefit organizations which aim to build such a climate. In addition to legal questions (is this allowed?), and economic questions (what do we gain?) this requires that people in organizations also engage with moral questions (what does this make us?) when making strategic decisions and developing organizational procedures (see also Box 1.1).

Box 8.4: Regulating Behavior and Culture

After the global financial crisis of 2008, there was broad consensus that changes were needed in the banking sector. No longer should it be allowed for financial professionals to become rich by cheating their customers, while relying on tax payers to bail them out in case they ran into problems. In addition to increased regulation and monitoring, reforms of the professional behavior and culture characterizing the sector seemed in order (Ho, 2009; Luyendijk, 2015).

Although there was wide consensus that something needed to be done, it was not so clear how to approach such a change. The Dutch Banking Association (NVB) made a valiant effort by being the first in the world to introduce a mandatory banker's oath. A formal pledge to act responsibly and mind their clients' interests had to be taken by all existing and new professionals working in finance, from bank teller to high level executive. Starting

January 1st, 2015, financial service organizations were responsible for taking and registering these pledges from over 90,000 professionals.

Initially this effort was ridiculed in the media. Clearly this was 'just a cosmetic PR exercise', as fines imposed in the financial sector were dismissed as 'chicken feed' by wealthy professionals. At the same time, however, commentaries acknowledged that other regulators – for instance in the UK – were limited in what they could do to eliminate perverse behaviors or irresponsible conduct because they had no legal basis for doing so (Aitken, 2014).

The banker's oath was only part of a broader effort of the Dutch regulator to transform the culture and behavior in the sector. The Dutch Central Bank (DNB) joined forces with the Financial Market Authority (AFM) in pioneering a new approach to this issue (Conley et al., 2019). They sought collaboration with behavioral scientists and invested in building teams of experts who could expand their methods for supervising behavior and culture in financial organizations (De Nederlandsche Bank, 2015). Gradually the regulators started specifying features that characterize a 'healthy' organizational culture. They developed concrete tools to monitor and assess progress made in culture transformations, and made public the results of these examinations in reports, case studies and brochures (AFM, 2017, 2020; Van Steenbergen et al., 2019a).

The investment in knowledge exchange appears to pay off. Compliance officers and other professionals participate in masterclasses teaching them to use the methods and tools that were developed to instigate and monitor culture changes. Complementing 'hard' regulation and the threat of sanctions with these 'softer' forms of regulation is seen as a constructive way to help professionals move forward. During the past years, regulators of other sectors in the Netherlands (such as the Consumer and Market Authority ACM) as well as financial regulators in Europe, the US, and Australia have expressed an interest in learning from these pioneering efforts, and have started to recruit behavioral experts to support their own regulatory efforts.

8.3.1 *Overcoming Shame and Guilt*

Misbehavior in organizations does not necessarily result from a deliberate intention to cheat, steal, or commit fraud. Of course thieves and criminals do exist and they should be punished when breaking the law. Even if people recognize some of their own dark traits in villains it does not mean they see them as realistic or attractive role models (Krause & Rucker, 2020). Yet there is a grey area where 'normal' people can come to act in ways that are seen as morally questionable. What they do transcends the common norms of decent and socially responsible behavior, even if is not against the letter of the law. Intervening in such a gradual and perhaps unintentional process requires a careful approach.

Alerting people to the undesirable implications of their behavior involves highlighting the negative moral implications of their choices. While this may seem the best way to convince them that change is needed, our analysis reveals that it also imposes identity threat and causes feelings of shame and guilt. Such emotional responses can even be triggered when the moral transgressions were made by others in the team or organization (Doosje & Branscombe, 2003; Tangney & Dearing, 2002). The experience of these particular emotions is bound to raise denials or justifications, or to cite external reasons that stand in the way of moral improvement (Gausel & Leach, 2011; Giner-Sorolla, 2012; Zhang & Chen, 2016; Zhang et al., 2019). This makes people defensive, especially when core group values are at stake. This was revealed by studying responses of self-identified Catholics to allegations of child sexual abuse by a Catholic priest (see also Box 2.2). High identifiers in particular, prioritized extending loyalty to their religious group over addressing the issues that were raised. They chose to disbelieve allegations of child abuse, and defend the abuser (Minto et al., 2016). This points to a more general pattern, where the identity implications of being confronted with past moral failures cause people to hide or deny such problems instead of addressing them.

Experimental research reveals that confronting people with their moral obligations, and reminding them of their shortcomings in the moral domain only compounds the problem. It raises negative emotions and induces a state of physiological threat – indicated by specific patterns of heart rate and blood pressure increases. These responses reveal that people are strongly affected and deeply care about the criticism levelled at them. At the same time the identity threat they experience is so severe that they do not know how to successfully cope with the situation (Does et al., 2012; Kouzakova et al., 2014; Van der Lee et al., 2017).

To be able to engage with the notion that change is needed, people first have to *overcome* these negative emotional and physiological responses. The way in which moral critique is voiced and the context in which moral appeals are made can help them do this. Research shows that even small shifts in how such critique is communicated can have far-reaching implications. For instance, the identity threat can be alleviated when critique of *actions* that can be changed (you did not handle that well) is separated from disapproval of people's *identity,* which seems more enduring and essential (you are an immoral person; Conway & Peetz, 2012). One way of doing this is to highlight how these actions show up a lack of *competence* (that was not very smart) instead of indicating flawed *moral* judgments (that was irresponsible; Pagliaro et al., 2011). Accordingly, organizations aiming to prevent unethical behavior in the workplace should not just appeal to the desire to do what is morally right. They should also redesign tasks, and promote incentives and decision processes to make this the smart thing to do, and educate people that this is the way to be successful in the organization (Zhang et al., 2014).

Further, feelings of threat and defensive responses can be reduced by focusing on *future improvement opportunities* instead of continuing to criticize people for past transgressions (Van der Lee et al., 2016). This not only applies when considering personal shortcomings, but also when confronted with moral failures of other group members that impact upon one's social identity. It was visible, for instance, when people were asked to reflect on the national problem of continuing discrimination in the workplace. Here, people revealed less physiological stress and generated more suggestions for change and improvement when they were reminded of the future ideal to offer equal employment opportunities - instead of admonishing them about failing the obligation to treat people fairly (Does et al., 2011; Does et al., 2012). Likewise, informing students about past incidents of plagiarism and academic fraud in their institution and discipline was only found to raise threat and defensive responses. Yet students were quite willing to consider how fraud might have happened and what could be done to prevent similar issues in the future after being offered an opportunity to improve the negative image of their group (Van der Toorn et al., 2015).

Nudging people towards moral improvement – instead of provoking defensive responses - requires some measure of forgiveness for past transgressions. A perspective on redemption is needed to provide them with new opportunities to enact and affirm key moral values (Woodyatt & Wenzel, 2013; Woodyatt et al., 2017). In an organizational context, making these opportunities very practical can help people bridge the gap between their values and good intentions on the one hand, and their behaviors on the other (Smith & Kouchaki, 2018a). It can be achieved for instance by not only encouraging them to commit to shared moral goals, but also requesting that they specify how these can be achieved, and challenging them to reflect on what can be learned from prior failures (Kouchaki & Smith, 2020). These are concrete strategies that compliance officers, supervisory boards and external regulators may implement to broaden their impact on the transformation and moral improvement of organizations.

8.3.2 Being Open to Learning From Errors

The ethical climate in the organization can also benefit or suffer from the way errors are dealt with. In any work setting, errors can be made as a result of unplanned deviations from standard procedures or incorrect decisions caused, for instance by lack of time or knowledge. This sets errors apart from fraud or intentional misconduct. Yet the way such unintentional lapses and mistakes are *dealt with* characterizes aspects of the workplace climate that are important for development and learning (Frese & Keith, 2015; Van Dyck et al., 2005). Moral issues often result not from mistakes that are made, but from attempts to cover them up, or avert responsibility. Organizations that manage to be open about and learn from errors create opportunities for moral improvement. A survey of over 5000 members of the US adult working population indicated the importance of such an organizational climate to curb and prevent misbehavior: it allows organizations to quickly detect and correct behavioral transgressions once these occur (Kaptein, 2011b). It is not self-evident that this happens. Major banks in Australia take an average of 1726 days (more than 4.5 years) to identify significant breaches of the law, a report of the Australian Securities and Investments Commission concluded (ASIC, 2018).

The ability to quickly detect, analyze and correct things that do not go according to plan, and a willingness to actively share this knowledge to prevent future problems, allows organizations to learn from errors that are made, even if these can never be fully avoided. This approach characterizes an open and safe work environment. It can facilitate workplace discussions about practical implications of important rules and regulations, and thus help prevent and overcome work practices that are ethically flawed (Victor & Cullen, 1988).

Many organizations hope to *prevent* errors. They offer rules to specify what is allowed and what is forbidden, and blame and punish those who do not abide by these rules (see Fig. 8.2: Dealing with errors). However, as noted before, unforeseen circumstances may arise, and other factors such as lack of time and fatigue (perhaps stemming from performance pressures) may prevent employees from following intended procedures. When individuals are held accountable and mistakes are not allowed, employees fear a negative performance evaluation or reduction of career opportunities should their failures come to light (Gelfand et al., 2011). Such fears tempt them to deny and cover up problems that arise, allowing the consequences of small lapses to get out of hand instead of addressing and correcting them quickly. This prevents the organization from curbing further damage of such mishaps and does not help to improve inadequate procedures (Edmondson, 1999, 2003). Post-hoc analyses of disasters due to 'human error' often reveal such a pattern. After the explosion at the nuclear power plant in Chernobyl in 1986, for instance, precious time was lost because those involved all prioritized face-saving strategies instead of acknowledging that mistakes were made and taking action to curb further escalation of the disaster.

Acknowledging that mistakes are made and may be inevitable does not necessarily imply that errors should be accepted and justified because nothing can be done to prevent them. Instead, making sure that errors that do occur are routinely reported and evaluated without assigning blame, helps employees and work teams to understand common pitfalls and encourages them to develop strategies to circumvent these. In medical teams as well as in the aviation industry, this approach to 'error management' allows for quick responses that substantially reduce the damage due to errors made, with fewer lives lost as a result (Edmondson, 1999, 2003). More generally, this approach to workplace errors makes people more willing to take responsibility for

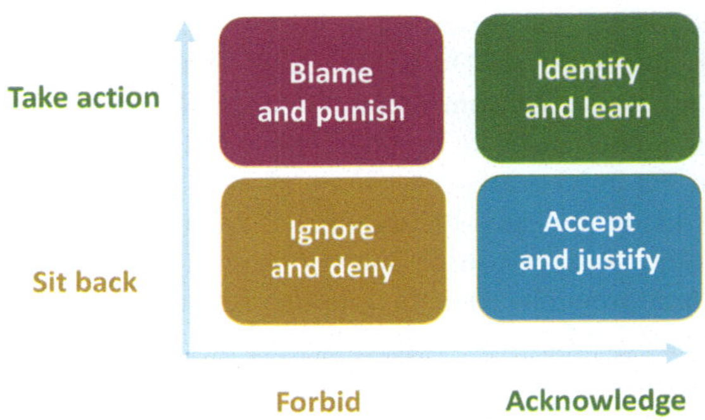

Fig. 8.2 Dealing with errors. Distinguishes between four common approaches to performance errors in organizations. The most constructive approach is to acknowledge that errors are bound to occur, while taking action to identify the origin and nature of these errors - as a way of learning from them

inviting feedback, as well as reporting and correcting flaws in the actions, services and products of themselves and their co-workers (Gronewold et al., 2013; Hofmann & Mark, 2006; Nembhard & Edmondson, 2006; Scholten & Ellemers, 2016). Research has found this only benefits the performance of the teams and organizations in question (Frese & Keith, 2015; Keith & Frese, 2011; Van Dyck et al., 2005).

Implementing this approach takes time and humility in trying to make incremental improvements instead of only addressing big issues. Developing an error management culture is only possible when daily routines include the consideration of smaller errors and what can be learned from them (Homsma et al., 2007; Sitkin, 1992). Once employees become convinced there is added value in also reporting smaller issues, incident registrations often suggest that problems increase. This is a common concern, for instance in the medical sector, where the general public does not always understand that incident numbers initially seem to go up when 'blame free reporting procedures' are first introduced. Yet the very fact that high performing teams were also the ones that reported many errors was the key observation that started the research program leading to current insights on error management cultures (Edmondson, 1999).

Further, employees need to know that their efforts to document what went wrong are not made in vain. This means that the organization needs to invest time to truly understand and address their concerns (Cannon & Edmondson, 2005). Indeed, employees will not continue to report and discuss problems they encounter unless the organization is willing to take action in order to improve (Heimbeck et al., 2003; Keith & Frese, 2008). Feedback about the added value of their reporting efforts can be provided for instance by sharing which incidents led to system changes, conveying at the same time that those who identify and report such errors do not suffer in terms of organizational standing or are seen as less loyal to the team (Masson & Fritsche, 2019). This was one of the concrete recommendations that emerged from in an in-depth analysis comparing 13 organizations in the financial service sector in the way they handled work-related errors (Van Steenbergen et al., 2019a). Here one of the interviewees commented *"The list [with reports of errors] is not read as a list of people who make the most mistakes, but as people who are the sharpest at detecting errors. It is immediately clear that it is not there to shame people as it includes some highly regarded traders."* (p. 67).

The same study also revealed how important it is for team and organizational leaders to offer positive examples (see also Chap. 3), for instance by openly talking about their own failures and how they were able to turn these into learning opportunities (Van Steenbergen et al., 2019a; see also Cannon & Edmondson, 2001; Rybowiak et al., 1999).

8.3.3 *Taking Pride in Doing What's Right*

Throughout this book we have argued that social identities can overrule personal endorsements of moral principles, and impact on what people consider to be right and wrong in the workplace (see also Ellemers, 2017; Ellemers & Van der Toorn,

2015; Kish-Gephart et al., 2010a). As a result, the organizational climate can enhance or diminish the moral behavior of individual workers depending on whether it encourages ethical and responsible behavior, or implicitly invites rule breaking and fraud. This can have far-reaching implications for the organization. For instance, a study of sales representatives revealed that those who experienced the work climate as more ethical had more trust in their supervisors, were more committed to the organization, and were less likely to leave for another job (DeConinck, 2011). In general, the ethical climate communicates the organization's commitment to shared values and impacts on the willingness and ability of individual workers to identify with the organization (Carr et al., 2003; Willis et al., 2019).

An organization can build a strong identity around features that are central, enduring, and distinctive (Gioia et al., 2013). This goes beyond formal value endorsements or mission statements, and has to permeate strategic decision making, organizational practices and everyday work experiences (see Box 8.5: Bank of Australia and Handelsbanken). Indeed, even when the organization values their individual contributions, achievements or attributes, people are unlikely to feel safe and committed unless the organization treats everyone fairly and respectfully (Rogers & Ashforth, 2017; see also Chap. 4). This explains the impact of displaying care for workers and clients, as a way to enact important values and principles (Barnett & Schubert, 2002; Dickson et al., 2001). A strong sense of identity and shared purpose also guards against unproductive rivalry in the workplace (Landkammer et al., 2019). People are more willing to connect their identity to the organization when they can endorse the distinctive purpose and legacy in terms of its role and contributions to society (see also Anderson, 1999; Aquino et al., 2006).

Box 8.5: Bank Australia and Swedish Handelsbanken

The widespread nature of banking scandals across the world make it tempting to think such problems are inherent to the sector (Duran, 2018; Knaus, 2019). Despite their perverse effects, incentive payment and high rewards are seen as essential tools to attract and motivate the best talents. But is this really true? Is the focus on individual and company earnings the only way for financial businesses to survive, or are alternative approaches possible?

Bank Australia is a customer-owned cooperative credit society that merged with other cooperative banks and credit unions. It was named Bank Australia in 2015, and became a certified Benefit Corporation in 2020. As a member of the Global Alliance for Banking on Values, it pledges to act responsibly by using the money put up by their customers to contribute to sustainable economic, social and environmental development. This ambition goes beyond getting certification for the social responsibility of their financial products. Additionally, the bank contributes to society by retaining jobs in Australia, running a carbon neutral organization, and allocating part of its profit to the funding of community projects for housing developments, environmental conservation and renewable energy. It does not invest in fossil fuels, live animal export, gambling, arms industry, and tobacco. The commitment of the bank to 'clean money' was emphasized during the Australian banking crisis by advertising the organization as "the bank Australia needs" (https://www.bankaust.com.au/).

Their morally responsible practices contribute to broader social causes but still lead to profits for the bank and its customers. This goal is achieved by developing products and credit plans for individual customers, not corporate clients. Further, customers are given a voice in the investments and policies of the bank. In return for their deposits, customers are rewarded with competitive rates and low fees, made possible by the profits made through management of the investments (Verghis, 2019). In 2019, this bank made a healthy profit of 22,9 million Australian Dollars and had a capital adequacy ratio of 16.4% (Bank Australia, 2019). It provides a prime example of how banks can do things differently and still be successful.

In Europe, Swedish Handelsbanken offers a different example. Like Bank Australia, Handelsbanken aims to minimize environmental and climate impact and invest in green initiatives, and shows a modest, but steady financial success, based on low-risk, cost-aware and long-term business relationships. However, their business structure is fundamentally different from traditional banks. The organization is highly decentralized. Branch managers have a mandate to adjust their business plan according to the needs of the local community. They all work according to the 'church-tower principle': business is only conducted with customers you know, because you can see them from the top of the local church tower (The Economist Newspaper, 2009). The focus on local customer relationships together with sustainability goals proves a highly effective commercial policy.

Long-term business relationships with customers and employees are supported by the absence of bonuses. All employees from cleaner to executive have a fixed salary, with profit shares being invested by a staff-owned foundation to increase the bank's pension fund (Smith, 2014). This reward structure makes it easier to decide on loans and advice on the basis of customer needs, not on short term profit for the bank. This unique strategy does not only satisfy the customer, but also contributes to the stability and financial growth of the bank. It allows the bank to attract talent away from competitors that focus on high rewards, and partly explains the continued success of the bank even during the global financial crisis (Handelsbanken, 2018). Although some local offices were closed down due to the increasing digitization of banking services, the network of branches is still considered as the backbone and key asset of the bank.

A special role is assigned to managers and team leaders in setting the tone in defining the moral identity of the organization (Ellemers et al., 2004; Platow et al., 2017; see also Chap. 3). A meta-analysis comparing effects of 35 study samples revealed that leader endorsement of moral norms and social values only predicts moral behavior in the organization, when leaders also *act in accordance* with these guidelines – displaying 'behavioral integrity' (Simons et al., 2015). Another meta-analysis summarizing results from over 100 samples comprising close to 30,000 research participants revealed that ethical leadership increases trust and reduces counterproductive work behaviors (Ng & Feldman, 2015). For instance, a study of over 900 employees and their managers employed at different organizations in the USA found that the likelihood that managers and team leaders came late without permission or took home resources from work was mirrored in the behavior of their team members (Mayer et al., 2009). Such visible role modeling was found to be more important than clarity of ethical standards. Everyday experiences with managers that allow workers to behave ethically, discuss ethical issues and reinforce ethical behavior, were all associated with decreased incidence of unethical behavior among employees (Kaptein, 2011b; see also Mayer et al., 2012).

Similar conclusions can be drawn from a study surveying over 10,000 employees working at different companies and industries in the USA (Treviño et al., 1999). Their impressions of how their company dealt with legal and ethical issues did not depend on how compliance programs were set up or what these entailed. Instead, the decisive factor was whether or not these programs were systematically followed through in the way the company dealt with different stakeholders. Only when employees could see with their own eyes that ethical behavior was noted and rewarded by company leaders did they believe that this was considered important. If this was the case, employees indicated less unethical behavior in the organization and more awareness of legal issues. This made them more supportive of organizational decisions, but also prompted them to seek advice from others in the firm, be willing to deliver bad news to management, and to report ethical violations (Treviño et al., 1999). An in-depth study among military personnel (Hannah et al., 2011), likewise revealed that leaders who visibly endorse ethical standards inspire moral courage among their followers. This helps them to refuse to follow assignments that go against key ethical principles, and withstand peer pressure to neglect important rules.

This influence works both ways. In addition to such top-down role modeling, bottom-up ethical reminders and endorsements can also highlight and reinforce shared moral values that define the identity of the organization and the way people work together (Ashforth et al., 2020; Weaver, 2006). For instance, research found that employee endorsements of moral values prevented supervisors from making unethical requests from subordinates (e.g. sending misleading messages to an opposing team, misrepresenting information for decision making) and made them less likely to do so themselves (Desai & Kouchaki, 2017). Another study of over 2500 US Army soldiers stationed in Iraq, likewise found that shared beliefs, storytelling and displays of exemplary behaviors at the team level influenced displays of moral courage. Knowing the ethical guidelines that were supported by their peers prompted soldiers, for instance, to challenge others who mistreated civilians, damaged private property, defied rules or falsified reports (Schaubroeck et al., 2012). Thus, on the workfloor too, displays of moral courage benefit the process of identity transformation towards moral improvement.

8.4 Conclusion: Integrating Moral Concerns

Standard approaches to misbehavior in organizations - such as the fraud triangle - attribute breaches of legal and ethical guidelines to individual character flaws and deliberate decision making. Common attempts to prevent and regulate this invoke the three quick fixes: changing the individuals, changing the rules and changing incentives (see Chap. 1). This approach may be indispensable to avoid villains and punish criminals, but it does not necessarily help understand how good people can come to do bad things.

Throughout this book we have argued for a more integrated approach to moral behavior in organizations. We focused on the social identities people have in the workplace and the identity threats they experience when considering whether and how work practices they engage in might be considered morally deficient (see Chap. 2). In each chapter we have addressed specific strategies that allow people to cope with such threats and restore a sense of moral identity. We have reviewed evidence from research showing how these identity management strategies preclude more fundamental changes that might lead to moral improvement. The recurring message is that formal and explicit measures taken to implement and guard moral standards are likely to fail as long as seemingly innocent organizational practices implicitly continue to justify and condone morally questionable outcomes (see Fig. 1.3).

The implicit norms embedded in 'standard business practices', can include celebrating leaders who ignore important guidelines (see also Chap. 3) by imposing performance targets that prevent careful quality control (see also Chap. 4), ignoring workers who offer a different perspective (see also Chap. 5), tempting workers to ignore safety regulations (see also Chap. 6), or generally failing to take into account the interests of different stakeholders (see also Chap. 7). An important implication of this is that attempts to redress such problems will have to go beyond removing or sanctioning the specific individuals who displayed unacceptable behavior. Instead, a broader reconsideration of structures, incentives, and everyday decisions is needed to ensure that moral guidelines are taken into account as a matter of course – not only in theory, but also in practice.

This is a choice not every organization is willing to make. In this final chapter we have indicated what organizations and the people in them can do to build an ethical climate at work. Treating each other with respect, constructively engaging with critical views and concerns, and learning from things that went wrong all seem relatively straightforward recommendations. Yet these good intentions are quite challenging to follow through, as they require people to overcome feelings of shame and guilt, be open and constructive about errors, and to take pride in being helped to do what is morally right.

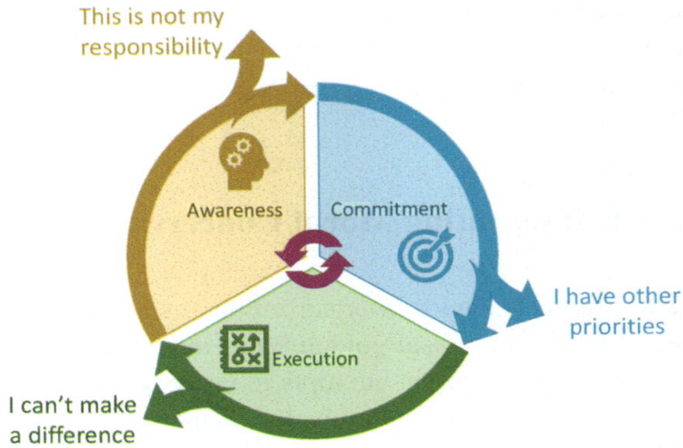

Fig. 8.3 Following through on good intentions. Figure shows the three interrelated steps that need to be taken to achieve moral improvement. First, people need to acknowledge improvements that are needed, and recognize that they too are responsible for making this happen (Awareness). Second, they have to be motivated to realize their moral ambitions, to the extent that these will be prioritized before other goals (Commitment). Third, they have to develop skills and opportunities needed to follow through on their good intentions, driven by the conviction that they can make a difference (Execution). At every step of the way, moral discomfort tempts people to abandon their good intentions, because they deflect responsibility to others, focus on other priorities, or feel unable to make a difference

Many of the pitfalls and hazards we have reviewed in this book come about because 'standard procedures' make it difficult for people in organizations to follow through on good intentions. The success in integrating moral concerns in everyday practices depends on three interrelated mechanisms (see Fig. 8.3: Following through on good intentions). First, people have to acknowledge the moral implications of 'standard procedures'. Second, they have to become motivated to address these. Third, they have to find practical ways of doing this. At every step of the way, it is easy to become distracted, and adopt one of the many strategies available for those attempting to manage their feelings of moral identity threat.

After becoming aware of moral implications of one's actions, it is still possible to deflect responsibility. For instance by morally excluding or neglecting the concerns, needs, and outcomes of those affected by one's actions. Once moral goals have been specified, this doesn't imply that people actually commit to these goals. Seeking moral elevation through the good deeds of others, justifying lack of change by pointing to other important outcomes, or taking symbolic actions as strategies towards moral licensing or moral cleansing all allow people to commit to moral goals, without reconsidering their priorities. Even when moral improvement is prioritized, it is not self-evident that people are able to execute their good intentions. This also depends on the circumstances they face and their conviction that they will be able to achieve change. Nothing is more discouraging than the belief that one's actions will not make a difference.

Improving the moral identity of the organization only becomes possible when people within it keep on the ball, by acknowledging *and* taking responsibility for moral implications of their actions, committing to moral improvement *and* prioritizing this before other goals, as well as doing everything they can to act in line with their moral intentions. It is not rocket science, but becoming a more moral organization requires continued alertness, commitment to difficult choices, and the determination to make a difference.

Recommended Reading

Den Nieuwenboer, N. A., & Kaptein, M. (2008b). Spiraling down into corruption: A dynamic analysis of the social identity processes that cause corruption in organizations to grow. *Journal of Business Ethics, 83*(2), 133–146. https://doi.org/10.1007/s10551-007-9617-8

Kish-Gephart, J. J., Harrison, D. A., & Treviño, L. K. (2010b). Bad apples, bad cases, and bad barrels: Meta-analytic evidence about sources of unethical decisions at work. *Journal of Applied Psychology, 95*, 1–31. https://doi.org/10.1037/a0017103

Near, J. P., & Miceli, M. P. (2016b). After the wrongdoing: What managers should know about whistleblowing. *Business Horizons, 59*, 105–114. https://doi.org/10.1016/j.bushor.2015.09.007

Smith, I. H. & Kouchaki, M. (2018b). Moral humility: In life and at work. *Research in Organizational Behavior, 38*, 77–94. https://doi.org/10.1016/j.riob.2018.12.001

Van Steenbergen, E., Van Dijk, D., Christensen, C., Coffeng, T., & Ellemers, N. (2019b). Learn to build an error management culture. *Journal of Financial Regulation and Compliance, 28*(1), 57–73. https://doi.org/10.1108/JFRC-12-2018-0156

References

Adams, J. S., Tashchian, A., & Shore, T. H. (2001). Codes of ethics as signals for ethical behavior. *Journal of Business Ethics, 29*(3), 199–211. https://doi.org/10.1023/A:1026576421399

AFM. (2020, June 29). *Bewust belonen en waarderen: Een oproep aan de sector op basis van onderzoek bij banken, verzekeraars en financieel dienstverleners.*. Retrieved from: https://www.afm.nl/nl-nl/professionals/nieuws/2020/juni/bewust-belonen-waarderen

AFM. (2017, Oct). *Learning from errors; towards an error management culture Insights based on a study in the capital markets*. Retrieved from: https://www.afm.nl/en/professionals/onderwerpen/gedrag-cultuur-publicaties

Aitken, R. (2014, Dec 23). Dutch bankers swearing an oath to god…whatever next? *Forbes*. Retrieved from: https://www.forbes.com/sites/rogeraitken/2014/12/23/dutch-bankers-swearing-an-oath-to-god-whatever-next/?sh=56262938a9f3

Ambrose, M. L., & Cropanzano, R. (2003). A longitudinal analysis of organizational fairness: An examination of reactions to tenure and promotion decisions. *Journal of Applied Psychology, 88*(2), 266. https://doi.org/10.1037/0021-9010.88.2.266

Anand, V., Ashforth, B. E., & Joshi, M. (2004). Business as usual: The acceptance and perpetuation of corruption in organizations. *Academy of Management Perspectives, 18*(2), 39–53. https://doi.org/10.5465/ame.2004.13837437

Anderson, P. (1999). Perspective: Complexity theory and organization science. *Organization Science, 10*(3), 216–232. https://doi.org/10.1287/orsc.10.3.216

Andreoli, N., & Lefkowitz, J. (2009). Individual and organizational antecedents of misconduct in organizations. *Journal of Business Ethics, 85*(3), 309. https://doi.org/10.1007/s10551-008-9772-6

Anvari, F., Wenzel, M., Woodyatt, L., & Haslam, S. A. (2019). The social psychology of whistleblowing: An integrated model. *Organizational Psychology Review, 9*(1), 41–67. https://doi.org/10.1177/2041386619849085

Aquino, K., Tripp, T. M., & Bies, R. J. (2006). Getting even or moving on? Power, procedural justice, and types of offense as predictors of revenge, forgiveness, reconciliation, and avoidance in organizations. *Journal of Applied Psychology, 91*(3), 653. https://doi.org/10.1037/0021-9010.91.3.653

ASIC. (2018). Review of selected financial services groups' compliance with the breach reporting obligation, *Australian Securities and Investments Commission Report 594*. Retrieved from: https://download.asic.gov.au/media/4879889/rep594-published-25-september-2018.pdf

Ashforth, B. E., & Anand, V. (2003). The normalization of corruption in organizations. In R. M. Kramer & B. M. Staw (Eds.), *Research in organizational behavior: An annual series of analytical essays and critical reviews* (pp. 1–52). Elsevier Science Ltd.. https://doi.org/10.1016/S0191-3085(03)25001-2

Ashforth, B. E., & Johnson, S. A. (2001). Which hat to wear? The relative salience of multiple identities in organizational contexts. In M. A. Hogg & D. J. Terry (Eds.), *Social identity processes in organizational contexts* (pp. 31–48). Psychology.

Ashforth, B. E., & Schinoff, B. S. (2016). Identity under construction: How individuals come to define themselves in organizations. *Annual Review of Organizational Psychology and Organizational Behavior, 3*, 111–137. https://doi.org/10.1146/annurev-orgpsych-041015-062322

Ashforth, B. E., Schinoff, B. S., & Brickson, S. L. (2020). "My company is friendly", "Mine's a rebel": Anthropomorphism and shifting organizational identity from "what" to "who". *Academy of Management Review, 45*, 29–57. https://doi.org/10.5465/amr.2016.0496

Bagozzi, R. P., & Lee, K. H. (2002). Multiple routes for social influence: The role of compliance, internalization, and social identity. *Social Psychology Quarterly*, 226–247. https://doi.org/10.2307/3090121

Bandura, A., Barbaranelli, C., Caprara, G. V., & Pastorelli, C. (1996). Mechanisms of moral disengagement in the exercise of moral agency. *Journal of Personality and Social Psychology, 71*(2), 364. https://doi.org/10.1037/0022-3514.71.2.364

Bank Australia. (2019). *Financial Report 2019*. Retrieved from https://www.bankaust.com.au/globalassets/assets/reporting-governance%2D%2Dpolicies/corporate%2D%2Dfinancial-reports/2019/2019-financial-report.pdf

Barnes, C. M., Schaubroeck, J., Huth, M., & Ghumman, S. (2011). Lack of sleep and unethical conduct. *Organizational Behavior and Human Decision Processes, 115*, 169–180. https://doi.org/10.1016/j.obhdp.2011.01.009

Barnett, T., & Schubert, E. (2002). Perceptions of the ethical work climate and covenantal relationships. *Journal of Business Ethics, 36*(3), 279–290. https://doi.org/10.1023/A:1014042613106

Barnett, T., & Vaicys, C. (2000). The moderating effects of individual's perceptions of ethical work climate on ethical judgments and behavioral intentions. *Journal of Business Ethics, 27*, 351–362. https://doi.org/10.1023/A:1006382407821

Barsky, A. (2008). Understanding the ethical cost of organizational goal-setting: A review and theory development. *Journal of Business Ethics, 81*(1), 63–81. https://doi.org/10.1007/s10551-007-9481-6

Bjørkelo, B., & Matthiesen, S. B. (2011). Preventing and dealing with retaliation against whistleblowers. In D. Lewis & W. Vandekerckhove (Eds.), *Whistleblowing and democratic values*. (ebook). International Whistleblowing Research Network.

Brady, A. M., Malone, A. M., & Fleming, S. (2009). A literature review of the individual and systems factors that contribute to medication errors in nursing practice. *Journal of Nursing Management, 17*(6), 679–697. https://doi.org/10.1111/j.1365-2834.2009.00995.x

Brass, D. J., Butterfield, K. D., & Skaggs, B. C. (1998). Relationships and unethical behavior: A social network perspective. *Academy of Management Review, 23*(1), 14–31. https://doi.org/10.5465/amr.1998.192955

Briscoe, F., & Gupta, A. (2016). Social activism in and around organizations. *The Academy of Management Annals, 10*(1), 671–727. https://doi.org/10.5465/19416520.2016.1153261

Brody, R. G., Melendy, S. R., & Perri, F. S. (2011). Commentary from the American Accounting Association's 2011 annual meeting panel on emerging issues in fraud research. *Accounting Horizons, 26*, 153–160. https://doi.org/10.2308/acch-50175

Buchholz, A. K. (2012). SAS 99: Deconstructing the fraud triangle and some classroom suggestions. *Journal of Leadership, Accountability, and Ethics, 9*, 109–118.

Butterfield, K. D., Trevin, L. K., & Weaver, G. R. (2000). Moral awareness in business organizations: Influences of issue-related and social context factors. *Human Relations, 53*(7), 981–1018. https://doi.org/10.1177/0018726700537004

Callahan, D. (2004). *The cheating culture: Why more Americans are doing wrong to get ahead.* Harcourt Inc.

Cannon, M. D., & Edmondson, A. C. (2001). Confronting failure: Antecedents and consequences of shared beliefs about failure in organizational work groups. *Journal of Organizational Behavior: The International Journal of Industrial, Occupational and Organizational Psychology and Behavior, 22*(2), 161–177. https://doi.org/10.1002/job.85

Cannon, M. D., & Edmondson, A. C. (2005). Failing to learn and learning to fail (intelligently): How great organizations put failure to work to innovate and improve. *Long Range Planning, 38*(3), 299–319. https://doi.org/10.1016/j.lrp.2005.04.005

Carpenter, T. D., & Reimers, J. L. (2005). Unethical and fraudulent financial reporting: Applying the theory of planned behavior. *Journal of Business Ethics, 60*(2), 115–129. https://doi.org/10.1007/s10551-004-7370-9

Carr, J. Z., Schmidt, A. M., Ford, J. K., & DeShon, R. P. (2003). Climate perceptions matter: A meta-analytic path analysis relating moral climate, cognitive and affective states, and individual level work outcomes. *Journal of Applied Psychology, 88*(4), 605. https://doi.org/10.1037/0021-9010.88.4.605

Carroll, R. (2019, July 2). Nick Leeson: lucrative new life of banking's most notorious rogue. *The Guardian.* Retrieved from https://www.theguardian com/business/2019/jul/02/nick-leeson-new-life-banking-notorious-rogue

Chambers, C. R., & Baker, W. E. (2020). Robust Systems of Cooperation in the presence of rankings: How displaying prosocial contributions can offset the disruptive effects of performance rankings. *Organization Science, 31*(2), 287–307. https://doi.org/10.1287/orsc.2019.1296

Cialdini, R. B., & Goldstein, N. J. (2004). Social influence: Compliance and conformity. *Annual Review Psychology, 55*, 591–621. https://doi.org/10.1146/annurev.psych.55.090902.142015

Cohen-Charash, Y., & Mueller, J. S. (2007). Does perceived unfairness exacerbate or mitigate interpersonal counterproductive work behaviors related to envy? *Journal of Applied Psychology, 92*, 666–680. https://doi.org/10.1037/0021-9010.92.3.666

Conley, J. M., Smeehuijzen, L., Williams, C. A., & Rupp, D. E. (2019). Can soft regulation prevent financial crises?: The Dutch Central Bank's supervision of behavior and culture. *Cornell International Law Journal, Faculty Publications.* 484. https://scholarship.law.unc.edu/faculty_publications/484

Conroy, S., Henle, C. A., Shore, L., & Stelman, S. (2017). Where there is light, there is dark: A review of the detrimental outcomes of high organizational identification. *Journal of Organizational Behavior, 38*(2), 184–203. https://doi.org/10.1002/job.2164

Conway, P., & Peetz, J. (2012). When does feeling moral actually make you a better person? Conceptual abstraction moderates whether past moral deeds motivate consistency or compensatory behavior. *Personality and Social Psychology Bulletin, 38*, 907–919. https://doi.org/10.1177/0146167212442394

Cramwinckel, F. M., Van Dijk, E., Scheepers, D., & Van den Bos, K. (2013). The threat of moral refusers for one's self-concept and the protective function of physical cleansing. *Journal of Experimental Social Psychology, 49*(6), 1049–1058. https://doi.org/10.1016/j.jesp.2013.07.009

Cressey, D. R. (1973). *Other people's money: A study in the social psychology of embezzlement.* Patterson Smith Publishing Corporation.

Cullen, J. B., Victor, B., & Bronson, J. W. (1993). The ethical climate questionnaire: An assessment of its development and validity. *Psychological Reports, 73*(2), 667–674. https://doi.org/10.2466/pr0.1993.73.2.667

Culture eats strategy for breakfast. (2017, May 23). Retrieved from https://quoteinvestigator.com/2017/05/23/culture-eats/

Dahling, J. J., & Gutworth, M. B. (2017). Loyal rebels? A test of the normative conflict model of constructive deviance. *Journal of Organizational Behavior, 38*(8), 1167–1182. https://doi.org/10.1002/job.2194

Deal, T. E., & Kennedy, A. A. (1982). *Corporate cultures: The rites and rituals of corporate life*. Penguin. https://doi.org/10.1016/0007-6813(83)90092-7

DeConinck, J. B. (2011). The effects of ethical climate on organizational identification, supervisory trust, and turnover among salespeople. *Journal of Business Research, 64*(6), 617–624. https://doi.org/10.1016/j.jbusres.2010.06.014

De Nederlandsche Bank. (2015). *Supervision of behavior and culture: Foundations, practice, and future developments*. Retrieved from: https://www.dnb.nl/en/supervision/055_Gedragencultuur/index.jsp

Den Nieuwenboer, N. A., & Kaptein, M. (2008a). Spiraling down into corruption: A dynamic analysis of the social identity processes that cause corruption in organizations to grow. *Journal of Business Ethics, 83*(2), 133–146. https://doi.org/10.1007/s10551-007-9617-8

Desai, S. D., & Kouchaki, M. (2017). Moral symbols: A necklace of garlic against unethical requests. *Academy of Management Journal, 60*(1), 7–28. https://doi.org/10.5465/amj.2015.0008

Dickson, M. W., Smith, D. B., Grojean, M. W., & Ehrhart, M. (2001). An organizational climate regarding ethics: The outcome of leader values and the practices that reflect them. *The Leadership Quarterly, 12*(2), 197–217. https://doi.org/10.1016/S1048-9843(01)00069-8

Dobbin, F., & Kalev, A. (2019). The promise and peril of sexual harassment programs. *Proceedings of the National Academy of Sciences, 116*(25), 12255–12260. https://doi.org/10.1073/pnas.1818477116

Does, S., Derks, B., & Ellemers, N. (2011). Thou shall not discriminate: How emphasizing moral ideals rather than obligations increases whites' support for social equality. *Journal of Experimental Social Psychology, 47*, 562–571. https://doi.org/10.1016/j.jesp.2010.12.024

Does, S., Derks, B., Ellemers, N., & Scheepers, D. (2012). At the heart of egalitarianism: How equality framing shapes cardiovascular challenge vs. threat in whites. *Social Psychology and Personality Science, 3*, 747–753. https://doi.org/10.1177/1948550612438924

Doosje, B., & Branscombe, N. R. (2003). Attributions for the negative historical actions of a group. *European Journal of Social Psychology, 33*(2), 235–248. https://doi.org/10.1002/ejsp.142

Dorminey, J., Fleming, A. S., Kranacher, M. J., & Riley, R. A. (2010). Beyond the fraud triangle. *The CPA Journal*, 17–23.

Doyle, E., Frecknall Hughes, J., & Summers, B. (2013). An empirical analysis of the ethical reasoning of tax practitioners. *Journal of Business Ethics, 114*, 325–339. https://doi.org/10.1007/s10551-012-1347-x

Duffy, M. K., Scott, K. L., Shaw, J. D., Tepper, B. J., & Aquino, K. (2012). A social context model of envy and social undermining. *Academy of Management Journal, 55*(3), 643–666. https://doi.org/10.5465/amj.2009.0804

Duffy, M. K., Shaw, J. D., & Schaubroeck, J. M. (2008). Envy in organizational life. In R. H. Smith (Ed.), *Envy: Theory and research* (pp. 167–189). Oxford University Press.

Dungan, J., Waytz, A., & Young, L. (2015). The psychology of whistleblowing. *Current Opinion in Psychology, 6*, 129–133. https://doi.org/10.1016/j.copsyc.2015.07.005

Dungan, J. A., Young, L., & Waytz, A. (2019). The power of moral concerns in predicting whistleblowing decisions. *Journal of Experimental Social Psychology, 85*, 103848. https://doi.org/10.1016/j.jesp.2019.103848

Duran, P. (2018, March 23). *Australia's big banks broke laws and failed public, inquiry reveals*. Retrieved from https://www.reuters.com/article/us-australia-banks-inquiry/australias-big-banks-broke-laws-and-failed-public-inquiry-reveals-idUSKBN1GZ17R

Edmondson, A. C. (1999). Psychological safety and learning behavior in work teams. *Administrative Science Quarterly, 44*, 350–383. https://doi.org/10.2307/2666999

Edmondson, A. C. (2003). Speaking up in the operating room: How team leaders promote learning in interdisciplinary action teams. *Journal of Management Studies, 40*(6), 1419–1452. https://doi.org/10.1111/1467-6486.00386

Edwards, M. A., & Roy, S. (2017). Academic research in the 21st century: Maintaining scientific integrity in a climate of perverse incentives and hypercompetition. *Environmental Engineering Science, 34*(1), 51–61. https://doi.org/10.1089/ees.2016.0223

Eidelman, S., & Biernat, M. (2003). Derogating black sheep: Individual or group protection? *Journal of Experimental Social Psychology, 39*(6), 602–609.

Ellemers, N. (2013). Connecting the dots: Mobilizing theory to reveal the big picture in social psychology (and why we should do this). *European Journal of Social Psychology, 43*, 1–8. https://doi.org/10.1002/ejsp.1932

Ellemers, N. (2017). *Morality and the regulation of social behavior: Groups as moral anchors*. Routledge. https://doi.org/10.4324/9781315661322

Ellemers, N. (2021). Science as collaborative knowledge generation. *British Journal of Social Psychology, 60*(1), 1–28. https://doi.org/10.1111/bjso.12430

Ellemers, N., De Gilder, D., & Haslam, S. A. (2004). Motivating individuals and groups at work: A social identity perspective on leadership and group performance. *Academy of Management Review, 29*(3), 459–478. https://doi.org/10.5465/amr.2004.13670967

Ellemers, N., & Jetten, J. (2013). The many ways to be marginal in a group. *Personality and Social Psychology Review, 17*, 3–21. https://doi.org/10.1177/1088868312453086

Ellemers, N., & Van der Toorn, J. (2015). Groups as moral anchors. *Current Opinion in Behavioral Sciences, 6*, 189–194. https://doi.org/10.1016/j.copsyc.2015.08.018

Eriksson, K., Strimling, P., & Coultas, J. C. (2015). Bidirectional associations between descriptive and injunctive norms. *Organizational Behavior and Human Decision Processes, 129*, 59–69. https://doi.org/10.1016/j.obhdp.2014.09.011

EY. (2020). *Is this the moment of truth for corporate integrity? Global Integrity Report 2020.* Retrieved from https://assets.ey.com/content/dam/ey-sites/ey-com/en_gl/topics/assurance/assurance-pdfs/ey-global-integrity-report-survey-respondents.pdf

Fehr, E., & Rockenbach, B. (2003). Detrimental effects of sanctions on human altruism. *Nature, 422*(6928), 137–140. https://doi.org/10.1038/nature01474

Feldman, Y. (2018). *The law of good people: Challenging states' ability to regulate human behavior*. Cambridge University Press. https://doi.org/10.7591/cornell/9781501709203.001.0001

Fortado, L. (2015, Oct 22). Kweku Adoboli: a rogue trader's tale. *Financial Times*. Retrieved from https://www.ft.com/content/0fa0b42a-783a-11e5-a95a-27d368e1ddf7

Frese, M., & Keith, N. (2015). Action errors, error management and learning in organizations. *Annual Review of Psychology, 66*, 661–687. https://doi.org/10.1146/annurev-psych-010814-015205

FSB. (2018). *Resolution report: "Keeping the pressure up". Seventh report on the implementation of resolution reforms.* Retrieved from https://www.fsb.org/wp-content/uploads/P151118-1.pdf

Gausel, N., & Leach, C. W. (2011). Concern for self-image and social image in the management of moral failure: Rethinking shame. *European Journal of Social Psychology, 41*(4), 468–478. https://doi.org/10.1002/ejsp.803

Gelfand, M. J., Frese, M., & Salmon, E. (2011). Cultural influences on errors: Prevention, detection and management In D. A. Hogmann & M. Frese (Eds.), *Errors in organizations* (pp. 273–315). Routledge.

Giner-Sorolla, R. (2012). *Judging passions: Moral emotion in persons and groups*. Psychology Press. https://doi.org/10.4324/9780203123874

Gino, F., Schweitzer, M. E., Mead, N. L., & Ariely, D. (2011). Unable to resist temptation: How self-control depletion promotes unethical behavior. *Organizational Behavior and Human Decision Processes, 115*(2), 191–203. https://doi.org/10.1016/j.obhdp.2011.03.001

Gioia, D. A., Patvardhan, S. D., Hamilton, A. L., & Corley, K. G. (2013). Organizational identity formation and change. *The Academy of Management Annals, 7*(1), 123–193. https://doi.org/10.5465/19416520.2013.762225

Gordon, A. (2020, June 25). Is this the moment of truth for corporate integrity? *EY.* Retrieved from https://www.ey.com/en_gl/forensic-integrity-services/is-this-the-moment-of-truth-for-corporate-integrity

Gorsira, M., Steg, L., Denkers, A., & Huisman, W. (2018). Corruption in organizations: Ethical climate and individual motives. *Administrative Sciences, 8*(1), 1–19. https://doi.org/10.3390/admsci8010004

Grandey, A. A., Ferris, D. L., & Melloy, R. C. (2018). A dual signal model of pride displays in organizations. *Research in Organizational Behavior, 38*, 153–168. https://doi.org/10.1016/j.riob.2018.11.004

Greve, H. R., Palmer, D., & Pozner, J. E. (2010). Organizations gone wild: The causes, processes, and consequences of organizational misconduct. *The Academy of Management Annals, 4*(1), 53–107. https://doi.org/10.5465/19416521003654186

Gronewold, U., Gold, A., & Salterio, S. E. (2013). Reporting self-made errors: The impact of organizational error-management climate and error type. *Journal of Business Ethics, 117*(1), 189–208. https://doi.org/10.1007/s10551-012-1500-6

Hamington, M. (2009). Business is not a game: The metaphoric fallacy. *Journal of Business Ethics, 86*(4), 473–484. https://doi.org/10.1007/s10551-008-9859-0

Handelsbanken. (2018). *Sustainability Report 2018.* Retrieved from https://www.handelsbanken.com/shb/inet/icentsv.nsf/vlookuppics/investor_relations_en_hallbarhetsred_2018_eng/%24file/hallbarhetsred_2018_eng.pdf

Hannah, S. T., Avolio, B. J., & Walumbwa, F. O. (2011). Relationships between authentic leadership, moral courage, and ethical and pro-social behaviors. *Business Ethics Quarterly, 21*(4), 555–578. https://doi.org/10.5840/beq201121436

Haslam, S. A., & Reicher, S. D. (2012). Contesting the "nature" of conformity: What Milgram and Zimbardo's studies really show. *PLoS Biology, 10*(11), e1001426. https://doi.org/10.1371/journal.pbio.1001426

Heffernan, M. (2014). Lose the competition. *RSA Journal, 160*(5558), 40–43.

Heimbeck, D., Frese, M., Sonnentag, S., & Keith, N. (2003). Integrating errors into the training process: The function of error management instructions and the role of goal orientation. *Personnel Psychology, 56*, 333–361. https://doi.org/10.1111/j.1744-6570.2003.tb00153.x

Henik, E. (2008). Mad as hell or scared stiff? The effects of value conflict and emotions on potential whistle-blowers. *Journal of Business Ethics, 80*(1), 111–119. https://doi.org/10.1007/s10551-007-9441-1

Ho, K. (2009). *Liquidated: An ethnography of Wall Street.* Duke University Press. https://doi.org/10.1215/9780822391371

Hofmann, D. A., & Mark, B. (2006). An investigation of the relationship between safety climate and medication errors as well as other nurse and patient outcomes. *Personnel Psychology, 59*(4), 847–869. https://doi.org/10.1111/j.1744-6570.2006.00056.x

Homan, M., Haslam, S. A., Steffens, N. K., & Reicher, S. D. (in press). Support for corporate corruption: Blind obedience or engaged followership?

Homsma, G. J., Van Dyck, C., De Gilder, D., Koopman, P. L., & Elfring, T. (2007). Overcoming errors: A closer look at the attributional mechanism. *Journal of Business and Psychology, 21*(4), 559–583. https://doi.org/10.1007/s10869-007-9041-1

Hornsey, M. J., & Imani, A. (2004). Criticizing groups from the inside and the outside: An identity perspective on the intergroup sensitivity effect. *Personality and Social Psychology Bulletin, 30*(3), 365–383. https://doi.org/10.1177/0146167203261295

Hoyt, C. L., Price, T. L., & Poatsy, L. (2013). The social role theory of unethical leadership. *The Leadership Quarterly, 24*(5), 712–723. https://doi.org/10.1016/j.leaqua.2013.07.001

Jackson, J. C., Gelfand, M., De, S., & Fox, A. (2019). The loosening of American culture over 200 years is associated with a creativity–order trade-off. *Nature Human Behaviour, 3*(3), 244–250. https://doi.org/10.1038/s41562-018-0516-z

Jackson, R. W., Wood, C. M., & Zboja, J. J. (2013). The dissolution of ethical decision-making in organizations: A comprehensive review and model. *Journal of Business Ethics, 116*(2), 233–250. https://doi.org/10.1007/s10551-012-1459-3

Jordan, A. H., & Monin, B. (2008). From sucker to saint: Moralization in response to self-threat. *Psychological Science, 19*(8), 809–815. https://doi.org/10.1111/j.1467-9280.2008.02161.x

Kaptein, M. (2008). Developing and testing a measure for the ethical culture of organizations: The corporate ethical virtues model. *Journal of Organizational Behavior: The International Journal of Industrial, Occupational and Organizational Psychology and Behavior, 29*(7), 923–947. https://doi.org/10.1002/job.520

Kaptein, M. (2011a). From inaction to external whistleblowing: The influence of the ethical culture of organizations on employee responses to observed wrongdoing. *Journal of Business Ethics, 98*(3), 513–530. https://doi.org/10.1007/s10551-010-0591-1

Kaptein, M. (2011b). Understanding unethical behavior by unraveling ethical culture. *Human Relations, 64*(6), 843–869. https://doi.org/10.1177/0018726710390536

Kassem, R., & Higson, A. (2012). The new fraud triangle. *Journal of Emerging Trends in Economics and Management Sciences, 3*, 191–195.

Keith, N., & Frese, M. (2008). Effectiveness of error management training: A meta-analysis. *Journal of Applied Psychology, 93*(1), 59. https://doi.org/10.1037/0021-9010.93.1.59

Keith, N., & Frese, M. (2011). Enhancing firm performance and innovativeness through error management culture. In *Handbook of organizational culture and climate* (Vol. 9, pp. 137–157) https://doi.org/10.4135/9781483307961.n9

Kelman, H. C. (1974). Further thoughts on the processes of compliance, identification, and internalization. *Perspectives on Social Power*, 125–171. https://doi.org/10.4324/9781315129693-6

Kilduff, G. J., & Galinsky, A. D. (2017). The spark that ignites: Mere exposure to rivals increases Machiavellianism and unethical behavior. *Journal of Experimental Social Psychology, 69*, 156–162. https://doi.org/10.1016/j.jesp.2016.10.007

Kilduff, G. J., Galinsky, A D., Gallo, E., & Reade, J. J. (2016). Whatever it takes to win: Rivalry increases unethical behavior. *Academy of Management Journal, 59*(5), 1508–1534. https://doi.org/10.5465/amj.2014.0545

Kish-Gephart, J. J., Harrison, D. A., & Treviño, L. K. (2010a). Bad apples, bad cases, and bad barrels: Meta-analytic evidence about sources of unethical decisions at work. *Journal of Applied Psychology, 95*, 1–31. https://doi.org/10.1037/a0017103

Knaus, C. (2019, Feb 4). *Banks may face criminal charges after final royal commission report*. Retrieved from https://www.theguardian.com/australia-news/2019/feb/04/banks-may-face-criminal-charges-after-final-royal-commission-report

Knoll, M., & Van Dick, R. (2013). Do I hear the whistle…? A first attempt to measure four forms of employee silence and their correlates. *Journal of Business Ethics, 113*(2), 349–362. https://doi.org/10.1007/s10551-012-1308-4

Kouchaki, M., & Desai, S. D. (2015). Anxious, threatened, and also unethical: How anxiety makes individuals feel threatened and commit unethical acts. *Journal of Applied Psychology, 100*(2), 360–375. https://doi.org/10.1037/a0037796

Kouchaki, M., Dobson, K. S., Waytz, A., & Kteily, N. S. (2018). The link between self-dehumanization and immoral behavior. *Psychological Science, 29*(8), 1234–1246. https://doi.org/10.1177/0956797618760784

Kouchaki, M., Feldman, Y., & Gino, F. (2015). Expressive effects of ethical codes: An experimental survey of US employees' interpretation, understanding and implementation of institutional ethical policies. *Inequality, Trust and Ethics Conference: London 2015*. Retrieved from https://ssrn.com/abstract=2607591

Kouchaki, M., & Gino, F. (2016). Memories of unethical actions become obfuscated over time. *Proceedings of the National Academy of Sciences., 113*(22), 6166–6171. https://doi.org/10.1073/pnas.1523586113

Kouchaki, M., Gino, F., & Feldman, Y. (2019). The ethical perils of personal, communal relations: A language perspective. *Psychological Science, 30*(12), 1745–1766. https://doi.org/10.1177/0956797619882917

Kouchaki, M., & Kray, L. J. (2018). "I won't let you down:" Personal ethical lapses arising from women's advocating for others. *Organizational Behavior and Human Decision Processes, 147*, 147–157. https://doi.org/10.1016/j.obhdp.2018.06.001

Kouchaki, M., & Smith, I. H. (2020). Building an ethical career. *Harvard Business Review, 98*(1), 135–139.

Kouchaki, M., Smith-Crowe, K., Brief, A. P., & Sousa, C. (2013). Seeing green: Mere exposure to money triggers a business decision frame and unethical outcomes. *Organizational Behavior and Human Decision Processes, 121*(1), 53–61. https://doi.org/10.1016/j.obhdp.2012.12.002

Kouzakova, M., Harinck, F., Ellemers, N., & Scheepers, D. (2014). At the heart of a conflict: Cardiovascular and self-regulation responses to value versus resource conflicts. *Social Psychological and Personality Science, 5*(1), 35–42. https://doi.org/10.1177/1948550613486673

Krause, R. J., & Rucker, D. D. (2020). Can bad be good? The attraction of a darker self. *Psychological Science, 31*(5), 518–530. https://doi.org/10.1177/0956797620909742

Landkammer, F., Winter, K., Thiel, A., & Sassenberg, K. (2019). Team sports off the field: Competing excludes cooperating for individual but not for team athletes. *Frontiers in Psychology, 10*. https://doi.org/10.3389/fpsyg.2019.02470

Lucas, K., & Fyke, J. P. (2014). Euphemisms and ethics: A language-centered analysis of Penn State's sexual abuse scandal. *Journal of Business Ethics, 122*(4), 551–569. https://doi.org/10.1007/s10551-013-1777-0

Luyendijk, J. (2015). *Swimming with sharks: My journey into the world of the bankers*. Guardian Faber Publishing.

Martin, K. D., & Cullen, J. B. (2006). Continuities and extensions of ethical climate theory: A meta-analytic review. *Journal of Business Ethics, 69*, 175–194. https://doi-org.proxy.library.uu.nl/10.1007/s10551-006-9084-7

Martinson, B. C., Anderson, M. S., & De Vries, R. (2005). Scientists behaving badly. *Nature, 435*(7043), 737–738. https://doi.org/10.1038/435737a

Marques, J., Abrams, D., & Serôdio, R. G. (2001). Being better by being right: Subjective group dynamics and derogation of in-group deviants when generic norms are undermined. *Journal of Personality and Social Psychology, 81*(3), 436–447. https://doi-org.proxy.library.uu.nl/10.1037/0022-3514.81.3.436

Masson, T., & Fritsche, I. (2019). Loyal peripherals? The interactive effects of identification and peripheral group membership on deviance from non-beneficial ingroup norms. *European Journal of Social Psychology, 49*(1), 76–92. https://doi.org/10.1002/ejsp.2501

Mayer, D. M., Aquino, K., Greenbaum, R. L., & Kuenzi, M. (2012). Who displays ethical leadership, and why does it matter? An examination of antecedents and consequences of ethical leadership. *Academy of Management Journal, 55*(1), 151–171. https://doi.org/10.5465/amj.2008.0276

Mayer, D. M., Kuenzi, M., & Greenbaum, R. L. (2010). Examining the link between ethical leadership and employee misconduct: The mediating role of ethical climate. *Journal of Business Ethics, 95*(1), 7–16. https://doi.org/10.1007/s10551-011-0794-0

Mayer, D. M., Kuenzi, M., Greenbaum, R. L., Bardes, M., & Salvador, R. B. (2009). How low does ethical leadership flow? Test of a trickle-down model. *Organizational Behavior and Human Decision Processes, 108*(1), 1–13. https://doi.org/10.1016/j.obhdp.2008.04.002

McCauley, C. (1989). The nature of social influence in groupthink: Compliance and internalization. *Journal of Personality and Social Psychology, 57*(2), 250. https://doi.org/10.1037/0022-3514.57.2.250

Miceli, M. P., & Near, J. P. (1989). The incidence of wrongdoing, whistle-blowing, and retaliation: Results of a naturally occurring field experiment. *Employee Responsibilities and Rights Journal, 2*(2), 91–108. https://doi.org/10.1007/BF01384940

Minto, K., Hornsey, M. J., Gillespie, N., Healy, K., & Jetten, J. (2016). A social identity approachh to understanding responses to child sexual abuse allegations. *PLoS One, 11*(4), 1–15. https://doi.org/10.1371/journal.pone.0153205

Misangyi, V. F., Weaver, G. R., & Elms, H. (2008). Ending corruption: The interplay among institutional logics, resources, and institutional entrepreneurs. *Academy of Management Review, 33*(3), 750–770. https://doi.org/10.5465/amr.2008.32465769

Monin, B. (2007). Holier than me? Threatening social comparison in the moral domain. *Revue Internationale de Psychologie Sociale, 20*, 53–68.

Monin, B., Sawyer, P. J., & Marquez, M. J. (2008). The rejection of moral rebels: Resenting those who do the right thing. *Journal of Personality and Social Psychology, 95*(1), 76. https://doi.org/10.1037/0022-3514.95.1.76

Mooijman, M., & Graham, J. (2018). Unjust punishment in organizations. *Research in Organizational Behavior, 38*, 95–106. https://doi.org/10.1016/j.riob.2018.10.001

Mooijman, M., Van Dijk, W. W., Van Dijk, E., & Ellemers, N. (2017). On sanction-goal justifications: How and why deterrence justifications undermine rule compliance. *Journal of Personality and Social Psychology, 112*(4), 577. https://doi.org/10.1037/pspi0000084

Moore, C. (2015). Moral disengagement. *Current Opinion in Psychology, 6*, 199–204. https://doi.org/10.1016/j.copsyc.2015.07.018

Moore, C., & Gino, F. (2013). Ethically adrift: How others pull our moral compass from true North, and how we can fix it. *Research in Organizational Behavior, 33*, 53–77 https://doi.org/10.1016/j.riob.2013.08.001

Morrison, E. W., & Milliken, F. J. (2000). Organizational silence: A barrier to change and development in a pluralistic world. *Academy of Management Review, 25*(4), 706–725. https://doi.org/10.5465/amr.2000.3707697

Near, J. P., & Miceli, M. P. (2008). Wrongdoing, whistle-blowing, and retaliation in the US government: What have researchers learned from the Merit Systems Protection Board (MSPB) survey results? *Review of Public Personnel Administration, 28*(3), 263–281. https://doi.org/10.1177/0734371X08319153

Near, J. P., & Miceli, M. P. (2016a). After the wrongdoing: What managers should know about whistleblowing. *Business Horizons, 59*, 105–114. https://doi.org/10.1016/j.bushor.2015.09.007

Neesham, C., & Gu, J. (2015). Strengthening moral judgment: A moral identity-based leverage strategy in business ethics education. *Journal of Business Ethics, 131*(3), 527–534. https://doi.org/10.1007/s10551-014-2483-2

Nembhard, I. M., & Edmondson, A. C. (2006). Making it safe: The effects of leader inclusiveness and professional status on psychological safety and improvement efforts in health care teams. *Journal of Organizational Behavior, 27*, 941–966. https://doi.org/10.1002/job.413

Ng, T. W., & Feldman, D. C. (2015). Ethical leadership: Meta-analytic evidence of criterion-related and incremental validity. *Journal of Applied Psychology, 100*(3), 948. https://doi.org/10.1037/a0038246

O'Fallon, M. J., & Butterfield, K. D. (2012). The influence of unethical peer behavior on observers' unethical behavior: A social cognitive perspective. *Journal of Business Ethics, 109*(2), 117–131. https://doi.org/10.1007/s10551-011-1111-7

Packer, D. J. (2008). On being both with us and against us: A normative conflict model of dissent in social groups. *Personality and Social Psychology Review, 12*, 50–73. https://doi.org/10.1177/1088868307309606

Packer, D. J., & Chasteen, A. L. (2010). Loyal deviance: Testing the normative conflict model of dissent in social groups. *Personality and Social Psychology Bulletin, 36*(1), 5–18. https://doi.org/10.1177/0146167209350628

Pagliaro, S., Ellemers, N., & Barreto, M. (2011). Sharing moral values: Anticipated ingroup respect as a determinant of adherence to morality-based (but not competence-based) group norms. *Personality and Social Psychology Bulletin, 37*(8), 1117–1129. https://doi.org/10.1177/0146167211406906

Pagliaro, S., Presti, A. L., Barattucci, M., Giannella, V. A., & Barreto, M. (2018). On the effects of ethical climate(s) on employees' behavior: A social identity approach. *Frontiers in Psychology, 9*, 1–10. https://doi.org/10.3389/fpsyg.2018.00960

Peterson, D. K. (2002). The relationship between unethical behavior and the dimensions of the ethical climate questionnaire. *Journal of Business Ethics, 41*(4), 313–326. https://doi.org/10.1023/A:1021243117958

Pike, B. E., Kilduff, G. J., & Galinsky, A. D. (2018). The long shadow of rivalry: Rivalry motivates performance today and tomorrow. *Psychological Science, 29*(5), 804–813. https://doi.org/10.1177/0956797617744796

Pinder, C. C., & Harlos, K. P. (2001). Employee silence: Quiescence and acquiescence as responses to perceived injustice. In K. M. Rowland & G. R. Ferris (Eds.), *Research in personnel and human resources management* (pp. 331–369). JAI. https://doi.org/10.1016/S0742-7301(01)20007-3

Pinto, I. R., Marques, J. M., Levine, J. M., & Abrams, D. (2010). Membership status and subjective group dynamics: Who triggers the black sheep effect? *Journal of Personality and Social Psychology, 99*(1), 107–119. https://doi-org.proxy.library.uu.nl/10.1037/a0018187

Platow, M. J., Haslam, S. A., & Reicher, S. D. (2017). The social psychology of leadership. In S. G. Harkins, K. D. Williams, & J. M. Burger (Eds.), *Oxford library of psychology. The Oxford handbook of social influence* (pp. 339–357). Oxford University Press.

Pornari, C. D., & Wood, J. (2010). Peer and cyber aggression in secondary school students: The role of moral disengagement, hostile attribution bias, and outcome expectancies. *Aggressive Behavior: Official Journal of the International Society for Research on Aggression, 36*(2), 81–94. https://doi.org/10.1002/ab.20336

Ramamoorti, S. (2008). The psychology and sociology of fraud: Integrating the behavioral sciences component into fraud and forensic accounting curricula. *Issues in Accounting Education, 23*(4), 521–533. https://doi.org/10.2308/iace.2008.23.4.521

Reckard, S. E. (2013, Dec 21). Wells Fargo's pressure-cooker sales culture comes at a cost. *Los Angeles Times*. Retrieved from https://www.latimes.com/business/la-fi-wells-fargo-sale-pressure-20131222-story.html

Rogers, K. M., & Ashforth, B. E. (2017). Respect in organizations: Feeling valued as "we" and "me". *Journal of Management, 43*(5), 1578–1608. https://doi.org/10.1177/0149206314557159

Rullo, M., Monaco, S., Giannini, F., Livi, S., & Presaghi, F. (2019). In the name of truth: People's reactions to ingroup and outgroup members who self-disclose a severe error. *The Social Science Journal, 56*(3), 421–424. https://doi.org/10.1016/j.soscij.2018.07.003

Rybowiak, V., Garst, H., Frese, M., & Batinic, B. (1999). Error orientation questionnaire (EOQ): Reliability, validity, and different language equivalence. *Journal of Organizational Behavior: The International Journal of Industrial, Occupational and Organizational Psychology and Behavior, 20*(4), 527–547. https://doi.org/10.1002/(SICI)1099-1379(199907)20:4<527::AID-JOB886>3.0.CO;2-G

Saini, A., & Martin, K. D. (2009). Strategic risk-taking propensity: The role of ethical climate and marketing output control. *Journal of Business Ethics, 90*(4), 593–606. https://doi.org/10.1007/s10551-009-0063-7

Sandström, U., & Van den Besselaar, P. (2018). Funding, evaluation, and the performance of national research systems. *Journal of Informetrics, 2*, 365–384. https://doi.org/10.1016/j.joi.2018.01.007

Schaubroeck, J. M., Hannah, S. T., Avolio, B. J., Kozlowski, S. W., Lord, R. G., Treviño, L. K., … Peng, A. C. (2012). Embedding ethical leadership within and across organization levels. *Academy of Management Journal, 55*(5), 1053–1078. https://doi.org/10.5465/amj.2011.0064

Schaubroeck, J. M., & Lam, S. S. (2004). Comparing lots before and after: Promotion rejectees' invidious reactions to promotees. *Organizational Behavior and Human Decision Processes, 94*(1), 33–47. https://doi.org/10.1016/j.obhdp.2004.01.001

Schein, E. H. (1996). Culture: The missing concept in organization studies. *Administrative Science Quarterly*, 229–240. https://doi.org/10.2307/2393715

Schminke, M., & Wells, D. (1999). Group processes and performance and their effects on individuals' ethical frameworks. *Journal of Business Ethics, 18*(4), 367–381. https://doi.org/10.1023/A:1005785628264

Schneider, B., Ehrhart, M. G., & Macey, W. H. (2013). Organizational climate and culture. *Annual Review of Psychology, 64*, 361–388. https://doi.org/10.1146/annurev-psych-113011-143809

Scholten, W. W. (2018). *Banking on team ethics: A team climate perspective on root causes of misconduct in financial services*. Ipskamp.

Scholten, W. W., & Ellemers, N. (2016). Bad apples or corrupting barrels? Preventing traders' misconduct. *Journal of Financial Regulation and Compliance, 24*, 366–382. https://doi.org/10.1108/JFRC-06-2016-0051

Schuchter, A., & Levi, M. (2016). The fraud triangle revisited. *Security Journal, 29*, 107–121. https://doi.org/10.1057/sj.2013.1

Shapiro, D. M. (2011). Better understanding accounting fraud. *The Journal of Corporate Accounting and Finance*, 61–64. https://doi.org/10.1002/jcaf.20690

Simha, A., & Cullen, J. B. (2012). Ethical climates and their effects on organizational outcomes: Implications from the past and prophecies for the future. *Academy of Management Perspectives, 26*(4), 20–34. https://doi.org/10.5465/amp.2011.0156

Simons, T., Leroy, H., Collewaert, V., & Masschelein, S. (2015). How leader alignment of words and deeds affects followers: A meta-analysis of behavioral integrity research. *Journal of Business Ethics, 132*(4), 831–844. https://doi.org/10.1007/s10551-014-2332-3

Sitkin, S. B. (1992). Learning through failure: The strategy of small losses. In B. M. Staw & L. L. Cummings (Eds.), *Research in organizational behavior* (pp. 231–266). JAI Press.

Sivertsen, G. (2017). Unique, but still best practice? The Research Excellence Framework (REF) from an international perspective. *Palgrave Communications, 3*(1), 1–6. https://doi.org/10.1057/palcomms.2017.78

Slingerland, W. (2018). *Network corruption: when social capital becomes corrupted: Its meaning and significance in corruption and network theory and the consequences for (EU) policy and law* (Doctoral dissertation). Vrije Universiteit Amsterdam.

Smith, D. W. (2014, May 28). *Handelsbanken: A different kind of bank.* Retrieved from https://www.wearesalt.org/the-swedish-bank-that-is-not-all-money-money-money/

Smith, I. H., & Kouchaki, M. (2018a). Moral humility: In life and at work. *Research in Organizational Behavior, 38*, 77–94. https://doi.org/10.1016/j.riob.2018.12.001

Soltani, B. (2007). *Auditing: An international approach.* Prentice Hall-Pearson Education.

Soltani, B. (2014). The anatomy of corporate fraud: A comparative analysis of high profile American and European corporate schandals. *Journal of Business Ethics, 120*, 251–274. https://doi.org/10.1007/s10551-013-1660-z

Spears, R. (2021). Social influence and group identity. *Annual Review of Psychology, 72*. https://doi.org/10.1146/annurev-psych-070620-111818

Stellar, J. E., & Willer, R. (2014). The corruption of value: Negative moral associations diminish the value of money. *Social Psychological and Personality Science, 5*(1), 60–66. https://doi.org/10.1177/1948550613484770

Strelan, P., & Boeckmann, R. J. (2006). Why drug testing in elite sport does not work: Perceptual deterrence theory and the role of personal moral beliefs. *Journal of Applied Social Psychology, 36*(12), 2909–2934. https://doi.org/10.1111/j.0021-9029.2006.00135.x

Suh, I., Sweeney, J. T., Linke, K., & Wall, J. M. (2018). Boiling the frog slowly: The immersion of C-suite financial executives into fraud. *Journal of Business Ethics*, 1–29. https://doi.org/10.1007/s10551-018-3982-3

Sun, J., & Goodwin, G. (2019). Do people want to be more moral? *PsyArXiv.* https://doi.org/10.31234/osf.io/9gux6

Sutherland, E. H. (1949). *White collar crime.* LexisNexis.

Tai, K., Narayanan, J., & McAllister, D. J. (2012). Envy as pain: Rethinking the nature of envy and its implications for employees and organizations. *Academy of Management Review, 37*, 107–129. https://doi.org/10.5465/amr.2009.0484

Takeover of Porn and Gambling Customers is a Great Embarrassment to ING. (2020, Nov 13). *News1.* Retrieved from. https://www.news1.news/2020/11/takeover-of-porn-and-gambling-customers-is-a-great-embarrassment-to-ing.html

Tangney, J. P., & Dearing, R. L. (2002). Gender differences in morality. In R. F. Bornstein & J. M. Masling (Eds.), *Empirical studies in psychoanalytic theories, Vol. 10. The psychodynamics of gender and gender role* (pp. 251–269). American Psychological Association. https://doi.org/10.1037/10450-007

Tappin, B. M., & McKay, R. T. (2017). The illusion of moral superiority. *Social Psychological and Personality Science, 8*(6), 623–631. https://doi.org/10.1177/1948550616673878

Täuber, S., & Van Zomeren, M. (2012). Refusing intergroup help from the morally superior: How one group's moral superiority leads to another group's reluctance to seek their help. *Journal of Experimental Social Psychology, 48*, 420–423. https://doi.org/10.1016/j.jesp.2011.08.014

Taylor, A. (2020, Jan 15). Leaked Boeing emails show slippery slope of a bad compliance culture. *The FCPA Blog.* Retrieved from https://fcpablog.com/2020/01/15/leaked-boeing-emails-show-slippery-slope-of-a-bad-compliance-culture/

Tenbrunsel, A. E., & Messick, D. M. (1999). Sanctioning systems, decision frames, and cooperation. *Administrative Science Quarterly, 44*(4), 684–707. https://doi.org/10.2307/2667052

Tenbrunsel, A. E., Rees, M. R., & Diekmann, K. A. (2019). Sexual harassment in academia: Ethical climates and bounded ethicality. *Annual Review of Psychology, 70*, 245–270. https://doi.org/10.1146/annurev-psych-010418-102945

The Economist Newspaper. (2009, May 16). *Back at the branch: More Swedish lessons for the banking industry*. Retrieved from https://www.economist.com/special-report/2009/05/16/back-at-the-branch

Treviño, L. K., Weaver, G. R., Gibson, D. G., & Toffler, B. L. (1999). Managing ethics and legal compliance: What works and what hurts. *California Management Review, 41*(2), 131–151. https://doi.org/10.2307/41165990

Turner, J. C. (1991). *Social influence*. Thomson Brooks/Cole Publishing.

Uddin, N., & Gillett, P. R. (2002). The effects of moral reasoning and self-monitoring on CFO intentions to report fraudulently on financial statements. *Journal of Business Ethics, 40*(1), 15–32. https://doi.org/10.1023/A:1019931524716

Umphress, E. E., Bingham, J. B., & Mitchell, M. S. (2010). Unethical behavior in the name of the company: The moderating effect of organizational identification and positive reciprocity beliefs on unethical pro-organizational behavior. *Journal of Applied Psychology, 95*(4), 769–780. https://doi.org/10.1037/a0019214

Van der Lee, R., Ellemers, N., & Scheepers, D. (2016). Mastering moral misery: Emotional and coping responses to intragroup morality (vs. competence) evaluations. *Cognition and Emotion, 30*, 51–65. https://doi.org/10.1080/02699931.2015.1050357

Van der Lee, R., Ellemers, N., Scheepers, D., & Rutjens, B. T. (2017). In or out? How the perceived morality (vs. competence) of prospective group members affects acceptance and rejection. *European Journal of Social Psychology, 47*(6), 748–762. https://doi.org/10.1002/ejsp.2269

Van der Toorn, J., Ellemers, N., & Doosje, B. (2015). The threat of moral transgression: The impact of group membership and moral opportunity. *European Journal of Social Psychology, 45*, 609–622. https://doi.org/10.1002/ejsp.2119

Van Dyck, C., Baer, M., Frese, M., & Sonnentag, S. (2005). Organizational error management culture and its impact on performance: A two-study replication. *Journal of Applied Psychology, 90*, 228–1240. https://doi.org/10.1037/0021-9010.90.6.1228

Van Dyne, L., Ang, S., & Botero, I. C. (2003). Conceptualizing employee silence and employee voice as multidimensional constructs. *Journal of Management Studies, 40*(6), 1359–1392. https://doi.org/10.1111/1467-6486.00384

Van Rooij, B., & Fine, A. (2018). Toxic corporate culture: Assessing organizational processes of deviancy. *Administrative Sciences, 8*(3), 23. https://doi.org/10.3390/admsci8030023

Van Steenbergen, E. F., & Ellemers, N. (2021). The social and organizational psychology of compliance: How organizational culture impacts on (un)ethical behavior. In D. D. Sokol & B. Van Rooij (Eds.), *Cambridge handbook of compliance*. Cambridge University Press.

Van Steenbergen, E. F., Van Dijk, D., Christensen, C., Coffeng, T., & Ellemers, N. (2019a). Learn to build an error management culture. *Journal of Financial Regulation and Compliance, 28*(1), 57–73. https://doi.org/10.1108/JFRC-12-2018-0156

Van Yperen, N. W., Hamstra, M. R., & Van der Klauw, M. (2011). To win, or not to lose, at any cost: The impact of achievement goals on cheating. *British Journal of Management, 22*, S5–S15. https://doi.org/10.1111/j.1467-8551.2010.00702.x

Vaughan, D. (1999). The dark side of organizations: Mistake, misconduct, and disaster. *Annual Review of Sociology, 25*, 271–305. https://doi.org/10.1146/annurev.soc.25.1.271

Vecchio, R. P. (2000). Negative emotion in the workplace: Employee jealousy and envy. *International Journal of Stress Management, 7*, 161–179. https://doi.org/10.1023/A:1009592430712

Vecchio, R. P. (2005). Explorations in employee envy: Feeling envious and feeling envied. *Cognition & Emotion, 19*(1), 69–81. https://doi.org/10.1080/02699930441000148

Verghis, S. (2019, July 25). *Understanding the 'clean money' movement.* Retrieved from https://www.sbs.com.au/topics/article/2019/06/12/understanding-clean-money-movement%3Futm_medium%3Dpartnerships%26utm_source%3Dsbs%26utm_campaign%3Dclean%2Bmoney%26utm_content%3Dbra_pl_awa_dir_nat_q1_cm

Victor, B., & Cullen, J. (1988). The organizational bases of ethical work climates. *Administrative Science Quarterly, 33*(1), 101–125. https://doi.org/10.2307/2392857

Vincent, L. C., & Kouchaki, M. (2016). Creative, rare, entitled, and dishonest: How commonality of creativity in one's group decreases an individual's entitlement and dishonesty. *Academy of Management Journal, 59*(4), 1451–1473. https://doi.org/10.5465/amj.2014.1109

Wakeman, S. W., & Moore, C. (2018). Rewarding deviants: Unethical behavior as a signal of one's communal value. *Academy of Management Proceedings, 1* https://doi.org/10.5465/AMBPP.2018.240

Warren, D. E., & Smith-Crowe, K. (2008). Deciding what's right: The role of external sanctions and embarrassment in shaping moral judgments in the workplace. *Research in Organizational Behavior, 28*, 81–105. https://doi.org/10.1016/j.riob.2008.04.004

Weaver, G. R. (2006). Virtue in organizations: Moral identity as a foundation for moral agency. *Organization Studies, 27*(3), 341–368. https://doi.org/10.1177/0170840606062426

Weibel, A., Den Hartog, D. N., Gillespie, N., Searle, R., Six, F., & Skinner, D. (2016). How do controls impact employee trust in the employer? *Human Resource Management, 55*(3), 437–462. https://doi.org/10.1002/hrm.21733

Wellcome. (2020). *What researchers think about the culture they work in*. Retrieved from https://wellcome.org/sites/default/files/what-researchers-think-about-the-culture-they-work-in.pdf

Willis, L., Reynolds, K. J., & Lee, E. (2019). Being well at work: The impact of organizational climate and social identity on employee stress and self-esteem over time. *European Journal of Work and Organizational Psychology, 28*(3), 399–413. https://doi.org/10.1080/1359432X.2019.1587409

Wilson, B. M., Harris, C. R., & Wixted, J. T. (2020). Science is not a signal detection problem. *Proceedings of the National Academy of Sciences, 117*(11), 5559–5567. https://doi.org/10.1073/pnas.1914237117

Wolfe, D. T., & Hermanson, D. R. (2004). The fraud diamond: Considering the four elements of fraud. *The CPA Journal*, 38–42. https://doi.org/10.1016/S1361-3723(04)00065-X

Wolfe, S., Worth, M., Dreyfus, S., & Brown, A. J. (2014). *Whistleblower protection rules in G20 countries: The next action plan*. Transparency International Australia.

Woodyatt, L., & Wenzel, M. (2013). Self-forgiveness and restoration of an offender following an interpersonal transgression. *Journal of Social and Clinical Psychology, 32*(2), 225–259. https://doi.org/10.1521/jscp.2013.32.2.225

Woodyatt, L., Wenzel, M., & Ferber, M. (2017). Two pathways to self-forgiveness: A hedonic path via self-compassion and a eudaimonic path via the reaffirmation of violated values. *British Journal of Social Psychology, 56*(3), 515–536. https://doi.org/10.1111/bjso.12194

Woolston, C. (2019). PhD's: The tortuous truth. *Nature, 575*, 403–406. https://doi.org/10.1038/d41586-019-03459-7

Zhang, J. W., & Chen, S. (2016). Self-compassion promotes personal improvement from regret experiences via acceptance. *Personality and Social Psychology Bulletin, 42*, 244–258. https://doi.org/10.1177/0146167215623271

Zhang, T., Gino, F., & Bazerman, M. H. (2014). Morality rebooted: Exploring simple fixes to our moral bugs. *Research in Organizational Behavior, 34*, 63–79. https://doi.org/10.1016/j.riob.2014.10.002

Zhang, Y., He, B., Huang, Q., & Xie, J. (2020). Effects of supervisor bottom-line mentality on subordinate unethical pro-organizational behavior. *Journal of Managerial Psychology, 35*(2), 419–434. https://doi.org/10.1108/JMP-11-2018-0492

Zhang, Y., Yam, K. C., Kouchaki, M., & Zhang, J. (2019). Cut you some slack? An investigation of the perceptions of a depleted employee's unethicality. *Journal of Business Ethics*, 1–11. https://doi.org/10.1007/s10551-017-3690-4

Zhong, C. B., Liljenquist, K., & Cain, D. M. (2009). Moral self-regulation: Licensing and compensation. In D. De Cremer (Ed.), *Psychological perspectives on ethical behavior and decision making* (pp. 75–89). Information Age Publishing.

Zhou, J., & Heim, D. (2016). A qualitative exploration of alcohol use among student sportspeople: A social identity perspective. *European Journal of Social Psychology, 46*(5), 581–594. https://doi.org/10.1002/ejsp.2195

Zyglidopoulos, S. C., & Fleming, P. J. (2008). Ethical distance in corrupt firms: How do innocent bystanders become guilty perpetrators? *Journal of Business Ethics, 78*(1–2), 265–274. https://doi.org/10.1007/s10551-007-9378-4

Correction to: The Human Factor in Organizational Change

Correction to:
Chapter 6 in: N. Ellemers, D. de Gilder, *The Moral Organization: Key Issues, Analyses, and Solutions*
https://doi.org/10.1007/978-3-030-84175-1_6

The content in box 6.3 in chapter 6 has been inadvertently printed incorrectly which has now been updated as given below per the author request.

Theranos was a high tech company founded by Stanford dropout Elizabeth Holmes. She was able to inspire and commit experienced business people (such as Rupert Murdoch, the Walton family), jaded politicians (such as Henry Kissinger, George Shultz) and well-connected private investors (such as Carlos Slim) to support her vision (see also Asher-Shapiro, 2019). The ambition was to develop the technology to offer quick, inexpensive, and non-invasive medical diagnoses for a number of diseases by analyzing only one drop of blood on-site.

The company developed a production site in Silicon Valley, and hired many hardware and software developers to create innovative solutions to realize the promises that were made. However, Theranos started selling its products before procedures were tested or approved by regulators, and medical experts maintained it was simply not possible to achieve what was promised. Yet, the initiative successfully attracted billions of dollars as startup capital, and persuaded US pharmacy store chain Walgreens to offer the 'disruptive' but non-existent service to customers at their stores (Carreyrou, 2018).

Analyses emphasize that even former employees of the company voiced their doubts and concerns about the feasibility of the project to responsible managers time and again. However, the pressure to deliver, the ambition to disrupt the industry and the strong belief that medical problems could be overcome through innovative high-tech solutions made investors, and clients, politicians and managers deaf to such concerns. In the end, inevitably everything fell apart, revealing large scale deception of all stakeholders: patients, jobs and investors, when the company went bankrupt (see Gibney et al., 2019).

The updated original version of this chapter can be found at
https://doi.org/10.1007/978-3-030-84175-1_6

N. Ellemers, D. de Gilder, *The Moral Organization: Key Issues, Analyses, and Solutions*, https://doi.org/10.1007/978-3-030-84175-1_9

Index

N. Ellemers, D. de Gilder, *The Moral Organization: Key issues, analyses, and solutions*, https://doi.org/10.1007/978-3-030-84175-1

D

G

H

I

R

The manufacturer's authorised representative in the EU is Springer Nature Customer Service Centre GmbH, Europaplatz 3, 69115 Heidelberg, Germany. If you have any concerns regarding our products, please contact ProductSafety@springernature.com

Printed and bound by CPI Group (UK) Ltd, Croydon, CR0 4YY
30/09/2026
02225498-0013